The Handbook
of Variable
Income Annuities

Founded in 1807, John Wiley & Sons is the oldest independent publishing company in the United States. With offices in North America, Europe, Australia, and Asia, Wiley is globally committed to developing and marketing print and electronic products and services for our customers' professional and personal knowledge and understanding.

The Wiley Finance series contains books written specifically for finance and investment professionals as well as sophisticated individual investors and their financial advisors. Book topics range from portfolio management to e-commerce, risk management, financial engineering, valuation, and financial instrument analysis, as well as much more.

For a list of available titles, visit our Web site at www.WileyFinance.com.

The Handbook of Variable Income Annuities

JEFFREY K. DELLINGER

WILEY

John Wiley & Sons, Inc.

For general information about our other products and services, please contact our Customer Care Department within the United States at (800) 762-2974, outside the United States at (317) 572-3993, or fax (317) 572-4002.

Wiley also publishes its books in a variety of electronic formats. Some content that appears in print may not be available in electronic books. For more information about Wiley products, visit our web site at www.wiley.com.

Jeffrey K. Dellinger is president of Longevity Management Corporation. He is a Fellow of the Society of Actuaries and a member of the American Academy of Actuaries. The viewpoints expressed herein are those of Longevity Management Corporation, not of the latter two professional actuarial organizations.

Library of Congress Cataloging-in-Publication Data:
Dellinger, Jeffrey K.
    The handbook of variable income annuities / Jeffrey K. Dellinger.
        p.   cm. — (Wiley finance series)
    Includes index.
    ISBN-13 978-0-471-73382-9 (cloth)
    ISBN-10 0-471-73382-2 (cloth)
  1. Variable annuities.   2. Retirement income.   I. Title   II. Series.
    HG8790.D45 2006
    368.3'75—dc22

                                                            2005016329

Printed in the United States of America.

10 9 8 7 6 5 4 3 2 1

To Robert and Margaret Dellinger,
my parents

and

To Orvis and Clela Dellinger,
my grandparents

Contents

Preface

Individual retirement security is a multifaceted subject of great importance. The unstoppable demographics of a large number of U.S. citizens transitioning from the accumulation phase of their economic lives to the distribution phase, the lessening percentage of workers covered by defined benefit pension plans, and the uncertain future of a U.S. Social Security program where relatively fewer workers must support relatively more retirees prompt the need for greater private-sector focus on retirement security.

Excellent product vehicles already exist to help individuals achieve retirement security on a basis greater than they could achieve by themselves. Such solutions are used today only to a minuscule degree relative to their potential. Several reasons account for this. First, the mere existence of such solutions is not well known to the average retiree or average individual transitioning toward the years where drawing income from accumulated assets will begin. Second, individuals are properly apprehensive about employing specific retirement income solutions because they've worked decades to amass their nest eggs; they want to avoid any mistakes that could cause them to need to return to work during advanced years when they would prefer not to do so or might be physically unable to do so. Third, financial advisers must feel comfortable enough with such solutions to explain them to clients; and such solutions must be congruent with financial advisers' need to receive ongoing compensation for providing ongoing counsel.

Individuals must make very real decisions regarding such factors as:

- Flexibility to change their retirement security program as their needs and situations change.
- Accessibility to their accumulated assets.
- Ability of their funds to provide income as long as they live, regardless of how long that is.
- Preferability of a stream of retirement income known with complete precision at the start of their income period—the stream may be level

or may increase periodically by a fixed dollar amount or fixed percentage, but it is known with 100% certainty at the outset.
■ Preferability of a stream of retirement income that displays some volatility
yet may offer greater potential to keep pace with or outpace inflation.

These are very real trade-offs for which individuals must make decisions. Not making a conscious decision is still making one—the individual
simply receives the default outcome. Those who enter retirement without a
plan experience Brownian motion—a sequence of incoherent, self-annulling,
and directionless steps.

The purpose of this book is to share in a hopefully understandable way
with the general reader some individual financial security programs for
which much advanced thinking has been done by people across a multitude
of disciplines in a number of countries, some even spanning back to prior
centuries. Only through an awareness of such programs do they even
become part of the potential retirement security solution set for an individual. Only through a relatively complete understanding of a solution can an
individual (or his or her adviser) *comfortably* proceed with it.

Actuarial, investment, and legal topics—all important to variable retirement income—are often shrouded in an aura of mystique. This text attempts
to shed light on matters that heretofore may have appeared secret, mysteri-
ous, and cryptic.

Like Dorothy discovers when she, the lion, the scarecrow, and the tin
woodsman encounter the great and powerful wizard of Oz, the scenario
isn't nearly as scary once you fully understand the mechanics behind it. The
French might exclaim "Voilà!" ("There it is!") as concepts underlying the
optimization of their finances during retirement years sequentially and systematically unfold.

This book is written for a wide audience. First and foremost, it is
designed to share a few comprehensible solutions that for millions of people may play an extremely important role in optimizing their personal
retirement security. Like any financial tool, such solutions are to be used
only to the degree appropriate. They may be totally inappropriate for some
people, appropriate for a small portion of the retirement assets of some, and
appropriate for a large portion of the retirement assets of others. The book
strives to ensure that possible solutions are understood to a degree that
most readers feel they have a sufficiently firm grasp of them to make informed decisions and could articulate their reasons to others. Graphics are
used to visually (and, hopefully, vividly) illustrate important concepts.

Second, the book is written for a variety of others. It takes the general
concepts to a greater level of analytical rigor and technical depth for those
who want to more fully understand the logical processes underlying these

solutions, offering references for those who want to take their understanding to an even higher degree and become "retirement income connoisseurs." It lets you "see the DNA" of immediate variable annuities. Do-it-yourselfers with an analytical or technical bent may enjoy a more detailed understanding of concepts that serve as the underpinnings for certain retirement security solutions. The mere presence of such explanations should give great comfort and assurance to readers who choose to make their own decisions about their personal retirement security but aren't inclined to know every last detail as long as they understand the general concepts and know that the underlying formulas are transparently exposed and verifiable by others, such as actuaries, finance professors, investment professionals, and mathematicians. (While the book uses the words "*retirement security* solutions," it is recognized that some people choose to or need to work during "traditional" retirement years. Thus, perhaps "*personal financial security* solutions" during years 50+ may more precisely describe the subject matter.)

Lord Kelvin eloquently decreed, "I often say that when you can measure what you are speaking about, and express it in numbers, you know something about it; but when you cannot measure it, when you cannot express it in numbers, your knowledge is of a meager and unsatisfactory kind."[1] The precise and economical language of mathematics will therefore appear. For those so inclined, sufficient formulas will be provided to allow individuals to make whatever changes they desire in assumptions to ascertain the degrees to which these change the results. A limited glance at the beauty, precision, and elegance of the mathematics supporting retirement income appears—a touch of its artistic grandeur.

Financial mathematics peculiar to annuities—such as projecting and discounting life-contingent annuity payment streams—are covered in detail, while financial mathematics affecting annuities but not unique to them are covered in less detail, with the focus being on showing where these concepts come into play in the world of income annuities. Nonetheless, descriptions and explanations absent the complex quantitative technicalities are provided first so that all readers may gain the benefit of concepts to make informed decisions about whether and to what degree they should capitalize on the solutions presented for their personal situation.

"The work of science is to substitute facts for appearances and demonstrations for impressions" is the motto of the Society of Actuaries, attributable to John Ruskin.[2] To a large extent, this book attempts to be scientific by providing demonstrations that are reproducible and verifiable by others, while recognizing that financial security in retirement is part science, part art: real science with a dash of black cat.

Outside our feeble minds is a vast world possessing an orderly structure often amenable to description by mathematical laws. We humans, with our rudimentary little brains freshly evolved from the brains of beasts, have—particularly in the last two millennia, from the geometry of the Greeks to the calculus of Newton and Leibniz—fashioned the logical framework for sound longevity insurance programs and then clothed that framework with scientifically gathered population data. This basic genetic structure of longevity risk management has evolved (for the better) through periodic mutations, adapting to environmental advances in law, investments, and even computer science.

Financial advisers may benefit from a fuller understanding of particular retirement security solutions described herein, including sales ideas. While there's a popular perception that retirement is synonymous with "carefree living" in one's "golden years," the contrasting, cold, hard reality is that many current retirees lead a troubled financial existence and many future retirees are grotesquely unprepared. Many retirees' lifestyles have deteriorated since they stopped working and they expect them to get bleaker, even with self-imposed austerity programs. Others use terms such as "just making ends meet," "struggling to get by," or "in a precarious position." There may be nothing more ghastly to some people than running out of money at a point in their lives where they are unable to work and losing their independence, with all decisions affecting their quality of life—where they will live, how they will eat, who will provide their medical care—in the hands of others. If a financial adviser performs a retirement needs analysis for a client couple and determines that their savings, pension, and Social Security benefits are inadequate to allow them to maintain their standard of living should they survive beyond "normal" ages, is it malpractice if an instrument is available through which the couple could eliminate that problem, and they are not advised to consider it?

Psychological factors play an influential role in retirement income decisions. Individuals have a natural and high risk aversion to running out of money in their old age, but they will act in advance on this risk aversion only if they themselves are aware of or an adviser convincingly makes them aware of the likelihood and magnitude of this contingency. Some will indeed prematurely exhaust their life savings and desperately wish they could rewind their lives and arrange entry into a program to safeguard against this. Individuals, societies, and government policy makers with virtually unlimited current wants yet finite resources are often unwilling to take advance steps necessary to protect themselves from adverse future events, including economic misfortune, even if highly projectable; and they take remedial actions only immediately before or when disaster strikes. Exactly because individuals often illogically discount risks far into the future, it is imperative to impress on them early the severity of the risk of destitution and the availability of the protective umbrella of longevity insurance to avert it. When elders become destitute, profound social and economic consequences ensue, including intergenerational conflict because other generations must support them, either privately or through government programs.

Because the current generation of elderly has a higher percentage that participated in defined benefit pension plans and has Social Security benefits relative to their working-period incomes that are higher than is likely for the next generation, they have been to some degree insulated from longevity risk, effectively hiding it. Workers today have not in large scale witnessed their grandparents or parents running out of money, so they underappreciate the risk, believing that magically everything will work out fine as it did for their predecessors—a belief often belied by hard analysis.

It is often easier to inspire the heart through sentiment than it is to teach the mind a mathematical truth. As such, appropriate methods are sometimes needed to motivate people to act in their own best economic self-interest. For variable income annuities to gain popularity in greater breadth requires appealing to emotions as well as to logic. A fuller understanding of what these financial instruments can accomplish aids in development of such emotion-based appeals. Liberation from fear of outliving one's accumulated wealth can offer psychic fulfillment, on which certain individuals place a high value. Experiential simulation in which retirees are shown a movie featuring themselves in several future simulated environments might facilitate more future-oriented thinking, improving their judgment about the value of inflation protection, longevity insurance, and so on. "Monte Carlo" financial projection illustrations, showing a variety of possible future outcomes, start to get at this, albeit in a less emotional way.

Insurance personnel—actuaries, consultants, product developers, product managers, sales managers, wholesalers, corporate officers, and even insurance company boards of directors (whose backgrounds and expertise often are outside the insurance realm)—may benefit from this book. Investment managers—whether they are individuals investing for themselves, plan fiduciaries investing for others, or insurance company portfolio managers—may derive benefit from a fuller understanding of the nature of the liabilities with which they are being asked to pair assets. Accountants, attorneys, estate planners, and other experts to whom individuals turn for help to financially plan the final decades of life will benefit. Financial security trade association members may glean a different perspective on topics with which they already have a degree of familiarity. Those on either side of the heretofore politically radioactive Social Security privatization debate may gain increased awareness of issues related to their position. Politicians, policy makers, and aides engaged in retirement security issues—public or private—will gain a more comprehensive picture.

This book escapes neat categorization. It can be a tool kit and reference manual for all individuals concerned with optimally managing assets they plan to use to support themselves in retirement—important in an era where retirement is increasingly becoming self-funded. It can be used as a textbook by educational institutions and financial credentialing programs. It can be used as a sales-idea generator by financial advisers, sales managers, wholesalers, or sales-illustration software designers. It can be used by trade associations to help governmental bodies—federal tax-law writers, securities agencies, and state insurance departments—better understand the nature of certain financial products to help them make well-informed decisions. It can be offered as an educational tool by organizations that assist seniors, such as AARP. It can be used as a blueprint by insurance companies already in or seeking to enter the retirement income markets. It can be used by those in a variety of special situations, from attorneys and judges tasked with determining the lost value of lifetime income to an injured party to charitable organizations whose members have a philanthropic intent and wish to make a current gift yet still be assured of lifetime income. In short, the book is useful to anyone whose inquisitiveness and imagination can extend the realm of applications to which the financial security solutions illustrated herein can be directed.

The book, if nothing else, pulls together in one place information from a kaleidoscope of disciplines—mathematics, investments, law, demography, biology, economics, taxation, marketing, distribution, psychology—the fascinating interplay of which is important to the understanding of variable income annuities. This is very much a topic that successively builds on prior knowledge, for which we owe our predecessors. British physicist and mathematical savant Isaac Newton recognized this building process and this debt to forebears when he proclaimed, "If I have seen further [than certain other men], it is by standing upon the shoulders of giants." Assembling information in one entity from multiple fields related to variable income annuities may facilitate a richer understanding and a more robust perspective that will enable interested parties to further advance the field.

For the past 20 years, the author has heard that the "magnificent tidal wave" of variable immediate annuity purchases is "5 years away." Some common misperceptions retard the ascendancy of what for many retirees should be a component of their financial plan. This book attempts to rectify nebulous mushy thinking about variable immediate annuities by articulating with a meaningful degree of precision—even exactitude—what they are, why they work, and how they might be used. It puts hard data and mathematical proof ahead of gut feelings. The book accentuates enduring concepts such as mathematical truths while granting less emphasis to transitory matters such as current accounting treatment of a specific transaction.

In this spirit, the hope is that information contained herein may be a small contribution—a beacon for development—toward heralding an era of greater awareness and use of a retirement income concept and instrument that for some will truly be the difference between the specter of destitution and the coziness of financial security. Mere mention of this product in the general media should make consumers more comfortable about purchasing it—much like retail mutual funds one generation ago—than they would be if they were irrevocably channeling their savings into a product with which they have no familiarity. While this solution to longevity risk is highly advanced in terms of development, it is embryonic in terms of growth in usage. Like the mighty oak that sleeps in the acorn, the trajectory of variable income annuities appears inevitable: An aging population, many with too few savings to last a lifetime, who are now offered a way to have those savings last a lifetime—a way that has no comparable competition—will trigger escalated use of variable income annuities. Victor Hugo's observation, "There's no force in the world so great as an idea whose hour has struck!" may well apply here.

The author admits up front that while the majority of prose contained in the book is descriptive in an educational way, the book is not totally devoid of the author's personal viewpoints. Decades of experience with this subject matter result in numerous observations and perspectives the author gladly shares.

The confluence of events mentioned in the opening paragraph makes the subject matter an imperative read for serious students of retirement security—their own or that of others. Powerful, well-conceived, fully transparent solutions exist with a regulatory and legal framework to support them. Only if people understand these solutions can they feel comfortable using them to whatever degree optimizes their personal financial situation.

The solutions described herein apply equally well (although not identically) to assets inside tax-qualified defined contribution plans (such as 401(k) savings and profit-sharing plans, 403(b) tax-deferred annuity plans, and IRAs) and to assets individuals may have saved on their own in mutual funds, stocks, bonds, certificates of deposit, or other financial instruments outside the umbrella of tax-qualified plans.

Proper perspective on financing retirement income is imperative. Extraordinary longevity is not a *certainty* for which one *saves*; it is a *risk* against which one *insures*. This change in worldview represents a profound transition in human perspective. Someday this solution may seem obvious to virtually everyone. Yet progress toward this perspective is not inevitable; it will come through the tireless efforts of those knowledgeable souls willing to clearly and compellingly articulate to others why this perspective yields the optimal solution to specific retirement income objectives.

While the book describes several financial security solutions of specific categories, it does not promote products of any specific company. It does, however, offer suggestions as to the factors that prospective users of specific solutions should consider as they make their own choices. This volume seeks to be information-rich in that its content reveals actionable steps for those who wish to optimize their own retirement income and offers depth and robustness sufficient to lead to more advanced development of the illustrated concepts by those so inclined.

All economic institutions and financial systems within their stewardship are devised by human beings. Money—anything which by general consent can be exchanged for a commodity or service—is a useful invention of man, serving as a medium of exchange, a standard of value, and a store of wealth. Most of us choose to store part of our hours of labor in the form of money—a claim check to be exchanged for goods and services years from now. When so viewed, it makes eminently good sense that we spend some time learning how we might most intelligently deploy our stored labor so that we achieve our objectives, which may well include maximizing the goods and services we may procure subject to the caveats that the flow of income allowing this is endless in each of our lifetimes and the pattern of income favors over time a constant or rising standard of living.

"I returned, and saw under the sun, that the race is not to the swift, nor the battle to the strong, neither yet bread to the wise, nor yet riches to men of understanding, nor yet favor to men of skill; but time and chance happeneth to them all," asserts Ecclesiastes 9:11. This biblical wisdom illustrates that millennia ago it was understood that random events can play a significant role in determining the lives of individuals. While actuarial science, investment theory, statistics, the development of insuring diversifiable financial risk by pooling and risk transfer, and the advent of derivative products to manage nondiversifiable risk all serve to help mankind cope with longevity risk better than at any time in human history, there remain elements of chance.

Yet the ability to hedge future uncertainty regarding the adequacy of one's accumulated assets to sustain him or her for the whole of life improves as one's knowledge of the tools and options available to help cope with this risk grows. As Louis Pasteur noted, "chance favors only the prepared mind." Your financial future is malleable rather than immutable. To an extent, your financial destiny, even distantly, is amenable to your control.

"Education is the best provision for old age," according to Aristotle. Best wishes for an enjoyable, intriguing, provoking, frightening, and motivating exploratory experience learning concepts that most people would never have occasion to contemplate but that hold genuine potential to meaningfully enhance your financial security and standard of living during retirement years.

JEFFREY K. DELLINGER

June 2006
Fort Wayne, Indiana

Overview

The aging of the population provides a new challenge for the cohort of the U.S. populace nearing retirement age: Having accumulated assets during their working years, their risk of dying too soon to provide financially for those dependent on them is being replaced by their risk of living too long, depleting their wealth, and becoming financially dependent on others. Annuities help Americans cope with this risk.

Americans' fierce independence and self-reliance produce in them a strong aversion to depleting their accumulated savings and becoming dependent on their children, relatives, friends, or the government in their old age. Income annuities provide a very real, favorable, and sound solution to this issue.

The Internal Revenue Code provides tax incentives to encourage Americans to use annuities to manage this risk. In the United States, authority to assume this risk and alleviate it for individuals is vested in insurance companies. A reasoned, regulatory framework of reserving, reporting, and on-site examining exists to ensure that obligations associated with assumption of these risks by insurers are met. State guaranty associations and their funds provide an additional safety net for fixed-income annuities, whereby any licensed insurer on the verge of trouble is aided to the extent necessary by assessments imposed on other insurers writing the same type of business in the same state.

Annuitants pay a premium and in exchange receive regular, periodic annuity benefits regardless of how long they live. Similarly situated annuitants—those with the same age, sex, and type of annuity option—receive identical annuity benefits for an identical premium. Some annuitants may survive only a few months, whereas others may survive many decades, living well beyond age 100. Insurance companies, through their pooling of mortality risk function, ensure that the premium collected and the reserves held for benefits not yet paid are sufficient to provide a lifetime of annuity benefits for all customers who elect life-contingent annuity options—those for which benefit payments are contingent on the survival of the annuitant.

The benefits of fixed annuities, if scheduled to remain level in all years, provide less and less purchasing power for an annuitant as the years progress. To combat this shortcoming of fixed annuities, variable annuities were created.

The premiums for variable annuities are deposited into various funding options, such as a common stock fund, and the annuity benefit payments depend on the performance of the assets in these underlying funds. The idea is that common stock performance, while it does not move in lockstep with inflation, may be better able to help protect the annuitant from the ravages of inflation than a fixed annuity would. Asset allocation across bond, stock, money market, and other funds is made based on the annuitant's risk tolerance and time horizon.

While a lifetime of annuity benefit payments is guaranteed, the level of those payments in a variable annuity is not guaranteed; rather, it fluctuates with the performance of the fund or funds chosen by the annuity contract owner. One chapter of this book describes the process by which initial and subsequent variable annuity benefits are determined. While individuals and their financial advisers may appreciate what a variable annuity can achieve in the way of risk mitigation and optimizing use of one's retirement savings, it is only through a more complete understanding of how these instruments function that a high degree of comfort is achieved.

It only makes sense that after accumulating a retirement nest egg for decades, significant thought should go into how this money will be returned to the person who saved it. The profundity of this decision and its impact on final decades of life are easily underestimated.

A knowledge base exists to help individuals make optimal decisions for their particular situations. Rather than relying on mysticism, feeling, or intuition to make such decisions, empirical study, rational analysis, scholastic approach, and scientific knowledge expertly applied are likelier to yield an optimal outcome. This volume attempts to convey some measure of the latter method.

The Handbook
of Variable
Income Annuities

CHAPTER 1

Retirement Income Basics

It is better to have a permanent income than to be fascinating.
                                        –Oscar Wilde, Irish dramatist

A GAME

At a carnival, you're presented with the game shown in Figure 1.1. Sixty-four balls will be dropped from a chute one at a time. They bounce off the pins—with equal chance of bouncing right or left—as gravity pulls them down until they land in one of seven bins. There are 63 white balls and one gray ball. You win a prize if you correctly guess where the gray ball will land. You win another prize if you guess the shape the balls will form across the bins once all balls have been dropped.

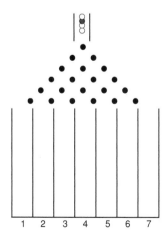

FIGURE 1.1   Carnival Game

1

Where do you guess the gray ball will land? What shape do you believe the balls will form across the bins once they have all dropped?

We'll come back to these two questions later. As you'll see, the answers to these two questions have a profound effect on your financial security during retirement. In fact, the game you just played may be analogous to the most important decision you'll need to make regarding your retirement savings—a decision that could well influence your quality of life, especially during advanced years.

YOUR RETIREMENT

You save for decades toward your retirement. You want the freedom and the peace of mind that come from knowing you're financially secure. Yet even if you've achieved your retirement savings goal at the point you retire, you still need to ensure that this will provide sufficient income regardless of how long you live.

There are a number of ways to try to make your nest egg sustain you for the rest of your life. Some of these ways require active investment management on your part. Some require you to estimate how long you may live, and they prove inadequate if you live longer. Some programs lack flexibility. Others can fail to adequately protect you against inflation.

To further complicate matters, you may have a variety of individual investments, such as individual stocks and bonds. You may have a variety of investments where your money is pooled with others, such as mutual funds and variable annuities. You may have money in tax-qualified plans, such as 401(k)s and individual retirement accounts (IRAs).

There are solutions to the challenge of meeting your retirement income needs. Some date back centuries, while variations on the basic approach are so new or novel as to have U.S. patents or patents pending on them. The important thing is to understand the basic rationale of each approach and the related factors as to why each approach might be right or wrong for you.

Before one can truly appreciate the quantum leap such solutions provide, it's helpful to understand more conventional retirement income approaches.

SELF-MANAGEMENT

One option to provide yourself with retirement income is to create a plan where you select a retirement period you wish to cover, such as 20 or 30 years. You then determine how you want to allocate your assets across different investment classes, such as large cap stocks, international stocks, and corporate bonds. Finally, you determine the monthly income you'd like and choose a rate of inflation that you expect so your monthly income can give you constant purchasing power. Computer software exists that will then tell you the probability that your plan will work; that is, it tells you the likelihood that your plan will provide you with the desired periodic (generally monthly) income over the retirement period and that you will not run out of money.

There are shortfalls with such a program. First, it involves active management on your part, which you may or may not enjoy doing during your retirement years. For example, you might need to structure your portfolio so it generates income uniformly throughout the year rather than irregularly, such as with semiannual bond coupons. Second, you may outlive the selected retirement period. Third, the assumptions you make, such as inflation rate, may prove inadequate.

There are additional challenges you face. For example, a software program that simply assumes a constant rate of return for any asset class, such as large-cap U.S. stocks, over your retirement period can be misleading— when the equity market is down, you will need to sell a greater number of shares at depressed prices to produce your desired income. If this scenario is not contemplated by the planning model, you could exhaust your retirement income well in advance of your target retirement period, in contrast to what the model showed.

To date, many individuals have chosen this self-management approach because it offers one enormously appealing feature: *control.* Nonetheless, the do-it-yourself approach can carry many risks.

FIXED ANNUITIES

Dictionaries define *annuity* as "... a sum of money payable yearly or at other regular intervals."[1] A "fixed annuity" can provide guaranteed lifetime income for you or for you and another person,[2] typically a spouse. It is called a "fixed annuity" because the monthly[3] income benefits are totally known at the time you start your annuity. These benefits can be level, such as $4,000 per month; or they can increase by a fixed percentage each year, such as $4,000 initially, increasing by 5% per year. Either way, the amount of every future income benefit is fully known at the outset.

In essence, a fixed annuity is *longevity insurance.* It provides lifetime income *no matter how long you live.* Unlike automobile insurance, homeowner's insurance, health insurance, life insurance, and disability insurance, longevity insurance is the one form of insurance you actually *hope* to use!

Because undue longevity is a risk, not a certainty, it is an event that should be insured against rather than saved for. Exactly as one does not accumulate a side fund equal in amount to a new house in the event of fire, one does not totally self-finance the risk of undue longevity. Because the proper perspective on financing retirement income is so important, it will be repeated here: Extraordinary longevity is not a *certainty* for which one *saves;* it is a *risk* against which one *insures.*

This is the critical difference between a self-management program described earlier and a fixed annuity. In the self-management program, you can run out of money and be left destitute.[4] With a fixed annuity, you can't run out of money because you receive guaranteed lifetime income.[5]

THE GAME REVISITED

Remember the carnival game? In which bin did you predict the gray ball would land? What shape did you predict the balls would form across the bins once they had all dropped?

Figure 1.2 shows how one trial of the game looked after it was played.

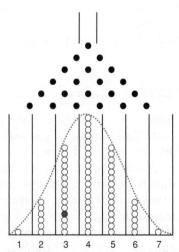

FIGURE 1.2 One Carnival Game
Outcome

Did you guess the gray ball would fall into Bin 3? If you did, you were just lucky. While any ball, including the gray ball, has a tendency to end up somewhere among the middle bins, it could have landed in any of the seven bins on any trial of the game.[6]

Did you guess the shape the balls would form across all bins after they had dropped? You can predict this in advance with a much higher degree of certainty than the behavior of any single ball.[7]

What does this game have to do with your retirement security? Plenty. While we can't predict exactly where the single gray ball will land in any trial of the game, we can predict with greater certainty the collective shape all balls will make. Similarly, while we can't predict how long one individual will survive, we can predict the survival pattern for a large group of people.

As a result, by pooling a large number of people with retirement income needs together, providing each with lifetime income is safely achievable because the pattern of survival for the group as a whole is known. In contrast, the survival of a single individual is unknown. He or she could survive only a short time, an average time, or a very long time—just as the gray ball could on any trial land in any of the seven bins.

It is this very element of predictability that allows a person with retirement income needs who participates with a group of similar people to enjoy retirement security unachievable on his or her own. This is why an annuity can provide retirement security superior to a self-management program.

While any group of people—a church group, a neighborhood association, a club—could pool its longevity risk in this way, it would still need someone to calculate the monthly benefits each person could receive and still be sure enough money would remain in the pool to pay annuity benefits to the last surviving annuitant. The group would need to manage the investments. It would need to administer the monthly benefit payments and tax reporting and to draft the contracts that spell out the terms of the arrangement for each member, and so on.

Annuity companies perform this same mortality risk pooling function. They make it easy for retirees to shed themselves of longevity risk by performing all the aforementioned functions. They make it less expensive because by operating in many geographic territories they achieve economies of scale. They make it safer because they operate under a regulatory framework that ensures adequate reserves to fund all future annuity benefits. They make the longevity risk transfer process more efficient because of the greater number of annuitants that form the annuitant pool, which results in actual experience being closer and closer to that expected with less chance for year-to-year deviations in mortality experience that can occur with a smaller group; and they can therefore work with smaller margins built into pricing to cope with adverse deviations. They make it easier since like-minded individuals wishing to free themselves from longevity risk do not have to find one another, belong to some common organization, or live in close proximity.

FIXED ANNUITIES REVISITED

Fixed annuities can cover one or more lives. They can provide level benefits or benefits that increase by a predetermined dollar amount or predetermined percentage each year.[8]

With the simplest type, a single premium is exchanged for a series of contractually guaranteed lifetime payments, which cease at death. This form provides maximum monthly income.

Some people prefer to know that they or their beneficiaries will receive at least a certain amount of income from their fixed annuity. One option is to elect a lifetime annuity that guarantees that at least a certain number of years of income benefits will be paid (typically 5 to 30 years). Another lifetime income option guarantees that at least as much will be paid out in monthly income benefits as was applied to purchase the annuity.[9] As would be expected, these forms of lifetime annuities with additional guarantees provide lower monthly income than annuities without them.

All forms of annuities offer the same present value of benefits; that is, there are no annuity options that are more valuable than any other for a given amount of premium. It is merely a matter of personal preference.

As we will quantify later, the actual return on investment experienced by any single annuitant in the pool of annuitants will depend on how long he or she survives. The important point is that at the time an annuitant applies the premium to the purchase of an annuity, he or she has purchased the contractual right to a stream of retirement income identical in present value to every other similarly situated person participating in the program. In that sense, every annuitant derives equal protective value. Each annuitant is assured of lifetime income and has transferred mortality risk that he or she was less suited to absorb on an individual basis to a program that pools mortality risk and is thereby better suited to absorb on a group basis.

Fixed annuities offer one enormously appealing feature: *guaranteed lifetime income.* Enjoying an income you can't outlive may make fixed annuities superior to a self-managed retirement program where you can run out of money.

Nonetheless, in order to achieve an income you can't outlive, with fixed annuities you (1) may not be adequately protected against *inflation;* and (2) you have to give up *access*—the premium used to purchase the fixed annuity is no longer accessible by you,[10] and you have no say over how your money is invested.

VARIABLE ANNUITIES

Like fixed annuities, variable annuities can cover one or more lives. Also like fixed annuities, many benefit choices are available, including the *inexhaustible* lifetime income option, which provides the maximum monthly income, and options that also include payments guaranteed to be made for a certain period of time or include various refund options.

What chiefly distinguishes variable annuities from fixed annuities is that with variable annuities the annuity contract owner (1) determines how the money will be invested and (2) bears the risks and rewards of those investments via changes in the amounts of the monthly retirement income checks, which fluctuate with fund performance.

In contrast, the entity underwriting a *fixed* annuity (typically an insurer) controls how those funds will be invested and bears the risks and rewards of those investments, since the dollar amount of benefit payments to the annuitant is guaranteed.

With variable annuities, the single premium is invested in one or more "subaccounts"[11] chosen by the contract owner. These may include domestic and international common stock funds, bond funds, money market funds, and specialty funds (e.g., real estate investment trusts, sector funds).

In contrast to fixed annuities with level (i.e., nonincreasing) benefits, variable annuities offer contract owners the prospect of a retirement income that protects purchasing power. For example, common stock fund returns, while not moving in lockstep with inflation, offer the possibility of returns over the course of one's retirement that may offset or more than offset the corrosive effects of inflation.

To see just how sinister that nemesis inflation can be, Figure 1.3 shows that a 60-year-old with $50,000 of annual living expenses will become a

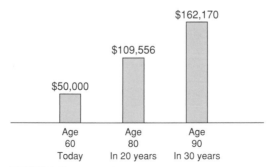

FIGURE 1.3   Annual Living Expenses at 4% Inflation Rate

90-year-old with over $162,000 of annual living expenses at a 4% infla-
tion rate.

Another way to view inflation is to contrast a fixed amount of income,
such as might be generated by a fixed annuity, with the real purchasing
power it provides in each future year. Figure 1.4 illustrates how a fixed
income of $50,000 at age 60 decreases in real purchasing power at a 4%
inflation rate. While a fixed income annuity with level benefit payments
provides a stable amount of income, it virtually assures a progressively dete-
riorating standard of living.

Monthly retirement income benefits fluctuate with the performance of
the underlying subaccount(s) chosen by the contract owner. In more modern contracts, the contract owner at any time may reallocate the percentage
each subaccount contributes toward a 100% total, where the weighted performance determines income benefits.[12]

Chapter 4 shows how the progression of monthly benefits is calculated.
In short, the contract owner picks a benchmark rate of return (often 3%,
4%, or 5%). If subaccount performance for the period equals that benchmark rate of return, the benefit payment remains level. To the extent subaccount performance for the period exceeds the benchmark return, benefits
rise. As a result, the lower the level of benchmark return chosen, the lower
the initial benefit but the steeper the rise of future benefits. Similarly, if subaccount performance for the period is less than the benchmark return, benefits decrease.

As with a fixed annuity, all forms of a variable annuity offer the same
present value of benefits; that is, there are no annuity options that are more
valuable than any other for a given amount of premium. It is merely a matter of personal preference. Given that one objective of a variable annuity is

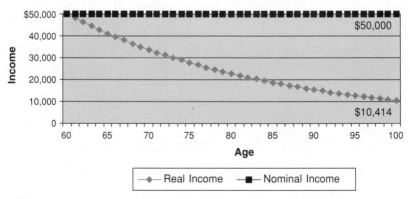

FIGURE 1.4   Fixed Annuity Income

to provide increasing benefit payments to offset or more than offset infla-tion, the variable annuity stands the better chance of achieving this objec-tive the lower the benchmark return chosen.

Note that while the level of monthly benefits fluctuates with subac-count performance, the annuitant is still guaranteed lifetime income. While the variable annuity contract owner assumes investment risk, the insurer assumes mortality risk; that is, the insurer guarantees that even if it has adverse mortality experience and annuitants survive longer than expected (e.g., due to unforeseen medical advances), this will have no effect on the benefits of any annuitants. Just as with fixed annuities, with variable annuities contract owners transfer mortality risk from themselves to the insurer. This often provides enormous peace of mind because, as was shown earlier, mortality is uncertain for any one individual who is thus ill-equipped to manage this risk, but it is much more certain for a large pool of individuals.

In the United States private sector (i.e., outside the Social Security sys-tem), there are only two ways to receive guaranteed lifetime income: through an annuity and through a defined benefit pension plan. Many peo-ple don't participate in a defined benefit pension plan.[13] For those who do, the benefits tend to be fixed in amount rather than being able to increase as with a variable annuity. Traditional defined benefit pension plan benefits are governed by a formula based on salary and years of service.

Even for those who participate in a defined benefit pension plan, the retirement income benefits may prove inadequate. For example, an individ-ual may have only a few years of service with the employer sponsoring the plan. An individual may have worked with three different employers over the course of a career—say, for 15 years each, from age 20 to age 65—each with a defined benefit plan. Unfortunately, benefits are based on final aver-age salary with *each* employer; so, at retirement, one of the individual's three pensions is based on a salary from 30 years ago and another from a salary 15 years ago. Such job mobility reduces defined benefit pension plan income to a small fraction of what would have been provided for the same number of years of service with a single employer.

Even those lucky few who did participate in defined benefit plans and have some level of guaranteed lifetime income—at a level established by a plan formula beyond their control—may still have a need for supplemental lifetime income to maintain their standard of living. This can only be achieved through an annuity.

Certain tax-qualified plans, such as IRAs and 401(k)s, have "required minimum distribution" rules that govern how money is distributed back to you. In contrast, non-tax-qualified annuities give you control over how and when you take retirement income. More important, the progression of income benefits from an annuity tends to correspond with retirement income needs in a manner superior to that of Internal Revenue Service (IRS) required minimum distribution arrangements.

For example, Figure 1.5 compares the progression of retirement income benefits of a generic immediate variable annuity (IVA) lifetime income option with those under an IRS required minimum distribution (RMD) program. The same fund is used for both cases and is assumed to return 8% each year. This is based on a $100,000 account value for a male, age 70. The IRS RMD program illustrated uses the age recalculation method.

In this example, note that while the variable annuity lifetime income option provides benefits that tend to increase over time—more in line with what one's actual retirement needs might be—the IRS RMD option produces benefits that increase initially but then decline. While a variety of investment arrangements (e.g., mutual funds, certificates of deposit, individual stocks in a self-directed IRA) can be used in conjunction with the IRS RMD option, only an annuity can provide the more desirable benefit pattern on a basis guaranteed to last a lifetime.

Note that this illustration assumes a constant 8% rate of return for both distribution options. In reality, returns will fluctuate from period to period, making for a less smooth benefit progression. Nonetheless, this illustrates the critical point: While IRS RMD options or other options from alternative investment vehicles may produce retirement income that "lasts a lifetime" in some fashion—albeit perhaps in a declining fashion, leaving critically reduced income in advanced years—only annuities can provide the more attractive (and appropriate) benefit progression of the nature shown in Figure 1.5.

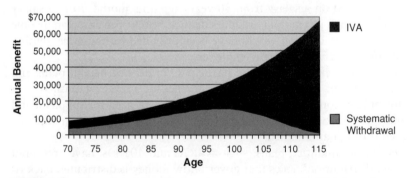

FIGURE 1.5 Immediate Variable Annuity versus Systematic Withdrawal (Based on Annuity 2000 Basic Mortality Table, 3% AIR, 8% fund performance.)

To date, variable annuities have been the superior private sector retirement income option. They provide:

- Income guaranteed to last a lifetime (for one or more individuals).
- Potential inflation hedge.
- Ability to reallocate among subaccounts, the performance of which determines monthly income benefits.
- Variety of optional guarantee and refund features (e.g., 10 years of guaranteed benefits regardless of survivorship, refund to beneficiary at death of annuitant of excess of annuity units used to purchase annuity over those paid out in monthly income benefits, etc.).

While perhaps ranking below certain colossal events in human history, such as the shift from barbarism to civilization, the invention of the variable income annuity is epochal in that it genuinely offers billions of people around the globe the opportunity to enjoy a more financially secure, more worry-free experience during the final decades of life.

Equally important, the timing of the introduction of the variable income annuity is fortuitous. The current generation of lives truly differs from predecessors. In *Future Shock*,[14] Alvin Toffler suggests dividing the last 50,000 years of man's existence into lifetimes of approximately 62 years each. There have been about 800 such lifetimes. The first 650 were spent in caves. Only during the most recent 70 did writing even exist. Only during the last 6 lifetimes did masses of mankind see a printed word. Only during the last 4 lifetimes has it been possible to measure time with any precision. Only in the last 2 lifetimes has anyone anywhere used an electric motor. Only during the present lifetime has the vast majority of all goods used in daily life been developed. Truly, the current generation differs vastly from its predecessors in terms of opportunities and technologies of which it can avail itself if it has the financial resources during the final decades of life to access these.

SHORTCOMING OF SIMPLIFIED RETIREMENT INCOME PROJECTIONS

Retirement income projections premised on a single rate of return are oversimplified, misleading, and dangerous. Let's look at an example that covers a fixed period of 10 years. The same inadequacy that appears here extends to lifetime annuities.

Suppose you have $100,000, are looking to invest it yourself in a variety of asset classes, plan to take equal annual withdrawals at the end of each year, and want to fully dissipate the account at the end of 10 years. You invest pri-

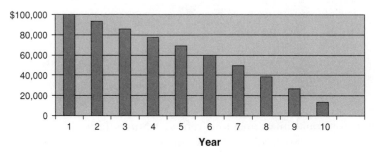

FIGURE 1.6   Beginning-of-Year Values

marily in stock and bond funds that historically have together averaged an 8% return per year. Figure 1.6 shows the beginning-of-year (BOY) values.

As a result, you assume an 8% return. An amortization table like that in Table 1.1 proves that annual end-of-year (EOY) withdrawals of $14,902.95 fully liquidate your original $100,000 over 10 years.

If your investments uniformly return the 8% you assumed each year, everything works out perfectly. Suppose, however, that while your investments return 8% *on average*[15] over the 10-year period, they happen to earn 10% less than this during the first five years and 10% more than this during the second five years. In this case, if you take the same $14,902.95 annual withdrawal, you run out of money after seven years. In fact, in year seven, you only get a year-end payment of $8,590.11. See Figure 1.7.

What went wrong? The model that assumed a static 8% rate of return was fallible. Even though 8% may have been an average rate of return over

TABLE 1.1   Amortization

Year	BOY Value	Appreciation	Payment	EOY Value
1	$100,000.00	$8,000.00	$14,902.95	$93,097.05
2	93,097.05	7,447.76	14,902.95	85,641.87
3	85,641.87	6,851.35	14,902.95	77,590.27
4	77,590.27	6,207.22	14,902.95	68,894.54
5	68,894.54	5,511.56	14,902.95	59,503.15
6	59,503.15	4,760.25	14,902.95	49,360.46
7	49,360.46	3,948.84	14,902.95	38,406.34
8	38,406.34	3,072.51	14,902.95	26,575.90
9	26,575.90	2,126.07	14,902.95	13,799.03
10	13,799.03	1,103.92	14,902.95	0.00

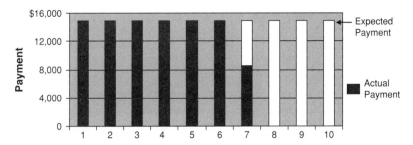

FIGURE 1.7 Actual versus Expected Payments

your 10-year holding period, your portfolio earned less than 8% during the early years when it applied to the higher account value you still had remaining and earned more than 8% during the later years when it applied to the much smaller account value remaining. As a result, your intended withdrawal program produced insufficient appreciation in the early years to keep it solvent.

Had the good investment experience occurred first—annual returns 10% more than you assumed during the first five years and annual returns 10% less than you assumed during the second five years—you would have successfully been able to receive your $14,902.95 payment every year for 10 years and still have a positive ending balance of $38,827.03.

A more credible approach is to use *stochastic*[16] simulations based on historical means, variances, and covariances of asset class returns. The distribution of results of, say, 1,000 scenarios modeled presents a more realistic picture of results you might expect. By its very nature of producing a variety of possible future scenarios predicated on historical information, it conveys that a specific dollar level of withdrawal will leave a residual balance at the end of the 10-year period in some cases, might exactly deplete the balance at the end of 10 years, and will prematurely deplete the fund in some cases.

Mathematicians speak of the "probability of ruin."[17] This is the percentage chance that your funds will be exhausted prior to the end of your target period. "Probability of ruin" and its complement, "probability of success," are based on assumptions input into the mathematical model as to mean returns per asset class, tendencies for returns to deviate from the mean, and interactions between asset classes.

While the preceding illustration covers a 10-year period, retirement horizons typically cover several decades. The chance of experiencing multiple economic downturns is greater over this longer horizon. As a result, retirement projections using static rates of return increasingly fail to reflect probability of ruin over longer periods relative to stochastic simulations.

SHORTCOMINGS OF TRADITIONAL RETIREMENT INCOME APPROACH

A traditional approach to applying retirement savings to the generation of retirement income is to use a chart similar to the one shown in Table 1.2. A new retiree selects a rate of investment return that he feels is reasonable and selects a time horizon over which he wishes the initial amount of retirement assets to sustain him. He then determines from the chart how much he can withdraw at the beginning of each month so that his initial amount will be exactly dissipated at the end of the chosen time period.

Shortcomings of this traditional approach include:

- The retiree still runs out of income if he survives beyond the time horizon he selects, unnecessarily subjecting himself to longevity risk.
- The retiree suffers less purchasing power every year, as long as the inflation rate is anywhere above zero.
- The retiree totally self-finances the risk of undue longevity, whereas because undue longevity is not a *certainty* for which one saves but rather a *risk* against which one insures, his approach to financing retirement income both unnecessarily leaves him exposed to the possibility of outliving his income and having less income in retirement than was otherwise possible.

The approach in Table 1.2 reveals a picture of retirement income planning of . . . yesteryear.

TABLE 1.2 Amount You Can Receive Monthly from a $100,000 Initial Sum

Investment Return*	Amount to Withdraw at Beginning of Each Month to Exactly Dissipate Principal and Interest at End of Time Horizon							
0%	$1,667	$ 833	$ 556	$ 417	$ 333	$ 278	$ 238	$ 208
2	1,749	918	642	504	422	368	330	301
4	1,832	1,006	734	600	522	472	437	412
6	1,917	1,097	831	704	632	587	557	537
8	2,001	1,191	934	814	749	710	686	670
10	2,087	1,287	1,040	929	872	839	820	809
12	2,173	1,386	1,150	1,049	999	972	958	950
14	2,259	1,487	1,263	1,171	1,129	1,108	1,097	1,092
Time Horizon	5 years	10 years	15 years	20 years	25 years	30 years	35 years	40 years

*Annual effective rate of interest.

RETIREMENT INCOME BASICS SUMMARY

Structuring a retirement income program requires consideration of many factors. Many individuals do not participate in any retirement program that offers them lifetime income. For those individuals who do, such a program may provide inadequate income, requiring supplementation.

Due to mortality unpredictability for any given individual, it is challenging to create and self-manage one's own retirement income program. If an individual survives longer than expected, she may exhaust her financial resources and be left destitute or dependent on family or government safety net programs. If an individual chooses to avoid this situation by spending only the interest on her retirement savings and leaving principal intact, she will have a lower income and commensurately lower standard of living than could otherwise be had.

Due to mortality predictability for a large group of individuals, a well-designed process exists that overcomes these obstacles. It guarantees lifetime income and lets the retiree/annuitant spend all of her interest and safely spend down her principal, resulting in a higher standard of living. Indeed, as we shall see in Chapter 6 on the mechanics of such a program, it is even better than this. In addition to income derived from one's own principal and interest or appreciation thereon, the annuitant population—especially the subpopulation surviving to more advanced ages—also enjoys something called "survivorship benefits."

Fixed annuities provide lifetime income with benefits fully known at time of entry into the annuity program. Retirement income benefits may be level in amount or increase (typically annually) by a constant dollar amount or constant percentage.

Variable annuities provide lifetime income with benefits that fluctuate based on performance of the investment subaccounts chosen by the annuity contract owner relative to a benchmark rate of return chosen by the annuity contract owner.

Benefit amounts for both fixed and variable annuities are *definitely determinable* at point of entry into the program. For fixed annuities, they are determinable as to exact dollar amount. For variable annuities, they are determinable as to the exact number of annuity units payable on each benefit date.

CHAPTER 2

Annuity Categorization

an • nu • ity *(&-'nü-&-tE, &-'nyü-&-tE)*, noun, plural *annuities*
  1. *a sum of money payable yearly or at other regular intervals*
  2. *the right to receive an annuity*
  3. *a contract or agreement providing for the payment of an annuity [Middle English* annuite, *from Middle French* annuité, *from Medieval Latin* annuitat-, annuitas, *from Latin* annuus, *yearly]*

  —*Merriam-Webster Online Dictionary*[1]

DEFERRED VERSUS IMMEDIATE ANNUITIES

Immediate annuities are those for which periodic benefit payments to the annuitant commence on purchase of the annuity.[2] These are sometimes known by their acronyms SPIA for a single premium immediate annuity issued on a fixed payout basis and SPIVA for a single premium immediate variable annuity issued on a variable payout basis.

> *Annuity derives from the Latin word* annuus, *meaning yearly.*

  Deferred annuities are those for which periodic benefit payments to the annuitant may commence at some future date. Deferred annuity contract owners may typically elect to take their money in a lump sum if they desire, rather than as a series of periodic benefit payments.

LIFE-CONTINGENT VERSUS
NON-LIFE-CONTINGENT ANNUITIES

Another distinction can be made among immediate annuities. *Life-contingent annuities* are those for which the payment is contingent on the survival of the annuitant. For example, a lifetime annuity for a single annuitant is an example of a life-contingent annuity.

In the United States, the regulatory framework is such that the insurance industry uniquely offers life-contingent annuities. The banking and securities industries are not permitted to underwrite mortality risk. As a result of these distinctive franchise rights, one might expect an enormous flow of retirement assets into the life insurance industry over the next several decades.

Life-contingent annuities can be subdivided into *single life annuities* and *joint life annuities*. Joint life annuities can be established so that on the death of the primary annuitant (typically the one who saved up the money to purchase the annuity) or on the death of either annuitant, the benefit amount is reduced because one person can live less expensively than two. Such annuities can either cost less than a joint life annuity that continues to provide 100% of the benefit paid when both lives were surviving or cost the same but provide a higher benefit while both annuitants are alive. The full gamut of annuity benefit options will be defined later, with commentary on which options appeal to annuitants who value certain characteristics.

Non-life-contingent annuities are those for which benefit payments are made irrespective of the continuing survival or nonsurvival of the annuitant(s). An immediate annuity that pays $40,000 per year for 20 years is an example of a non-life-contingent annuity. The $40,000 annual payment will be paid no matter what. It will be paid to the annuitant if surviving, otherwise to the beneficiary.[3]

TAX-QUALIFIED VERSUS
NON-TAX-QUALIFIED ANNUITIES

Tax-qualified (Q) annuities are generally those to which the U.S. Internal Revenue Code permits contributions to be made on a pretax basis. Because neither the principal nor any appreciation have been taxed, all monies withdrawn from the contract—whether via partial withdrawals, full surrender, or periodic annuity benefits—are fully taxable.

Non-tax-qualified (NQ) annuities are generally those to which contributions are made on an after-tax basis. Because the principal has been taxed once, it is withdrawn tax-free from the account, and only appreciation is taxable.

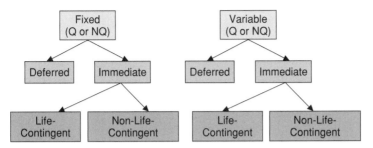

FIGURE 2.1   Categorization Summary

For both tax-qualified and non-tax-qualified deferred annuities, the U.S. Internal Revenue Code provides tax deferral on contract appreciation (the so-called "inside build-up") for all years until money is withdrawn from the contract. Taxation will be described in a later chapter.

SUMMARY

Annuity categorizations are summarized in Figure 2.1. Additional classifications include:

- Single, periodic, or flexible premium products.
- Two-tier fixed deferred annuities—a lower crediting rate applies to account value taken as a lump sum, while a higher crediting rate applies to account value used to generate an immediate annuity.
- Modified guarantee annuities—annuities that guarantee a rate of interest for a fixed term where the guarantee may be modified by a market value adjustment (positive or negative) for premature withdrawals or surrenders before the end of the term.
- Equity-indexed annuities—annuities that guarantee an interest crediting rate typically lower than traditional fixed deferred annuities but that may also credit to the account value some percentage of upside return in a generally well-known stock market index.

CHAPTER 3

Immediate Fixed Annuity Mechanics (Non-Life-Contingent)

Do you mean to come to want in your old age...?
Why don't you make over your property? Buy an annuity...,
and make your life interesting to yourself and everybody else.
        —Charles Dickens, *Martin Chuzzlewit,* 1843–1844

APPROACH

The greatest value that annuities provide resides in the distribution phase (as opposed to the accumulation phase). As explained in Chapter 1, lifetime income options provide a solution to the challenge of optimally using one's retirement savings to maximize income while assuring oneself that such income will never be exhausted. Therefore, special emphasis will be placed on immediate annuity lifetime income options.

In particular, the greatest value that immediate annuities provide resides with immediate variable annuities. Before explaining their mechanics, it is instructive to explain the mechanics behind immediate fixed annuities. They are simpler. An understanding of these will provide a helpful building block toward the understanding of immediate variable annuity mechanics.

One may accumulate retirement savings that will eventually be applied to the purchase of an immediate annuity either inside a deferred annuity contract or outside of it in, say, stocks, bonds, or mutual funds. The annuity or nonannuity accumulation vehicle may be either inside or outside the umbrella of a tax-qualified account such as an individual retirement account (IRA). There are justifications both for accumulating retirement savings funds inside the deferred annuity contract that will eventually be used to provide lifetime income (e.g., gaining familiarity and comfort with the subaccounts and investment managers) and for accumulating such funds separate and apart from an annuity contract (e.g., to take advantage of lower capital gains tax rates or to invest in low-cost index funds without the additional deferred annuity-related charges).

Deferred annuities may be used as a retirement savings accumulation vehicle. State laws generally require deferred annuity owners to receive periodic annuity income based on the greater of the "conversion rates" shown in the back of the deferred annuity contract or the conversion rates currently in effect at the time the contract owner exchanges his or her single premium (i.e., deferred annuity account value) for a series of periodic retirement income benefits. "Conversion rates" are simply the factors that "convert" a single premium into a periodic retirement income amount, based on characteristics including the annuitant's age, sex, annuity option selected, state of residence, and market (tax-qualified or non-tax-qualified). The process of converting a deferred annuity account value into an immediate annuity goes by the dreadful and very consumer-unfriendly term "annuitization."

We now begin to draw back the curtain to reveal the inner workings of an immediate fixed annuity. The reason is simple. Immediate annuity prospects are understandably reluctant to irrevocably part with a portion of their retirement savings in exchange for a guarantee of lifetime income or even income for a fixed period of time unless they can see how the program works, that its underlying logic is financially sound, and that meaningful legal and regulatory frameworks are in place to ensure that guaranteed payments are met.

FIXED ANNUITY PAYOUT[1]

Suppose you are the individual tasked with determining how much annuity benefit to pay for a given premium. In annuity companies, this work is performed by pricing actuaries.[2]

An annuitant wishes to purchase a fixed single premium immediate annuity that will pay $1,000 at the beginning of each year for 10 years. You look at yields currently available on a portfolio of fixed-income securities[3,4] that will replicate this payout pattern and use that information to arrive at a present value, which is called the net premium.

This net premium, together with interest it earns before it is paid out, is exactly sufficient to provide the annuity benefit payments, as well as administrative expenses, profit, and taxes.

For example, suppose you can purchase a 10-year fully amortizing mortgage yielding 8% that exactly replicates this payout stream. You determine that a 1% spread between the earned rate on this asset and the credited rate on the reserve—that portion of the premium that has not yet been paid out in the form of periodic benefits—is adequate to cover expenses and meet your earnings goals.

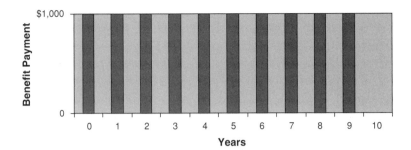

Net Premium = Present value of $1,000 payable at beginning of
year for 10 years

$$= \$1,000 \, \ddot{a}_{\overline{10}|\,.07}$$

$$= \$7,515.23$$

FIGURE 3.1 Fixed Annuity Payout

Discounting the ten $1,000 payments at 7%, you arrive at the net premium of $7,515.23. (See Figure 3.1.) (The strange symbol under the graph in Figure 3.1 is not an Egyptian hieroglyph but rather international actuarial notation, a system adopted in 1898 by the International Congress of Actuaries, which is a condensed way to say in symbols what is said in words on the top line.) You then add whatever loading is necessary to cover acquisition expenses, such as financial adviser commissions and contract issue costs, to arrive at the gross premium you will charge your customer.

In Chapter 4, we extend this exercise to immediate variable annuities. For those interested, further information related to asset-liability management for immediate fixed annuities appears in the following section.

IMMEDIATE FIXED ANNUITY
ASSET-LIABILITY MANAGEMENT

The process of pairing a collection of assets appropriate for the characteristics of the liabilities assumed goes by the name of "asset-liability management" (ALM) and is a field unto itself. For example, a *dedicated portfolio* consisting exclusively of "A" rated corporate bonds could be constructed so that the redemption values of bonds maturing in the current year plus coupon income from both bonds maturing in the current year and bonds maturing in later years exactly replicate (i.e., cash-flow match) the projected annuity payouts plus administrative expenses plus profit plus taxes.

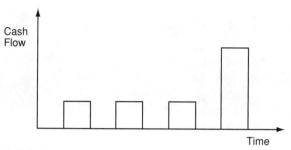

FIGURE 3.2   Single Bond

The cash flow pattern of a single bond looks like the graph in Figure 3.2. Thus the cash flow pattern of a four-bond portfolio looks like the graph in Figure 3.3.

Such a declining pattern of cash flows is consistent with the graph of projected payments for a lifetime annuity shown in Figure 4.4, since fewer annuitants survive each year to be entitled to benefit payments.

Alternatively, (1) a fully amortizing mortgage with no prepayment allowed or (2) coupons stripped from a bond might exactly match the level annuity outflows of a non-life-contingent fixed-period immediate annuity.

Note that an asset portfolio that *cash-flow matches* the projected liability stream is also by definition *duration matched* (both as to total duration and partial or key rate durations), where "duration" is used in the technical sense described in the next section—as a measure of bond price sensitivity to interest rate changes. Such "asset-liability *matching*" was an

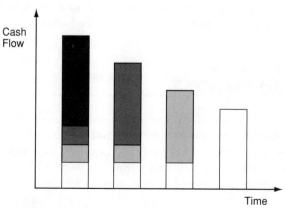

FIGURE 3.3   Four-Bond Portfolio

early version of ALM, which then broadened into "asset-liability *management*," where similar techniques reduce asset-liability mismatch risk even without exact cash-flow matching. For example, other, less restrictive, approaches can be used—match the total asset duration to the total liability duration, but only require cash-flow matching for the first 24 months of the multidecade projection.

Insurers often segment their general account assets into smaller portfolios, where a specific asset portfolio will be paired with a collection of product liabilities sharing similar characteristics (e.g., immediate fixed annuities). This allows for superior internal product-line management, asset/liability management, hedging, reinsurance, and financial reporting—especially with regard to an earnings-by-source analysis. It's still the case that all general account assets back all general account liabilities, but such general account segmentation facilitates improved internal product management.

A statement of investment policy exists for each such portfolio, describing product liabilities to be backed, allowable asset classes, minimum and maximum percentages of the portfolio that may be allotted to each asset class, allowable credit quality distribution, target duration and average life of the asset portfolio, liquidity needs, derivative policy, approving bodies, names of product (liability) and portfolio (asset) managers, and date of most recent investment policy version. Maximum dollar amounts that may be invested in securities of any one issuer across all general account asset portfolio segments are also common. Periodic surveillance for compliance with investment policy constraints is performed, with borderline or noncompliant items highlighted (encrimsoned) in reports.

Sophisticated approaches can be used to manage immediate fixed annuities, which lend themselves excellently to quality asset-liability management because the liabilities are highly predictable due to the irrevocable nature of the election to purchase an immediate annuity. Life-contingent liabilities are projectable with a high degree of precision, while non-life-contingent liabilities are projectable with total precision.

In contrast, deferred fixed annuities and certain optional features available with them lend themselves to a lower quality of asset-liability management because behavioral parameters—like timing and amount of partial withdrawals, full surrenders, and optional benefit utilization—are less predictable, being subject to policyholder and financial adviser behavior that with varying degrees of sensitivity can be influenced by the economy (e.g., interest rate movements), new products, regulatory or tax changes, and so on. Such behavioral parameters are absent with immediate fixed annuities.

Sophisticated optimization techniques that can be applied to various investment problems include linear programming (LP) and quadratic programming. The simplex algorithm, introduced by George Dantzig in the late 1940s, can be used to compute a solution to an LP problem, that is, a problem that maximizes a specific linear function while satisfying a given constraint set of inequalities. In 1952, Dr. Harry Markowitz first used quadratic programming to systematically create optimum investment portfolios, showing how to select from a universe of individual securities and how to weight those selections in constructing portfolios.

For immediate fixed annuities, one desires to construct a mathematical model to structure that combination of fixed income securities from the available universe that replicates the immediate annuity payout obligations plus expenses plus profit at least cost subject to constraints enunciated in the statement of investment policy. In practice, the large-scale computational procedures that solve this classic investment problem of fulfilling a prescribed schedule of payouts are handled by a computer program. To avoid capital gain or loss recognition and/or to minimize transaction costs, an insurer may wish to include certain existing holdings in its constraint set when modeling the optimal asset portfolio toward which it seeks to move.

Assurance of liability fulfillment (assuming acceptable default experience) is achieved with passive "buy-and-hold" investment management once an exact-match asset portfolio is established. To the extent the acceptable asset universe contains fixed-income securities that offer higher yields but do not exactly cash-flow match the liabilities, a balance must be struck between the objectives of precise matching and least-initial-cost portfolio. For example, if one could purchase a nonmatching asset portfolio at lower cost—where even at a 0% reinvestment rate applied to bonds that mature before they are needed to fund an annuity payout the prescribed liability stream could be fulfilled—then one might define the "optimal" portfolio to be other than a precise match.

As the reinvestment rate is liberalized, more—and, hence, potentially lower cost—asset portfolios fulfill the prescribed liability schedule. If the reinvestment assumption is not met in actual practice, there will be deficits and additional costs for which a special reserve fund might be initially established. If the reinvestment assumption is more than met in actual practice, such excess funds could result in net takeouts and lower the cost.

It is preferable to focus on lowest market cost for the matching portfolio rather than on highest "portfolio yield." A "portfolio yield" computed as the weighted average of the yields of the individual securities in the portfolio fails to recognize their varying maturities. As a result, some high-yield portfolios so calculated cost more than the optimal portfolio. This situation can be overcome by using the "internal rate of return" or "true cash flow yield" that equates the entirety of fixed-income portfolio cash flows with the purchase price.

"Spread management" financial reporting investigates the "spread" between earned rate on assets and credited rate on immediate fixed annuity reserves. Asset yields should be quoted on a consistent basis (e.g., annual effective yield, semiannual bond equivalent yield), and that basis should be identical to that for the reserve liabilities. Asset yields should reflect any early payment vulnerability attributable to call or prepayment options (e.g., by using the "option-adjusted yield").

While an asset portfolio well-matched to a projected immediate fixed annuity liability stream can be virtually left on mechanical autopilot, changing yield curve shapes and levels over time may offer a new optimal portfolio. If cost savings are sufficiently large and the insurer is willing to engage in some degree of active investment management, opportunities for additional takeouts may arise.

With immediate fixed annuities, the underlying mortgage investments can become nonperforming and the underlying bonds can default, wiping out the margin that insurers hope to achieve between the interest rate they earn on these investments and the interest rate they credit to the underlying immediate annuity reserve, which is the present value of annuity benefits not yet paid out. Because lifetime immediate fixed annuities often span multidecade periods, insurers need to feel comfortable that the credit quality of their fixed-income assets underlying the reserves is sufficiently high to weather the several business cycle downturns that are likely to occur over this much time.

Because of the frequently long duration of immediate fixed annuity benefits, it may be impossible to cash-flow match assets and liabilities. For example, some annuity contracts will have benefit liabilities extending 50 years into the future, while fixed-income assets supporting them typically run 30 years or less. While prudent investment portfolio managers invest long and with as much call protection as possible, if interest rates decline, then bonds may be called and mortgages prepaid, leaving the assets to be reinvested at lower interest rates unable to support the annuity obligations; that is, there exists reinvestment risk.

As a result, using a level reserve valuation interest rate forever may prove inadequate. Immediate fixed annuity pricing, therefore, generally grades down the interest assumption after a period of years to some ultimate level. National Association of Insurance Commissioners (NAIC) Actuarial Guideline IX-B[5] addresses this same issue on the reserving front by a commissioner's reserve valuation method called the graded interest rate method, which requires all benefits to be reserved using graded interest rates.

Immediate fixed annuities are liabilities of the *general account* of an insurer. As mentioned earlier, while general account assets are often segmented into asset portfolios intended to back liabilities sharing similar characteristics, it is still the case that all assets of the general account back all liabilities of the general account. If an insurer becomes financially troubled due to, say, excessive claims in its disability income and life insurance lines, that would also impact its ability to meet its obligated payments to immediate fixed annuity policyholders.

Assets inside a *separate account* of the insurer are insulated from liabilities of the insurer other than those for which the separate account assets are expressly intended to provide. This may give greater claims-paying comfort to an immediate variable annuity customer than to an immediate fixed annuity customer. In contrast, state guaranty associations cover immediate fixed annuities backed by the general account but not immediate variable annuities backed by a separate account, which may give greater comfort to an immediate fixed annuity customer.

Note that an insurer offering both life insurance and immediate annuities has a natural mortality hedge: Greater-than-expected deaths in the life insurance business that would lead to greater-than-expected claim costs could be fully or partially offset by greater-than-expected deaths in its life-contingent immediate annuity business, which results in mortality gains and the freeing up of assets previously paired with immediate annuity reserves that can now be used to pay the greater-than-expected life insurance claims.

Similarly, fewer-than-expected deaths would make the immediate annuity business less profitable and the life insurance business more profitable. This "natural hedge" or "mortality immunization" only occurs to the extent that (1) the greater-than-expected or fewer-than-expected deaths affect the life insurance and immediate annuity businesses to a comparable degree, recognizing the immediate annuity population may be older than the insured life population and therefore may not be equally impacted by whatever event(s) changed actual mortality experience from expected and (2) immediate annuity business and life insurance business share the "right" in-force balance.

DURATION

While a full exposition of the concept of *duration* is beyond the scope of this book, it will be briefly described because of its importance to immediate fixed annuity ALM.

Duration is a summary measure that provides a first-order approximation of the price sensitivity of bonds (and other fixed-income securities) to interest rate movement. Its use in attempting to immunize the ability of a fixed-income portfolio to meet a prescribed series of payment obligations such as exist with immediate fixed annuities against interest rate changes (i.e., yield curve movement) is superior to focusing on "term to maturity." Duration is one important tool for measuring and managing interest rate risk.

In 1938, Frederick Macaulay developed the concept of duration as he searched for a summary measure of the "length" of a bond that would better explain bond price behavior relative to interest rate changes than did "term to maturity." Macaulay advocated a weighted average of the time to each bond payment—both coupons and principal—with the weights being the present value of each such payment as a percent of the total present value of all payments. Macaulay used the yield to maturity of the bond to discount all payments. He thus defined duration (D) as:

$$D = \frac{\displaystyle\sum_{k=1}^{n} \frac{kC_k}{(1+i)^k} + \frac{nP_n}{(1+i)^n}}{\displaystyle\sum_{k=1}^{n} \frac{C_k}{(1+i)^k} + \frac{P_n}{(1+i)^n}} \qquad (3.1)$$

where D = duration

C_k = coupon payment at time k

P_n = principal payment at time n (maturity)

i = yield to maturity

Duration is measured in units of years. Duration decreases with the passage of time. For a zero-coupon bond (and only for a zero-coupon bond), duration equals term to maturity. For a coupon-bearing bond, duration is always shorter than term to maturity.

Bond coupon size affects duration. Duration decreases as coupon size increases, since more bond value is paid sooner.

Duration decreases as yield to maturity increases, since a higher interest rate used for discounting places relatively more value on nearer-term payments and relatively less value on longer-term payments.

In 1952, British actuary F. M. Redington attempted to determine what allocation of assets would minimize the probability of losses for the liabilities of a life insurer from changes in market interest rates. His more rigorous approach involved calculating first derivatives of the values of the assets and the liabilities with respect to interest rates. Redington coined the term *immunization* to signify that the assets were invested in a manner so as to make the value of the existing block of business immune to a change in market interest rates. Effectively, Redington stated that immunization occurs when *duration of assets equals duration of liabilities.*

In 1973, Michael Hopewell and George Kaufman calculated the differential of the price P of a bond with respect to the interest rate i to derive the relationship:

$$\frac{dP}{P} = -D\frac{di}{1+i} \qquad (3.2)$$

For relatively low interest rates, $1 + i \approx 1$, so this reduces to the approximation:

$$\frac{dP}{P} \approx -D \cdot di \qquad (3.3)$$

In terms of first differences, this becomes:

$$\frac{\Delta P}{P} \approx -D \cdot \Delta i \qquad (3.4)$$

In words, equation 3.4 says that the percentage change in the price of a bond approximately equals the bond duration times the change in interest rate. For example, a bond with a four-year duration would change (decrease) in value approximately 4% for each 1% rise in interest rate. The negative sign indicates that a rise in interest rates decreases bond value, while a fall in interest rates increases bond value. This is the well-known inverse relationship between bond price and interest rates.

Equation 3.4 shows clearly an important fact: The longer the duration, the greater the proportional price volatility for a given change in interest rate (where interest rate equals yield to maturity).

The price of a bond is the discounted value of future payments, where the discount rate for each payment depends on the time until payment. For a given market price, the *yield to maturity* of the bond is that single interest rate that equates price with the discounted value of future cash payments.

If the yield curve were perfectly flat, the yield to maturity would equal each of the discount rates. Since this is not generally the case, changes in the yield to maturity and changes in discount rates for each payment are not the same. A variety of changes in the discount rates—due to all sorts of bends and shifts in the yield curve—can produce a given change in yield to maturity. The approximate equation 3.4 is an accurate measure of the proportional change in bond price only for changes in the yield to maturity. It is *not* an accurate measure of the proportional change in bond price for any pattern of discount rates that produce the same average discount rate, since the different patterns may result in different yields to maturity.

The Macaulay duration mentioned earlier—derived by computing the first derivative of bond price with respect to yield to maturity—holds only for a process in which a flat term structure of discount rates shifts randomly by the same amount (up or down) for all payments, preserving the flatness. While Macaulay's approach was groundbreaking and tractable and facilitated greatly improved understanding of empirical bond price data, the process of interest rate changes to which it applies with accuracy is limited, since real-world interest rate changes are other than a level shift up or down across the term spectrum.

Different assumptions about the stochastic process by which discount rates for different time points—the term structure of interest rates—change lead to different derivations of a duration measure. These durations are also weighted averages of the time to each payment, like Macaulay's formula, but are more complex. If the real-world stochastic process governing interest rate changes differs from the one an investor predicts, his calculated portfolio duration may be shorter than or longer than that actually needed to create an immunizing portfolio; that is, he bears "stochastic process risk." Corporate bonds are subject to a second stochastic process risk related to defaults.

Another criticism of Macaulay duration is that the stochastic process associated with it is not free of riskless arbitrage opportunities. This notion will be explored in a later section on options.

Volatility of bond price may be viewed as price risk. Since the greater the duration of a bond, the greater the change in price for a given change in interest rate, duration may be viewed as an index of bond price risk—much as "beta" (to be defined later in the book) is an index of stock price risk.

Duration, under any formula, is a proxy for price risk only for relatively small changes in interest rates. As a first derivative measure, duration D only provides information about the relationship of bond price P to interest rates i in the local neighborhood of i_0, the point at which the tangent line to the true, nonlinear bond price curve is drawn. The absolute value of the slope of the tangent line is the duration, as shown in Figure 3.4.

The larger the change in interest rates, the more the straight line diverges from the true bond price curve. As a result, the error introduced by applying equation 3.4 increases with larger changes in interest rates.

Incorporating higher-order terms (i.e., second derivative and beyond) that capture the nonlinearity can reduce the margin of error. Nonetheless, the gist of the matter remains: Duration is a useful (albeit imperfect) measure of the price volatility of bonds and other fixed-income securities for small changes in interest rates.

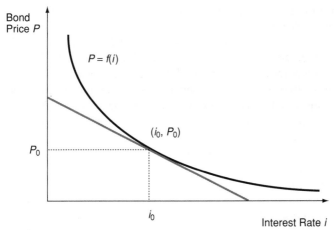

FIGURE 3.4   Duration

The duration D of a portfolio is equal to the weighted average of the durations of the individual bonds that comprise it, with weights based on the prices P of the bonds. For example, the duration of a two-bond portfolio is:

$$D = \frac{P_1 D_1 + P_2 D_2}{P_1 + P_2}$$

As a result, a portfolio of coupon-bearing bonds with a particular duration is effectively equivalent to a single zero-coupon bond of identical duration—which is its term to maturity.

If an investor believes interest rates will be lower than the market consensus as expressed in the term structure of interest rates, he may choose to purchase an asset portfolio with a duration longer than that of the immediate fixed annuity liabilities he's obligated to meet. If he's right, the gain from the price appreciation of the bonds he must sell early will exceed the lost income from reinvestment at lower yields of bonds that matured before being needed to meet annuity obligations; that is, if he sets $D_{\text{Assets}} > D_{\text{Liabilities}}$ and interest rates fall, he wins. This is no longer immunization but rather an active duration strategy where the investor seeks to achieve a higher return and assumes greater risk to do so.

Similarly, if an investor believes interest rates will be higher than the market consensus as expressed in the term structure of interest rates, he may choose to purchase an asset (A) portfolio with a duration shorter than that of the immediate fixed annuity liabilities (L) he's obligated to meet. If he's right, the income gains from reinvesting the coupons and maturing bonds before they're needed to meet annuity obligations will exceed the capital losses on unmatured bonds that are sold to meet annuity obligations; that is, if he sets $D_A < D_L$ and interest rates rise, he wins. Again, this is not immunization but an active duration strategy that should only be pursued if an investor's interest rate forecast is different from the market forecast embedded in the initial term structure of interest rates.

Risk-averse investors will adopt a posture closer to (imperfect) immunization; that is, where $D_A = D_L$. Slightly less risk-averse investors will devise a "stop loss" active duration strategy that only allows asset duration and liability duration to mismatch up to a predetermined degree.

Including futures contracts for the purchase of bonds (long position) lengthens duration of the asset portfolio. Including futures contracts for the sale of bonds (short position) shortens it. Interest rate options also may be used to sculpt asset portfolio duration. For example, opposite of what happens to bond prices, interest rate put options *increase* in value when interest rates rise and therefore have negative duration, which when added to the asset portfolio will shorten the duration.

Immediate fixed annuity writers employ cash flow testing actuaries who analyze the ability of asset portfolios associated with blocks of such business to withstand a variety of future interest rate scenarios. To the extent an insurance company has assets and liabilities that are not equally interest sensitive (i.e., $D_A \neq D_L$), it incurs interest rate risk. Surplus formulas are established to guard against interest rate risk to a specified level.[6]

The greater the difference between D_A and D_L for the insurance enterprise, the greater the potential swings in net worth (NW), since equation 3.4 for a block of fixed annuity business can be extended to the entire company. Noting that equation 3.4 can be rewritten as $\Delta P \approx -D \cdot P \cdot \Delta i$, we have:

$$
\begin{aligned}
\Delta NW &= \Delta(A - L) \\
&\approx (-D_A \cdot A \cdot \Delta i) - (-D_L \cdot L \cdot \Delta i) \\
&\approx -(D_A - D_L) \cdot A \cdot \Delta i
\end{aligned}
\qquad (3.5)
$$

since we assume the two sides of the balance sheet—assets (A) and liabilities inclusive of net worth (L)—are equal at the beginning.

Just as we saw for the active duration investor earlier, because interest rate changes affect the price of long-duration portfolios more than short-duration portfolios, a rise in interest rates will depress the price of an insurance company's assets more than its liabilities if $D_A > D_L$, reducing its net worth.

Conversely, if interest rates fall when $D_A > D_L$, the price of an insurance company's assets will elevate more than its liabilities, increasing its net worth.

Recall that the price versus interest rate relationship is nonlinear. The degree of nonlinearity is measured by a second derivative characteristic of the bond price versus interest rate relationship called *convexity*. A straight line has zero convexity. The upward curvature of the bond price function $P = f(i)$ in Figure 3.4 is said to exhibit *positive* convexity.

Total duration is a measure of bond price sensitivity to a change in interest rate; that is, total duration measures the impact of a shock to the *total* yield curve on *all* bond payments, both coupons and redemption principal. *Partial duration* or *key rate duration* measures the impact on bond price of a shock to the yield curve at *one particular point*. This allows analysis of the relative impact on bond price—or on the value of cash flows of any security or liability—of changes at various points along the yield curve, which may guide one's understanding of where risk exposure is greatest and where countermeasures are most beneficial. The sum of partial durations is total duration.

DURATION EXAMPLE

Consider a two-year corporate bond with a face value of $1,000 carrying coupons at an 8% nominal semiannual rate issued at par. Cash flows payable to the lender are:

Time (yrs)	Cash Flow
0.5	$ 40
1.0	40
1.5	40
2.0	1,040

The *yield to maturity* is the single interest rate that if earned uniformly over the entire period equates the cash flow series with the bond price (P).

$$P = 40 \cdot (1 + i)^{-0.5} + 40 \cdot (1 + i)^{-1.0} + 40 \cdot (1 + i)^{-1.5}$$
$$+ 1,040 \cdot (1 + i)^{-2.0} \tag{3.6}$$

The yield to maturity, i, that satisfies equation of value 3.6 is 8.16% expressed as an annual effective interest rate or 8.00% expressed as a nominal semiannual interest rate.

While the derivation is deferred until Chapter 6, the relationship between a nominal semiannual interest rate $i^{(2)}$ and an annual effective interest rate i is given by the formula:

$$\left(1+\frac{i^{(2)}}{2}\right)^{2}=1+i \tag{3.7}$$

The following equivalency chart shows the relationship in equation 3.7 for $i = 8.16\%$, as well as for 1% higher and 1% lower, since we wish to investigate the impact on bond price if we shock the interest rate (i.e., yield to maturity) up 1% or down 1%.

Nominal Semiannual Rate $i^{(2)}$	Annual Effective Rate i
7.04%	7.16%
8.00	8.16
8.96	9.16

Actual bond prices, if we shock the flat annual effective yield curve up 1% or down 1% from its 8.16% level, and the first differences of these bond prices are:

i	P	ΔP
7.16%	$1,017.69	
		$17.69
8.16	1,000.00	
		17.22
9.16	982.78	

Looking at first differences, the percentage change in bond price per 1% change in yield to maturity is 1.769% as rates fall and 1.722% as rates rise.

We now calculate the duration D of this bond by recalling the earlier approximation equation 3.3 and rewriting it in an equivalent form:

$$\frac{dP}{di}\approx-D\cdot P \tag{3.8}$$

and calculating

$$\frac{dP}{di}=\left[-0.5\cdot40\cdot(1+i)^{-1.5}\right]+\left[-1.0\cdot40\cdot(1+i)^{-2.0}\right]$$
$$+\left[-1.5\cdot40\cdot(1+i)^{-2.5}\right]+\left[-2.0\cdot1{,}040\cdot(1+i)^{-3.0}\right]$$

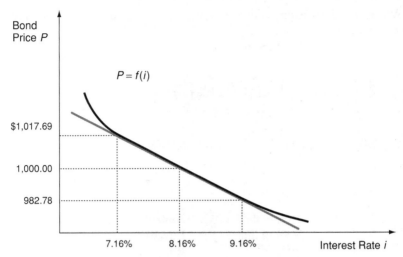

FIGURE 3.5   Duration and Convexity of Two-Year Bond

At the annual effective interest rate point $i = 8.16\%$, we have $dP/di =$ $-1,745.14$. Since $P = \$1,000$, this approximate equality gives $D \approx 1.745$; that is, the proportional change in bond price per 1% absolute change in yield level is about 1.745%.

This duration estimate aligns reasonably well with *actual* bond price changes in the preceding list, where a 1% fall raises the bond price 1.769% and a 1% rise lowers the bond price 1.722%.

Figure 3.5 shows that the slope of the line tangent to the curve that plots bond price against interest rate at the 8.16% yield to maturity point is such as to produce a 1.745% change in bond price for a 1% change in interest rate.

Note that a 1% interest rate reduction leads to a bigger percentage change in bond price than 1.745%, meaning the bond price curve is *increasing* in steepness as interest rates fall. Note also that a 1% interest rate increase leads to a smaller percentage change in bond price than 1.745%, meaning the bond curve is *decreasing* in steepness as interest rates rise.

A security has positive convexity if a 1% rate reduction leads to a price increase larger than the corresponding decrease if the rate rises 1%. This is the case with this two-year bond. Thus, this bond has positive convexity.

A final note: In the preceding example, we actually used *modified duration* from equation 3.3, defined as

$$D_{\text{modified}} = \frac{-1}{P} \cdot \frac{dP}{di}$$

$$= \frac{-1}{1,000} \cdot -1,745.14$$

$$= 1.745$$

The *Macaulay duration* of the two-year bond example, D_{Macaulay}, as defined by equation 3.1, is 1.8875 years. The Macaulay duration differs from the modified duration by the factor $(1 + i)$, where i is the yield to maturity:

$$D_{\text{Macaulay}} = D_{\text{modified}} \cdot (1 + i)$$

$$= 1.74514 \cdot (1 + 0.0816)$$

$$= 1.8875$$

CHAPTER 4

Immediate Variable Annuity Mechanics (Non-Life-Contingent)

I do not know whether, upon the whole, it would not be more advisable to do something for their mother while she lives, rather than for them—something of the annuity kind I mean. My sisters would feel the good effects of it as well as herself. A hundred a year would make them all perfectly comfortable.

—Jane Austen, *Sense and Sensibility*, 1811

APPROACH

Suppose the next customer wants an annuity that provides a first annual payment of $1,000 but at all times would like the portion of the premium not yet paid out in benefits to be invested in the stock market. The customer realizes that the next nine payments after the first cannot be guaranteed to be $1,000 each, as with a fixed annuity, but is willing to assume this risk in hopes of receiving an income stream superior to what could be obtained through an immediate fixed annuity.

As in Chapter 3, you are the pricing actuary for the insurer. You now have a very different task. With the fixed annuity, you knew the return on the assets was 8% per year. With this variable annuity, you don't know what the return on the assets now invested in common stocks will be, and it's highly unlikely that the return will be uniform each year throughout the annuity payout period.

As a result, you decide to *assume* an interest assumption, such as 5%. You recognize up front that your assumption will not always (if ever!) be

---

This chapter is extracted in part from the VARDS Executive Series report, "The Mechanics of Variable Annuitization," by Jeffrey K. Dellinger © 1994. Reprinted with the permission of Morningstar, Inc.

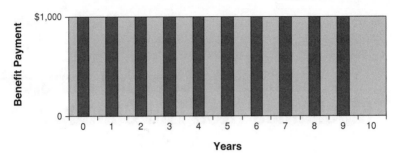

Net Premium = Present value of $1,000 payable at beginning of
                   year for 10 years

$\qquad$ = $1,000\ \ddot{a}_{\overline{10}|\,.05}$ (assume variable fund returns 5%/year)

$\qquad$ = $8,107.82

FIGURE 4.1   Variable Annuity Payout

correct. Thus, you also need to incorporate a compensating mechanism
whenever actual investment experience differs from what you assumed.

Discounting the stream of annuity benefit payments shown in Figure
4.1 at 5% produces a net premium of $8,107.82. Again, you may add in
whatever loading is necessary to cover acquisition expenses and profit to
arrive at the gross premium. This same process is valid whether we are discussing a true single premium immediate variable annuity (SPIVA) purchased with "fresh, new, outside" money or a variable annuitization of an
existing deferred annuity contract.

Suppose the portfolio of common stocks purchased with this premium
actually provided a level 5% return each year. Then we could afford to pay
out exactly $1,000 on each annuity payment date because that was exactly
what we assumed the return would be; that is, if the net premium were used
to create a common stock fund that returned 5% annually for the term of the
annuity payout and we paid the annuitant $1,000 on each annuity payment
date, the fund would be exactly depleted with the final $1,000 payment.

If, however, the fund performed better than 5% per year, we could pass
this better-than-anticipated return through to the annuitant in the form of
higher annuity benefit payments. Conversely, if the fund performed worse
than 5% per year, we would likewise need to pass this investment experience through to the annuitant in the form of lower annuity benefit payments. This is apparent in the graph in Figure 4.2.

Since 5% was assumed in this example to be the rate at which the fund
would perform, it is known as the "assumed investment rate," or AIR. The
AIR is the rate of return that if earned uniformly throughout the payout

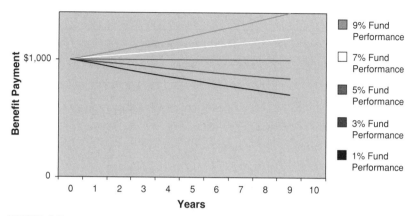

FIGURE 4.2   Benefit Payment at Various Fund Performance Levels

period would produce a level series of annuity benefit payments. While AIR is the terminology the insurance industry has used for decades, one can equally well replace this with more consumer-friendly terms, such as "benchmark rate," "hurdle rate," or "target return."

Whatever it is called, it merely represents the rate of return used in determining the initial benefit payment and also the measuring stick against which future subaccount experience will be compared to determine if benefit payments are to rise, remain level, or fall. These adjustments ensure the solvency of the program, whereby the underlying fund is exactly exhausted upon payment of the final annuity benefit. The impact on benefit payments of how the subaccount actually performs relative to what was assumed appears below:

> *Subaccount performance > AIR* → *Benefit payments increase*
> *Subaccount performance = AIR* → *Benefit payments level*
> *Subaccount performance < AIR* → *Benefit payments decrease*

Table 4.1 simply shows in tabular form the information contained in Figure 4.2.

To ensure that prospective IVA contract owners receive an unbiased picture of how annuity benefit payments fluctuate, Section 50.8 of New York State Insurance Department Regulation 47 stipulates that any illustration of benefit payments based on fund performance above the AIR must be accompanied by an illustration of benefit payments based on fund performance equidistant below the AIR.

TABLE 4.1 5% AIR, $1,000 First Payment

	Fund Performance				
Year	1%	3%	5%	7%	9%
0	$1,000.00	$1,000.00	$1,000.00	$1,000.00	$1,000.00
1	961.90	980.95	1,000.00	1,019.05	1,038.10
2	925.26	962.27	1,000.00	1,038.46	1,077.64
3	890.01	943.94	1,000.00	1,058.24	1,118.69
4	856.11	925.96	1,000.00	1,078.40	1,161.31
5	823.49	908.32	1,000.00	1,098.94	1,205.55
6	792.12	891.02	1,000.00	1,119.87	1,251.48
7	761.95	874.05	1,000.00	1,141.20	1,299.15
8	732.92	857.40	1,000.00	1,162.94	1,348.64
9	705.00	841.07	1,000.00	1,185.09	1,400.02

To ensure that illustrated future annuity benefit payments don't appear overly rosy, the same New York regulation says hypothetical rates of return cannot exceed 8% without the approval of the Superintendent of Insurance.

Because of a desire to ensure that illustrations are not misleading, the Securities and Exchange Commission (SEC) and the National Association of Securities Dealers (NASD) have rules that in most cases preclude any projections of future performance for registered securities products, including variable annuities. NASD Conduct Rule 2210 (Communications with the Public) (d)(1)(D) reads:

> *Communications with the public may not predict or project performance, imply that past performance will recur or make any exaggerated or unwarranted claim, opinion or forecast. A hypothetical illustration of mathematical principles is permitted, provided that it does not predict or project the performance of an investment or investment strategy.*[1]

New York Regulation 47 similarly provides that illustrations of benefits payable under a separate account annuity contract shall not include projections of past investment experience into the future or attempted predictions of future experience.

Because the purchase of a variable income annuity typically constitutes an irrevocable election, because a potentially significant portion of a retiree's assets may be involved, and because a full understanding of and reasonable expectations for the series of retirement income benefits that might evolve can be best served by numerical examples showing the annuity benefit streams that would emerge under different future fund performance levels, rules that formerly precluded any such illustrations have been liberalized. This seemed an imperative step for the growth of the product. Variable income annuity prospectuses or their Statement of Additional Information (SAI) counterparts, for example, now contain such illustrations.

Section 50.8 of New York Insurance Department Regulation 47, for example, permits the use of hypothetical rates of return, clearly designated as such, to illustrate possible levels of variable annuity payments, provided use of such hypothetical rates does not conflict with applicable SEC requirements.

ANNUITY UNITS

Mechanically, an insurer handles the transaction described in Figure 4.1 as follows. It determines the present value at 5% of a payment of 1 at the beginning of the year (BOY) for 10 years. (It can be 1 dollar, 1 unit, etc.) Since every dollar behaves like every other dollar, we can work with a payment of 1 and know that if we want the present value for a payment of 100, for example, we just need to multiply the result by 100.

This present value (PV) is 8.1078—if we have a net premium of $8.1078, we can pay $1 initially and on each future payment date if the fund performs at the AIR of 5%. If we have twice as much net premium, about $16.22, we can pay $2 initially and on each future payment date. If we have $1,000 of net premium, we can pay $123.34.

AIR	PV of 1 @ BOY for 10 years	Initial Payout Rate per $1,000 of Net Premium
5%	8.1078	$\dfrac{1,000}{8.1078} = \$123.34$

This is how variable annuity benefits are typically quoted: the initial periodic benefit per $1,000 of premium. Only the initial benefit payment is known with certainty. The rest all fluctuate with the performance of the underlying fund(s) chosen. Premium is usually after state premium tax, if any. Some companies factor premium tax implicitly into their loadings rather than charging it explicitly against the premium before application of the initial payout rate per $1,000.

Since this annuitant has 8.1078 thousands of net premium and the initial payout rate is $123.34 per thousand, the initial benefit payment is $1,000.

Annuitant has $8,107.82 of net premium.

First payment = Number of 1000s of net premium × Payout rate per $1,000

$$= 8.1078 \times \$123.34$$

$$= \$1,000.00$$

If the first payment is $1,000 and the annuity unit value is $2.00 on the date the annuity commences, there will be $1,000/$2.00, or 500, *annuity units* paid on each benefit payment date.

$$\text{First payment} = \$1,000.00$$

$$\text{Annuity unit value} = \$2.00$$

$$\text{Number of annuity units per payment} = \frac{\$1,000.00}{\$2.00} = 500 \text{ units}$$

The number of annuity units paid on each annuity benefit payment date remains constant. The annuity unit value changes as investment subaccount performance fluctuates. It is this change in annuity unit value that causes annuity benefit payments to fluctuate.

Accumulation unit values measure the performance of the subaccount during the accumulation phase of a deferred annuity contract. These represent realized and unrealized capital gains, dividend and interest income, mortality and expense risk charges, asset management fees, and so on.

Annuity unit values are used during the payout phase of the annuity contract. These reflect the same components as the accumulation unit values, but they back out the AIR. This is because the annuitant was already given credit for the AIR in the construction of the initial payout rate per $1,000.

To see this, suppose that a 0% interest assumption had been used to discount the annuity benefit payments. This would have resulted in a higher present value and thus a lower payout rate per $1,000. By having used a 5% interest assumption, a lower present value resulted, which produced a higher payout rate per $1,000. Thus, the annuitant has already received credit for the 5% fund performance, and this must be backed out of the annuity unit value to avoid double counting it.

Equation 4.1, known as a *recursion formula,* is used to determine the next annuity unit value from the last one. The annuity unit value increases by the actual fund performance and then the AIR is backed out.

$$\text{Annuity unit value}_{t+1} = \text{Annuity unit value}_{t} \times \frac{1 + \text{Subaccount performance}}{1 + \text{AIR}} \qquad (4.1)$$

For example, if the subaccount performed at 10% during year 1, the annuity unit value would increase from $2.00 to $2.00 × 1.10/1.05, or $2.0952. The first annuity benefit payment is 500 units at $2.00 per unit, for a payment of $1,000. The second annuity benefit payment is 500 units at $2.0952 per unit, for a payment of $1,047.60. In this example, the variable annuity payout did its job: providing an increasing benefit payment to help the annuitant offset the ravages of inflation.

Example: Subaccount performs at 10% during year 1.

$$\text{Annuity unit value}_1 = \$2.00 \times \frac{1.10}{1.05}$$
$$= \$2.0952$$

$$\text{Annuity payment 1} = 500 \text{ units} \times \$2.00/\text{unit}$$
$$= \$1,000.00$$

$$\text{Annuity payment 2} = 500 \text{ units} \times \$2.0952/\text{unit}$$
$$= \$1,047.60$$

This example assumes the premium is allocated to one investment subaccount, the performance of which governs annuity benefit payments. If the premium is allocated to more than one subaccount, the same process holds. The premium is simply first divided among subaccounts in whatever portions the annuity owner chooses.

While this example assumed annual retirement income benefits, the same process holds for more frequent annuity benefit payments. Monthly benefits are the most popular. For example, if there are 30 days between payments, the algorithm used to determine the next annuity unit value from the last one is:

$$\text{Annuity unit value}_{t+1} = \text{Annuity unit value}_t$$
$$\times \frac{1 + \text{Subaccount performance}}{(1 + \text{AIR})^{30/365}} \quad (4.2)$$

Example: Subaccount performs at 1% during first month.

$$\text{Annuity unit value}_1 = \$2.00 \times \frac{1.01}{1.05^{30/365}}$$
$$= \$2.0119$$

$$\text{Annuity payment 1} = 500 \text{ units} \times \$2.00/\text{unit}$$
$$= \$1,000.00$$

$$\text{Annuity payment 2} = 500 \text{ units} \times \$2.0119/\text{unit}$$
$$= \$1,005.95$$

Annuity unit values are typically calculated once per business day after the close of stock exchanges. Those annuity unit values will determine annuity benefit payments to some annuitants, those whose benefits are based on that "valuation date" each payment period. (In the future, if subaccounts are valued several times per day or, ultimately, continuously—because stock exchanges at some future point may be open 24 hours a day—then insurance companies will likely pick one time of day to determine annuity unit values.)

Thus, in general, the recursion formula that describes the progression of annuity unit values is:

$$\text{Annuity unit value}_{t+1} = \text{Annuity unit value}_t$$
$$\times \frac{1 + \text{Subaccount performance}}{(1 + \text{AIR})^{n/365}} \qquad (4.3)$$

where n = number of days between valuation periods

For example, $n = 1$ for two successive business days and $n = 3$ over a typical weekend (i.e., with no Friday or Monday holiday). The denominator in the exponent will be 366 in leap years.

"Subaccount performance" in equation 4.3 reflects (1) dividends, interest, realized and unrealized capital gains and losses, investment expenses, and taxes associated with the underlying investment fund as a percentage of fund assets and (2) daily asset charges (e.g., mortality and expense risk charge) at the variable annuity subaccount level. Formulaically:

$$\text{Subaccount performance}_t = \frac{\text{II}_t + \text{CAP}_t - \text{EXP}_t}{\text{R}_{t-1}} - \text{Daily asset charges}$$

where   II = investment income = dividends + interest accrued or paid
CAP = realized and unrealized capital gains (positive) and losses (negative)
EXP = investment expenses and taxes, if any, on underlying investment fund
R = reserve for annuities in payout phase + account value for annuities in accumulation phase

Note that the reserve in the denominator is that from the close of the prior day (and includes all prior-day transactions to the related subaccount, such as money entering through new premiums and transfers into the subaccount and money exiting through partial withdrawals, full surrenders, and transfers out of the subaccount); that is, subaccount performance is reflective of the change in value that day as a percentage of assets that began the day.

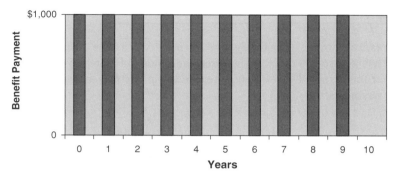

FIGURE 4.3   Fixed Annuity Payout

The same process holds for life-contingent annuity benefit options. Only the projected payout stream used as the starting point differs. For example, while Figure 4.3 shows the 10-year fixed period benefit we've been discussing, Figure 4.4 shows the projected benefit stream for a life-only annuity to a female, age 65; that is, if an insurer sold life annuities paying $1 per annum to a cohort of 1,000 females, age 65, this is the series of annuity benefits it would expect to make if actual subaccount performance equaled the AIR. Equivalently, Figure 4.4 represents the projected benefit payments to one female, age 65, of $1,000 per annum if living. Projected benefit payments of $1 per annum are discounted at the AIR to arrive at the present value, and this amount is divided into $1,000 to arrive at the initial payout rate per $1,000 for a single life annuity.

As with the 10-year fixed period annuity, the initial benefit amount for the life annuity is divided by the annuity unit value at that time. The result is the number of annuity units payable on that first payment date and all future payment dates.

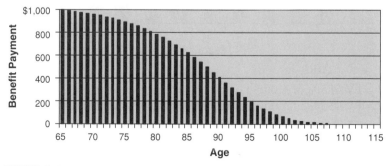

FIGURE 4.4   Life Annuity Option (female age 65, life only)

VARYING THE AIR

In the example we've been following, we used 5% as the AIR. Suppose instead that we use 3% or 7%. The three equations in Figure 4.5 show that the higher the assumed investment rate, the lower the present value of the annuity payments.

AIR	PV of 1 @ BOY for 10 Years	Initial Payout Rate per $1,000 of Net Premium
3%	8.78611	$\dfrac{\$1,000}{8.78611} = \$113.82$
5%	8.10782	$\dfrac{\$1,000}{8.10782} = \$123.34$
7%	7.51523	$\dfrac{\$1,000}{7.51523} = \$133.06$

The lower the present value of the annuity payments, the higher is the resulting value when this is divided into $1,000. The end result is that the higher the AIR, the higher the initial payout rate per $1,000.

To see this graphically, the same premium needed to fund an initial benefit payment of $1,000 when a 5% AIR is assumed will produce $923 using a 3% AIR or $1,079 using a 7% AIR.

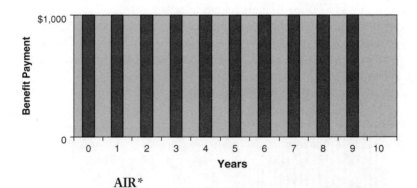

AIR*

8,786.11 = PV @ 3% of 1,000 payable at beginning of year for 10 years
8,107.82 = PV @ 5% of 1,000 payable at beginning of year for 10 years
7,515.23 = PV @ 7% of 1,000 payable at beginning of year for 10 years

*Assumed investment rate.

FIGURE 4.5 Variable Annuity Payout

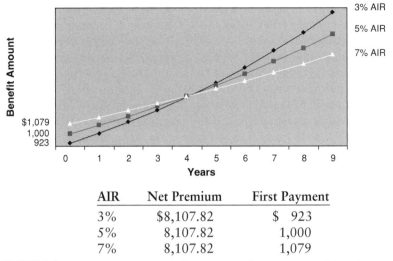

AIR	Net Premium	First Payment
3%	$8,107.82	$ 923
5%	8,107.82	1,000
7%	8,107.82	1,079

FIGURE 4.6   Annuity Payments (subaccount performance = 12%/year)

When using a 7% AIR, however, the common stock subaccount (or other subaccount) must now perform at 7% rather than 5% just to keep annuity benefit payments level; that is, with a 7% actual return on the common stock subaccount, an annuity with a 7% AIR will have benefit payments that remain level, while an annuity with a 5% AIR will have benefit payments that increase.

Figure 4.6 compares annuity benefit payments at three different AIRs when actual subaccount performance is 12% per year. The lower the AIR, the lower the initial benefit payment, but the steeper the increase in the curve of future annuity benefit payments.

Insurers may offer only one AIR in a variable annuity contract, or they may offer annuitants a choice of AIRs. For customers who must choose from a selection of AIRs, there is no "right" choice. All benefit payment streams are actuarially equivalent. Some begin high and increase slightly, while others begin low and increase rapidly; but all have an identical value on a discounted basis (provided the discounting is done at a rate equal to the subaccount performance).

If an insurer offers multiple AIRs within one variable annuity contract, then:

■ It must educate prospective annuitants on the ramifications of their choice. Customers may elect the highest AIR either because they don't understand the process and blindly think the choice with the highest initial payout is the best or because they do understand the process and simply want more money sooner with a less rapid increase later.

■ It must calculate and administer multiple sets of annuity unit values, one per subaccount for each AIR.

IVA contract owners elect an AIR only once, at contract inception. The AIR chosen continues in effect thereafter. (While some recent IVA offerings permit a midstream change in AIR, these remain in the minority.)

Remember that the goal of an immediate variable annuity is to provide an increasing stream of retirement income payments to the annuitant. The higher the AIR, the harder it is to achieve this goal because the "hurdle rate" at which the subaccount must perform is higher. As a result, the National Association of Insurance Commissioners' (NAIC) Model Variable Annuity Regulation stipulates that the AIR "shall not exceed 5% except with the approval of the Commissioner."[2]

Section 50.6(a)(1) of New York State Insurance Department Regulation 47 states that the smallest annual rate of investment return that would have to be earned on separate account assets so that the dollar amount of variable annuity payments would not decrease is 6.5%. This is *before* product fees and charges (e.g., mortality and expense risk charge) are reflected. For example, 1.5% in charges would equate with a 5% AIR.

Whether one AIR or multiple AIRs are offered, the insurer needs some time between when it calculates the annuity unit value to determine the benefit payment amount for that period and when it can actually get the amount to the annuitant either in the form of a hard-coded check[3] or through electronic deposit into the customer's bank account.

The *valuation date* is the date on which funds are valued and annuity unit values are calculated. The *payment date* is the date the dollar benefit reaches the annuitant. For example, if the prospectus lists the valuation date as 14 days prior to the payment date, then an annuitant desiring receipt of benefit payments on the fifteenth of the month will have those payments based on annuity unit values as of the first of the month.

Table 4.2 simply shows the same information as appears in Figure 4.6. Note the crossover point between year four and year five. In year four, annuity benefit payment amounts in descending order are the 7% AIR annuity, the 5% AIR annuity, and the 3% AIR annuity. In year five, the order is reversed with the 3% AIR annuity now providing the highest benefits followed by the 5% AIR annuity and lastly the 7% AIR annuity.

The performance of the underlying fund(s) chosen by the annuitant and the annuitant's longevity—not the AIR—ultimately determine the degree of financial benefit to the annuitant.

TABLE 4.2 Annual Benefit Payments
(actual fund performance = 12%/year)

Year	AIR 3%	5%	7%
0	$ 922.80	$1,000.00	$1,078.85
1	1,003.43	1,066.67	1,129.27
2	1,091.11	1,137.78	1,182.03
3	1,186.45	1,213.63	1,237.27
4	1,290.12	1,294.54	1,295.09
5	1,402.85	1,380.84	1,355.60
6	1,525.43	1,472.90	1,418.95
7	1,658.72	1,571.09	1,485.26
8	1,803.66	1,675.83	1,554.66
9	1,961.26	1,787.55	1,627.31

VOLATILITY OF VARIABLE ANNUITY INCOME

Illustrations to this point assume subaccount performance at one uniform level year after year. This lends clarity to understanding how annuity benefits change when subaccount performance is higher than, equal to, or lower than the AIR.

Lest the reader be left with the impression that variable annuity income always follows some smooth course like those in Figure 4.6, Figure 4.7 shows the series of benefit payments based on a 100% allocation to a Standard & Poor's (S&P) 500 index[4] subaccount. The first monthly annuity

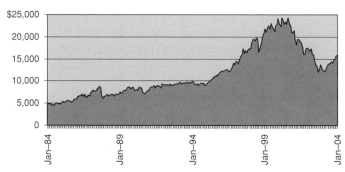

FIGURE 4.7 Variable Income Annuity Monthly Benefits (S&P 500; 4% AIR)

payment is $5,000 and the valuation date is the first business day of January 1984. Annuity benefits thereafter are valued on the first business day of each month. Values are for a hypothetical immediate variable annuity product using a 4% AIR and no expenses for either the IVA product or the underlying S&P 500 fund.

The above benefits could be associated with any form of annuity option—life-contingent or non-life-contingent—that pays an initial $5,000 monthly benefit and runs for at least the period shown.

IMMEDIATE VARIABLE ANNUITY VERSUS SYSTEMATIC WITHDRAWALS

Immediate Variable Annuity

Advantages	Disadvantages
■ Income guaranteed to last a lifetime.	■ No "account value" to draw on for financial emergencies.
■ Variety of payout options.	■ Irrevocable election.
■ Immediate annuity tax treatment.	
■ Compliance with IRS minimum distribution rules.	

With an *immediate variable annuity*, the premium is surrendered to the insurance company in exchange for a promise by the insurer to pay regular, periodic income guaranteed to last a lifetime (assuming the payout option chosen is life-contingent), although the level of that income is not guaranteed. With a *systematic withdrawal program* from a deferred annuity, the owner maintains an active deferred annuity contract. The systematic withdrawal service is simply a convenient means for making withdrawals from this active account. The contract owner can merely submit a form once to commence a series of withdrawals rather than being required to submit a form every time a withdrawal is desired. A systematic withdrawal program can similarly be established where the underlying savings instrument is a retail mutual fund.

An immediate variable annuity provides the more favorable immediate annuity tax treatment to annuities in the non-tax-qualified market, those having a positive cost basis. A variety of annuity payout options is available and can be set up to comply with IRS minimum distribution rules so no further concerns or calculations are involved on the part of the annuitant after IVA contract inception.

As the decision to purchase an immediate variable annuity is irrevocable (at least after the "free look" period), the decisions whether to purchase an IVA, how much premium to apply, and what annuity option should be elected are important. The irrevocable nature of the annuity may be perceived negatively, and, if so, this must be overcome in the sales process. The same is true due to the fact that there is no "account value" on which to draw in times of financial emergencies.

Allowing such access could result in mortality anti-selection. Annuitants who find they have a life-threatening illness would want to withdraw as much money as possible from the fund, leaving it less able to provide for those annuitants who survive to very advanced ages. This would defeat one of the main purposes of immediate annuities, which is "insurance against living too long" and outliving one's income. Non-life-contingent fixed-period immediate variable annuities could theoretically be commutable, although, depending on the commutation formula, the insurer might give up the asset charges it could have earned had the annuity persisted. One insurer offers more attractive annuity payout rates if a customer waives the commutability privilege.

Retirement savings might be applied to an immediate variable annuity to cover known, ongoing expenses that occur during retirement years. Retirement savings earmarked for large, ad hoc expenses (home purchases, car purchases, vacations, and the like) might best be kept outside of an immediate variable annuity.

Systematic Withdrawal

Advantages	Disadvantages
■ Account value to draw on as needed.	■ May deplete or outlive income.
■ Variety of distribution options.	■ Withdrawals receive "interest out first" tax treatment.
■ Compliance with IRS minimum distribution rules.	
■ Revocable election.	

Systematic withdrawal leaves an active account value that can be drawn on as needed, offers a variety of distribution options that can ensure compliance with IRS required minimum distribution rules, and is a revocable election. The chief disadvantage is that the owner may deplete the account and outlive the income payments provided by systematic withdrawals.

Depending on the situation, the systematic withdrawal may be taxed "interest out first" like any other withdrawal from a recent deferred annuity contract rather than receiving the more favorable immediate annuity tax treatment. Systematic withdrawals might be subject to the 10% penalty tax on premature distributions if not properly established.

Figure 4.8 compares immediate variable annuity income benefits to systematic withdrawal income benefits. The same fund is used for both cases and is assumed to return 8% each year. The IVA is based on a $100,000 premium and a straight life annuity for a male age 70, using Annuity 2000 Basic Table mortality and a 3% AIR. Systematic withdrawals are similarly based on a $100,000 starting value and are determined for a tax-qualified defined contribution plan (e.g., IRA) participant age 70 using IRS minimum distribution requirements effective as of 2004. Both approaches assume annual payments made at the beginning of the year.

In this example, the IVA provides higher income in all years. Even though both programs use the same fund returning 8% every year, the IRS minimum distributions provide decreasing amounts of income at advanced ages, an undesirable result.

Note how an immediate variable annuity may provide a series of benefits that increase with advancing age, with no possibility of being terminated due to exhaustion of an individual's personal account.

In contrast, note how alternative savings vehicles may provide a decreasing series of benefits at advanced ages under certain IRS required minimum distribution rules—even though investment performance is identical to that in the immediate variable annuity.

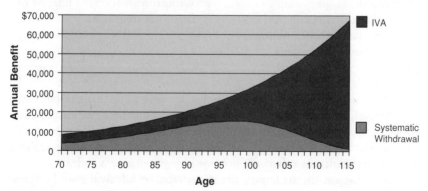

FIGURE 4.8   Immediate Variable Annuity Benefit and Pattern Are Superior to Systematic Withdrawal

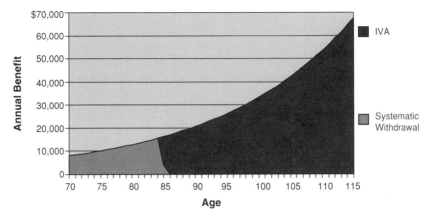

FIGURE 4.9 Immediate Variable Annuity Income Inexhaustibility Is Superior to Systematic Withdrawal

The systematic withdrawal program provides a residual account balance for the beneficiary at the death of the owner, whereas the IVA does not.

Figure 4.9 compares annual income from the same straight life annuity for a male age 70 purchased by a $100,000 premium with annual income of identical amounts from a systematic withdrawal program. Using systematic withdrawal, a reduced final payment is made at age 85 and the account is fully depleted. No income at ages 86 and beyond exists.

REVERSE DOLLAR COST AVERAGING

Immediate variable annuities offer a desirable characteristic in that by definition they pay a benefit based on a specific number of annuity units every period. If the annuity unit value goes down, the payment goes down. If it goes up, the payment goes up.

In contrast, withdrawing a fixed dollar amount each period from an alternative investment vehicle, such as a mutual fund or a deferred variable annuity, results in an undesirable characteristic that might be called "reverse dollar cost averaging." In traditional dollar cost averaging while one is accumulating savings, one invests the same dollar amount each period—automatically buying more shares when the price is low and fewer shares when the price is high.

If one withdraws the same dollar amount each period during the liquidation phase, he or she sells more shares when the price is low and sells fewer shares when the price is high—exactly the opposite of what one would like to do. Again, this phenomenon is avoided automatically with immediate variable annuities.

This phenomenon often *can* be avoided with alternative liquidation vehicles. To the extent ownership interests can be expressed in units rather than dollars—such as in mutual fund shares or individual common stock shares—instructions to systematically liquidate the holdings via regular, periodic sales of the same number of shares allows avoidance of the undesirable reverse dollar cost averaging characteristic.

OWNER CONTROL AFTER IVA PURCHASE

"Loss of control" historically was terminology used when IVA prospects described important factors in their decision to purchase or not purchase an IVA. "Loss of access to a lump sum withdrawal" is a more accurate descriptor, since the owner still exercises several elements of control:

- The right to reallocate percentages among subaccounts, the performance of which determines annuity benefit payments—via either automatic rebalancing or ad hoc reallocations—and to do so on a tax-free basis.
- The right to change a beneficiary, unless the owner previously designated a beneficiary as irrevocable.
- The right to vote on proxy matters associated with the investment funds underlying the variable annuity subaccounts.

The IVA contract owner controls the initial allocation and any subsequent reallocations among the subaccounts, the performance of which determines annuity benefit payments; that is, while purchase of an immediate variable annuity is an irrevocable election, the election of which subaccount or subaccounts will determine the benefit payments is not. For example, an owner may initially elect a variable payout based 50% on the performance of a growth fund and 50% on the performance of a bond fund. The owner may later switch to an allocation where the payments are based 60% on a growth and income fund, 30% on a bond fund, and 10% on an international equity fund.

A reallocation will trigger a communication by the insurer to the owner. This notification will indicate the new number of annuity units per subaccount on which future payments will be based. The insurer reallocates assets in an amount equal to the reserve among the subaccounts in proportion to the new percentages on which future annuity payments will be based. Both to constrain administrative expenses and to minimize disruption to fund performance, insurers may limit reallocations to a specific number per year.

If an insurer offers a combination variable and fixed immediate annuity, (1) reallocations from one variable subaccount to another are allowed, (2) reallocations from one variable subaccount to a fixed payout are sometimes allowed, but (3) reallocations from a fixed payout to a variable subaccount are generally disallowed to prevent interest rate (disintermediation) risk to the insurer. For example, if a contract owner switches wholly or partially from a variable payout to a fixed payout, the insurer buys a portfolio of fixed-income assets (e.g., bonds, mortgages) that replicate the payout pattern. If the owner wanted to switch back into a variable subaccount after interest rates had risen substantially, this could force the insurer to sell the bonds and mortgages at capital losses to raise the cash to transfer into the variable subaccounts. The insurer would be forced to absorb those losses because they were part of a guaranteed, fixed payout and not part of a variable subaccount where negative experience would have been passed through to the annuitant. It is important to note that the fixed, guaranteed portion of a combination variable and fixed payout is constant and does not fluctuate with interest rates that the insurer may be crediting to the fixed account in a combination variable and fixed deferred annuity contract.

IVA contract owners control beneficiary designations at and after purchase. Unless the owner voluntarily chose to make a previous beneficiary designation irrevocable, the owner may make a different beneficiary designation post-issue.

IVA contract owners have a say in proxy issues associated with the investment funds related to their contract. For example, due to performance, compliance, or other issues, it may be desirable to substitute one fund for another. (The SEC has an interest in ensuring any such "deletions and substitutions" are in the best interest of registered product contract owners.) Investment management policies might be modified to take advantage of new opportunities. Affected IVA owners retain the right to vote on these and similar issues. Additional subaccounts may be added to an IVA product by the insurer periodically without the need for contract owner approval, since contract owners reserve the right to avail themselves or not avail themselves of such new investment options.

The financial security system is conceptually envisioned in Figure 4.10.

Conceptually, each of the owner-annuitants sits outside the glass-walled polygon. They can reach inside the glass wall through flexible gloves to reallocate the assets in the amount of the reserve associated with their account among the various subaccounts available to them. Their allocations and the performance of the subaccounts they have currently chosen govern their annuity benefit payments. While the owner-annuitants control and move funds in the amount associated with their contract, they cannot pull them through the glass wall, which ensures that adequate funds remain inside the glass to pay lifetime income, since construction of this financial

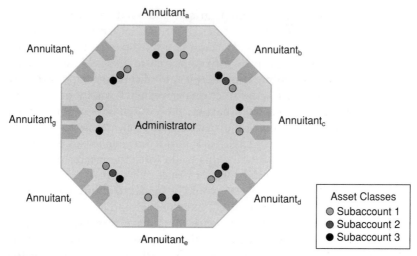

FIGURE 4.10   Conceptual Depiction of Financial Security System

security system assures that other participants cannot make unauthorized excess extractions beyond those to which they are contractually entitled.

Note that the glass wall is transparent in the sense that publicly available financial reports show the aggregate dollar amount of separate account assets and liabilities. Typically, however, the dollar amount of reserve associated with any one particular contract is not visible to the contract owner-annuitant, lest the individual perceive he has access to such sum or his beneficiaries perceive the sum at the time of his death is due them. Rather, the owner-annuitant reallocates by electing different subaccounts and/or different percentages associated with each subaccount that will govern his annuity income, as opposed to reallocating dollar amounts among subaccounts.

The program administrator sits inside the glass-walled polygon. Only he has the access key to get inside. New net premiums add to the total assets inside. The program administrator pays the periodic annuity benefits due annuitants, pays death claims to beneficiaries, reallocates reserves released by deceased annuitants to survivors via survivorship credits, and makes fine-tuning adjustments (plus or minus) to the total assets in the pool as emerging mortality experience dictates.

CHAPTER 5

Annuity Payout Options

Forewarned, forearmed; to be prepared is half the victory.
—Miguel de Cervantes Saavedra, *Don Quixote*,
1547–1616

HISTORY

Annuities, extraordinarily popular in modern times, trace their origin back to the Roman empire (27 B.C.–A.D. 395). In the emperor's time, Roman citizens would make a one-time payment to the *annua*. In exchange, the contract promised a stream of annual stipends for a fixed period of time or for life. A Roman, Domitius Ulpianus, created the first life table for computing the estate values of annuities a decedent might have purchased on the lives of others. Because uncertainty about length of life is an omnipresent source of risk—spanning time and geography—it is not surprising that the history of annuities spans millennia. Even the writings of the 1800s of Charles Dickens and Jane Austen reference annuities as seen in the opening quotations of the previous two chapters.

Annuity contracts, ancient or new, must define precisely the *annuity payout option*—the nature of annuity benefits and the conditions under which they will be paid. Annuity payout options provide a variety of ways to receive income. There is no one best or right or wrong option to select. They are all *actuarially equivalent* in value—the purchaser is entitled to select from any of the available annuity options, where every available option is equal in present value when discounted at the actual investment return experienced by the subaccount(s) chosen.[1]

The insurer issuing the annuity is indifferent as to which annuity option is elected. All options are premised on a common set of assumptions about mortality, expenses, and other factors that determine conversion rates. While some insurers might prefer annuity options that tend to last longer (e.g., joint

59

and survivor annuities, single life annuities with long certain periods), dissipate the reserve more slowly, and as a result leave a greater reserve on deposit against which the insurer extracts a margin,[2] there is no annuity option that is richer or less rich than others on a present value basis.

ANNUITY OPTIONS

Your annuity is sort of your personal pension. You exchange a single premium for periodic retirement income. The annuity option you choose defines the terms under which the income is paid. The following list shows immediate variable annuity options, grouped into single life annuities, joint life annuities, and non-life-contingent annuities; their definitions are given in the subsequent text.

Annuity Options
Single Life

- Life only
- Life with N years certain[3]
- Unit refund
- Modified unit refund
- Installment refund
- Modified installment refund
- Temporary life annuity
- Reversionary annuity

Joint Life

- Joint and $X\%$ to survivor
- Joint and $X\%$ to survivor with N years certain
- Joint and $X\%$ to secondary annuitant
- Joint and $X\%$ to secondary annuitant with N years certain
- Joint life annuity with pop-up provision
- Reversionary annuity

Non-Life-Contingent

- Installments for a designated period

Single Life Options

Single Life Annuity   Annuity income will be provided for the lifetime of the annuitant, no matter how long that may be. Annuity income stops on death of the annuitant. This option is also known as a "straight life" or a "life only" annuity.

Single Life Annuity with *N* Years Certain   Annuity income will be provided for *N* years, regardless of survival of the annuitant. After *N* years, annuity income will be provided for the lifetime of the annuitant (10 and 20 are common values for *N*). This option is also known as an "*N* years certain and continuous annuity." It is actually a combination of a non-life-contingent "installments for a designated period of *N* years" annuity option (described later) and an *N*-year deferred single life annuity option (just described).

Unit Refund   Annuity income will be provided for the lifetime of the annuitant. The number of annuity units purchasable by the net premium is determined by dividing the net premium by the annuity unit value at time of purchase. For example, if the net premium is $100,000 and the annuity unit value is 5.00, then the result is 20,000 units. On each annuity payment date, the dollar value of a constant number of annuity units is paid. Let's assume the dollar value of 100 annuity units is paid monthly. The beneficiary will receive on the annuitant's death a lump-sum dollar amount equal to 20,000 annuity units less 100 annuity units per monthly payment already made to the annuitant. If the annuitant had received 50 monthly payments before his death, the beneficiary would receive the value of 20,000 – (50 × 100), or 15,000, annuity units. If the value of 20,000 annuity units or more had already been paid to the annuitant while living, no payment is due the beneficiary. In this example, 20,000 annuity units will have been paid after 16 years and 8 months.

Effectively, this ensures that the net premium applied to purchase the contract is returned in benefit payments, except that the total of the benefit payments returned reflects gains and losses attributable to subaccount performance and thus may be more or less than the original net premium. This option guarantees that "units" will be refunded rather than an absolute amount of "dollars." (The immediate *fixed* annuity payout option analogue, called cash refund, guarantees return of the original net premium in dollars.)

If the annuitant were previously invested in the same variable annuity contract during the *deferred* variable annuity phase and if product-related fees and charges are identical during the *accumulation* phase and payout phase, there is an equivalent way to view and to administer a unit refund annuity. The number of *accumulation* units purchasable by the net premium will be determined. The number of accumulation units represented by each future annuity payment will be determined and subtracted from this total. If at the time of the annuitant's death there remains a positive number of accumulation units, the value of these will be paid in one lump sum to the beneficiary. This equivalency should come as no surprise, since using either this accumulation unit approach or the previous annuity unit approach guarantees that at least as much as was applied to purchase the immediate annuity will be returned in the form of benefit payments, with the caveat that such return reflects the impact of subaccount performance.

Modified Unit Refund   This is the same as the unit refund option, except that some percentage (1%–99%) of the annuity units originally purchased by the net premium is guaranteed to be returned (in terms of "units") rather than 100%. A modified unit refund allows the contract owner to "dial in" a guaranteed return of annuity units anywhere between 0% (life only option) and 100% (unit refund option).

Historically, an immediate fixed annuity option analogous to this type of benefit was used in conjunction with contributory defined benefit pension plans—those funded partly by the employee and partly by the employer. This benefit ensured that 100% of the *employee's* contribution was returned either in pension payments or a lump-sum death benefit to the beneficiary.

Installment Refund   Annuity income will be provided for the lifetime of the annuitant. The number of annuity units purchasable by the net premium will be determined by dividing the net premium by the annuity unit value at time of purchase. On each annuity payment date, the dollar value of a constant number of annuity units is paid. If at the time of the annuitant's death, the number of annuity units paid out is less than the number of annuity units initially purchasable, annuity benefit payments will continue to the beneficiary until the cumulative number of annuity units paid out equals the number initially purchasable.

Effectively, this ensures that the net premium applied to purchase the contract is returned in benefit payments, except that the total of the benefit payments returned reflects gains and losses attributable to subaccount performance and thus may be more or less than the original net premium. This option guarantees that "units" will be refunded rather than an absolute amount of "dollars."

The unit refund option defined earlier is identical to this installment refund option, except that the former pays the beneficiary any death benefit in one lump sum, whereas the latter pays it in continuing installments. Recognizing the time value of money and the fact that any death benefit is paid in full earlier under a unit refund option, for a given amount of premium, annuity income will be slightly higher under an installment refund option than under a unit refund option.

Just as with the unit refund option, the installment refund option also can equivalently be viewed and administered on the basis of accumulation units. The number of accumulation units purchasable by the net premium will be determined. The number of accumulation units represented by each future annuity payment will be determined and subtracted from this total. If at the time of the annuitant's death there remains a positive number of accumulation units, annuity payments will continue to the beneficiary until these units are exhausted.

The installment refund option can be closely approximated by a judicious choice of certain period under a life annuity with certain period option. For example, if the installment refund option will return all annuity units purchased by the premium after, say, 12 years and 2 months of annuity benefits, virtually the same result is achieved by electing a life annuity with 12 years certain.

Modified Installment Refund   This is the same as the installment refund option, except that some percentage (1%–99%) of the annuity units originally purchased by the net premium is guaranteed to be returned (in terms of "units") rather than 100%.

A modified installment refund allows the contract owner to "dial in" a guaranteed return of annuity units anywhere between 0% (life only option) and 100% (installment refund option).

***N* Year Temporary Life Annuity**   Annuity income will be provided for the shorter of *N* years or the life of the annuitant.

Reversionary Annuity   Lifetime annuity income will be provided to the annuitant, if alive, on expiration of an *N*-year period. For example, lifetime income will be provided to the annuitant, if still alive, on expiration of 10 years. This is effectively an *N*-year deferred life annuity. (*Note:* If the annuitant dies within the *N*-year period, no annuity benefit is payable.)

Joint Life Options

Joint and *X*% to Survivor   Annuity income will be provided while both the annuitant and the joint annuitant are living. After the death of either the annuitant or the joint annuitant, annuity income will be provided for the lifetime of the survivor at *X*% (0%–100%) of the income level payable while both were alive. Annuity income stops when both the annuitant and joint annuitant are no longer living.

Joint and *X*% to Survivor with *N* Years Certain   This is the same as the joint and *X*% to survivor option, except that payments are guaranteed to be made for *N* years regardless of the survival of the annuitant or the joint annuitant. While annuity payments for *N* years are guaranteed to be made, contract language defines whether after the first death within *N* years, annuity income will be paid at the full level that was in effect when both were alive—dropping to $X\%$ only after the certain period expires—or immediately revert to the reduced level $(X\%)$ payable when only one is alive.

Joint and $X\%$ to Secondary Annuitant   Annuity income will be provided for the lifetime of the primary annuitant. Should the primary annuitant predecease the secondary annuitant, lifetime income at a reduced level $(X\%)$ will continue for the remaining lifetime of the secondary annuitant.

Joint and $X\%$ to Secondary Annuitant with N Years Certain   This is the same as the joint and $X\%$ to secondary annuitant option, except that payments are guaranteed to be made for N years regardless of the survival of the primary annuitant or secondary annuitant. While annuity payments for N years are guaranteed to be made, contract language defines whether after the death of the primary annuitant within N years, annuity income will be paid at the full level or at the reduced level $(X\%)$ for the remainder of the N-year period.

Joint Life Annuity with Pop-up Provision   Annuity income will be provided for as long as the primary annuitant, the secondary annuitant, or both survive. Should the secondary annuitant predecease the primary annuitant, annuity income will pop up thereafter to the level the primary annuitant could have had if he or she had originally elected a single life-only annuity. (*Note:* This is actually a special case of a joint and $X\%$ to survivor option, where $X = 100$ if the primary annuitant dies first and $X > 100$ if the secondary annuitant dies first.)

Reversionary Annuity (Joint Life)   Lifetime annuity income will be provided to the annuitant, if alive, beginning on the death of a second life. For example, lifetime annuity income will be provided to a wife, if still alive, beginning on the death of her husband. (*Note 1:* If the annuitant predeceases the second life, no annuity benefit is payable. *Note 2:* While this arrangement can be defined totally in terms of annuities, it can also be thought of as insurance because a death triggers payment as with life insurance; only here, the death benefit is paid as a lifetime annuity rather than in a lump sum.)

Non-Life-Contingent Option

Installments for a Designated Period   Annuity income will be provided for a fixed period of N years regardless of the survival of the annuitant. If the annuitant dies within the N-year period, remaining payments will be made to the beneficiary. (Immediate *fixed* annuities include a second non-life-contingent option, called installments of a designated amount, which pays a fixed dollar amount each period. The net premium determines how long the installments of a designated dollar amount will be paid, and there is usually a partial final benefit payment. Immediate variable annuities do not offer the installments of a designated dollar amount option because the benefit each period is based on a number of annuity units, whose values fluctuate, rather than on a fixed number of dollars.)

Additional Aspects of Annuity Options

Not all single premium immediate variable annuity (SPIVA) contracts offer all annuity options. Other annuity options could be made available. For example, it is possible for a joint life annuity to cover three or more lives, such as a husband, a wife, and either a parent or a child in their care. Theoretically, virtually any annuity option imaginable could be priced and made available, provided there are reasonably reliable statistics on which to base a projection of expected benefit payments. For that matter, an annuity can be priced to pay as long as at least any one of a German shepherd, a human, and a penguin are alive, provided credible mortality statistics exist! Myriad "designer" annuities custom-tailored to an individual's special needs are achievable, although insurers prefer to offer a finite set of annuity options and to automate administration of these.

Since life insurance is generally forbidden in the individual retirement account (IRA) market,[4] any custom-designed immediate annuity options would need to temper the magnitude of any embedded life insurance elements. These might be restricted to levels similar to those found in "unit refund," "installment refund," or "life with period certain" options. In tax-qualified markets, the length of the certain period is restricted to ensure that the individual to whom preferential tax treatment (i.e., deferral) was granted during the accumulation phase is the same individual expected to derive the majority of retirement income value during the distribution phase.

Annuity benefits that "back-end" the majority of annuity payments might not qualify for immediate annuity tax treatment, which calls for substantially equal benefit payments. Customizable immediate variable annuity benefit options can be offered, provided they don't run afoul of any securities or state insurance regulations.

Immediate fixed annuities most often tend to provide level income or income that increases annually by a predetermined dollar amount (linear growth) or by a predetermined percentage (exponential growth). Fixed annuities where the income increases annually according to an index such as the Consumer Price Index (CPI) historically have not generally been offered, primarily because of the uncertainty of the level of future benefit payments the insurer would need to fund with the original single premium. Recent offerings in investments available to support an investment strategy underlying inflation-indexed immediate fixed annuities are making such a product more readily available.

Of course, immediate variable annuity payments fluctuate with the performance of the subaccounts in which the owner elects to invest. One typically thinks about subaccount performance equal to the assumed investment rate (AIR) providing a level series of annuity benefits. One could equally well think about it as a 3% AIR product providing annuity benefits that increase by about 2% annually if a level 5% return is achieved; that is, someone desiring an immediate variable annuity where benefits increase about 2% per year if a level 5% return is achieved need only elect a 3% AIR rather than a 5% AIR. (Actually, such benefit payments would increase annually by 1.05/1.03, or 1.94%, rather than by 2% if the 5% subaccount performance were achieved.)

In addition to annuity option, an annuity owner typically has other choices, including benefit payment frequency and AIR:

■ **Benefit Payment Frequency.** Annual, semiannual, quarterly, and monthly payment modes are most frequently offered. Any other payment frequency could be offered,[5] such as the biweekly mode with which individuals often received a paycheck during active working years. Benefit frequency could theoretically increase to the point where payments were continuous, and the most technical mathematical treatises regarding annuities include the study of continuous annuity payments as well as real-world discrete ones.
■ **AIR.** AIRs of 3% to 5% are common. Nonintegral AIR values, such as 3.5%, are sometimes offered. AIR values greater than 5% require state insurance commissioner approval in some states. A 7% AIR is about as high as is typically seen.

Figure 5.1 portrays the major immediate annuity classification factors.

CONSIDERATIONS IN SELECTING AN ANNUITY OPTION

Logically, selection of a refund annuity and inclusion of a certain period with a lifetime annuity are hard to justify. The objective of an immediate variable annuity is to provide maximum periodic income guaranteed to last a lifetime. A single "life only" annuity achieves this objective. If the annuitant has a dependent spouse, a "joint and X% to survivor" annuity achieves it, where $X < 100$ because there will be some level of expense reduction on the first death.

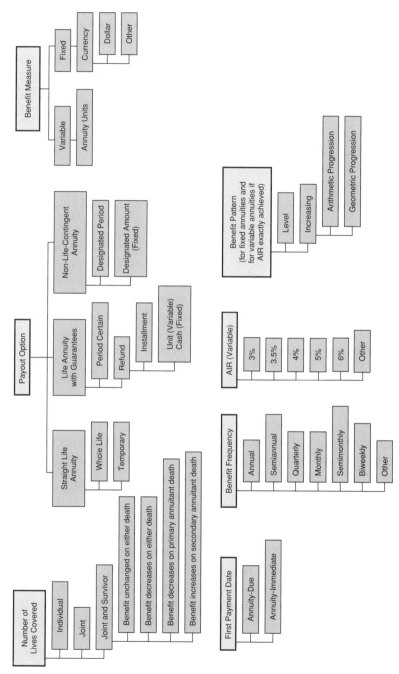

FIGURE 5.1 Classification of Single Premium Income Annuities

Psychologically, immediate variable annuity purchasers often are more comfortable attaching a certain period or some form of refund feature, which diminishes their income. If leaving assets to a beneficiary is an objective, this may be accomplished more efficiently by life insurance and other financial instruments.

In tax-qualified markets where 100% of distributions in any form are taxable, one might question the suitability of an immediate life annuity with a certain period. Effectively, the immediate annuity premium is applied to the purchase of two sequential annuities. The first commences immediately and is a non-life-contingent annuity for the length of the certain period. The second commences at the end of the certain period and is a deferred lifetime annuity.

If an individual were merely to make regular, periodic withdrawals from the investment accumulation vehicle (e.g., deferred annuity, mutual fund) for a period of time equal to the length of the certain period he would otherwise have elected, he suffers no tax disadvantage; yet should he die during this interval, his beneficiary receives the fund corpus. If he survives to the end of the certain period, he may purchase a life-only annuity at that point.

If instead such individual originally elects a life with period certain annuity and dies within the certain period, he seemingly unnecessarily forfeits the present value of the deferred lifetime annuity. That said, there are some reasons to consider an immediate life annuity with a certain period in the tax-qualified market. First, there is simplicity, as the full transaction is completed at once rather than in multiple steps, potentially important if the owner may become physically or mentally unable to manage his affairs at a later date. Second, the portion of the premium applied to the deferred lifetime annuity accumulates with benefit of both interest and survivorship during the deferral period, resulting in a higher annuity benefit than if it merely accumulates with benefit of interest outside the immediate annuity and is applied to the purchase of a life annuity at the time the certain period would have expired had a life with period certain annuity initially been elected. As with any investment decision, an individual's unique facts and circumstances—especially age and length of certain period—must be evaluated. If the annuitant is relatively young (e.g., female age 60) and the certain period is relatively short (e.g., 5 years), then the benefit reduction by including a certain period is relatively small, and there is relatively less income lost if the annuitant alternatively takes withdrawals from an investment accumulation period for 5 years and then elects a life-only annuity. If the annuitant is relatively old (e.g., male age 75) and the certain period is relatively long (e.g., 15 years), then the benefit reduction by including a certain period is relatively large, and there is relatively more income lost if the annuitant alternatively takes withdrawals from an investment accumulation period for 15 years and then elects a life-only annuity.

In the non-tax-qualified market, original election of a "life with period certain annuity" at least offers the more favorable immediate annuity tax treatment (i.e., each payment consists of a nontaxable return of principal element and a taxable appreciation element), rather than the "100% taxable interest out first, followed by principal" tax treatment associated with withdrawals from some investment vehicles other than immediate annuities, such as deferred annuities.

In lieu of using a certain period in conjunction with a lifetime annuity in tax-qualified markets, individuals might consider electing regularly scheduled (e.g., monthly) withdrawals that pay the greater of a fixed dollar amount—possibly with some annual percentage increase (e.g., 3%)—or the IRS required minimum distribution. At the end of the period that otherwise would have served as their certain period, they can apply the remaining proceeds to the purchase of a single life or joint life immediate variable annuity.

Such an approach, however, may result in the undesired "reverse dollar cost averaging" phenomenon described in Chapter 4. Thus, a fixed number of accumulation units (for a deferred variable annuity) or a fixed number of shares (for a retail mutual fund) might be liquidated each period rather than withdrawing a fixed dollar amount.

Yet another option is to apply some retirement savings to the purchase of a single life or joint life immediate variable annuity with no certain period or refund feature, while leaving the remainder in its current savings vehicles, making withdrawals as needed (or as required by the IRS) to supplement the annuity, and keeping that portion available to meet liquidity needs. This allows retirees to receive the maximum possible lifetime income from the annuity, which was the whole point of saving money for retirement. Such higher income could mean extra vacations, dining out more frequently, or similar improved quality-of-life benefits—with greater comfort spending current income, knowing that exhaustion of income is not a concern.

Tax law incentives currently under consideration to encourage purchase of lifetime annuities could alter tax treatment of nonqualified immediate annuities, tax-qualified immediate annuities, or both. Any such change could alter one's decisions regarding the use of certain periods in conjunction with lifetime annuities in tax-qualified markets.

That said, different annuity options provide solutions to different real-world needs. Here are sample reasons that specific options might be selected:

- *I'm a single person with no dependents. What option might I consider?* Perhaps a "life only" annuity. This maximizes your income. Since you needn't cover any dependents, attaching some type of refund feature or guaranteed number of payments—which would reduce your income— may not be important to you.

■ *I'm a widow with no dependents. I'd like a reasonably high level of income, but I'd feel just awful knowing that if I were to die shortly after purchasing an immediate annuity, no further benefits would be paid.*
You might consider a "life with N years certain" annuity, where N is perhaps 5 or 10, since you expressed a desire for a reasonably high level of income. Although you have no dependents, you'll need to name a beneficiary with this option to receive any benefits due after your death. (It can be a church or a charity as well as a natural person.)

■ *Lifetime income interests me, but I'd feel more comfortable buying a variable income annuity if I knew that either I or my beneficiary would get at least as much out of it as I put into it.*
You might consider a unit refund or an installment refund option. This ensures that you and your beneficiary will collectively receive as many units back as were originally purchased. Note that the value of those units fluctuates based on the performance of the subaccounts you choose; so while you are not guaranteed to get back at least as many dollars as you put into it, you will receive at least the value associated with all of the units you originally purchased.

The installment refund option will provide higher income than the unit refund option. This is because it is more expensive to pay out the residual, if any, to the beneficiary in one lump sum than in continuing installments. (A lump sum has a higher present value at time of purchase than several installments that occur later than the lump sum and, therefore, have a lower discounted value. As a result, more of your original premium is needed to fund that lump sum, resulting in lower annuity benefits for the unit refund option than for the installment refund option.)

■ *I want to ensure that my wife and I receive income for the rest of our lives. If only one of us is around, we can probably get by on 75% of what we need when we're both alive.*
Consider a "joint and 75% to survivor" option. This provides annuity payments while you, your spouse, or both are surviving. Because the annuity benefit payments drop to 75% of their original level on the first death, the annuity benefits payable while you are both alive are higher than if you elect a "joint and 100% to survivor" option. You may also attach a guaranteed number of payments to this option, although the higher the number of guaranteed payments, the lower your monthly benefits will be.

■ *I'm in a quandary. In addition to myself, I'd like to cover my spouse with an annuity. But I know that makes the annuity benefits lower than if I just had a single life annuity on myself. Yet if I buy a joint life annuity covering both of us and my spouse predeceases me, I'll end up with less annuity income than I could have had if I'd have just purchased a single life annuity for myself. Effectively, I'll feel badly that I made the wrong annuity option decision should my spouse predecease me.*

A "joint life annuity with a pop-up provision" is just what you need. If your spouse predeceases you, the annuity benefit pops up to the level you could have had originally had you elected a single life annuity on yourself. Because of this, the annuity benefit payable while you are both alive is less than what a "joint and 100% to survivor" option pays. Yet this pop-up option ensures you can't make the wrong decision (as you define it), since if your spouse predeceases you, you'll end up with the same annuity income as if you'd elected a single life-only annuity on yourself.

For example, you know you can receive an initial monthly variable payout of $1,000 under a life-only annuity covering only yourself. Alternatively, you can cover both yourself and your spouse under a joint life annuity with an initial variable payout of $800. You know you'll have buyer's remorse if you elect the joint life annuity and your spouse predeceases you. You'll feel you made the wrong decision, since you'll forgo the difference—$200 per month initially, thereafter adjusted by subaccount performance—you could have had if you had elected the single life-only annuity. You'll needlessly have given up $200 per month to ensure lifetime income for your spouse, which is lost money if she predeceases you.

A solution to this dilemma is to elect a "joint and survivor with a pop-up provision" option initially paying $780 per month. (Actual relative dollar amounts between the single life only, the joint and survivor, and the joint and survivor with pop-up provision options will depend on the issue ages of the two individuals.) If you die first, your spouse continues to receive the same $780 per month as when you were both alive (adjusted for subaccount performance), meeting your desire to protect her under a joint lifetime income program. If your spouse predeceases you, your monthly benefit pops up to the same level as would have occurred had you originally elected the $1,000 single life annuity on yourself.

Some annuitants view the preceding situation, where a spouse predeceases them and they end up receiving less in annuity income than if they had originally elected a single life annuity on themselves, as having to forever pay a "phantom insurance premium." They view the difference between the higher monthly single life benefit on themselves and the lower monthly joint life benefit on both of them as an "insurance premium" assessed every month that ensures their spouse will receive lifetime income if they—the primary annuitant—die first. The buyer in the example absolutely wished to avoid paying this "insurance premium" to guarantee lifetime income to a spouse who predeceased him.

A sales concept called "pension maximization" is occasionally touted as a means to deal with this same issue. The primary annuitant is advised to (1) elect a life-only annuity in order to receive the maximum level of pension income and (2) purchase a life insurance policy on himself so that should he predecease his spouse, the insurance death benefit paid can be applied to purchase a single life annuity on the spouse. The economics of this should be investigated for any particular case. It is noteworthy that two products—annuity and life insurance—are sold, resulting in two sales commissions payable, two sets of state premium tax, and two sets of DAC tax (defined in Chapter 10), the expense of which may reduce value to the end consumer.

Insurance products tend to be more heavily loaded than annuity products, making their introduction into this combined sales concept less likely to result in value superior to that achievable with the annuity alone. Additionally, to the extent that annuities introduce conservatism into pricing by assuming people live longer than they actually do, that serves to make any life-insurance-like characteristics embedded in the annuity attractively priced.

In some pension plan situations, the "joint and survivor" annuity option is less than the actuarial equivalent of the single "life only" annuity because of inclusion of simplified formulas regarding benefits under optional forms of annuity. Those situations may lend themselves to a greater likelihood that the pension maximization concept could be viable. A numerical comparison of all the economics of such a transaction should still be investigated for any particular case.

IMMEDIATE VARIABLE ANNUITY PROSPECTS

Are you a candidate for an immediate variable annuity? If you are nearing retirement age, desire a potential hedge against inflation, want guaranteed lifetime income—possibly to cover both you and your spouse—like the ability to control the asset classes in which you invest, value the ability to change your investment mix periodically or simply rebalance it to your target asset allocation and do either on a tax-free basis, you are the typical immediate variable annuity prospect.

If you have assets in retirement savings programs like IRAs or 401(k)s that you have always mentally earmarked for truly using to provide income during retirement years, you may well be an immediate variable annuity candidate.

If you don't have a defined benefit pension plan that will provide you with guaranteed lifetime income—or even if you do but the pension alone is insufficient to meet your income needs—you may be a potential immediate annuity variable owner.

If you consider yourself to be in average health or above average health or if you have a family history of favorable longevity, you may be a candidate. If your health is below average but you are still concerned about outliving your income, you may be a candidate for an immediate variable annuity, particularly one with some form of refund feature or guaranteed number of payments. You may be a candidate for a medically underwritten immediate variable annuity (described in Chapter 13) that provides a higher benefit level in recognition of health impairments.

If you have so few assets that it is challenging to get by day to day, you might not be a suitable candidate for an immediate annuity, as you may need those assets for emergency purposes, and placing them into an immediate variable annuity puts your principal beyond reach.

If you have so many assets that you can safely live off just the interest or dividends that they generate, you may not need an immediate variable annuity—which lets those with more modest wealth effectively spend down their principal safely without ever running out. Nonetheless, because of a positive correlation between wealth, education, and longevity, you may expect to derive a good rate of return[6] from an immediate variable annuity (IVA) due to outliving the majority of annuitants in the pool and benefiting from the forfeitures of those annuitants who predecease you as their reserves are released and redistributed among the survivors. Access to the highest-quality medical care, high education, and awareness of and compliance with longevity-conducive lifestyles suggest the wealthy class may well be able to capitalize on IVAs.

The preceding two paragraphs suggest there is a midrange "sweet spot" of net worth (inclusive of the present value of any pensions, including Social Security) that makes individuals the most likely candidates to be immediate variable annuity owners. Below this range, liquidity needs prevail. Above this range, quality of life is not greatly enhanced by assurance of lifetime income or the higher income that derives from the capacity of immediate variable annuities to spend down principal safely, making the income stream higher than that produced by interest only leaving principal intact.

While only an imprecise guideline and individual circumstances will dictate exceptions, people retiring with financial assets ranging from $300,000 to $3,000,000 may be candidates for IVA ownership. While again only a crude guideline, 20% to 50% of those financial assets might be applied to the purchase of IVAs. The purchase(s) should be large enough to make the longevity insurance so procured meaningful but still balancing this with the need for some measure of liquid assets held outside the IVA. Individuals nearing or at retirement age with moderate to high levels of disposable income and a strong savings propensity characterize the IVA target market.

Young people may also sometimes be prospective immediate variable annuity owners or, if not owners, annuitants. For example, parents who desire to leave money to children who would be ineffective stewards of a lump sum might consider naming in a will or as beneficiary of a life insurance policy a trustee who is to purchase an immediate variable annuity for the benefit of the children, who will be the annuitants. Especially when many decades of life likely await them, an immediate variable annuity, with its ability to invest all or a portion in instruments with a historical track record of besting inflation, makes sense.

Anyone who doesn't want to spend 30 or so years in retirement constantly worrying that he or she will outlive his or her income is an IVA candidate. Who knows—this freedom from worry may be conducive to longevity in itself!

If you are a variable income annuity candidate, your "decision set" is comprised of the following:

- Buy/don't buy.
- IVA product/insurance company/investment manager.
- Annuity option.
- Optional secondary guarantees, if any.
- Subaccount selection/percentage allocation.
- Rebalancing.
- Service options/direct deposit of benefit payments/electronic receipt of prospectus and updates.

VALUE EQUIVALENCE OF ANNUITY OPTIONS

Annuity options are generally *equivalent* in value—every available option is equal in present value when discounted at the actual investment return experienced by the subaccount(s) chosen. For example, the present value of each of the three different series of annuity payments shown in Figure 4.6 and Table 4.2—and reproduced in Figure 5.2—(one series each at 3% AIR, 5% AIR, and 7% AIR) at the 12% actual rate of return experienced is $8,107.82.

Since each individual may have a different time value of money, discounting the series of benefit payments provided by different annuity options

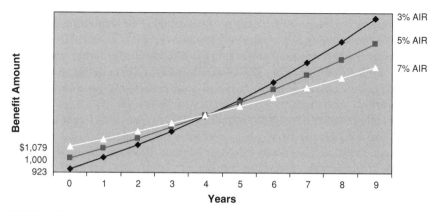

FIGURE 5.2 Annuity Payments (subaccount performance = 12%/year)

may result in unequal present values when discount factors other than a uniform discount rate equal to the actual investment return are used. For example, a customer's time value of money may mimic that of a (typically monotonically increasing) yield curve.

Discounting using a traditionally shaped, positively sloping yield curve vector[7] will produce greater present values for annuity options that provide the most income in the early years (e.g., those based on a higher AIR). This is because the discount rate for these payments will be lower than the discount rate for later payments, resulting in a higher present value.

This varying utility of money could alter individuals' preferences for various AIRs; that is, the annuity options to them, particularly with respect to different AIRs, may not be perceived as value-equivalent.

Recall that a low AIR produces a steeper curve of future benefit payments, while a high AIR produces a flatter curve of future benefit payments. As a result, an individual might feel that because electing a high AIR produces higher benefit levels early and because she associates a lower interest rate with these under her own personal time value of money, this offers her a benefit stream with a higher present value.

It's all a matter of personal choice. The main job of an IVA is to provide an income that one can't outlive. It's second most important job is to provide a hopefully increasing series of benefits that allow one to keep up with or to beat inflation. The lower the AIR elected, the better the chance the IVA will succeed at keeping pace with inflation.

People living more healthful lives may prefer a low AIR since they expect to live a long time and expect to need higher benefit amounts down the road. Those living less healthful lives may prefer a higher AIR so they get "more money sooner" since they're less certain whether they'll be around well down the road. Thus, actual mortality experience may differ by AIR chosen, although this is generally not reflected in establishing IVA payout rates.

While here we've chosen to compare relative value of different payment streams by discounting to arrive at present values, relative value comparisons may equally be achieved by accumulating different payment streams to arrive at future values. For life-contingent annuity options, one's perception of probabilities of survival as well as one's personal time value of money factor into one's assignment of value to different payment streams.

CHAPTER 6

Annuitant Populations and Annuity Present Values

The years of our life are threescore and ten, or even by reason of strength fourscore.

—Psalm 90:10

opulation dynamics have long been studied by actuaries, demographers, economists, census takers, and numerous others. Thomas Malthus, an English economist, wrote in 1798 *An Essay on the Principle of Population.* The Malthusian perspective was that human populations grow geometrically, that this is faster than the earth is able to provide subsistence, and that these two items need to experience comparable growth. Since humans tend not to invoke "preventative checks" by limiting their population size voluntarily, destructive "positive checks" of famine, disease, poverty, and war restore the necessary equilibrium through population reduction.

CATEGORIZATION AND CHARACTERISTICS

Annuities are often categorized as *individual annuities* or *group annuities.* An individual annuity is typically a one-on-one sale between a financial adviser and a client. The individual decides to apply a single premium to the purchase of an immediate variable annuity (IVA). This is a voluntary election.

In contrast, a group annuity can be for the benefit of members of a specific organization—employer, association, and so on. The terms of the retirement savings program might be such as to require the application of the member's account value to the purchase of a lifetime annuity. This is a forced election.

As a result, one would correctly expect a difference in mortality exhibited by these two groups. For individual annuities, an individual will generally only select a lifetime annuity if the person considers himself or herself to be in good health and expects to live at least as long as an "average" person. In contrast, those in the group annuity pool will be comprised of those in excellent health, those in average health, and those in poor health. As a group, they therefore will not be expected to survive as long as a similar collection of individual annuitants, that is, with the same age and sex distribution.

Different populations will exhibit different mortality characteristics. These differ by age, sex, height, weight, tobacco use, alcohol use, medical conditions, geographic region, education level, avocations, wealth, and a host of other factors. Yet to simplify the application process, typically no underwriting is done with relation to immediate annuities. Rather, prospective annuitants are simply classified into one of two large categories: individual or group.

More precise underwriting[1] could be done and in some cases is done. This can result in higher annuity benefits issued to individuals in poorer health, recognizing their shorter expected period of receiving annuity payments. These are known as "substandard" annuities. One way to make the adjustment is to "rate up" the annuitant in age; for example, treat a seriously ill 65-year-old as a 72-year-old.

Some potential underwriting criteria are forbidden by law. For example, race cannot typically be a factor. Some states (e.g., Montana) and some situations (e.g., an annuity falling under the umbrella of an employer-sponsored plan under ERISA—the Employee Retirement Income Security Act of 1974) preclude the use of gender as an underwriting factor. As a result, "unisex" annuity rates are used; that is, the same benefit results from the same premium, regardless of sex.

For such unisex immediate annuity business, an insurer needs to evaluate the likely male/female ratio. For example, if males can transfer out of an employer-sponsored ERISA program to an individual retirement account (IRA) and therefore be able to receive higher sex-distinct annuity payouts available to males—who don't survive as a class as long as females—then the insurer may assume that they will and set the unisex rate based on a 0% male, 100% female mix assumption.

In most countries (with at least five exceptions), females live longer than males. Biological and behavioral reasons appear in scientific literature to explain why this is so. There are more males than females at the moment of conception, yet one hundred years later females greatly outnumber males. *Why* female mortality rates by age are lower than for males is intriguing; but *that* they are lower is what is of immediate consequence when pricing variable income annuities. To the extent the biological or behavioral factors causing the differences may be modified in the future to narrow the gap, mortality improvement factors ultimately may be impacted.

POPULATION MATHEMATICS

One needs to be able to quantify how populations behave in order to ensure the solvency of any immediate annuity program. The first step is to measure historical mortality rates for the types of individuals expected to constitute the annuitant population. A *mortality rate* is simply the probability that a person of a certain age and sex will die within the next year.

For example, the probability that a 65-year-old male will die within one year of his 65th birthday might be 1%. Using international actuarial notation, mortality rates are expressed as q_x, where q denotes the probability of death and x represents age. (Age can be variously defined as "age last birthday," "age nearest birthday," or "age next birthday.") In this example, $q_{65} = 0.01$.

On the flip side, we can say the probability that a 65-year-old male will survive one year from his 65th birthday is 99%. Survival rates are expressed as p_x, where p denotes probability of survival. In this example, $p_{65} = 0.99$.

A person must either survive or die during the year, with 100% probability. By definition,

$$p_x + q_x = 1$$

Suppose we start with 1,000 males age 65. We call such a group a *cohort*. We call the number of lives starting the process the *radix*.

Define the number of lives l age x beginning the year by l_x. Here, $l_{65} = 1,000$.

Define the number of deaths d at age x by d_x. Then

$$d_x = l_x \cdot q_x$$

The number dying during year of age x equals the number starting the year times the mortality rate. Here, $d_{65} = l_{65} \cdot q_{65} = 1,000 \cdot 0.01 = 10$; that is, 1% of the original 1,000 age 65 males died before turning 66.

Regarding notation, multiplication shall be indicated either by a dot ($\cdot$) or by adjacent multiplicands, reserving an "x" to denote annuitant age. While the dot product or Euclidean inner product of vectors shares this same dot notation, here it simply conveys multiplication.

The number of lives beginning age $x + 1$ equals the number beginning age x minus deaths at age x:

$$l_{x+1} = l_x - d_x$$

So $l_{66} = l_{65} - d_{65} = 1,000 - 10 = 990$.

Equivalently, the number of lives beginning age $x + 1$ equals the number beginning age x times the probability of surviving from age x to age $x + 1$:

$$l_{x+1} = l_x \cdot p_x$$

Here $l_{66} = l_{65} \cdot p_{65} = 1{,}000 \cdot 0.99 = 990$.
To summarize:

$$p_x + q_x = 1, \text{ or } q_x = 1 - p_x$$
$$d_x = l_x - l_{x+1}, \text{ or } l_{x+1} = l_x - d_x$$
$$d_x = l_x \cdot q_x$$
$$l_{x+1} = l_x \cdot p_x, \text{ or } p_x = \frac{l_{x+1}}{l_x}$$

where l_x = number of lives age x
   d_x = number of lives age x dying before age $x + 1$
   p_x = probability of life age x surviving to age $x + 1$
   q_x = probability of life age x dying before age $x + 1$

We now know how to calculate a table showing how many lives of the original 1,000 65-year-old males will survive into each future year. Just as we calculated 990 will survive to age 66, we can calculate how many will survive to age 67, 68, 69, and so on. All we need to know to do this is the table of q_x values, known as a mortality table.

We can graphically portray this same information, as in Figure 6.1. Each bar shows how many of the original 1,000 65-year-olds survive to the beginning of each future year. This is an l_x graph for males based on a mortality table called the Annuity 2000 Basic Table. An l_x graph is called a *survivorship curve*.

A mnemonic is to visualize a group of l_x lives, currently age x, as a totem pole of height l_x. The totem pole travels to the right as time progresses and the group gets older. The survivorship curve descends on the group, so that they die as the curve touches them.[2] See Figure 6.2.

An arbitrarily large number of annuitants (1,000 here) is chosen. It is the *ratios* that are important, such as the ratio l_{95}/l_{65}, which tells the proportion of 65-year-olds who started the program still being alive at age 95 to qualify for an annuity payment that year. Because only *ratios* are important, it is immaterial whether we assume 1,000 lives begin the program or 1,000,000 lives.

The mortality table and resultant survivorship curve are important to an immediate annuity program. The program sponsor—whether it be a church group, a community, or an insurer—needs to project the future annuity payments it expects to make. If actual mortality experience comes reasonably

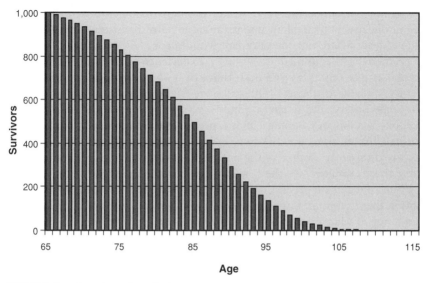

FIGURE 6.1   Annuitant Population

close to projected, the program should remain solvent and fulfill its mission of providing lifetime income to all participants.

While it may sound cold or morbid, from a solvency perspective, it doesn't matter which annuitants die early and which survive to the most advanced ages. The program succeeds if actual mortality collectively mimics that projected, regardless of where any specific individual's experience may fall.

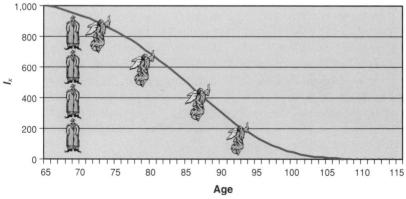

FIGURE 6.2   Survivorship Curve l_x

Think back to Chapter 1. Recall the balls dropped down the chute. They collectively formed an understandable pattern. At the same time, we didn't know where the one gray ball would drop.

Similarly, the immediate annuity experience—the l_x graph or a d_x graph—is like that. One can even think of it as a sort of "cosmic game of chance," where for those 1,000 males age 65, certain of them fall in the d_{65} bin while others land in the d_{95} bin. It's as if there were a population lattice, like the one in Chapter 1 that reproduces the bell-shaped curve of the normal distribution; but the pins in this population lattice are arranged slightly differently so that as the balls fall through them they produce a d_x curve that translates into the l_x survivorship curve in Figure 6.1.[3]

Such debates on predestination, cosmic chance, or the reason why some land in the d_{65} bin and others in the d_{95} bin are better left to philosophers. In a letter to Max Born in 1926, Albert Einstein commented, "At any rate, I am convinced that He [God] does not play dice."

To succeed, immediate variable annuity programs need only concern themselves with probability of mortality and probability of survival and how these change over time, not with metaphysical explanations of how such probabilities come to be.

It is interesting that the graph in Figure 6.2 is shaped like the downward side of a hill, which suggests a physics analogy. Individuals spend their lives, perhaps up through age 65, storing up their own "potential energy" as they build up their hill of retirement savings assets. At that point, they start down the hill, with a liquidation of their retirement savings assets, turning the stored "potential energy" into "kinetic energy," where the assets work for them to buy the goods and services they need, as current employment income is often absent. See Figure 6.3.

Tables 6.1 and 6.2 and Figures 6.4, 6.5, and 6.6 illustrate selected survival probabilities.

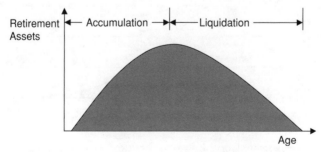

FIGURE 6.3   Accumulation and Liquidation Phases

TABLE 6.1 Probability* That a 65-Year-Old Today Will Reach Age Shown

| | Percentage | |
Age	Male	Female
70	93%	96%
75	83	89
80	68	79
85	49	62
90	30	41
95	13	19
100	4	6
105	1	1

*Values are based on Johansen, Robert J., 1998. Annuity 2000 Mortality Tables. Transactions, Society of Actuaries, 1995–96 Reports. © 1998 Society of Actuaries. Values are rounded to the nearest 1%.

Percentages in the table are associated with 65-year-olds today who consider themselves sufficiently healthy to purchase an immediate annuity.

TABLE 6.2 Probability* That *At Least One* Member of a 65-Year-Old Couple Today Will Reach Age Shown

Age	Percentage
70	100%
75	98
80	93
85	81
90	58
95	30
100	10
105	2

*Values are based on Johansen, Robert J., 1998. Annuity 2000 Mortality Tables. Transactions, Society of Actuaries, 1995–96 Reports. © 1998 Society of Actuaries. Values are rounded to the nearest 1%.

Percentages in the table are associated with 65-year-olds today who consider themselves sufficiently healthy to purchase an immediate annuity.

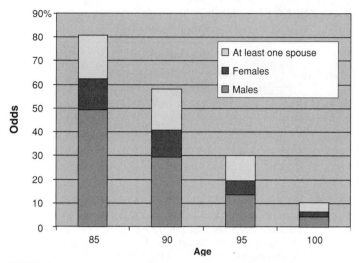

FIGURE 6.4   Odds of 65-Year-Olds Living to Various Ages
Source: Johansen, Robert J., 1998. Annuity 2000 Mortality Tables.
Transactions, Society of Actuaries, 1995–96 Reports. © 1998
Society of Actuaries.

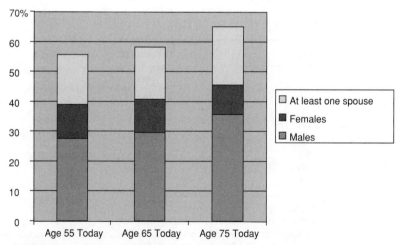

FIGURE 6.5   People Who Will Live to Age 90
Source: Johansen, Robert J., 1998. Annuity 2000 Mortality Tables.
Transactions, Society of Actuaries, 1995–96 Reports. © 1998 Society of
Actuaries.

I am long on ideas, but short on time. I expect to live to be only about a hundred.

—Thomas Alva Edison

- Colonel Harland Sanders actively began franchising Kentucky Fried Chicken at age 65.
- Ronald Reagan held his fourth summit meeting with Mikhail Gorbachev at age 77.
- Frank Lloyd Wright created the New York Guggenheim Museum at age 80.
- Thomas Edison applied for a patent at age 83.
- Michelangelo was an active artist at age 88.

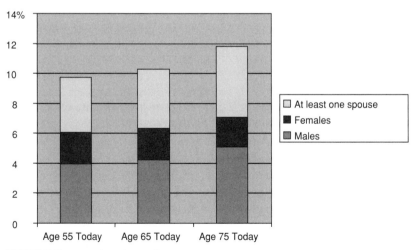

FIGURE 6.6 People Who Will Live to Age 100
Source: Johansen, Robert J., 1998. Annuity 2000 Mortality Tables. Transactions, Society of Actuaries, 1995–96 Reports. © 1998 Society of Actuaries.

ANNUITY MATHEMATICS (LIFE-CONTINGENT)

Now that we know how to project how many annuitants will be alive in each future year to receive payments, how do we determine how much money we need up front to make those payments? For simplicity, assume we pay $1 annually at the start of each year to each surviving annuitant. Since every dollar behaves like every other, if we want to pay, say, $1,000 at the start of each year, we simply multiply our result by 1,000.

In the first year, we need $1,000 to pay $1 to each of the initial 1,000 65-year-old males. In the second year, we need $990 to pay $1 to each of the 990 survivors.

We assume the premium we receive up front will be invested so as to return a uniform percentage—the assumed investment rate (AIR)—in every future year. We know that it won't do this exactly and that the variable annuity payments will fluctuate to the extent of any deviation, but we still make this assumption.

Suppose the AIR is 5%. As a result, we need $990 discounted at 5%, or $990/1.05 = $942.86, up front in order to make annuity payments to the 66-year-olds one year from now.[4]

We repeat this process for all future years and sum the results. This is the net present value (NPV) of the annuity, that amount needed to fund all future payments.

Let i be the AIR. Let $v = 1/(1 + i)$ be the factor that discounts a payment of $1 one year hence at interest rate i.

Then the net present value, the amount we need at program inception to generate all future annuity benefit payments to all annuity program participants, is:

$$\text{NPV}^{\text{All}} = l_{65} + l_{66} \cdot v + l_{67} \cdot v^2 + l_{68} \cdot v^3 + \cdots$$

If we want to know the NPV per program participant, we need to divide by l_{65}, the number of lives starting the program:

$$\text{NPV}^{\text{Participant}} = \frac{l_{65}}{l_{65}} + \frac{l_{66}}{l_{65}} \cdot v + \frac{l_{67}}{l_{65}} \cdot v^2 + \frac{l_{68}}{l_{65}} \cdot v^3 + \cdots$$

$$= 1 + p_{65}v + {}_2p_{65}v^2 + {}_3p_{65}v^3 + \cdots$$

where ${}_np_x$ = probability life age x survives n years

We could go ahead and sum this series each time we need it. There exists a shortcut methodology for such calculations. While it's no big deal to have a computer calculate this series today, in the precomputer era, this shortcut was important.[5] Here's how it works:

Define D_x as $l_x \cdot v^x$.

Define N_x as $\sum_{k=x}^{\omega-1} D_k = D_x + D_{x+1} + D_{x+2} + \cdots + D_{\omega-1}$, where ω is the *terminal age* of the mortality table. Then

$$\frac{N_x}{D_x} = \frac{D_x + D_{x+1} + D_{x+2} + \cdots + D_{\omega-1}}{D_x}$$

$$= \frac{D_x}{D_x} + \frac{D_{x+1}}{D_x} + \frac{D_{x+2}}{D_x} + \cdots + \frac{D_{\omega-1}}{D_x}$$

$$= \frac{l_x v^x}{l_x v^x} + \frac{l_{x+1} v^{x+1}}{l_x v^x} + \frac{l_{x+2} v^{x+2}}{l_x v^x} + \cdots + \frac{l_{\omega-1} v^{\omega-1}}{l_x v^x}$$

$$= 1 + \frac{l_{x+1} v}{l_x} + \frac{l_{x+2} v^2}{l_x} + \cdots + \frac{l_{\omega-1} v^{\omega-x-1}}{l_x}$$

$$= 1 + p_x v + {_2}p_x v^2 + \cdots + {_{\omega-x-1}}p_x v^{\omega-x-1}$$

We can create a table of D_x and N_x values once (for each AIR) and then use it to more easily calculate the NPVs we'll need.

$\ddot{a}_x$ is international actuarial notation (i.e., a shorthand or condensed way of saying the same thing) for the present value of a life annuity to a life age x with annual payments of 1, where the dieresis (¨) indicates payments are made at the *beginning* of the period. Thus,

$$\ddot{a}_x = \frac{N_x}{D_x}$$

That's all there is to calculating the NPV necessary to fund a lifetime immediate variable annuity to a male age 65.

As we saw in the opening chapters, the first immediate variable annuity payment is determined by dividing the net premium by $\ddot{a}_x$. This makes sense because if, say, the net premium were \$12 and $\ddot{a}_x$ = \$12, then we have just enough to pay \$1 per period. If the net premium were \$120 and $\ddot{a}_x$ = \$12, we'd have enough to pay \$10 per period.

The difference between the gross premium (GP) and the net premium (NP) is usually defined as follows:

$$\text{GP} \cdot (1 - \text{Load}) = \text{NP} \quad \text{or} \quad \text{GP} = \text{NP}/(1 - \text{Load})$$

The load is typically a "percentage of premium" charge used to cover acquisition expenses, such as wholesaler compensation, financial adviser sales compensation, policy issuance, record setup, and the like, as well as state premium tax, if applicable.

FIGURE 6.7 Premium Conversion to Initial Benefit

Insurance companies typically consider their actuarial assumptions used to price immediate variable annuities—mortality rates, initial and ongoing expense assumptions, average contract size, federal income tax rates, deferred acquisition cost (DAC) tax rates, wholesaling allowances, and the like—to be proprietary information. External constituencies typically only see the resultant conversion factors that show the initial variable annuity benefit per $1,000 of premium.

Product expense and profit loads are invisible to both financial advisers and annuity contract owners. The initial variable annuity benefit per $1,000 of net premium is quoted, and 100% of the net premium is applied to this payout rate.

External constituencies don't see what's in the "black box" between the premium and the initial benefit amount (see Figure 6.7), nor do they need to in order to make an informed decision. For example, if Company A used more aggressive mortality assumptions but more conservative expense assumptions while Company B used more conservative mortality assumptions but more aggressive expense assumptions and both arrived at the same initial annuity benefit for the same premium, then it is inconsequential to the prospective IVA purchaser that they arrived at the same offer by different means. The prospective purchaser has all the necessary information to make an informed buying decision.

ANNUITY MATHEMATICS (NON-LIFE-CONTINGENT)

While life-contingent annuity payout options tend to fulfill the need for lifetime income in an optimal fashion, non-life-contingent fixed-period annuity options for IVAs also exist.

Fixed-Period Annuity Payout

The present value of a fixed-period annuity payout option that runs for a period of n years regardless of the survival or nonsurvival of the annuitant can be calculated as shown below. Let i be the AIR. Let $v = 1/(1 + i)$ be the factor that discounts a payment of 1 one year hence at interest rate i.

The present value of an annual annuity of 1 (one dollar, one unit, etc.) with first payment made at the beginning of the first year, designated $\ddot{a}_{\overline{n}|}$, can be calculated on a seriatim basis as shown in equation 6.1. An annuity with payments at the *beginning* of each period is called an annuity-due. (Since every dollar behaves like every other dollar, we calculate an annuity of 1. If we want to know the present value of an annuity where each payment is 100, we simply multiply the result by 100.)

$$\ddot{a}_{\overline{n}|} = 1 + v + v^2 + \ldots + v^{n-2} + v^{n-1} \tag{6.1}$$

A shortcut calculation exists. The terms of equation 6.1 are in geometric progression and form a *geometric series*. To find an expression for the sum of the geometric series, first we multiply both sides of equation 6.1 by $-v$, which results in equation 6.2.

$$-v\,\ddot{a}_{\overline{n}|} = -v - v^2 - v^3 - \cdots - v^{n-1} - v^n \tag{6.2}$$

Then we add equations 6.1 and 6.2:

$$
\begin{aligned}
\ddot{a}_{\overline{n}|} - v\,\ddot{a}_{\overline{n}|} &= 1 + (v - v) + (v^2 - v^2) + \cdots + (v^{n-1} - v^{n-1}) - v^n \\
(1 - v)\,\ddot{a}_{\overline{n}|} &= 1 - v^n \\
\ddot{a}_{\overline{n}|} &= \frac{1 - v^n}{1 - v} \quad (v \neq 1)
\end{aligned}
\tag{6.3}
$$

Analogously, the present value of an annuity-immediate, $a_{\overline{n}|}$, with payments at the *end* of each period is:

$$a_{\overline{n}|} = \frac{1 - v^n}{i}$$

The formula for $a_{\overline{n}|}$ can be derived by general reasoning. If an amount of 1 is invested at rate i, it will provide a series of payments of i per annum for n years and will remain intact at the end of this period. The present value of the future payments this unit of 1 will generate therefore equals:

- The value of an annuity of i per annum for n years, or $i a_{\overline{n}|}$, plus
- The value of a single payment of 1 at the end of n years, or v^n.

Thus,

$$1 = i a_{\overline{n}|} + v^n$$

$$a_{\overline{n}|} = \frac{1 - v^n}{i}$$

Again, as with life-contingent annuities, the first immediate variable annuity payment is determined by dividing the net premium by $\ddot{a}_{\overline{n}|}$ (or $a_{\overline{n}|}$). Tables in Appendixes M and N show values of $\ddot{a}_{\overline{n}|}$ and $a_{\overline{n}|}$, respectively, for various values of n at common AIRs.

Perpetuity

A *perpetuity* is an annuity where payments continue forever. It is the infinite extension of an n-year fixed-period annuity. An example of a perpetuity is the dividend on a preferred stock with no redemption provision.

The present value of a perpetuity-due, denoted $\ddot{a}_{\overline{\infty}|}$, is:

$$\ddot{a}_{\overline{\infty}|} = 1 + v + v^2 + \cdots \qquad (6.4)$$

We know from equation 6.3 that the partial sum, $\ddot{a}_{\overline{n}|}$, of the first n terms of this infinite geometric series is:

$$\frac{1 - v^n}{1 - v}$$

If the sequence $\ddot{a}_{\overline{1}|}, \ddot{a}_{\overline{2}|}, ..., \ddot{a}_{\overline{n}|}, ...$ of partial sums converges, and if $\lim_{n \to \infty} \ddot{a}_{\overline{n}|} = \ddot{a}_{\overline{\infty}|}$, then the sum of the infinite series is defined to be $\ddot{a}_{\overline{\infty}|}$.

If $v < 1$, then v^n gets closer and closer to 0 as n gets large. In fact, v^n can be made to approximate 0 as closely as we wish by taking n large enough. It follows that:

$$\lim_{n \to \infty} \ddot{a}_{\overline{n}|} = \lim_{n \to \infty} \frac{1 - v^n}{1 - v}$$

$$= \frac{1}{1 - v}$$

Analogously, the present value of a perpetuity-immediate, denoted $a_{\overline{\infty}|}$, is:

$$\lim_{n \to \infty} a_{\overline{n}|} = \lim_{n \to \infty} \frac{1 - v^n}{i} = \frac{1}{i}$$

Reversing course, if we know the present value of a perpetuity-due, $\ddot{a}_{\overline{\infty}|}$, the present value of an annuity-due for a fixed period of n years can be determined:

$$\ddot{a}_{\overline{n}|} = 1 + v + v^2 + \cdots + v^{n-1}$$

$$= \sum_{k=0}^{\infty} v^k - \sum_{k=n}^{\infty} v^k$$

$$= \frac{1}{1 - v} - v^n \sum_{k=0}^{\infty} v^k$$

$$= \frac{1}{1 - v} - v^n \frac{1}{1 - v}$$

$$= \ddot{a}_{\overline{\infty}|} - v^n \ddot{a}_{\overline{\infty}|}$$

$$= \ddot{a}_{\overline{\infty}|} (1 - v^n)$$

As a numerical example of a perpetuity, we know the present value of a perpetuity-due of 1 is:

$$\ddot{a}_{\overline{\infty}|} = 1 + v + v^2 + \cdots$$

$$= \frac{1}{1-v}$$

Suppose the interest rate i is 5%. Then,

$$\ddot{a}_{\overline{\infty}|} = \frac{1}{1 - \dfrac{1}{1.05}} = 21$$

With an initial value of 21, it is clear that we can pay 1 at the beginning of the year, have 20 left over, which—at 5% interest—will grow back to 21 at the beginning of the next year; and the process repeats.

Thus, if we want to pay a perpetuity of 1 annuity unit per year at the beginning of the year using a 5% AIR and starting with an annuity unit value of 1.000, we need \$21.

Similarly, if we want to pay a perpetuity of 1 annuity unit per year at the end of the year using a 5% AIR and starting with an annuity unit value of 1.000, we need $1/i = 1/0.05 = \$20$. Thus, \$20 at 5% will grow to \$21 at year-end, we can pay \$1, begin the second year also with \$20, and the process repeats.

Fixed-Period Annuities Payable More Frequently Than Once a Year

Annual "effective" interest rates are those for which interest is paid once a year. "Nominal" interest rates are those for which interest is paid more frequently than once a year.

Define the *nominal rate of interest* payable m times per year as $i^{(m)}$. A nominal rate of interest $i^{(m)}$ is an annual rate payable $m$thly, where the rate of interest is $i^{(m)}/m$ for each mth of a year. For example, a nominal rate of 4% payable quarterly denotes an interest rate of 1% per quarter; $i^{(4)}/4 = 1\%$.

If 1 is invested at the start of a year, interest during the first mth of a year is the principal, 1, times the interest rate, $i^{(m)}/m$, or $i^{(m)}/m$. During the second mth of a year, interest is the new balance, $1 + i^{(m)}/m$, times the interest rate $i^{(m)}/m$, or $(1 + i^{(m)}/m) \cdot i^{(m)}/m$. This produces a balance at the end of the second mth of a year of:

$$(1 + i^{(m)}/m) + (1 + i^{(m)}/m)i^{(m)}/m = (1 + i^{(m)}/m)^2$$

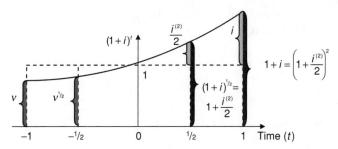

FIGURE 6.8 Nominal and Effective Rates of Compound Interest

Proceeding in a similar fashion, the year-end balance is $(1 + i^{(m)}/m)^m$. Because the year-end balance is also $1 + i$, we have

$$1 + i = (1 + i^{(m)}/m)^m$$

which yields the following relationships:

$$i = (1 + i^{(m)}/m)^m - 1$$
$$i^{(m)} = m[(1 + i)^{1/m} - 1]$$

For example, a nominal rate of 4% payable quarterly equates to an annual effective rate of 4.06%:

$$0.0406 = (1 + .04/4)^4 - 1$$

Figure 6.8 shows relationships between the discount factor v, effective interest rate i, and nominal interest rate $i^{(2)}$.

While not absolutely essential to an understanding of fixed-period annuities payable more frequently than once per year—since such present values can be expressed exclusively in terms of an annual effective interest rate i, or, equivalently, the discount factor $v = 1/(1 + i)$—such an understanding both allows for simpler formulas and reduces confusion over the interest rate that serves as an AIR for variable income annuities.

Annuity-Immediate

The present value, $a_{\overline{n}|}^{(m)}$, of an n-year fixed-period annuity-immediate with m payments per year and effective interest rate i is shown in equation 6.5.

The annuity pays $1/m$ at the end of each mth of a year for a total annual payment of 1.

$$
\begin{aligned}
a_{\overline{n}|}^{(m)} &= \frac{1}{m}[v^{1/m} + v^{2/m} + \cdots + v^{(mn-1)/m} + v^{n}] \\
&= \frac{1}{m}\left[\frac{v^{1/m} - v^{n+1/m}}{1 - v^{1/m}}\right] \\
&= \frac{1 - v^{n}}{m[(1+i)^{1/m} - 1]} \\
&= \frac{1 - v^{n}}{i^{(m)}}
\end{aligned}
$$

(6.5)

Note the following relationship between the present value of an annuity-immediate with one payment per year and an annuity-immediate with m payments per year:

$$
a_{\overline{n}|}^{(m)} = \frac{i}{i^{(m)}} a_{\overline{n}|}
$$

Thus, if one has a table of annuity present values, $a_{\overline{n}|}$, one can quickly derive $a_{\overline{n}|}^{(m)}$.

Values of $a_{\overline{n}|}^{(m)}$ appear in Appendix N.

Annuity-Due

Analogously, the present value, $\ddot{a}_{\overline{n}|}^{(m)}$, of an annuity that pays $1/m$ at the *beginning* of each $m$thly period for n years is:

$$
\begin{aligned}
\ddot{a}_{\overline{n}|}^{(m)} &= \frac{1}{m}[1 + v^{1/m} + v^{2/m} + \cdots + v^{n-1/m}] \\
&= \frac{1 - v^{n}}{m(1 - v^{1/m})}
\end{aligned}
$$

Another derivation is to note that since each payment is made one $m$thly period earlier, the present value must be $(1 + i)^{1/m}$ times that for an annuity with end-of-period payments:

$$
\begin{aligned}
\ddot{a}_{\overline{n}|}^{(m)} &= (1+i)^{1/m} a_{\overline{n}|}^{(m)} \\
&= \frac{1 - v^{n}}{m(1 - v^{1/m})}
\end{aligned}
$$

As the number of payments m each year grows larger and larger, the interval of time between payments grows smaller and smaller. The limiting case is where the frequency of payments becomes infinite; that is, payments are made continuously.

While one does not hand out annuity benefits on a continuous basis in practice, a continuous annuity is of interest. For example, it can be used to approximate annuities with a high payment frequency, such as daily. It serves as a double check, since the present value of an annuity-immediate converges toward the present value of a continuous annuity from below it with increasing m. The present value of an annuity-due converges toward the present value of a continuous annuity from above it with increasing m. This convergence is visible in the tables in Appendix M.

Force of Interest

To fully understand continuous annuities, it is helpful to first understand the *force of interest*. An effective rate of interest i measures interest over one year. A nominal rate of interest $i^{(m)}$ is a measure of interest paid over $m$ths of a year. We can continue this progression in the study of interest by looking at interest over infinitesimally small intervals of time.

Consider the intensity with which interest operates at a particular moment of time. This measure is called the *force of interest*.

Define an *accumulation function* $a(t)$ that represents the accumulated value at time t ($t \geq 0$) of a principal investment of 1. One common accumulation function is *simple interest*, where $a(t) = 1 + it$, for $t \geq 0$. Note that this is a *linear* function.

Another common accumulation function is *compound interest*, where $a(t) = (1 + i)^t$, for $t \geq 0$. Note that this is an *exponential* function.

Graphs of simple interest and compound interest appear in Figure 6.9; $a(0) = 1$ and $a(1) = 1 + i$ for both simple interest and compound interest. The simple interest accumulation function exceeds compound interest on the interval $(0, 1)$. On the interval $(1, +\infty)$, the compound interest accumulation function exceeds the simple interest function. In all the annuity calculations thus far and from this point on, compound interest is assumed.

In Figure 6.9, the slope of the tangent line to the accumulation function $a(t)$ at any point t_0 is given by the derivative at that point, $a'(t_0)$. But as the accumulated value increases with time, the rate of change increases simply because there is more value in the fund. For example, note that the tangent line to the compound interest curve would get progressively steeper as we move to the right—even though the formula responsible for fund growth tells us that interest for any year is consistently equal to i times the beginning-of-year fund value.

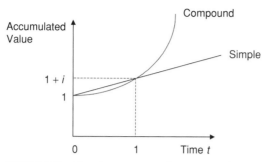

FIGURE 6.9   Simple Interest and Compound Interest

Thus, the derivative alone is an unacceptable measure of the instantaneous rate of interest because it depends on the amount in the fund at time t. We remedy this by "normalizing" the measure by dividing $a'(t)$ by the amount in the fund at time t, namely $a(t)$. This measure, the force of interest, is denoted by δ_t. It measures the intensity with which interest operates at time t, expressed as a rate independent of the amount in the fund.

$$\delta_t = \frac{a'(t)}{a(t)}$$

where δ_t is an instantaneous measure of interest at time t expressed as an annual rate. The instantaneous rate of interest δ_t may be viewed as the fundamental rate, where an interest rate found by measurement for any other time period merely expresses the results of the instantaneous rate by relating the effect of its operation to a given interval of time.

For the compound interest function $a(t) = (1 + i)^t$, we have

$$\delta_t = \frac{d/dt(1+i)^t}{(1+i)^t}$$

$$= \frac{(1+i)^t \log_e (1+i)}{(1+i)^t}$$

$$= \log_e (1+i)$$

where $\log_e$ is the natural logarithm

Since δ_t is constant and does not depend on t, we can omit the subscript and state that for compound interest:

$$\delta = \log_e (1 + i)$$

Taking the antilogarithm of both sides,

$$e^{\delta} = 1 + i$$

Equation 6.6 relates the measures of interest (effective, nominal, and instantaneous):

$$1 + i = \left[1 + \frac{i^{(m)}}{m} \right]^m = e^{\delta} \tag{6.6}$$

Continuous Fixed-Period Annuity

Denote by $\bar{a}_{\overline{n}|}$ the present value of an annuity payable continuously for n years, where the total amount paid each year is 1. Then

$$\bar{a}_{\overline{n}|} = \int_0^n v^t dt$$

$$= \frac{v^t}{\log_e v} \Big|_0^n$$

$$= \frac{1 - v^n}{\delta}$$

since $\log_e v = \log_e [1/(1 + i)] = \log_e 1 - \log_e (1 + i) = 0 - \delta = -\delta$.

Varying Benefit Annuities

Thus far the annuities considered pay *level* benefits (1) if they are an immediate fixed annuity or (2) if the AIR is exactly achieved and they are an immediate variable annuity. We now consider annuities that pay *varying* benefits, again (1) if an immediate fixed annuity or (2) if the AIR is exactly achieved under an immediate variable annuity.

The total present value of a *varying* annuity can be determined by calculating the present value of each individual benefit separately and summing the results. For annuity benefits that form an *arithmetic progression* or a *geometric progression*, we derive simplified formulas.

An *arithmetic progression* is one where given the first benefit b_1 and common difference d, succeeding terms in the sequence are obtained by the rule

$$b_{n+1} = b_n + d, \quad n = 1, 2, 3, \ldots$$

A *geometric progression* is one where given the first benefit b_1 and common ratio r, succeeding terms in the sequence are obtained by the rule

$$b_{n+1} = b_n \cdot r, \quad n = 1, 2, 3, \ldots$$

Payments Vary in Arithmetic Progression

Consider an annuity where benefits begin at B and increase by D each year. Assume benefits are payable annually at the end of the year for n years. See Figure 6.10.

(Assume all benefit payments are greater than zero; that is, B is positive and D can be positive or negative, provided that the final payment $B + (n - 1)D > 0$.)

Let S be the sum of the terms in equation 6.7. We'll calculate $(1 + i)S$, then subtract equation 6.7 from equation 6.8.

$$S = Bv + (B + D)v^2 + (B + 2D)v^3 + \cdots + [B + (n - 2)D]v^{n-1}$$
$$+ [B + (n - 1)D]v^n \tag{6.7}$$

$$(1 + i)S = B + (B + D)v + (B + 2D)v^2 + \cdots + [B + (n - 2)D]v^{n-2}$$
$$+ [B + (n - 1)D]v^{n-1} \tag{6.8}$$

$$\overline{iS = B + D(v + v^2 + v^3 + \cdots + v^{n-1}) - Bv^n - (n - 1)Dv^n}$$
$$= B(1 - v^n) + D(v + v^2 + v^3 + \cdots + v^{n-1} + v^n) - nDv^n$$

Therefore,

$$S = B\frac{1 - v^n}{i} + D\frac{a_{\overline{n}|} - nv^n}{i}$$

$$= Ba_{\overline{n}|} + D\frac{a_{\overline{n}|} - nv^n}{i} \tag{6.9}$$

This formula gives the present value S for benefit payments that vary in arithmetic progression.

For example, the present value of a 20-year annuity-immediate at 3% interest of benefit payments that begin at 1,000 and increase 50 per year, as shown in Figure 6.11, is:

$$S = 1{,}000\,a_{\overline{20}|} + 50\frac{a_{\overline{20}|} - 20v^{20}}{0.03} = 21{,}217.41$$

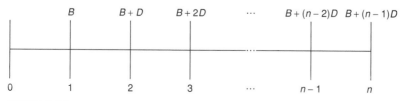

| | B | $B + D$ | $B + 2D$ | $\cdots$ | $B + (n-2)D$ | $B + (n-1)D$ |

FIGURE 6.10   Payments Varying in Arithmetic Progression

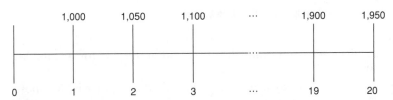

FIGURE 6.11 Arithmetic Progression Numerical Example

Note that benefits in Figure 6.11 would be those for (1) a fixed annuity at 3% interest or (2) a variable annuity if the 3% AIR were exactly realized, when the annuity under observation is one where benefits are projected to vary in arithmetic progression if the AIR is precisely met.

For an annuity-due, all benefit payments are received one year earlier. Thus, the present value of an annuity-due with benefits in arithmetic progression is the present value of an annuity-immediate adjusted for interest of one year. Multiplying equation 6.9 for S by $(1 + i)$ and simplifying, we have the following value for an annuity-due with benefits in arithmetic progression:

$$(1+i)S = B\ddot{a}_{\overline{n}|} + D\frac{\ddot{a}_{\overline{n}|} - nv^{n-1}}{i}$$

Payments Vary in Geometric Progression

Consider an annuity where benefits begin at B and increase by the common ratio $(1 + c)$ each year. Assume benefits are payable annually at the end of the year for n years. See Figure 6.12.

Present value $= B[v + (1 + c)v^2 + (1 + c)^2v^3 + \cdots + (1 + c)^{n-1}v^n]$

$\qquad\qquad\qquad\qquad\qquad\qquad\qquad\qquad\qquad$ (6.10)

$\qquad\quad = Bv\{1 + [(1 + c)v] + [(1 + c)v]^2 + \cdots + [(1 + c)v]^{n-1}\}$

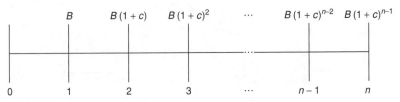

FIGURE 6.12 Payments Varying in Geometric Progression

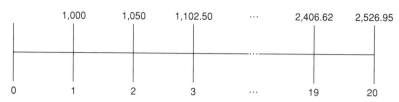

FIGURE 6.13 Geometric Progression Numerical Example

In the opening section on fixed-period annuity payouts, we showed in equation 6.3 that the sum of the first n terms of a geometric progression with ratio r is $(1 - r^n)/(1 - r)$. Thus,

$$\text{Present value} = Bv\frac{1-[(1+c)v]^n}{1-[(1+c)v]}$$

$$= B\frac{1}{1+i} \cdot \frac{1-[(1+c)/(1+i)]^n}{1-[(1+c)/(1+i)]} \qquad (6.11)$$

$$= B\frac{1-[(1+c)/(1+i)]^n}{i-c}$$

While equation 6.11 is undefined if $i = c$, this simply implies the factor $[(1 + c)v] = [(1 + c)/(1 + i)]$ in equation 6.10 equals 1, in which case the present value is simply Bvn.

For example, the present value of a 20-year annuity-immediate at 3% interest of benefit payments that begin at 1,000 and increase 5% per year, as shown in Figure 6.13, is:

$$\text{Present value} = 1,000\frac{1-[(1.05)/(1.03)]^{20}}{0.03-0.05} = 23,453.33$$

As expected, the present value of an annuity that increases 5% geometrically exceeds the present value of an annuity that increases 5% arithmetically. See Figure 6.14.

In general, _geometrically increasing_ variable income annuities—where the annuity benefit increases by a certain percentage if the AIR is exactly met—are not available. This is because a comparable benefit progression can be achieved via judicious choice of AIR.

For example, suppose we have a standard IVA with a 3% AIR where annuity benefits remain level if the AIR is met. In the scenario of an actual 7% net investment return, we know:

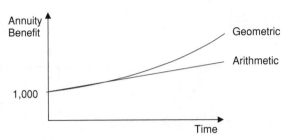

FIGURE 6.14   Present Value of Geometrically
Increasing Annuity Exceeds Present Value of
Comparable Arithmetically Increasing Annuity

$$\text{Second annual benefit}^{\text{Level}} = \text{First annual benefit} \cdot \frac{1.07}{1.03}$$

$$\approx \text{First annual benefit} \cdot 1.04$$

Now suppose an IVA has a 7% AIR, but annuity benefits increase at a compound annual rate of 4% if the AIR is exactly met. Suppose that in the first year the actual net investment return of the subaccount(s) elected is again 7%. Then,

$$\text{Second annual benefit}^{\text{Increasing}} = \text{First annual benefit} \cdot 1.04$$

$$\cdot \frac{1 + \text{Investment return}}{1 + \text{AIR}}$$

$$= \text{First annual benefit} \cdot 1.04 \cdot \frac{1.07}{1.07}$$

$$= \text{First annual benefit} \cdot 1.04$$

The benefit progression of the 3% AIR annuity in this example is about the same as the benefit progression of the 7% AIR annuity where benefits increase by 4% if the AIR is met. (An actual investment return of 7.12% for both IVAs and a 7.12% AIR for the 4% increasing annuity would produce *exactly* a 4% increase in second annual benefit in both situations.)

The first approach—the "traditional" one—makes the product simpler, since *all* movement in annuity benefit level is attributable to net subaccount performance relative to the AIR.

ANNUITY MATHEMATICS II (LIFE-CONTINGENT)

In the Annuity Mathematics (Life-Contingent) section earlier in this chapter, we looked at the basics of life-contingent annuities, namely single straight life annuity options with annual payments. Here, we investigate other annuity payout options, benefit modes more frequent than annually, and annuities that cover more than one life.

Pure Endowments

Since l_x is the number of lives beginning year of age x and since l_{x+n} is the number of lives beginning year of age $x + n$, then l_{x+n}/l_x represents that portion of the original group of l_x lives that survive to begin year of age $x + n$. We denote this probability p that a life age x will survive n years by $_np_x$:

$$_np_x = \frac{l_{x+n}}{l_x}$$

If a life age x is to receive a payment of K at the end of n years if he is then living, such a deferred payment is called an *n-year pure endowment of K*. The present value is $K \cdot v^n \cdot {}_np_x$, where v is the discount factor.

The present value at age x of an *n-year pure endowment (E) of 1* is denoted by $_nE_x$:

$$_nE_x = v^n \cdot {}_np_x = v^n \cdot \frac{l_{x+n}}{l_x}$$

Recall our earlier introduction to *commutation functions*, where $D_x = v^x \cdot l_x$. Then,

$$_nE_x = v^n \cdot \frac{l_{x+n}}{l_x} = \frac{v^{x+n}}{v^x} \cdot \frac{l_{x+n}}{l_x} = \frac{D_{x+n}}{D_x}$$

$_nE_x$ is the *net single premium* at age x for an *n-year pure endowment of 1*. Ignoring expenses, it represents the single premium a life age x makes now in exchange for a payment of 1 by the insurer n years from now if he is still alive.

For example, consider the net single premium for a 65-year-old male for a 20-year pure endowment of $1,000 using the Annuity 2000 Mortality Table and 5% interest. Using the D_x column for 5% in Appendix G-3, we have:

$$1,000 \,_{20}E_{65} = 1,000 \frac{D_{85}}{D_{65}} = 1,000 \frac{74.4098}{372.5131} = 199.75$$

Note that in this same table, $l_{65} = 8,880.6752$ and $l_{85} = 4,706.7425$. Suppose each of the 8,880.6752 lives at age 65 contributes 199.75 to a fund that grows at 5% interest for 20 years, at which time the accumulated value is distributed equally among the survivors. There should be exactly enough to provide 1,000 to each of them:

Original group of 65-year-olds	8,880.6752
Contribution	× 199.75
Initial fund	1,773,922.22
Accumulated at 5% for 20 years	× $(1.05)^{20}$
Accumulated value after 20 years	4,706,743.76
Survivors at age 85	÷ 4,706.7425
Share per survivor	1,000.00

Note that interest at 5% alone would cause each original participant's 199.75 to accumulate after 20 years to 530.00, *with benefit of interest*. Because each survivor is also entitled to a share of the forfeitures of those who die before age 85, each original participant's 199.75 accumulates after 20 years to 1,000.00, with benefit of interest *and survivorship*.

Figure 6.15 illustrates the higher accumulated value attributable to this pooling approach where a fund accumulates with both *benefit of interest* and *benefit of survivorship*.

$_{n}E_{x}$ accumulates over n years with benefit of interest and survivorship to 1. Thus, $1/_{n}E_{x}$ is an n-year accumulation factor for interest and survivorship, since $_{n}E_{x} \cdot (1/_{n}E_{x}) = 1$.

$$199.75 \cdot 1.05^{20} \cdot \frac{l_{65}}{l_{85}} = 199.75 \cdot 2.653 \cdot 1.887 = 1,000.00$$

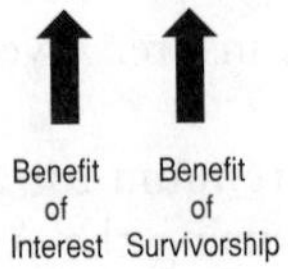

Benefit of Interest   Benefit of Survivorship

FIGURE 6.15 Benefit of Interest and Survivorship

Conversely, 1 discounts over n years with interest and survivorship to $_nE_x$. Thus, $_nE_x$ is an n-year discount factor for interest and survivorship, since $1 \cdot (_nE_x) = {_nE_x}$.

Annuity Payout Options: Single Life with Annual Benefits

A single life annuity with annual payments of 1 commencing at the end of one year can be viewed as a series of pure endowments. Its present value, a_x, is:

$$a_x = {_1E_x} + {_2E_x} + {_3E_x} + \cdots + {_{\omega-x-1}E_x}$$

$$= \sum_{t=1}^{\omega-x-1} {_tE_x} \qquad (6.12)$$

$$= \sum_{t=1}^{\omega-x-1} \frac{D_{x+t}}{D_x}$$

Earlier, we defined $N_x = \sum_{k=x}^{\omega-1} D_k = D_x + D_{x+1} + D_{x+2} + \cdots + D_{\omega-1}$. Equation 6.12 then becomes:

$$a_x = \frac{N_{x+1}}{D_x}$$

Commutation function values for N_x and D_x at common AIRs are given in Appendix G. N_x commutation columnar values are easily calculated by summing D_x values from the oldest age backward to the youngest age. This definition of N_x makes it clear that $N_x = N_{x+1} + D_x$.

Another annuity option is an *n-year temporary life annuity*. Rather than continuing payments as long as the annuitant survives as in the preceding single life annuity, benefits are again payable if the annuitant survives but only for a maximum period of n years.

The present value of an annual n-year temporary life annuity of 1, denoted $a_{x:\overline{n}|}$, is:

$$a_{x:\overline{n}|} = \sum_{t=1}^{n} {_tE_x} = \sum_{t=1}^{n} \frac{D_{x+t}}{D_x} = \frac{N_{x+1} - N_{x+n+1}}{D_x}$$

Another annuity option is an *n-year deferred life annuity*. This is a life annuity where payments during the first *n* years are excluded. If the annuitant survives from age x to age $x + n$, and payments are made annually at the end of the year, he will receive his first payment one year later, if surviving. The present value, denoted $_{n|}a_x$, is:

$$_{n|}a_x = \sum_{t=n+1}^{\omega-x-1} {}_tE_x = \frac{1}{D_x} \sum_{t=n+1}^{\omega-x-1} D_{x+t} = \frac{N_{x+n+1}}{D_x}$$

Since the combination of an *n*-year temporary life annuity and an *n*-year deferred life annuity produces a life annuity, it should come as no surprise that the sum of the present values of the former produces the present value of the latter:

$$\frac{N_{x+1} - N_{x+n+1}}{D_x} + \frac{N_{x+n+1}}{D_x} = \frac{N_{x+1}}{D_x}$$

$$a_{x:\overline{n}|} \qquad + \quad _{n|}a_x \quad = \quad a_x$$

An *n-year deferred k-year temporary life annuity* excludes the first *n* years of payments, then makes annual payments at the end of each year for *k* years if the annuitant survives. The present value, denoted $_{n|k}a_x$, is:

$$_{n|k}a_x = \sum_{t=n+1}^{n+k} {}_tE_x = \frac{1}{D_x} \sum_{t=n+1}^{n+k} D_{x+t} = \frac{N_{x+n+1} - N_{x+n+k+1}}{D_x}$$

An annuity like those just described, having payments made at the *end* of each payment period (here one year), is labeled *annuity-immediate*. An annuity for which a payment is made at the *beginning* of each payment period is labeled *annuity-due*.

For example, a life annuity-due with annual payments of 1 (where the first payment is made at the beginning of each year) makes an instant payment of 1 and then has the same payment schedule as a life annuity-immediate with annual payments of 1. Thus, the present value (PV) of a life annuity-due, denoted $\ddot{a}_x$, is:

$$\ddot{a}_x = 1 + a_x = 1 + \frac{N_{x+1}}{D_x} = \frac{N_x}{D_x}$$

Summary of Life-Contingent Annuities with Annual Payments of 1

Annuity Payout Option	Annuity-Due PV	Annuity-Immediate PV
Life annuity	$\ddot{a}_x = \dfrac{N_x}{D_x}$	$a_x = \dfrac{N_{x+1}}{D_x}$
n-year temporary life annuity	$\ddot{a}_{x:\overline{n}\rvert} = \dfrac{N_x - N_{x+n}}{D_x}$	$a_{x:\overline{n}\rvert} = \dfrac{N_{x+1} - N_{x+n+1}}{D_x}$
n-year deferred life annuity	$_{n\rvert}\ddot{a}_x = \dfrac{N_{x+n}}{D_x}$	$_{n\rvert}a_x = \dfrac{N_{x+n+1}}{D_x}$
n-year deferred k-year temporary life annuity	$_{n\rvert k}\ddot{a}_x = \dfrac{N_{x+n} - N_{x+n+k}}{D_x}$	$_{n\rvert k}a_x = \dfrac{N_{x+n+1} - N_{x+n+k+1}}{D_x}$

Annuity Payout Options: Single Life with Benefits Payable More Frequently Than Annually

Life-contingent annuities are typically payable more frequently than once a year, with monthly benefits being quite common. In general, we can evaluate annuities payable m times per year, where 1, 2, 4, and 12 are customary values for m.

We will continue to assume total payments of 1 per year. An annuity-immediate with m payments per year will pay $1/m$ at equal $m$thly intervals. The first benefit of $1/m$ is payable at age $x + 1/m$, the next at age $x + 2/m$, and so forth, contingent on the survival of the life age x at issue.

The present value of a life annuity-immediate of 1 payable m times per year is denoted $a_x^{(m)}$. Its present value is given by:

$$a_x^{(m)} = \frac{1}{m}\left(\frac{l_{x+1/m}}{l_x} \cdot v^{x+1/m} + \frac{l_{x+2/m}}{l_x} \cdot v^{x+2/m} + \cdots \right)$$

$$= \frac{1}{m}\sum_{t=1}^{\infty} \frac{D_{x+t/m}}{D_x}$$

$$= \frac{1}{m}\sum_{t=1}^{\infty} {}_{t/m}E_x$$

The upper limit of the summation is technically $m(\omega - x)$, but for brevity it is written here as ∞ since $D_{x+t/m} = 0$ for all terms where $t \geq m(\omega - x)$ since there are no survivors there.

If l_x is described by a mathematical formula, then $a_x^{(m)}$ may be evaluated precisely. In actual practice, such is usually not the case and the value of

$$\sum_{t=1}^{\infty} D_{x+t/m}$$

must be approximated.

The approximation in equation 6.13 is by far the one most frequently used:

$$a_x^{(m)} \approx a_x + \frac{m-1}{2m} \tag{6.13}$$

A precise derivation of this approximation formula is provided in the following section.

Derivation of Approximation Formula for Present Value of Annuities Payable More Frequently Than Annually

Approach

So the reader may understand where this is leading, the approximation formula used is the first two terms of *Woolhouse's formula*, which derives from the *Euler-Maclaurin formula*, which derives from the *Taylor series*.

Taylor Series

Consider a function f as a power series in $(x - a)$; that is,

$$f(x) = \sum_{n=0}^{\infty} c_n (x-a)^n$$
$$= c_0 + c_1(x-a) + c_2(x-a)^2 + \cdots + c_n(x-a)^n + \cdots \tag{6.14}$$

Suppose the radius of convergence of this power series is R, meaning that on the interval $(a - R, a + R)$ the power series converges for each value of x and the series represents a number that is the sum of the series. This power series defines the function $f(x)$, where the domain of f includes all values of x for which the power series converges, namely those values of x in the interval $(a - R, a + R)$.

If we repeatedly differentiate the function $f(x)$, where the nth derivative is denoted $f^{(n)}(x)$, we have

$$f^{(1)}(x) = c_1 + 2c_2(x-a) + 3c_3(x-a)^2 + 4c_4(x-a)^3 + \cdots + nc_n(x-a)^{n-1} + \cdots$$

$$f^{(2)}(x) = 2c_2 + 2 \cdot 3c_3(x-a) + 3 \cdot 4c_4(x-a)^2 + \cdots + (n-1) \cdot nc_n(x-a)^{n-2} + \cdots$$

$$f^{(3)}(x) = 2 \cdot 3c_3 + 2 \cdot 3 \cdot 4c_4(x-a) + \cdots + (n-2) \cdot (n-1) \cdot nc_n(x-a)^{n-3} + \cdots$$

and so on. If we let $x = a$ in the power series, we find

$$c_0 = f(a) \quad c_1 = f^{(1)}(a) \quad c_2 = \frac{f^{(2)}(a)}{2!} \quad c_3 = \frac{f^{(3)}(a)}{3!}$$

In general,

$$c_n = \frac{f^{(n)}(a)}{n!}$$

where $n! = n \cdot (n-1) \cdot (n-2) \cdots 2 \cdot 1$
$ 0! \equiv 1$

Substituting these c_n values into the power series $f(x)$ shown in equation 6.14, we have

$$\sum_{n=0}^{\infty} \frac{f^{(n)}(a)}{n!}(x-a)^n = f(a) + f^{(1)}(a)(x-a) + \frac{f^{(2)}(a)}{2!}(x-a)^2 + \cdots + \frac{f^{(n)}(a)}{n!}(x-a)^n + \cdots$$

This is called the *Taylor series* of f at a.

In the special case where $a = 0$, we have

$$\sum_{n=0}^{\infty} \frac{f^{(n)}(0)}{n!}x^n = f(0) + f^{(1)}(0)x + \frac{f^{(2)}(0)}{2!}x^2 + \cdots + \frac{f^{(n)}(0)}{n!}x^n + \cdots$$

This is called the *Maclaurin series*.

For example, if $f(x) = e^x$, then $f^{(n)}(x) = e^x$ for all x. Therefore, $f^{(n)}(0) = 1$ for all n. The Maclaurin series for e^x is given by

$$1 + x + \frac{x^2}{2!} + \frac{x^3}{3!} + \cdots + \frac{x^n}{n!} + \cdots$$

We say the function $f(x) = e^x$ is given by the *Taylor* (or *Maclaurin*) series expansion.[6]

Euler-Maclaurin Formula

The Euler-Maclaurin formula describes the sum of a function, $\Sigma f(x)$, over a certain range in terms of the integral of the function, $\int f(x)\, dx$, over the same range plus adjustment terms. The adjustment terms are based on derivatives at the endpoints of the range.

To derive this formula, some notation from numerical analysis regarding finite differences is helpful.

1. Define $\Delta f(x)$ as the *first difference* of a function $f(x)$ found by subtracting successive functional values:

$$\Delta f(x) = f(x + 1) - f(x)$$

Differences of $f(x)$ arranged in a tabular format create a *difference table,* like Table 6.3.

Δ is the *forward difference operator,* which applied to a function changes it into another function.

2. Define the *shifting operator* $Ef(x)$ as

$$Ef(x) = f(x + 1) \tag{6.15}$$

Thus,

$$\Delta f(x) = f(x + 1) - f(x) = Ef(x) - f(x) \tag{6.16}$$

In terms of operators that can be applied to a generic function $f(x)$, we have

$$\Delta \equiv E - 1 \tag{6.17}$$

and

$$E \equiv 1 + \Delta \tag{6.18}$$

The "1" in equations 6.17 and 6.18 is the *identity operator,* which leaves the function unchanged.

Analogous to the need in calculus to find *antiderivatives* in order to integrate, in numerical analysis one needs to find *antidifferences* to perform summations.

TABLE 6.3   Difference Table

x	$f(x)$	$\Delta f(x)$
0	$f(0)$	
		$\Delta f(0)$
1	$f(1)$	
		$\Delta f(1)$
2	$f(2)$	
		$\Delta f(2)$
3	$f(3)$	

To evaluate $\sum_{x=a}^{b} f(x)$, we seek a function $F(x)$ such that $\Delta F(x) = f(x)$. Then,

$$f(a) = F(a + 1) - F(a)$$
$$f(a + 1) = F(a + 2) - F(a + 1)$$
$$f(a + 2) = F(a + 3) - F(a + 2)$$
$$\cdots$$
$$f(b - 1) = F(b) - F(b - 1)$$
$$f(b) = F(b + 1) - F(b)$$

Summing both sides produces

$$\sum_{x=a}^{b} f(x) = \sum_{x=a}^{b} \Delta F(x) = F(x)\Big|_{a}^{b+1} = F(b+1) - F(a) \qquad (6.19)$$

3. Define Σ as the *summation operator*. From equation 6.19, we see that $\Sigma \Delta F(x) = F(x)$, using correct limits of summation. In terms of operators, $\Sigma \Delta \equiv 1$. We can also say $\Delta^{-1} \equiv \Sigma$, so that differencing and summation can be viewed as inverse operators.

4. Define D as the *derivative operator*. Note that an operator can be applied more than once. For example, since $Ef(x) = f(x + 1)$, we have $Ef(0) = f(1)$, $E^2 f(0) = f(2)$, and $E^x f(0) = f(x)$.
   Recall the *Maclaurin series* for the function $f(x)$:

$$f(x) = \sum_{n=0}^{\infty} \frac{f^{(n)}(0)}{n!} x^n = f(0) + f^{(1)}(0)x + \frac{f^{(2)}(0)}{2!} x^2 + \cdots + \frac{f^{(n)}(0)}{n!} x^n + \cdots$$

Expressed in terms of operators on $f(0)$, this becomes

$$E^x = 1 + x \cdot D + \frac{x^2}{2!} \cdot D^2 + \frac{x^3}{3!} \cdot D^3 + \cdots$$
$$= e^{xD}$$

(since the earlier example showed the form of the Maclaurin series for e^x). Thus,

$$E \equiv 1 + \Delta \equiv e^{D}$$

implying

$$D \equiv \log_e(1 + \Delta) \equiv \log_e E$$

5. Derivation: Then, the summation of a function $f(x)$ is given by

$$\sum f(x) = \Delta^{-1} f(x)$$

$$= (e^D - 1)^{-1} f(x)$$

$$= \left(D + \frac{D^2}{2!} + \frac{D^3}{3!} + \frac{D^4}{4!} + \cdots \right)^{-1} f(x) \quad \text{(by series expansion)}$$

$$= \left(D^{-1} - \frac{1}{2} + \frac{D}{12} - \frac{D^3}{720} + \cdots \right) f(x) \quad \text{(by division)}$$

$$= \int f(x)dx - \frac{1}{2}f(x) + \frac{1}{12}f^{(1)}(x) - \frac{1}{720}f^{(3)}(x) + \cdots$$

(6.20)

Recall from equation 6.19 that if we can find a function $F(x)$ such that $\Delta F(x) = f(x)$, then

$$\sum_{x=a}^{b} f(x) = \sum_{x=a}^{b} \Delta F(x) = F(x)\Big|_a^{b+1} = F(b+1) - F(a)$$

We know that the terms to the right of the equal sign in equation 6.20 constitute such a function $F(x)$, so the summation $\sum f(x)$ from $x = 0$ to $x = n - 1$ equals the terms to the right of the equal sign evaluated from $x = 0$ to $x = n$:

$$\sum_{x=0}^{n-1} f(x) = \int_0^n f(x)dx - \frac{1}{2}\left[f(n) - f(0)\right] + \frac{1}{12}\left[f^{(1)}(n) - f^{(1)}(0)\right]$$

$$- \frac{1}{720}[f^{(3)}(n) - f^{(3)}(0)] + \cdots$$

Adding $f(n)$ to both sides produces the more customary form of the *Euler-Maclaurin formula*:

$$\sum_{x=0}^{n} f(x) = \int_0^n f(x)dx + \frac{1}{2}\left[f(n) + f(0)\right] + \frac{1}{12}\left[f^{(1)}(n) - f^{(1)}(0)\right]$$

$$- \frac{1}{720}[f^{(3)}(n) - f^{(3)}(0)] + \cdots$$

Woolhouse's Formula

The whole point of this exercise is that we wish to calculate the present value of a life annuity with payments more frequently than annually, where there are m payments per year. This, however, depends on discounting for survivorship payments at intervals smaller than the annual mortality rates given in a mortality table. One algorithm to accomplish this is *Woolhouse's formula.*

Suppose we have functional values (i.e., mortality rates) tabulated at integral points $x = 0, 1, 2, \ldots, n$. Each of the n intervals is divided into m subintervals (see Figure 6.16). There are $n \cdot m$ subintervals.

Woolhouse's formula will express the sum of a function at the $m$thly points as m times the sum at the integral points plus some adjustment terms. Since the sum at $m$thly points has m times as many terms as the sum at integral points, this seems sensible.

From the Euler-Maclaurin formula, we know

$$\int_0^n f(x)dx = [f(0) + f(1) + \cdots + f(n)] - \frac{1}{2}[f(n) + f(0)] - \frac{1}{12}[f^{(1)}(n) - f^{(1)}(0)]$$
$$+ \frac{1}{720}[f^{(3)}(n) - f^{(3)}(0)] - \cdots$$

(6.21)

Heretofore we have implicitly assumed an *interval of differencing* of 1. We assumed functional values were tabulated one unit apart, so we defined the first forward difference

$$\Delta f(x) = f(x + 1) - f(x)$$

More generally, we may let the *interval of differencing* be c, whereby

$$\underset{c}{\Delta} f(x) = f(x + c) - f(x)$$

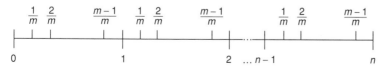

FIGURE 6.16   Subdivision of Intervals

If we repeat the approach to the derivation of the Euler-Maclaurin formula for interval of differencing $c = 1/m$, it becomes

$$m\int_0^n f(x)dx = [f(0) + f(1/m) + f(2/m) + \cdots + f(n)] - \frac{1}{2}[f(n) + f(0)]$$

$$-\frac{1}{12m}[f^{(1)}(n) - f^{(1)}(0)] + \frac{1}{720m^3}[f^{(3)}(n) - f^{(3)}(0)] - \cdots$$

(6.22)

If we multiply equation 6.21 by m, we can equate the right-hand side of equation 6.21 with the right-hand side of equation 6.22 to find

$$[f(0) + f(1/m) + f(2/m) + \cdots + f(n)] = m[f(0) + f(1) + \cdots + f(n)]$$

$$-\frac{m-1}{2}[f(n) + f(0)] - \frac{m^2 - 1}{12m}[f^{(1)}(n) - f^{(1)}(0)]$$

$$+\frac{m^4 - 1}{720m^3}[f^{(3)}(n) - f^{(3)}(0)] - \cdots$$

This is *Woolhouse's formula.*

Applying Woolhouse's Formula

To determine $a_x^{(m)}$, the present value of a life annuity-immediate of 1 payable m times per year at the rate of $1/m$ per payment, we wish to calculate the following sum:

$$a_x^{(m)} = \frac{1}{m}\left(\frac{l_{x+1/m}}{l_x} \cdot v^{1/m} + \frac{l_{x+2/m}}{l_x} \cdot v^{2/m} + \cdots\right)$$

$$= \frac{1}{m}\sum_{t=1}^{\infty}\frac{D_{x+t/m}}{D_x}$$

$$= \frac{1}{mD_x}\sum_{t=1}^{\infty}D_{x+t/m}$$

We can apply Woolhouse's formula. Note that since we're calculating an annuity-*immediate* here, we wish to calculate $f(1/m) + f(2/m) + \cdots + f(n)$ and, thus, the $f(0)$ term is subtracted.

$$a_x^{(m)} = \frac{1}{mD_x} \sum_{t=1}^{\infty} D_{x+t/m}$$

$$= \frac{1}{mD_x} \left[\sum_{t=0}^{\infty} D_{x+t/m} - D_x \right]$$

$$= \frac{-1}{m} + \frac{1}{mD_x} \left[\sum_{t=0}^{\infty} D_{x+t/m} \right]$$

$$= \frac{-1}{m} + \frac{1}{D_x} \left[\sum_{t=0}^{\infty} D_{x+t} - \frac{m-1}{2m}(D_\infty + D_x) \right.$$

$$\left. -\frac{m^2-1}{12m^2} \left(\frac{dD_\infty}{dx} - \frac{dD_x}{dx} \right) + \cdots \right]$$

Recalling that the upper limit of the summation has been symbolized by ∞, $D_\infty = D_\omega = 0$. To find the derivative of D_x, we have from calculus

$$\frac{dD_x}{dx} = v^x \cdot \frac{dl_x}{dx} + l_x \cdot \frac{dv^x}{dx}$$

Let us define a new term, μ_x, called the *force of mortality* (which will be described in detail later in this chapter) as $\mu_x = -l_x'/l_x$. We then have $dl_x/dx = -l_x\mu_x$. The derivative of v^x is $v^x \log_e v = -v^x\delta$. Making these substitutions, we have

$$a_x^{(m)} = \frac{-1}{m} + \frac{1}{D_x} \left[\sum_{t=0}^{\infty} D_{x+t} - \frac{m-1}{2m} D_x \right.$$

$$\left. -\frac{m^2-1}{12m^2} \{0 - [v^x \cdot (-l_x\mu_x) + l_x \cdot (-v^x\delta)]\} + \cdots \right]$$

$$= \frac{N_x}{D_x} - \frac{m+1}{2m} - \frac{m^2-1}{12m^2}(\mu_x + \delta) + \cdots$$

$$= \frac{D_x + N_{x+1}}{D_x} - \frac{m+1}{2m} - \frac{m^2-1}{12m^2}(\mu_x + \delta) + \cdots$$

$$= a_x + \frac{m-1}{2m} - \frac{m^2-1}{12m^2}(\mu_x + \delta) + \cdots$$

The approximation given by truncating this series after the first two terms is the one we sought to derive and the one most commonly used:

$$a_x^{(m)} \approx a_x + \frac{m-1}{2m}$$

ALTERNATE DERIVATION OF APPROXIMATION FORMULA FOR PRESENT VALUE OF ANNUITIES PAYABLE MORE FREQUENTLY THAN ANNUALLY

After enduring the preceding proof of the value of $a_x^{(m)}$ and the approximation given by the first two terms of this infinite series, hopefully it won't be too disconcerting to find that the same formula results simply by assuming linearity between D_x and D_{x+1}!

If D_{x+1} is linear for $0 \leq t \leq 1$, then the functional value at each $m$thly point is given by $D_{x+1} = (1 - t) \cdot D_x + t \cdot D_{x+1}$, whence

$$
\begin{aligned}
\sum_{t=1}^{m} D_{x+t/m} &= \frac{m-1}{m} D_x + \frac{1}{m} D_{x+1} \\
&\quad + \frac{m-2}{m} D_x + \frac{2}{m} D_{x+1} + \cdots \\
&\quad + \frac{1}{m} D_x + \frac{m-1}{m} D_{x+1} \\
&\quad + 0 \cdot D_x + 1 \cdot D_{x+1} \\
&= \frac{D_x}{m}\left[1 + 2 + \cdots + m - 1\right] + \frac{D_{x+1}}{m}\left[1 + 2 + \cdots + m\right] \\
&= \frac{D_x}{m}\frac{[(m-1)\cdot m]}{2} + \frac{D_{x+1}}{m}\frac{[m\cdot(m+1)]}{2} \\
&= \frac{m-1}{2} D_x + \frac{m+1}{2} D_{x+1}
\end{aligned}
$$

The present value of a lifetime series of annual payments of 1 at the rate of $1/m$ per $m$thly period is

$$a_x^{(m)} = \frac{1}{m} \sum_{t=1}^{\infty} \frac{D_{x+t/m}}{D_x}$$

$$= \frac{1}{mD_x} \sum_{t=0}^{\infty} \left[\frac{m-1}{2} D_{x+t} + \frac{m+1}{2} D_{x+t+1} \right]$$

$$= \frac{m-1}{2m} \ddot{a}_x + \frac{m+1}{2m} a_x$$

$$= \frac{m-1}{2m} (1 + a_x) + \frac{m+1}{2m} a_x$$

$$= a_x + \frac{m-1}{2m}$$

A sample D_x curve appears in Figure 6.17, which suggests that the assumption that D_{x+t} is a linear function for $0 \le t \le 1$ is more appropriate in the earlier years following issue at "traditional" IVA issue ages—which fortunately have a higher present value impact—than in later years.

Because of the "concave upward" nature of the D_x curve, to the extent a linear function is assumed for D_x between successive integral values D_x and D_{x+1} in lieu of a concave upward function, the approximation for $a_x^{(m)}$ will tend to result in slight overstatement.[7] This should not be surprising, since if three terms are used rather than two in the infinite series representation for $a_x^{(m)}$, such third term is negative.

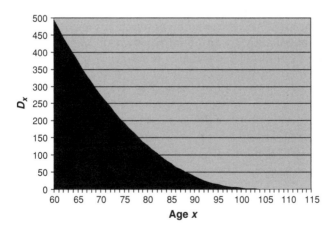

FIGURE 6.17 D_x Curve
(Annuity 2000 Mortality Table, Male, 5%)

Formulas for temporary and deferred life-contingent annuities payable m times per year can be derived from the approximation formula for $a_x^{(m)}$ and are therefore approximations as well.

The present value of an n-year deferred life annuity-immediate payable m times per year is given by

$$
\begin{aligned}
{}_{n|}a_x^{(m)} &= {}_nE_x \cdot a_{x+n}^{(m)} \\
&\approx {}_nE_x \cdot \left(a_{x+n} + \frac{m-1}{2m} \right) \\
&\approx {}_{n|}a_x + \frac{m-1}{2m} \cdot {}_nE_x
\end{aligned}
$$

The present value of an n-year temporary life-contingent annuity-immediate payable m times per year can be expressed as

$$
\begin{aligned}
a_{x:\overline{n|}}^{(m)} &= a_x^{(m)} - {}_{n|}a_x^{(m)} \\
&\approx \left(a_x + \frac{m-1}{2m} \right) - \left({}_{n|}a_x + \frac{m-1}{2m} \cdot {}_nE_x \right) \\
&\approx a_{x:\overline{n|}} + \frac{m-1}{2m}\left(1 - {}_nE_x \right)
\end{aligned}
$$

Present value formulas for single life annuity-*due* options payable m times per year are quickly derived by noting that they differ from annuity-*immediate* options only by an initial payment of $1/m$. The formula for a single life-only annuity-due payable m times per year is

$$
\begin{aligned}
\ddot{a}_x^{(m)} &= \frac{1}{m} + a_x^{(m)} \\
&\approx \frac{1}{m} + \left(a_x + \frac{m-1}{2m} \right) \\
&\approx \frac{1}{m} + \left(\ddot{a}_x - 1 + \frac{m-1}{2m} \right) \\
&\approx \ddot{a}_x - \frac{m-1}{2m}
\end{aligned}
$$

The present value of an n-year deferred life annuity-due payable m times per year is

$$_{n|}\ddot{a}_x^{(m)} = {}_nE_x \cdot \ddot{a}_{x+n}^{(m)}$$

$$\approx {}_nE_x \cdot \left(\ddot{a}_{x+n} - \frac{m-1}{2m} \right)$$

$$\approx {}_{n|}\ddot{a}_x - \frac{m-1}{2m} \cdot {}_nE_x$$

The present value of an n-year temporary life annuity-due payable m times per year is

$$\ddot{a}_{x:\overline{n}|}^{(m)} = \ddot{a}_x^{(m)} - {}_{n|}\ddot{a}_x^{(m)}$$

$$\approx \left(\ddot{a}_x - \frac{m-1}{2m} \right) - \left({}_{n|}\ddot{a}_x - \frac{m-1}{2m} \cdot {}_nE_x \right)$$

$$\approx \ddot{a}_{x:\overline{n}|} - \frac{m-1}{2m}\left(1 - {}_nE_x \right)$$

A summary of formulas for selected life-contingent annuity options with benefit payment frequency greater than once per year (expressed in terms of commutation functions) follows.

Annuities-Immediate

$$a_x^{(m)} \approx \frac{N_{x+1} + \dfrac{m-1}{2m} D_x}{D_x}$$

$$_{n|}a_x^{(m)} \approx \frac{N_{x+n+1} + \dfrac{m-1}{2m} D_{x+n}}{D_x}$$

$$a_{x:\overline{n}|}^{(m)} \approx \frac{N_{x+1} - N_{x+n+1} + \dfrac{m-1}{2m}(D_x - D_{x+n})}{D_x}$$

Annuities-Due

$$\ddot{a}_x^{(m)} \approx \frac{N_x - \frac{m-1}{2m}D_x}{D_x}$$

$$_n|\ddot{a}_x^{(m)} \approx \frac{N_{x+n} - \frac{m-1}{2m}D_{x+n}}{D_x}$$

$$\ddot{a}_{x:\overline{n}|}^{(m)} \approx \frac{N_x - N_{x+n} - \frac{m-1}{2m}(D_x - D_{x+n})}{D_x}$$

If we modify the usual notation to define

$$N_x^{(m)} = N_x - \frac{m-1}{2m}D_x$$

we can rewrite the preceding annuity-due formulas more concisely:

$$\ddot{a}_x^{(m)} \approx \frac{N_x^{(m)}}{D_x}$$

$$_n|\ddot{a}_x^{(m)} \approx \frac{N_{x+n}^{(m)}}{D_x}$$

$$\ddot{a}_{x:\overline{n}|}^{(m)} \approx \frac{N_x^{(m)} - N_{x+n}^{(m)}}{D_x}$$

Appendixes G (male) and H (female) show commutation function values (called "commutation columns") for AIRs of 3%, 4%, 5%, and 6%. The $N_x^{(12)}$ values that appear in Appendixes G and H are calculated using the preceding definition for $N_x^{(m)}$.

Annuity benefits may be other than strictly an annuity-due, with benefits paid at the beginning of each period, or strictly an annuity-immediate, with benefits paid at the end of each period. An annuity company may allow an IVA applicant to select one of several standardized dates of the month to receive benefit payments or may allow any date of the month to be chosen.

For example, if the premium is paid on the first of the month and the IVA applicant wishes to receive annuity benefits on the sixteenth of each month, then *all* benefit payments (not just the first one) fall 15 days later than calculated under an annuity-due formula. Therefore, all benefits are increased by multiplying by a factor of $(1 + \text{AIR})^{15/365}$. Technically, there should also be an adjustment for mortality. In the interest of simplicity, the mortality adjustment is usually ignored as negligible.

CONTINUOUS LIFE-CONTINGENT ANNUITIES

Previously, we studied non-life-contingent continuous annuities payable for a fixed period of n years, with present value denoted $\bar{a}_{\overline{n}|}$. Analogously, as the payment frequency m becomes infinite, the result is a life-contingent continuous annuity, with present value denoted $\bar{a}_x$.

The continuous annuity is to be regarded as one that pays benefits continuously throughout the year such that the total annual payment is 1. While clearly not commercially available, continuous annuities help promote understanding of theory underlying annuities, particularly in a limiting sense.

$$
\begin{aligned}
\bar{a}_x &= \lim_{m \to \infty} a_x^{(m)} \\
&= \lim_{m \to \infty} \frac{1}{m} \sum_{t=1}^{\infty} {}_{t/m}E_x \\
&= \int_0^{\infty} {}_tE_x \, dt \\
&= \frac{1}{D_x} \int_0^{\infty} D_{x+t} \, dt \\
&= \int_0^{\infty} v^t {}_tp_x \, dt
\end{aligned}
\tag{6.23}
$$

As a reminder, even though the symbol ∞ appears as the upper limit of each integrand for simplicity, the upper limit is the end of the life span according to the mortality table used. The function being integrated is therefore defined on a closed interval. Thus, contrary to first appearance, these are not improper integrals—those with an infinite interval of integration.

The formulas for $\bar{a}_x$ in equation 6.23 are incalculable unless the l_x function is of a form permitting the integrations to be performed, which is atypical. Approximation methods may be used. For example, hearkening back to our series representation for $a_x^{(m)}$ and letting m become infinite yields these approximations:

$$\bar{a}_x = \lim_{m \to \infty} a_x^{(m)}$$

$$= \lim_{m \to \infty} \left[a_x + \frac{m-1}{2m} - \frac{m^2-1}{12m^2}(\mu_x + \delta) + \cdots \right]$$

$$\approx a_x + \frac{1}{2} - \frac{1}{12}(\mu_x + \delta)$$

$$\approx a_x + \frac{1}{2}$$

(6.24)

Distinctive commutation functions can be defined to facilitate calculation of present values of continuous life-contingent annuities:

$$\bar{D}_x = \int_0^1 D_{x+t} dt$$

$$\bar{N}_x = \sum_{t=0}^{\infty} \bar{D}_{x+t}$$

$$= \int_0^\infty D_{x+t} dt$$

Thus,

$$\bar{a}_x = \frac{\bar{N}_x}{D_x}$$

If we assume D_{x+t} is linear for $0 \le t \le 1$, then

$$\bar{D}_x = \int_0^1 D_{x+t} dt \approx \frac{1}{2}(D_x + D_{x+1})$$

As a result,

$$\bar{N}_x \approx \frac{1}{2}(N_x + N_{x+1}) = \frac{1}{2}D_x + N_{x+1}$$

Using these approximations reproduces the approximate value of $\bar{a}_x$ derived in equation 6.24:

$$\overline{a}_x = \frac{\overline{N}_x}{D_x}$$

$$\approx \frac{\frac{1}{2}D_x + N_{x+1}}{D_x}$$

$$\approx a_x + \frac{1}{2}$$

The same three annuities for which present value formulas were provided earlier—life only, n-year deferred, and n-year temporary—have these *continuous annuity analogues*:

Life only:
$$\overline{a}_x = \int_0^\infty v^t {}_t p_x dt = \frac{\overline{N}_x}{D_x}$$

n-year deferred:
$${}_{n|}\overline{a}_x = \int_n^\infty v^t {}_t p_x dt = \frac{\overline{N}_{x+n}}{D_x}$$

n-year temporary:
$$\overline{a}_{x:\overline{n}|} = \int_0^n v^t {}_t p_x dt = \frac{\overline{N}_x - \overline{N}_{x+n}}{D_x}$$

VARYING LIFE-CONTINGENT ANNUITIES

We previously discussed non-life-contingent immediate variable annuities, the payments of which vary in a predetermined fashion if the AIR is exactly met; that is, benefits increase arithmetically or geometrically. In analogous fashion, life-contingent immediate variable annuities can also be established so as to have payments vary in a predetermined fashion if the AIR is exactly met. The formulas are equally applicable to life-contingent immediate fixed annuities.

An immediate annuity can be designed with virtually any series of benefit levels imaginable. Variations in benefit levels need not be formula driven or uniform in amount or rate, nor need they occur with any specific frequency. This is because whether variations are regular or irregular, present values may always be determined from first principles by viewing the benefit stream as a series of pure endowments and summing it.

In certain cases where variations follow a uniform pattern or happen to be the sum or difference of common annuity forms, relatively simple formulas may be derived to express present values of such varying annuities. For example, a life annuity that pays a benefit of 1 for 10 years and 2 thereafter can be expressed as the combination of a life annuity and a 10-year deferred life annuity.

A life annuity in which annual payments increase in arithmetic progression of 1 at age $x + 1$, 2 at age $x + 2$, 3 at age $x + 3$, and so forth, is called an *increasing life annuity*, denoted by $(Ia)_x$. Its present value can be determined by the summation in equation 6.25. Because the payment pattern can be expressed as a life annuity plus a one-year deferred life annuity plus a two-year deferred life annuity, and so on, its present value is also expressed by equations 6.26 and 6.27.

$$(Ia)_x = \sum_{t=1}^{\infty} t v^t \, _t p_x \qquad\qquad (6.25)$$

$$(Ia)_x = \sum_{t=0}^{\infty} \, _{t|} a_x \qquad\qquad (6.26)$$

$$(Ia)_x = \sum_{t=0}^{\infty} \frac{N_{x+t+1}}{D_x} \qquad\qquad (6.27)$$

Much like we defined the commutation function N_x as the sum of D_x values, let us now define the commutation function S_x as the sum of N_x values:

$$S_x = \sum_{t=0}^{\infty} N_{x+t}$$

The present value of the *increasing life annuity* can now be rewritten as

$$(Ia)_x = \frac{S_{x+1}}{D_x}$$

Values of S_x can be found in Appendixes G and H. In commercial practice, an immediate annuity that follows an annual benefit pattern of 1, 2, 3, ... (or a multiple such as $10,000; $20,000; $30,000; ...) is unusual. A retiree electing a fixed immediate annuity might desire benefits that increase in arithmetic progression more on the order of 1, 1.05, 1.10, 1.15, ... While immediate variable annuity benefits could equally well be set up to increase if the AIR were exactly met, this is uncommon. Rather, benefit fluctuations tend to be wholly attributable to subaccount performance deviating from the AIR.

A life annuity that begins at 1, increases at the rate of 1 per year, and then levels off when the annual benefit reaches n is identical to layering n deferred annuities. Thus, its present value, denoted $(I_{\overline{n}|}a)_x$, is so calculated:

$$(I_{\overline{n}|}a)_x = \sum_{t=0}^{n-1} {}_{t|}a_x$$

$$= \sum_{t=0}^{n-1} \frac{N_{x+t+1}}{D_x} \qquad (6.28)$$

$$= \frac{S_{x+1} - S_{x+n+1}}{D_x}$$

If, rather than payments of n continuing for life as just shown, we allow for only one payment of n after which all benefits cease, we have an *n-year temporary increasing life annuity*. Annual benefits of 1, 2, 3, ..., n are paid if the annuitant is surviving, and then they stop. The present value, denoted $(Ia)_{x:\overline{n}|}$, can be derived by subtracting an n-year deferred life annuity with benefit payments of n from equation 6.28:

$$(Ia)_{x:\overline{n}|} = (I_{\overline{n}|}a)_x - n \cdot {}_{n|}a_x$$

$$= \frac{S_{x+1} - S_{x+n+1} - nN_{x+n+1}}{D_x} \qquad (6.29)$$

Increasing life annuities-due can be determined in similar fashion to the annuities-immediate represented in equations 6.25 to 6.29. For example, the present value of an increasing life annuity-due is given by

$$(I\ddot{a})_x = \frac{S_x}{D_x}$$

Decreasing life annuity (Da) formulas can similarly be generated. For example, an *n-year temporary decreasing life annuity* that begins with a benefit of n, decreases by 1 each year, and ends with a final payment of 1 is equivalent to the sum of n level temporary annuities, the first lasting one year, the second lasting two years, and the nth lasting n years.

$$(Da)_{x:\overline{n}|} = \sum_{t=1}^{n} a_{x:\overline{t}|}$$

$$= \sum_{t=1}^{n} \frac{N_{x+1} - N_{x+t+1}}{D_x}$$

$$= \frac{nN_{x+1} - (S_{x+2} - S_{x+n+2})}{D_x}$$

Increasing life annuities (Ia) with payments more frequent than annually can be handled in similar fashion. For example, an increasing life annuity with m payments per year with total annual payments of 1, 2, 3, ... in succeeding years has the present value $(Ia)_x^{(m)}$ shown in equation 6.30. This formula assumes that m equal payments are made in any given year, with the benefit level stepping up only once annually. This increasing life annuity has benefits equal to a series of deferred life annuities, and its formula so reflects.

$$
\begin{aligned}
(Ia)_x^{(m)} &= \sum_{t=0}^{\infty} {}_{t|}a_x^{(m)} \\[2mm]
&\approx \sum_{t=0}^{\infty} \frac{N_{x+t+1} + \dfrac{m-1}{2m}D_{x+t}}{D_x} \\[2mm]
&\approx \frac{S_{x+1} + \dfrac{m-1}{2m}N_x}{D_x}
\end{aligned}
\tag{6.30}
$$

Let the progression of benefits be such that not only are benefits payable m times per year but the *rate* of benefit payments increases m times per year. For example, assume the increasing annuity is payable at the rate of $1/m$ per year at the end of the first $1/m$ years, at the rate of $2/m$ at the end of the second $1/m$ years, and so on.

For an annuity issued to a life age x, the first payment is due at time $x + 1/m$ in the amount of $1/m^2$, because the annual rate of payment is $1/m$ and the period covered is $1/m$ years. Similarly, the second payment is due at time $x + 2/m$ in the amount of $2/m^2$, because the annual rate of payment is $2/m$ and the period covered is $1/m$ years. The present value of this annuity, denoted $(I^{(m)}a)_x^{(m)}$, is

$$
(I^{(m)}a)_x^{(m)} = \frac{1}{D_x} \sum_{t=1}^{\infty} \frac{t}{m^2} D_{x+t/m}
$$

Using Woolhouse's formula, we can expand this summation into a series. Using this series as far as the term involving the first derivative as an approximation, we have

$$
(I^{(m)}a)_x^{(m)} \approx (Ia)_x + \frac{m^2-1}{12m^2}
$$

If the frequency of payment m becomes infinite, we have continuous varying annuities. For the increasing life annuity for which the rate of payment is constant within any given year, there is a continuous annuity that pays at the rate of 1 per year in the first year, 2 per year in the second year, and so on. Its present value, denoted $(I\overline{a})_x$, is the sum of deferred level continuous annuities:

$$(I\overline{a})_x = \sum_{t=0}^{\infty} {}_{t|}\overline{a}_x$$

$$= \sum_{t=0}^{\infty} \frac{\overline{N}_{x+t}}{D_x}$$

$$= \frac{\overline{S}_x}{D_x}$$

where $\overline{S}_x \equiv \sum_{t=0}^{\infty} \overline{N}_{x+t}$

The present value of an annuity that is payable continuously and increases continuously and the benefit level of which is at the rate of t per year at the exact moment of attaining age $x + t$ is

$$(\overline{I}\overline{a})_x = \int_0^{\infty} t v^t {}_t p_x dt$$

$$= \frac{1}{D_x} \int_0^{\infty} t D_{x+t} dt \qquad (6.31)$$

Because the continuously payable, continuously increasing annuity shown in equation 6.31 is the infinite counterpart of $(I^{(m)}a)_x^{(m)}$, we can approximate the value of the former by taking the limit of the latter:

$$(\overline{I}\overline{a})_x = \lim_{m \to \infty} (I^{(m)}a)_x^{(m)}$$

$$\approx \lim_{m \to \infty} \left[(Ia)_x + \frac{m^2 - 1}{12m^2} \right]$$

$$\approx (Ia)_x + \frac{1}{12}$$

Life Annuity with a Term Certain

Single life annuities may provide the additional stipulation that benefit payments will be provided for a fixed number of years irrespective of the survival or nonsurvival of the annuitant; that is, benefit payments will be provided for the longer of a fixed period of time or the life of the annuitant.

Such annuities go by the names of "life annuity with n years certain" or "n-year certain and continuous annuity." The word *continuous* in the latter name shouldn't be confused with *continuously payable annuities*, $\bar{a}_x$, discussed earlier.

Periods of 10 and 20 years certain are common. Some companies offer certain periods in increments of 5 years. Other companies offer certain periods of any integral number of years.

Life annuities with a term certain are equivalent to a non-life-contingent fixed period annuity followed by a life annuity. Thus, the present value, denoted in equation 6.32 by the net premium P, for a life with n years certain annuity-immediate of 1 per annum payable $m$thly and issued to a life age x is

$$P = a_{\overline{n}|}^{(m)} + {}_{n|}a_x^{(m)} \tag{6.32}$$

Installment Refund Annuity

The installment refund annuity is a special case of a life annuity with a term certain. For an installment refund annuity, the length of the term certain is judiciously chosen so as to ensure that the gross premium is returned.

Denote the gross premium G and the expense loading factor h so that the net premium available for investment is $P = G \cdot (1 - h)$. If it were to so happen that the gross premium G were an exact multiple of the annual annuity benefit of 1, then the present value of such an installment refund annuity would be

$$G \cdot (1 - h) = a_{\overline{G}|}^{(m)} + {}_{G|}a_x^{(m)}$$

The above situation is virtually never the case—except by rare coincidence—but it illustrates the nature of the installment refund annuity.

When G is not an exact multiple of the annual annuity benefit of 1, one approach is to define a function

$$f(G) = a_{\overline{G}|}^{(m)} + {}_{G|}a_x^{(m)} - G \cdot (1 - h)$$

and solve for the value of G such that $f(G) = 0$. There is an integer n such that $f(n) > 0$ and $f(n + 1) < 0$. Using linear interpolation, an approximate value of G is then given by

$$G \approx n + \frac{f(n)}{f(n) - f(n+1)}$$

In actual practice, should the annuitant die before annuity benefits have been paid that cumulatively sum to G, the series of annuity benefits will continue under the same pattern as when the annuitant was living, although there may be a *partial* final payment so the sum returned precisely totals *G*.

It should be defined by the insurer and conveyed to the contract owner whether at a minimum the entire gross premium will be returned, the entire gross premium net of any state premium tax will be returned, or some other amount will be returned.

When dealing with immediate *fixed* annuities, the installment refund annuity ensures that a specific dollar amount will be returned. When dealing with immediate *variable* annuities, the installment refund annuity ensures that a specific number of units will be returned. The dollar amount guaranteed to be returned therefore may be more, the same, or less than the gross premium—the units purchased are guaranteed to be returned. Investment experience may cause the cumulative dollar value of the fluctuating series of variable income benefits—the number of which such payments are guaranteed—to differ from the gross premium.

Unit Refund Annuity

A *cash refund annuity* is one form of life-contingent immediate *fixed* annuity. We shall study it first, so that its variable counterpart, the *unit refund annuity*, will naturally follow and be more easily understood. A *cash refund annuity* differs from an installment refund annuity only in the manner in which any residual value due the beneficiary following the death of the annuitant is paid.

In the installment refund annuity, residual value is paid to the beneficiary in continuing installments. In a cash refund annuity, residual value is paid in one lump sum. As a result, the same premium purchases a slightly higher periodic annuity benefit under the installment refund option, since under the cash refund option, the benefit due the beneficiary is paid sooner and the time value of money difference is reflected in annuity pricing.

A cash refund annuity promises lifetime income to the annuitant with the additional proviso that at least the gross premium used to purchase the annuity will be returned. The cumulative total of annuity benefits plus the value of any death benefit will at least equal the gross premium.

Note that the promise is a *return of the gross premium*. It is not a return of the gross premium with interest (although conceptually such an annuity could be constructed, at a higher price or lower benefit).

To determine the relationship between premium and annuity benefit level, it is helpful to view a cash refund annuity as a combination of (1) a life annuity and (2) insurance equal at any point in time to the excess of the gross premium over cumulative annuity benefits already paid. The insurance element disappears once cumulative annuity benefits received equal or exceed the gross premium.

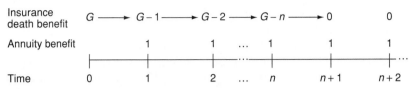

FIGURE 6.18   Cash Refund Annuity Combines Insurance and Annuity Benefits

Denote the gross premium G and the expense loading factor h so that the net premium available for investment is $P = G \cdot (1 - h)$. First, consider a cash refund annuity-immediate with annual payments of 1, issued to a life age x. The net single premium equals the present value of the life annuity plus the present value of the death benefit.

The present value of the life annuity is a_x. The death benefit begins with a value of G and reduces by 1 each year. If G falls between two successive integers so that $n < G < n + 1$, a death benefit will exist for $n + 1$ years.

To determine the present value of the decreasing amounts of insurance depicted in the timeline in Figure 6.18, we shall digress and define in the tinted box insurance commutation functions, just as we did annuity commutation functions.

Life Insurance

Annuity payments are contingent on the *survival* of a life. *Insurance* payments are contingent on the *death* of a life.

We shall consider an insurance consisting of a death benefit of 1, payable at the end of the year of death of a specific individual called the *insured*. *Term insurance* pays a death benefit only if death occurs within a limited period of time.

Let $A^1_{x:n|}$ denote the present value for term insurance of 1 covering n years issued to a life age x. The present value, or net single premium, is

$$A^1_{x:n|} = v q_x + v^2 {}_{1|}q_x + v^3 {}_{2|}q_x + \cdots + v^n {}_{n-1|}q_x \qquad (6.33)$$

where ${}_{t|}q_x = d_{x+t} / l_x$ represents the probability of death deferred t years into the future of a life originally age x, and the 1 written above the x in the subscripted compound symbol suffix $x:n|$ indicates that the event is determined upon the prior failure of that element (i.e., here, death of a life originally age x must occur first before the second element, expiration of n years, occurs).

Each term in the expression $A^1_{x:\overline{n}|}$ represents the probability of death in a specific year multiplied by the present value of a payment of 1 at the end of that year. By substituting the preceding definition of $_{t|}q_x$ into equation 6.33 for $A^1_{x:\overline{n}|}$, we have

$$A^1_{x:\overline{n}|} = \sum_{t=0}^{n-1} v^{t+1} {}_{t|}q_x = \frac{1}{l_x} \sum_{t=0}^{n-1} v^{t+1} d_{x+t}$$

Whole life insurance is merely term insurance for which the term extends to the end of the mortality table. As a result, insurance is payable whenever death occurs, that is, the term $n = \omega - x$. Making this substitution, the present value of whole life insurance, A_x, is given by

$$A_x = \sum_{t=0}^{\infty} v^{t+1} {}_{t|}q_x = \frac{1}{l_x} \sum_{t=0}^{\infty} v^{t+1} d_{x+t}$$

where $\infty = \omega - x - 1$.

Two new commutation functions will allow us to simplify the expressions for life insurances. Define C_x and M_x as

$$C_x \equiv v^{x+1} d_x$$

$$M_x \equiv \sum_{t=0}^{\infty} C_{x+t}$$

Then

$$A^1_{x:\overline{n}|} = \frac{1}{l_x} \sum_{t=0}^{n-1} v^{t+1} d_{x+t}$$

$$= \frac{1}{v^x l_x} \sum_{t=0}^{n-1} v^{x+t+1} d_{x+t}$$

$$= \frac{1}{D_x} \sum_{t=0}^{n-1} C_{x+t}$$

$$= \frac{M_x - M_{x+n}}{D_x}$$

and

$$A_x = \frac{M_x}{D_x}$$

Life Insurance with a Varying Death Benefit

Consider insurances that provide an increasing or decreasing death benefit rather than a level benefit of 1. A new commutation function will again aid in formula simplification. Define R_x as:

$$R_x \equiv \sum_{t=0}^{\infty} M_{x+t} = \sum_{t=0}^{\infty} (t+1)C_{x+t}$$

An increasing whole life insurance that provides a death benefit of 1 in the first year, 2 in the second year, 3 in the third year, and so forth, has a present value, denoted $(IA)_x$, given by

$$(IA)_x = vq_x + 2v^2{}_{1|}q_x + 3v^3{}_{2|}q_x + \cdots$$

$$= \frac{1}{l_x} \sum_{t=0}^{\infty} (t+1)v^{t+1}d_{x+t}$$

$$= \frac{1}{D_x} \sum_{t=0}^{\infty} (t+1)C_{x+t}$$

$$= \frac{R_x}{D_x}$$

A whole life insurance that provides a death benefit that increases by 1 for n years and remains constant thereafter has a present value given by

$$(I_{\overline{n}|}A)_x = \frac{R_x - R_{x+n}}{D_x}$$

An *increasing term insurance* that provides a death benefit of 1 in the first year, 2 in the second year, and so forth, and covers a period of n years has a present value given by

$$(IA)^1_{x:\overline{n}|} = \frac{R_x - R_{x+n} - nM_{x+n}}{D_x}$$

A *decreasing term insurance* that provides a death benefit of n in the first year, $n-1$ in the second year, and so forth, and covers a period of n years has a present value given by

$$(DA)^1_{x:\overline{n}|} = \frac{nM_x - (R_{x+1} - R_{x+n+1})}{D_x} \tag{6.34}$$

The present value of the death benefit that starts at G and decreases by 1 per year is a decreasing term insurance. If G happened to be an integer, we would merely substitute G for n in equation 6.34 for decreasing term insurance.

Recalling that n is the greatest integer in G, $G - n$ represents a fraction of 1 that remains as the amount of insurance during the policy year that begins at attained age $x + n$ (see timeline in Figure 6.18). The present value of an insurance in the amount of $G - n$ at attained age $x + n + 1$ and thereafter must therefore be subtracted. Thus, the present value of a *decreasing term insurance* that provides a death benefit of G in the first year, $G - 1$ in the second year, $\ldots$, $G - n$ in the nth year, and zero thereafter is given by

$$\frac{G \cdot M_x - (R_{x+1} - R_{x+n+1}) - (G - n) \cdot M_{x+n+1}}{D_x}$$

$$= \frac{G \cdot (M_x - M_{x+n+1}) - (R_{x+1} - R_{x+n+1} - n \cdot M_{x+n+1})}{D_x}$$

For a *cash refund annuity*, the net premium equals the present value of the life annuity plus the present value of the decreasing term insurance, yielding this equation:

$$(1 - h)G = \frac{N_{x+1}}{D_x} + \frac{G \cdot (M_x - M_{x+n+1}) - (R_{x+1} - R_{x+n+1} - n \cdot M_{x+n+1})}{D_x}$$

Solving for G, we have

$$G = \frac{N_{x+1} - (R_{x+1} - R_{x+n+1} - n \cdot M_{x+n+1})}{(1 - h)D_x - (M_x - M_{x+n+1})} \tag{6.35}$$

Because n is the greatest integer in G, values of n must be tried until a consistent value of G is found.

Now that we have studied the *cash refund* option associated with an immediate fixed annuity, the *unit refund* option associated with an immediate variable annuity follows naturally. A *cash refund annuity* promises lifetime income to the annuitant with the additional proviso that at least the gross premium used to purchase the annuity will be returned. A *unit refund annuity* promises lifetime income to the annuitant with the additional proviso that at least the number of annuity units purchasable by the gross premium at policy inception will be returned.

Thus, the same formula for the gross premium G for the cash refund annuity (equation 6.35) applies equally to the unit refund annuity. For example, if the annuity unit value happened to be 1.00 at policy inception, a gross premium of G would be sufficient to fund an annual lifetime annuity benefit of 1 annuity unit plus decreasing term insurance that starts at G annuity units and declines by 1 annuity unit per year.

Values of commutation functions C, M, and R for AIRs of 3%, 4%, 5%, and 6% appear in Appendixes I and J.

We now extend our study of cash refund (for immediate fixed annuities) and unit refund (for immediate variable annuities) options to annuities with benefits payable m times per year. We know the present value of the life annuity is $a_x^{(m)}$, which we approximate by

$$a_x^{(m)} \approx \frac{N_{x+1}}{D_x} + \frac{m-1}{2m}$$

The death benefit associated with the decreasing term insurance element decreases by $1/m$ at the end of each mth part of a year. Again, letting n be the greatest integer in G, the death benefit extends over n complete years and over a partial final year.

Our expression for a cash refund or a unit refund annuity will be simplified if we make the assumption of a *uniform distribution of deaths* (UDD)[8] during any year of age; that is, if benefits are payable monthly, we will assume that 1/12 of all deaths occurring during the year of attained age $x + t$ to attained age $x + t + 1$ occur in each monthly benefit period.

From age $x + t$ to $x + t + 1/m$, the death benefit is $G - t$. The present value at age x of such a death benefit under a UDD assumption is

$$\frac{(G-t) \cdot C_{x+t}}{mD_x}$$

In the subsequent age interval $x + t + 1/m$ to $x + t + 2/m$, the death benefit is $G - t - 1/m$. The present value at age x is

$$\frac{(G-t-1/m) \cdot C_{x+t}}{mD_x}$$

Continuing in this fashion, the present value of the death benefit for the full age interval $x + t$ to $x + t + 1$ is

$$\frac{C_{x+t}}{mD_x}\sum_{j=0}^{m-1}\left(G-t-\frac{j}{m}\right)=\frac{C_{x+t}}{mD_x}\left[mG-mt-\frac{m(m-1)}{2m}\right]$$

$$=\frac{C_{x+t}}{D_x}\left[G-t-\frac{m-1}{2m}\right]$$

To find the present value of the death benefit for the first n years, those in which the annuitant's age at the beginning of the year runs from x to $x+n-1$, we have

$$\sum_{t=0}^{n-1}\frac{C_{x+t}}{D_x}\left[G-t-\frac{m-1}{2m}\right]=\frac{1}{D_x}\left[\left(G-\frac{m-1}{2m}\right)\cdot(M_x-M_{x+n})-\left(\sum_{t=0}^{n-1}t\cdot C_{x+t}\right)\right] \quad (6.36)$$

Because

$$R_x=\sum_{t=0}^{\infty}M_{x+t}=\sum_{t=0}^{\infty}(t+1)C_{x+t}$$

we know that the final term in equation 6.36 can be expressed as

$$\sum_{t=0}^{n-1}t\cdot C_{x+t}=\sum_{t=0}^{n-1}(t+1)C_{x+t}-\sum_{t=0}^{n-1}C_{x+t}$$

$$=\sum_{t=0}^{\infty}(t+1)C_{x+t}-\sum_{t=n}^{\infty}(t+1)C_{x+t}-(M_x-M_{x+n})$$

$$=R_x-\sum_{k=0}^{\infty}(n+k+1)C_{x+n+k}-(M_x-M_{x+n}) \qquad (\text{let } k=t-n)$$

$$=R_{x+1}-n\sum_{k=0}^{\infty}C_{x+n+k}-\sum_{k=0}^{\infty}(k+1)C_{x+n+k}+M_{x+n}$$

$$=R_{x+1}-nM_{x+n}-R_{x+n}+M_{x+n}$$

$$=R_{x+1}-R_{x+n}-(n-1)M_{x+n}$$

Thus, the present value of the death benefit in the first n years is given by

$$\frac{1}{D_x}\left\{\left(G-\frac{m-1}{2m}\right)\cdot(M_x-M_{x+n})-\left[R_{x+1}-R_{x+n}-(n-1)M_{x+n}\right]\right\}$$

We must add to this the present value of the death benefit for the final partial year that begins at attained age $x+n$.

The death benefit at the beginning of year of age $x + n$ is the fraction $G - n$. Let r denote the greatest integer in the ratio $(G - n)/(1/m)$. The present value of the final partial year of insurance is given by

$$\frac{C_{x+n}}{mD_x} \sum_{j=0}^{r} \left(G - n - \frac{j}{m} \right) = \frac{C_{x+n}}{mD_x} \left[(r+1)(G-n) - \frac{r(r+1)}{2m} \right]$$

$$= \frac{(r+1)C_{x+n}}{mD_x} \left(G - n - \frac{r}{2m} \right)$$

Bringing it all together, we equate the net single premium with the present value of the life annuity and the present value of the decreasing term insurance:

$$(1-h)G \approx \frac{N_{x+1}}{D_x} + \frac{m-1}{2m} + \frac{1}{D_x} \left\{ \left(G - \frac{m-1}{2m} \right) \cdot \left(M_x - M_{x+n} \right) \right.$$

$$\left. - \left[R_{x+1} - R_{x+n} - (n-1)M_{x+n} \right] \right\}$$

$$+ \frac{(r+1)C_{x+n}}{mD_x} \left[G - n - \frac{r}{2m} \right]$$

We solve for G and get

$$G = \frac{\alpha}{\beta} \tag{6.37}$$

where $\alpha = N_{x+1} + \dfrac{m-1}{2m}(D_x - M_x + M_{x+n}) - [R_{x+1} - R_{x+n} - (n-1)M_{x+n}]$

$$- \frac{r+1}{m}\left(n + \frac{r}{2m}\right)C_{x+n}$$

$$\beta = (1-h)D_x - (M_x - M_{x+n}) - \frac{r+1}{m}C_{x+n}$$

Since both n and r depend on the value of G, trial values of n and r are applied until a consistent value of G is achieved.

Prior to the advent of high-speed computers, the calculation for G was somewhat simplified through the elimination of the variable r by assuming that $r = 0, 1, 2, \ldots, m - 1$. For example, if we assume $r = 0$, then we may understate the premium because we omit some present value of the final partial year of term insurance. If we assume $r = m - 1$, then we may also understate the premium because we include the present value of a negative death benefit in the latter part of the final partial year of term insurance.

Modified Unit Refund Annuity

As with the unit refund annuity, with the modified unit refund annuity, we shall first consider its immediate fixed annuity counterpart, which is the modified cash refund (MCR) annuity. The modified unit refund annuity will then naturally follow.

The *modified cash refund annuity* has its genesis in contributory pension plans, those to which employees make contributions. A modified cash refund annuity in such a contributory pension plan context provides:

- A life annuity.
- A lump-sum death benefit equal to the excess, if any, of the accumulated value of *employee* contributions as of the commencement date of the pension over the sum of the pension payments provided (without interest) up to the point of death.

For example, if an employee's accumulated value at the commencement date of the pension is K and the annuity is \$1 per annum payable monthly, then the death benefit is K at annuity inception, $K - \$1/12$ after one monthly payment, $K - \$2/12$ after two monthly payments, and so on. The death benefit is zero once the sum of annuity payments equals or exceeds K.

The rationale behind a contributory pension plan offering a modified cash refund annuity option is that under a life-only option, an employee might lose all or some of his or her own contributions by early death after retirement. Thus, while employees might have a life-only annuity option as one of their alternate choices, it generally is not the automatic or default option.

The present value of the modified cash refund death benefit (PVDB) to a life age x at commencement of the pension where annuity benefits are payable $m$thly is

$$PVDB_x = \sum_{t=0}^{mK-1} {}_{t/m}p_x \cdot {}_{1/m}q_{x+t/m} \cdot v^{t+1/m} \left(K - \frac{t+1}{m} \right)$$

where ${}_{t/m}p_x$ = probability that a life age x will survive t/m years

       ${}_{1/m}q_{x+t/m}$ = probability that a life attained age $x + t/m$ will die in the following $1/m$ year

We will make the traditional assumption that the MCR death benefit is payable at the end of the year of death. If accumulated employee contributions at annuity commencement are an integral multiple n of the annual annuity benefit of \$1, we have for the present value of the death benefit

$$PVDB_x = \sum_{t=0}^{mn-1} {}_{t/m}p_x \cdot {}_{1/m}q_{x+t/m} \cdot v^{[t/m]+1}\left(n - \frac{t+1}{m}\right)$$

where $[t/m]$ signifies the largest integer in t/m

Again assuming uniform distribution of deaths, the present value of the death benefit becomes

$$\sum_{t=0}^{n-1}\sum_{j=0}^{m-1}\frac{1}{m}\frac{d_{x+t}}{l_x}v^{t+1}\left(n-t-\frac{j+1}{m}\right) = \sum_{t=0}^{n-1}\frac{1}{m}\frac{C_{x+t}}{D_x}\sum_{j=0}^{m-1}\left(n-t-\frac{j+1}{m}\right)$$

$$= \sum_{t=0}^{n-1}\frac{1}{m}\frac{C_{x+t}}{D_x}\left[m(n-t)-\frac{m+1}{2}\right]$$

$$= \frac{1}{D_x}\left[n(M_x - M_{x+n}) - (M_{x+1}-M_{x+n})\right.$$

$$\left. - \cdots - (M_{x+n-1}-M_{x+n})\right]$$

$$- \frac{m+1}{2m}\cdot\frac{M_x - M_{x+n}}{D_x}$$

$$= \frac{1}{D_x}\left[nM_x - R_{x+1} + R_{x+n+1} - \frac{m+1}{2m}M_x\right. \qquad (6.38)$$

$$\left. + \frac{m+1}{2m}M_{x+n}\right]$$

$$= \frac{1}{D_x}\left[nM_x - \left(R_x - \frac{m-1}{2m}M_x\right)\right.$$

$$\left. + \left(R_{x+n} - \frac{m-1}{2m}M_{x+n}\right)\right]$$

$$= \frac{nM_x - R_x^{(m)} + R_{x+n}^{(m)}}{D_x}$$

where $R_x^{(m)} \equiv R_x - \dfrac{m-1}{2m}M_x$

Note that in equation 6.38, the computation of the death benefit, we assumed annuity benefits were payable at the *beginning* of each *m*thly period. Therefore, for consistency, we need to reflect an annuity-*due*. The present value of the life annuity-due of $1 payable *m*thly is given by

$$\ddot{a}_x^{(m)} \approx \frac{N_x}{D_x} - \frac{m-1}{2m}$$

$$\approx \frac{N_x^{(m)}}{D_x}$$

where $N_x^{(m)} \equiv N_x - \dfrac{m-1}{2m} D_x$

Finally, we add the present value of the life annuity to the present value of the death benefit to arrive at the present value of the *modified cash refund annuity*:

$$\frac{N_x^{(m)} + nM_x - R_x^{(m)} + R_{x+n}^{(m)}}{D_x} \tag{6.39}$$

One method for determining the present value of the modified cash annuity if accumulated employee contributions at annuity commencement are *not* an integral multiple of the annual annuity benefit of $1 is to find such nonintegral values of *n* by interpolation.

The *modified unit refund* option associated with immediate variable annuities uses the same net single premium as shown in equation 6.39. The difference in interpretation is that the number of annuity units purchasable at policy inception with the employee's accumulated contributions is guaranteed to be returned. The dollar value returned may be more than, the same as, or less than the employee's applied contributions, depending on how annuity unit values fluctuate during the initial period where the annuity units purchased by the employee's contributions are being returned.

While contributory pension plans prompted the creation of the modified cash (unit) refund option, their application is not limited to such plans. By using this same formula, an IVA contract owner can "dial in" any percentage of his premium for which he wishes to have that percentage of his total annuity units purchasable at contract inception returned, from 0% to 100%. At the extreme ends of the spectrum, 0% is equivalent to a single life only annuity; 100% is equivalent to a unit refund annuity.

Just as there exists a modified unit refund annuity, a similar approach may be used to generate a modified installment refund annuity. The difference resides in whether the death benefit is paid in one lump sum or in continuing installments. The modified installment refund annuity consists of a life annuity with a certain period of a length that returns the desired percentage of the premium. At the extreme ends of the spectrum, 0% is equivalent to a single life only annuity; 100% is equivalent to an installment refund annuity.

Another View of Modified Unit Refund Annuity

As the frequency of benefit payment m approaches infinity (∞), the modified cash refund annuity becomes a continuously payable life annuity plus a death benefit payable immediately at the moment of death.

The present value of the MCR annuity is a function of n as defined above; that is, accumulated employee contributions at annuity commencement are an integral multiple n of the annual annuity benefit. Thus, we'll call this present value of the MCR annuity $M(n)$.

$$M(n) = \bar{a}_x + \int_0^n (n-t)\,_t p_x \mu_{x+t} v^t dt$$

The second term represents the present value of the death benefit. In words, it sums at each point from time 0 to time n the value of the death benefit at that point, which is $(n - t)$, times the probability a life originally age x survives t years, times the probability that the life succumbs to the force of mortality[9] μ at time $x + t$, times the discount factor v^t.

The first derivative with respect to n is

$$M'(n) = \lim_{h \to 0} \frac{1}{h} \left[\int_0^{n+h} (n+h-t)\,_t p_x \mu_{x+t} v^t dt - \int_0^n (n-t)\,_t p_x \mu_{x+t} v^t dt \right]$$

$$= \lim_{h \to 0} \frac{1}{h} \left[\int_n^{n+h} (n-t)\,_t p_x \mu_{x+t} v^t dt + h \int_0^{n+h} {}_t p_x \mu_{x+t} v^t dt \right]$$

$$= \int_0^n {}_t p_x \mu_{x+t} v^t dt$$

$$= \bar{A}^1_{x:\overline{n}|}$$

where $\bar{A}^1_{x:\overline{n}|}$ is the symbol for an n-year term insurance payable at the moment of death.

The second derivative with respect to n is

$$M''(n) = {}_n p_x \mu_{x+n} v^n$$

The Maclaurin series expansion is given by

$$M(n) = M(0) + nM^{(1)}(0) + \frac{n^2}{2!} M^{(2)}(0) + \frac{n^3}{3!} M^{(3)}(0) + \cdots$$

$$= \overline{a}_x + n \cdot 0 + \frac{n^2}{2} \mu_x + \cdots$$

Thus, using terms as far as the second derivative yields the approximation given by

$$M(n) \approx \overline{a}_x + \frac{\mu_x n^2}{2} \qquad (6.40)$$

This expression suggests that the MCR annuity approximately equals the present value of a continuous life annuity plus a death benefit with present value of $\mu_x \cdot n^2/2$.

A geometrical interpretation is consistent with the approximation formula in equation 6.40. Figure 6.19 shows that the MCR death benefit decreases uniformly from n at annuity inception to zero n years later. Recall that the MCR death benefit is given by

$$\int_0^n (n-t) \, {}_t p_x \mu_{x+t} v^t dt$$

The factor μ_{x+t} increases exponentially with time. (For example, we will later explore Makeham's Law: $\mu_x = A + Bc^x$.) The product ${}_t p_x \cdot v^t$ decreases exponentially with time. (Recall $v = 1/(1 + i) < 1$.) Thus, if we consider the

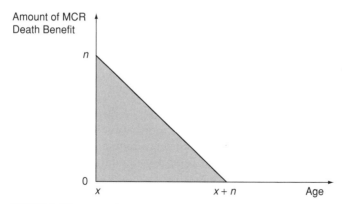

FIGURE 6.19 Modified Cash Refund Death Benefit

impact of time t increasing the initial value μ_x as approximately offset by the factor $_tp_x \cdot v^t$ serving to decrease it, we have

$$_tp_x\mu_{x+t}v^t \approx \mu_x$$

Therefore, the MCR death benefit is approximately given by

$$\mu_x \cdot \int_0^n (n-t)dt = \mu_x \cdot \frac{n^2}{2}$$

The value of the MCR death benefit is thus approximated by the area of the triangle, $n^2/2$, times the force of mortality at policy inception, μ_x, or roughly the amount of the payoff times the likelihood of the payoff.

Relationship of Immediate Annuity to Life Insurance

While this volume is dedicated to immediate annuities, it is interesting to note that immediate annuities bear a precise relationship to life insurance. For example, if we let A_x denote the present value of whole life insurance that pays a benefit of 1 at the end of the year of death, the relationship is given by

$$A_x = v\ddot{a}_x - a_x$$

The term $v\ddot{a}_x$ represents the present value of an annuity that pays v to the annuitant at the beginning of each year if she is alive. Because v grows over a period of one year to 1, paying v at the start of the year is equivalent to paying 1 at the end of the year for any year the annuitant completes. The term a_x represents the present value of an annuity that pays 1 at the end of each year if she is alive. Thus, the difference between these two annuities is a single payment of 1 at the end of the year of death. This is exactly the benefit paid by the whole life insurance, so its present value, A_x, is the same.

Using Annuity Mortality to Price Life Insurance Elements of Immediate Annuities

It is common practice to use only one mortality table for all elements that determine the present value of an immediate annuity. Some immediate annuity payout options—such as unit refund—contain a life insurance component. Traditionally, the same mortality assumptions used to ascertain the present value of the immediate annuity component of the total present value are also used to ascertain the present value of the life insurance component.

To the extent that there is any conservatism in the annuity mortality assumptions—by assuming lengthier lives than actually anticipated through smaller q_x values, such as those in statutorily required mortality tables used for statutory reserve valuation—this actually introduces an element of liberalism in the present value of the life insurance component; that is, it may understate its present value.

To the extent this phenomenon occurs in pricing—in the setting of the net or gross single premium for an annuity option—this makes the premium less adequate to fund the combination package of life annuity and life insurance benefits than perhaps was perceived. The favorable news is that the present value of the life annuity component tends to be meaningfully larger than the present value of the insurance component, likely making any conservatism introduced into the former outweigh the resultant liberalism that occurs in the latter. For example, recall the alternate view of the modified cash refund annuity. The present value of the MCR annuity is approximated by

$$M(n) \approx \overline{a}_x + \frac{\mu_x n^2}{2}$$

Suppose the annual pension is 1. Suppose also that the accumulated contributions of the employee are 4. Assume the pensioner wishes to commence his annuity at age 65.

The present value $\overline{a}_x$ can be approximated by letting the frequency of payments per year m become infinite in the formula for $a_x^{(m)}$:

$$\overline{a}_x \approx \lim_{m \to \infty} a_x^{(m)}$$
$$\approx \lim_{m \to \infty} \left[\frac{N_{x+1}}{D_x} + \frac{m-1}{2m} \right]$$
$$\approx a_x + \frac{1}{2}$$

Using the Annuity 2000 Basic Table for males at 7% interest, we have

$$\overline{a}_{65} \approx 9.527 + \frac{1}{2} \approx 10.027$$

We can similarly estimate μ_{65} from the same mortality table. (If l_x is defined only by the values in a mortality table where the underlying mathematical law is unknown, exact values of $\mu_x = -l_x'/l_x$ are indeterminable, and approximations must be used.)

Numerous methods exist for approximating μ_x. Since here we only care about the general order of magnitude, we shall use one of the simplest approximate differentiation formulas (accurate for second-degree polynomials):

$$f'(x) \approx \frac{f(x+h) - f(x-h)}{2h}$$

Letting $h = 1$, we have

$$\mu_x = -\frac{l'_x}{l_x} \approx -\frac{l_{x+1} - l_{x-1}}{2l_x} \approx \frac{l_{x-1} - l_{x+1}}{2l_x}$$

Using the Annuity 2000 Basic Table, we have

$$\mu_{65} \approx 0.0105 \approx 0.01$$

Then, the approximate value of the death benefit component of the MCR annuity is

$$\frac{\mu_x}{2} n^2 \approx \frac{0.01}{2} \cdot 4^2 \approx 0.08$$

Thus, with a life annuity present value of approximately 10 and a death benefit present value of approximately 0.1, any conservatism introduced into annuity mortality rates that produces liberalism if the same mortality rates are used to value the life insurance component should not present a pricing issue. Given that the present value ratio of the annuity to the life insurance is 100 to 1, the death benefit component adds only a relative 1% to the value of the life annuity when determining the total present value of the MCR annuity. Even in annuity payout options containing stronger life insurance elements—such as a full cash (unit) refund annuity option—there should not be a pricing issue.

Complete Annuities

A *complete annuity*, also called an *apportionable annuity*, is an annuity that provides for a final payment at death proportional to the time elapsed since the last payment. In contrast, a *curtate annuity*, vastly more common, does not provide any final fractional annuity benefit of this nature.

The present value of a complete life annuity-immediate of 1 per year payable $m$thly is denoted $\mathring{a}_x^{(m)}$. The present value of a complete life annuity differs from the present value of a curtate life annuity only by the present value of the proportionate payment at death:

$$\overset{\circ}{a}_x^{(m)} \approx a_x^{(m)} + \frac{1}{2m} \overline{A}_x$$

Since each periodic payment is $1/m$ and since, on average, death occurs midway between payment dates, the fractional final payment is approximated by $1/2m$. The fact that this amount is payable immediately on death indicates that it represents a continuous insurance payable at the moment of death, with present value $\overline{A}_x$, in the amount $1/2m$.

Insurance payable at the moment of death, originally issued to a life age x, has a present value given by

$$\overline{A}_x = \int_0^\infty {}_t p_x \mu_{x+t} v^t dt \tag{6.41}$$

In words, it sums at each instantaneous point from time 0 to time $\omega - x$ (denoted in equation 6.41 by ∞) the value of the death benefit at that point, which is 1, times the probability a life originally age x survives t years, times the probability that the life succumbs to the force of mortality μ at time $x + t$, times the discount factor v^t.

The present value $\overline{A}_x$ can be approximated using several approaches. Perhaps the simplest is to assume that total deaths for any year are concentrated in the middle of the year of age. Insurance is thus paid, on average, half a year earlier when paid at the moment of death than when paid at the end of the year of death. As a result,

$$\overline{A}_x \approx (1+i)^{\frac{1}{2}} A_x$$

POPULATION THEORY

Mathematics is sometimes subdivided between "pure mathematics," focusing more on theory, and "applied mathematics," focusing more on applications. Actuarial science is one branch of applied mathematics.[10] Demography is one specialized branch of actuarial science that focuses on the analysis of population statistics.

Some mortality functions basic to demography are helpful to a fuller understanding of annuity mathematics. We begin by defining three new functions. How each helps us understand characteristics of a population of interest will become evident shortly.

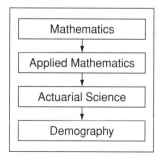

1. $L_x = \int_x^{x+1} l_y \, dy = \int_0^1 l_{x+t} \, dt$

2. $T_x = \int_x^\infty l_y \, dy = \int_0^\infty l_{x+t} \, dt = \sum_{y=x}^\infty L_y = \sum_{t=0}^\infty L_{x+t}$

3. $Y_x = \int_x^\infty T_y \, dy = \int_0^\infty T_{x+t} \, dt$

Total Future Lifetime

The total future lifetime, T_x, of the l_x lives now age x is given by

$$T_x = \int_x^\omega l_t \, dt$$

Geometrically, this is the area under the survivorship curve l_x shown in Figure 6.20.

Although the fact that T_x represents the total future lifetime of the l_x lives now age x may be readily apparent from the definition, there is an alternative way to show that T_x represents the total number of years lived by these l_x lives from age x until death. The term $l_y \mu_y \, dy$ represents the number of lives that die at the moment of attaining age y. Each of these lives has lived $y - x$ years since age x. Thus, the number of years lived by the entire group subsequent to age x is given by

$$
\begin{aligned}
\int_x^\infty (y - x) l_y \mu_y \, dy &= \int_x^\infty (y \cdot l_y \mu_y - x \cdot l_y \mu_y) \, dy \\
&= [-y l_y - T_y + x l_y]_{y=x}^{y=\infty} \\
&= x l_x + T_x - x l_x \\
&= T_x
\end{aligned}
\tag{6.42}
$$

L_x represents the number of years lived between age x and age $x + 1$ by the l_x lives. This is apparent from the definition of L_x. Again, we can look

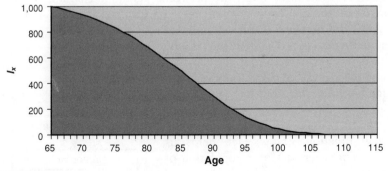

FIGURE 6.20   Survivorship Curve l_x

at an alternative view. If we change the upper limit in the integrand in equation 6.42 from ∞ to $x + 1$ and recall that the number of lives that die at the moment of attaining age y is given by $l_y \mu_y dy$, it will indicate the number of years lived between age x and age $x + 1$ by those who die during this period:

$$\int_x^{x+1} (y-x) l_y \mu_y dy = \int_x^{x+1} \left(y \cdot l_y \mu_y - x \cdot l_y \mu_y \right) dy$$
$$= \left[-y l_y - T_y + x l_y \right]_{y=x}^{y=x+1}$$
$$= \left[-(x+1) l_{x+1} - T_{x+1} + x l_{x+1} \right]$$
$$\quad - \left[-x l_x - T_x + x l_x \right]$$
$$= T_x - T_{x+1} - l_{x+1}$$
$$= L_x - l_{x+1}$$

Of the l_x members who began the period, l_{x+1} survived the entire one-year period. Thus, to the number of years lived between age x and age $x + 1$ by those who die during this period, namely $L_x - l_{x+1}$ as we just showed, we must add l_{x+1} years, one year for each of the l_{x+1} lives who lived one full year between age x and age $x + 1$. The sum is the expected result, L_x.

The symbol T_x represents the total future lifetime of the l_x lives now age x. Therefore, Y_x represents the total future lifetime of those age x and older.

Values of the functions L_x, T_x, and Y_x based on the Annuity 2000 Mortality Table are given in Appendix K (males) and Appendix L (females).

When we only have a mortality table and the precise mortality law underlying it is unknown, we must resort to approximate integration to derive L_x, T_x, and Y_x values. A common approach is the *trapezoidal rule*, reflecting that the area under a function $f(x)$ between any two successive domain values x_n and x_{n+1} is approximated by a trapezoid, as illustrated in Figure 6.21.

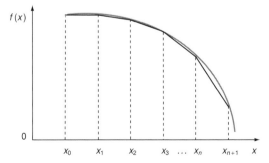

FIGURE 6.21   Area Under $f(x)$ Approximated by Trapezoids

The area of a trapezoid in the unit subinterval x_n to x_{n+1} is $\frac{1}{2} [f(x_n) + f(x_{n+1})]$.

Numeric values for the L_x, T_x, and Y_x functions as they appear in Appendixes K and L are calculated using the trapezoidal rule to approximate the integrals:

$$L_x \approx \frac{1}{2}(l_x + l_{x+1}) \approx l_x - \frac{1}{2}d_x$$

$$T_x \approx \frac{1}{2}l_x + \sum_{y=x+1}^{\infty} l_y$$

$$Y_x \approx \frac{1}{2}T_x + \sum_{y=x+1}^{\infty} T_y$$

The trapezoidal rule is a better approximation in the center section of the mortality table where the l_x curve is more linear; it is a worse approximation at both ends of the mortality table where the l_x curve is less linear. More sophisticated approximate integration formulas may be used at the very low and very high ages.

Central Death Rate

Earlier in this volume, we defined the ratio of d_x to l_x as the mortality rate q_x: q_x is the ratio of deaths during year of age x to the number of lives at the beginning of year of age x.

By its definition, L_x represents the mean value of the function l_y between x and $x + 1$. We now define the ratio of d_x to L_x as the *central death rate* m_x: m_x is the ratio of deaths during year of age x to the average number of surviving lives during the age interval x to $x + 1$. It relates the number of deaths to the mean value of l_x over the age interval x to $x + 1$.

The central death rate m_x bears this approximate relationship to the mortality rate q_x:

$$m_x \equiv \frac{d_x}{L_x}$$

$$\approx \frac{d_x}{l_x - \frac{1}{2}d_x}$$

$$\approx \frac{q_x}{1 - \frac{1}{2}q_x}$$

The central death rate, when its definition is expressed in integral form, suggests information about the force of mortality:

$$m_x \equiv \frac{d_x}{L_x}$$

$$= \frac{\int_0^1 l_{x+t} \cdot \mu_{x+t} dt}{\int_0^1 l_{x+t} dt}$$

This expression makes it clear that the central death rate, m_x, is the weighted mean of the force of mortality, μ_x, over the interval age x to age $x + 1$. The weights are the number of lives attaining age $x + t$ at each point in the interval $0 \le t \le 1$. If such weighted average value of the force of mortality can be estimated by $\mu_{x+\frac{1}{2}}$, this suggests that m_x is approximately equal to $\mu_{x+\frac{1}{2}}$.

The same result can be achieved through the following approach. From the definition of $L_x = \int_x^{x+1} l_y dy$, it follows that

$$L'_x = l_{x+1} - l_x = -d_x$$

If we make the assumption of uniform distribution of deaths between age x and age $x + 1$, we have

$$L_x \approx l_{x+\frac{1}{2}}$$

Thus,

$$m_x \equiv \frac{d_x}{L_x}$$

$$= \frac{-L'_x}{L_x}$$

$$\approx \frac{-l'_{x+\frac{1}{2}}}{l_{x+\frac{1}{2}}}$$

$$\approx \mu_{x+\frac{1}{2}}$$

MORTALITY IMPROVEMENT

There is some terminal age beyond which humans in the population under study do not survive. This terminal age, called ω (the Greek omega), is the last age shown in the mortality table.

While mortality data at very advanced ages is scant relative to younger ages, 120 years is roughly the maximum life span any human tends to achieve.[11] While humans in their 70s, 80s, and 90s are living longer than they did previously—the q_x for each of those ages is lower than it was in earlier times—demographers haven't seen the *maximum life span* change for centuries.

While medical advances may enable elderly individuals to survive more years than previously—sometimes in admittedly feeble states—it is still the case that no one lives beyond some maximum life span. Studies into aging will tell us whether this implies that a maximum number of cell divisions are programmed into our bodies before they become incapable of reproducing further (the so-called "Hayflick limit"[12]) possibly because telomeres (specks of DNA that cap the ends of chromosomes) wear out, whether increasing loss of organ reserve with age (due to nature setting the rate of enzymatic repair[13] of DNA at less than the rate of damage from normal metabolism and environmental agents so animals can accumulate mutations and evolve) eventually forbids restoration to vigor after a health threat, or whether maximum life span is attributable to some other array of factors. We know caloric restriction and lower body temperature slow aging; clues like these may someday yield definitive answers about the complex process of aging.

Clearly, there are leading causes of death for the individual annuitant population—cardiovascular disease, cancer, and so on. When mortality rates associated with one or more such major causes of death show substantial decreases, it is precisely such events that are likely to have the most dramatic impact on mortality improvement factors. Sharp declines in cardiovascular disease mortality, for example, may be achieved preventatively by controlling heart disease risk factors or clinically through more effective emergency practices (e.g., diagnostic and surgical techniques) and long-term care for cardiovascular disease patients.

Mortality improvement in the first half of the twentieth century derived mainly from progress against infectious, acute diseases, chiefly benefiting younger ages. Mortality improvement in the last half of the twentieth century derived more from progress against chronic disorders of the older ages, such as ischemic heart disease, which are financially more important in an annuity table. Greater awareness and control of hypertension, changes in cigarette smoking habits postponing chronic obstructive pulmonary disorders, advanced emergency and follow-up care for heart attack victims, promotion of salutary lifestyles[14] by encouraging exercise and controlling risk factors like high cholesterol and saturated fat diets to combat heart disease, and improved cancer treatments are partial causative factors of mortality improvement.

Medical literature[15] demonstrates that further significant disease reduction is achievable by eliminating lifestyle-related, controllable risk factors, including tobacco use, alcohol abuse, obesity, physical inactivity, high blood pressure, high blood cholesterol, low fruit and vegetable intake, illicit drugs, unsafe sex, and iron deficiency. These examples show that the ages with the highest mortality improvement factors change over time and that specific events and health care trends cause mortality improvement factors (MIF) for the same age to be nonuniform over time—hence, the need for ongoing mortality studies.

Cause-of-death records with consistent coding instructions for the annuitant subpopulation—as already exists for the general population— would provide guidance as to relative strength of various mortality hazards, producing more informed estimates of prospective MIF changes as cures and more efficacious treatments emerge. Notably, events reducing or delaying heart disease and cerebrovascular disease would have significant impact, as these collectively constitute a meaningful portion of advanced age death rates. For example, two causes, acute myocardial infarction and chronic ischemic heart disease, account for two-thirds of total cardiovascular deaths and one-third of deaths from all causes.[16] At more advanced ages, cardiovascular disease significantly exceeds cancer as a cause of death.

The advent of Medicare and Medicaid programs may also play a role in mortality improvement, making medical treatment more accessible to those at "typical" annuitant ages, thereby increasing their awareness of their medical conditions. The inception of these programs and their funding, the ensuing wider spread of access and, therefore, diagnoses and treatment, and the greater resultant activity levels of affected individuals— healthful in itself—may synergistically yield mortality improvement.

A historical look at life expectancy suggests that modern demographic history can be divided into three epidemiological eras:[17]

1. *Age of Pestilence and Famine.* Life expectancy in this pre-1650 era fluctuated between 20 and 40 years. Infectious diseases such as diarrhea, influenza, plague, pneumonia, smallpox, and tuberculosis were major killers, especially among youth and childbearing women. Mortality rates were high and stagnant.
2. *Age of Receding Pandemics.* From 1650 to World War I, life expectancy increased to about 50 years. Higher incomes and improved public health measures such as sanitation ameliorated the most deadly infectious diseases. Fewer deaths at young ages with correspondingly more survivors at old ages began the shift from death due to infectious disease to death due to chronic disease.
3. *Age of Degenerative Diseases of Affluence.* Life expectancy in developed countries during the twentieth century rose from about 50 years to 70 years. Medical knowledge and care reduced death by infectious diseases, further shifting the major causes of death to chronic diseases, such as heart disease, stroke, and cancer.

Other observers[18] suggest the beginning of a fourth epidemiological era, the *Age of Delayed Degenerative Diseases*. While major causative factors of mortality will continue to be chronic degenerative diseases, medical and lifestyle changes will shift the age distribution of deaths from these causes toward older ages.

Clearly, general population mortality rates are inappropriate for use in IVAs because they reflect no self-selection and because meaningful differences in important factors—such as income levels and geographic distribution—exist between the general population and the subset of IVA purchasers. Because mortality improvement factors measure *change* in mortality, not mortality itself, general population MIFs are more likely to extend to the IVA subpopulation, with adjustments as necessary to the extent causal factors affect these two socioeconomic groups differently.

The result of mortality rates improving (i.e., becoming lower) over time yet with no change in maximum life span is a "squaring of the mortality curve"—the shape of the l_x curve shown earlier in Figure 6.1 might look like the shapes projected for 25 and 50 years from now that appear in Figure 6.22.

The graph in Figure 6.22 represents the Annuity 2000 Basic Mortality Table for males, with mortality improvement for 25 years and for 50 years based on Projection Scale G (defined in Table 6.4). The shape of the curve bulges increasingly toward the upper right-hand corner of the box, making it more "squared off"; that is, the curve moves progressively closer to the shape of the rectangular box that contains it. As a result, this view of future evolution, where mortality rates decline at advanced ages but the terminal age ω remains biologically constrained at or near its current level, is sometimes also called "rectangularization."

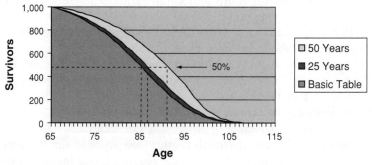

FIGURE 6.22   Squaring of Mortality Curve

TABLE 6.4 Mortality Improvement Factors

Age	Projection Scale G MIF (Males)	Projection Scale G MIF (Females)
5–9	1.50%	1.50%
10–14	0.25	1.00
15–19	0.20	0.50
20–24	0.10	0.50
25–29	0.10	0.75
30–34	0.75	1.25
35–39	1.00	2.25
40–44	2.00	2.25
45–49	1.75	2.00
50–54	1.75	2.00
55–59	1.50	1.75
60–64	1.50	1.75
65–69	1.50	1.75
70–74	1.25	1.75
75–79	1.25	1.50
80–84	1.25	1.50
85–89	1.25	1.50
90–94	1.00	1.25

Source: Derivation of 1983 Table *a*, *Transactions of the Society of Actuaries*, 33, 721. © 1982 Society of Actuaries.
Note: The Annuity 2000 Mortality Tables use 100% of male Projection Scale G and 50% of female Projection Scale G.[19]

It is interesting that the terminal age ω changes little. While a 65-year-old 25 years from now can expect to enjoy more future years of life than a 65-year-old today, it may still be the case that the greatest age to which anyone ever lives may remain virtually unchanged. More precisely, while *life expectancy* for any given attained age x may increase, *maximum life span* for the population may not.

Mortality improvement is not the same for males as for females. Mortality improvement differs also by age. For a more general U.S. population, whose mortality differs from the annuitant population whose members deem themselves sufficiently healthy to purchase an annuity, males age 65 to 84 show annual mortality improvement around 1.50%, and males age 85 and over show mortality improvement of about 0.50%. Females age 65 to 84 show mortality improvement of about 0.50%, and those age 85 and over about 0.20%.[20]

Note in Figure 6.22 the horizontal dotted line indicating the 50% survival age at which half of the original cohort has died and half survive. The age at which this occurs—as seen on the horizontal axis—continues to increase with time; yet the maximum age to which people survive remains unchanged. This shows graphically that life expectancy as of age 65 increases,[21] while maximum life span does not.

For a variety of reasons, mortality in the United States does tend to improve over time; that is, q_x values tend to decrease. They do not decrease by a uniform percentage for all ages and for both sexes, but they do decrease. Table 6.5 shows the extent of the relative decrease over time for various levels of mortality improvement.

While we celebrate the marvelous—even miraculous—improvements in medical care, we also must be vigilant regarding the resultant long-term economic consequences. To keep the annuity program solvent and to keep encroachment on targeted profit margins at bay, such mortality improvement needs to be recognized. This is especially important since the annuity payout can span multiple decades. Small inadequacies in mortality assumptions each year can cumulatively result in a magnified effect because of the compounding of such inadequacies over a multidecade payout period. Barring "reserve strengthening" by truing up reserves for projected annuity benefits along the way, the shortfall of the fund to prove adequate to pay benefits to the last surviving annuitant could be large. While such reserve

TABLE 6.5 Mortality Improvement Factor Impact over Time

MIF	Relative Reduction in Mortality Rate, End of 25 Years	Relative Reduction in Mortality Rate, End of 50 Years
0.25%	6.1%	11.8%
0.50	11.8	22.2
0.75	17.2	31.4
1.00	22.2	39.5
1.25	27.0	46.7
1.50	31.5	53.0
1.75	35.7	58.6
2.00	39.7	63.6
2.25	43.4	67.9
2.50	46.9	71.8

strengthening comes from the insurance company surplus, it is important to recognize that nonparticipating IVA contracts already issued cannot be modified to counteract emerging mortality improvement. An insurer only gets one chance to handle mortality improvement, and that is at point of sale via the amount of premium collected.

While mortality improvement associated with defined benefit pension plans can be handled by higher future employer contributions, and mortality improvement associated with Social Security can be handled by higher taxpayer contributions or adjustments to the benefit formula, no post-issue corrective mechanisms to adjust for higher-than-expected mortality improvement for IVAs exist—other than possibly via transfer of shareholder wealth held in an insurer's surplus account to policyholders. Thus, while biomedical technologies that slow senescence and are capable of being administered to and effective in a large portion of the population do not currently exist, it may be more important to project mortality improvement that anticipates this possibility in individual immediate annuities than in public or private defined benefit pension plans or Social Security.

For life-contingent IVAs with long certain periods, the effect of underestimating future mortality improvement is moderated. This is because such an annuity option is a combination of a non-life-contingent fixed-period annuity followed by a deferred life annuity and nearer-term payments associated with the non-life-contingent annuity have a relatively higher present value impact since the discounting process assigns to earlier payments more value than later payments. Mortality improvement factors, however, still affect (1) the present value of the life annuity as of the point it commences and (2) the mortality rates associated with years of age during the deferral period through which this present value is discounted.

To quantify mortality improvement, mortality improvement factors are used, specific to each age and sex. Call these MIFs. If, say, a 65-year-old female had a 3% probability of dying during the next year in 2005, we would say $q_{65} = 0.03$. Yet statistical studies might suggest that female-age-65 mortality is improving on a relative basis by 1% per year.

To reflect this, in 2006 we would expect a 65-year-old female to have a probability of dying equal to 99% of 3%, or 2.97%.

In general,

$$q_x^{\text{Year } N+1} = q_x^{\text{Year } N} \times (1 - \text{MIF})$$

In our example,

$$q_{65}^{2006} = q_{65}^{2005} \times (1 - 0.01)$$

Repeating the process, in 2007 we might expect another 1% relative mortality improvement. We'd have

$$q_{65}{}^{2007} = q_{65}{}^{2006} \times (1 - 0.01) = q_{65}{}^{2005} \times (1 - 0.01)^2$$

In general,

$$q_x{}^{\text{Year } N + k} = q_x{}^{\text{Year } N} \times (1 - \text{MIF})^k$$

This formula assumes the mortality rate for age x improves annually on a relative basis by the constant mortality improvement factor for a k-year projection period; that is, mortality is modeled as the product of the mortality rate for a base year multiplied by a reduction factor, which follows an exponential decay. Of course, the mortality improvement factor for a given age and sex combination needn't be one uniform scalar in all years. Rather, a vector of mortality improvement factors could be employed, resulting in the formula

$$q_x{}^{\text{Year } N+k} = q_x{}^{\text{Year } N} \times (1 - \text{MIF}_N) \times (1 - \text{MIF}_{N+1})$$
$$\times (1 - \text{MIF}_{N+2}) \times \cdots \times (1 - \text{MIF}_{N+k-1})$$

To assess the sensitivity of annuity present values to MIFs, Table 6.6 shows the present value (PV) of an annual life-only annuity-due at 5% interest for a male age 65 using the Annuity 2000 Basic Mortality Table, using a 1%/year MIF, and using a 2%/year MIF. For example, for a 1% per year MIF, age 65 mortality rate is used from the Annuity 2000 Basic Mortality Table, the age 66 mortality rate is projected one year at 1%, the age 67 mortality rate is projected two years at 1%, and so on. Under this so-called "generational" approach, mortality improvement is incorporated into the pricing or valuation process by adjusting each mortality rate applied to a given individual for mortality improvement to the future year in which the mortality rate is applied.

The terminology "reduction rates" rather than "mortality improvement factors" is sometimes used in conjunction with official population

TABLE 6.6 Annuity PV Sensitivity to MIF

	PV of Male Age 65 Life-Only Annuity ($\ddot{a}_{65}$)	PV Relative to 0% MIF
A2000 Basic Table	12.278	100.0%
A2000 Basic Table with 1%/year MIF	12.673	103.2
A2000 Basic Table with 2%/year MIF	13.107	106.8

projections such as those produced by the U.S. Bureau of the Census for the Old Age Survivors and Disability Insurance (OASDI) program or by the United Kingdom Government Actuary's Department for the U.K. Social Security System. A *reduction rate* is defined for each age as the complement of the ratio between two consecutively observed mortality rates for that age. As in the preceding example of a 65-year-old female having a 3% observed mortality rate in one year and a 2.97% rate in the next, the reduction rate equals 1 − (2.97%/3.00%), which is 0.01, or 1%. Because the size of the population and its constitution by age and sex are so important in such official projections, fertility and migration are essential factors in modeling in addition to mortality.

Reduction rates in such official projections are not merely the result of a mechanical extrapolative process; they also rely on expert opinion. U.S. 1995-based official projections that support the ultimate reduction rates are accompanied by this text:

> *Future reductions in mortality will depend upon such factors as the development and application of new diagnostic, surgical, and life-sustaining techniques, the presence of environmental pollutants, improvements in exercise and nutrition, the incidence of violence, the isolation and treatment of causes of disease, improvements in prenatal care, the prevalence of cigarette smoking, the misuse of drugs (including alcohol), the extent to which people assume responsibility for their own health, and changes in our conception of the value of life. After considering how these and other factors might affect mortality, we postulated three alternative sets of ultimate annual percentage reductions in death rates by sex, age group, and cause of deaths for years after 2020.[22]*

The graph of mortality improvement factors in Figure 6.23 exhibits remarkable irregularities. The lack of smoothness in mortality rates projected using such a scale results in potential inconsistencies. For example, one may start with a smooth base mortality table with increasing values of q_x, but the accumulated effect of mortality-improvement-factor projections could create an anomaly whereby mortality rates would decline with age, especially over long projection periods. If the plausibility of the projected values appears suspect, this may be attributable to a propagation of errors caused by MIFs for two successive ages differing too radically. Smoothing of mortality improvement factors themselves or the resultant projected mortality rates may be needed, although end users of projected mortality rates typically prefer "goodness of fit" over "smoothness." While graduating mortality rates to form a smooth progression is based on an intuitive belief that the true rates form a smooth sequence, such an intuitive belief is supported by empirical evidence.

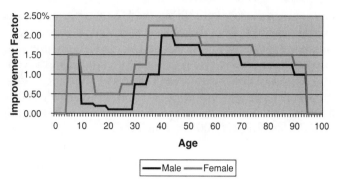

FIGURE 6.23 Mortality Improvement Factors by Age
(Projection Scale G)

Modeling mortality rate trends at postretirement ages occasionally causes some commentators to postulate that much of the mortality improvement to ever be realized has been realized. Research-based evidence strongly suggests mortality rates continue to decline at a reasonably steady rate, in which case comments that mortality improvement factors will decline and grade to zero are misconceived.

Modeling mortality improvement factors at advanced ages is made difficult due to both inaccuracies in available data (e.g., when were centenarians *really* born?) and variability due to small exposures to risk (i.e., scant data). Data reliability problems as to exact date of birth for advanced age individuals include lack of birth records, low literacy levels, functional or cognitive disability making it impossible to report one's own age and needing to rely on knowledge of others, and mistakes in completing census and other age-collection surveys.

Theoretically, for any given annuity option, the annuity payout rates representing the first variable annuity payment for each $1,000 of net premium should be different (i.e., slightly lower) each year for a given age and sex combination. This is wholly attributable to the slight change in mortality assumptions as specified by the mortality improvement factors. Since the cohort beginning at age x in each successive year can be expected to draw a slightly longer series of annuity benefit payments, each payment needs to be slightly less if the present value of the series of annuity payments is to remain unchanged.

Such annuity payout rates are termed "dynamic," as opposed to "static." Sometimes one immediate variable annuity table needs to be created that will be used for several years, such as in the back of a deferred variable annuity contract, making it impractical to use truly dynamic payout rates. In such instances, the payout rates may be based on mortality rates projected several years into the future, which may be a little too conservative for annuitants purchasing immediate variable annuities in the first few years and a little too liberal for annuitants purchasing beyond the presumed starting date to which mortality rates were projected but perhaps being adequate on average.

Another common practice to handle such mortality improvement by using only one static table is to employ "age setbacks" for each 5-, 10-, or 20-year date of birth cohorts. For example, those annuitants electing an immediate variable annuity at age 65 who were born between 1940 and 1959 might use the payout rates per $1,000 of net premium in the table as is. Those annuitants electing an immediate variable annuity at age 65 who were born between 1960 and 1979 might be required to use a "one-year age setback"; that is, they might be required to use the age 64 payout rates. This younger assumed age results in a longer expected payout period and, therefore, a lower series of benefits, accomplishing virtually the same effect as a truly dynamic set of variable payout rates.

For example, a_{64} is 14.072 and a_{65} is 13.640, using the male Annuity 2000 Basic Table and a 3% AIR. If it were believed that the appropriate action for a specific situation were to project 1.25% annual mortality improvement for 7½ years, then $a_{65}^{Projected}$ is equal to 14.068. This age 65 value on a projected basis is nearly equivalent to the age 64 value on an unprojected basis, implying that a one-year age setback could accomplish virtually the same effect.

Continuing this approach, a_{63} is 14.500 using the male Annuity 2000 Basic Table and a 3% AIR. Projecting 1.25% annual mortality improvement for 15 years produces $a_{65}^{Projected}$ equal to 14.495. Thus, a two-year age setback accomplishes virtually the same effect. If an insurer felt uniform 1.25% annual mortality improvement at ages 65 and older were appropriate for a specific application, it could (as a reasonable approximation) employ a one-year age setback for each 7½ year-of-birth cohort. The insurer would want to investigate the reasonableness of this approximation across the range of ages for which it expects to sell annuities.

The use of mortality improvement factors becomes especially critical when conversion factors are contained in *deferred* annuity contracts, showing the dollar amount of the first variable annuity payment for each $1,000 of accumulated value. These conversion factors promised to deferred variable annuity owners may span well over half a century. For example, if a 25-year-old school teacher makes a first deposit into a deferred variable annuity contract today, starts receiving retirement income at age 65, and lives until age 100, the conversion factors must be satisfactory to cover mortality improvements over the 40-year accumulation period and the 35-year liquidation period—a total of 75 years.

Future mortality rates may not be a mere extrapolation of past mortality-rate trends. Events—cancer cure, gene therapy, artificial organs, organ regeneration—may cause a point of discontinuity where future mortality rates are expected to differ materially from past rates in a positive way, at least for the subpopulation of interest. On the flip side, recent trends in childhood and adult obesity, new diseases, and the global reemergence of communicable diseases may materially affect mortality rates in a negative way. Similarly, terrorism that produces mass destruction caused not by the vicissitudes of nature but by the malevolence of other human beings may negatively affect mortality rates. (As some jokingly say when pointing out its dynamic rather than static nature, "Mortality is not dead!")

The point is that annuity writers have to make *some* assumptions as to these occurrences. These assumptions will prove adequate or inadequate depending on future events. Predicting mortality far into the future is not a sure thing but rather a conjecture. Actuaries who set these assumptions for variable income annuities know that the universe will fail to conform to their assumptions. The only question is by how much!

Credibility theory[23] deals with the issue of assigning weights to how much mortality-rate assumptions should be based on past experience and how much on expectations for the future, especially where events suggest a change from the past trend. As long as conditions remain relatively stable, past history may suggest future experience, accomplished via standard statistical techniques such as linear extrapolation or regression or exponential smoothing. In the real world, trends change, and previous experience may be a poor indicator of future experience. Projection of turning points is challenging.

Credibility theory has been used in areas of insurance where there is a high rate of claims and a short pricing horizon, such as property/casualty insurance. Its use with life insurance and annuities is more recent due to their lower rate of claims and long pricing horizons.

Sensitivity testing allows an assessment of the degree to which various mortality improvement assumptions impact annuity present values and, therefore, benefit payments. Stochastic mortality modeling offers insight into the economics of longevity insurance.

An indication of the cumulative impact of mortality improvement over prior eras can be seen by these statistics on 5-year-old boys and girls, based on the Annuity 2000 Basic Mortality Table:

- For 5-year-old boys, 87.6% of their deaths will occur at ages 65 and older.
- For 5-year-old girls, 92.8% of their deaths will occur at ages 65 and older (see Figure 6.24).

A line graph showing the distribution of age at death for a beginning group comprised of 5-year-old females appears in Figure 6.25.

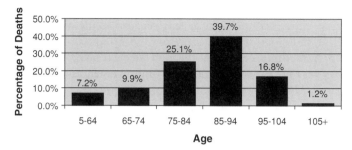

FIGURE 6.24 Deaths by Age for a Group of 5-Year-Old Females
Source: Annuity 2000 Basic Mortality Table.[24]

Agricultural innovations permitting improved nutrition, engineering innovations resulting in improved and more sanitary living and working spaces, medical innovations resulting in improved immunization programs to ward off disease and in antibiotic therapies to combat disease, and productivity improvements that permitted rising incomes that made such health care accessible contributed to mortality improvement—as characterized by the single-point summary measure known as "life expectancy"—during the world industrialization of the 1900s.

Mortality improvement is expected to continue, and mortality improvement factors will reflect this. Actual mortality improvement does not occur at a uniform rate in all years, even though this is an assumption almost universally employed. Sometimes Thomas Malthus's destructive "positive

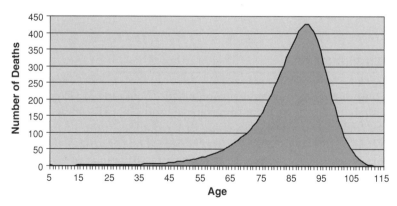

FIGURE 6.25 Distribution of Age at Death for a Group of 10,000 5-Year-Old Females
Source: Annuity 2000 Basic Mortality Table.[25]

checks" (such as new diseases like SARS or AIDS; even old diseases, like influenza epidemics; war; earthquakes; nuclear reactor accidents; or biological, chemical, or radiological terrorism) slow the progression or even yield retrogression. Sometimes new breakthrough medical advances speed the progression. As year-to-year actual mortality improvement factors may be jerkily arrhythmic, MIF studies generally encompass multiyear periods.

That mortality improvement will continue into the indefinite future seems plausible, although many projectionists slow the improvement over time; that is, their MIFs reduce with advancing decades of their progression. Reasons include the line of thinking that it will be hard for the twenty-first century to replicate the extraordinary advances of the twentieth century or that improvements must necessarily be smaller as some biological limits are approached.

Because of the long-range nature of IVA liabilities—which often span multiple decades—mortality improvement projections are critical pricing assumptions. The impact is especially pronounced for immediate annuities where benefits increase with time (as opposed to being level), since the benefits at the advanced ages become so large, making the projected number of annuitants still alive to receive them so critical. Immediate fixed annuity benefits can increase with time, such as with annuity payout options where the benefits are guaranteed to increase, say, 3% or 5% each year. (While such increases may be referred to as a cost-of-living adjustment, or COLA, this terminology is often reserved for nonuniform increases in annuity benefits tied to some particular version of the Consumer Price Index.) As mentioned earlier, immediate variable annuity benefits could similarly be designed so that if the AIR were met, the benefits would increase by a certain degree each year—as opposed to the traditional approach of level benefits if the AIR is met.

THE AGING PROCESS

Eternal youth has been a dream of mankind for thousands of years. Spanish explorer Juan Ponce de Leon discovered Florida in 1513 while searching for the fountain of youth—an elixir that would keep the body young forever. While historically medical research focused on geriatrics—the study of the physiology and pathology of characteristic afflictions of old age—there has recently been an enormous upturn in true aging research.

There is no easy definition of *aging*. In general, it's a loss of function with time. Events associated with aging occur at cellular, genetic, and molecular levels.

The Human Genome Project and tools and techniques evolving from that effort accelerated the biological knowledge revolution, including

> *I have come on account of my ancestor Utanapishtim, who…was*
> *given eternal life. About Death and Life I must ask him!*
> —*Gilgamesh*, The Epic of Gilgamesh,
> *Tablet IX, 2000* B.C.

research into the aging process. Research into life processes may, after thousands of years of false promises about discovering the "fountain of youth," genuinely offer the prospect of slowing the aging process.

Pursuit of the secret of immortality is the quest of Gilgamesh, adventurer and king of Uruk, in mankind's first recorded epic, carved on clay tablets in Babylonia 4,000 years ago. Fearing death, Gilgamesh seeks eternal life by making a perilous journey across the Waters of Death to visit the only two immortal humans, alive since before the Great Flood. Given two chances for immortality, Gilgamesh blunders both and returns to Uruk.

Such has been the fate of the pursuit of longer life span since antiquity.[26] Despite the cumulative research and knowledge gathering in the entirety of human history, nobody today outlives the longest-lived Romans, Greeks, or Sumerians over whom King Gilgamesh ruled. Yet, in the 1900s, two of mankind's three classic dreams—(1) travel to the moon or planets, (2) transmutation of metals, and (3) life span extension—were realized. Perhaps the 2000s will mark accomplishment of the third.

We know that "biological age" differs from "chronological age" because some humans age faster than others, yet we sell annuities based on "chronological age," primarily due to lack of good markers for determining "biological age." Theories on aging—evolutionary, biochemical wear and tear, neuroendocrine, immune system, free radical, and so on—abound.

The disparity between chronological age and biological age is most pronounced in individuals suffering from a disease called *progeria*, or advanced aging. This affliction is characterized by an adolescent of 10 or 12 years old who effectively dies of old age. Senility, arteriosclerosis, baldness, and wrinkled skin are characteristics of this unusual disease that condenses nine decades of biological age into one decade of chronological age.

Dr. Francis Collins, Director of the National Human Genome Research Institute, predicts, "By 2030, major genes responsible for the aging process in humans will likely have been identified, and clinical trials with drugs to retard the process may well be getting underway."

While there may be no genes for aging, genes may still regulate the speed and the expression of the deteriorative process that occurs after reproductive maturity, leading to loss of function that we call aging. We can add and remove genes at will—instead of being restricted to modifications that arrive through Darwin's evolutionary process.[27] To the extent the result is to pull back the throttle on the deteriorative-process regulator, the possibility of human life span extension—perhaps dramatically—should not be rejected as implausible.

As a result, in contrast to the view of future evolution where mortality rates decline at advanced ages but the terminal age ω remains biologically constrained at or near its current level, an alternative view of future evolution is emerging whereby extension of maximum life span (beyond the value of ω today, around 120 years) is a possibility. Under this alternative view, rather than "rectangularization" of the mortality curve there is a "right shift."

Ramifications for variable income annuities (and retail immediate fixed annuities, pension plan obligations, and Social Security obligations) are clear. If the aging process falls within control of biomedical sciences and biological forces governing life processes and aging thereby fall within the influence of humanity, annuity income will need to cover longer periods than anticipated by mortality improvement factors in use today. The slowing or reversal of the aging process could prove calamitous for immediate annuity writers.

Reserve strengthening will be necessary for annuities previously sold. Pricing will need to be altered for annuities to be sold in the future. If annuitants live longer because of maximum life span extension as well as lower mortality rates, then the cumulative effect of inflation over these extra years will be greater. Should inflation continue and should equity investments continue to be a primary means to cope with inflation, then variable income annuities may be even more protective and valuable—by providing potentially increasing benefits that keep pace with or outpace the effects of these longer periods of corrosive inflation—relative to fixed income annuities.

Mortality is generally considered a *diversifiable* risk. The greater the number of homogeneous exposure units in a given underwriting category, the more certain the aggregate actual experience tends to be—such as for an entire variable income annuitant pool—according to the law of large numbers. Yet unexpectedly large mortality improvement factor advancement is a *nondiversifiable* risk.

The risk of common stock investing is diversifiable through greater numbers of stocks—with progressively smaller security-specific risks—up to the point where the entire market constitutes the asset pool, as in a total stock market index. Beyond that point, it is nondiversifiable in that general economic conditions affect all or a large part of the entire market. Similarly, mortality risk is diversifiable through greater numbers of annuitants—with progressively smaller annuitant-specific risks—and beyond that point, it is nondiversifiable in that general biological conditions affect all or a large part of the entire market of annuitants.

One may infer that earnings of variable income annuity issuers may be more volatile in the future as actual annuitant mortality holds greater potential to differ from expected. Unexpectedly high mortality improvement factors could result in losses attributable to this pricing component. On the flip side, large-scale terrorism events (e.g., biological, radiological) and/or large-scale natural disasters (e.g., earthquakes, new viruses) producing high mortality—especially at more advanced ages—could produce large mortality gains for variable income annuity issuers.

Like any other business, variable income annuity issuance is not without risk—even when run by very bright, ethical, well-educated people relying on a solid database of historical experience. The point is simply that future actual-to-expected (A/E) mortality ratios for annuitants may be more volatile than has historically been the case. While investment performance affects IVA writer revenues and corporate tax rates and regulatory requirements affect their expenses, the A/E ratio is a risk metric of very high interest to IVA practitioners.

This may increase the importance for insurance companies to offer both life insurance and annuities, which are natural hedges. Insurers offering both life insurance and immediate annuities enjoy some level of immunization against mortality risk, akin to immunization typically considered in the investment world through asset/liability management techniques, such as key rate duration matching. Their risk on life insurance business is insureds "dying too soon." Their risk on immediate annuity business is annuitants "dying too late."

As a consequence, more or fewer deaths than expected result in gains in one line of business and losses in the other. While the sizes of the books of these two business lines might not be such as to have exactly offsetting economic impact, some level of immunization against the risk that actual mortality experience may differ from pricing assumptions is achieved. To the extent an insurer is unable to achieve the desired balance of mortality risk immunization naturally through the relative amount of sales and in-force business of each, it can sculpt the retention of mortality risk through judicious use of reinsurance[28] and/or securitization of mortality risks, effectively creating a "mortality immunization" trading market.

As has occurred with the automobile, the airline, and savings and thrift industries, should cataclysmic events befall annuity issuers—such as a miraculous medical advance that greatly, broadly, and instantaneously positively benefits longevity—and Congress deems their ability to meet obligations in the public interest, government intervention in some form (e.g., temporary financial assistance) is a possibility, though by no means a duty.

At that point, new IVA product offerings might shift to a *participating* basis, where some level of mortality risk is guaranteed to be covered by the insurer in the way of conservative mortality assumptions used in IVA pricing and, to the extent better actual mortality experience emerges, IVA contract owners will share in this experience through higher benefits, either higher future benefits or perhaps a "13th monthly check" each year. Effectively, participating variable annuity benefit levels reflect evolving mortality experience patterns as well as investment experience; that is, the recursion formula that relates one periodic annuity benefit to the next contains both an investment experience factor and a mortality experience factor.

Variable income annuities will become increasingly necessary if, as the adage of a 1960s space-travel television character goes, people wish to "live long and prosper." Unlike science fiction, however, the scientific, intellectual pursuit of the aging process—what it is, and how to retard or arrest it—is receiving considerable attention. Reduced mortality rates seem inevitable. While understanding of the aging process remains in a rudimentary stage, scientists increasingly recognize extension of maximum life span as a possibility.

Physicians and researchers study centenarians (people one hundred years old or older) in an effort to better understand the factors—genetic, social, and environmental—that contribute to their aging well. Centenarians (see Figure 6.26) appear to age slowly and to delay or altogether escape

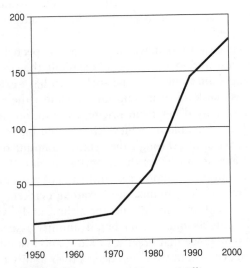

FIGURE 6.26 Centenarians per Million People in the United States
Source: U.S. Census Bureau.

Alzheimer's disease, cancer, heart disease, stroke, and similar maladies normally associated with aging.

We do not stand on the threshold of "curing death." Rather, a more likely scenario is a delay in onset of chronic diseases of old age. As Mason Cooley, U.S. aphorist, phrases this, "Mortality: not acquittal but a series of postponements is what we hope for."

Immortality, if achievable, has profound ramifications. Inevitability of death is central to religion, retirement planning, and a sense of urgency to accomplish life goals. Finite natural resources, at least on earth, would be strained. Social order would be altered. The world would no longer lose its most experienced members, allowing for contributions to science and the arts by people whose talents and abilities expand with agelessness. Theologians and philosophers may address questions about why eternal lives are worth living.

AGING THEORIES, BIOMARKERS, AND TELOMERES

People age biologically at different rates even though they all age chronologically at one uniform rate. As a result, some people enjoy excellent health and mental acuity while identically aged others exhibit pronounced physical and cognitive deterioration. Counting years is not as accurate a predictive method for the distribution of future longevity as assessments using biological-age measures. Such physical gauges of condition are called biomarkers of aging. Research areas as to potential biomarkers of aging include cell replication rate, changes in circulating hormones, and immunological markers.

Major theories on aging share the viewpoint that aging is a consequence of the cumulative hurtful effects of random events. The *wear-and-tear theory* advocates that years of damage to molecules within cells accumulate and eventually kill the cells and their hosts. Toxins and radiation, including ultraviolet light, repeatedly damage the DNA that makes up human genes. While the human body repairs DNA damage, the repairs are sometimes incomplete (allowing evolution) and sometimes inaccurate.

Like hard tips on shoelaces, human chromosomes have "end caps" of DNA called telomeres that shorten with each cell division. When they reach a critically short length, the cells can no longer divide. Telomere loss leads to DNA damage. Adding the enzyme telomerase to cell cultures repairs shortened telomeres and appears to maintain cells in a youthful state.

Normal cell metabolism produces toxic free radicals. Antioxidants within the cells neutralize dangerous free radicals. The *free radical theory* proposes that those free radicals that escape the cleanup process cause oxidative damage to DNA that accumulates over time and that may be a direct cause of aging.

The ancient *rate-of-living theory* suggests that humans possess some essential substance that once fully consumed causes death or that they only get a finite number of breaths or heartbeats. Since calorie restriction appears to prolong life, some quip that there's greater validity to the notion that people each get a specific "pile of food" at birth, and once it's consumed they die, than there is to the notion of finite breaths or heartbeats, which has little evidential support.

The *cross-linking theory* says that with age, DNA, proteins, and other molecules develop improper bonds or cross-links to one another. The needless cross-links reduce the elasticity or mobility of proteins. Damaged proteins are traditionally broken down by enzymes called proteases, but the presence of cross-links inhibits the activity of proteases. The damaged, unnecessary proteins consequently remain and cause problems, possibly including skin wrinkling, cataracts, and atherosclerosis. That cross-link-inducing compounds cause young tissue to resemble old tissue and that cross-link-preventing compounds may delay cataract formation suggests that cross-linking may be a component of aging, although it may or may not be a primary cause.

Genetic mutations in germ cells—egg or sperm—will pass on to future generations. Genetic mutations in somatic cells—the rest of human bodily cells not having reproduction as a principal function—only affect the present generation and do not pass on. While most bodily cell mutations will be corrected and eliminated, those that are not corrected and eliminated accumulate, eventually causing cell malfunction and cell death. The *somatic mutation theory* suggests that this process is a vital part in the aging process. The DNA of mitochondria, the cellular powerhouses that convert energy into a useful form, accumulate somatic mutation errors with age, and their age-related decline in functioning may be an important factor in aging.

Telomeres—bits of DNA at the tips of the 46 chromosomes inside the nucleus of almost all human cells—shorten each time a cell divides. Cell division (called *mitosis*) is essential because many bodily cells must be replaced over time, for example, skin cells and digestive tract cells. When a cell's telomeres reach a critically short length, the cell can no longer replicate. It ultimately malfunctions, and some even die. The cell begins to fail as it enters this stage of growth arrest known as replicative senescence. Telomere shortening may be a type of genetic biological clock that may lend insight into the aging process and cancer. Some liken telomeres to a fuse that grows progressively shorter and finally detonates a cellular time bomb that disrupts a cell's internal structures and functions.

That telomeres relate to *cellular* aging has been known for decades. More recent studies link telomeres to *human* aging. That telomeres are linked to human disease and mortality, as either a cause or a symptom, suggests they may be a physical biomarker of aging. One study showed that the shorter the telomeres of white blood cells, the greater the risk of certain cancers. Another study found that participants with shorter blood cell telomeres died four to five years earlier and were vastly more likely to die of heart disease and infectious disease than were participants with longer telomeres.

Shortened telomeres are associated with a number of age-related diseases and have been identified in a variety of cells, including blood, muscle, skin, cardiovascular, and central nervous system. Telomere shortening depends not only on the number of divisions a cell has experienced but also on the amount of oxidative damage it has suffered, such as from normal metabolism—those physical and chemical processes involved in maintenance of life. People with progeria, the premature aging syndrome previously discussed that causes young children to age so rapidly that they die of old age in their teens, have exceptionally short telomeres.

Cells need their protective telomeres for cell division, because they prevent important genetic information from being lost during cell division. Telomeres also protect chromosome ends from appearing broken, where such perceived breakage triggers one of two biological repair responses: (1) fixing a broken DNA end by copying the sequence from a similar unbroken DNA molecule (known as recombination) or (2) joining together two broken ends.

Senescence, the stage where cells stop reproducing, is related to telomere length. Adding telomerase, an enzyme that lengthens telomeres, to cells allows them to reproduce indefinitely. In most human cells, telomerase is turned off, causing telomeres to shorten as they continue to divide. In almost 90% of cancer cells, telomerase is present, effectively rewinding the cellular clock by lengthening telomeres, replacing fragments of DNA lost during normal cell division. While most human cells can only divide a finite number of times (30 to 50 times in the laboratory), if telomerase stops telomere shortening and because telomerase is present in most cancer cells, then, in theory, cancer cells can live forever.

While the entire aging process may not be explained solely by telomere shortening, this area is fertile ground for research on aging and disease.

FORCE OF MORTALITY

Because projecting the series of future annuity benefits if the AIR is exactly achieved—and because this depends on the mortality assumptions used—is so critical to the setting of the conversion factors, the pricing of the annuity in terms of establishing the mortality and expense and administrative (M&E&A) charge, and the ongoing mortality studies to see how close actual mortality experience is to that assumed, we will study this in more detail.

Just as our initial principal of 1 is subject to the incremental effect of the *force of interest* δ, an original cohort of l_x lives is subject to the decremental effect of the *force of mortality* μ.

The intensity with which mortality is operating at each moment in time varies. The force of mortality is a measure of this instantaneous variation.

Consider the survivorship curve $1/11 \cdot \sqrt{121 - x}$ and a beginning group (radix) of 1,000 lives so that $l_x = 1,000 \cdot 1/11 \cdot \sqrt{121 - x}$. (See Figure 6.27.)

The slope of the tangent line to l_x is given by the derivative of l_x with respect to x.

$$l'_x = \frac{-1,000 \cdot 1/11 \cdot 1/2}{\sqrt{121 - x}} = \frac{-500/11}{\sqrt{121 - x}}$$

At age 57, the derivative l'_{57} is

$$l'_{57} = \frac{-500/11}{8} \approx -5.68$$

At age 57, l_x decreases by about 5.68 lives per year. (The symbol $\approx$ denotes approximate equality.)

Had we started with 2,000 lives, the same approach would show that at age 57, l_x decreases by about $2 \cdot 5.68$, or 11.36, lives per year. As a result, this measure of the force with which mortality is operating at any point in time is unsatisfactory, since it depends on the number of lives surviving at any one time.

To remedy this, we again "normalize" the measure by dividing by the number of lives surviving at any time, namely l_x. The measure is then independent of the number of lives attaining age x. To give this index a positive value, we also multiply by -1. Thus, the *force of mortality* μ_x is defined as

$$\mu_x = -\frac{l'_x}{l_x} \tag{6.43}$$

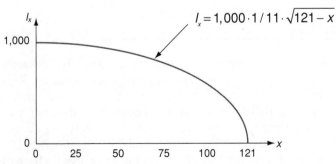

FIGURE 6.27   Survivorship Curve

In the preceding example,

$$\mu_{57} = -\frac{(-5.68)}{l_{57}} = \frac{5.68}{8,000/11} \approx 0.0078$$

The symbol μ_x represents the (instantaneous) force of mortality *at the exact moment* of attaining age x; μ_x is expressed as an *annual rate*. And l_x can be expressed as a function of μ_x. Since

$$\frac{d}{dx}\log_e l_x = \frac{1}{l_x} \cdot \frac{dl_x}{dx}$$

we can rewrite equation 6.43 for μ_x as

$$\mu_x = -\frac{d}{dx}\log_e l_x$$

Renaming x by t and integrating both sides from time $t = 0$ to time $t = x$, we have

$$\int_0^x \mu_t dt = -\int_0^x \frac{d}{dt}\log_e l_t dt$$

$$= -\log_e l_t \Big]_0^x$$

$$= -(\log_e l_x - \log_e l_0)$$

$$= -\log_e \frac{l_x}{l_0}$$

Thus,

$$l_x = l_0 \cdot e^{-\int_0^x \mu_t dt}$$

In words, the number of surviving lives at any time x equals the initial number of lives brought forward x years on which the varying force of mortality operates continuously.

Note the duality with the force of interest, where the accumulated value at any time x equals the initial principal brought forward x years on which the force of interest operates continuously.

Similarly, i represents the annual effective rate of interest resulting from the force of interest δ over a one-year period, while q_x represents the annual effective rate of mortality resulting from the force of mortality μ operating over a one-year period. The instantaneous rate of mortality μ may be viewed as the fundamental rate, where a mortality rate found by measurement for any other time period merely expresses the results of the instantaneous rate by relating the effect of its operation to a given interval of time.

MORTALITY LAWS

"A law explains a set of observations; a theory explains a set of laws," John Casti, U.S. mathematician and author, notes. We observe actual mortality data and seek to derive an explanatory law consistent with a set of observations. In the past three hundred years, substantial improvement has been made in the development of mathematical formulas that generate mortality rates progressively more consistent with observed data.

Survivorship curves typically resemble the basic shape illustrated in Figure 6.28. Because number of deaths per unit of time are high at both ends of the life span—in the first few days following birth and at very advanced ages—there are at least two *inflection points:* those points where the graph is concave downward immediately to the left of the point and concave upward immediately to the right (or vice versa).

Phrased in calculus terminology, a point (c, l_c) is an inflection point if the second derivative l''_x is less than zero if x is less than c and l''_x is greater than zero if x is greater than c; or if the second derivative l''_x is greater than zero if x is less than c and l''_x is less than zero if x is greater than c.

For example, the second bend point, or inflection point, which usually occurs at around age 80 or age 90, reflects a deceleration in the rate of mortality value increase. At least two points of inflection make it challenging to fit a simple formula to the curve. See Figure 6.28.

The survivorship curve l_x is a continuous function of x, defined on the closed interval $[0, \omega]$, that decreases from l_0 to zero.

In 1724, Abraham de Moivre proposed representing l_x as a straight line:

$$l_x = l_0\left(1 - \frac{x}{\omega}\right)$$

While de Moivre recognized this to be merely an approximation, it did simplify calculations and he advised this approach be limited to the center portion of the mortality curve.

In 1825, English mathematician Benjamin Gompertz approached the subject by focusing on μ_x, where his hypothesis may be stated as

$$\mu_x = Bc^x$$

Gompertz's approach appears equivalent to assuming the force of mortality increases in geometric progression. His formula for μ_x implies this formula for l_x:

$$l_x = \frac{l_0 \cdot g^{c^x}}{g}$$

where $\log_e g = -B/\log_e c$

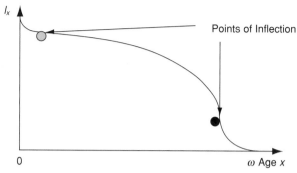

FIGURE 6.28   Inflection Points of Function l_x

Gompertz acknowledged, "It is possible that death may be the consequence of two generally coexisting causes: the one, chance, without previous disposition to death or deterioration; the other, a deterioration, or increased inability to withstand destruction."[29] Gompertz's law of mortality, however, only accounts for the latter cause.

In 1860, to Gompertz's formula British actuary William M. Makeham[30] added the former cause—what we might call "accidental" deaths—to result in a formula that may be expressed as

$$\mu_x = A + Bc^x$$

Makeham's formula for μ_x implies this formula for l_x:

$$l_x = \frac{l_0}{g} \cdot s^x \cdot g^{c^x}$$

where $\log_e s = -A$
    $\log_e g = -B/\log_e c$

Makeham's formula (or law), while quite similar, improved Gompertz's formula meaningfully. Because the formulas involve parameters (e.g., A, B, c), they do not uniquely define one mortality table but rather an infinite family of them. Once numerical values are selected for the parameters and a radix chosen, a unique mortality table is defined.

For example, if we let $A = 0.00235$, $B = 10^{-5}$, and $c = 1.109$, and choose a radix of 10,000 for age 50, Makeham's law produces the l_x curve graphed in Figure 6.29. For comparison, the l_x curve based on the Annuity 2000 Mortality Table for males is graphically reproduced in Figure 6.30. A graph of the difference between these two tables, using a different scale, is shown in Figure 6.31.

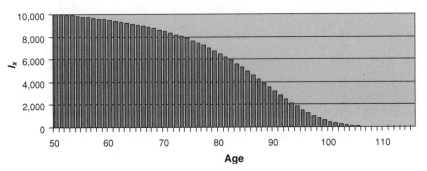

FIGURE 6.29   Makeham's Law: l_x Values

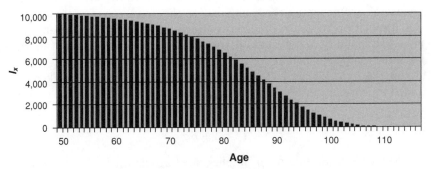

FIGURE 6.30   Annuity 2000 Mortality Table (males): l_x Values

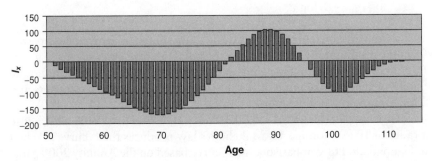

FIGURE 6.31   Difference in l_x Values between Makeham's Law and Annuity 2000 Mortality Table

Note how well this three-parameter Makeham formula approximates the Annuity 2000 Mortality Table. Between ages 50 and 86, the relative difference is less than 2% of the Annuity 2000 Mortality Table; between ages 50 and 96, the relative difference is less than 3.2%.

This "goodness of fit" test suggests Makeham's hypothesis may have some validity, especially at ages most important for immediate annuities. That the force of mortality strongly appears to increase in geometric progression when chance accidents are discarded may have implications for biologists, biogerontologists, and others studying the aging process, who may seek explanatory factors that would result in a geometric progression. Theories of aging also need to explain the paradoxical situation of the mortality deceleration to the right of the second (black) inflection point in Figure 6.28, possibly progressing to the extent that a *mortality plateau* is observed, where increasing death rates characteristic of aging may disappear and mortality rates may level off at some ultimate level. Even in 1867, Makeham noted that for humans "the rapidity of increase in death rate decelerated beyond age 75."[31]

Makeham proposed a second law with the hypothesis that a constant factor, an arithmetically increasing factor, and a geometrically increasing factor comprise the force of mortality:

$$\mu_x = A + Dx + Bc^x$$

As we will see in the section on formula-based mortality tables, "goodness of fit" of mortality rates generated by mathematical formulas with real-world, observed mortality data may be enhanced by splicing together multiple formulas, each of which describes unique characteristics of one segment (i.e., age bracket) of the mortality table.

MORTALITY TABLES

Periodic, large-scale, intercompany[32] mortality studies of individual and group annuitants are performed. These constitute some or all of the raw data from which annuitant mortality tables are ultimately constructed. Mortality tables, contrary to wishful thinking, don't fall from the sky and aren't divined by omniscient sages on mountaintops. Rather, methodologies for conducting mortality studies, compiling mortality data, measuring actual mortality, and creating mortality tables are well defined.[33] Note that different mortality tables result for different populations under study, such as life insureds versus annuitants.

Mortality rates produced by raw mortality data are smoothed via a mathematical process known as "graduation." (Methods of graduation include "Jenkins' fifth-difference modified osculatory interpolation formula," "Karup-King four-point formula," and "Whittaker-Henderson Type A and Type B formulas.") There is a well-known trade-off between "smoothness" and "goodness of fit" when constructing annuitant mortality tables. The results form the bases used for establishing annuity prices and reserves; for example, the mortality rates coming out of the studies (appropriately adjusted for this purpose) are promulgated as the required mortality assumptions to be used in determining statutory reserves, that conservatively determined pot of money calculated to be adequate to provide for all future annuitant claims—the present value of future benefits (PVFB).

Such statutory valuation tables—because of their protective capital adequacy function—take the mortality rates resulting from the study of actual experience and then introduce a loading factor to establish the desired degree of conservatism. For example, to introduce conservatism of 10%,

$$q_x^{\text{Statutory valuation}} = q_x^{\text{Actual experience}} \times (1 - 0.10) \qquad (6.44)$$

The statutory q_x values are 10% lower than the q_x values suggested by actual experience. Because the q_x values are lower, by definition the p_x values are higher (recall $p_x + q_x \equiv 1$, where the symbol "$\equiv$" represents a tautology, a statement that is by definition true). Higher p_x values reflect higher probabilities of survival, a longer period over which annuity benefits will be paid, and therefore a higher present value, or reserve. Thus, if one insurance company happens to sell immediate annuities to a population subset that happens to enjoy exceptional longevity with mortality rates 10% below the general annuitant population, the statutory reserves will still prove adequate for that company.

If a company sells too little immediate annuity business for its experience to mimic that of a large group of annuitants, it needs to hold reserves at a higher level, such as through a method like the 10% mortality rate loading in equation 6.44. Just as a single individual looks to join a pool of similarly situated individuals to form an effective risk-reducing annuity program, an annuity company also needs to have enough annuitants in the pool to feel comfortable that its projected stream of benefit payments—and the reserve that is the present value of such a stream—is reasonably accurate.

This safety margin may serve to cover not only variations in mortality experienced by a single company but also variations between different annuity payout options (e.g., refund versus nonrefund), year to year mortality fluctuations, variations between different kinds of contracts (e.g., immediate fixed annuities, immediate variable annuities, matured deferred annuities), and future improvements in annuitant mortality beyond that assumed by a given set of mortality improvement factors.

When mortality assumptions used for pricing immediate variable annuities are determined starting with the most recent valuation tables, such conservatism needs to be backed out if the most realistic mortality rates are desired to be used. In the preceding example, this is achieved by merely dividing all the statutory valuation q_x rates by 0.9, or $(1 - 0.10)$.

If statutory reserves are predicated on mortality assumptions more conservative than those used in pricing, the resultant statutory reserve can exceed the net premium the insurer collects to fund the immediate variable annuity. As a consequence, some of the insurer's formerly free surplus needs to be set aside to result in adequate statutory reserves. This phenomenon is known as "statutory surplus strain." (On immediate fixed annuities, a valuation interest assumption more conservative than a pricing interest assumption can cause the same occurrence; that is, the "strain" can be attributable to the valuation interest assumption as well as to the valuation mortality assumption. The term *surplus strain* describes any insurance transaction where funds collected are insufficient under statutory accounting guidelines to cover liabilities established.)

The same intercompany mortality experience studies can be used to determine mortality improvement factors, the MIFs. Indeed, MIF tables are periodically produced by organizations such as the Society of Actuaries. Because such periodic mortality studies involve different companies, different amounts of mortality exposures, and similar but different lines of business (e.g., immediate annuities, deferred annuities reaching their maturity date and being automatically annuitized, annuities resulting from life insurance settlement options, structured settlements, etc.), a sharp review is required to distinguish genuine mortality improvements from "statistical noise" differences attributable to data gathering and, when used, risk selection and classification practices.

Insurance companies conduct experience studies to measure their own individual annuitant mortality against that expected in their pricing. The results are stated as "actual to expected ratios," or A/E ratios; q_x^{Actual} values are compared to q_x^{Expected}.

An A/E ratio equal to one implies that real-world experience exactly matches the experience that the insurer assumed. (It's unusual when the universe conforms to assumptions actuaries lay out for it! They know their assumptions will always be wrong, but they try to minimize the degree of deviation.)

An A/E ratio less than one implies that the insurer's mortality assumptions are inadequate; that is, fewer annuitants died than anticipated. Conversely, an A/E ratio greater than one implies the insurer's mortality assumptions are more than adequate—more annuitants died than expected.

In contrast, for life insurance products, an A/E ratio less than one implies that the insurer's mortality assumptions are more than adequate—fewer insureds died than anticipated. An A/E ratio greater than one implies the life insurance mortality assumptions are inadequate—more life insureds died than expected.

Annuity writing companies and life insurance writing companies may introduce a profit margin into each of the mortality, expense, and investment components. Alternatively, they may choose to use, say, a best estimate of actual mortality and expense components and introduce all profit margin through the investment component. The end results may be similar either way, although if mortality and expense values are relatively more constant and investment values are relatively more volatile, quicker crude earnings analyses may be facilitated by needing to investigate only the investment component, rather than all three components.

The A/E ratios are calculated for each age and sex combination as well as in total for the specific unit of business under study. The unit might be all business issued during a certain time period, all business issued under one specific set of mortality assumptions, all business written in a geographic region or by a certain distribution office or channel, and so on.

Actual mortality may deviate from expected (that is, A/E ratio ≠ 1) due to bad original mortality assumptions, a class of annuitants different from that expected buying the product, antiselection by buyers or their representatives who buy certain options from one insurer and other options from another, mortality improvement at rates other than anticipated, random fluctuation, radical medical improvement (e.g., cancer cure, use of stem cells or other progenitor cells that can mature into any of the body's 200 or so cell types and that allow an individual to reproduce any of his own organs that are failing), catastrophe (e.g., war, earthquakes, epidemics, nuclear reactor destruction, tsunamis), and so on.

Annuity writing companies may also look at actual annuitant mortality experience in quinquennial (5-year) or decennial (10-year) age groupings. While the A/E ratio for one specific age and sex may be out of line, if the A/E ratio for the more data-rich quinquennial age grouping including that age is appropriate, it is less likely the insurer will go to the trouble and expense of refining mortality rates that impact rate manuals, sales quotation and illustration software, and reserving and other systems. Investigating actual to expected annuitant mortality experience in quinquennial or decennial age groupings may be particularly useful and appropriate at young ages and at very advanced ages where mortality exposure data may be sparse.

The A/E ratios can also be and are calculated based on the type of annuity option elected. As would be expected, only those who consider themselves in superior health tend to elect a "straight life only" annuity option with no refund feature or guaranteed period. Those who consider themselves in average or perhaps subaverage health or whose ancestral longevity record is not the best might tend to elect annuity options with stronger refund or guarantee features. If the spouse were in poor health, a couple might not elect a joint and survivor annuity option.

Some degree of self-selection is to be expected. Rational people act in their own best economic self-interest and try to achieve the mortality anti-selection that best benefits them. If the same mortality assumptions are used for all annuity options, one would expect the A/E ratio to be lower for "straight life only" options and higher for options with rich refund or guarantee features.

Experience studies also reveal A/E ratios that differ between single-life annuities and joint-life annuities. There are a variety of reasons for this. Some may be real, such as that married couples may live longer than the single elderly. Others may simply be a matter of underreporting of deaths, such as when there is a "joint and 100% to survivor" annuity option where annuity payments are deposited electronically into the annuitants' checking account each month. Because the payment doesn't change at the first death, the surviving annuitant doesn't think to notify the insurer about the death of the other joint annuitant, typically the spouse. As a result, the A/E study reflects an artificially low value, since that death went unreported. The underreporting also results in the insurer holding too high a reserve. Since the present value of future benefits now should be based on only one life instead of two, the reserve should be reduced.

To ensure they don't continue annuity payments beyond the point of contractual obligation, insurers perform an audit function to verify periodically the continuing survival of annuitants. They reserve the right to do so via language in immediate variable annuity contracts.

Bank accounts frozen on death, Social Security death benefit payments made to a person with the annuitant's Social Security number, and other clues exist suggesting that an annuitant may be deceased. Periodic letters from insurers to annuitants—particularly the most elderly of annuitants—are sometimes used, simply requiring a signature as verification of continuing survival. Businesses exist that will perform this annuitant-survival audit function for immediate annuity and pension sponsors.

To the extent payments were made beyond those to which the now deceased annuitant was contractually entitled, an attempt is generally made to recover overpayments. How overpayments will be treated is typically defined in the contract and prospectus (sometimes overpayments are collected with interest). Finally, the case moves to the department within the insurance company where death claims are processed.

In the "tales from the crypt" realm, there is the story of an annuitant who became incapacitated so as to be unable to affix his signature to endorse his annuity benefit checks. The insurer supposedly agreed to accept his thumb print as evidence of ongoing survival. The legend is that following the death of the annuitant, his wife pickled his thumb so as to continue endorsing the checks!

MORTALITY TABLE CONSTRUCTION

Mortality table construction involves a defined period of observation of a defined population segment. The constructor of the table ultimately wishes to create a fraction. The numerator of the fraction is the number of lives that leave the defined group due to the cause being measured. While a variety of sources of decrement (e.g., death, disability, recovery, retirement, withdrawal, marriage) may result in a human life exiting the original classification under observation—for which multiple-decrement tables may be created—here we shall concern ourselves exclusively with the decrement of mortality and the single-decrement table it spawns. The denominator of the fraction is the mortality *exposure*—the annual units of human life subject to death within the defined period of observation.

Although simple in concept, there are a number of details to address in terms of execution. For example, tabulating rules must define whether the observation period is a calendar year, a year that begins on an annuity policy anniversary, a birthday-to-birthday year, or some other period of observation. They must define whether the group being observed is closed or is open to new entrants during the observation period. They must define age, such as age last birthday, age nearest birthday, or age next birthday.

The study must define whether a "select and ultimate" mortality table or an "aggregate" mortality table is desired. An aggregate mortality table will include experience of all annuitant lives irrespective of the length of time since policy issue. In contrast, a select mortality table by definition requires a separate study based on issue age.

Mortality functions such as q_x—the probability that a life age x will not survive to age $x + 1$—represent *annualized* measures. In the construction of mortality tables, it becomes necessary to evaluate probabilities that are not annualized. For example, an annuitant may enter the observation group in a mortality study at age 65¼. Because of this, the assumption as to the pattern of mortality in a time interval less than one year becomes important, with different assumptions producing different mortality rates.

Each of the 116 or so ages within an annuitant mortality table has some true, underlying pattern of mortality within its unit length, which may differ by age. Some reasonably accurate assumption about this mortality pattern, or distribution of deaths within a unit interval, is needed if the resultant mortality table is to be representative of observed experience.

To the extent various assumptions as to distribution of deaths within a unit interval, each of which is logically "reasonable," produce numerical probability values that are quite similar, though not identical, the choice of such assumption may consider convenience in conducting the study rather than just considerations of accuracy. Theoretically, there exist an infinite number of alternative assumptions that may describe mortality patterns within the unit interval. For example, $_tq_x$ $(0 \leq t \leq 1)$ may be represented by any function $f(t)$ such that $f(0) = 0$ and $f(1) = q_x$.

Three particular assumptions regarding the pattern of mortality within the unit age interval tend to be of highest interest. These are (1) uniform distribution of deaths, (2) Balducci hypothesis, and (3) constant force of mortality. We briefly review each. Following the review of these three approaches, the application of this information will make evident the need for this prerequisite study. It will be seen that the assumption chosen affects the determination of mortality exposure—the denominator of the desired fraction—and therefore affects mortality rates—the total fraction.

Uniform Distribution of Deaths

Uniform distribution of deaths (UDD) assumes that deaths occur uniformly between any two consecutive ages. In algebraic terms, UDD assumes

$$_tq_x \equiv t \cdot q_x$$

where $0 \leq t \leq 1$

This simple assumption asserts, for example, that the probability of death of a life age x within ⅓ of a year is ⅓ as great as that over a full one-year interval:

$$_{1/3}q_x = \tfrac{1}{3} q_x$$

It similarly asserts that if n deaths occur over a one-year period in the group under observation for lives age x at the start of the period, then exactly one death will occur in each of the n equal subintervals that comprise the year.

The uniform distribution of deaths assumption asserts that the function $f(t) = {_tq_x}$ is linear on the interval $0 \leq t \leq 1$.

$$f(t) = {_tq_x} = mt + c$$

Because $_0q_x = 0$, this indicates that $c = 0$. Because $_1q_x = q_x$, this indicates that $m = q_x$. Thus,

$$f(t) = {}_tq_x = q_x \cdot t + 0 = t \cdot q_x$$

Because UDD assumes that deaths occur uniformly throughout the unit age interval, this implies that the l_x curve between age x and age $x + 1$ is a straight line. This can be validated as

$$l_{x+t} = l_x \cdot {}_tp_x$$
$$= l_x \cdot (1 - {}_tq_x)$$
$$= l_x \cdot (1 - t \cdot q_x)$$
$$= l_x - t \cdot d_x$$

Therefore, the entire l_x curve becomes a connected series of straight lines. The force of mortality under the UDD assumption is

$$\mu_{x+t} = -\frac{l'_{x+t}}{l_{x+t}}$$

$$= -\frac{(-d_x)}{l_x - t \cdot d_x} \qquad (6.45)$$

$$= \frac{q_x}{1 - t \cdot q_x}$$

Thus, the force of mortality μ_{x+t} is an increasing function of t for $0 \le t \le 1$—within any unit age interval—under the UDD assumption. This is a reasonable assumption for the vast majority of points on the mortality curve.

Note, however, that the force of mortality function μ_x is discontinuous under UDD when we look at an interval wider than the unit age interval. From the definition of μ_{x+t} in equation 6.45, for the unit interval age x to age $x + 1$, we have a right endpoint value of $\mu_{x+1} = q_x/p_x$. For the unit interval age $x + 1$ to age $x + 2$, we have a left endpoint value of $\mu_{x+1} = q_{x+1}$. These two values for μ_{x+1} are generally unequal, resulting in an overall μ_x function that is discontinuous under UDD.

Balducci Hypothesis

In 1920, Italian actuary Gaetano Balducci proposed a pattern of mortality over the unit age interval:

$$_{1-t}q_{x+t} \equiv (1-t) \cdot q_x$$

where $0 \le t \le 1$

Balducci asserted that the function $f(t) = {}_{1-t}q_{x+t}$ is linear on the interval $0 \le t \le 1$; that is,

$$f(t) = {}_{1-t}q_{x+t} = mt + c$$

Because $_1q_x = q_x$, this indicates that $c = q_x$. Because $_0q_{x+1} = 0$, this indicates that $m = -q_x$. Thus,

$$f(t) = {}_{1-t}q_{x+t} = -q_x \cdot t + q_x = (1-t) \cdot q_x$$

Unlike the UDD assumption, the Balducci hypothesis is not associated with a simple verbal description.

To investigate the force of mortality under the Balducci hypothesis, we first derive an expression for l_{x+t}:

$$_{1-t}p_{x+t} = \frac{l_{x+1}}{l_{x+t}} = 1 - {}_{1-t}q_{x+t} = 1 - (1-t)q_x$$

so

$$l_{x+t} = \frac{l_{x+1}}{1-(1-t)q_x} \cdot \frac{l_x}{l_x}$$

$$= \frac{l_x \cdot l_{x+1}}{l_x - (1-t)d_x}$$

$$= \frac{l_x \cdot l_{x+1}}{l_{x+1} + t \cdot d_x}$$

where $0 \le t \le 1$

The force of mortality under the Balducci hypothesis is

$$\mu_{x+t} = -\frac{l'_{x+t}}{l_{x+t}}$$

$$= \frac{\dfrac{l_x \cdot l_{x+1} \cdot d_x}{(l_{x+1} + t \cdot d_x)^2}}{\dfrac{l_x \cdot l_{x+1}}{l_{x+1} + t \cdot d_x}}$$

$$= \frac{d_x}{l_{x+1} + t \cdot d_x}$$

$$= \frac{q_x}{p_x + t \cdot q_x}$$

$$= \frac{q_x}{1 - (1-t) \cdot q_x}$$

where $0 \le t \le 1$

Note that the Balducci hypothesis produces the somewhat disturbing result of a force of mortality μ_{x+t} that *decreases* over the unit interval $0 \le t \le 1$. This decrease, however, takes place only *within* unit age intervals; μ_x values still increase with advancing age across the entire age spectrum. Clearly, the μ_{x+t} function is discontinuous at endpoints of unit intervals.

Constant Force of Mortality

The third pattern of mortality within the unit age interval is that of a constant force of mortality. Because the force of mortality increased within the unit age interval under UDD and decreased within the unit age interval under the Balducci hypothesis, the constant force of mortality assumption is intermediate to these two distribution of deaths assumptions.

The constant force of mortality assumption is simply

$$\mu_{x+t} \equiv \mu$$

where $0 \le t \le 1$

Because the force of mortality is constant within a unit age interval but generally increases with advancing age, the force of mortality function μ_x in the case of the constant force of mortality assumption is discontinuous as well.

Comparison of Three Pattern-of-Mortality Assumptions

As already noted, over the unit age interval x to $x + 1$, the force of mortality increases under uniform distribution of deaths, is constant under constant force of mortality, and decreases under the Balducci hypothesis. While Figure 6.32 reflects this, the figure exaggerates the differences to make them more visually evident. The μ_{x+t} curves for a unit interval at most ages tend to be more horizontal than those shown for UDD and Balducci.

It would appear that μ_{x+t} curves under UDD and Balducci are mirror images, being symmetric about a vertical line extending upward from age $x + \frac{1}{2}$. This is true because

$$\mu_{x+t}^{\text{UDD}} = \mu_{x+1-t}^{\text{Balducci}} = \frac{q_x}{1 - t \cdot q_x}$$

where $0 \le t \le 1$

As a result, these two curves intersect at $t = \frac{1}{2}$.

Total area under the three curves is identical.

$$\int_0^1 \mu_{x+t}^{\text{UDD}}\,dt = \int_0^1 \mu_{x+t}^{\overset{\text{Constant}}{\underset{\text{force}}{}}}\,dt = \int_0^1 \mu_{x+1}^{\text{Balducci}}\,dt$$

Because of this, if the μ_{x+t} curves for UDD and Balducci were linearly increasing and linearly decreasing, respectively (i.e., forming an "**X**" shape),

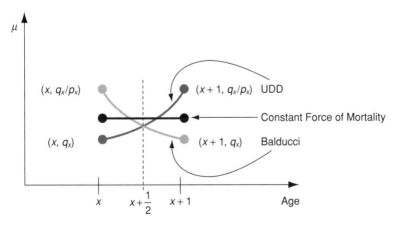

FIGURE 6.32 Relative Magnitudes of Force of Mortality μ_{x+t} Based on Different Pattern-of-Mortality Assumptions for a Unit Age Interval

then all three curves would intersect at $(x + \frac{1}{2}, \mu_{x+\frac{1}{2}})$. Because in actuality μ_{x+t} curves under UDD and Balducci are concave upward, $\mu_{x+\frac{1}{2}}$ under constant force of mortality exceeds $\mu_{x+\frac{1}{2}}$ under UDD and Balducci.

Now look at the l_{x+t} function under the three patterns of mortality. The l_x and l_{x+1} values are independent of the three assumptions under study regarding the nature of the l_{x+t} function at intermediate points. Thus, these three l_{x+t} functions share common endpoints. See Figure 6.33.

Earlier we saw that under UDD, $l_{x+t} = l_x - t \cdot d_x$ for $0 \leq t \leq 1$, so this l_{x+t} function is linear, as shown in Figure 6.33.

Under the Balducci hypothesis, we saw that

$$l_{x+t} = \frac{l_x \cdot l_{x+1}}{l_{x+1} + t \cdot d_x}$$

where $0 \leq t \leq 1$

Because l'_{x+t} is less than 0 and l''_{x+t} is greater than 0, it follows that l_{x+t} is a decreasing hyperbola that is concave upward, as shown in Figure 6.33.

Recall from the discussion regarding the force of mortality that

$$l_x = l_0 \cdot e^{-\int_0^x \mu_y dy}$$

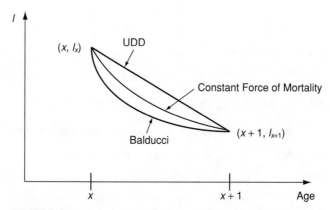

FIGURE 6.33 Relative Magnitudes of Survivorship Function l_{x+t} Based on Different Pattern-of-Mortality Assumptions for a Unit Age Interval

Thus,

$$_np_x = \frac{l_{x+n}}{l_x} = \frac{l_0 \cdot e^{-\int_0^{x+n} \mu_y dy}}{l_0 \cdot e^{-\int_0^{x} \mu_y dy}} = e^{-\int_x^{x+n} \mu_y dy} = e^{-\int_0^{n} \mu_{x+t} dt}$$

Now looking at Figure 6.32 illustrating values of μ_{x+t}, we see that for $0 < n < 1$

$$\int_0^n \mu_{x+t}^{\text{UDD}} dt < \int_0^n \mu_{x+t}^{\overset{\text{Constant}}{\text{force}}} dt < \int_0^n \mu_{x+1}^{\text{Balducci}} dt$$

Therefore,

$$e^{-\int_0^n \mu_{x+t}^{\text{UDD}} dt} > e^{-\int_0^n \mu_{x+t}^{\overset{\text{Constant}}{\text{force}}} dt} > e^{-\int_0^n \mu_{x+t}^{\text{Balducci}} dt}$$

making

$$_np_x^{\text{UDD}} > {_np_x^{\overset{\text{Constant}}{\text{force}}}} > {_np_x^{\text{Balducci}}}$$

and thus

$$l_{x+n}^{\text{UDD}} > l_{x+n}^{\overset{\text{Constant}}{\text{force}}} > l_{x+n}^{\text{Balducci}}$$

This results in the relative magnitude of the l_{x+t} function as expressed in Figure 6.33. Using the three pattern-of-mortality assumptions, Figure 6.33 immediately reveals that the anticipated number of deaths in the first half of a year of age is largest under the Balducci hypothesis, next largest under the constant force of mortality assumption, and smallest under the UDD assumption.

The UDD assumption by definition assumes an equal number of deaths in each half of the year. Because the l_{x+t} curve falls off most rapidly under Balducci, it shows the highest number of deaths in the first half of the year. The constant force of mortality assumption produces an l_{x+t} curve intermediate to the other two.

Reflecting back on the μ_{x+t} graph in Figure 6.32, this is the expected result. The force of mortality operates most heavily early in the year under Balducci, producing the highest expected number of deaths early in the year.

Table 6.7 summarizes selected characteristics resulting from the three assumptions regarding patterns of mortality at points interior to a unit age interval.

TABLE 6.7 Summary of Functions Resulting from Pattern-of-Mortality Hypotheses on a Unit Age Interval

	Uniform Distribution of Deaths (UDD)	Balducci	Constant Force of Mortality
	Hypothesis: $_tq_x = t \cdot q_x$ $(0 \le t \le 1)$	Hypothesis: $_{1-t}q_{x+t} = (1-t) \cdot q_x$ $(0 \le t \le 1)$	Hypothesis: $\mu_{x+t} = \mu$ $(0 \le t \le 1)$
l_{x+t}	$l_x - t \cdot d_x$	$\dfrac{l_x \cdot l_{x+1}}{l_{x+1} + t \cdot d_x}$	$l_x \cdot e^{-\mu t}$
$_tq_x$	$t \cdot q_x$	$\dfrac{t \cdot q_x}{1-(1-t) \cdot q_x}$	$1 - e^{-\mu t}$
$_{1-t}q_{x+t}$	$\dfrac{(1-t) \cdot q_x}{1 - t \cdot q_x}$	$(1-t) \cdot q_x$	$1 - e^{-\mu(1-t)}$
μ_{x+t}	$\dfrac{q_x}{1-t \cdot q_x}$	$\dfrac{q_x}{1-(1-t) \cdot q_x}$	μ
μ_x	q_x	$\dfrac{q_x}{p_x}$	μ
μ_{x+1}	$\dfrac{q_x}{p_x}$	q_x	μ
Form of l_{x+t}	Linear	Decreasing hyperbola	Decreasing exponential
Form of μ_{x+t}	Increasing hyperbola	Decreasing hyperbola	Constant

Mortality Exposure Determination

We now make evident the rationale for study of the three assumed patterns of mortality on the unit interval. First, it should be noted that numerical values calculated under these three assumptions produce relatively minor variation in results. For example, q_{65} equals 0.007017 for a female when using the Annuity 2000 Basic Table. Using Table 6.7, we find the following values for $_{3/4}q_{65+1/4}$ in Table 6.8:

TABLE 6.8 Numerical Examples of $_{1-t}q_{x+t}$

	Uniform Distribution of Deaths (UDD)	Balducci	Constant Force of Mortality
$_{¾}q_{65+¼}$	0.005272	0.005263	0.005267

Given the closeness of the three values—at least for ages in the first few decades following "normal" retirement ages, when IVAs are often purchased—practical considerations may govern more heavily than accuracy considerations in choice of unit-interval mortality pattern assumption. As you may surmise, one of these three assumptions is virtually universally applied in mortality table construction with the reason being practical considerations. Exactly which one is about to be revealed.

Consider the time line from age x to age $x + 1$ in Figure 6.34. A lives were under observation at exact age x. N lives, the new entrants, entered the group under observation at age $x + s$. W lives, the withdrawals, exited the group under observation at age $x + t$. D lives, the deaths, were observed among lives while members of the group under observation. B lives remained in the group under observation at age $x + 1$. Thus, the arithmetical equation

$$A + N - W - D = B$$

clearly holds.

Note that if one or more of the W lives died after exiting the group under observation, such number is *excluded* from the number of deaths D; that is, any person who withdrew at age $x + t$ and died before age $x + 1$ is not counted as a death because the person was not a member of the group under observation at the time of death.

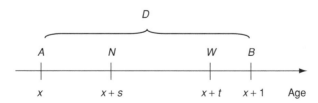

FIGURE 6.34 Time Line for Group of Lives under Observation

We seek to determine the value of q_x, the mortality rate for a life age x over the unit age interval x to $x + 1$. Effectively, we wish to solve the equation

$$A \cdot q_x + N \cdot {}_{1-s}q_{x+s} - W \cdot {}_{1-t}q_{x+t} = D$$

The uniform distribution of deaths assumption, the Balducci assumption, and the constant force of mortality assumption lead to these expressions of this equation:

UDD $$A \cdot q_x + N \cdot \frac{(1-s)q_x}{1-s \cdot q_x} - W \cdot \frac{(1-t)q_x}{1-t \cdot q_x} = D$$

Balducci $$A \cdot q_x + N \cdot (1 - s)q_x - W \cdot (1 - t)q_x = D$$

Constant Force
of Mortality $$A \cdot q_x + N[1 - (1 - q_x)^{1-s}] - W[1 - (1 - q_x)^{1-t}] = D$$

Solving for q_x using Balducci yields

$$q_x = \frac{D}{A + N(1-s) - W(1-t)}$$

Hearkening back to Figure 6.34, we see that the denominator in the preceding equation is logical. The A lives were subject to mortality risk for a full year, and the N lives were subject to mortality risk for the fractional part $1 - s$ of a year. The W lives were not members of the group and, therefore, were not subject to mortality risk for the fractional part $1 - t$ of a year. As an example, if $A = 100$, $N = 30$, $W = 20$, $s = \frac{1}{3}$, $t = \frac{3}{4}$, and $D = 5$, then

$$q_x = \frac{5}{100 + 30(1 - \frac{1}{3}) - 20(1 - \frac{3}{4})} = \frac{5}{115}$$

In contrast, solving for q_x using the UDD assumption or the constant force of mortality assumption results in more complex equations, for example, equations whose solutions demand iterative techniques or series expansion. While certainly of lesser significance in an era of low-cost automated computing, it is still the case that the more attractive tractability under the Balducci hypothesis makes it the preferred assumption for mortality table construction.

If in a unit-age interval during an observation period there are multiple new entrant points and/or multiple withdrawal points, the q_x calculations under UDD or constant force of mortality become increasingly complex, whereas complexity for the Balducci hypothesis does not materially change.

We can define the mortality rate q_x as the ratio of deaths D to *exposure E*:

$$q_x = \frac{D}{A + N(1-s) - W(1-t)} = \frac{D}{E}$$

Determination of the number of deaths D in the group under observation between ages x and $x + 1$ is straightforward. It is the *exposure E* on which the assumption of patterns of mortality on a unit-age interval focuses.

In addition to greater calculation simplicity, Balducci is also of greater value because, when observing a group for the purpose of constructing a mortality table, the probability $_{1-t}q_{x+t}$—which the Balducci hypothesis simplifies so well—is encountered more frequently than the probability $_tq_x$—which the UDD assumption simplifies so well.

It is important to note that while in calculating E a deduction of the fraction $1 - t$ of a year is made for the W lives that withdraw, no such adjustment is made for the deaths D that occur at one or more points during the year. While at first glance it might seem that on death no further exposure is contributed and deaths should be treated in a manner consistent with withdrawals, a simple example will show this approach to be implausible.

Suppose two lives exact age x are observed. Both survive one-half year and then die. If we treat deaths the same as withdrawals, we have $q_x = D/E = 2/1 = 200\%$. Barring resurrection and a second death for both in the same year, it is well agreed that a mortality rate cannot exceed 100%!

The reality is that the exposure formula E was derived directly from the equation associated with the time line diagram, namely,

$$A \cdot q_x + N \cdot {_{1-s}q_{x+s}} - W \cdot {_{1-t}q_{x+t}} = D$$

and when the formulas derived earlier under the Balducci hypothesis for each of the q terms were substituted, the result was

$$q_x = \frac{D}{A + N(1-s) - W(1-t)} = \frac{D}{E}$$

The derivation produces no subtractive term for deaths in the denominator. This tells us that the number of deaths D must be placed at the end of the unit age interval, as shown in Figure 6.35.

Because no subtractive term exists for deaths in the calculation of exposure E, deaths contribute exposure to the end of the unit-age interval for purposes of calculating q_x. Even if one of the A members exact age x dies only one day into the observation period, exposure is contributed until age $x + 1$—nearly a full year after death. This is a straightforward mathemati-

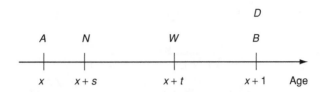

FIGURE 6.35 Placement of Deaths D on Exposure Time Line for q_x Determination under Balducci Hypothesis

cal consequence of the choice of assumption regarding pattern of mortality on the unit-age interval. Clearly, this remedies the improper approach that resulted in a mortality rate in excess of 100%.

For the same reason, if one of the A members exact age x dies one day into the observation period and the observation period for the mortality study ends at midyear, exposure is contributed until year-end, even though this is beyond the defined end of the study. Again, this should not be found disquieting but rather a straightforward mathematical consequence of our selection of an intra-age mortality pattern assumption.

One may state the same thing in slightly different language. When a life enters a group under observation for purposes of a mortality study, she bears a specific amount of *potential* exposure for the age interval she enters and for all subsequent age intervals. When she exits the observed group, a negative adjustment is made in the way of *cancelled* exposure. Cancellation is effective immediately for withdrawals. Cancellation is effective for deaths, but only for age intervals subsequent to the one in which death actually occurs. Total exposure contributed by a life to a particular age interval is the excess of potential over cancelled exposure.

Now that the mathematical foundation for mortality table construction is established, in actual practice what remains is to tabulate often massive quantities of data, ensuring that exposures are allocated to appropriate unit age intervals. A table of ungraduated (i.e., nonsmoothed or "raw") mortality rates is the resultant output.

CONSIDERATIONS IN MORTALITY TABLE SELECTION

When selecting a mortality table to use for pricing IVAs, annuity companies need to look at the experience data on which a mortality table is premised. For example, the 1983 Table *a* is an individual annuity valuation table. Indeed, the more recent Annuity 2000 Mortality Table—also an individual annuity valuation table—is based on the 1983 Table *a*, projected forward. The 1983 Table *a* appears in Appendix S. Its predecessor, the 1971 Individual Annuitant Mortality Table (1971 IAM), appears in Appendix R.

Individual annuities included in a mortality study, such as is the case with the 1983 Table *a*, may arise from individual immediate annuities, matured deferred annuities, and life income settlements. To the extent an annuity company wishes to apply such a base mortality table or a variation thereof to IVA pricing, it may wish to determine whether this application might result in a higher degree of self-selection, that is, a greater percentage of healthy and extra-healthy lives forming the pool. This could occur because for immediate annuity purchases, the candidates may evaluate their own health right at the point of making the purchase decision. In contrast, individuals who purchased deferred annuity contracts many years earlier and received an individual annuity as an automatic event on reaching the maturity age stated in the contract might include more of a mixture of extra-healthy, healthy, and less-healthy lives.

Mortality studies focus on the ratio of actual to expected deaths by amounts of annual income rather than by number of contracts (i.e., deaths associated with larger contracts are more heavily weighted, rather than all deaths counting equally). This is because (1) mortality experience differs by level of annual income and (2) the financial effect of annuitant mortality clearly depends on amount of annual income, not number of contracts. Annuity writers' mortality gains or losses aren't dictated by just how many annuitants die but rather by the amounts of annual income no longer payable to those who die (and therefore whose reserves are released—or, in the case of annuities with a guarantee or refund feature still active, whose reserves are reduced).

Due to this same self-selection process, immediate nonrefund annuities (e.g., single life-only annuities) will exhibit lower mortality rates than immediate refund annuities (e.g., unit refund, installment refund, and life with certain period). As a result, when source data includes refund and nonrefund immediate annuities, matured deferred annuities, and life settlement options—as is the case with the 1971 IAM (Individual Annuity Mortality) Table and 1983 Table *a*—the resultant mortality rates (with their 10% loading removed) may be inappropriate for calculating single premiums for immediate annuities. This is because that is not the objective of these tables. The objective of those constructing these tables—and the Annuity 2000 table—is to develop an annuity mortality table that is "safe" for the reserve *valuation* of all types of individual annuities. These tables include suitable margins relative to aggregate current experience to provide a degree of safety.

These mortality tables to be used in reserve valuation are the *minimum* valuation standard for all types of individual annuities. If they are not representative of the mix of business of a particular annuity writer, it is incumbent on the valuation actuary to determine an appropriate reserving basis at least as strong as the minimum standard and applied on a consistent basis.

The mix of refund and nonrefund immediate annuities, matured deferred annuities, and life settlement options (i.e., death claims, maturities, and surrenders) comprising the source data for an intercompany mortality study may fluctuate from one study to the next. Adjustments are necessary to keep the percentage contribution from each type of business constant between studies to ensure that any mortality trends truly exist and are not merely attributable to measuring a different mix of source data.

Because of the self-selection process, mortality rates of immediate annuities are lower for a life age x that just purchased the IVA contract than for a life age x that purchased the same contract, say, 10 years earlier. This introduces the concept of "select" and "ultimate" mortality. Self-selection is evident by lower mortality rates in early durations under immediate annuity contracts.

If an individual voluntarily purchases a life-contingent IVA (or elects a life-contingent IVA in lieu of a lump-sum distribution or non-life-contingent distribution from a defined contribution plan), the result of this self-selection process is that the collection of such lives does not constitute a random group but rather a *select* group, the members of which have initially satisfied themselves as to a health status that suggests to them that such a purchase may be expected to be economically favorable.

Assume that the effect of self-selection wears off over 10 years; that is, the difference in mortality rates is negligible between a life with attained age x that purchased the contract 10 years earlier and a life with attained age x that purchased the contract 20 years earlier.

Actuarial notation to denote the number of lives beginning year of age x within the select period is $l_{[x]}$, the [ ] being the symbol to denote "select." If experience suggests, say, a 10-year select period for immediate annuity purchasers at age 65, then the progression of lives comprising such a cohort is denoted $l_{[65]}, l_{[65]+1}, l_{[65]+2}, l_{[65]+3}, \ldots, l_{[65]+9}, l_{75}, l_{76}, \ldots$ "Ultimate" annuitant mortality rates—those beyond the "select" period—are signified by the usual l_x notation, such as l_{75} and l_{76} in this example.

Because the effect of selection wears off with each year since policy inception, this tendency may be expressed mathematically by a series of inequalities:

$$q_{[x]} < q_{[x-1]+1} < q_{[x-2]+2} < \cdots$$

To gain a sense of magnitude of potential selection effects, Table 6.9 compares the present value (a_x) of an annuity of \$1 per year paid at the end

TABLE 6.9   Effect of Selection on Annuity Present Values

- Select mortality assumed equal to 85% and 90% of Annuity 2000.
- Select mortality grades up to ultimate mortality over 10-year period.
- 5% AIR.

Age at Issue	a_x on Annuity 2000 (1)	85% Select Mortality		90% Select Mortality	
		a_x (2)	(2) ÷ (1) (3)	a_x (4)	(4) ÷ (1) (5)
Males					
60	12.991	13.062	100.5%	13.038	100.4%
65	11.603	11.705	100.9	11.671	100.6
70	10.075	10.220	101.4	10.172	101.0
75	8.501	8.694	102.3	8.629	101.5
Females					
60	13.929	13.977	100.3	13.961	100.2
65	12.617	12.685	100.5	12.663	100.4
70	11.107	11.205	100.9	11.172	100.6
75	9.411	9.555	101.5	9.507	101.0

of the year with and without selection effects. Where selection effects are present in this example, "select" mortality rates are assumed over the first 10 years of policy durations after issue. "Select" mortality is equal to 85% and 90% of Annuity 2000 Mortality Table rates, grading up uniformly toward "ultimate" mortality over 10 years—at 1.5% per year and 1.0% per year for the 85% and 90% assumed select mortality, respectively.

The selection effect can be material because (1) the selection effect occurs at the beginning of the annuity payout period; (2) the result is a greater number of surviving lives projected to receive benefits; and (3) when discounting a series of future benefit payments, nearer-term payments have a relatively greater impact on present value than farther-term payments. A comparison of annuity present values due to such selection effect appears in Table 6.9.

While such percentage increases in annuity present value may initially appear minor, it must be remembered that in the United States the variable annuity business is quite competitive. Thus "economic value added" (EVA) by an IVA sale—the present value of distributable earnings discounted at the insurer's cost of capital as a percentage of gross premium received—can be a low number. The variable annuity business is a low-margin, high-volume business. As a result, an increase in actual cost (i.e., present value) to the insurer of providing variable income benefits by a few percent that is unaccounted for in the pricing process due to failure to recognize or adequately recognize the effects of selection can meaningfully detract from "value added" by an IVA sale.

Individual annuity valuation tables have historically not been "select-and-ultimate" tables, but rather "aggregate" tables: The valuation mortality rate for a life age x makes no distinction between a life who just purchased an immediate annuity at age x and one who has attained age x but purchased an immediate annuity decades ago. Individual annuity valuation tables, therefore, include all contract durations, mixing "select" rates and "ultimate" rates.

The Annuity 2000 table is an aggregate mortality table, reflecting a combination of "select" and "ultimate" rates. The select rates are lower than those in the Annuity 2000 table and the ultimate rates are higher. Thus, aggregate rates depend on the relative mix of (1) mortality exposures in the select period, (2) how far such exposures are into the select period, and (3) mortality exposures in the ultimate period. Select mortality grades into ultimate mortality, and a selection period of 10 years is consistent with statements of informed observers.

While use of aggregate rates is certainly safer than using only ultimate mortality, if a particular annuity writer believes it will have a substantially higher proportion of new, select, annuity business than that used to develop the valuation table, the valuation actuary should make suitable adjustments, holding a reserve in excess of the *minimum* valuation standard.[34] Similarly, if product development and pricing actuaries unload and project the valuation mortality table for use as a pricing mortality table, they should also make suitable adjustments.

The degree of selection—as evidenced by the progression of $l_{[x]}, \ldots, l_{[x]+n}$ values relative to $l_x, \ldots, l_{x+n}$ values—can be influenced by tax law. To the extent tax law provides incentives to encourage private-sector life-contingent immediate annuities, the portion of the U.S. population availing themselves of these protective devices should increase. The resultant inclusion of less-healthy lives that would not have purchased IVA instruments absent encouraging tax policy serves to narrow, but not close, the gap between select mortality and ultimate mortality. In addition to lessening self-selection, inclusion of such incremental IVA purchasers—some with less-than-stellar health—could also reduce the rate of annuitant mortality improvement or even shift aggregate annuitant mortality rates higher.

Annuitant mortality is higher for contracts written in the tax-qualified annuity markets than for those written in the non-tax-qualified annuity market; that is, there is more self-selection in the non-tax-qualified market where such purchases may provide retirement income supplemental to some other primary retirement income source(s). Prospective non-tax-qualified IVA purchasers may evaluate their health status more closely before purchasing a contract, whereas tax incentives may play a stronger role and health status a weaker role in tax-qualified markets.

In summary, self-selection is evidenced by:

- Lower overall mortality for annuitants versus nonannuitants (aggregate mortality).
- Lower mortality in early immediate annuity contract durations (select and ultimate mortality).
- Lower mortality for straight lifetime annuity options versus annuity options containing certain periods or refund features (installment refund, unit refund).
- Lower mortality in non-tax-qualified market.

Because a select-and-ultimate mortality table may be necessary for use in pricing IVAs, the format of one with a 10-year select period appears in Table 6.10A. The $l_{[x]}$ column represents the number of lives that at inception of their IVA contracts are age x. The $l_{[x]+1}$ column represents the number of survivors at age $x + 1$ of the $l_{[x]}$ lives that purchased an IVA contract one year earlier. The progression continues through $l_{[x]+9}$. The select symbol [ ] is absent in the l_{x+10} column because the effect of selection is assumed to wear off by that point—l_{x+10} represents the number of survivors of the $l_{[x]}$ lives that purchased an IVA 10 years earlier, the number of survivors of the $l_{[x-1]}$

TABLE 6.10A Select-and-Ultimate Mortality Table (*l* values)

[x]	$l_{[x]}$	$l_{[x]+1}$	$l_{[x]+2}$	$l_{[x]+3}$	$l_{[x]+4}$	$l_{[x]+5}$	$l_{[x]+6}$	$l_{[x]+7}$	$l_{[x]+8}$	$l_{[x]+9}$	l_{x+10}	x+10
60												70
61												71
62												72
63												73
64												74
65												75
66												76
67												77
68												78
69												79
70												80
71												81
72												82
73												83
74												84
75												85

lives that purchased an IVA 11 years earlier, and so on. This l_{x+10} column constitutes the *ultimate* portion of the *select-and-ultimate* mortality table; l_{x+11} is located directly beneath l_{x+10} in the *ultimate* column. One reads the *select* values from $l_{[x]}$ through $l_{[x+9]}$ horizontally, then reads the *ultimate* values $l_{x+10}, l_{x+11}, \ldots$ vertically. As an example, in the first row of Table 6.10A for a new 60-year-old annuitant (that is, $x = 60$), one traces the select values $l_{[60]}, l_{[61]}, \ldots, l_{[69]}$ horizontally across the top row and then traces the ultimate values $l_{70}, l_{71}, l_{72}, \ldots$ vertically down the last column. (See Table 6.10B for d values and Table 6.10C for q values.)

Select commutation functions can be calculated from the *select* portion of the mortality table for use in calculating present values of life-contingent annuities. For example, if the select period is 10 years, the formulas for D values are

$$D_{[x]+t} = v^{x+t} \cdot l_{[x]+t} \qquad \text{for } 0 \le t < 10$$

$$D_{x+t} = v^{x+t} \cdot l_{x+t} \qquad \text{for } t \ge 10$$

N values are determined by summing D values for each issue age:

$$N_{[x]+t} = \sum_{k=t}^{9} D_{[x]+k} + \sum_{k=10}^{\omega-x-1} D_{x+k} \qquad \text{for } 0 \le t < 10$$

$$N_{x+t} = \sum_{k=t}^{\omega-x-1} D_{x+k} \qquad \text{for } t \ge 10$$

TABLE 6.10B　　Select-and-Ultimate Mortality Table (d values)

$[x]$	$d_{[x]}$	$d_{[x]+1}$	$d_{[x]+2}$	$d_{[x]+3}$	$d_{[x]+4}$	$d_{[x]+5}$	$d_{[x]+6}$	$d_{[x]+7}$	$d_{[x]+8}$	$d_{[x]+9}$	d_{x+10}	$x+10$
60												70
61												71
62												72
63												73
64												74
65												75
66												76
67												77
68												78
69												79
70												80
71												81
72												82
73												83
74												84
75												85

TABLE 6.10C Select-and-Ultimate Mortality Table (q values)

$[x]$	$q_{[x]}$	$q_{[x]+1}$	$q_{[x]+2}$	$q_{[x]+3}$	$q_{[x]+4}$	$q_{[x]+5}$	$q_{[x]+6}$	$q_{[x]+7}$	$q_{[x]+8}$	$q_{[x]+9}$	q_{x+10}	$x+10$
60												70
61												71
62												72
63												73
64												74
65												75
66												76
67												77
68												78
69												79
70												80
71												81
72												82
73												83
74												84
75												85

An annual *n*-year deferred life annuity-immediate has a present value described by

$$_{n|}a_{[x]} = \frac{N_{[x]+n+1}}{D_{[x]}} \qquad \text{for } n < 9$$

$$_{n|}a_{[x]} = \frac{N_{x+n+1}}{D_{[x]}} \qquad \text{for } n \geq 9$$

While the theoretical constructs underpinning development of an immediate annuitant mortality table for pricing or reserve valuation are well understood, it is clearly not the case that every annuity company arrives at the same end result. While scientific analysis can carry the process so far, business decisions made within a host of constraints (e.g., practicality, administrability, regulation, competition, sales volume) dictate the annuity purchase rates actually offered to the public. A variety of ways of handling acquisition expenses (policy issue, sales compensation, premium tax, and DAC tax), ongoing maintenance expenses (annuity benefit payments, tax reporting), and terminal expenses (death claim processing) specifically related to an IVA line of business—as well as how an annuity company handles the allocation of overhead expenses among business lines and what specific level of profitability it targets—similarly impact annuity purchase rates.

Valuation mortality tables tend to be sex-distinct rather than unisex. One reason is simply that the male/female proportions for a particular annuity company may differ from those on which a merged gender valuation table is based. Another reason is that even if the male/female proportions are appropriate today (say 50%/50%), they may become inappropriate at some later date because males do not live as long as females, resulting in a different mix (say 40%/60%)—even if no new business is written.

Mortality rates at very advanced ages, such as over 100, are based on a relatively small number of lives, so less confidence is placed in them. Rather, a smooth (cubic) curve was used in the 1983 Table *a* (and therefore in the Annuity 2000 table) to grade mortality rates from age 97 (where there was more "reliable" data) to age 115, the terminal age chosen, with q_{115} equal to 1. For annuities purchased at "customary" ages of 60 to 70, projected payments at ages above 100 have little impact on present values.

One researcher postulates that mortality rates above age 100 may level off between 30% and 40%, rather than continually increase. Research from 1939 suggests that mortality rates asymptotically approach an ultimate plateau of about 0.44 for women and 0.54 for men.[35] Future advanced-age mortality studies will either support or refute these hypotheses.

FORMULA-BASED MORTALITY TABLES

The adventure of humankind's marvelous struggle to understand the laws governing the world has inspired a number of noteworthy attempts to capture the nature of human mortality expressed as a mathematical formula. It would be convenient if all attained-age mortality-rate values in a mortality table could be expressed by one mathematical formula, appropriately parameterized. This would speed the process of answering numerous questions about the population of interest.

Gompertz's law assumes an exponential function for the force of mortality:

$$\mu_x = Bc^x = e^{\alpha + \gamma x}$$

where $B = e^{\alpha}$
       $c = e^{\gamma}$

The formula implies that the probability of dying increases at a constant exponential rate as age increases. The law effectively describes exponential aging.

Studies show that Gompertz's law matches up reasonably well with empirical mortality data between the ages of 30 and 90. That this is so suggests implications about and lends insight into biophysical processes,

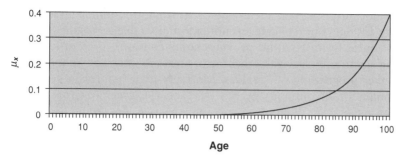

FIGURE 6.36 Force of Mortality μ_x under Gompertz's Law

although those will not be described here. Studies also show decreasing values of B over time, reflecting mortality improvement.

Just as life expectancy is a single summary measure by which different mortality tables can be compared, the Gompertz parameters B and c form another basis for comparison.

Graphically, the force of mortality μ_x under Gompertz's law with parameters $B = 0.000049$ and $c = 1.094$ (as associated with the 1971 Individual Annuity Mortality Table for males[36]) appears in Figure 6.36.

Since Gompertz's law, $\mu_x = Bc^x = e^{\alpha + \gamma x}$, is an exponential function, applying the natural logarithmic (ln) transformation produces the linear equation $\ln \mu_x = \alpha + \gamma x$—a straight line. The same information graphed in Figure 6.36 appears in Figure 6.37, the only difference being that the natural logarithm of the force of mortality—rather than μ itself—appears as the dependent variable on the vertical axis.

At least to date, population questions where l_x assumes a specific analytic form are rarely considered. Rather, l_x is axiomatically presumed to possess certain characteristics—for example, it is monotonically decreasing—but applications involving l_x simply tend to use a set of discrete values.

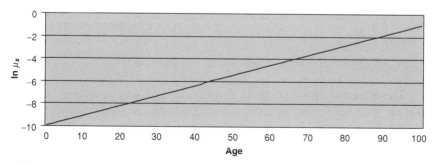

FIGURE 6.37 Force of Mortality $\ln \mu_x$ under Gompertz's Law

It is not surprising that a reasonable mathematical formula (at least that we know of) does not replicate an entire mortality table across the full spectrum of ages. Even if nature provides some constant force of mortality working against our survival, other factors serve to interrupt what might be a smoother progression of l_x values. Mortality improvement factors alone cause points of discontinuity every five years whenever the factor for one five-year age bracket differs from a contiguous one. Accidental death rates tend to be more of an addition to nonaccidental death rates, rather than some specific percentage of them, and may be greater at the more physically active young adult ages.

A more complex mathematical formula that does a better job of replicating an entire mortality table may well include the Gompertz formula and the Makeham formula as special cases.[37]

As mentioned earlier, one of the disadvantages of independently projecting age-specific mortality rates into the future is the possibility of obtaining an irregular shape to the mortality curve at some point beyond the base year. If a mathematical curve, appropriately parameterized, could fit the whole range of ages well, this could preserve a logical mortality pattern over the projection period.

While de Moivre, Gompertz, and Makeham took notable earlier attempts at this approach, in 1980 Heligman and Pollard[38] proposed an eight-parameter mathematical curve that has the capability to represent different patterns of mortality specific to each stage of the human life span. The Heligman-Pollard (H-P) equation is

$$\frac{q_x}{p_x} = A^{(x+B)^C} + D \cdot e^{-E(\ln x - \ln F)^2} + GH^x$$

where A is approximately q_1, the age 1 mortality rate
  B indicates the location of q_0 in the interval $(q_1, 0.5)$
  C reflects the speed of infant mortality decline
  D reflects the severity of the "accident hump"
  E measures the spread of the "accident hump"
  F indicates the location of the "accident hump"
  G denotes the initial level of old-age mortality
  H reflects the rate of increase of old-age mortality

The tripartite terms of the H-P equation represent mortality behavior in three specific life stages: infancy, young adulthood, and maturity.

While "accident" is a cause of death that is often represented by a constant add-on to age-based mortality rates, there is an "accident hump" in young adulthood (i.e., teenage years).

Further analysis of the H-P formula continues. The third term of the H-P formula represents a Gompertz law, which is not generally a good representation of mortality at very advanced ages. While observed mortality data at very advanced ages remains the scantest, current thinking is that mortality rates do not progress monotonically toward unity (i.e., $q_\omega = 1$) but rather reach a peak and level off at some plateau at the highest ages.

LAW OF LARGE NUMBERS

Life is more interesting because it holds some unknowns. If everything in nature were entirely predictable and all natural laws were known and unchanging, this static nature without variation would prove less fascinating. In 1703, mathematician Gottfried von Leibniz told scientist Jakob Bernoulli that nature does work in patterns, but "only for the most part.[39]" The rest—the unpredictable part—is what lends interest to observing nature.

Financial security programs, such as variable income annuities, however, can operate more efficiently if the "unpredictable part"—the variability of results—can be minimized. A concept related to this degree of variability is the *Law of Large Numbers*. (A proof of the Law of Large Numbers appears in Appendix P.)

If we were to toss a fair coin a large number of times and count the number of heads that we observe, it seems that the number of heads divided by the number of coin tosses should be close to ½. In fact, it seems the more times we toss the coin, the closer this ratio should be to ½.

We cannot say with certainty that the ratio will ever be ½. We can, however, show that the probability it differs from ½ by any small amount tends to zero the more times we toss the coin. This is a special case of the Law of Large Numbers.

The Law of Large Numbers is a concept from the mathematical field of probability theory. For those interested, here is a precise statement of this theorem:

Suppose that X_1, X_2, ..., X_k, ... is a sequence of independent, identically distributed random variables, each with mean μ and variance σ^2. Define the new sequence of X_i values by

$$\bar{X}_n = \frac{1}{n}\sum_{i=1}^{n} X_i$$

where $n = 1, 2, 3, ...$

Then, $\lim_{n \to \infty} P\left(\left|\bar{X}_n - \mu\right| > \varepsilon\right) = 0$, *for any* $\varepsilon > 0$.

While a seemingly technical distinction, it is important to note that the Law of Large Numbers does not say that the average is necessarily getting closer to ½ with every additional flip of the coin. Rather, it says that with increasing flips of the coin, the probability tends to zero that the average differs from ½ by more than some small chosen number, however small that number may be.

What does this have to do with immediate variable annuities? Plenty. Think of the fair coin. We know that it possesses the characteristic that on average a toss will result in heads one-half the time. We can repeat the experiment of tossing the coin as many times as we like. From this sample of results, we can draw an inference as to the true underlying rate, although the sample results of our limited experiment may differ from the exact underlying rate.

Similarly, there is some set of actual mortality rates at any point in time for a specific population cohort that sampling approximates and calls a mortality table. The sample data may be that for immediate variable annuitants and comes from actual insurance company mortality experience data of companies issuing immediate variable annuities.

Insurance companies track their actual experience to compare against the mortality experience they assumed in pricing, that is, in their determination of the number of annuity units to pay each benefit period based on the single premium applied. It is in the interest of both insurers and annuitants for such mortality experience data to be shared industrywide.[40] This helps ensure that annuitants don't pay too much because the mortality rates assumed were unduly conservative and don't pay too little so that the fund will become insolvent before the final annuitant dies.

While members of a church group, a neighborhood association, or other small group could conceptually safeguard one another against living too long and outliving their accumulated assets by pooling their mortality risks and forming their own immediate annuity pool, too small a group of participants can produce actual mortality experience that deviates significantly from the mortality rates assumed in determining benefit payments. Just as a pool of annuitants can provide better longevity risk protection than a single individual can, a large group can provide better longevity protection than a small one. Risk diffusion is enhanced as an ever-larger group of relatively homogeneous exposure units is pooled.

The Law of Large Numbers informs us of the propensity for results to tend toward the true underlying mortality rates approximated by an experience-based mortality table with smaller and smaller probability of deviation the larger the annuitant pool.

If the l_x graph in Figure 6.1 reflects expected annuitant mortality that an insurer assumes in pricing will play out in real-world future experience,

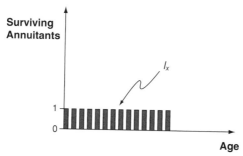

FIGURE 6.38   Actual l_x Curve for Only One Annuitant

it is clear that if there is only one annuitant, the shape of the actual l_x curve will be materially different, looking like Figure 6.38.

It is only through the addition of ever-greater numbers of annuitants that the shape of the actual annuitant survival curve will be more closely approximated by the expected annuitant survival curve.

In a sense, the entry of an individual into an immediate annuitant pool is like a chemical reaction in which both parties are transformed—and beneficially so. The individual successfully lays off his or her longevity risk. The annuitant pool, by virtue of the Law of Large Numbers, continues its march toward more closely reflecting the true underlying mortality rates. It is symbiosis.

For some people, the point at which they discover why the pooled approach can protect individuals from outliving their assets in a fashion superior to attempting to do so on one's own is a *"Eureka!"* moment. Still for others, the notion of having *any* portion of their assets inaccessible to them is an insurmountable psychological hurdle, even after explanation that this is a price for the very protection that will allow them to live more comfortably and securely.

LIFE EXPECTANCY

One of the great misconceptions about immediate annuities is that insurers calculate an annuitant's life expectancy and then determine the present value of an annuity for that period of time to arrive at the cost for a life annuity.[41] While some may find this shocking, annuity writers don't even calculate life expectancy. There is no need to do so.

Recall the earlier l_x graphs, such as Figure 6.1. If investment performance equals the AIR and if each annuitant purchases an identical single

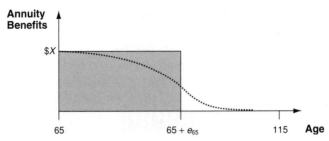

FIGURE 6.39 Annuity Benefit Comparison for (1) Life-Contingent Annuity and (2) Non-Life-Contingent Annuity for Fixed Period Equal to Life Expectancy

"life only" annuity, then these graphs show the pattern of projected aggregate benefits the annuity writer must pay. They start high, monotonically decrease, and terminate by the terminal age ω.

It is *not* the case that insurers make a flat, level payment every month to each annuitant until he or she hits his or her life expectancy and then make zero payments thereafter, which would look like the gray box in Figure 6.39. Rather, the payment pattern (for an immediate fixed annuity or for an immediate variable annuity where subaccount performance equals the AIR) mimics the dotted l_x curve in Figure 6.39.

Exactly what is life expectancy? It represents the mean (average) future lifetime at age x.

Life expectancy for a life age x is represented by the term e_x using international actuarial notation. The mathematical definition[42] of life expectancy e_x is given by

$$e_x = \frac{1}{l_x}\sum_{t=1}^{\infty}l_{x+t} = \sum_{t=1}^{\infty}{}_tp_x$$

This definition is called the *curtate* expectation of life.

It is interesting that expectation of life is a special case of a life annuity where the interest rate is zero. Recall the formula for the present value of a life annuity, a_x, and note that when the interest rate i equals 0, we have v equal to $1/(1+i)$, or 1, producing

$$a_x = vp_x + v^2{}_2p_x + v^3{}_3p_x + \cdots$$

$$= \sum_{t=1}^{\infty}{}_tp_x \quad (\text{when } i=0)$$

$$= e_x$$

The *complete* expectation of life $\mathring{e}_x$ is defined as

$$\mathring{e}_x = \frac{1}{l_x} \int_0^\infty l_{x+t} dt = \int_0^\infty {}_t p_x dt$$

Similarly, complete expectation of life is a special case of a continuously payable life annuity of 1 per annum where the interest rate i is zero:

$$\overline{a}_x = \int_0^\infty v^t {}_t p_x dt$$

$$= \int_0^\infty {}_t p_x dt \qquad (\text{when } i = 0)$$

$$= \mathring{e}_x$$

Both definitions may be interpreted as representing the mean future lifetime at age x—e_x includes only full years of lifetime and ignores final fractional years of life, whereas $\mathring{e}_x$ includes the complete future lifetime. On average, $\mathring{e}_x$ exceeds e_x by one-half year:

$$\mathring{e}_x \approx e_x + \frac{1}{2}$$

Life expectancy e_x changes as x changes; that is, as one ages, life expectancy decreases. It is not the case that life expectancy decreases by one each year. That would suggest that a group of lives age x would have no remaining life expectancy at all once e_x years elapsed and the annuitants reached their life expectancy as it was calculated as of the start of the immediate annuity. Yet they do have some positive life expectancy remaining at that point, so clearly life expectancy cannot decrease uniformly by one year with each passing year but must decrease by something less. This is exactly what happens.

As examples, complete life expectancy for males and females at various attained ages is shown in Table 6.11, based on an individual annuitant mortality table called the Annuity 2000 Basic Table.

When life expectancy is mentioned without further description—such as in news articles comparing life expectancy among different countries or life expectancy in the same country at different points in time—it is implied that this means life expectancy at age 0. For example, the Centers for Disease Control and Prevention (CDC) reported that for the U.S. general population, "The gap between male and female life expectancy closed from 5.4 years in 2002 to 5.3 years in 2003, continuing a trend toward narrowing since the peak gap of 7.8 years in 1979. Record-high life expectancies were found for white males (75.4 years) and black males (69.2 years), as well as for white females (80.5 years) and black females (76.1 years)."[43]

TABLE 6.11 Life Expectancy at Attained
Age x (years)

x	Male	Female
60	23.64	26.53
65	19.55	22.17
70	15.76	18.02
75	12.41	14.14
80	9.55	10.70
85	7.19	7.82
90	5.36	5.62
95	3.98	4.13
100	2.88	3.04

Source: Annuity 2000 Basic Table.

This closing of the gap between male and female general population mortality is consistent with that for individual annuitant mortality. In constructing the Annuity 2000 Mortality Table, 100% of Projection Scale G male mortality improvement factors were used, whereas only 50% of Projection Scale G female mortality improvement factors were used, the end result of which is a similar narrowing of the male and female mortality gap as reflected by this individual annuitant mortality table.

Higher life expectancy values in the United States over the past few centuries are in part attributable to reduced infant mortality rates. Just during the twentieth century, general population life expectancy at age 0 in the United States rose from 47 years at the beginning of the century to over 75 years at the end.[44]

Life expectancy at older ages also increased. General population life expectancy at age 65 in the United States rose from 12 years to 17 years. At age 85, it rose from 4 to 6 years.[45] Note that these life expectancy values for the general population are lower than comparable values for the self-selected, healthier annuitant population shown in Table 6.11. Similar life expectancy trends characterize national populations in the developed world. Note that life expectancy alone tells us nothing about whether additional years of life represent healthy states or states of moderate to severe frailty.

While an annuity writer can calculate e_x from the mortality table q_x values it uses to price immediate variable annuities, it has no need to do so and generally doesn't. Sometimes life expectancy is calculated, however, when one wants to understand via some singular index measure how one mortality table compares to another. In particular, life insurers might be interested in comparative life expectancies at age 30, e_{30}, whereas immediate annuity writers might be interested in comparative life expectancies at age 65, e_{65}. Clearly, however, mortality tables contain more robust information than is encapsulated in the single value called "life expectancy."

Note that life expectancy is defined in such a way as to represent the *mean*. To derive a different measure, the *median*—that time at which exactly 50% of the original group of l_x lives is surviving and 50% has died—one seeks the age m such that l_m/l_x equals 50%. For example, using the Annuity 2000 Mortality Table for males, we find that of an original group of l_{65} lives, 50% are alive as of age 85.77, assuming uniform distribution of deaths; that is, $l_{85.77}/l_{65}$ equals 50%.

Comparing measures, e_{65} is 19.95 years, $\mathring{e}_{65}$ is 20.45 years, and median survival at male age 65 is 20.77 years.

Life expectancy represents the *mean* future lifetime at age x. It is often incorrectly stated that life expectancy is the future lifetime until the point where 50% of the original group is surviving and 50% is not; such a statistic is characterized by the *median* future lifetime. (See Figure 6.40.)

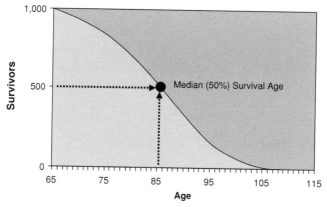

FIGURE 6.40 Median Future Lifetime of Annuitant Population

As an example, it so happens that life expectancy for a male age 52 under the Annuity 2000 Basic Table is 30.000 years; that is, $e_{52} = 30$. The present value of an annual annuity-immediate of $1 per year for 30 years at 5% is $15.37; that is, $a_{\overline{e_{52}}|} = a_{\overline{30}|} = \$15.37$. The present value of a lifetime annual annuity-immediate of $1 per year at 5% is $14.57; that is, $a_{52} = \$14.57$.

In this case, it takes $15.37 to provide an annuity of $1 per annum that lasts for a fixed period equal to life expectancy and $14.57 to provide an annuity of $1 per annum that lasts for life. To think about this in terms of annual income for a given single premium, a $100,000 single premium would provide $6,506 annually for a fixed period equal to life expectancy or $6,863 annually for life.

Think about the incredible power of that statement. It says that an individual age x can apply a fixed sum of money and generate—either through self-management or immediate annuity purchase—an income stream that will run for a fixed period of time equal to mean (average) future lifetime of all similarly situated individuals age x, after which the fund is fully depleted and payments stop, with no further income payments occurring should this particular individual's future lifetime prove longer than the average future lifetime. Or the same individual age x can apply a *smaller* sum of money and generate—through an immediate annuity purchase—an income stream of equivalent magnitude that will run for his *entire life*.

In addition to the expectation function relating to the lifetime annuity, which is by far the version of greatest interest, there are expectation functions relating to other annuity forms. The curtate and continuous *temporary expectations of life*, respectively, are defined by

$$e_{x:\overline{n}|} = \sum_{t=1}^{n} {}_tp_x \quad \text{and} \quad \overset{\circ}{e}_{x:\overline{n}|} = \int_0^n {}_tp_x dt$$

The proof that an annuity for a fixed period of time equal to life expectancy costs more (i.e., has a higher present value) than a lifetime annuity (that is, $a_{\overline{e_x}|} > a_x$ whenever the assumed interest rate $i > 0$) is given in the next section.

Mathematical Proof

$$a_{\overline{e_x}|} > a_x \text{ When } i > 0$$

Recall earlier in the section on life expectancy that the statement was made that the present value of a life annuity (at any positive rate of interest) is smaller than the present value of an annuity with benefit payments of the same amount made for a fixed period of time equal to life expectancy. The upshot of this is that a given single premium can therefore provide higher benefits under a lifetime annuity than under a fixed-period annuity that runs for life expectancy as calculated at policy issue. This section provides the mathematical proof of this assertion.

Assertion: $a_{\overline{e_x}|} > a_x$ when $i > 0$

Proof: Express the value of life expectancy e_x as the sum of an integer n and a fraction f, $0 \le f < 1$:

$$e_x = \sum_{t=1}^{\infty} {}_t p_x = n + f$$

The non-life-contingent fixed-period annuity, with present value $a_{\overline{e_x}|}$, pays 1 at the end of each year for n years and makes a final partial payment at time $n + f$ years.

$$\text{Final partial payment} = \frac{(1+i)^f - 1}{i}$$

Note that, as expected, the final partial payment is 0 if $f = 0$, is 1 if $f = 1$, and increases at intermediate points. The proof that a non-life-contingent fixed-period annuity with fractional term $n + f$ produces a final payment of $[(1 + i)^f - 1]/i$ at the end of $n + f$ years appears in Appendix Q.

The final payment $[(1 + i)^f - 1]/i$ is very close to f at typical interest rates. So it seems logical that if we discount the final payment for a period of $n + f$ years back to inception of the annuity, it will have a greater present value than if we discount f for a longer period of $n + 1$ years. Thus, we can show that

$$v^{n+f} \cdot \frac{(1+i)^f - 1}{i} \ge v^{n+1} \cdot f$$

This inequality is needed early in the proof. Its derivation will immediately follow the proof of the main assertion, presented here.

For $n \ne 0$, we have

$$a_{\overline{e_x}|} = a_{\overline{n+f|}}$$

$$= a_{\overline{n|}} + v^{n+f} \cdot \frac{(1+i)^f - 1}{i}$$

$$\geq a_{\overline{n|}} + v^{n+1} \cdot f$$

$$= a_{\overline{x:n+1|}} + \sum_{t=1}^{n} v^t (1 - {}_t p_x) + v^{n+1} (f - {}_{n+1} p_x)$$

$$> a_{\overline{x:n+1|}} + v^{n+1} \left[\sum_{t=1}^{n} (1 - {}_t p_x) + (f - {}_{n+1} p_x) \right]$$

$$= a_{\overline{x:n+1|}} + v^{n+1} \left[n + f - \sum_{t=1}^{n+1} {}_t p_x \right]$$

$$= a_{\overline{x:n+1|}} + v^{n+1} \left[\sum_{t=1}^{\infty} {}_t p_x - \sum_{t=1}^{n+1} {}_t p_x \right]$$

$$= a_{\overline{x:n+1|}} + v^{n+1} \left[\sum_{t=n+2}^{\infty} {}_t p_x \right]$$

$$\geq a_{\overline{x:n+1|}} + \sum_{t=n+2}^{\infty} v^t {}_t p_x$$

$$= a_x$$

We desire to show that

$$v^{n+f} \cdot \frac{(1+i)^f - 1}{i} \geq v^{n+1} \cdot f$$

which is equivalent to

$$v^f \cdot \frac{(1+i)^f - 1}{i} \geq v \cdot f$$

or

$$1 - v^f \geq i \cdot v \cdot f$$

Both functions $g(f) = 1 - v^f$ and $h(f) = i \cdot v \cdot f$ have a functional value of zero at $f = 0$ and a functional value of $1 - v = 1 - 1/(1 + i) = i/(1 + i) = i \cdot v$ at $f = 1$. See Figure 6.41.

The function $h(f)$ is linear between $f = 0$ and $f = 1$, and $g(f)$ is a continuous, monotonically increasing, concave downward function on the interval $[0, 1]$. To see this, we show the first derivative of g to be positive and the second derivative to be negative.

$$g'(f) = -\ln v \cdot v^f > 0$$

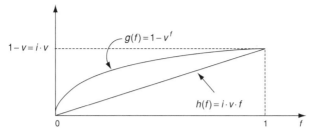

FIGURE 6.41   Comparison of $1 - v^f$ and $i \cdot v \cdot f$

since $v < 1$, $\ln v < 0$, so $-\ln v > 0$.

$$g''(f) = -(\ln v)^2 \cdot v^f < 0$$

Since g and h share common functional endpoints on the interval $[0, 1]$, both are continuous and monotonically increasing, and h is linear while g is concave downward, $g \geq h$, as illustrated in Figure 6.41.

Q.E.D. ■

(*quod erat demonstrandum*—signifies the conclusion of a proof; from Latin, "which was to be demonstrated or proved")

Figure 6.42 shows actual values of $g(f)$ and $h(f)$ on the vertical axis for values of f on the horizontal axis. A high interest rate i of 500% was used to amplify the comparative nature of the two functions:

$$g(f) = 1 - v^f$$

$$h(f) = i \cdot v \cdot f$$

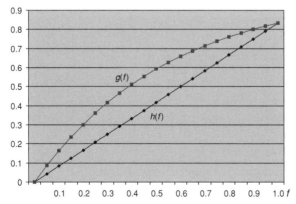

FIGURE 6.42   Comparison of $1 - v^f$ and $i \cdot v \cdot f$ for $i = 500\%$

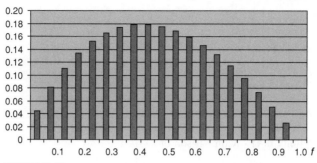

FIGURE 6.43   Excess of $g(f)$ over $h(f)$ on Interval $[0, 1]$

Figure 6.43 shows the difference in functional values, $g(f) - h(f)$, corresponding to Figure 6.42.

Geometric Illustration

$$\bar{a}_{\overline{\mathring{e}_x}|} > \bar{a}_x \text{When } i > 0$$

In this section, we present a less rigorous—but equally convincing—geometric proof that the present value of a non-life-contingent fixed-period annuity covering a period equal to life expectancy is greater than the present value of a life annuity.

Recall that the present value of a life annuity of 1 per annum payable continuously is

$$\bar{a}_x = \int_0^\infty v^t \,_t p_x dt$$

When the interest rate i is zero, then

$$v = 1/(1 + i) = 1$$

and

$$\bar{a}_x = \int_0^\infty \,_t p_x dt = \frac{l}{l_x} \int_0^\infty l_{x+t} dt = \frac{T_x}{l_x}$$

Recall the definition of complete expectation of life:

$$\mathring{e}_x = \int_0^\infty \,_t p_x dt = \frac{l}{l_x} \int_0^\infty l_{x+t} dt = \frac{T_x}{l_x}$$

The present value of a non-life-contingent fixed-period annuity of 1 per annum to an initial group of l_x lives for a period equal to their complete life expectancy as of age x at 0% interest is the area under the rectangle in Figure 6.44. The l_x lives (the rectangle height) will each receive a total of $\overset{\circ}{e}_x$ (the rectangle width) in annuity benefits, for a total of $l_x \cdot \overset{\circ}{e}_x = T_x$.

The present value of a life annuity of 1 per annum to an initial group of l_x lives at 0% interest is the area under the l_y survivorship curve. l_x lives will each receive a total of $\overline{a}_x$ in annuity benefits, for a total of $l_x \cdot \overline{a}_x = T_x$.

As a result, the area of the gray rectangle in Figure 6.44 equals the area under the l_y curve (both equal T_x). This implies that the area inside the gray rectangle and above the l_y curve, denoted by α, equals the area outside the rectangle and below the l_y curve, denoted by β.

This tells us what we already knew: At interest rate i of 0%, the present value of a continuous life annuity $\overline{a}_x$ equals the complete life expectancy $\overset{\circ}{e}_x$ and both equal T_x/l_x.

The new viewpoint to be garnered, however, is to recognize that, regardless of interest rate, the gray rectangle and the l_y curve illustrate the annuity benefit payments under a fixed-period annuity that spans a period equal to complete life expectancy and a life annuity, respectively. We know that the total payments made in either case to an initial group of l_x lives is T_x and that the areas under both the gray rectangle and l_y curve are identical.

Thus, at any positive rate of interest (i.e., $i > 0\%$), it is clear that the present value of the fixed-period annuity exceeds the present value of the life annuity because under the former, the annuity payments are made earlier. This shorter period of discounting results in a higher present value.

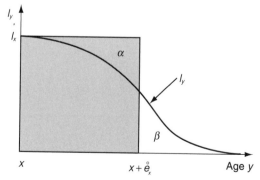

FIGURE 6.44 Comparison of Continuous Life Annuity with Continuous Non-Life-Contingent Fixed-Period Annuity Payable for a Period Equal to Complete Life Expectancy

Because the single premium P is precisely the amount needed to fund an immediate annuity benefit B with a present value a, $P = B \cdot a$, that is, we have the relationship $P/a = B$.

Since $\overline{a}_{\overline{\mathring{e}_x}|} > \overline{a}_x$ when $i > 0$, for the same premium P, the annuity benefit B_0 under the fixed-period annuity for complete life expectancy will be less than the annuity benefit B_1 under the life annuity.

Looking afresh at Figure 6.44, it is clear that some portion of annuity benefits overlap between the two annuities under study. This portion will have an identical present value regardless of interest rate.

The difference in present value will be wholly attributable to—and exactly equal to—the excess in present value of the segment denoted by α over the present value of the segment denoted by β.

Related Geometrical Interpretation

We now greatly simplify the prior situation where we had l_x lives with immediate annuities payable continuously. Suppose instead we only have two lives age 60, each of whom receives an annual annuity-immediate of \$1. We know that one will live 10 years to age 70, receiving 10 annual payments and dying immediately following receipt of the 10th \$1 payment. The other will live 30 years to age 90, receiving 30 annual payments and dying immediately following receipt of the 30th \$1 payment. The darker shaded areas in Figure 6.45 represent life annuity payments.

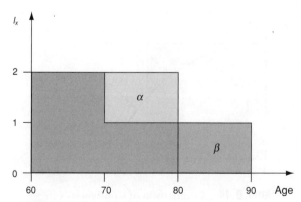

FIGURE 6.45   Comparison of Discrete Life Annuity with Discrete Non-Life-Contingent Fixed-Period Annuity Payable for a Period Equal to Life Expectancy

Life expectancy is then 20 years, to age 80. If instead of a life annuity we pay both people a non-life-contingent fixed-period annuity covering a period equal to life expectancy, we simply move the β rectangle over the α rectangle.

Clearly, the two life annuities pay the same total annuity benefits as the two fixed-period annuities. While α and β both represent \$10 of payments, those in α are more valuable because they are made earlier. Thus, the fixed-period annuity covering life expectancy has the greater present value.

Let's explore the difference in present value between the fixed-period annuity for life expectancy and the life annuity. We saw in the previous section that the difference in present value is wholly attributable to—and exactly equal to—the present value of payments in the α segment over the present value of payments in the β segment.

The present value at annuity inception of α benefits is the present value of a 10-year fixed-period annuity, deferred 10 years. The present value of β benefits is the present value of a 10-year fixed-period annuity, deferred 20 years. The difference is shown by

$$\text{PV of } \alpha \text{ benefits} - \text{PV of } \beta \text{ benefits} = v^{10} \cdot \frac{1-v^{10}}{i} - v^{20} \cdot \frac{1-v^{10}}{i}$$

$$= \frac{v^{10} - 2v^{20} + v^{30}}{i} \tag{6.46}$$

Figure 6.46 shows the excess of the present value of α benefits over the present value of β benefits—and therefore the excess of the present value of the fixed-period annuity covering life expectancy over the present value of the life annuity—at various interest rates.

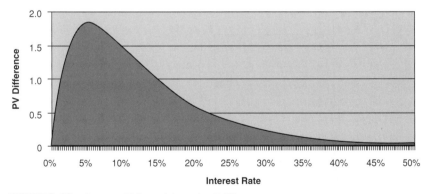

FIGURE 6.46 Present Value of Annuity Differences

The difference in present values of the two annuities peaks when the interest rate is around 5.25% in this particular example, where $q_{70} = 0.5$ and $q_{90} = 1.0$ and all other $q_x = 0$.

We know the excess in present value is 0 when i is 0%. It is also clear from equation 6.46 that the excess in present value approaches zero as i approaches infinity (∞). Yet we know that at any positive rate of interest, a difference in present value exists. Thus the difference in present values begins at zero, increases until its maximum value,[46] and then asymptotically approaches zero.

Another Related Geometrical Interpretation

We can use this same diagrammatic form to illustrate a life annuity with n years certain. Note on the horizontal axis in Figure 6.47 that we have replaced $x + \mathring{e}_x$ with $x + n$.

A life annuity with benefits guaranteed for n years is represented by the sum of the areas θ and α (which together comprise the gray rectangle) plus the area β.

The n years certain guarantee is represented by the area α. If α were perfectly triangular—where its l_y curve hypotenuse were a straight line—then its area would equal one-half times its base n times its height h, or $nh/2$.

If the triangle were of the same shape (i.e., a "similar triangle") regardless of the value of n, then its height h would bear some constant relation to its width n. Let $h = kn$, where k is a constant. Then the area of $\alpha = (k/2) \cdot n^2$. See Table 6.12.

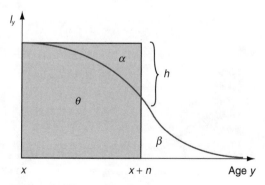

FIGURE 6.47   Continuous Life Annuity with n Years Certain

TABLE 6.12 Area of α

n	$(k/2) \cdot n^2$
10	$50\,k$
20	$200\,k$
30	$450\,k$

The essence is this: Under a continuous life annuity, the cost of guaranteeing a number of years certain varies *approximately* with the square of the number of years in the guarantee period.

If α were perfectly triangular, then the cost of adding a 20-year certain period and a 30-year certain period would be 2^2, or 4, and 3^2, or 9 times, respectively, the cost of adding a 10-year certain period.

Concededly, the veracity of this "rule of thumb" varies with age and length of certain period, since (1) the closeness of the shape of the α segment to a triangle and (2) the consistency in relationship of height h to width n do as well. See Table 6.13 for an example.

The present values of a single life annuity with 0, 10, 20, and 30 years certain issued at age 65 with annual payments of $1 at the end of the year appear in Table 6.14. For females, the cost of adding a 20-year certain period and a 30-year certain period are 4.0 and 9.0 times the cost of adding a 10-year certain period, respectively, as the aforementioned "rule of thumb" predicts. For males, the cost of adding a 20-year certain period and a 30-year certain period are 3.7 and 7.4 times the cost of adding a 10-year certain period, respectively.

TABLE 6.13 Comparison of Approximate and True Costs of Guaranteeing a Number of Years Certain

Female Age 65 Annual payments of $1 at end of year	
Present value of life annuity	12.617
Present value of life annuity with 10 years certain	12.941

Present value of life annuity with 7 years
   certain using approximation rule for
   area of α
	$12.617 + 49\% \cdot (12.941 - 12.617)$
	$= 12.776$

True value	12.782

Source: Based on Annuity 2000 Mortality Table and 5% interest.

TABLE 6.14   Present Value of Annuity
(Annual Payments of $1 at End of Year)

	Female Age 65	Male Age 65
Life only	12.617	11.603
Life and 10 years certain	12.941	12.127
Life and 20 years certain	13.917	13.561
Life and 30 years certain	15.549	15.495

Source: Based on Annuity 2000 Mortality Table and 5% interest.

AGE DISTRIBUTION HISTOGRAMS

How the U.S. population—current and future projected—is constituted of
people of various ages is often depicted in the form of a histogram like those
shown in Figures 6.48, 6.49, and 6.50. In statistics, a *histogram* is a graph-

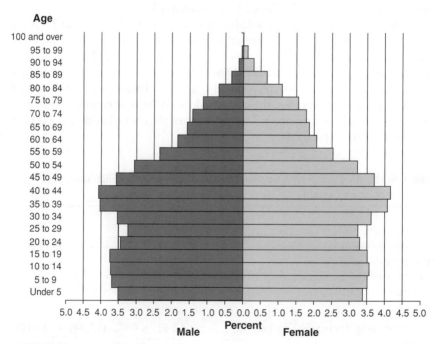

FIGURE 6.48   (NP-P2) Projected Resident Population of the United States as of
July 1, 2000, Middle Series
Source: National Projections Program, Population Division, U.S. Census Bureau,
Washington, D.C. 20233.

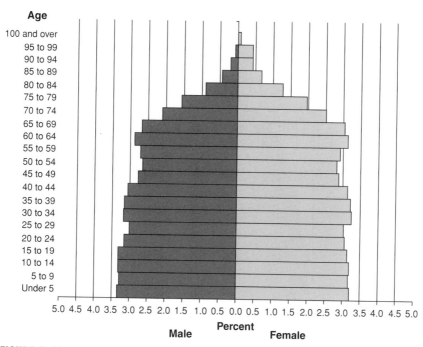

FIGURE 6.49 (NP-P3) Projected Resident Population of the United States as of July 1, 2025, Middle Series
Source: National Projections Program, Population Division, U.S. Census Bureau, Washington, D.C. 20233.

ical representation of a frequency distribution, where the widths of the contiguous horizontal bars are proportional to the frequency of the class. The following population histograms for Year 2000 (Figure 6.48) and projected for Year 2025 (Figure 6.49) and for Year 2050 (Figure 6.50) are from the U.S. Census Bureau.

There is a bit of a "pig in the python" effect in the middle of the Year 2000 histogram relative to the smoother projected Year 2050 histogram. This has important implications for the U.S. Social Security system, for the workforce, and for financial institutions looking to capitalize on retirement savings and retirement income market opportunities.

The U.S. Census Bureau projects the population for each of the age bands shown in Figure 6.51 as of Year 2025 and as of Year 2050 for comparison with actual Year 2000 values. This has important implications for the target market of prospective IVA purchasers. There will be 45 million more people over age 50 in 2025 than there were in 2000. There will be 72 million more people over age 50 in 2050 than there were in 2000.

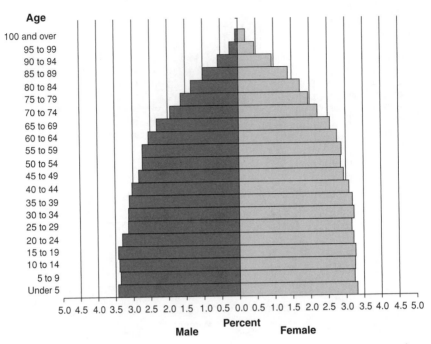

FIGURE 6.50 (NP-P4) Projected Resident Population of the United States as of July 1, 2050, Middle Series
Source: National Projections Program, Population Division, U.S. Census Bureau, Washington, D.C. 20233.

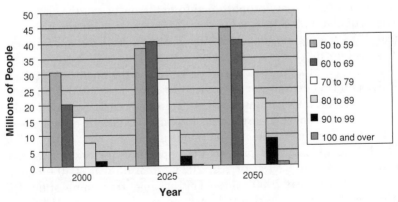

FIGURE 6.51 Changes in U.S. Population Demographics

MORTALITY TABLE AS SURVIVORSHIP MODEL

While a mortality table may represent a historical record tracing the survival of l_0 lives from birth until death, it can also be viewed (with projections as appropriate) as the survivorship model for a newly born group of l_0 lives. We now interpret the mortality table this way and view characteristics of this closed block of lives.

From the earlier section on life expectancy, we know that for those members of the closed block of lives who survive to age x, their average age at death will be $x + \overset{\circ}{e}_x$, since $\overset{\circ}{e}_x$ represents average future lifetime as of age x.

Because each of the l_x lives has already lived x years, their total past lifetime is $x \cdot l_x$ years. Their total future lifetime is given by T_x. Thus, total lifetime is given by $x \cdot l_x + T_x$. If we divide this total lifetime by the number of lives, l_x, in the group being observed, we have

$$\text{Average total lifetime} = \frac{x \cdot l_x + T_x}{l_x}$$

$$= x + \frac{T_x}{l_x}$$

$$= x + \overset{\circ}{e}_x$$

Since average total lifetime for a person age x is the same thing as average age at death, we see that this derivation produces the same common sense result described in the second paragraph of this section.

We can derive the average age at death for those who survive to age x but die before age $x + n$. The number of such persons in an original group of l_x lives is given by

$$\int_x^{x+n} l_y \mu_y \, dy = l_x - l_{x+n}$$

The total of the ages at death of such persons who die between ages x and $x + n$ is given by[47]

$$\int_x^{x+n} y l_y \mu_y \, dy = \left[-y l_y - T_y \right]_x^{x+n}$$
$$= -(x+n) l_{x+n} - T_{x+n} + x l_x + T_x$$

Thus, the average age at death for those who survive to age x but die before age $x + n$ is

$$\frac{-(x+n) l_{x+n} - T_{x+n} + x l_x + T_x}{l_x - l_{x+n}} = x + \frac{T_x - T_{x+n} - n l_{x+n}}{l_x - l_{x+n}}$$

On reflection, this is exactly to be expected. Each of the original l_x lives already survived x years. The total future lifetime between ages x and $x + n$ is $T_x - T_{x+n}$. Since we are only interested in lives that die between ages x and $x + n$, we must subtract n years for each of the l_{x+n} lives that survive the period, or nl_{x+n}.

There are numerous purposes for which we may wish to view the mortality table as a survivorship model. As one example, it may aid in the evaluation of immediate variable annuities versus alternative retirement income distribution vehicles. As another example, it may reveal a host of characteristics of a population of interest, especially if we can view the population as being approximately stationary.

STATIONARY POPULATION

Suppose that a population experiences l_0 annual births, that these births are uniformly distributed throughout the year, and that deaths occur exactly in accordance with the mortality table. Assume there is no migration into or emigration out of the population. After a period of years at least equal to the terminal age of the mortality table, it can be shown that the total population remains stationary and that the age distribution is constant.

That the population remains stationary means that each life exiting the population by death is simultaneously replaced by a new life entering the population by birth.

That the age distribution remains constant means that each life age x that leaves this age group either by death or by attaining age $x + 1$ is simultaneously replaced by a life entering this age group by leaving age $x - 1$ and attaining age x.

If l_0 annual births are uniformly distributed throughout each year, then in any fraction of a year t, there will be tl_0 births. There will be l_x lives that attain age x in any year, survivors of the births that occurred x years earlier. Since births are uniformly distributed throughout the year, it follows that in any fraction t of a year, tl_x lives will attain age x.

Exploring incidence of death, we note that the tl_y lives attaining age y in any fraction of a year t are subject to the force of mortality μ_y. The number of lives dying at age y during the interval of time t is given by $tl_y\mu_y dy$. Thus, the number of lives dying between ages x and $x + 1$ during any fraction of a year t is given by

$$\int_x^{x+1} tl_y\mu_y dy = td_x$$

For t equal to 1, we see that total deaths during the year equal d_x. Because deaths during any fraction t of a year equal that same fraction of total deaths for the year td_x, we see that deaths are uniformly distributed over the year.

The number of total deaths at all ages in the population over a time interval t is given by

$$\int_0^{\omega} tl_y \mu_y dy = tl_0$$

The number of births during any interval t is tl_0, and the number of deaths during any interval t is tl_0. Thus, the population is indeed stationary. Further, since the time interval t can be arbitrarily small, we can deduce that each life exiting the population by death is simultaneously replaced by a life entering the population by birth.

Of the lives that have attained integral age x but not age $x + 1$, during a time interval t the number of lives that leave age group x by attaining age $x + 1$ is tl_{x+1}. The number of lives that leave age group x by death during a time interval t is td_x. The total decrement to age group x during time interval t is $tl_{x+1} + td_x = tl_x$.

The total increment to age group x during time interval t attributable to lives entering from the prior age group is tl_x. The total decrement to age group x during time interval t attributable either to lives exiting to the next age group or to death is also tl_x, as we just showed. Thus, the total population by age—and hence the age distribution—remains constant. Again, because we may construe the time interval t to be arbitrarily small, we may deduce that any time a life exits age group x by death or by attaining age $x + 1$, it is simultaneously replaced by a life entering age group x from the immediately preceding age group. As a result, the number of lives at age x in this (stationary) population is constant.

The number of lives attaining exact age $x + t/m$ in any time interval $1/m$ is $l_{x+t/m}/m$. This approximates the number of lives between age $x + t/m$ and age $x + (t + 1)/m$ at any time. The number of lives between age x and age $x + 1$ is therefore given by

$$\lim_{m \to \infty} \sum_{t=0}^{m-1} \frac{1}{m} l_{x+t/m} = \int_0^1 l_{x+t} dt = L_x$$

In the context of a stationary population, the mortality functions have the following interpretations:

- L_x is the constant number of lives between ages x and $x + 1$.
- T_x is the constant number of lives in the population age x and over.
- l_x is the number of lives attaining age x in any year.
- d_x is the number of deaths between ages x and $x + 1$ in any year.
- l_0 is the number of births in any year.
- l_0 is the number of deaths in any year.

A census of our stationary population would at any time show the information just given. The number of lives age x in the census would be L_x. The number of lives age x and over would be T_x. The total population would be T_0. Because the population is stationary, the particular yearly period used to conduct the census enumeration is immaterial.

While a stationary population is admittedly an artificial construct, it can serve as a model for solving demographic problems where the population is approximately stationary and has a relatively stable age distribution. For example, consider the subpopulation of lives age x and older. For this subpopulation, we have this information:

- Number of subpopulation members $= T_x = \int_x^\infty l_y\,dy$

- Total past lifetime before age x $= x \cdot T_x$

- Total past lifetime from age x to current age
$$= \int_x^\infty (y - x) l_y\,dy$$
$$= \left[-yT_y - Y_y + xT_y \right]_x^\infty$$
$$= Y_x$$

- Total future lifetime
$$= \int_x^\infty T_y\,dy$$
$$= Y_x$$

- Total lifetime of T_x persons age x and older $= xT_x + 2Y_x$

- Average attained age of T_x persons age x and older
$= x +$ average past lifetime after age x
$$= x + \frac{Y_x}{T_x}$$

- Average attained age of full population $= \dfrac{Y_0}{T_0}$

- Average age at death of T_x persons age x and older

$$= \frac{xT_x + 2Y_x}{T_x}$$

$$= x + \frac{2Y_x}{T_x}$$

- Average age at death of full population $= \dfrac{2Y_0}{T_0}$

Note that $2Y_0/T_0$, the average age at death of the present members of the full population, exceeds T_0/l_0, the average age at death for newly born lives. This is because deaths occurring at ages prior to the attained ages of members of the present population are excluded from the former group and included in the latter group.

So far, we have viewed population characteristics for a group between ages x and $x + 1$ and a group age x and over. Extension to any subset of the population now living between ages y_1 and y_2 is straightforward:

- Number of subpopulation members $\quad = \int_{y_1}^{y_2} l_y dy \qquad (6.47)$

- Total past lifetime $\quad = \int_{y_1}^{y_2} y l_y dy \qquad (6.48)$

- Total future lifetime $\quad = \int_{y_1}^{y_2} T_y dy \qquad (6.49)$

- Total lifetime $\quad = \int_{y_1}^{y_2} (y l_y + T_y) dy \qquad (6.50)$

- Average attained age $\quad = \dfrac{\text{Total past lifetime}}{\text{Number of members}}$

- Average age at death $\quad = \dfrac{\text{Total lifetime}}{\text{Number of members}}$

Suppose we wish to find the total past lifetime since age 65 for persons now living between ages 70 and 80. We modify the above "total past lifetime" integrand slightly to find

$$\int_{70}^{80} (y - 65) l_y dy = 70T_{70} + Y_{70} - 80T_{80} - Y_{80} - 65(T_{70} - T_{80})$$

When investigating population members whose deaths occur under particular circumstances, the two variables of range of current age $y_1 \le y \le y_2$

and death within a certain time interval $t_1 \leq t \leq t_2$ emerge, resulting in a double integral specification of the solution. For example, the following properties are associated with that subpopulation whose members are now living and are between ages y_1 and y_2 and who will die within the time interval t_1 and t_2 years into the future:

■ Number of members $= \int_{y_1}^{y_2} \int_{t_1}^{t_2} l_{y+t} \mu_{y+t} dt dy$ (6.51)

■ Total past lifetime $= \int_{y_1}^{y_2} \int_{t_1}^{t_2} y \cdot l_{y+t} \mu_{y+t} dt dy$ (6.52)

■ Total future lifetime $= \int_{y_1}^{y_2} \int_{t_1}^{t_2} t \cdot l_{y+t} \mu_{y+t} dt dy$ (6.53)

■ Total lifetime $= \int_{y_1}^{y_2} \int_{t_1}^{t_2} (y+t) \cdot l_{y+t} \mu_{y+t} dt dy$ (6.54)

In equations 6.51 to 6.54, the first integration with respect to t sums deaths among those now age y, and the second integration with respect to y sums these values for all y in the interval $y_1 \leq y \leq y_2$.

As an example, we will let the subpopulation be those persons now living between ages 60 and 70 who will die before age 90. We will find the number of members and their total lifetime.

■ Number of members $= \int_{60}^{70} \int_0^{90-y} l_{y+t} \mu_{y+t} dt dy$

$$= \int_{60}^{70} \left[-l_{y+t} \right]_0^{90-y} dy$$

$$= \int_{60}^{70} (l_y - l_{90}) dy$$

$$= \left[-T_y - y l_{90} \right]_{60}^{70}$$

$$= T_{60} - T_{70} - 10 l_{90}$$

■ Total lifetime $= \int_{60}^{70} \int_0^{90-y} (y+t) \cdot l_{y+t} \mu_{y+t} dt dy$

$$= \int_{60}^{70} \left[-(y+t) l_{y+t} - T_{y+t} \right]_0^{90-y} dy$$

$$= \int_{60}^{70} (y l_y + T_y - 90 l_{90} - T_{90}) dy$$

$$= \left[-y T_y - 2Y_y - 90 y l_{90} - y T_{90} \right]_{60}^{70}$$

$$= 60 T_{60} + 2Y_{60} - 70 T_{70} - 2Y_{70} - 10(90 l_{90} + T_{90})$$

It is noteworthy that if $t_1 = 0$ and $t_2 = \infty$, then equations 6.51 to 6.54 degrade to equations 6.47 to 6.50 given previously. This is expected, since it removes any specified circumstances regarding time of death.

MULTILIFE ANNUITIES

Heretofore, the focus on life-contingent annuities has exclusively pertained to those covering only a single life. We now extend earlier concepts and theory to the case of annuities involving more than one life.

For a group of k lives with ages $x_1, x_2, \ldots, x_k$, survival of this collective group entity certainly occurs if all members continue to survive. We can define failure of group survival however we choose: when the first death occurs, when the last death occurs, or anywhere in between.

Consider a joint life annuity payable as long as all annuitants survive. The joint life status $(x_1 x_2 \cdots x_k)$ continues to exist as long as all lives (x_1), (x_2), ..., (x_k), survive where the symbol (x) denotes "a life aged x." In this instance, the existence of the group is defined to terminate on the first death.

For ease in development of theory underlying multilife annuities, we make the assumption that probabilities of survival for lives involved in the multilife annuity status are *independent*. This is not perfectly true in every case, since annuitants who are related or who engage in shared activities may be exposed to the same mortality hazards—common automobile accident, contagion, and so on. Similarly, death rates among widows and widowers in the first year following death of a spouse are higher than normal, again making the assumption of independence of deaths less than purely true.[48]

Denote the probability that the joint life status $(x_1 x_2 \cdots x_k)$ will survive n years by $_n p_{x_1 x_2 \cdots x_k}$. Because joint life survival is defined to require survival of all the individual component member lives and because survival probabilities among these lives are assumed to be independent, we have

$$_n p_{x_1 x_2 \cdots x_k} = _n p_{x_1} \cdot _n p_{x_2} \cdots _n p_{x_k}$$

The probability that the joint life status will fail within n years is

$$_n q_{x_1 x_2 \cdots x_k} = 1 - _n p_{x_1 x_2 \cdots x_k}$$

The probability that the joint life status will fail in the $(n + 1)$th year is

$$_{n|} q_{x_1 x_2 \cdots x_k} = _n p_{x_1 x_2 \cdots x_k} - _{n+1} p_{x_1 x_2 \cdots x_k}$$

The present value of an immediate annuity paying 1 at the end of each year as long as the joint life status $(x_1 x_2 \cdots x_k)$ is surviving is:

$$a_{x_1 x_2 \cdots x_k} = \sum_{t=1}^{\infty} v^t {}_t p_{x_1 x_2 \cdots x_k}$$

Joint life counterparts of single life functions simply replace single life probabilities with joint life probabilities. For example,

$$e_{xy} = \sum_{t=1}^{\infty} {}_t p_{xy}$$

$$\bar{a}_{wxy} = \int_0^{\infty} v^t {}_t p_{wxy} dt$$

Let the joint life counterpart of the formula ${}_n p_x = l_{x+n}/l_x$ be

$$_n p_{x_1 x_2 \cdots x_k} = \frac{l_{x_1 + n : x_2 + n : \ldots : x_k + n}}{l_{x_1 x_2 \cdots x_k}} \tag{6.55}$$

where the terms on the right side of the equation are yet to be defined.

We know that

$$\begin{aligned}
_n p_{x_1 x_2 \cdots x_k} &= {}_n p_{x_1} \cdot {}_n p_{x_2} \cdots {}_n p_{x_k} \\
&= \frac{l_{x_1 + n} l_{x_2 + n} \cdots l_{x_k + n}}{l_{x_1} l_{x_2} \cdots l_{x_k}}
\end{aligned} \tag{6.56}$$

From equations 6.55 and 6.56, we see that

$$\frac{l_{x_1 + n : x_2 + n : \ldots : x_k + n}}{l_{x_1 x_2 \cdots x_k}} = \frac{l_{x_1 + n} l_{x_2 + n} \cdots l_{x_k + n}}{l_{x_1} l_{x_2} \cdots l_{x_k}}$$

which intimates that we define the joint life function $l_{x_1 x_2 \cdots x_k}$ as the product of a constant c and the single life functions $l_{x_1} l_{x_2} \ldots l_{x_k}$, whence

$$l_{x_1 x_2 \cdots x_k} = c l_{x_1} l_{x_2} \cdots l_{x_k}$$

The constant of proportionality c is in practice some power of 10^{-1}, to scale down numerical values to the desired order of magnitude.

Joint life definitions for q and d are given by

$$q_{x_1 x_2 \cdots x_k} = 1 - p_{x_1 x_2 \cdots x_k}$$

$$= \frac{l_{x_1 x_2 \cdots x_k} - l_{x_1 + 1 : x_2 + 1 : \ldots : x_k + 1}}{l_{x_1 x_2 \cdots x_k}}$$

$$= \frac{d_{x_1 x_2 \cdots x_k}}{l_{x_1 x_2 \cdots x_k}}$$

where $d_{x_1 x_2 \cdots x_k} = l_{x_1 x_2 \cdots x_k} - l_{x_1 + 1 : x_2 + 1 : \ldots : x_k + 1}$

Note that the assumption of independence of survival rates among lives in a joint life status makes the cumbersome collection of joint life mortality rates by observing multiple collections of lives unnecessary. Rather, single life mortality rate tables may still be constructed and then applied in the manner described by equation 6.56 to derive joint-life survival probabilities.

Recall that for a single life status, the *force of mortality* is given by

$$\mu_{x+t} = -\frac{l'_{x+t}}{l_{x+t}}$$

$$= -\frac{d \log_e l_{x+t}}{dt}$$

We extend this to a joint life status:

$$\mu_{x_1 + t : x_2 + t : \ldots : x_k + t} = -\frac{l'_{x_1 + t : x_2 + t : \ldots : x_k + t}}{l_{x_1 + t : x_2 + t : \ldots : x_k + t}}$$

$$= -\frac{d \log_e l_{x_1 + t : x_2 + t : \ldots : x_k + t}}{dt}$$

Recalling that $l_{x_1 + t : x_2 + t : \ldots : x_k + t}$ may be expressed in terms of single life l_x values, we have

$$\mu_{x_1 + t : x_2 + t : \ldots : x_k + t} = -\frac{d \log_e c l_{x_1 + t} l_{x_2 + t} \cdots l_{x_k + t}}{dt}$$

$$= -\frac{d \log_e l_{x_1 + t}}{dt} - \frac{d \log_e l_{x_2 + t}}{dt} - \cdots - \frac{d \log_e l_{x_k + t}}{dt}$$

$$= \mu_{x_1 + t} + \mu_{x_2 + t} + \cdots + \mu_{x_k + t}$$

In other words, the joint life force of mortality equals the sum of the individual single life forces of mortality.

Joint life commutation functions are defined analogously to their single life counterparts:

$$D_{x_1 x_2 \ldots x_k} \equiv v^{(x_1 + x_2 + \ldots + x_k)/k} l_{x_1 x_2 \ldots x_k}$$

$$N_{x_1 x_2 \ldots x_k} \equiv \sum_{t=0}^{\infty} D_{x_1 + t : x_2 + t : \ldots : x_k + t}$$

$$S_{x_1 x_2 \ldots x_k} \equiv \sum_{t=0}^{\infty} N_{x_1 + t : x_2 + t : \ldots : x_k + t}$$

Note that the exponent $(x_1 + x_2 + \cdots + x_k)/k$ is such that an increase of one year of age for each of the k lives produces an increase of unity in the exponent. The analogy with the single life counterpart is clear.

Formulas for present values of multilife annuities parallel their single life counterparts. The present value of an immediate annuity paying 1 at the end of each year as long as the joint life status $(x_1 x_2 \cdots x_k)$ is surviving is:

$$a_{x_1 x_2 \ldots x_k} = \sum_{t=1}^{\infty} v^t {}_t p_{x_1 x_2 \ldots x_k}$$

$$= \frac{N_{x_1 + 1 : x_2 + 1 : \ldots : x_k + 1}}{D_{x_1 x_2 \ldots x_k}}$$

It may be the case that different mortality tables are appropriate for different lives comprising the multilife status $(x_1 x_2 \ldots x_k)$. For example, standard mortality may be appropriate for all annuitants except the kth annuitant, who, due to impaired health, is subject to a substandard mortality table. If we let l^* denote that the value of l is taken from the substandard mortality table, then the joint life functions will reflect the dual mortality basis if

$$l_{x_1 x_2 \ldots x_k} = c \cdot l_{x_1} \cdot l_{x_2} \cdots l_{x_{k-1}} \cdot l^*_{x_k}$$

LAST SURVIVOR ANNUITIES

Thus far, we have focused on a group of k lives with ages $x_1, x_2, \ldots, x_k$, where failure of this collective group entity was defined to occur on the first death of any member. We now shift our focus to defining failure of this collective group entity as occurring when the last survivor dies. Even insurance parlance uses the very terminology "last survivor"—or, synonymously, "joint and survivor"—when discussing a multilife status that fails to exist only on the death of its final member.

The symbol $(\overline{x_1 x_2 \cdots x_k})$ denotes a group of k lives with ages $x_1, x_2, \ldots, x_k$ that comprise a "last survivor" status. As long as at least one of the individual component single life statuses $(x_1), (x_2), \ldots, (x_k)$ that comprise the group remains alive, the group continues to exist.

In contrast, we previously were discussing the "joint life" status, denoted $(x_1 x_2 \cdots x_k)$, where the group fails to exist on the first death. The absence of a horizontal bar over the status indicates "joint life," while the presence of a horizontal bar indicates "last survivor."

The probability that the last survivor status will survive for n years is

$$
\begin{aligned}
{}_n p_{\overline{x_1 x_2 \cdots x_k}} &= 1 - (1 - {}_n p_{x_1})(1 - {}_n p_{x_2}) \cdots (1 - {}_n p_{x_k}) \\
&= ({}_n p_{x_1} + {}_n p_{x_2} + \cdots + {}_n p_{x_k}) \\
&\quad - ({}_n p_{x_1 x_2} + {}_n p_{x_1 x_3} + \cdots + {}_n p_{x_{k-1} x_k}) \\
&\quad + ({}_n p_{x_1 x_2 x_3} + {}_n p_{x_1 x_2 x_4} + \cdots + {}_n p_{x_{k-2} x_{k-1} x_k}) \\
&\quad - ({}_n p_{x_1 x_2 x_3 x_4} + \cdots + {}_n p_{x_{k-3} x_{k-2} x_{k-1} x_k}) \\
&\quad + \cdots \\
&\quad + (-1)^{k+1} {}_n p_{x_1 x_2 \cdots x_k}
\end{aligned}
$$

The probability that the last survivor status will survive for n years is the complement of the probability that all lives will die within n years.

The probability that the last survivor status $(\overline{x_1 x_2 \cdots x_k})$ will fail within n years is

$$
{}_n q_{\overline{x_1 x_2 \cdots x_k}} = 1 - {}_n p_{\overline{x_1 x_2 \cdots x_k}}
$$

The probability that the last survivor status $(\overline{x_1 x_2 \cdots x_k})$ will fail in the $(n + 1)$th year is

$$
{}_{n|} q_{\overline{x_1 x_2 \cdots x_k}} = {}_n p_{\overline{x_1 x_2 \cdots x_k}} - {}_{n+1} p_{\overline{x_1 x_2 \cdots x_k}}
$$

Note that the probability that the last survivor status will survive for n years as given earlier may be expressed more succinctly as follows:

$$
\begin{aligned}
{}_n p_{\overline{x_1 x_2 \cdots x_k}} &= \sum {}_n p_{x_1} - \sum {}_n p_{x_1 x_2} + \sum {}_n p_{x_1 x_2 x_3} \\
&\quad - \sum {}_n p_{x_1 x_2 x_3 x_4} + \cdots + (-1)^{k+1} {}_n p_{x_1 x_2 \cdots x_k}
\end{aligned}
$$

where summations cover all possible combinations of lives taken one at a time, two at a time, three at a time, and so forth. Note the absence of horizontal bars on the right side of the equation. This tells us that probabilities of survival of a last survivor status can be expressed in terms of single life and joint life probabilities.

The last survivor cases of two lives and three lives are then

$$_n p_{\overline{xy}} = \sum {}_n p_x - {}_n p_{xy} = {}_n p_x + {}_n p_y - {}_n p_{xy}$$

$$_n p_{\overline{wxy}} = \sum {}_n p_w - \sum {}_n p_{wx} + {}_n p_{wxy} = {}_n p_w + {}_n p_x + {}_n p_y - {}_n p_{wx} - {}_n p_{wy} - {}_n p_{xy} + {}_n p_{wxy}$$

Related functions can be expressed in the expected way:

$$_n q_{\overline{xy}} = 1 - {}_n p_{\overline{xy}}$$

$$= 1 - \left({}_n p_x + {}_n p_y - {}_n p_{xy} \right)$$

$$= {}_n q_x + {}_n q_y - {}_n q_{xy}$$

$$= \sum {}_n q_x - {}_n q_{xy}$$

This pattern extends to the formulas for present values of annuities. Consider a last survivor immediate annuity of 1 paid at the end of each year to a life age x and a life age y. Such an annuity payout option is commonly called "joint and 100% to survivor."

$$a_{\overline{xy}} = \sum_{t=1}^{\infty} v^t {}_t p_{\overline{xy}}$$

$$= \sum_{t=1}^{\infty} v^t \left({}_t p_x + {}_t p_y - {}_t p_{xy} \right)$$

$$= a_x + a_y - a_{xy}$$

$$= \sum a_x - a_{xy}$$

The present value of a last survivor immediate annuity of 1 paid at the end of each year to a life age w, a life age x, and a life age y similarly produces the expected result:

$$a_{\overline{wxy}} = \sum_{t=1}^{\infty} v^t {}_t p_{\overline{wxy}}$$

$$= \sum_{t=1}^{\infty} v^t \left({}_n p_w + {}_n p_x + {}_n p_y - {}_n p_{wx} - {}_n p_{wy} - {}_n p_{xy} + {}_n p_{wxy} \right)$$

$$= a_w + a_x + a_y - a_{wx} - a_{wy} - a_{xy} + a_{wxy}$$

$$= \sum a_w - \sum a_{wx} + a_{wxy}$$

The expression in the preceding equation for $a_{\overline{wxy}}$ can be checked by noting the annuity payments provided when different numbers of annuitants are surviving. When all three are surviving, each annuity contributes a payment of 1, so the total payment is $1 + 1 + 1 - 1 - 1 - 1 + 1 = 1$. When two are surviving, the first cluster of three annuities contributes a payment of 2, the second cluster of three annuities contributes a payment of –1, and the final triple life annuity contributes a payment of 0, for a total of 1. When only one is surviving, only one annuity in the first cluster of three annuities contributes a payment of 1, with all other annuities contributing 0.

The joint life status $(x_1 x_2 \cdots x_k)$ and the last survivor status $(\overline{x_1 x_2 \cdots x_k})$ so far have been defined where the component parts of the group are single life statuses $(x_1), (x_2), \ldots, (x_k)$. The joint life status and last survivor status can also relate to groups of component statuses that are not single lives.

For example, $a_{\overline{wx}:\overline{yz}}$ is the present value of an annuity payable during the *joint* existence of the *last survivor* of (w) and (x) and the *last survivor* of (y) and (z). This is called a *compound status*. This particular compound status happens to be a *joint* status of which the component parts are themselves *last survivor* statuses.

This compound status can be expressed in terms of single life and joint life functions:

$$a_{\overline{wx}:\overline{yz}} = \sum_{t=1}^{\infty} v^t \, {}_t p_{\overline{wx}:\overline{yz}}$$

$$= \sum_{t=1}^{\infty} v^t \, {}_t p_{\overline{wx}} \cdot {}_t p_{\overline{yz}} \qquad \text{[Both status } (\overline{wx}) \text{ and status } (\overline{yz}) \text{ must survive.]}$$

$$= \sum_{t=1}^{\infty} v^t ({}_t p_w + {}_t p_x - {}_t p_{wx})({}_t p_y + {}_t p_z - {}_t p_{yz})$$

$$= \sum_{t=1}^{\infty} v^t ({}_t p_{wy} + {}_t p_{wz} + {}_t p_{xy} + {}_t p_{xz} - {}_t p_{wxy} - {}_t p_{wxz} - {}_t p_{wyz} - {}_t p_{xyz} + {}_t p_{wxyz})$$

$$= a_{wy} + a_{wz} + a_{xy} + a_{xz} - a_{wxy} - a_{wxz} - a_{wyz} - a_{xyz} + a_{wxyz}$$

More general multilife annuities exist. For example, it was mentioned that for a group of k lives with ages $x_1, x_2, \ldots, x_k$, survival of this collective group entity can be defined to occur if *all* members continue to survive (joint life), if *any* member continues to survive (last survivor), or any condition in between these extremes.

One example of a condition in between these extremes is an annuity that provides a benefit as long as there are at least h survivors out of the original group of k lives. Letting h equal 2 and k equal 3, the formula for the present value of an annuity paying 1 at the end of each year *at least 2* annuitants are surviving is:

$$a^2_{\overline{wxy}} = a_{wx} + a_{wy} + a_{xy} - 2a_{wxy} \qquad (6.57)$$

In equation 6.57, the expression for $a^2_{\overline{wxy}}$ can be checked by noting the annuity payments provided when different numbers of annuitants are surviving. When any two or all three are surviving, the total payment is 1. When zero or one are surviving, the total payment is 0.

Another example of a condition in between the extremes is an annuity that provides a benefit if there are *exactly h* survivors out of the original group of *k* lives. Letting *h* equal 1 and *k* equal 3, the formula for the present value of an annuity paying 1 at the end of each year there is exactly 1 survivor of the original group of 3 lives is:

$$a^{[1]}_{\overline{wxy}} = a_w + a_x + a_y - 2(a_{wx} + a_{wy} + a_{xy}) + 3a_{wxy} \qquad (6.58)$$

Note that this is actually an immediate annuity with a deferred first payment, where deferral occurs until two annuitants die, leaving exactly the one survivor, the condition on which annuity benefit payment is predicated.

Again, in equation 6.58, the expression for $a^{[1]}_{\overline{wxy}}$ can be verified by noting the annuity payments provided when different numbers of annuitants are surviving. It can be seen that the annuity functions to the right of the equal sign contribute a total payment of zero if 0, 2, or 3 annuitants are alive and a total payment of 1 if 1 annuitant is alive.

While not described here, there is a standard, methodical approach to derive formulas for multilife annuities where payments are made (1) if exactly *h* of *k* lives are surviving and (2) if at least *h* of *k* lives are surviving.

Regarding notation, a horizontal bar above a subscripted suffix indicates annuity benefits are based on *survivors* and not on *joint lives*. The number of survivors is listed over the right end of the bar. If the number of survivors, say *h*, is enclosed in brackets (e.g., [*h*]), this means *exactly h* survivors. If no brackets appear, this means *at least h* survivors. If no number of survivors is listed above the horizontal bar, this implies unity, which means *at least one survivor*.

CONTINGENT ANNUITIES

The multilife statuses studied so far make no distinction as to the order of death of the component lives. For example, the joint life status (*wxy*) terminates on the first death, regardless of whether the first death is that of (w), (x), or (y).

Contingent functions depend on a specified order of death. For example, an immediate annuity where the benefit level depends on the order of death of the annuitants is a contingent function.

We know that to determine the present value of an annuity, we project the series of expected annuity benefits based on survival probabilities. We then discount the series for interest. Since the discounting for contingent annuities is the same as has already been studied, what remains is to understand the survival probabilities associated with multilife statuses where order of death matters.

For two annuitants of the same age and sex, the exercise is trivial. The probability that a specific one of them will die first is ½. The probability that the specific life will die first and within n years is $\frac{1}{2} \cdot {}_n q_{xx}$, where ${}_n q_{xx}$ represents the probability that the joint lifetime ends within n years and ½ is the likelihood that failure was caused by death of the specific life.

Consider two lives of unequal ages x and y. The probability that (x) will die before (y) and within one year is:

$$q^1_{xy} = \int_0^1 {}_t p_{xy} \mu_{x+t} dt$$

$$= \frac{1}{l_{xy}} \int_0^1 l_{x+t:y+t} \mu_{x+t} dt \tag{6.59}$$

The expression in equation 6.59 denotes the probability that the joint-life status (xy) will fail within one year because of the death of (x). The differential ${}_t p_{xy} \mu_{x+t} dt$ represents the probability that the joint life status (xy) will survive to time t and then (x) will die at the moment of attaining age $x + t$.

Other contingent probabilities naturally follow by changing the limits of integration. As examples, the probability that (x) will die before (y) and within n years and the probability that (x) will die before (y) in the $(n + 1)$th year are, respectively,

$$_n q^1_{xy} = \int_0^n {}_t p_{xy} \mu_{x+t} dt$$

$$_{n|} q^1_{xy} = \int_n^{n+1} {}_t p_{xy} \mu_{x+t} dt$$

The probability that the specified life (x) will die *second* and within one year is given by

$$q^2_{xy} = \int_0^1 {}_t p_x (1 - {}_t p_y) \mu_{x+t} dt$$

$$= \int_0^1 {}_t p_x \mu_{x+t} dt - \int_0^1 {}_t p_{xy} \mu_{x+t} dt \tag{6.60}$$

$$= q_x - q^1_{xy}$$

On reflection, the result in equation 6.60 is intuitively obvious: $q_x = q^1_{xy} + q^2_{xy}$. If (x) dies within one year, he or she will either die first or second!

Similarly, the probability that (x) will die second and during the $(n+1)$th year is given by

$$_{n|}q^2_{xy} = \int_n^{n+1} {}_tp_x(1 - {}_tp_y)\mu_{x+t}dt$$

$$= \int_n^{n+1} {}_tp_x\mu_{x+t}dt - \int_n^{n+1} {}_tp_{xy}\mu_{x+t}dt$$

$$= {}_{n|}q_x - {}_{n|}q^1_{xy}$$

Note that (y) may die anytime during the first n years or may predecease (x) in the $(n+1)$th year.

The probability that a specific single life status (w) will be the first, second, and third, respectively, to fail among three lives (w), (x), and (y) is given by

$$_{\infty}q^1_{wxy} = \int_0^{\infty} {}_tp_{wxy}\mu_{w+t}dt$$

$$_{\infty}q^2_{wxy} = \int_0^{\infty} {}_tp_w \cdot {}_tp^{[1]}_{xy}\mu_{w+t}dt$$

$$= \int_0^{\infty} {}_tp_w({}_tp_x + {}_tp_y - 2{}_tp_{xy})\,\mu_{w+t}dt$$

$$= {}_{\infty}q^1_{wx} + {}_{\infty}q^1_{wy} - 2{}_{\infty}q^1_{wxy}$$

$$_{\infty}q^3_{wxy} = \int_0^{\infty} (1 - {}_tp_x)(1 - {}_tp_y)\,{}_tp_w\mu_{w+t}dt$$

$$= {}_{\infty}q_w - {}_{\infty}q^1_{wx} - {}_{\infty}q^1_{wy} + {}_{\infty}q^1_{wxy}$$

$$= 1 - {}_{\infty}q^1_{wx} - {}_{\infty}q^1_{wy} + {}_{\infty}q^1_{wxy}$$

Regarding notation, when a numeral, say h, appears over one status of a subscripted suffix containing several statuses, this indicates that the function is determined by that particular status being the hth to fail. For example, $_{\infty}q^2_{wxy}$ refers to the contingency that (w) will be the second life to fail of the three lives.

REVERSIONARY ANNUITIES

A *reversionary annuity* is an annuity that begins on the failure of one status (S) if a second status (T) is then in existence. Annuity benefits continue thereafter during the existence of (T).

A simple example is an immediate life annuity to a person age x where benefits are deferred n years, denoted $_{n|}a_x$. The completion of n years is the failing status ($\overline{n}|$), on which the annuity commences to the annuitant originally age x if still alive, making (x) the second status.

Where the failing status involves life contingencies, reversionary annuities are one form of *contingent annuities*, discussed in the prior section. The most basic form of reversionary annuity is where an annuity of 1 per year is payable to a life now age x beginning at the end of the year of death of a life now age y. This is an annuity to (x) after (y).

The present value of this annuity is:

$$a_{y|x} = \sum_{t=1}^{\infty} v^t {}_t p_x (1 - {}_t p_y)$$

$$= a_x - a_{xy}$$

Annuity payments are made at the end of each year that (x) is alive and (y) is not. The formula clearly reveals this reversionary annuity to be equivalent to a life annuity to (x) with payments omitted during the joint lifetime (xy).

Regarding notation, a vertical bar separating the elements of a subscripted suffix indicates a reversionary function. The status after the bar follows the status before the bar. For example, $a_{y|x}$ is an annuity on the life of (x) after the death of (y), as the preceding example illustrates.

In general, whatever the failing status (S) on which an annuity to the surviving status (T) happens to be, the same form of expression holds:

$$a_{S|T} = a_T - a_{ST} \tag{6.61}$$

For example, if (S) is a fixed period of n years ($\overline{n}|$) and (T) is the single life status (x), then the n-year deferred single life annuity $_{n|}a_x$ mentioned earlier can be evaluated using equation 6.61, the basic form for a reversionary annuity:

$$a_{\overline{n}||x} = a_x - a_{x:\overline{n}|}$$

As another example, if (S) is the single life status (w) and (T) is the joint life status (xy), then

$$a_{w|xy} = a_{xy} - a_{wxy}$$

Another, more advanced, example is where (S) is the last survivor status $(\overline{wx})$ and (T) is the single life status (y). Then a life annuity payable to (y) following the death of the last survivor of (w) and (x) is expressed as

$$a_{\overline{wx}|y} = a_y - a_{\overline{wx}:y}$$

$$= a_y - (a_{wy} + a_{xy} - a_{wxy})$$

The most basic form of reversionary annuity shown in equation 6.61 involving annual payments has the following counterpart when the benefit frequency is m times per year and begins at the end of the mth part of the year in which (y) dies:

$$a_{y|x}^{(m)} = a_x^{(m)} - a_{xy}^{(m)}$$

If m approaches ∞, we have the following reversionary annuity involving continuous payments:

$$\overline{a}_{y|x} = \overline{a}_x - \overline{a}_{xy}$$

This is the present value of an annuity of 1 per annum with benefits to (x) beginning at the moment of death of (y). Benefits are payable continuously throughout the remaining lifetime of (x).

A reversionary annuity where the benefit frequency is m times per year but the benefit begins $1/m$ years from the moment of death of (y) has this present value:

$$\hat{a}_{y|x}^{(m)} = \int_0^\infty v^t {}_tp_{xy}\mu_{y+t}a_{x+t}^{(m)}dt$$

It is interesting that although known as reversionary *annuities*, they may also be viewed as *insurances* because benefits commence on failure of a specified status, a hallmark of an insurance. That this is so becomes explicitly evident when we rewrite a continuously payable reversionary annuity in an equivalent form:

$$\overline{a}_{y|x} = \int_0^\infty v^t {}_tp_x(1 - {}_tp_y)\,dt$$

$$= \int_0^\infty \int_0^t v^t {}_tp_x \, {}_rp_y\mu_{y+r}dr\,dt \quad (\text{since } 1 - {}_tp_y = \int_0^t {}_rp_y\mu_{y+r}dr)$$

$$= \int_0^\infty \int_r^\infty v^t {}_tp_x \, {}_rp_y\mu_{y+r}dt\,dr \quad (\text{inverting order of integration}) \qquad (6.62)$$

$$= \int_0^\infty {}_rp_y\mu_{y+r} \cdot {}_r|\overline{a}_x dr$$

$$= \int_0^\infty v^r {}_rp_{xy}\mu_{y+r} \cdot \overline{a}_{x+r}dr$$

The contingent insurance form of the reversionary annuity is clearly visible here. The final equality reflects the present value of the probability that the joint status (xy) survives, then (y) succumbs to the instantaneous force of mortality, at which moment a continuous life annuity becomes payable to (x). In comparison, the expression for a life insurance of 1 payable at the moment of death of (y) is

$$\bar{A}_y = \int_0^\infty v^r {}_r p_y \mu_{y+r} dr \qquad (6.63)$$

Reversionary annuities may have conditions premised on *issue date* of the contract or premised on *date of death* of the failing status. We first look at reversionary annuities with conditions premised on issue date.

An *n-year temporary reversionary annuity*, denoted $a_{y|x:\overline{n}|}$ or ${}_n a_{y|x}$, is an annuity to (x) after (y) with the proviso that no payments be made after n years from the issue date. The present value is given by

$$a_{y|x:\overline{n}|} = a_{x:\overline{n}|} - a_{xy:\overline{n}|}$$

An *n-year deferred reversionary annuity*, denoted $a_{\overline{y:\overline{n}|}|x}$ or ${}_{n|}a_{y|x}$, is an annuity to (x) after (y) with the proviso that no payments be made within n years from the issue date. The present value is given by

$$a_{\overline{y:\overline{n}|}|x} = a_x - a_{x:\overline{y:\overline{n}|}}$$
$$= a_x - a_{xy} - a_{x:\overline{n}|} + a_{xy:\overline{n}|}$$
$$= {}_{n|}a_x - {}_{n|}a_{xy}$$

We next look at reversionary annuities with conditions premised on the date of death of the failing status.

An annuity to (x) commencing n years after the death of (y) has present value

$$\sum_{t=1}^\infty v^{n+t} {}_{n+t}p_x (1 - {}_t p_y) = \frac{D_{x+n}}{D_x}(a_{x+n} - a_{x+n:y})$$
$$= \frac{D_{x+n}}{D_x} a_{y|x+n} \qquad (6.64)$$

An annuity to (x) payable only for n years after the death of (y) is a temporary annuity. Its payments are equivalent to those of a normal reversionary annuity less the reversionary annuity given by equation 6.64, where payments to (x) are deferred until n years after the death of (y). Thus, its present value is so constructed:

$$a_{y|x} - \frac{D_{x+n}}{D_x} a_{y|x+n}$$

We next look at an n years certain and life thereafter annuity-due of 1 per annum payable $m$thly to (x) that commences on the death of (y). To determine its present value, we hearken back to equation 6.62, where we showed explicitly that reversionary annuities may also be viewed as insurances. To determine the present value of just the deferred life annuity portion following the n-year certain period, we simply replace the continuous annuity in equation 6.62 with a deferred life annuity:

$$\int_0^\infty v^r {}_r p_{xy} \mu_{y+r} \cdot {}_{n|}\ddot{a}_{x+r}^{(m)} dr \tag{6.65}$$

The present value of the n-year certain period payments is

$$\ddot{a}_{\overline{n}|}^{(m)} \cdot \overline{A}_y \tag{6.66}$$

where $\overline{A}_y$ is as defined by equation 6.63, and the product represents the present value of an n-year annuity-due payable $m$thly beginning at the moment of death.

The sum of equations 6.65 and 6.66 is the total present value of the annuity described earlier: an n years certain and life thereafter annuity-due of 1 per annum payable $m$thly to (x) that commences on the death of (y). This particular reversionary annuity also goes by the name of *whole life insurance with continuous installments*. (The terminology can be confusing. This is not an annuity payable continuously; that is, it does not involve an $\overline{a}_x$ term. Rather, it derives its name from the fact that an "n-years certain and life annuity" also goes by the name "n years certain and continuous annuity.")

Under the *term insurance with continuous installments* counterpart to the reversionary annuity described in the previous paragraph, the annuity benefit to (x) is payable only if (y) dies in the first k years. The present value of just the deferred life annuity portion following the n-year certain period is

$$\int_0^k v^r {}_r p_{xy} \mu_{y+r} \cdot {}_{n|}\ddot{a}_{x+r}^{(m)} dr \tag{6.67}$$

The present value of the n-year certain period payments is

$$\ddot{a}_{\overline{n}|}^{(m)} \cdot \overline{A}_{y:\overline{k}|}^1 = \ddot{a}_{\overline{n}|}^{(m)} \cdot \int_0^k v^r {}_r p_y \mu_{y+r} dr \tag{6.68}$$

The sum of equations 6.67 and 6.68 is the total present value of the term insurance with continuous installments annuity.

LAST-SURVIVOR ANNUITY WITH POP-UP PROVISION

As a refresher, we rewrite here the following definition of this annuity option described in Chapter 5:

Joint Life Annuity with "Pop-Up" Provision *Annuity income will be provided for as long as the primary annuitant, the secondary annuitant, or both survive. Should the secondary annuitant predecease the primary annuitant, annuity income will pop up thereafter to the level the primary annuitant could have had if he or she had originally elected a single life annuity. (Note: This is actually a special case of a Joint and X% to Survivor option, where X = 100 if the primary annuitant dies first and X > 100 if the secondary annuitant dies first.)*

Recall that the impetus for creation of this form of annuity option is to provide one solution for the quandary of a prospective IVA purchaser who must choose between electing a "single life only" annuity on himself that provides a higher benefit or a "last survivor" annuity covering himself and his spouse that provides a lower benefit. He wishes to avoid "buyer's remorse" should his spouse predecease him and he feel he elected the "wrong" annuity option, ending up with less income than he could have had if he had originally chosen the "single life only" annuity on himself. He wishes to avoid paying what he views as a "phantom insurance premium" in the way of ongoing reduced annuity benefits that accompany the last survivor option should the second life he wished to cover predecease him.

To purchase a single life annuity covering only himself and paying 1 per annum at the end of each year, he would need to apply a net premium $P = a_x$. To purchase a last survivor option having a present value of $a_{\overline{xy}} = a_x + a_y - a_{xy}$ with the same premium P would—because it provides payments as long as either of *two* people survive—produce a lower annual benefit payment B, where

$$B = \frac{P}{a_{\overline{xy}}}$$

What the prospective purchaser desires is an annuity that provides an annual benefit B' ($B' < B$) while both he and his spouse are alive or while only his spouse is alive but that "pops up" to an annual benefit of 1 should his spouse predecease him. Thus, applying the same premium P that he could alternatively use to purchase a single life annuity of 1 on himself, he may now create the exact form of annuity he desires with a benefit B' that satisfies the following equation:

$$P = B'(a_{xy} + a_{x|y}) + 1 \cdot a_{y|x}$$
$$= B'(a_{xy} + a_y - a_{xy}) + 1 \cdot (a_x - a_{xy})$$
$$= B' a_y + a_x - a_{xy}$$

Since we defined $P = a_x$, we can solve for B':

$$B' = \frac{a_{xy}}{a_y}$$

Thus, the "last survivor option with a pop-up provision" purchasable with a net premium $P = a_x$ provides a life annuity of B' to the spouse (y) and a reversionary life annuity of 1 to (x) after the death of (y).

INCREASINGLY IMPORTANT CONCEPT IN TOUGH ECONOMIC TIMES

Mortality risk pooling through immediate variable annuities increases in importance in tough economic times. This is because as an individual's retirement asset portfolio has shrunk and has become increasingly incapable of generating the necessary income to maintain a comparable standard of living through the years ahead, the portion of immediate variable annuity income payments attributable to the mortality component becomes ever more meaningful. For example, if a prospective retiree's assets were exclusively or nearly exclusively invested in the stock market in 2000, they likely were significantly reduced in value by 2003. The amount of monthly retirement income the remaining assets could generate on their own is, by definition, less than the amount of monthly retirement income the remaining assets could generate on their own plus the amount of monthly retirement income generated by the mortality pooling benefit of an immediate variable annuity.

This is a critically important fact, whether one wishes to fully examine the mathematical wizardry proving it or not. Thus, it will be repeated here: *The amount of monthly lifetime retirement income a given sum of assets can generate is, by definition, lower than the amount achievable by investing the same sum identically inside an IVA.*

This is because the "reserve" attributable to a deceased annuitant who no longer requires the "longevity insurance" afforded by the immediate variable annuity is reallocated to the remaining, surviving members of the annuitant pool who do require it.

Consider ten 90-year-old citizens of Annuiland, that unique and fictitious country where all its citizens survive to age 90 and all are deceased by age 100. Amazingly, exactly 10% of each starting cohort of 90-year-old Annuilanders dies each year on the day before their next birthday (see Table 6.15).

Each Annuilander tends to have saved enough money to carry him or her through to about age 95. On their common 90th birthday, 10 Annuilanders agree to pool their retirement savings of $100,000 each. On the last day of each year, a retirement income check will be sent to each surviving member.

One member graciously agrees to administer the program at no charge. They collectively agree on a 5% assumed investment rate (AIR). Each member will receive the value of 21,946.5244 annuity units on the last day of each year, if then surviving.

They decide to set the annuity unit value at $1.00 at the start of the program. The $1,000,000 they collectively invest earns *exactly* 5% over the entire 10-year life of the program. As a result, the annuity unit value constantly remains at $1.00. Since the number of annuity units paid each period to a member stays constant, this means each annuity payment (equal to the number of annuity units paid times the annuity unit value on the valuation date) also stays constant over the entire 10-year program.

While a_{90} could be calculated using commutation functions where $a_{90} = N_{91}/D_{90}$, it can always be calculated from first principles by summing

TABLE 6.15 Annuiland Mortality Characteristics

Age	l_x	p_x	q_x
90	10	9/10 = 0.9000	1/10 = 0.1000
91	9	8/9 = 0.8889	1/9 = 0.1111
92	8	7/8 = 0.8750	1/8 = 0.1250
93	7	6/7 = 0.8571	1/7 = 0.1429
94	6	5/6 = 0.8333	1/6 = 0.1667
95	5	4/5 = 0.8000	1/5 = 0.2000
96	4	3/4 = 0.7500	1/4 = 0.2500
97	3	2/3 = 0.6667	1/3 = 0.3333
98	2	1/2 = 0.5000	1/2 = 0.5000
99	1	0/1 = 0.0000	1/1 = 1.0000
100	0		

in seriatim fashion the annual benefit payment of 1 times the appropriate discount factor times the probability of survival:

$$a_{90} = 1/1.05 \times 1 + 1/1.05^2 \times 0.9 + 1/1.05^3 \times 0.8 + 1/1.05^4 \times 0.7$$
$$+ 1/1.05^5 \times 0.6 + 1/1.05^6 \times 0.5 + 1/1.05^7 \times 0.4 + 1/1.05^8$$
$$\times 0.3 + 1/1.05^9 \times 0.2 + 1/1.05^{10} \times 0.1$$

$$= 4.5565$$

$$100,000/4.5565 = 21,946.5244$$

Each member receives $21,946.52 on each annual payment date, which is the last day of the year before the next birthday. Immediately after receiving this payment, the one member of the group that fate has dictated to die that year passes away.

Let's look at the whole program, shown in Table 6.16. Each surviving member receives an annual payment of $21,946.52. The plan works perfectly in that the last breath of the last surviving annuitant and the fund are exhausted simultaneously. Every survivor continues to get the absolutely maximum possible annual benefit payment that the fund can support, while still guaranteeing it will remain solvent for the entire program in order to support its goal.

Total payments of $1,207,058.84 are comprised of $1,000,000 of principal and $207,058.84 of appreciation. Each annual payment pays out all investment earnings of that year plus some principal. The program, properly constructed, systematically spends down principal in exactly the optimal fashion to maximize annual income while keeping the program solvent. In contrast, any individual who goes it alone outside an annuity program can't know how much principal can be safely spent down each year.

Note that had any one member decided to go it alone and not participate in the program, she would have exhausted her personal fund after about five payments.[49] See Table 6.17.

Effectively, the "forfeitures" of those who die are reallocated to support ongoing benefit payments to those who survive. This "survivorship" element of each benefit payment allows the benefit payments to longer-term survivors to be higher than they would be if members could rely only on benefit payments attributable to their own original principal and investment earnings thereon.

Table 6.17 is proof of that, since the member who opted not to participate in the program ran out of income in about five years and is left impoverished, whereas her twin sister who participated is assured to receive continuing benefit checks for life since she enjoys the "survivorship" element of the annuity program. Even though the portfolio of securities inside

TABLE 6.16 Annuiland IVA Program

Time	Age	BOY* Fund	Investment Earnings	EOY† Fund before Payments	Payments	EOY Fund after Payments
0	90	$1,000,000.00	$ 50,000.00	$1,050,000.00	$ 219,465.24	$830,534.76
1	91	830,534.76	41,526.74	872,061.49	197,518.72	674,542.77
2	92	674,542.77	33,727.14	708,269.91	175,572.20	532,697.72
3	93	532,697.72	26,634.89	559,332.60	153,625.67	405,706.93
4	94	405,706.93	20,285.35	425,992.28	131,679.15	294,313.13
5	95	294,313.13	14,715.66	309,028.79	109,732.62	199,296.17
6	96	199,296.17	9,964.81	209,260.98	87,786.10	121,474.88
7	97	121,474.88	6,073.74	127,548.62	65,839.57	61,709.05
8	98	61,709.05	3,085.45	64,794.50	43,893.05	20,901.45
9	99	20,901.45	1,045.07	21,946.52	21,946.52	0.00
10	100	0.00	0.00	0.00	0.00	0.00
			$207,058.84		$1,207,058.84	

*BOY = Beginning of year.
†EOY = End of year.

TABLE 6.17 Annuilander Self-Funding Income

Time	Age	BOY* Fund	Investment Earnings	EOY[†] Fund before Payments	Payments	EOY Fund after Payments
0	90	$100,000.00	$ 5,000.00	$105,000.00	$21,946.52	$83,053.48
1	91	83,053.48	4,152.67	87,206.15	21,946.52	65,259.62
2	92	65,259.62	3,262.98	68,522.61	21,946.52	46,576.08
3	93	46,576.08	2,328.80	48,904.89	21,946.52	26,958.36
4	94	26,958.36	1,347.92	28,306.28	21,946.52	6,359.76
5	95	6,359.76	317.99	6,677.74	6,677.74	0.00
6	96	0.00	0.00	0.00	0.00	0.00
7	97	0.00	0.00	0.00	0.00	0.00
8	98	0.00	0.00	0.00	0.00	0.00
9	99	0.00	0.00	0.00	0.00	0.00
10	100	0.00	0.00	0.00	0.00	0.00
			$16,410.36		$116,410.36	

*BOY = Beginning of year.
[†]EOY = End of year.

the IVA performs identically to the same portfolio of securities outside the IVA, IVA benefits continue for those who survive beyond the point where withdrawals exhaust the non-IVA account.

In difficult economic times when financial projections portend a precarious future, being a participant in such an immediate variable annuity program is all the more important. This is because one's own principal and appreciation are increasingly insufficient to meet one's lifetime income needs. Participating in an immediate variable annuity program allows an additional layer of retirement income on top of this—income attributable to value reallocated to the survivors that was previously held as a reserve for now-deceased annuitants.

If the difficult economic times result from poor stock market performance, a participant can change the allocation of subaccounts the performance of which dictates his or her level of income. For example, he or she may choose to allocate relatively more to a Treasury bond subaccount, high-quality corporate bond subaccount, and/or money market subaccount.

Of course, any allocation or reallocation among subaccounts should be appropriate for the annuitant's long-term interests. A risk tolerance questionnaire is one tool used to determine an appropriate asset allocation. Responses to the questionnaire suggest an asset allocation pie chart, where each pie slice represents a particular asset class. The final step is the selection of individual subaccounts to fill each pie slice to the appropriate level.

While the owner of the immediate variable annuity may reallocate among subaccounts without it being a taxable event, frequent changes or "market timing" generally don't yield superior returns. Financial advisers often suggest the annuitant maintain a balance across multiple asset classes appropriate for the annuitant's risk tolerance and investment horizon.

Frequent reallocation among subaccounts may actually reduce returns *for that particular investor* because such frequent movement may be more emotion-based, where greed and fear alternate in causing suboptimal trading behavior, for example, allocating more to an asset class that has had a run-up and may now be overvalued and allocating less to an asset class that has suffered a decline and may now be undervalued—exactly the opposite of what unemotional, logic-driven thought might suggest.

Frequent reallocation among subaccounts can actually reduce returns *for all investors* in those subaccounts because such activity results in higher trading expenses and higher cash levels held by the fund underlying the subaccount. As a result, most insurers limit the frequency of reallocations allowed per year.

Such investment considerations are the subject of the next chapter.

CHAPTER 7

Immediate Variable
Annuity Subaccounts

*October. This is one of the peculiarly dangerous months to
speculate in stocks. Others are November, December, January,
February, March, April, May, June, July, August, and September.*
                                                    –Mark Twain

OVERVIEW OF SUBACCOUNTS

Immediate variable annuity contracts typically offer a variety of subaccounts into which the contract owner may allocate the premium. These may
be common stock subaccounts (large cap, mid cap, small cap, sector, specialty, domestic, international), bond subaccounts (government, corporate,
long-term, medium-term, short-term), money market subaccounts, balanced subaccounts, real estate subaccounts, and so on.

Premium allocated to a specific subaccount of the immediate variable
annuity (IVA) contract is in turn invested in an underlying investment fund.
While similar to publicly available mutual funds, these investment funds are
specifically created for use in variable annuity and variable life insurance
products.

Publicly available retail mutual funds may in most instances not be used
in conjunction with variable annuity products, due to a 1981 IRS ruling
prohibiting this. While IRS private letter rulings may not be used as precedent, a 1998 IRS private letter ruling allowed a variable annuity fund of
retail mutual funds, provided customers aren't able to control the choice
of which retail mutual funds appear in this fund-of-funds format.

The underlying investment funds may be managed by the investment
arm of the issuing insurer, by independent asset management companies,

or by a combination of both. While the earliest variable annuities only had one account to which all premium was allocated—typically a relatively conservative common stock fund—the trend has been toward each variable annuity having an increasingly greater number of subaccounts—sometimes dozens.

While early variable annuities tended to rely on a single investment manager, the trend has been toward multimanager products; that is, the same variable annuity offers numerous subaccounts managed by numerous investment management companies.

Some insurance companies go one step further and include one consistent collection of subaccounts and investment managers in registered products across all their product lines, such as variable universal life insurance, variable annuities, and 401(k) market savings products. This common fund lineup approach offers multiple benefits:

- Only a single set of subaccounts with which wholesalers and financial advisers need to become familiar.
- Greater insurance company influence on investment managers, since each subaccount has more assets than if it appeared in only one product.
- Improved cross-selling of multiple products offered by one insurer to a single client, although this occurs only to the extent that the products share the same target markets (e.g., affluent, middle class, workplace, etc.).
- Higher probability of garnering "shelf space" with large brokerage firms, which may prefer to work with only a half-dozen major insurers each of which offers a broad product range.

Some financial advisers prefer IVA subaccounts of load fund investment managers—those whose retail mutual fund offerings contain product expense loads used to compensate financial advisers for selling those mutual funds. Financial advisers may be more familiar with load fund investment managers because those operating under a sales commission model tend to sell funds of only such firms. (Financial advisers operating under a fee-based model may also work with no-load retail mutual funds, which also tend to be available to consumers for direct purchase.) For financial advisers operating under a sales commission model, if clients like their experience with one or more load fund investment managers with subaccounts inside the IVA, such clients may be inclined to purchase retail mutual funds of the same investment manager, which can generate additional sales commissions for the adviser.

Subaccounts derive their name because they are component parts of a "separate account." A "separate account" is established and registered with the Securities and Exchange Commission (SEC). The account is "separate" in that it is apart from and distinguishable from an insurer's "general account."

In the United States, the business of insurance is currently state regulated.[1] Insurance companies have a federally granted monopolistic franchise to issue life-contingent immediate annuities.

There is movement toward optional federal chartering in order to improve efficiency and speed to market for new products.[2] Currently, an insurer might have to abide by 50 different sets of rules and product versions in order to offer a product nationwide, since each state insurance department may require its approval and compliance with all aspects of insurance laws of that state before approving a product for sale. The National Association of Insurance Commissioners (NAIC) has as one of its goals increased uniformity of product rules and requirements across states.

The insurer's state of domicile has insurance laws that dictate which investments are permissible for the insurer to make for its general account and in what quantities. This is attributable to the historical bent of insurance companies to offer product guarantees of a nature that demanded a reasonably high degree of "safe" investing, for example, use of a high proportion of fixed-income securities such as bonds and mortgages.

These rules would be too restrictive to allow a product like an immediate variable annuity, in which a customer may wish to allocate a large proportion—up to 100%—of the premium to a common stock fund.[3] As a result, these products are managed out of a separate account. The separate account registration statement describes the investment policies to be employed.

Use of a separate account actually provides additional security for owners of separate account products. This is because separate account assets are largely believed to be insulated from liabilities associated with products for which the assets backing them are housed in the general account. (Some state insurance statutes specifically mention this; others are silent.)

Investment funds underlying variable annuity products may be *passively* managed or *actively* managed. Among those that are passively managed, *index* funds attempt to replicate the performance of a specific index, such as the Standard & Poor's (S&P) 500 or Down Jones Wilshire 5000. Because the target contents of such funds are defined by formula, the funds avoid expenses of investment research analysts, multiple portfolio managers, trips to meet with company managements, higher trading commissions associated with higher portfolio turnover rates, and so on. Effectively, the funds look to provide a "market" return, where the type of index defines the market.

In contrast, actively managed investment funds look to produce returns superior to the market through a variety of means, such as technical analysis, fundamental analysis, proprietary models, and the like. Actively managed funds therefore have higher expenses. To beat passively managed funds, higher-cost, actively managed funds need to produce sufficiently higher gross fund performance so as to more than offset the incrementally greater costs of active management.

By definition, actively managed funds must *collectively* underperform passively managed index funds. This is because there are a finite amount of securities of the type in which a specific fund may invest. Taken in aggregate, actively managed funds must then produce the market return minus their higher management expenses, whereas passively managed funds must collectively produce the market return minus their lower management expenses.

Historical evidence rejects the hypothesis that the stock market is inefficient in placing proper valuations on securities and that active investment management can exploit those inefficiencies. Of 355 stock mutual funds in 1970, only 41%, or 147, survived to 2003. If an average annual return of ±1% of the unmanaged S&P 500 Index is defined as being roughly equivalent to the index, then 280 funds (79%) either failed or underperformed the index, 52 funds (15%) were equivalent, and 23 funds (6%) outperformed it. If an average annual return of ±2% of the unmanaged S&P 500 Index is defined as being roughly equivalent to the index, then 98% of funds failed, underperformed it, or were equivalent; that is, only 2% of actively managed funds outperformed an unmanaged index.[4]

Because hard data spanning a one-third century measurement period show that active fund management systematically fails to add shareholder value (i.e., the problem resides with the approach itself rather than with fund managers who execute it), proponents of indexing make the case against the search for the needle in the haystack and believe investors are better served by owning—via an index fund—the market haystack itself. Index fund proponents find higher expenses of active management unnecessarily confiscatory.

Another benefit of index funds is that they avoid securities *overlap*. For example, if an IVA contract owner makes use of, say, three domestic common stock subaccounts, a given security might be owned by two or even all three. Higher concentrations in specific securities can result, with less diversification than would have been achieved simply by investing in an index fund. If an IVA owner invested, say, in a Dow Jones Wilshire 5000 Total Market Index[5] subaccount and a total international stock index subaccount, he or she could achieve significant diversification at low cost with zero securities overlap for the common stock component of the IVA holdings.

Because of the potentially multidecade period that an immediate variable annuity may span, product expenses, including investment management expenses, are important. The potentially lengthy period covered means that small expense differences are magnified through compounding.

Different people—investment portfolio managers included—may assess the value of any specific asset quite differently. Financial economics says that despite various perceptions of value by different individuals, the market price is the medium of exchange, making it the uniquely sensible value.

TYPOLOGY OF VARIABLE ANNUITY SUBACCOUNTS

The prospectus states the investment objective of a fund and describes certain investment policies that will be used to try to achieve that objective. There is no guarantee that the objective will be achieved.

"Capital appreciation" is a typical objective of common stock funds. "Current income" is an objective that receives greater emphasis in bond funds. "Capital preservation" is one usual objective of money market funds.

Investment subaccounts can be categorized as stock subaccounts, fixed-income subaccounts, and the catchall category "other." A *style box grid* (see Figure 7.1) is one common representation for stock subaccounts and fixed-income subaccounts (bonds, mortgages, cash equivalents).

Columns in the *stock fund style box* represent "styles" of investing. Value-oriented stocks are those a portfolio manager believes are currently undervalued and will rise in price as their worth is recognized by the market. Growth-oriented stocks are those of companies a portfolio manager believes will experience sales, earnings, and market share growth faster than the general economy and faster than the average for the industry. Stocks in the "blend" column include (1) a mix of value-oriented and growth-oriented stocks and (2) single stocks that exhibit both value and growth characteristics.

Rows in the stock fund style box represent sizes of the companies issuing the securities, where "cap" is short for "capitalization." Large cap

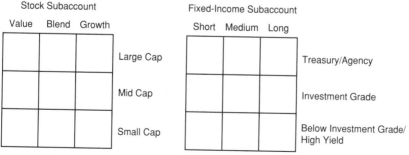

FIGURE 7.1 Stock Subaccount and Fixed-Income Subaccount Style Boxes

stocks can be defined as those above a certain market capitalization, mid cap stocks are those within a specified market capitalization range, and small cap stocks are those below this range. Because market capitalizations fluctuate constantly, the three rows are sometimes alternatively defined by percentages rather than by absolute dollars. For example, large cap stocks might be those in the top 70% of market capitalizations of actively traded domestic stocks, mid cap stocks being the next 20%, and small cap stocks the remaining 10%.

Each column, row, and cell has its own characteristics that tend to distinguish it. For example, large cap value stocks may be more "defensive," performing relatively better than large cap growth stocks in bear markets. In the opposite corner, small cap growth stocks tend to exhibit more price volatility (some would say with prices darting like a mouse on espresso!).

Columns in the *fixed-income style box* represent interest rate sensitivity. "Duration" in its technical investment sense[6] is typically used, rather than length of maturities of securities. Short-duration fixed-income investments exhibit the least sensitivity in price to fluctuations in interest rates, while long-duration fixed-income investments exhibit the most sensitivity.

Rows in the fixed-income style box represent credit quality of the entity issuing the security. Higher credit quality securities (e.g., Treasury securities issued by the U.S. government, which has the power to generate tax revenue to pay off its debt; or securities of corporate issuers whose ability to repay debt as measured by their "coverage ratio," defined as earnings available for payment of bond charges divided by amount of bond charges, is high) tend to be less risky and offer relatively lower rates of return. Lower credit quality securities tend to be riskier and commensurately offer relatively higher rates of return, since these are associated with higher default rates— less certainty that all interest due will be paid or that principal will be fully repaid. Higher initial gross yields (e.g., before recognition of any later defaults) can usually be achieved by assuming more duration risk (i.e., investing in more highly interest-rate-sensitive instruments), more credit risk (i.e., investing in lower credit quality), more call or prepayment risk (i.e., investing in instruments that may be repaid early), and more liquidity risk (i.e., investing in less liquid instruments).

Different organizations use different definitions for their style box grids, so one must be careful when making comparisons. For example, rather than the fixed-income rows being "Treasury/Agency, Investment Grade, and Below Investment Grade," as in the grid in Figure 7.1, the rows could be defined as "High Quality (Treasury, AAA, AA), Medium Quality (A, BBB), and Low Quality (BB and lower)."

For the average fixed-income investor, the salient points are

1. If bond coupon payments and principal repayments are viewed as weights on a horizontal wooden plank, the single point at which you could place a pencil vertically under the plank and balance it is akin to the notion of "duration" for that bond (although the actual definition also recognizes present values of those payments).
2. The higher the duration, the more the price of the bond fluctuates up or down with decreases or increases in interest rates, respectively.

A precise, detailed explanation of duration appears in Chapter 3.

"Other" subaccounts outside the realm of domestic stock and fixed-income subaccounts include

- International subaccounts.
- Sector subaccounts, which concentrate on one industry sector (e.g., health care, utilities).
- Balanced subaccounts, which look to strike a particular balance of stock, fixed-income, and cash-equivalent securities.
- Managed subaccounts, where the portfolio manager selects and periodically redetermines the desired mix of stock, fixed-income, and cash-equivalent securities based on his outlook of relative value.
- Specialty subaccounts, such as real estate investment trusts (REITs).

Within any specific style box cell, investment substyles may be employed. Substyle approaches include "contrarian" and "growth at a reasonable price (GARP)."

Style box grids are by no means the only way to categorize securities. For example, stocks alone can also be categorized as blue chip stocks, growth stocks, emerging growth stocks, income stocks, cyclical stocks, defensive stocks, and speculative stocks.

A variable annuity subaccount may be required by its definition in the prospectus to adhere to one specific style box cell at all times. A variable annuity subaccount may also be such as to migrate among two or more style box cells, while remaining true to its investment objective stated in the prospectus. Thus, while a specific style box cell may represent the location that describes where the subaccount most frequently resides or currently resides, it is helpful for an annuitant to understand the degree of investment latitude the subaccounts she's considering have as she contemplates an appropriate asset allocation.

Once an asset allocation appropriate for the annuitant's risk tolerance and time horizon is selected and established, it is advisable to leave it unperturbed. Constant focus on daily investment returns may cause investors to

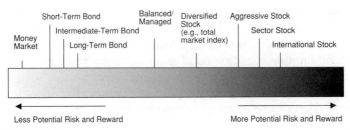

FIGURE 7.2   Subaccount Types

feel the need to be proactive and to trade in and out of subaccounts with frequency, typically leading to suboptimal results as trading becomes more emotion-based, much like Caesar regarded Cassius in Shakespeare's *Julius Caesar*: "He thinks too much: such men are dangerous."

It is more relaxing—and usually more profitable in the long term—simply to recognize that asset allocation is the dominant factor driving investment results, to establish an appropriate asset allocation, and to adhere to it. It is, however, generally recommended to rebalance periodically (e.g., annually or when an asset class gets 5% to 10% away from target allocation).

Variable annuity writers frequently offer prospects or contract owners visual help in ascertaining relative levels of risk among offered subaccounts by displaying a pyramid with lower risk/lower return investment classes at the base and higher risk/potentially higher return investment classes nearer the peak. The risk-reward spectrum is sometimes displayed as a horizontal bar (as in Figure 7.2), with lower risk investments toward one end and higher risk toward the other.

It is important that bond subaccount investors understand the difference between a bond subaccount and a bond. When one buys a single bond and holds it to maturity, there is a specific time at which the investor will have her principal fully returned (assuming no default), which makes a single bond a *debt* investment. When one invests in a bond subaccount, with the expectation of gain, there is no one time at which the investor is guaranteed to have her principal returned, which makes a bond subaccount an *equity* investment.

NUMBER OF SUBACCOUNTS AND CONSIDERATIONS IN SUBACCOUNT SELECTION

While variable annuities originally only contained one subaccount, around 1980 a movement started to offer multiple subaccounts. Different investment management companies were involved in managing the funds underlying the subaccounts for a given variable annuity. IVA contract owners now enjoyed diversification among funds and fund managers within the same product.

Legal concerns about the number of subaccounts permitted within a variable annuity centered on the issue of "investor control." The insurer is considered the owner of the variable separate account for federal tax purposes. If, instead, variable annuity contract owners were considered owners of the variable separate account assets, income and gains would be includable in their gross income annually rather than being tax-deferred.

Years ago, the IRS published rulings saying that variable annuity contract owners will be considered to own separate account assets if they possess "incidents of ownership" of those assets, such as the ability to exercise "investment control" over the assets. This originally limited the number of subaccounts per IVA product to just a handful. During the 1990s, the number of subaccounts per product skyrocketed, with some variable annuities offering 50 or 75.

IRS Revenue Ruling 2003-91 acknowledges that 20 investment subaccounts can be offered under a variable annuity contract without causing the contract owner to be treated as owner of the underlying assets. Offering more than 20 is not a violation of "investor control" restrictions per se, but contract designs that stay within 20 appear to be within a "safe harbor."

More was not necessarily better. The large number of subaccount choices in a product overwhelmed some prospective purchasers. While financial advisers could keep up with a smaller number of subaccounts— knowing issues, why investment performance for the prior quarter was what it was—it became impossible to stay knowledgeable about a large number.

Variable annuity prospectuses, which include both product information and information pertaining to each specific fund within the product, mushroomed in size. The number of annuity unit values to administer increased drastically. If a product had 50 funds the investment management of which was spread over 15 different companies, each such company realized it might only get a single-digit percentage of product assets. This tempered investment management company enthusiasm to participate in some products.

In the early 2000s, there is slight movement toward fewer subaccounts in registered products. A more manageable number of investment choices can actually improve product appeal. Regardless of how many subaccount choices existed, it was common for a variable annuity contract owner to use only three of them. Such a triad might consist of a common stock subaccount for growth, a bond subaccount for preservation of capital and income, and an equity-income subaccount for a degree of income and growth.

The underlying investment funds of the variable annuity separate account must meet diversification requirements prescribed by Treasury

Department regulation.[7] Insurers, in order to provide initial asset diversification, may initially participate in the separate account for a limited period of time by contributing "seed money" and later withdrawing this—either wholly or in gradual installments—once contract owner deposits and premiums can adequately support investment diversification.

Because an IVA purchase is typically an irrevocable election and because access to principal other than through regularly scheduled periodic income payments is generally unavailable, it is important for the contract owner to be comfortable with the investment manager(s) in the product.

Index funds inside an IVA allow contract owners to know what to expect in the way of investment performance; that is, owners can expect each index fund to perform quite similarly to—but not exactly identically to—the index the performance of which it is attempting to duplicate.

As mentioned earlier, index funds are passively managed funds, meaning their contents as to both issuing companies of the securities and percentages of each security held look to mimic that of the underlying index. The index can be a domestic stock index, an international stock index, a bond index, a REIT index, or any other index involving a well-defined basket of securities.

Index funds tend to have lower investment management expenses associated with them than actively managed funds do. This is because index funds do not require research analysts; they incur a lower number of transaction expenses, since their contents remain relatively stable and have low turnover; and they require only a single portfolio manager.

Index fund performance isn't usually identical to the index. Because the index itself is an unmanaged basket of securities, it reflects no administration expenses in its performance numbers. In contrast, an index fund does incur transaction and administration expenses; and, to the extent it does, its performance should typically be slightly lower than the index.

IVA contract owners may like the psychological comfort of indexed subaccounts because they know that the investment funds underlying the subaccounts that they choose, the performance of which determines their retirement income benefits, will perform at or nearly at the "market." To the extent they allocate a percentage to an S&P 500 Index subaccount, they feel reasonably comfortable that the return on the underlying fund will be close to that of the S&P 500 Index. There's no chance they'll handily beat the index, nor is there a chance they'll fall quite short of the index—as long as the underlying index fund is managed closely to its stated investment policy objective.

As with any investment, expenses matter. The less the return is diminished by high investment management expenses, high transactional expenses associated with large portfolio turnover rates, and high 12b-1 fees, the greater the return of the subaccount and thus the higher the retirement income benefits.

Indexed subaccounts thus have two important characteristics: (1) low cost and (2) virtual assurance that returns will approximate the index with little chance of substantially underperforming the market defined by the index.

Active portfolio management involves research, fundamental and/or technical analysis, trips to speak with company managements, and other methods where information, research, and experience are used to try to achieve a better performance result than a passively managed fund, whose contents are dictated by formula.

Active portfolio management may seek to overweight sectors that it sees as having more favorable prospects and to underweight others. It can then focus on individual security selections within any industry sector. Such portfolio construction that focuses first on industry sectors and second on specific securities is a "top down" approach. In contrast, "bottom up" portfolio construction focuses first on individual security selection. Either way, portfolio managers decide what and when to buy and what and when to sell.

Actively managed funds underlying IVA subaccounts tend to be more expensive due to the additional research and security selection activities. They also tend to have higher levels of trading activity—as revealed by the annual portfolio turnover rate—and incur the associated higher transactional expenses. Active portfolio management must outperform its benchmark (e.g., an index) by at least the amount of expenses it creates for the fund if it is to beat its benchmark.

While the higher portfolio turnover rate of actively managed funds may drive up fund expenses, annuity taxation currently is such that higher portfolio turnover does not present a tax issue because that portion of annuity payments that is taxable is taxed at the ordinary income tax rate. Thus, the effect of high turnover—causing more gains to be classified as short-term and therefore taxed at ordinary income rates rather than as long-term and taxed at lower capital gains rates—which is present for retail mutual funds in the non-tax-qualified market, does not come into play for annuities. As a consequence, investors wishing to employ both passive and active investment management might tilt their portfolios more toward active management in the IVA and more toward passive management in retail mutual funds.

Some investors prefer the lower cost and market performance of index funds. Others look to actively managed funds in hopes of outperforming the market.

There may be multiple classes of shares for a particular underlying investment fund available in registered annuity products. These may have different expense levels, including different levels of 12b-1 fees. They may be known as Class 1 and Class 2 shares, service class shares, and so on. Thus, while two IVA products may share an underlying fund of the same investment manager, it is not necessarily the case that the cost to the consumer associated with this fund is identical in both products.

Section 50.9 of New York Insurance Regulation 47 requires an insurer to mail at least once a year to every separate account annuity contract holder a statement of investments held in the separate account.

MODERN PORTFOLIO THEORY

The body of thought classified as modern portfolio theory stems from the historical inability of those concerned with investment analysis to express quantitatively risk and its relation to investment return. Modern portfolio theory focuses attention beyond the traditional evaluation of individual securities to overall portfolio composition. The tools of modern portfolio theory allow for more precise quantitative measurement of risks and returns and for development of optimal portfolios.

In 1952, Nobel Prize-winning economist Dr. Harry M. Markowitz produced a collection of propositions regarding rational investor behavior[8] that were the tenets of modern portfolio theory. Using quadratic programming, he provided a theoretical framework for systematically creating optimum portfolios. His approach showed how to select from a universe of individual securities and how to weight those selections in constructing portfolios. Purchases and sales of individual securities are meaningful only to the extent that they alter the overall risk-return aspects of the aggregate portfolio. Dr. Markowitz's landmark achievement was to shift the focus of attention to total portfolio risk rather than to individual securities in making investment process decisions.

The premise of Markowitz's work is that rational investors should have an aversion to absorbing greater risk without being compensated by an adequate increase in expected return—the mean of a probability distribution. Rational investors should prefer a portfolio with minimum deviation of returns about the mean. As a result, Markowitz defined *risk* as the variability of returns measured by the standard deviation of expected returns about the mean. The approach, called a "mean-variance portfolio optimization method," was the genesis of modern quantitative finance.

At last, portfolio investment risk was quantified after lacking such a dimension of risk, which previously made any statements of portfolio performance relatively meaningless. Any portfolio that outperformed the total stock market average may simply have had an aggressive investment manager who selected higher-risk stocks, such as those non-dividend-paying stocks that might maximize capital gains in a bull market without regard for the likelihood of greater downturns in a bear market.

Using this definition of risk and the assumed aversion to risk, Markowitz observed that investors should try to minimize deviations from the expected portfolio rate of return by diversifying the securities they own. Diversification can occur across asset classes (e.g., bonds, stocks, real estate, money markets) and again within asset classes (e.g., by holding securities of different companies).

Holding different security issues, however, doesn't significantly reduce variability if the timing, direction, and magnitude of their price fluctuations are similar—if their market prices exhibit high "positive covariance." Effective diversification is achieved only if the portfolio contains securities that do not fluctuate in a similar way. The result is that the variability of the portfolio rate of return becomes significantly less than the variability of individual securities in the portfolio.

This idea is easily illustrated in Figure 7.3 by a two-stock portfolio with equal amounts invested in each stock. In the upper graph of Figure 7.3, the two securities are perfectly positively correlated. When one stock moves either up or down, the other experiences the exact same change in timing, magnitude, and direction. Combining the two securities into a portfolio does not reduce the variance in total return. The variance of the portfolio return is identical to the variance in return of each of the two securities.

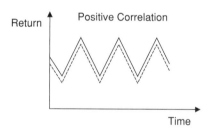

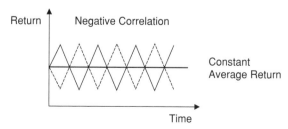

FIGURE 7.3 Two-Stock Portfolio with Positive Correlation and Negative Correlation

In the lower graph of Figure 7.3, the two securities are negatively correlated. When one stock moves either up or down, the other moves in exactly the opposite direction in the same proportion. Combining the two securities into a portfolio produces a constant average return, completely eliminating any variance in portfolio return.

The same concept is extendible to portfolios with more than two securities. For each security, its expected return, expected standard deviation, and covariance with each other security in the universe under consideration is determined. With this information, Markowitz showed how quadratic programming (performed by computer) could calculate a set of optimal portfolios.

The locus[9] of optimal portfolios, called the "efficient frontier," is denoted by the curve in Figure 7.4. Portfolio C is considered suboptimal because Portfolio A could produce the same expected return with lower risk (i.e., lower standard deviation), whereas Portfolio B could produce a higher expected return with the same degree of risk.

Individual investors will reach different decisions as to where on the risk-return spectrum of efficient portfolios they wish to fall. Individuals more interested in capital preservation and more consistent returns will choose a portfolio to the left end of the curve. Individuals more interested in investing aggressively by being willing to accept more variability in returns for higher but less certain returns will choose a portfolio to the right end of the curve.

A portfolio will not retain its efficient frontier status indefinitely. Periodic adjustments based on updated data are necessary. The calculations involved in rerunning the optimization program are simplified by relating the returns on each security to an index and thereby implicitly to each other security, rather than relating the returns on each security to the

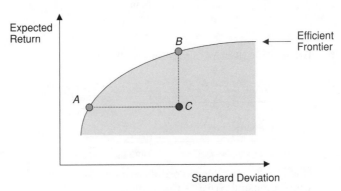

FIGURE 7.4 Efficient Frontier of Optimal Portfolios

returns on each other security, an approach that produces a huge number of covariances to track.

CAPITAL ASSET PRICING THEORY

Markowitz adjusted risk by moving along the efficient frontier of various portfolios of different individual securities. In contrast, capital asset pricing theory adjusts risk by borrowing or lending against a single optimal risky portfolio, which is the entire market of securities under consideration.

In Figure 7.5, point M represents the expected return and risk (variability) of the whole market, that is, the complete universe of available risky investments (as opposed to risk-free). Each security issue is weighted according to its share of total market value. The universe of securities is typically approximated by a surrogate index, since the actual universe of available securities is ever-changing.

In capital asset pricing theory, point M is the optimal risky portfolio because no other investment combination produces a better trade-off between return and risk.

Point R_f in Figure 7.5 represents the expected return on a risk-free asset for the period under consideration. Portfolios on the line segment R_fM represent the continuum of returns ranging from a portfolio consisting of 100% risk-free and 0% risky assets to a portfolio consisting of 0% risk-free and 100% risky assets, the latter portfolio mirroring the market.

To achieve an expected return in excess of the market along the line segment MZ, an investor borrows additional funds and invests those in the market, "leveraging" his portfolio. As illustrated in the figure, the returns so achieved will exceed those achieved by moving upward on Markowitz's efficient frontier.

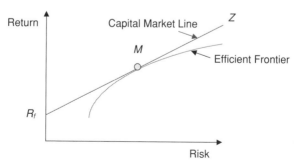

FIGURE 7.5 Capital Market Line

(Figure 7.5 is a simplification in that $R_f Z$ represents a straight line segment, inferring that investors can borrow at the risk-free rate. In reality, investors have to pay more for borrowed funds than the risk-free rate. This creates a downward bend point at M, making the rate of return investors can achieve by increasing risk less than that indicated by line segment MZ. Nonetheless, the concept of a capital market line remains valid.)

TOTAL MARKET RISK VERSUS
SECURITY-SPECIFIC RISK

William F. Sharpe divided risk into two elements: (1) *Market risk* is that portion of the price movement of an individual security or a particular portfolio that is attributable to movement of the market as a whole. (2) *Security-specific risk* is that portion of price movement unique to a specific security.

Market risk is a nondiversifiable risk. Security-specific risk is a diversifiable risk. Since not all companies respond to movement of the whole market with equal sensitivity, combining additional securities that are less than perfectly positively correlated can create a more diversified portfolio with lower risk.

Figure 7.6 measures the sensitivity of returns on a specific security to returns on the total market. It partitions the return on a specific security

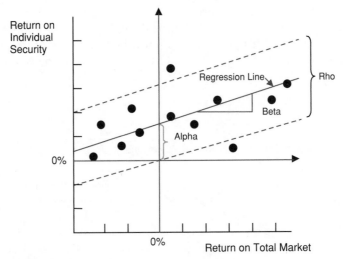

FIGURE 7.6   Regression Line of Individual Security Return as a Function of Total Market Return

(e.g., a common stock) into two components: (1) a market component and (2) a specific security component.

Each black dot on the chart represents the gain or loss in a particular month for a specific stock (as measured by the vertical axis) and the corresponding gain or loss on the entire market for the same period. A least-squares regression line is drawn based on 12 monthly observations.

"Beta" is the slope of the regression line, the amount of "rise" in individual stock return per unit of "run" in total market return. If the slope were at a 45-degree angle, beta would be 1.0, meaning that on average during the observation period a 1% total market return was accompanied by a 1% individual stock return. A shallower slope implies a beta less than 1.0, while a steeper slope implies a beta greater than 1.0. For example, a beta of 1.3 means that on average during the observation period, the stock moved up 1.3% for every 1.0% the total market moved up. It also means the stock moved down 1.3% for every 1.0% the total market moved down. Thus, high beta stocks are more volatile, while low beta stocks are more stable. Clearly, beta measures the price movement component of an individual stock that is attributable to total market movement.

"Alpha" shows where the regression line intercepts the vertical axis. It shows the average amount of price return of a specific stock independent of total market return; that is, it shows the average price return of a specific stock when total market return is 0%. Clearly, alpha measures the price movement component of an individual stock that is attributable solely to that specific stock. (*Note:* Returns on an individual stock are generally measured net of the risk-free rate of return.)

As an example, suppose that for a specific stock, alpha is 1% and beta is 1.3. If total stock market return for a given month were 2%, then the return for the specific stock predicted by the regression line is 3.6%. A 2% market return is on average associated with a 2.6% stock return (2% × 1.3 beta = 2.6%). Independent of market movement, the stock tends to produce a 1% return. Together this totals 3.6%.

Note that not all the black dots in Figure 7.6 fall directly on the regression line. Thus, the regression line merely represents an *average* relationship. "Rho" measures the degree to which individual black dot observations deviate from the regression line. "Rho" is the correlation coefficient; "rho squared" is the coefficient of determination. Rho equals 100% when all observations fall on the regression line. Rho equals 0% when there is a total absence of any linear relationship between return on the individual stock and return on the total market.

As increasingly more stocks are combined into a portfolio, rho moves toward 100%; that is, greater diversification brings the portfolio ever closer to the total market for that asset class. With increasingly more stocks, the return on the portfolio grows ever closer to the return on the total market. Ultimately, security-specific risk is eliminated, and only market risk remains.

One may expect positive alphas of some individual stocks to be offset by negative alphas of other individual stocks so that the alpha of the total diversified portion tends to zero. If this assumption is made—together with the assumption that portfolio rhos tend to zero with increasing diversification—then the portfolio return tends toward a function that only depends on beta: Portfolio return tends toward its beta times total market return.

Beta becomes the most important determinant of portfolio return within an investment manager's control (since he or she cannot control market movement). Also, the standard deviation of portfolio returns is a function of the beta of the portfolio and the standard deviation of total market returns. Thus, beta can be used to measure comparative riskiness of alternative portfolios. As a result, Sharpe's "market line" can be expressed as

$$R_p = R_f + \beta(R_m - R_f)$$

where R_p = portfolio return
R_f = risk-free return
β = portfolio beta
R_m = total market return

The end result is a "capital market line" graph identical in appearance to that shown earlier in Figure 7.5. The only distinction is that now "risk" on the horizontal axis is calibrated in terms of "portfolio beta," where it was previously calibrated by "standard deviation of return."

RANDOM WALK

Capital asset pricing theory sees markets as generally being in equilibrium, with no strong foresight as to direction and magnitude of change in the next instant. The next new event that drives trading activity cannot be successfully predicted from knowledge of prior events. As a result, stock price behavior resembles a random walk.[10]

(Brownian motion, originally the random motion caused by a great number of molecular collisions of physical microscopic particles suspended in a liquid or a gas, is of importance in continuous-time finance. Stock prices are usually assumed to follow a random walk. The discrete random walk process converges to Brownian motion; that is, Brownian motion is a limit of random walks.)

The random walk hypothesis for stock price movement assumes stocks trade in an efficient market, characterized by a large number of rational investors freely competing with each other. It suggests that information sufficiently meaningful to affect stock price is quickly accessible to knowledgeable investors, causing that information to be rapidly reflected in stock price.

The random walk and efficient market hypotheses imply that at any point in time the price of a security is the best estimate of its value and incorporates all available information (public and perhaps private). If strictly true, this implies that any attempts to outsmart the market are futile. (Recently, corporations have formed internal markets for such purposes as establishing sales projections, recognizing that market behavior inclusive of perspectives of a wide variety of individuals tends to be superior to one person, such as a sales manager who might otherwise have established an estimate alone.)

Exactly how strongly the random walk and the efficient market hypotheses hold has important ramifications for mutual fund and other investment managers. If they hold strongly, then investment managers should be unable to consistently forecast future prices of individual securities by such a large margin as to recover their research expenses, management fees, and commission expenses and still beat a passively managed index fund with an identical benchmark.

INVESTMENT RISK

Investment risk is not so cleanly measurable as might first appear. For example, in addition to price change over a measurement period, rate of return also includes any dividends or interest received during the period and should be included in any change in value measurement.

In Figure 7.7, investment *B* has a more volatile rate of return pattern than investment *A* does. If volatility alone were considered as a measurement of risk, investment *A* would be considered least risky. Since even the lowest returns on investment *B* exceed the highest returns on investment *A*, it would be difficult to say that *B* was the "riskier" investment. It is clearly the more "uncertain" investment, but not likely to be declared "riskier."

This example might suggest a risk measure that looks at reward in relation to variability. William F. Sharpe of Stanford University introduced one such measure in 1966. While he termed it the "reward-to-variability ratio," it is more commonly called the Sharpe Ratio.

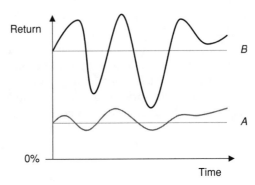

FIGURE 7.7 Magnitude and Variability of
Returns for Investment *A* and Investment *B*

If in Figure 7.7 the return curve for investment *B* were translated downward so that 60% of the time it exceeded *A* and 40% of the time it fell below *A*, the situation becomes less clear. Even though the majority of time the rate of return on *B* exceeds the rate of return on *A*, there are two troughs on *B* where the losses are very steep. Especially if *A* never involves a loss of principal and *B* sometimes involves a loss of principal, the decision as to which investment is "riskier" grows more complex. Thus, a more refined definition of risk should consider magnitude of possible losses along the way and not merely variability of returns.

Investors can always receive a guaranteed rate of interest and a guaranteed return of principal by investing in risk-free Treasury bills. As a result, it may be more appropriate to define a *loss* as occurring whenever the return on the alternative investment falls below this risk-free rate. Even if the alternative investment returned more than zero but less than the risk-free rate, economists would state this event involved an "opportunity loss." While absolute losses (i.e., loss of principal) tend to be more emotionally upsetting, the risk-free rate should often be the more appropriate frame of reference if Treasury investments are an allowable alternative in the investor's investment set.

Variable income annuity investors will receive periodic reports about the subaccounts in their product. These reports will contain a listing of assets held as well as summary statistics and perhaps investment manager commentary. Although investment management is—and must be—primarily outside the control of the IVA contract owner, the preceding primer that just scratches the surface of portfolio management may be helpful to the owner.

ACADEMIC RESEARCH AND ITS PRACTICAL
IMPLICATIONS FOR RETIREMENT INCOME

How the premium is divided among different asset classes (stocks, bonds, short-term instruments) may have a much greater impact on returns and therefore on retirement income than which particular annuity subaccounts are used.

The types of assets in which one invests (e.g., stocks, bonds, cash equivalents) dominate portfolio performance. Individual security selection and market timing play minor roles.

Total asset portfolio construction involves investment policy decisions and investment strategy decisions. *Investment policy* defines which asset classes to include and in what proportions. *Investment strategy* decisions may include temporarily overweighting certain asset classes and underweighting others (market timing) and selecting specific individual securities rather than investing in the asset class as a whole (security selection).

Academic research reported in *Financial Analysts Journal*[11] looked at benchmark returns of passively managed asset portfolios constructed of stock, bond, and cash market indexes in the same proportions as 91 large corporate pension plans. Actual plan returns were compared to benchmark returns.

Investment policy explained 93.6% of the variation in actual plan performance from benchmark performance. Investment policy and market timing collectively explained 95.3% of the variation. Investment policy and security selection collectively explained 97.8%. Effectively, policy explained 93.6% with timing, selection, and a combination effect explaining the residual.

Benchmark performance—investing in selected asset classes in selected proportions—explains 100% of itself. To the extent actively managed portfolios produced returns that differed from benchmark portfolio returns, the attribution chart in Figure 7.8 depicts the degree to which various factors explain the variation.

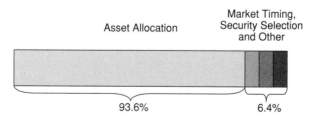

FIGURE 7.8 Variation in Actual Portfolio Performance from Benchmark Portfolio Performance

On average, active investment management produced annual returns 1.10% lower than the passively managed benchmark indexes. Market timing lost plans 0.66% per year, security selection lost plans 0.36% per year, and other factors lost plans 0.07% per year.

Performance attribution—attributing total asset portfolio performance to its component parts—implies from this research that the way asset classes as a whole perform and the proportion an investor allocates to each class explain in largest part portfolio return. Market timing and security selection play a smaller—and, on average, negative—role. (See Figure 7.9.) Hence, research supports the opening statement to this section—that how one spreads variable income annuity premium across asset classes has a more profound effect on retirement income than which particular subaccounts are chosen.

While common stocks and inflation don't move in lockstep, Figure 7.10 illustrates why—at least historically—having a common stock component in the allocation of subaccounts that drive variable income annuity benefit levels offers the potential for annuity benefits to keep up with or outpace inflation. The S&P 500 index[12] is an indicative measure of performance of large capitalization stocks. "Inflation" reflects the Consumer Price Index for All Urban Consumers, Seasonally Adjusted, as reported by the U.S. Department

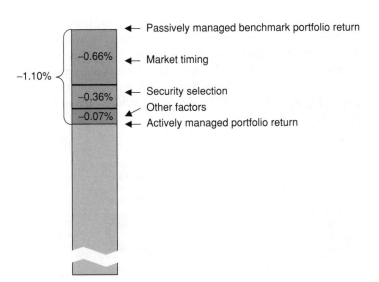

FIGURE 7.9 Effect of Active Investment Management for 91 Large Pension Plans

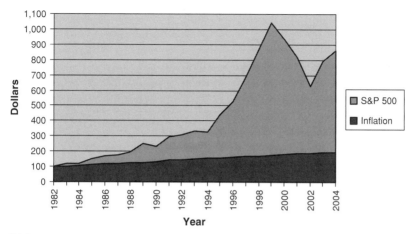

FIGURE 7.10 Stock Performance versus Inflation: Year-end 1982–2004

of Labor, Bureau of Labor Statistics. These two measures are compared assuming a $100 starting value at year-end 1982.

Suppose we estimate that over the retirement period of a particular individual, inflation will run about 4% per year. If the AIR is 5%, then it will require 9.2% annual subaccount performance to allow annuity benefit payments to rise with inflation—that is, to keep a constant level of purchasing power.

To see this, suppose an annuitant initially receives $1,000 per month. To keep pace with inflation, the monthly benefit one year later will need to be $1,040. The assumed investment rate (AIR) built into the payout is 5%; so if the subaccount performs only at 5%, the benefit will remain at $1,000. If the subaccount performs at 9.2%, the benefit will increase to $1,000·(1.092/1.05), or $1,040.

It would obviously take even higher investment performance if we assume a higher inflation rate or if the AIR were higher. A higher AIR may promote more variable income annuity sales because the initial benefit is more attractive, but it may also promote more discontented contract owners if investment performance isn't adequate. Because the world of investment managers revolves heavily around managing client expectations and then meeting or exceeding them, this is more readily accomplished with a lower AIR.

In the absence of a clear understanding by the buyer (and sometimes by the seller) of the impact that the AIR selection makes on the slope of future annuity benefits, a disproportionate number of annuitants may elect the highest AIR simply because it provides the highest initial benefit.

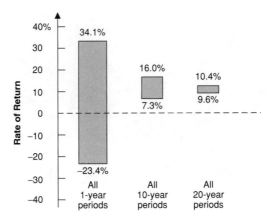

FIGURE 7.11 S&P 500 Range of Average Annual Returns 1983–2004[13]

Allocation of IVA premium to common stocks—especially small stocks—can increase volatility of annuity benefit levels in the short run due to the wide dispersion of annual common stock returns around the mean (see 1-year periods in Figure 7.11). Common stocks, however, historically have provided a reasonably attractive combination of average annual returns and volatility when viewed over a sufficiently long period, as may be the case with an investor's retirement horizon (see 10- and 20-year periods in Figure 7.11).

Diversification across asset classes affects both the risk—as measured by the variability of portfolio returns—and the reward—as measured by the mean rate of portfolio returns (see Figure 7.12).

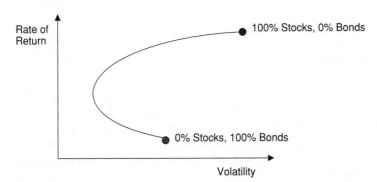

FIGURE 7.12 Asset Class Diversification Can Both Increase Return and Decrease Volatility

Figure 7.13 compares hypothetical performance of an all-stock portfolio, an all-bond portfolio, and a 60% stock/40% bond combination portfolio. As expected, the stock portfolio exhibits the greatest volatility of returns, the bond portfolio the least volatility, and the combination portfolio an intermediate volatility.

When modeling retirement income, it is important to recognize that results may differ between a liquidation program (where retirement income payments are regularly being made from the asset portfolio) and an accumulation program (where starting assets are left intact, with no withdrawals). For example, the stock/bond mix that optimizes the owner's return versus volatility relationship preference in the accumulation phase where assets are untouched may differ in the liquidation phase where assets are periodically withdrawn.

When modeling just the retirement income phase, results may also differ for a program where the original asset allocation persists unaltered and for a program with periodic rebalancing to a specific mix of stocks and bonds. Rebalancing can be by *time*—such as quarterly—or by *rule*—such as on any valuation date where any component of the asset mix deviates from its target allocation by more than X% (e.g., 10%).

It is possible to create software that illustrates, for a given portfolio of asset classes and for a given AIR, what the series of projected annuity benefits would look like based on the historical mean return and variance, with shaded areas indicating where returns within one, two, and three standard deviations would fall. Without guaranteeing any future performance, this illustration would allow IVA investors the opportunity to compare the patterns that might be expected to emerge (e.g., degree of dispersion of benefit levels within a 95% confidence interval) under different asset allocations and AIRs available to them. In other words, a probabilistic representation of their future experience based on historical means and variances of asset classes may serve as a guide to the performance that *might* be expected,

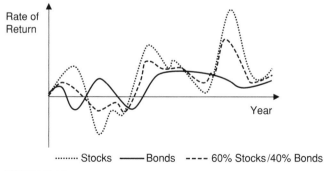

FIGURE 7.13 Comparative Volatility of Returns

based on a particular selection of subaccounts. Appropriate disclosure language that such a representation is not a guarantee but rather a guide based on historical characteristics of asset classes could be used.

Monte Carlo simulation is one such analytical tool for modeling uncertainty surrounding future variable income annuity benefits. Monte Carlo simulation is a mathematical modeling application that generates multiple future outcome scenarios based on assumptions regarding asset class mean returns, asset class volatility, and inter-asset class correlations. By creating a spectrum of possible retirement income scenarios—consistent with parameters drawn from historical data—variable income annuitants can gain a better perspective about possible outcomes of their AIR and subaccount decisions than they can from a deterministic model that reveals only a single, average outcome scenario.

Academic research and simulation studies validate the case for asset diversification as it applies to optimizing one's retirement income experience. For example, Milevsky and Robinson[14] state, "It appears that the lifetime probability of ruin for a consumption rate that is equal to the life annuity payout is at its lowest with a well-diversified portfolio." In particular, based on the Canadian mortality and capital markets data they used, they found that for a 65-year-old female the lowest probability of ruin occurs with an 80% stock/20% bond portfolio mix and for a 65-year-old male it is a 60% stock/40% bond mix.

Research continues regarding optimal investment strategy to minimize the probability of lifetime ruin. The goal is to determine the optimal investment strategy of an individual who targets a scheduled pattern of consumption and seeks to invest his or her finite wealth in a risky financial market in such a way as to minimize the probability of outliving that wealth. The importance of optimization is immense, as an American Council of Life Insurers report "found that seventy-one percent of the women and sixty percent of the men surveyed are concerned that it will be difficult to make their retirement savings last a lifetime."[15] *Optimization* is a branch of applied mathematical analysis that deals with techniques for finding extremal values of a function.

One researcher[16] approaches the problem by considering wealth w at time t as a function of a riskless bond, a risky stock account, income, and consumption. The research finds the minimum probability of ruin $\psi(w)$ if the optimal investment rule $\pi(w)$ telling how much to invest in the risky asset is followed. Results include the distribution of lifetime ruin given that ruin occurs and the distribution of wealth at time of death (i.e., bequest) given that ruin does not occur. A maximum consumption rate to target a given probability of lifetime ruin can be determined.

While risk theory generally defines *ruin* as wealth of zero, ruin can equally be defined as wealth falling below a specific level ($w_\alpha > 0$) before the individual dies, since one could feel ruined or impoverished before wealth hits zero. Thus, $\psi(w_\alpha) = 1$. At the other end of the spectrum, once an individual's wealth rises to a sufficiently high level, wealth can be totally invested in a riskless asset and still generate interest earnings that meet or exceed the targeted consumption level, at which point $\psi(w) = 0$.

This research is evolving, and future refinements will include annuities in the set of investments, a force of mortality that is allowed to vary with time, and more realistic models of stock- and bond-price processes. This early research offers the advantage of being amenable to analytical solutions. Relaxing some less realistic assumptions to better conform to real-world experience may offer optimal investment strategies that are only numerically obtainable.

The early research[17] provides (or confirms already known) insights into optimal investment strategy. For an individual who consumes at a constant (real) dollar rate (as opposed to, say, consuming a constant proportion of wealth), these insights hold:

- As wealth increases, the amount in the risky asset decreases to zero (since at some point interest on a riskless asset is sufficient to meet consumption).
- The higher the mortality rate, the lower the probability of lifetime ruin (since the probability of dying before exhausting wealth increases— implying that women with their lower mortality rates are more likely to experience ruin than men even if women invest optimally).
- The higher the volatility, the greater the probability of lifetime ruin (since more volatility increases the chance of falling short of investment goals).
- The greater the expected return of the risky asset over a riskless one, the lower the probability of ruin.
- The greater the consumption rate, the higher the probability of ruin.
- The higher the income from a job, pension, or Social Security, the lower the probability of ruin.
- The higher the mortality rate, the less should be invested in the risky asset (since an individual more likely to die need not invest as aggressively to sustain a given consumption rate as one with a longer expected time horizon).
- The higher the volatility, the less should be invested in the risky asset (since higher volatility increases the chance of wealth falling to the ruin level).
- The higher the consumption, the greater the amount that needs to be invested in the risky asset to sustain that consumption.
- The higher the income from a job, pension, or Social Security, the lower the amount that needs to be invested in the risky asset (since the income replaces part of the earnings the risky asset had to generate to sustain consumption).

CHAPTER 8

Rate of Return

Thrift is a wonderful virtue, especially in an ancestor.

−Anonymous

DEFINITION

Rate of return is defined as that single interest rate i that, if earned uniformly over an entire n-year period, would equate a single premium P with a series of annuity benefits B_k made at time k, where k equals $0, 1, 2, \ldots, n$. Thus, we can set up an *equation of value*.[1]

$$P = B_0 + \frac{B_1}{(1+i)} + \frac{B_2}{(1+i)^2} + \cdots + \frac{B_n}{(1+i)^n}$$

If we define the symbol v as $1/(1 + i)$, where the *discount factor* v "discounts" the value of a payment at the end of a year to its value at the beginning of the year, the *equation of value* becomes

$$P = B_0 + B_1 v + B_2 v^2 + \cdots + B_n v^n$$

Thus, if all annuity benefit payments are discounted at the rate of return, their present value will equal the premium. Equivalently, if the premium is accumulated at the rate of return and all annuity benefit payments are accumulated at the rate of return, both accumulated values will be identical at the end of the program.

When it comes to immediate variable annuities (IVAs), although rate of return is important, the more important thing is to ensure oneself of lifetime income.

EARLY DEATHS AND LATE DEATHS

On entry into the immediate variable annuity program, every annuitant has equal present value (PV) and equal protective value; that is, all are entitled to receive lifetime income. There is no way to know who will live to very advanced ages—and as a consequence receive a higher rate of return than could otherwise have been had with only their own assets—and who will die early into the program—and as a consequence receive a lower rate of return than could otherwise have been had with only their own assets.[2]

The more important fact is that by entering into the program, all members have gained the peace of mind and assurance that they can count on a lifetime income. Absent such entry, they risk surviving longer than their assets will support them. To not enter into the program is tantamount to saying, "I'd rather take the risk of self-financing my retirement income, living too long, and being destitute in my old age than take the risk of buying insurance, dying early, and receiving a lower rate of return on my assets than I could have had if I had been willing to go broke."

For those annuitants who would be devastated if they only received annuity benefits for a short period and then died, they can elect annuity options that provide any of multiple forms of additional guarantees. These can include various levels of refunds to beneficiaries in a lump sum, a continuing series of benefit payments to beneficiaries, or a continuing series of benefit payments to a joint annuitant.

Yet, as we'll see, an immediate annuity is designed to be "spent"; that is, it is an inefficient "wealth transfer" vehicle. Thus, one should not feel compelled to elect an annuity payout option with a high refund element or long guaranteed payout period—and accept the commensurately lower retirement income—in order to increase the probability that some of the immediate annuity value gets transferred to beneficiaries. Other nonannuity assets of the retiree are better suited for that purpose—individual stocks where the beneficiary receives a stepped-up cost basis at death of the annuitant, life insurance, and so on.

There is a common misconception about what happens to the money of those annuitants who die shortly after entry into an immediate variable annuity program: that this money then "belongs" to the insurance company. The reality is that the reserve released by those who die either early or late in the program is reallocated to provide annuity benefits to annuitants who continue to survive. Essentially, the "forfeitures" of those who die early allow annuity benefits to be made to those annuitants who survive longer—including surviving to periods longer than those for which their own retirement savings would have sustained them absent the program.

Indeed, if actual mortality experience matches up exactly with the mortality assumptions made by the insurer when determining the annuity benefits to pay, the insurer will experience neither a gain nor a loss attributable to mortality because 100% of forfeitures—the reserves released by deceased annuitants—will fund benefit payments to surviving annuitants. Quite simply, the living inherit exactly the assets of the deceased.

In such an instance where actual mortality experience matches up exactly with the mortality assumptions, the insurer would profit only by any revenue it received to administer the program over the expenses it incurred to manage it. Investment results—good or bad—are passed through to annuitants in the way of higher or lower annuity benefits.

Of course, the insurer offering the program is ultimately responsible for honoring its guarantees to annuitants. If the annuitant pool survives longer than expected, the insurer must periodically chip in additional funds. If the annuitant pool survives shorter than expected, the insurer will reap a mortality gain.

Valuations of an insurer's immediate annuity liabilities are performed at least annually. Monthly valuations are common. "Mortality adjustments" are made to ensure that the annuity assets held in a separate account are exactly adequate to provide for the annuity reserve liabilities. This "truing up" process ensures ongoing attention to the program and ensures that any shortfalls are made up immediately, not waiting until the end of the program where the fund would appear inadequate to support payments to the final few annuitants.

Of course, actual mortality experience and expected mortality experience will not be identical in all years, even if the mortality assumptions are quite good. Some random fluctuations will occur, likely resulting in some years of "mortality gains" and some years of "mortality losses."

ANNUILAND EXAMPLE

For a healthy person with a family history of longevity, an immediate variable annuity can be a good investment even if the person is sufficiently wealthy that he or she doesn't need longevity insurance. In the Annuiland example in Chapter 6, the longest survivor realized an 18% annual rate of return on his $100,000 deposit—even though the underlying investments only returned 5% year in and year out (see Table 8.1).

Said another way, an investor outside an annuity would have to realize an 18% rate of return year in and year out to generate the same 10 payments of $21,946.52. This is because the weighted average effect of survivorship credits was to add 13% to the 5% investment earnings.[3]

The large percentage losses for the annuitants who died after one, two, or three years could be avoided by electing some form of additional

TABLE 8.1 Annuiland Rates of Return—
Life Only Annuity

Number of Annual Payments	Rate of Return
1	−78%
2	−41
3	−18
4	−5
5	3
6	8
7	12
8	15
9	16
10	18

guarantees. For example, if a "life with 5 years certain" annuity option were elected by all 10 Annuilanders, the annual benefit would be $18,586.59, and the rates of return would be as shown in Table 8.2.

The "life only" annuity safeguarded against longevity risk and provided the maximum periodic benefit payments. The layering on of additional guarantees—which may have produced increased psychological comfort with the purchase decision—served to reduce the periodic benefit payments.

TABLE 8.2 Annuiland Rates of Return—
Life with Five Years Certain Annuity

Number of Annual Payments	Rate of Return
1	−2.4%
2	−2.4
3	−2.4
4	−2.4
5	−2.4
6	3.2
7	7.0
8	9.8
9	11.7
10	13.2

Taken to the extreme, all 10 Annuilanders could have elected a 10-year fixed-period annuity that paid 10 annual payments regardless of survival or nonsurvival. The first benefit for their $100,000 premium would have been $12,950.46. Again assuming subaccount performance perpetually equal to the 5% assumed investment rate (AIR), the next nine benefits would be of the same amount. Each annuitant (in combination with his or her beneficiary) would have experienced exactly a 5% rate of return. The $12,950.46 benefit level is less than that of any annuity option involving some life-contingent element, that is, requiring survival to qualify for one or more payments.

A "life only" option with an annual $21,946.52 benefit offers the highest payment, and a "10-year fixed-period" option with an annual $12,950.46 benefit offers the lowest payment. Life-contingent options with some level of additional guarantees (e.g., life with five years certain, unit refund) fall in between.

RATE OF RETURN EXAMPLE
USING REALISTIC MORTALITY RATES

The results in the Annuiland example are fairly dramatic because of the high hypothetical mortality rates—and therefore high survivorship credits—that we assigned to these very advanced ages. Yet if we look at an example using a reasonable set of assumptions,[4] we see that a similar effect exists. For example, for a 70-year-old male with a $100,000 premium electing an annual life only annuity with a benefit of $10,288.02 at the end of each year, the rates of return shown in Table 8.3 result. These illustrate the beneficial investment opportunity for extra-healthy lives. For example, if our age-70 annuitant survives to receive 25 annual benefit payments, he will realize a rate of return of 9.1% on his $100,000 premium, even though the investments returned only 5% year in and year out. Again, this shows that healthy (or lucky!) individuals may choose to purchase an immediate variable annuity strictly for its investment value, even if they are sufficiently wealthy so as not to need longevity insurance against outliving their wealth. In this example, the investor buoyed his annual rate of return by 4.1% over what would have been achieved by investing the same $100,000 in the same funds outside of the annuity.

(If the annuitant were related to Methuselah and lived forever and received an annual benefit of $10,288.02 *in perpetuity*, his rate of return on his $100,000 would be 10.288%. It would be as though he were receiving 10.288% interest on his $100,000 forever. This is why the rates of return in this example asymptotically approach 10.288% [see Figure 8.1].)

TABLE 8.3   Rate of Return—Life Only Annuity (70-year-old male)

Age	Number of Payments	Rate of Return	Age	Number of Payments	Rate of Return
70	1	−89.7%	93	24	9.0%
71	2	−62.4	94	25	9.1
72	3	−41.7	95	26	9.3
73	4	−28.0	96	27	9.4
74	5	−18.7	97	28	9.5
75	6	−12.3	98	29	9.6
76	7	−7.6	99	30	9.6
77	8	−4.1	100	31	9.7
78	9	−1.5	101	32	9.8
79	10	0.5	102	33	9.8
80	11	2.1	103	34	9.9
81	12	3.4	104	35	9.9
82	13	4.4	105	36	9.9
83	14	5.3	106	37	10.0
84	15	6.0	107	38	10.0
85	16	6.6	108	39	10.0
86	17	7.1	109	40	10.1
87	18	7.5	110	41	10.1
88	19	7.8	111	42	10.1
89	20	8.1	112	43	10.1
90	21	8.4	113	44	10.1
91	22	8.6	114	45	10.2
92	23	8.8	115	46	10.2

Assumptions:
• 5% AIR
• 5% Actual investment return
• Annuity 2000 Basic Table
• $100,000 premium
• $10,288.02 annual benefit (EOY)

One of the key criticisms by immediate variable annuity naysayers is that it is not a good investment choice if you happen to die fairly soon after purchase. The point is that it is an insurance program against living too long and outliving one's financial resources; an IVA is first and foremost an insurance instrument that happens to contain investment elements. Those who don't survive to a "normal" age don't need to make use of this longevity insurance; those who survive longer than average do.

One might question whether these naysayers also contend that life insurance isn't ever a good buy because you might live to age 100 and

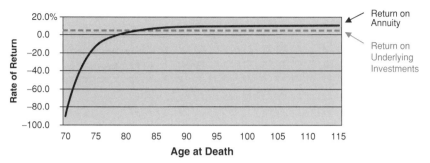

FIGURE 8.1   Rate of Return—Life Only Annuity (70-year-old male)
Assumptions:
- 5% AIR
- 5% Actual investment return
- Annuity 2000 Basic Table
- $100,000 premium
- $10,288.02 annual benefit (EOY)

thus wouldn't be getting a bargain by paying only a few life insurance premiums and then having your beneficiaries "enjoy" a quick claim! At younger ages, the greatest threat to family financial stability is premature death, a risk for which financial protection is achieved via *life* insurance. At older ages, the greatest threat to family financial stability is longevity, a risk for which financial protection is achieved via *living* insurance.

ANNUITY PRESENT VALUE DISTRIBUTIONS

One final way of viewing the preceding case of the 70-year-old male annuitant with a $100,000 premium electing a life only annuity with a 5% AIR where actual investment experience is also 5% is this: The present value (discounted at 5% interest but not discounted for survivorship) of the annuity benefits actually received is as shown in Table 8.4.

Graphically, the distribution of present values plotted against the percentage of annuitants receiving them is represented by the curve in Figure 8.2.

As would be expected, if we multiply the "PV of Annuity" by the "Percentage of Annuitants" surviving exactly long enough to receive the number of annuity payments associated with that present value for all data points and sum them, the result is $100,000, which is the premium. Although some annuitants die early and receive a present value of annuity payments less than their premium and some die late and receive a present

TABLE 8.4 Present Value of Annuity Benefits Received—Life Only Annuity (70-year-old male)

Age	Number of Payments	PV at 5%	Age	Number of Payments	PV at 5%
70	1	$ 9,798.11	93	24	$141,960.65
71	2	19,129.64	94	25	144,998.73
72	3	28,016.82	95	26	147,892.14
73	4	36,480.80	96	27	150,647.77
74	5	44,541.73	97	28	153,272.18
75	6	52,218.80	98	29	155,771.61
76	7	59,530.30	99	30	158,152.03
77	8	66,493.64	100	31	160,419.09
78	9	73,125.39	101	32	162,578.20
79	10	79,441.34	102	33	164,634.49
80	11	85,456.53	103	34	166,592.86
81	12	91,185.28	104	35	168,457.98
82	13	96,641.23	105	36	170,234.28
83	14	101,837.38	106	37	171,926.00
84	15	106,786.09	107	38	173,537.16
85	16	111,499.15	108	39	175,071.59
86	17	115,987.78	109	40	176,532.96
87	18	120,262.66	110	41	177,924.74
88	19	124,333.98	111	42	179,250.24
89	20	128,211.42	112	43	180,512.63
90	21	131,904.23	113	44	181,714.90
91	22	135,421.19	114	45	182,859.92
92	23	138,770.67	115	*	*

*Since payments are at end of year, no one remains alive at end of year 115 to receive payment.

value of annuity payments more than their premium, it is precisely the case that the *average* of the present values as weighted by the percentage of annuitants receiving each equals the premium.

(*Note:* "Premium" used here is the "net premium," which is the gross premium less premium tax, DAC tax [described in Chapter 10], and any front-end loads built into the conversion factors to cover acquisition expenses such as sales commissions and policy issue.)

Stated in statistical terms, the graph in Figure 8.2 shows the distribution of present values of annuity payments. The mean of the distribution is $100,000.

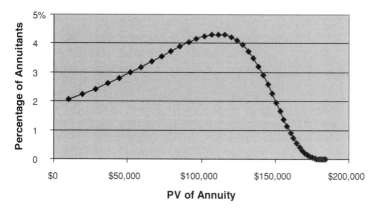

FIGURE 8.2   Distribution of Present Value of Life Annuity (male age 70)

(*Note:* "Present value" often denotes a series of payments discounted for interest. "Actuarial present value" often denotes a series of payments discounted for interest and survivorship. In this instance, annuity benefits stop when the annuitant is no longer surviving and therefore reflect survivorship. They are discounted for interest at 5%. As a result, the mean of $100,000 is also called the actuarial present value.)

Figure 8.2 pertains to the distribution of life annuity present values for a male age 70. Similar graphs for male age 50 and male age 90 appear in Figures 8.3 and 8.4, respectively. Note that Figures 8.2, 8.3, and 8.4 reflect different scales on both the horizontal and vertical axes. As expected, the younger age-50 annuitants have a distribution that shifts to the right of the age-70 annuitants because fewer die sooner with relatively smaller present values and more die later with relatively larger present values. For male age 90, the distribution shifts to the left as more annuitants die early with relatively smaller present values and fewer die later with relatively larger present values.

Additional information can be gleaned from the distribution of annuity present values graphed in Figures 8.2, 8.3, and 8.4. The *standard deviation* of the present value distribution is measurable. The *coefficient of dispersion*, which is the standard deviation divided by the mean, is measurable. The coefficient of dispersion is a numerical indicator of whether the underlying present value distribution is spread out or highly concentrated.

Another measure of the distribution of annuity present values is a form of *confidence interval*.[5] For example, to construct a 90% confidence interval, determine the present value excluding the lowest 5% of observed pres-

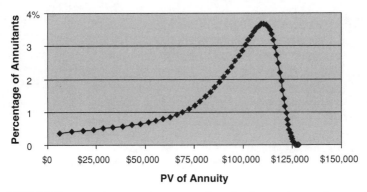

FIGURE 8.3 Distribution of Present Value of Life Annuity (male age 50)

ent values, then divide by the mean to express as a percentage. Next, determine the present value excluding the highest 5% of observed present values, and divide by the mean.

Consequently, we know that the present value of annuity payments for any individual lies between the low point and the high point of the confidence interval with 90% probability. The same approach can be used to derive any other confidence interval, for example, 75%.

In the mathematical field of statistics, "confidence interval" has a precise meaning from which the preceding approach deviates. To a statistician,

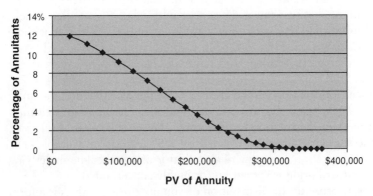

FIGURE 8.4 Distribution of Present Value of Life Annuity (male age 90)

the confidence interval tends to be an interval on the real number line within which a population parameter resides with given probability. The confidence intervals in the examples given here instead describe the range within which the annuity present value for one individual resides with a specific probability. The population parameters are *assumed,* and we seek to quantify the variation in a resultant measure—the ensuing annuity present values experienced by individual samples from the annuitant population.

Figure 8.5 compares the distributions of present values of an annual life annuity-immediate of $1 to males aged 50, 70, and 90 using the Annuity 2000 Basic Table and a 5% AIR, where the AIR is exactly achieved in real-world experience. Note that the distribution of annuity present values spreads out with increasing contract issue age; that is, at age 50 the distribution is more peaked—with a large number of data points near the peak—than occurs for age 70 or age 90. Coefficients of dispersion increase and 90% confidence intervals expand with increasing issue age. At high issue ages, there is less confidence that the mean provides a good estimate of the annuity present value because there is so much variation.

The distribution of present values for males of a given age tends to be more spread out than for females of the same age. In general, higher mor-

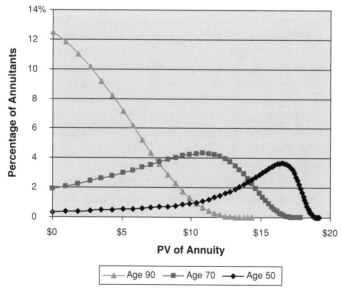

FIGURE 8.5 Distribution of Present Value of Life Annuity

tality subgroups (e.g., males relative to females, older people relative to younger) have broader dispersion of present values.

The distributions of annuity present values for a $1 annual life annuity-immediate to a male age 50 at various interest rates appear in Figure 8.6. These equally well represent immediate fixed annuities based on the three interest rates shown and immediate variable annuities where the three values represent the AIRs and the AIRs are exactly achieved in real-world experience.

The distribution of annuity present values is broader at lower interest rates and more compressed into a narrower distribution at higher interest rates. At progressively higher interest rates, the effect on the present value of living longer is reduced by the greater discount applied to future payments. Because the distribution of annuity present values is increasingly compressed into an ever-narrower spike at progressively higher interest rates—as measured by confidence intervals or coefficients of dispersion—one has significantly more confidence in statements regarding annuity present value.

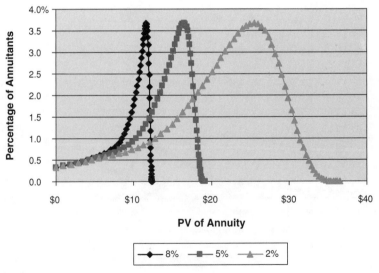

FIGURE 8.6 Distribution of Present Value of Life Annuity (male age 50)

ANNUITY PRESENT VALUE APPRAISALS

While most often a best *single-point* estimate of annuity present values—the mean of the distribution—is of interest, there are occasions where *variation* is of interest. For example, in a divorce settlement (known in actuarial evidence cases by the legal terminology "dissolution of marriage"), as assets are valued, the attorney for one party may wish to contend that a smaller present value than the mean of the distribution should be assigned to a life-contingent annuity asset (e.g., due to impaired health), whereas the attorney for the other party may wish to contend that a present value larger than the mean should be used.

While each case is decided independently, the argument is sometimes made that the actuarial present value (the mean of the distribution) applies to a *pool* of annuitants (some in better health, some in worse health) and that it can only be known in hindsight following death what the present value of *any one individual* is at time of marital dissolution, and therefore the mean of the distribution is the best single-point estimate of annuity present value and should be assigned to the asset. While one solution is simply to split all future annuity payments into two specified portions,[6] there is often a desire for the parties to have final resolution at time of marital dissolution rather than to continue to share ownership of certain assets; that is, total assets are valued and apportioned, with the annuity asset generally residing with a single owner.

Actuaries are sometimes engaged to provide expert testimony in appraising the right to future pension payments in divorce litigation, just as others appraise such community (marital) assets as a home or a family business. Some contend that the appraisal is designed to assign one reasonable present value to the asset rather than to try to predict which of the many present values across the distribution spectrum might be the one that will apply to one particular individual.

One divorce actuary[7] offers the following analogy to lawyers and judges to convey a distinction between appraisal and prediction: Marital assets include one ticket entitling the bearer to a single coin toss. If heads, the bearer receives $100,000. If tails, the bearer receives nothing. The mathematical expectation is $50,000, which most lawyers and judges find to be the fair market value of this asset. Suppose 1,000 appraisals of this kind are performed, and actual payouts are matched against the $50,000 appraisal. In all 1,000 cases, the actual payout differs from the appraised value by $50,000, since the only possible results are zero and $100,000. Does this infer all 1,000 appraisals are wrong because none of them predicted the correct payout?

The paradox may be resolved by pointing out that the accuracy of any single appraisal is entirely independent of whether it is borne out by that ticket bearer's experience. The extension to a pension appraisal in divorce litigation is the proposition that such a valuation based on mathematical expectation rather than on prediction cannot be measured by any single person's experience. While measuring means and variability of annuity present value distributions is appropriate for running a solvent immediate annuity program—where these parameters may be used for pricing, reserving, and surplus formula factor setting—at least one author contends that courts are best served when given a single figure, the actuarial present value, in marital dissolution litigation.

If one party to the divorce receives $50,000 in cash as a compensating asset while the other receives the ticket, it becomes clearer that perhaps more than the expected value of an asset matters in division of assets in a divorce. Risk related to the assets matters. Because the approach of giving one party $50,000 in cash and the other party the ticket guarantees a loser in every case, King Solomon might suggest each party share equal interest in the ticket; however, as previously mentioned, the parties often desire to avoid any future shared ownership.

Expected value receives much attention, while variation receives less. While different viewpoints may exist on how to value and divide assets— including future income streams that may depend on continuing survival— the divorce example is a useful illustration of considering variability of possible returns as well as the expected return. One noteworthy distinction in this example is that a pension was already in place, whereas a candidate considering voluntary purchase of an IVA is procuring longevity insurance that may not otherwise be in place or may be needed as a supplement. Thus, regardless of the variability of return that is dependent on how long the annuitant lives, transfer of the risk of outliving one's assets is achieved.

Variability of annuity present values is also of interest in establishing statutory reserves and risk-based capital (RBC) requirements. The aforementioned approach and measurement tools can be part of the collection of techniques for testing adequacy of reserves and RBC to withstand random fluctuations.

BENEFIT OF INVESTMENT VERSUS BENEFIT OF SURVIVORSHIP

Recall the example in Chapter 6 of a 20-year endowment where each member of a group of 65-year-olds pays a premium of $199.75, which grows at 5% annually. The survivors at age 85 share the fund equally, with each receiving $1,000.00. The *benefit of interest* alone grew each original member's share to $530.00. The *benefit of survivorship*—the paying of a benefit only to those who survived the 20-year period—produced the remainder of the growth to $1,000.00.

If we look at the benefit of survivorship for various one-year periods, from age x to age $x + 1$, we see how the benefit of survivorship increases with age. For example, the benefit of survivorship for a male age 65 using the Annuity 2000 Mortality Table is $l_{65}/l_{66} = 1/p_{65}$, or 1.01. Whatever investment subaccount rate of return is achieved is effectively supplemented by another 1% simply due to surviving the year. Note the term "effectively." It is still the case that benefits increase or decrease only by net investment performance above or below the AIR. The benefit of survivorship was already factored into the process when the projected series of benefits was discounted at the AIR at contract inception to arrive at the number of annuity units payable per period.

The point, however, is that, at advanced ages, the benefit of survivorship is generally much richer than the benefit of investment when viewing a variable income annuity as a series of endowments. For example, at male age 95, the benefit of survivorship is l_{96}/l_{95}, or 1.1936; that is, a 95-year-old electing an IVA would experience a 19.36% rate of return merely by surviving the year and being entitled to forfeitures from those who don't. At these advanced ages, the rate of return impact attributable to surviving the year generally exceeds the rate of return impact attributable to investment performance.

While early years contribute comparatively less to the benefit of survivorship and later years contribute comparatively more, the composite benefit can be determined. For instance, in the earlier example of a 70-year-old who purchases a lifetime annuity with $100,000 that experiences a uniform 5% rate of investment return, his composite return should he live to age 93 is 9%. The benefit of survivorship effectively served to add 4% annually to the 5% benefit of investment.

Another conceptual way to contrast benefit of investment with benefit of survivorship is this: Consider an investment fund to which three 65-year-olds each contribute an identical amount up front with no further contributions. A level annual withdrawal amount is set at a magnitude that will sustain payments to each of the three participants for 19 years—that is, with benefit of investment only—at which point the fund is exhausted. See Figure 8.7.

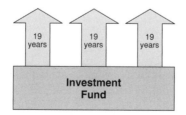

FIGURE 8.7   Benefit of Investment

Now, on the investment fund is overlaid an annuity structure that partitions payments emanating from an initial investment identical in size to that in Figure 8.7 in a precise way so as to offer a longer income stream exactly to those who need income longer. For example, suppose the three 65-year-olds survive 10, 20, and 30 years, respectively. The annuity overlay effectively serves as a "membrane" that "filters" payments from the investment fund so as to ensure that payments continue for the whole of life (see Figure 8.8). Equivalently stated, the annuity overlay serves to convert a program based on benefit of investment to a program based on benefit of investment and survivorship.

Note that in Figure 8.7 benefits were set at a level so as to be payable for 19 years. Suppose that for our three participants q_{75} is ⅓, q_{85} is ½, and q_{95} is 1 and all other q_x values are zero, resulting in one participant surviving 10 years, one 20 years, and one 30 years. Life expectancy, e_{65}, equals 20 years. We learned earlier that for any positive rate of return, the present value of an annuity for a fixed period equal to life expectancy exceeds the present value of an annuity payable for life. Thus, the same premium funds higher benefits for a lifetime annuity than it does for a fixed-period annuity equal in length to life expectancy. This point is illustrated in Figure 8.8.

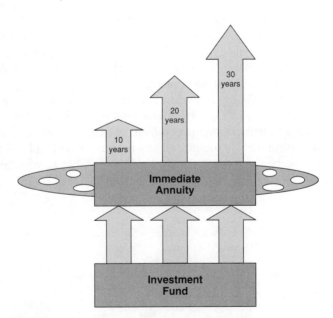

FIGURE 8.8   Benefit of Investment and Benefit of Survivorship

The premium P is sufficient to provide life-contingent benefits to the three participants who on average survive $1/3 \times (10 + 20 + 30)$, or 20 years. The same premium P would therefore be insufficient to provide non-life-contingent benefits of equivalent size for their 20-year life expectancies; as a result, it only funds benefits of identical amount for 19 years.

The annuity overlay that combines the benefit of survivorship with the benefit of investment partitions the fund proceeds in an equitable, fully pre-scribed manner that maximizes income to annuitants while ensuring the fund remains adequate to sustain the longest-surviving annuitant.

Because a variable income annuity can be viewed as a series of endow-ments—to which both benefit of investment and benefit of survivorship apply—the question of whether one finds the concept of a variable income annuity psychologically appealing or unappealing boils down to the answers to this series of questions:

- Would you be willing to deposit into a particular investment fund the same sum of money as 100 people your age and gender do, where the fund balance 10 years from now would be equally divided among the survivors?
- Would you be willing to participate in a second program, again deposit-ing into a particular investment fund the same sum of money as 100 people your age and gender do, where the fund balance 15 years from now would be equally divided among the survivors? (The sum of money to participate in this program is smaller than for the 10-year program.)
- Would you be willing to make that deposit for 20 years?
- Would you be willing to participate in one consolidated program in which you deposit a single sum of money equal to that for a collection of programs, like those described in the preceding three questions, that spans every year into the future from your current age to age 115?

If the answer to the last question is "yes," the person is psychologically predisposed to buying into the concept of mortality risk pooling and is a variable income annuity prospect. If the answer to the last question is "no," the person is opposed to the mortality risk pooling concept and is—at least unless persuaded to the contrary—not a variable income annuity prospect.

To see a variable income annuity as a series of endowments, consider a 65-year-old female who wishes to receive the value of 1 annuity unit at the beginning of each year for the rest of her life. Assuming a 4% AIR and using the Annuity 2000 Basic Mortality Table, we note that $\ddot{a}_{65}$ equals 14.617. Table 8.5 breaks this total single premium into its component annual endowments.

TABLE 8.5 Annual Life Annuity-Due for 65-Year-Old Female ($\ddot{a}_{65}$) Decomposed into Component Endowments

Year n	Age	$_nE_{65}$	Year n	Age	$_nE_{65}$	Year n	Age	$_nE_{65}$
0	65	1.000	17	82	0.373	34	99	0.022
1	66	0.955	18	83	0.343	35	100	0.016
2	67	0.911	19	84	0.313	36	101	0.012
3	68	0.868	20	85	0.284	37	102	0.008
4	69	0.827	21	86	0.256	38	103	0.006
5	70	0.787	22	87	0.228	39	104	0.004
6	71	0.749	23	88	0.202	40	105	0.003
7	72	0.711	24	89	0.176	41	106	0.002
8	73	0.674	25	90	0.152	42	107	0.001
9	74	0.638	26	91	0.130	43	108	0.001
10	75	0.603	27	92	0.109	44	109	0.000
11	76	0.569	28	93	0.091	45	110	0.000
12	77	0.535	29	94	0.074	46	111	0.000
13	78	0.501	30	95	0.060	47	112	0.000
14	79	0.469	31	96	0.047	48	113	0.000
15	80	0.436	32	97	0.037	49	114	0.000
16	81	0.405	33	98	0.029	50	115	0.000

Total of $_nE_{65}$ 14.617

Decomposed in this manner, the annuitant can see the portion of the single premium funding each future annuity benefit. In this way, she gains an exact sense for the nature of the program in which she's participating. For example, one can see that 56% of the premium goes to fund annuity benefits for the first 10 years, since the sum of the first 10 endowments is 8.120.

Each of the endowments includes both benefit of investment and benefit of survivorship. If the first 10 payments were guaranteed to be paid regardless of survivorship, as in a "life with 10 years certain" payout option, the first 10 payments would cost more, totaling 8.435, since these would receive no discounting for survivorship.

RATE OF RETURN METHODOLOGIES

In general (including outside the scope of immediate variable annuities), measurement of investment rates of return can be based on several asset valuation bases, such as cost, book, or market. Similarly, rates of return can be calculated using different methodologies, including dollar-weighted rate

of return and time-weighted rate of return. There is no one "right" investment return methodology. Rather, one must choose the methodology most
consistent with (or statutorily prescribed for) the application for which the
calculation is intended.

A *dollar-weighted rate of return* is calculated by considering the actual
level of assets and cash flow of the fund during the total period under observation. The dollar-weighted rate of return gives full weighting to the actual
value of assets and cash flow of the fund. It provides the actual rate of
return earned by the fund.

A *time-weighted rate of return* is calculated in a manner to eliminate the
effect of different asset levels and cash flow. It is considered a more appropriate measure of return for the purpose of comparing performance among
investment managers, since the assets under their stewardship are likely to
exhibit dissimilar starting levels and dissimilar cash flow patterns during the
period under observation. Time-weighted rates of return are almost always
used for comparison to standard indexes.

In order to ensure greater uniformity in methodology used by investment managers to calculate and report rates of return of various funds, the
Association for Investment Management and Research (AIMR) promulgated Global Investment Performance Standards (GIPS). These standards
list acceptable methods and effective dates for their required use.

Multiperiod returns should be geometrically (rather than arithmetically)
linked. For example, if a portfolio returns +10% the first year and −10%
the second year, the arithmetic average of the two years is 0%. Yet if $100
were invested at the start, there would be $100 × (1 + 0.10), or $110, at the
end of the first year and $110 × (1 − 0.10), or $99, at the end of the second
year. While the arithmetic mean return is 0%, the geometric mean return is
$[(1 + 0.10) \times (1 - 0.10)]^{1/2} - 1$, or −0.50%. Since the ending value of $99
is clearly less than the beginning value of $100, the arithmetic mean of
0% is a less reflective measure of return than the geometric mean of −0.50%.

The upshot is that since multiple rate-of-return methodologies exist,
any valid comparison must ensure that calculations are performed under a
uniform methodology.

RATE OF RETURN AND INFLATION

Rate of return should be considered relative to inflation. For example, a 7%
nominal rate of return might be comprised of 4% inflation plus a 3% real
rate of return; that is, an individual with $100 today could purchase
$100 worth of goods and services today. Alternatively, this individual
could invest at 7% and have $107 one year from now with which he could

> *The arithmetic makes it plain that inflation is a far more devastating tax than anything that has been enacted by our legislature. The inflation tax has a fantastic ability to simply consume capital. It makes no difference to a widow with her savings in a 5% passbook account whether she pays 100% income tax on her interest income during a period of zero inflation, or pays no income taxes during the years of 5% inflation. Either way, she is "taxed" in a manner that leaves her no real income whatsoever.*
> —*Warren Buffett*, Fortune, *May 5, 1977*

purchase equivalent goods and services then costing $104. Thus, the 7% return is meaningful only in the context of its relation to the inflation rate.

Recall that an objective of a variable income annuity is to provide income that helps keep pace with inflation. While variable income annuity benefits will not move in lockstep with inflation, they at least provide an opportunity to help cope with inflationary effects that is absent in fixed annuities or pensions that pay the same dollar amount of benefit in all years.

As one's perspective on inflation is often colored by its levels of the past few years while its effects on retirement income may span decades, it is helpful to view a graphic illustration of inflation rates over the past few decades, as in Figure 8.9. The graph is constructed from the Consumer Price Index (CPI) for All Urban Consumers: All Items, seasonally adjusted, published by the U.S. Department of Labor, Bureau of Labor Statistics. It reflects the year-over-year change in the CPI using January 1 values. While

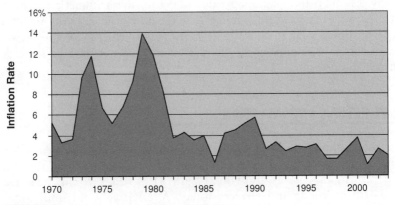

FIGURE 8.9 U.S. Annual Inflation 1970–2003

not a perfect representation of every individual's situation, it shows the relative change in price of a market basket of goods and services.

Importantly, the graph illustrates that rates of inflation are not uniform[8] and that there can be periods of extreme inflation, which have a meaningfully corrosive effect on a fixed level of income. While governmental monetary and fiscal policies may attempt to control inflation, it remains a risk for individuals with a potentially multidecade retirement horizon.

DEFLATION

Americans who lived during the Great Depression need little reminder that *deflation* (falling prices) has also occurred. In the early stages of falling prices, people with fixed incomes from fixed annuities find their lot improving. Their incomes are stable in dollars, and dollars will buy more.

People with variable incomes from variable annuities will find that their income tied to bond subaccounts increases because bonds rise in price in the early stages of deflation because they promise fixed income in dollars, which are growing more valuable. Variable annuitants will find their income tied to stock subaccounts sliding downhill because stocks represent partial ownership of business, and business is becoming less profitable as prices fall.

No one escapes the collapsing effects of *extreme* deflation. Wages and salaries are cut as businesses try to reduce expenses to adapt to falling income. Unemployment spreads. Production falls off with declining demand. Individuals and businesses become unable to meet payments on their debt. Bond and mortgage defaults mushroom. Common stock prices shrivel. Government revenues shrink as income and sales taxes fall off as business volume falls off. Land owners cannot pay real estate taxes, reducing government revenue further exactly when government expenses are rising as men and women require public assistance. If the deflation proceeds far enough, even government bonds are not safe from the extreme consequences of price collapse.

Inflation, too, creates its own set of challenges. As dollars buy less and less, people begin to favor tangible commodities—land, houses, gold—over paper assets, relying on physical goods rather than money to be their store of value. People are buying things and inflating prices, but wages and salaries do not rise as fast, the result being that workers grow poorer by the day. In the fixed-income investment markets, bonds and mortgages are heavily discounted, since people are less eager to agree to receive a fixed sum of money at a future time when that money will likely be of much less value. Lenders may foreclose, preferring property to their mortgages. Retirees receiving fixed incomes—through pensions or immediate fixed annuities—find that their money does not go very far. While inflation—especially extreme inflation—carries perils, inflation—and, in particular, mild inflation—is vastly preferred to the harsh consequences of a genuinely thorough deflation. As a result, economic policy makers are vigilant in guarding against delation.

There is no bomb-proof shelter that protects retirees from every economic scenario. Recent history suggests inflation to be a greater threat to retirees than deflation. Variable income annuities provide an opportunity superior to fixed income annuities for rates of return that help annuitants cope with the economic threat perceived to be more likely during their retirement horizon: inflation.

RATE OF RETURN AND TAXES

After-tax returns are what matter, since individuals only get to spend income net of taxes. As a result, any true comparison of alternative retirement income vehicles should be performed on an after-tax basis.

As described in Chapter 10 on annuity taxation, income derived from variable income annuities is currently taxed in the United States at ordinary income rates. This is true for IVAs in both tax-qualified and non-tax-qualified markets. Because of the welfare-enhancing benefits of immediate annuities—since they will keep some individuals from running out of money that otherwise would have—there is a movement toward encouraging the use of IVAs through tax incentives, which could change (improve) IVA taxation.

Certain conventional, non-mortality-contingent assets are currently taxed at lower rates. For example, long-term capital gains and dividends on common stock are currently taxed at rates below the ordinary income tax rate. Any retirement income comparisons using such assets need to account for the degree to which an individual might expect entitlement to such lower tax rates. For example, a stock mutual fund with high annual portfolio turnover rates may produce relatively more short-term capital gains taxed at ordinary income rates than long-term capital gains taxed at lower rates.

Each individual's tax situation differs. For example, different federal income tax brackets and different state and local income tax rates can make two identical IVA purchases produce different after-tax income.

Any comparison of a mortality-contingent asset, like an IVA, with a non-mortality-contingent asset, like a stock mutual fund, needs to recognize not only the *investment* element but also the *protection* element. A lower tax rate on a portion of a stock mutual fund may be a poor trade-off if longevity is such as to cause destitution at some point that could have been averted with a mortality-contingent asset.

CHAPTER 9

Reserves and Risk-Based Capital

The greatest of all gifts is the power to estimate things at their true worth.

—Francois de La Rochefoucauld

RESERVES

Insurance companies through the issuance of immediate variable annuities (IVAs) reduce risk in the economy by transferring risk from individuals, who, regardless of high intelligence or great investment knowledge, cannot safely absorb it simply because they can't know how long they'll live, to an insurance company facilitating a program for a large annuitant pool, where the aggregated nature increases predictability and makes the collective risk manageable. This is the quintessence of an immediate variable annuity company. Such a company, like any business, has a financial structure. This includes a balance sheet like the simplified one shown in Figure 9.1.

A *balance sheet* is a statement of assets (what the insurer owns), liabilities (what the insurer owes), and net worth (the difference). The largest liability for an insurer is its policy reserves.

Reserves are that pot of assets necessary to have on hand at any time so that, together with interest thereon and future premiums, there is enough money to pay projected claims. Positive reserves are a natural consequence of annuity premium inflows to an insurance company coming earlier in time than annuity benefit (claim disbursement) outflows.

ABC LIFE INSURANCE COMPANY
Balance Sheet
December 31, 2010

Assets		Liabilities	
Cash	1,000,000	Net Policy Reserves	105,000,000
Bonds	50,000,000	Policy Claims	2,000,000
Stocks	5,000,000	Taxes and Expenses	2,000,000
Mortgage Loans	50,000,000	Other Liabilities	1,000,000
Real Estate	5,000,000		
Policy Loans	10,000,000	Total Liabilities	110,000,000
Premiums Receivable	2,000,000		
Investment Interest			
Accrued	1,000,000	**Net Worth**	
Other Assets	1,000,000		
		Capital	3,000,000
		Surplus	12,000,000
		Total Net Worth	15,000,000
		Total Liabilities	
Total Assets	125,000,000	and Net Worth	125,000,000

FIGURE 9.1   Balance Sheet for ABC Life

While general accounting practice calls "reserves" any amounts set aside to provide for future losses—such as unfavorable judgments in pending litigation—the terminology "reserve" as used here will refer to the "benefit reserve," dedicated to providing future annuity benefit payments.

People commonly speak about reserves as if they were assets rather than liabilities. This can lead to confusion. To be clear, when the statement is made that an insurer has adequate reserves to cover its claims, what is more precisely meant is that there exist assets in an amount sufficient to offset the reserve liability.

By definition, a reserve equals the present value of future benefits (PVFB) minus the present value of future premiums (PVFP): Reserve = PVFB − PVFP. For an immediate annuity, there are no future premiums since it is traditionally a single premium product, that is, PVFP equals zero. As a result, the reserve is quite simply the present value of future annuity benefit payments projected to be made. These reserves depend on the same factors used in pricing the annuity: age, sex, annuity option, mortality rates, and assumed investment rate (AIR). An immediate annuity reserve can be determined at any time t by these equations:

$$\text{Reserve}_t = \text{PVFB}_t - \text{PVFP}_t$$
$$= \text{PVFB}_t - 0$$
$$= \text{PVFB}_t$$

Different reserves may be calculated for different purposes and different audiences. First, generally accepted accounting principles (GAAP) reserves are those of interest to stockholders, who view the situation as an ongoing business enterprise and who want to see a reasonably accurate (i.e., not conservative, not liberal) calculation of the reserve liability an insurer possesses to pay claims promised under terms of annuity contracts. Thus, GAAP accounting has as a primary objective the accurate reporting of the value of the insurance enterprise on a going-concern basis for the benefit of its owners and prospective owners, so reserve liabilities are valued on more of a "best estimate" basis.

Second, statutory reserves prepared for insurance regulators are calculated with some degree of conservatism, since one of the primary objectives of statutory insurance accounting is to safeguard insurer solvency. Because future, real-world experience may deviate from mere extrapolation of historical trends, statutorily determined reserves are defined conservatively to enhance the likelihood of achieving their solvency protection function. An insurer must hold reserves for immediate variable annuities in accordance with statutory provisions of insurance laws of each state.

Insurance companies annually file with state insurance commissioners financial statements prepared in accordance with state regulatory practices known as statutory accounting practices (SAP). Insurance company statutory financial performance information is reported by line of business, enabling examiners to determine if net income is comprised of profits in some business lines and losses in others—an important distinction given the long-term nature of annuity and insurance contracts.

Third, tax reserves are those used to determine liability for federal income tax determination purposes.

Accounting standards change over time. At the time of this writing, efforts are underway to establish internationally accepted accounting standards for insurance companies. The International Accounting Standards Board (IASB) will promulgate the standards, premised on "fair value" accounting. In the United States, the Financial Accounting Standards Board (FASB) and the Securities and Exchange Commission (SEC) set public accounting standards, which are likely to converge with international ones. U.S. GAAP accounting for life insurers today defers certain expenses (e.g., annuity product acquisition expenses spread over the life of the contract), and the reporting structure is based on matching revenues with expenses. International standards may be based on an asset/liability approach, where assets and liabilities are valued at market values. Since there is no such thing as a "market value" for insurance liabilities—because they are not actively traded in an open market—a stochastic actuarial modeled value will likely be used.

Because a finite amount of money flows into and out of the insurance company over the life of a block of business, cumulative earnings for the total period are identical under all approaches. The different sets of accounting rules rather reflect different partitioning of total earnings among reporting periods, affecting the *pattern* of earnings recognition.

Insurers are free to price and to offer immediate annuity products based on mortality assumptions more liberal than those required to calculate statutory reserves. To the extent that the net premium collected from an annuitant is then lower than the initial statutory reserve, the insurer must supply the difference.

If indeed actual mortality experience is what the insurer assumed in pricing, rather than the more conservative level assumed by statutory reserve setting, the additional funds the insurer supplied are gradually returned to the insurer's surplus account. Yet during the period these funds are tied up and unavailable for other corporate purposes, there is an opportunity cost to the insurer. The insurer in its product pricing, therefore, factors in a "rent assessment" for such use of capital.

Whereas insurers could use statutory reserve valuation mortality tables for pricing and thereby eliminate "surplus strain," this would result in uncompetitive annuity payout rates. Recall that valuation mortality is by definition conservative. Thus, insurers price by projecting annuity benefit payments based on *expected* mortality experience, discounting these at the AIR, recognizing that the resultant present value will be less than the initial required statutory reserve, and pricing in the "rent assessment" on that tied-up surplus that should be released gradually over time—since an IVA is a liquidation product and therefore its reserves on both pricing and reserving bases must converge to zero at the terminal age(s) of the mortality table(s). The progression of IVA statutory reserve values for a given contract don't uniformly (i.e., monotonically) decrease, since subaccount performance can at times increase the reserve more than annuity payments decrease it; but over the long run, clearly the reserves under the pricing and reserving bases must converge.

If large volumes of new immediate annuity business continue to be written, "surplus strain" persists. This could be a limiting factor for small-

or medium-sized insurers. There are multiple ways to address this issue, including raising additional capital (e.g., stock issuance); using less competitive payout rates, which reduce surplus strain on each such contract written; shutting off new sales; or reinsuring part of the business—existing business, future business, or both.

Mortality tables that are used to determine statutory reserves change periodically. The statutory mortality table to be applied to any specific immediate annuity generally is based on the contract issue date. The National Association of Insurance Commissioners (NAIC) adopts a new individual annuity mortality table. States then approve its use for determining the minimum standard of valuation for such contracts.

RISK-BASED CAPITAL

In addition to reserve liabilities, insurers also earmark surplus to provide additional assurance of being able to meet contractual obligations. Such allocated surplus becomes unavailable for other corporate purposes; so a product margin must be introduced to "pay rent" at a fair return on such surplus the product ties up.

Statutory reserves may be established on a basis sufficient to cover expected claims using some slightly conservative assumptions. For immediate variable annuities, this might involve mortality rates that are 10% lower than the best current information trended into the future might suggest. This has the effect of assuming annuitants will each survive longer, more annuity payments will be made, and the present value of future benefits— the reserve—is therefore higher.

When reserves and allocated surplus are collectively taken into account, the total may be adequate to cover a very high percentage (96–99%) of future scenarios that could possibly materialize. For example, unexpectedly high mortality-improvement factors resulting from a cancer cure might result in a series of annuity benefit payments that are lengthier yet still fundable from the combination of reserves and surplus. On the other hand, a genetic discovery that stops the aging process and allows annuitants (barring accidental deaths) to live hundreds of years might be an outlier scenario (less than 1% probability) that eventually would exhaust both the reserve and the surplus.

Technically, the minimum amount of surplus that an annuity company needs is the amount required to obtain and to maintain authority to operate as a life insurance company. In reality, surplus is established in relation to the insurer's obligations, where management allocates some portion of surplus to cover adverse experience, making that surplus unavailable for other corporate purposes.

"Risk-based capital" (RBC) is terminology used to allocate funds to guard against specific risks that could threaten insurer solvency. Risk-based capital is a measure of strength to withstand financial strain beyond that absorbed by reserves. Insurance companies may establish their own internal target surplus formulas. They might scientifically determine a formula that safeguards the enterprise to the desired degree. They may hold capital in excess of this amount—sometimes called "cosmetic surplus" or "redundant surplus"—if they deem it necessary or desirable to achieve specific claims-paying ratings from independent rating agencies. This may be achieved by grossing up an internally derived target surplus formula by a specific percentage to arrive at the desired capital level for ratings purposes. Such private rating agencies as A. M. Best, Fitch, Moody's, and Standard & Poor's design their own RBC formulas to evaluate insurance company capital adequacy, the end result of such a process being to assign insurers a quality rating.

Insurance supervision is primarily intended to ensure that insurers have the capacity to meet their obligations to pay claims to policyholders. Insurers are required to maintain sufficient assets to meet these obligations under a large range of—but not the totality of—possible future economic scenarios. This statutory minimum solvency requirement reduces the risk of failure.

A "fixed-ratio" model, where the amount of assets required to be held is a fixed percentage of some item from the insurer's balance sheet, is a simple approach used by some countries. In the United States, the NAIC regulatory RBC model is more refined and considers the relative degree of risks posed by different classes of insurance liabilities as well as risks posed by assets. (Note that a more refined formula does not by itself assure greater capital adequacy protective power than a coarser formula. The parameterization of the formulas and the particular mix of business lines involved play roles in addition to the granularity of the formulas.)

Traditionally, a "probability-of-ruin" approach was used to set RBC factors, where the level of capital is established so as to achieve a specific probability that assets will be greater than liabilities. This measure, however, fails to account for the *severity* of the insolvency. As a result, it is being supplanted by the more recently developed "expected policyholder deficit" (EPD) approach, which considers both probability of ruin and magnitude of deficit. The thinking is that RBC factors for different lines of insurance business, including annuities, should be set so as to equate their EPD ratios, defined as the ratio of the EPD to the liability, thereby setting the standard based on the average cost of insolvency. The EPD approach is now accepted as a basis for NAIC regulatory RBC formulas, although both probability-of-ruin and EPD approaches have their own advantages and disadvantages.

NAIC risk-based capital requirements evaluate the adequacy of statutory capital and surplus relative to investment, insurance, and business risks. The NAIC RBC formula defines the regulatory minimum amount of capital that a company must maintain to avoid regulatory action. Total adjusted capital is divided by the authorized control level of RBC—both defined by the NAIC—to arrive at the RBC ratio. Five levels of regulatory action may be triggered depending on the ratio:

1. **No Action** (RBC ratio > 200%).
2. **Company Action Level.** Insurer must submit a proposed corrective action plan to the regulator (150% ≤ RBC ratio < 200%).
3. **Regulatory Action Level.** Insurer must submit a proposed corrective action plan, although a regulator may issue a corrective order requiring compliance within a specific period (100% ≤ RBC ratio < 150%).
4. **Authorized Control Level.** Regulatory response is the same as for the regulatory action level, but the regulator may also take action to rehabilitate or liquidate the insurer (70% ≤ RBC ratio < 100%).
5. **Mandatory Control Level.** Regulator must rehabilitate or liquidate the insurer (RBC ratio < 70%).

Annuity companies typically hold some multiple of this amount of minimally required assets. Larger insurers tend to operate with a lower capital margin (the ratio of capital to assets) than smaller insurers with similar asset, liability, and business risks. This may be appropriate because larger insurers tend to exhibit more stable operating results.

The NAIC RBC ratio level provides an early warning signal to regulators regarding company solvency. A company that falls into the "No Action" level is not necessarily in strong financial condition; it merely means the company has not triggered a regulatory intervention level.

RBC formulas typically assign different weighting factors to the C1 to C5 components of risk, along with subcomponents of each category. RBC formulas also recognize the interplay (covariances) between risk components. "C" stands for "contingency," while "1" through "5" stand for the five major categories of types of contingency:

1. **C-1: Asset Depreciation.** For example, the risk that fixed-income investments will default before maturity or that common stock market values will fall.
2. **C-2: Pricing Inadequacy.** For example, the risk of actual claims experience more adverse than pricing assumptions, such as immediate annuitants surviving longer than expected.

3. **C-3: Interest Rate Risk.** For example, the risk of high fixed-deferred-annuity redemption requests due to rising interest rates and better fixed annuity crediting rates available elsewhere, forcing insurers to disinvest at market values lower than book values to raise the cash to pay surrendering contract owners (so-called "disintermediation risk"); another example is the risk of high cash inflows during low interest rate periods, where contractually guaranteed minimum crediting rates of fixed annuities exceed fixed-income investment yields (so-called "premium dump-in" risk).

4. **C-4: General Business Risk.** A catchall category that includes risk of mismanagement; lawsuits; fraud; regulatory changes; changes in tax law, including federal income tax rates; and so on.

5. **C-5: Foreign Exchange Risk.** For those insurers operating in multiple countries, the risk of exchange losses when profits are translated into the currency of the country of domicile of the headquarters or parent company.

Greater degrees of surplus are allocated the greater the claim volatility that might result in shocks to the system. Fairly low surplus factors are required for conventional immediate variable annuities because "annuitants don't live longer all at once," in staccato fashion; that is, if there is a major event affecting mortality, such as a cancer cure, this will result in greater payments than expected by the insurer over a long period of time. It is not the case that if mortality rates decline precipitously, then an unexpectedly large claim payment would need to be made instantly, the situation for which allocated surplus traditionally guards. If appropriate, reserve strengthening may be in order, under which the insurer (or state insurance commissioner) reassesses the outlook for projected immediate annuity payments and establishes additional reserves.

RESERVE LAWS AND GUIDELINES

The simplified, skeletal balance sheet shown in Figure 9.1 represents an insurer that only offers insurance and annuity products where assets are housed in its general account. For immediate variable annuities, assets in an amount at least equal to reserve liabilities are housed in a separate account.

Five selected documents provide variable annuity reserve guidance:[1]

1. **NAIC Model Variable Annuity Regulation.**[2] Article VI, Section 5, requires "the reserve liability for variable annuities shall be established

pursuant to the requirements of the Standard Valuation Law in accordance with actuarial procedures that recognize the variable nature of the benefits provided and any mortality guarantees."

2. **NAIC Model Standard Valuation Law (SVL).**[3] Section 5a generally requires use of the Commissioners' Annuity Reserve Valuation Method (CARVM), defined as the excess of the greatest present value of future guaranteed benefits provided for at the end of each contract year over the present value of any valuation considerations. (Looking only at discrete points in time, such as contract year-ends, is known as "curtate" reserve valuation; looking at all points in time, which is deemed more appropriate by some since there can be points of discontinuity immediately after a contract year-end, is known as "continuous" reserve valuation.) The CARVM can sometimes be challenging to apply due to the variable, nonguaranteed nature of benefits. The SVL applies more easily to valuation of fixed, guaranteed benefits.

3. **Actuarial Guideline XXXIII (AG33).** This represents the NAIC's interpretation of the CARVM and applies to all contracts subject to the CARVM that contain "elective benefits." AG33 requires "all guaranteed benefits potentially available under the terms of the contract must be considered . . . and . . . each integrated benefit stream available under the contract must be individually valued and the ultimate reserve established must be the greatest of the present values of these values." This guideline interprets the CARVM applications to annuity contracts with multiple benefits, involving development of "Integrated Benefit Streams" reflecting blends of more than one type of benefit. Currently, this applies primarily to deferred variable annuities since they are the ones that tend to offer multiple elective benefits. As competition breeds similar arrays of elective benefits during the payout phase, AG33 application will extend there.

4. **Actuarial Guideline XXXIV (AG34).** AG34 represents the NAIC's interpretation of the CARVM application to minimum guaranteed death benefits in variable annuity contracts. These must be included in the Integrated Benefit Streams used in calculating reserves under AG33. Again, while the current province of AG34 is primarily or exclusively deferred variable annuities, product development may extend death benefits beyond the traditional ones into immediate variable annuities.

5. **Actuarial Guideline XXXIX (AG39).** AG39, Reserving for Variable Annuities with Guaranteed Living Benefits, contains what many believe are temporary solutions to address reserve requirements associated with a class of additional fund performance guarantees layered—generally on an optional basis—onto base variable annuity contracts. Details about Guaranteed Payout Annuity Floors, the form of guaran-

teed living benefit most closely associated with immediate variable annuities, are described later in Chapter 18 on product development.

Statutory reserves for immediate variable annuities are typically set equal to the present value of future benefits under the payout option chosen. The PVFB is calculated using the AIR elected and the mortality table used to calculate the initial benefit payment, if this is consistent with state law. The discounted value of the projected series of annuity units to be paid is multiplied by the current annuity unit value to determine the dollar amount of the reserve.

In the last quarter of the nineteenth century, numerous insurance companies engaged in extravagance and disregard of policyholder rights, often becoming insolvent. In response, the New York legislature in 1905 passed a resolution appointing the Armstrong Committee to examine the affairs of life insurance companies doing business in the state of New York. Revised and strengthened life insurance laws were codified in the New York Insurance Code of 1906. As a result, New York has a reputation for the toughest, most stringent insurance laws—although much of what New York instituted served as precedent for other state insurance commissioners to adopt.

New York Insurance Code Section 4240(a)(5) states that no guarantee of the assets allocated to a separate account shall be made to a contract holder by the insurer unless the insurer shall submit annually to the superintendent an opinion of a qualified actuary that the assets and any risk charges payable from the assets make good and sufficient provision for the liabilities. A memorandum describing the calculations and assumptions is required.

New York State Insurance Department Regulation 47—NYCRR Part 50.6.(3)—required insurance companies issuing variable annuities to accumulate an "annuitant mortality fluctuation fund" in addition to the reserve, using a plan approved by the Superintendent of Insurance. Mortality losses were first charged against the "annuitant mortality fluctuation fund" until such fund was exhausted and then against a "special contingent reserve fund." The former was more in the nature of a reserve, in that it provided for some level of deviation of experience from pricing assumptions, while the latter was more in the nature of a partitioning of the insurer's surplus account, effectively representing a "special surplus fund" as contrasted with "unassigned surplus."

New York Insurance Law Section 4240(b)(2) stated that an insurer was to establish a special contingent reserve fund for a separate account that was to be not less than 2.5% of the value of the assets of the separate account, but not more than $750,000. It was to be used to defray an expense incurred in connection with a variable annuity contract where such expense was in excess of the contract holder's share of assets in the separate account.

While annuity accounting rules change with some frequency, the following three promulgations offer a flavor for the issues addressed:

1. **FASB 60.** Deferrable Expenses, GAAP for traditional products.
2. **FASB 97.** Universal life type products and investment contracts.
2. **AICPA Practice Bulletin 8.** Application of FASB 97.

MORTALITY ADJUSTMENTS

Reserves are effectively calculated assuming that a small portion of each annuitant will die each year and the remaining portion will survive. Of course, either an annuitant fully dies or fully survives—it's not a little of one and a little of the other.

As a result, mortality adjustments are made in the insurer's administration of the business. For those annuitants who die (with no refund or guarantee feature but only a straight life annuity option), the insurer's obligation to them is fully discharged, so their reserve is fully released.

For those who survive, the insurer's obligation to them is now slightly higher "because a little piece of them didn't die in the prior year," so a portion of the reserves released from deceased annuitants is added to the reserves for surviving annuitants. (Actually, the insurer must "true up" the reserves for surviving annuitants, regardless of whether the reserves released from deceased annuitants are adequate to do so.)

For annuitants who die with additional payments required to be made to joint annuitants or beneficiaries, the reserve is reduced to the appropriate level, being not entirely but only partially released. Again, the reserve equals the present value of future benefits, where those benefits are now the insurer's obligation to the joint annuitant, contingent annuitant, or beneficiary.

It is important to note that state insurance law generally requires that annuity unit values be unaffected by an insurer's actual mortality experience. Thus, if annuitants in general are living longer than expected or if it simply happens by random chance that fewer annuitants than expected died in a given year, the insurer ends up with a higher reserve requirement than anticipated. It is not the case that the mortality adjustments made to surviving annuitants can be made smaller or that adverse mortality experience can be reflected in lower annuity unit values that would make future annuity payments smaller. Indeed, this is the very mortality risk that an annuitant pays the insurance enterprise to absorb when the annuitant pays the "Mortality and Expense" (M&E) risk charge.

The "survivorship element" of immediate variable annuity payments is achieved by and made quite visible by this process of mortality adjustments, whereby reserves released from deceased annuitants are transferred to surviving annuitants in the pool—which is the very mechanism that allows annuity pool participants to collectively and safely achieve the guaranteed lifetime income unachievable on their own.

As there is frequently a statutory stipulation that adverse mortality experience may not impact the separate account contract owners, reserve adjustments are made (at least annually) to inject funds into the separate account to the extent of any mortality losses incurred during the year. These funds come from the general account of the insurer.

Mortality Adjustment Numerical Example

Let's look at the reserve record kept for one annuitant. We'll choose the longest survivor of the Annuiland group. Her original reserve is her $100,000 deposit. To this, we add investment earnings and subtract her payment for the year to arrive at the end-of-year (EOY) reserve.

Because our 10 annuitants are identical in terms of age and original deposit, they each have the same end-of-year-one reserve: $83,053.48. At this point, one annuitant dies. The reserve for her is released, as she no longer requires longevity insurance. The reserve held for her is sprinkled equally across reserves for the 9 survivors who still need longevity insurance.

To each of their $83,053.48 reserves is added ⅑ of the $83,053.48 reserve released, or $9,228.16. This produces an end-of-year adjusted reserve for each annuitant of $92,281.64.

Notice that at the start of the second year, there are nine annuitants with an adjusted reserve of $92,281.64. This makes the total reserve $830,534.76, exactly the beginning-of-year (BOY) fund value shown in Table 6.16 for the entire surviving annuitant pool. The process is repeated each year, with the results appearing in Table 9.1.

The longest surviving annuitant receives $219,465.24 in total payments. These are comprised of her $100,000 principal, $31,062.56 in earnings, and $88,402.68 of mortality adjustments—reserves that are released by other annuitants who predecease her and that are reallocated to her. The $31,062.56 in investment earnings is attributable both to her original principal and to mortality adjustments allocated to her.

We saw earlier that if the longest surviving annuitant had tried to go it alone and taken $21,946.52 annual payments, she would have been able to receive only five full payments and a partial sixth payment before running out of money. On her own, she would have received her $100,000 principal and $16,410 in earnings. From this and from information in the prior paragraph, we can see that while participating in the annuity program, she received her $100,000 principal and $16,410 in earnings, but also received $88,403 of mortality adjustments allocated to her and another $14,653 in

TABLE 9.1 Reserve Record of Longest Annuiland Survivor

Time	BOY Reserve	Earnings	Payments	EOY Reserve	Mortality Adjustment	EOY Adjusted Reserve*
0	$100,000.00	$5,000.00	$21,946.52	$83,053.48	$ 9,228.16	$92,281.64
1	92,281.64	4,614.08	21,946.52	74,949.20	9,368.65	84,317.85
2	84,317.85	4,215.89	21,946.52	66,587.21	9,512.46	76,099.67
3	76,099.67	3,804.98	21,946.52	57,958.13	9,659.69	67,617.82
4	67,617.82	3,380.89	21,946.52	49,052.19	9,810.44	58,862.63
5	58,862.63	2,943.13	21,946.52	39,859.23	9,964.81	49,824.04
6	49,824.04	2,491.20	21,946.52	30,368.72	10,122.91	40,491.63
7	40,491.63	2,024.58	21,946.52	20,569.68	10,284.84	30,854.52
8	30,854.52	1,542.73	21,946.52	10,450.73	10,450.73	20,901.45
9	20,901.45	1,045.07	21,946.52	0.00	0.00	0.00

*The reserve at the end of policy year t is called the *terminal* reserve; $_tV_x$ is the t-th year terminal reserve for a policy originally issued to a life age x using international actuarial notation.

earnings attributable to those mortality adjustments after they were allocated to her. It is these latter two items that produced the extra $103,056 that sustained her after she would have exhausted her own funds.

Note that while the longest surviving annuitant receives 5% in investment credits each year, her survivorship credits overwhelm these. For instance, in the first year, her EOY adjusted reserve is 11.1% higher because she received ⅑ (11.1%) of the reserve released by the deceased annuitant.

In the second year, her investment credit is again 5%, while her survivorship credit is 12.5%, since she received ⅛ (12.5%) of the reserve released by the deceased annuitant.

At younger ages, the investment credit is generally higher than the survivorship credit. At more advanced ages, the survivorship credit is generally higher than the investment credit. This is because the survivorship credit relates to the mortality rates, and mortality rates increase with age.

We discount the stream of annuity payments for both interest and survivorship to arrive at the present value of the annuity. This present value is divided into the net premium to determine the initial annuity benefit amount. Since we discount for interest and survivorship in calculating the present value—and the present value at the start of the annuity is the initial reserve—it only makes sense that we must accumulate for both interest and survivorship as we go the other direction in calculating the forward progression of reserve values. For example, in determining the level of annual benefit for the Annuilanders, we forecasted that only 90% of those who began the program at age 90 would still be alive on their 91st birthday. Since we discounted annuity payments for survivorship in that year by multiplying by 0.9, we similarly must accumulate for survivorship by dividing by 0.9. The EOY reserve is therefore divided by 0.9 to produce the EOY adjusted reserve.

The presence of a survivorship credit distinguishes an annuity from a "do-it-yourself" retirement income program that only includes one individual who can achieve investment credits but no survivorship credits. Survivorship credits are achievable only when two or more annuitants pool their mortality risk.

Again, it must be remembered that while we calculate a reserve for internal management purposes and external regulatory reporting purposes, annuitants have no access to this reserve—in order to safeguard the program against mortality anti-selection—and therefore are almost universally not told the level of the reserve attributable to their specific annuity obligation. A reserve is a technical accounting measure of the insurer's liability for future periodic annuity benefits due annuitants; it is *not* some accumulated surplus in excess of this fully available for release to beneficiaries on the annuitant's death.

Let's look at how the cumulative benefit paid to each of the 10 Annuilanders consists of original principal, appreciation, and survivorship credits (also known as "mortality adjustments" or "mortality credits"). See Table 9.2.

TABLE 9.2 Annuilander Benefits Decomposed into Principal, Appreciation, and Mortality Credit Components—Expressed in Dollars

Number of Benefits Paid Before Death	Cumulative Principal Paid	Cumulative Appreciation Paid* (Capital Gains, Dividends, Interest)	Cumulative Mortality Credits	Cumulative Benefits Paid
1	$16,946.52	$ 5,000.00	$ 0.00	$ 21,946.52
2	25,050.80	9,614.08	9,228.16	43,893.04
3	33,412.78	13,829.97	18,596.81	65,839.56
4	42,041.86	17,634.95	28,109.27	87,786.08
5	50,947.80	21,015.84	37,768.96	109,732.60
6	60,140.75	23,958.97	47,579.40	131,679.12
7	69,631.26	26,450.17	57,544.21	153,625.64
8	79,430.29	28,474.75	67,667.12	175,572.16
9	89,549.24	30,017.48	77,951.96	197,518.68
10	99,999.96	31,062.55	88,402.69	219,465.20

*Appreciation values are for appreciation on original principal plus appreciation on mortality credits (i.e., on reserves released by earlier deaths and reallocated to annuitant).

TABLE 9.3 Annuilander Benefits Decomposed into Principal, Appreciation, and Mortality Credit Components—Expressed in Percentages

Number of Benefits Paid Before Death	Cumulative Principal Paid	Cumulative Appreciation Paid* (Capital Gains, Dividends, Interest)	Cumulative Mortality Credits	Cumulative Benefits Paid
1	77.2%	22.8%	0.0%	100%
2	57.1	21.9	21.0	100
3	50.7	21.0	28.2	100
4	47.9	20.1	32.0	100
5	46.4	19.2	34.4	100
6	45.7	18.2	36.1	100
7	45.3	17.2	37.5	100
8	45.2	16.2	38.5	100
9	45.3	15.2	39.5	100
10	45.6	14.2	40.3	100

*Appreciation values are for appreciation on original principal plus appreciation on mortality credits (i.e., on reserves released by earlier deaths and reallocated to annuitant).

Note: Values shown are *percentages of cumulative benefits paid.* For example, the 77.2% in the first row does not mean that 77.2% of the principal of the annuitant who died at the end of the first year was returned to her, but rather that of her total benefits received, 77.2% of them were attributable to principal (i.e., premium) she paid, 22.8% to appreciation, and none to mortality credits. From Table 9.2, it can be seen that this annuitant only had 16.9% of her principal returned to her ($16,946.52/$100,000) prior to death, with the remainder being reallocated among survivors.

Perhaps it is more enlightening and revealing to reproduce Table 9.2 using percentages instead of dollars (Table 9.3), where cumulative benefits paid for each of the 10 annuitants are broken down into their component parts of principal, investment credits, and mortality credits. Note the increasingly dominant percentage of cumulative benefits attributable to mortality credits (rather than to investment credits) with increasing longevity.

IMMEDIATE VARIABLE ANNUITY RESERVE CALCULATIONS

The size of the "pot of assets" an insurer must hold at any point to be sufficient to cover all future retirement income obligations to annuitants (plus administrative expenses, taxes, and profit) must be determined. This is called the "reserve."

In general, the reserve at any point in time equals the present value of future benefits minus the present value of future premiums. For immediate annuities, there typically is only a single premium. As a result, the PVFP is zero.

Recall the formula:

$$\text{Reserve} = \text{PVFB} - \text{PVFP}$$

$$= \text{PVFB} - 0 \text{ (for single premium IVA)}$$

$$= \text{PVFB}$$

We denote the reserve at time t for an immediate annuity issued to a life age x by $_tV_x$. For an annuity that pays 1 (one unit, dollar, etc.) at the end of each year the annuitant is alive, the progression of reserve values is shown in Table 9.4.

The function $_tV$ provides *end-of-policy-year* reserve values, known as *terminal* reserves. For example, at the end of the first policy year, the first year terminal reserve, $_1V_x$, is a_{x+1}.

For simplicity, we can assume that expenses, taxes, and profit are covered out of the product charges and look only at the net investment return that governs the dollar amounts of periodic retirement income to the annuitant.

A *prospective* reserve calculation strictly looks forward to the future benefits that are projected to be paid and discounts them for interest and survivorship to arrive at a present value (see Figure 9.2). The reserve formula in Table 9.4 is a *prospective* formula.

A *retrospective* reserve calculation strictly looks backward and accumulates the original net premium less periodic benefit payments for interest and survivorship to arrive at an accumulated value. The recursion relation

TABLE 9.4 Reserve for Life Annuity-Immediate with Annual Payments of 1 Issued at Age x

Time	Reserve Symbol	Reserve Formula
0	$_0V_x$	$a_x = N_{x+1}/D_x$
1	$_1V_x$	$a_{x+1} = N_{x+2}/D_{x+1}$
2	$_2V_x$	$a_{x+2} = N_{x+3}/D_{x+2}$
...	...	...
t	$_tV_x$	$a_{x+t} = N_{x+t+1}/D_{x+t}$

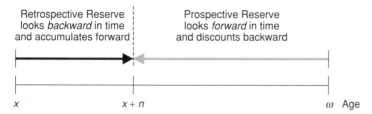

FIGURE 9.2   Reserve Calculation at Attained Age $x + n$

in the following formula shows how to derive the next reserve in the progression from the last one. This reserve formula is a *retrospective* formula.

$$\text{Reserve}_{t+1} = \frac{(\text{Reserve}_t - \text{Benefit}_t) \cdot (1 + i)}{p_{x+t}}$$

In words, this assumes the new reserve equals the old reserve less an annual annuity benefit paid at the start of the period brought forward to reflect *actual* subaccount performance at the rate i and one year of survivorship for a life of attained age $x + t$. Note that this recursion formula is for an annual annuity-due. For an annual annuity-immediate, the prior terminal reserve would first be updated for subaccount performance and survivorship, and then the benefit would be subtracted.

A retrospective definition of reserves expresses the reserve in terms of *past* premiums and *past* benefits. Retrospective formulas express the reserve as the excess of accumulated value of premium paid over accumulated value of annuity benefits provided. Since one *discounts* for interest and survivorship when deriving the present value used to establish the conversion factor at contract inception, it makes sense that one must *accumulate* for interest and survivorship as one moves forward in time.

The retrospective reserve calculation clearly shows how forfeitures (i.e., reserves released) by deceased annuitants are spread across surviving annuitants—and don't go to the insurer offering the annuity program, as is often misconstrued. Because the reserve progression as shown in the recursion relation includes a $1/p_{x+t}$ factor, the reserve at time $t + 1$ for the surviving annuitants is thereby increased by this factor. Whether the total reserve increases, remains the same, or decreases depends on the totality of survivorship, subaccount performance, and benefit level.

While the general concept is that reserves released by deceased annuitants are spread across surviving annuitants, in reality, this would happen exactly only by coincidence. The reserve formulas—retrospective or pro-spective—govern reserve determination at any time. Reserves released by deceased annuitants during any one reporting period may be less than ade-quate, exactly adequate, or more than adequate to bring reserves for surviv-ing annuitants to the proper level.

Because there is just one "correct" value for the current reserve given a specific set of mortality and interest assumptions, by definition, the pro-spective and the retrospective reserves must be identical. For example, we know the *prospectively* determined nth-year terminal reserve for a single life annuity-due of 1 originally issued at age x is

$$\ddot{a}_{x+n} = N_{x+n}/D_{x+n}$$

To *retrospectively* determine the same reserve, we accumulate the excess of the premium over the benefits provided:

$$\text{Accumulated Value of Premium} = \frac{P}{{}_nE_x} = \frac{\ddot{a}_x}{\dfrac{D_{x+n}}{D_x}} = \frac{\dfrac{N_x}{D_x}}{\dfrac{D_{x+n}}{D_x}} = \frac{N_x}{D_{x+n}}$$

$$\text{Accumulated Value of Benefits} = \frac{1}{{}_nE_x} + \frac{1}{{}_{n-1}E_{x+1}} + \frac{1}{{}_{n-2}E_{x+2}} + \cdots + \frac{1}{{}_1E_{x+n-1}}$$

$$= \frac{D_x}{D_{x+n}} + \frac{D_{x+1}}{D_{x+n}} + \frac{D_{x+2}}{D_{x+n}} + \cdots + \frac{D_{x+n-1}}{D_{x+n}}$$

$$= \frac{N_x - N_{x+n}}{D_{x+n}}$$

$$\begin{aligned}\text{Accumulated Value of Premium} - \\ \text{Accumulated Value of Benefits} &= \frac{N_x}{D_{x+n}} - \frac{N_x - N_{x+n}}{D_{x+n}} \\ &= \frac{N_{x+n}}{D_{x+n}} \\ &= \ddot{a}_{x+n}\end{aligned}$$

An equivalent view is to recognize that the value of the premium at any point in time must be equal to the value of the annuity benefits already pro-vided plus those promised for the future. Thus, at any time n ($0 \le n < \infty$),

Value of Premium = Value of Past Benefits + Value of Future Benefits

Value of Premium − Value of Past Benefits = Value of Future Benefits

$$\underbrace{\frac{N_x}{D_{x+n}} \quad - \quad \frac{N_x - N_{x+n}}{D_{x+n}}}_{\text{Retrospective Reserve}} \quad = \quad \underbrace{\frac{N_{x+n}}{D_{x+n}}}_{\text{Prospective Reserve}}$$

Note that for single premium immediate variable annuities, the prospective reserve is the more easily calculated, having the simpler formula. The reserve is simply the net single premium at the attained age for the future benefits to be provided. This present value of future annuity units to be paid can be determined, then multiplied by the current annuity unit value to arrive at the dollar amount of the reserve. Note that such methodology results in a reserve that reflects *actual* investment results to date and continued assumption of the AIR for future benefits.

When post-issue subaccount reallocations that determine periodic annuity benefits are made, a new reserve calculation must be performed. The total reserve remains the same, but the partial reserve per subaccount changes. The reserve calculation is the same as for a new issue, as the reserve can be thought of as a net premium at the time of reallocation to be applied to the annuity option as characterized at time of reallocation and using the annuitant's attained age. For example, if the original annuity option were "life with 10 years certain" at issue age 65 and if a subaccount reallocation were made three years later, the reserve would be calculated as a "life with 7 years certain" annuity at attained age 68. The new number of annuity units payable for each of the subaccounts chosen under the reallocation is calculated and conveyed to the contract owner. Shares are sold from and bought in the appropriate underlying funds to ensure synchronization between actual investments and those the performance of which the contract owner most recently instructed are to govern his periodic income.

Reserves are calculated periodically, usually monthly. Calculations are typically performed by an automated reserve calculation system known as a "valuation system," since it places a value on the insurer's liability to policyholders.

Thus, while policy year-end reserves, the *terminal* reserves, are illustrated in Table 9.4, in actual practice an insurer needs to derive reserves at fractional policy durations. While historically this was once done by linear interpolation between successive terminal reserves, the advent of computers facilitates more precise calculation.

Previous to the computer era, *mean* reserves, $_{t+1/2}V$, were particularly important. This was because when valuing the aggregation of an insurer's liabilities, a customary assumption was that on any particular valuation date, all policies issued between t and $t + 1$ years earlier were, on average, $t + \frac{1}{2}$ years old.

For single premium immediate variable annuities, the mortality adjustment process, where reserves are released or reduced by the death of an annuitant and reserves are increased to reflect the ongoing survivorship of other annuitants, occurs in conjunction with the reserve valuation cycle.

If assumed mortality experience is exactly met in real-world experience, as in the earlier Annuiland example, the reserves released on death are exactly sufficient in magnitude and timing when spread across the reserves for the survivors to bring those reserves up to the required level.

RESERVE EFFECT INTRODUCED BY OFFERING MULTIPLE SUBACCOUNTS

Variable annuities were first used in 1952 by the College Retirement Equity Fund (CREF), established by a special act of the New York legislature, to fund tax-qualified pension arrangements. State laws prohibited insurers from offering a class of products where the assets backing them were housed in a separate account segregated from general account assets. State insurance department regulatory approvals were necessary because when immediate variable annuities first were commercially available, there was only a single common stock investment fund per product to which 100% of a contract owner's premium was allocated. State insurance law limitations on common stock investments precluded holding such assets in the general account in quantities that would be necessary for fear that poor or volatile returns on this asset class could affect the capital base supporting fixed, guaranteed return products.

Because policyholders could lose money in a deferred variable annuity or could experience downward fluctuations in benefit payments under an immediate variable annuity if common stock performance were poor, insurance company officers[4] often felt that what their brethren developing such products were doing was heretical. After all, insurers had become known as bastions of safety and guarantees. Surely such wild ideas would harm this reputation!

Product advancements led to the offering of multiple subaccounts and multiple investment management companies inside a single immediate variable annuity focused on common stock, bond, money market, international stock, and other asset classes.

As a result, immediate variable annuity contract owners choose different collections of subaccounts the performance of which determine their retirement income benefits. Now when reserves are released or reduced by the death of an annuitant, it may well be the case that shares in funds underlying their specific collection of subaccounts need to be sold and shares in other funds underlying the specific collection of subaccounts chosen by surviving annuitants, whose reserves must be increased, need to be purchased.

This introduces a new element of volatility that can be to the benefit or the detriment of the insurer responsible for immediate variable annuity benefits. The value of the reserve released by a deceased annuitant may be inadequate, exactly adequate, or more than adequate to supplement the reserve of the surviving annuitants. In other words, even if mortality assumptions and subaccount performance assumptions are precisely realized in actual, real-world experience, the existence of multiple subaccounts with different investment performance presents an opportunity for gains or losses on the part of the insurer offering the product—a risk that didn't exist in the days of a single subaccount.

For example, suppose we have two 98-year-old Annuilanders, each of whom pays a $100,000 premium for a "life only" IVA with a 5% AIR. Because of their unique and magical mortality characteristic, where exactly one dies each year with absolute certainty—although no one knows in advance which one—right after receiving her annual, year-end annuity benefit, we have the following determination of initial benefit:

$$\text{Present Value of Annuity} = \frac{1}{1.05} \cdot (1) + \frac{1}{1.05^2} \cdot (0.5) = 1.4059$$

$$\text{Initial Benefit} = \frac{\text{Premium}}{\text{PV of Annuity}} = \frac{100,000}{1.4059} = \$71,129.03$$

$$\frac{\text{Number of Annuity}}{\text{Units per Payment}} = \frac{\text{First Benefit}}{\text{Annuity Unit Value at Inception}}$$

$$= \frac{\$71,129.03}{\$1.00} = 71,129.03$$

One Annuilander invests in a common stock subaccount that performs at +15% in both years. The other Annuilander invests in a bond subaccount that performs at +5% in both years. The stock subaccount and bond subaccount each begin with an annuity unit value of $1.00 at policy inception (see Table 9.5). Thus, each Annuilander will be paid the value of 71,129.03 annuity units on each benefit date.

TABLE 9.5   Annuity Unit Values

Subaccount	Time 0	Time 1	Time 2
Stock	1.0000	$1.15/1.05 = 1.0952$	$1.15^2/1.05^2 = 1.1995$
Bond	1.0000	$1.05/1.05 = 1.0000$	$1.05^2/1.05^2 = 1.0000$

At the end of the first year prior to annuity benefit payments, the total value of assets is $100,000 \cdot 1.05 + \$100,000 \cdot 1.15$, or \$220,000. Benefits are paid as follows:

$$\text{Annuilander in Stock Subaccount: Benefit} = 71,129.03 \cdot \frac{1.15}{1.05} = \$77,903.22$$

$$\text{Annuilander in Bond Subaccount: Benefit} = 71,129.03 \cdot \frac{1.05}{1.05} = \$71,129.03$$

Total Benefits Paid at End of Year 1 $\overline{\$149,032.25}$

End-of-first-year assets after benefit payments is $220,000 - \$149,032.25$, or \$70,967.75. At this point, the Annuilander invested in the bond subaccount dies. Her reserve is released and reallocated to the sole surviving annuitant, who remains 100% invested in the stock subaccount, to which all assets in the annuity program are now allocated.

At the end of the second year prior to annuity benefit payments, the total value of assets is $70,967.75 \cdot 1.15$, or \$81,612.91. Benefits are paid as follows:

$$\text{Annuilander in Stock Subaccount: Benefit} = 71,129.03 \cdot \frac{1.15^2}{1.05^2}$$

$$= \$85,322.58$$

It is clear that there are not enough assets to pay the annuity benefit. What happened? If both annuitants invest in the same subaccount, everything works fine. Here, one annuitant invested in the bond subaccount, which underperformed the stock subaccount. As a result, when the annuitant invested in the bond subaccount died, her reserve that was released was inadequate to bring total assets up to the level of the reserve needed for the surviving annuitant.

In actual practice, at the end of the first year immediately following the death of the first annuitant, the insurer would need to inject sufficient funds so as to bring assets in the underlying stock fund up to the level of the reserve for the surviving annuitant.

The point to be made, though, is that when more than one subaccount is available, the insurer may realize gains or losses even if every annuitant dies perfectly on schedule. This is because when the subaccounts perform at different levels, reserves released on death may be less than adequate or more than adequate to bring the total reserve to the right level.

Let's reverse the order of deaths and assume that the Annuilander invested in the stock subaccount dies first. The same $70,967.75 in assets exists at the end of the first year after benefit payments. This would grow in the bond subaccount during the second year to $70,967.75·1.05, or $74,516.14. Benefits are paid as follows:

$$\text{Annuilander in Bond Subaccount: Benefit } = 71,129.03 \cdot \frac{1.05^2}{1.05^2}$$
$$= \$71,129.03$$

There is $3,387.11 of assets in excess of that needed to pay the annuity benefit. This is because the reserve released by the deceased Annuilander invested in the stock subaccount was more than necessary to supplement the reserve for the surviving annuitant invested in the bond subaccount.

In actual practice, at the end of the first year immediately following the death of the first annuitant, the insurer would extract sufficient funds so as to bring assets in the underlying bond fund down to the level of the reserve for the surviving annuitant.

Through this process of periodic valuation of assets and liabilities, the two are equated. To the extent that total separate account assets exceed annuity reserve liabilities, the insurer extracts assets. To the extent that total separate account assets fall short of annuity reserve liabilities, the insurer injects assets.

When IVAs were first introduced and there was only one fund in which all assets were invested, this phenomenon was not an issue. With the advent of multiple subaccounts available for investment within the same IVA product, the potential for the insurer offering the product to experience investment-related gains and losses emerged even if investment performance matched pricing assumptions. Surplus should be allocated to the extent necessary to cover this form of experience deviation to the desired level of protection.

To the extent that the mortality assumptions used to determine statutory reserves are conservative—and recall that separate account assets must be at least as large as statutory reserves—any reserves released due to such conservative mortality assumptions may help offset any investment-related losses that may occur from the phenomenon in the preceding example.

There's no reason to believe that annuitants invested in lower-performing subaccounts will systematically tend to predecease annuitants invested in higher-performing subaccounts—unless annuitants who sense that their retirement horizon may be shorter invest more conservatively. Thus, over the long run, insurer investment-related gains and losses from the preceding phenomenon might counterbalance. Over the short run, there may be some volatility.

USE OF STATUTORY IMMEDIATE VARIABLE ANNUITY RESERVES IN PRODUCT DESIGN

We have already discussed the protective function of statutory reserves. There exist state insurance statutes that prescribe the (conservative) basis for statutory reserve determination. These ensure that if real-world experience is at least as favorable as the conservative assumptions (e.g., mortality rates) employed in determining the level of reserves, the insurer is holding sufficient assets to satisfy all of its immediate variable annuity obligations.

Annual reporting to state insurance departments, periodic examinations of insurers by state insurance regulators, and, for publicly traded companies, audits by independent external auditors are yet additional protective devices to safeguard the interests of IVA contract owners and annuitants.

An insurance investor looks at statutory earnings to assess whether they will be sufficient to support the level of new business growth desired without having to seek outside funding or reinsurance. An insurance investor looks at GAAP earnings because these are of primary interest to shareholders viewing the enterprise on a "going concern" basis.

Product development personnel of insurers—those who design and price immediate variable annuity product offerings—often rely on statutory accounting rules to govern their decisions. This is because finance theory tends to calculate measurements based on free cash flows. Under state insurance regulatory regimes, statutory accounting defines and governs free cash flows.

Distributable earnings equal *after-tax statutory earnings* plus *after-tax interest on required capital* plus *any decrease (or minus any increase) in required capital*. This is the measure of *free cash flows* available to an investor in this business. Insurers cannot dividend anything above such statutory earnings, with the exception of extraordinary dividends, which requires approval from the domiciliary state of the insurer.

Said another way, distributable earnings are amounts an insurer can distribute while still retaining the required capital to support ongoing operation. Distributable earnings are comprised of earnings calculated under the applicable regulatory accounting basis, adjusted by (1) retaining a portion of regulatory earnings or (2) releasing a portion of regulatory surplus, the end result of which is to arrive at capital and surplus levels appropriate to support ongoing operations of the insurer.

When one invests in a bond, for example, one determines the rate of return based on the future cash flows expected to be received. Similarly, when valuing an annuity manufacturing business, one predicates value on the free cash flows or distributable earnings expected to be received in the future.

An internal rate of return (IRR), which equates an initial (and possibly subsequent) investment of capital to manufacture a financial product having a specific design and price with its projected series of free cash flows, can be determined.[5] This IRR can be compared to the risk-free rate, the cost of capital, the return the company can earn on financial instruments, or some benchmark rate, such as 12% or 15%. A fundamental principle is that the capital investment in a block of business should be repaid at a yield commensurate with the risks inherent in the business.

This is much easier said than done. Options embedded in the assets and liabilities must be examined, which behave differently in various economic scenarios. Where policyholder control of elements exists, empirical data on policyholder behavior to parameterize some of the formulas precisely may be lacking.

Nonetheless, an evaluative framework for quantitatively determining optimal product design and product management strategies for maximizing the long-run wealth of an annuity writing enterprise exist. It often takes time, however, to fine-tune the assumptions needed by such models. Such models offer excellent guidance as to relative attractiveness of different strategies—high expected returns, minimal dispersion between highest and lowest possible returns across all scenarios modeled, and so on. Of course, one difficulty may be that the best strategies are unimplementable in a marketplace filled with competitors who may be unwisely employing their capital!

Product design and product management strategies impact the level of statutory reserves and RBC—two important elements affecting the IRR of a specific annuity product under consideration and, by extension, the collective financial results of the annuity writing enterprise.

SUBSTANDARD ANNUITY RESERVES

Immediate variable annuities may be written on lives in health sufficiently impaired to make adjustments in the pricing mortality table used. Such annuities are called "substandard annuities." Their characteristics will be more fully described in the section on substandard annuity underwriting in Chapter 13.

Insurers may use different approaches to recognize these health impairments when determining reserves. Approaches to calculate impaired life annuity reserves include these four bases:

1. **The annuitant's actual age and standard mortality** (the standard basis). This, however, likely results in a reserve meaningfully higher than the net premium. As a result, some of the insurer's surplus now must form the remainder of the reserve not covered by the net premium. This tying up of the insurer's surplus, or "surplus strain," needs to be reflected in the annuity pricing if the insurer is to realize its targeted IRR. The result is likely an uncompetitive premium.

2. **The "rated up" age on which pricing is premised and standard mortality.** This approach may presume that substandard mortality exists at all future durations, resulting in the least surplus strain among various approaches. Periodic review of the reserve may be in order. For example, if a 60-year-old receives an "age rate-up" to 80 as a result of impaired health and if the terminal age of the mortality table is 115, an unattended reserve progression would have the reserve grading to zero after about 35 years. Yet if by some chance the annuitant, then age 95, were still alive, clearly a positive reserve should be held.

3. **The actual age and substandard mortality.** The initial reserve so determined may be equivalent (or nearly so) to that under the second approach, but it avoids the possibility of a zero reserve while the annuitant is still alive. The substandard mortality used may be a multiple of standard mortality, or it may assume a constant number of extra deaths added at each attained age.

4. **The actual age and substandard mortality that grades into standard valuation mortality.** This reduces initial surplus strain while also recognizing that with the passage of time the health of such an annuitant who continues to survive may equate more closely with his or her peers, those who didn't have substantial impairment at time of issue but whose health may also have deteriorated with time.

Statutory reserve valuation clearly must comply with state valuation laws. For example, New York will not permit the second basis, involving permanent "age rate-up," but rather requires the fourth basis, where substandard annuity reserves grade into standard reserves.

NAIC Actuarial Guideline IX-A[6] describes minimum statutory reserves allowed for substandard annuities. It describes when and to what extent a substandard mortality table may be used to value reserves. Guideline

IX-A permits use of a substandard mortality table for benefits arising from court settlements, workers' compensation settlements, and settlements arising from long-term disability claims when the annuitant is the injured party. When substandard reserves are allowed, Guideline IX-A requires the *constant extra deaths method* mentioned earlier. Such substandard reserves must grade into standard reserves by the end of the standard mortality table. NAIC Actuarial Guideline IX-C allows substandard individual immediate annuity reserves on the same basis as that used for structured settlements.

INSURANCE COMPANY ABSORBS RISKS

The insurer offering an immediate variable annuity is exposed to certain risks, most notably and visibly *mortality* and *expense* risks. These are the "M" and "E" in the "M&E risk charge" mentioned earlier. While an insurer assesses an M&E risk charge and assumes mortality and expense risks, it is not necessarily the case that these charges are intended to cover exactly these risks. Rather, the insurer's product developers try to ensure that the totality of product fees and charges—its inflow items—cover claims due contract owners, expenses (including taxes), and profit—its outflow items.

The issuing insurer absorbs all mortality risk. If medical advances, a cancer cure, artificial organs, nutritional improvements, increased availability of donated organs for increased transplants, gene therapy slowing the aging process, infectious disease cures, heart disease cures, ability to grow one's own replacement organs from stem cells, highway safety, improved sanitation, improved health education, or any other life-extending trends or events should occur that would result in the insurer making annuity payments for a longer period than anticipated, this risk is borne by the insurer. While IVAs have an investment element, they are clearly insurance products due to complete mortality risk transference and are so regulated.

If the fund created with the premiums of all immediate variable annuity contract owners were exhausted, the insurer must pay all future annuity benefits out of its own pocket. (The fund would never be exhausted since periodic assessments of the insurer's liability would result in earlier reserve strengthening in recognition of the annuity payments being longer than anticipated.)

An insurer cannot go back and ask annuity customers for additional premiums because the conversion factors that translate a single premium into a periodic income benefit proved inadequate. Random fluctuation could cause that subset of annuitants forming the annuitant pool for any one insurer to have better than expected longevity. While statutory reserve requirements tend to cover reasonably large mortality experience deviations, it could still be the case that a combination of an unusually healthy annuitant pool and unexpected medical advances causes an insurer to experience higher annuity payment claims than assumed by pricing. In other words, the latter element of this combination expresses that higher than anticipated mortality improvement factors (MIFs) can occur.

Immediate annuity writers also absorb expense risks. They guarantee that they will not increase contract owner expense charges over the life of the contract. This is true even if postage costs to mail contracts, prospectuses, account statements, semiannual and annual reports of underlying fund performance, and annual income tax statements increase. This is true even if federal, state, or local governments impose more onerous and expensive reporting requirements on the insurer any time during the possibly multidecade life of an annuity contract. This is true even if Congress increases the insurer's corporate income tax rate, for example, if it raises taxes to pay for broader, more expensive, government-sponsored health care programs for seniors.

Insurers may choose to implement or may be forced by competition to provide additional and more convenient ways for IVA contract owners to manage their account, such as by providing an improved Internet self-service center or interactive voice response telephone system or by increasing the hours or days its call center representatives are available. Additional service features, such as automatic portfolio rebalancing, may be offered.

If the general economy suffers and stock and bond funds perform badly, the value against which the expense charge is assessed may be much smaller than expected, making the expense charge collected inadequate to cover the insurer's expenses.

Insurers—the counterparty to immediate variable annuity contracts— absorb bona fide risks, including marketing risk, mortality risk, investment risk, and regulatory risk. They may seek to manage certain of these risks through reinsurance or by also selling life insurance products, which are a natural hedge to the mortality risk embedded in immediate annuities. With immediate annuities, the insurer's risk is policyholders living too long, whereas with life insurance, its risk is policyholders living too short. In symbiotic combination, the offering insurer achieves a degree of mortality risk immunization.

In a utopian, quixotic world, all assumptions an annuity company uses to model its future business play out exactly in actual experience. In the real world, deviations exist, producing risk (i.e., uncertainty) that annuity companies seek to manage. A partial list of risks to which an immediate variable annuity issuer is exposed follows:

- **Financing.** The insurer bankrolls the front-end acquisition expenses. To the extent these exceed any front-end loadings built into pricing, the insurer hopes eventually to recover these expenses through asset-based charges (e.g., mortality, expense, and administration charges). To the extent these are predicated on mortality and asset performance assumptions, there is no guarantee the insurer will be able to recover these expenses.

■ **Fund Performance.** The underlying funds are assumed to perform at levels near some long-term measure of their performance; for example, in order to cover front-end expenses (policy issue, record setup), ongoing maintenance expenses (annuity benefit calculations, annuity benefit payments, tax statement preparation and mailing, reserve calculations), and back-end expenses (death claim calculations and processing), insurers make fund performance assumptions when establishing the level of charges they will assess as a percentage of the reserve. The insurer is subject to general economic and market conditions risks, as well as the risk that one or more investment managers may underperform.

■ **Asset Allocation.** Immediate variable annuity contract owners may allocate funds to lower-earning asset classes and/or may exhibit poor market timing as they reallocate among subaccounts, resulting in not only lower annuity benefits for themselves but also lower asset-based revenue for the insurer.

■ **Administration Costs.** Such costs may increase due to more services demanded, such as automatic portfolio rebalancing, without any concomitant increase in revenue. Increased federal- or state-mandated reporting requirements—to governmental agencies, contract owners, or both—could increase costs. Even if the insurer assumes some degree of annual net expense inflation (actual inflation minus productivity gains) in pricing, actual net inflation could exceed this.

■ **Corporate Federal Income Tax Rate.** This can increase over the often multidecade span of an annuity payout, yet policy charges are defined in the annuity contract and prospectus and are typically guaranteed not to increase.

■ **Tax-Qualified/Non-Tax-Qualified Business Mix.** To the extent an insurer offers identical payouts to these two markets by assuming a specific percentage of non-tax-qualified business subject to IRC Section 848 DAC (Deferred Acquisition Cost) tax and by spreading this cost over all business, the actual business mix must be such that the assumed percentage of non-tax-qualified business or something less materializes.

■ **Mortality Guarantees.** Immediate variable annuitants may live longer than expected and receive periodic retirement income payments longer than expected. It is immaterial whether this occurs from a healthier than expected cohort buying the insurer's product, from medical advancements, or from statistical aberration.

■ **Legal Challenges.** Changing securities laws, state insurance laws, tax laws, and attitudes about appropriate market conduct over the holding periods typical for IVA owners create opportunity for a variety of legal risks associated with immediate variable annuity products, sales, and administration.

- **Average Size.** An average premium size assumption is made in product pricing. If the average size is less than assumed (e.g., many small individual retirement accounts), there will not be as much asset-charge revenue generated per contract as expected to cover acquisition expenses and maintenance expenses.

RISK MEASURES AID IN CAPITAL REQUIREMENTS

Increasingly sophisticated approaches to refine reserve and risk-based capital determination to more accurately reflect risks inherent in assets, liabilities, or their interplay continue to evolve. A *quantile risk measure* is often used to set capital requirements for uncertain future liabilities. This may be a more reasonable approach for traditional variable income annuities, where investment risk is passed through to annuitants and mortality risk is such as to be unlikely to cause unexpectedly high and immediate claim demands.

This may be a less reasonable approach for some newer variable income annuities containing embedded investment options that leave some investment risk with the annuity company. Because these designs are more likely to spawn low-frequency, high-severity events (e.g., a precipitous stock market decline where the insurer guarantees an annuity benefit floor regardless of investment performance and may need to significantly and immediately increase reserves), a *dynamic conditional tail expectation* (CTE) *risk measure* may be more suitable for establishing capital requirements. Unlike the quantile risk measure, it does not ignore information in the tail of the loss distribution—a place that reflects adverse experiential events on a grander scale that are more likely to occur under newer IVA product designs.

The following section briefly describes risk measures that are helpful in establishing capital requirements appropriate for uncertain future events.

RISK MEASURES

A risk measure maps a profit-or-loss random variable to the real number line. Risk measures are commonly used to determine premiums and capital requirements for uncertain future liabilities such as variable income annuities.

The *quantile risk measure* with parameter α $(0 \leq \alpha < 1)$ is the α-quantile of the loss distribution; that is, if the continuous loss random variable is X $(X > 0)$ and the α-quantile random variable is denoted by $Q_\alpha(x)$, then

$$P\{X \leq Q_\alpha(x)\} = \alpha$$

In words, the probability that the random variable X takes on a value that is less than or equal to $Q_\alpha(x)$ is α. Setting capital requirements with this measure infers that capital will be sufficient to meet the liability with probability α.

The quantile risk measure has some shortfalls. For example, reliance on it promotes the offering by insurers of products with risks characterized by low-frequency, high-severity events. It ignores important information in the tail of the loss distribution, those events that occur with probability $1 - \alpha$.

The *conditional tail expectation risk measure* remedies this shortfall. The CTE risk measure with parameter α $(0 \leq \alpha < 1)$ for a continuous loss random variable X and quantile value $Q_\alpha(x)$ is defined as

$$\text{CTE}_\alpha(X) = E[X \mid X > Q_\alpha(x)]$$

In other words, the CTE risk measure is the expected value of the random variable X given that X is greater than $Q_\alpha(x)$. The capital requirement is adequate to cover the loss associated with the worst $(1 - \alpha)$ event, on average. For example, U.S. and Canadian insurance regulators may call for the projection of losses and the use of the CTE risk measure at the 95% level for the total capital requirement.

A current development is the extension of the *static* CTE risk measure into a *dynamic* CTE risk measure.[7] Such a dynamic risk measure gives a value for the capital to be held at the valuation date that considers not only the distribution of outcomes for the future loss as of the point the liability is ultimately discharged, but also considers intermediate capital requirements that recognize how the loss process has evolved to date. This allows a risk manager not to hold excessive capital if the risk evolves favorably to the company. This development is a current step in the evolution of analytical approaches to establishing capital requirements the purpose of which is to ensure than insurers hold total capital—in the form of reserves and allocated surplus collectively—that is sufficient to a high degree (but with less than complete certainty) to meet policyholder claim obligations, including the long-term obligations represented by variable income annuities.

RISK MEASURES AND ECONOMIC CAPITAL

An insurance company issuing immediate annuities desires to determine the optimal amount of economic capital that minimizes the economic cost of risk-bearing. As one example, actuarial reserves and RBC are two solvency buffers. An insurer looks to fulfill its future obligations to annuitants while holding the minimum amount of assets in the form of reserves and RBC that is consistent with its risk preferences. This leads to management by economic capital.

Premiums, economic capital, asset allocation, and other variables may be derived in an optimization procedure—such as one that minimizes economic cost or that maximizes profit subject to risk preference constraints. If one insurer sets its total economic capital buffer at the 90th percentile and another otherwise similarly situated insurer has a higher degree of risk aversion and sets its buffer at the 95th percentile, the different amounts of economic capital (investment) needed will produce a higher IVA premium for the second insurer if both insurers target an identical IRR.

Risk exposure and economic capital are trade-offs. Barring regulatory requirements, there is no unique level of economic capital for IVA writers. *Economic capital* is that amount an insurer should hold that is consistent with its risk preference—its level of desire to avoid ruin. *Regulatory capital* is the minimum amount an insurer is forced to hold.

There is a hierarchy between the concepts of risk measures and economic capital. First, an insurer determines a risk measure consistent with its risk preferences. Second, economic capital is derived from this risk measure.

Insurance companies with multiple business lines must determine how large total economic capital should be and then determine how to allocate this among business lines. Similarly, if multiple legal entities are involved, total economic capital may be determined first at the conglomerate level and then allocated among the various subsidiaries. Each subsidiary, however, also faces its own determination of a total economic capital level derived from its risk measure(s), which may or may not coincide with the allocation given it by managing officers of the conglomerate.

While reserves are calculated for individual product lines, it should be recalled that all general account assets of an insurer support all general account liabilities. As a result, aggregating reserve liabilities company-wide and testing the adequacy of assets to support the reserve liabilities in total is more meaningful than a similar exercise for a single product line.

The *total asset requirement* that consists of both reserves and required capital for an individual product line is a more relevant metric than reserves alone. The aggregate total asset requirement company-wide—premised on stochastic risk measurement—is even more meaningful. This requirement reflects natural hedges, such as the partial mortality hedge that results from offering both life insurance and immediate annuities.

From a solvency and risk management perspective, the level of total asset requirement is the essential metric. Where one draws the line between how much of the total asset requirement is comprised of an asset amount equal to the reserve and how much is comprised of the residual asset amount of risk-based capital is not as important a distinction on a pretax basis as it is on an after-tax basis.

From a taxation perspective, where one draws the line between how much of the total asset requirement consists of reserves and how much consists of residual RBC matters. This is because the level and timing of insurer taxation is in part premised on the definition of deductible tax reserves.

While current financial reporting rules require that a reserve be represented by a single number, this may not be the best representation of this risk metric. Especially when a multibillion dollar reserve value is stated to the nearest penny, it may confer to users of this information who are unfamiliar with the true nature of reserves more probability that the liability is concentrated at or around this single number than may actually be the case.

The goal of reserve setting is to put forth a representative value or range of values consistent with the objective of creating the reserve in the first place—best estimate, a targeted degree of conservatism for statutory valuation purposes, and so on. The reserve should be neither unduly liberal nor unduly conservative relative to its objective and one should not attribute greater weight to any single number proffered for the reserve than the distribution from which it is taken warrants.

A statutory total asset requirement that is protective to the same degree for different insurance companies is more likely achieved if it reflects the actual risks of each company rather than if it is based on a single, hard-coded formula. Equivalently stated, *principles-based* reserves and capital requirements that reflect risks peculiar to each insurer may be more appropriate than the older regime of *formula-based* reserves and capital requirements.

As one example, suppose an IVA offers a guaranteed floor benefit regardless of actual investment subaccount performance. Insurance Company A defines this benefit as a level floor equal to X% of the first annuity benefit. Insurance Company B defines this benefit as a "ratcheting" floor equal to Y% of the highest annuity benefit paid on any policy anniversary, including inception. Assume that Y is greater than X. Insurance Company B clearly offers the richer benefit, both because Y exceeds X and because the guaranteed floor potentially "ratchets up" rather than remains level.

The total asset requirement might be such that stochastic testing is required to determine CTE 90, the conditional tail expectation that averages the 10% worst results. This approach recognizes that the risk of the investment guarantee is in the tail of the loss distribution—actual subaccount performance being too low relative to the AIR to sustain annuity benefits at or above the guaranteed floor level. The reserve requirement might be CTE 65, the conditional tail expectation that averages the 35% worst results.

With equivalent or nearly equivalent assumptions employed by the valuation actuaries for Insurance Company A and Insurance Company B, the richer benefit for Company B will result in a higher reserve and a higher total asset requirement.

Desires to refine capital adequacy methodologies must be balanced with the costs—including generating and calibrating the stochastic scenarios and modeling perhaps millions of contracts over thousands of scenarios for a multidecade projection period.

CHAPTER 10

Immediate Variable Annuity Taxation

Friends ... and neighbors, the taxes are indeed very heavy, and if those laid on by the government were the only ones we had to pay, we might the more easily discharge them; but we have many others, and some much more grievous to some of us. We are taxed twice as much by our idleness, three times as much by our pride, and four times as much by our folly; and from these taxes the commissioners cannot ease or deliver us, by allowing an abatement.

—Benjamin Franklin,
Poor Richard's Almanac

IMMEDIATE VARIABLE ANNUITY INCOME TAXATION*

For federal income tax purposes, an *immediate annuity* is defined by Internal Revenue Code Section 72(u)(4) as an annuity that is purchased with a single premium or annuity consideration, with an annuity starting date no later than one year from date of purchase and that provides for a series of substantially equal[1] periodic payments to be made no less frequently than annually during the annuity period.[2]

Internal Revenue Code Section 72 and associated regulations govern personal federal income taxation of immediate variable annuities (IVAs).

---

*This section is extracted in part from the VARDS Executive Series report, "The Mechanics of Variable Annuitization," by Jeffrey K. Dellinger, © 1994. Reprinted with the permission of Morningstar, Inc.

Author's note: Because tax laws change and because the same transaction may receive different tax treatment depending on when the annuity contract was issued, it is advisable to consult a tax adviser regarding annuity-related tax issues.

These rules determine the portion of each annuity payment that is excludable from gross income as a return of the purchaser's investment in the annuity contract and the portion that is taxed as earnings on that investment.

For a tax-qualified annuity having zero cost basis, 100% of each immediate variable annuity benefit payment is taxable as ordinary income. A non-tax-qualified immediate variable annuity[3] contains a tax-excludable portion of each payment equal to the investment in the contract divided by the number of years over which it is expected annuity payments will be made.[4] Once the cost basis has been fully recovered, all future annuity benefit payments are fully taxable.[5]

If the annuity is to be paid for a fixed number of years, then the "expected number of years of payments" denominator in the tax-excludable portion calculation (investment in contract/expected number of years of payments) is simply that fixed number of years. If the annuity option is life-contingent (either single life or joint life), the expected number of years of annuity payments to be made is based on actuarial tables promulgated by the IRS. If annuity benefit payments are of a frequency other than monthly, adjustments to IRS actuarial tables are to be made. For example, for a 10-year fixed-period variable payout with a $60,000 cost basis, the annual excludable amount is $60,000/10, or $6,000.

$$\frac{\text{Investment in Contract}}{\text{Expected Number of Years of Payments}} = \text{Excludable Portion}$$

$$\frac{\$60,000}{10} = \$6,000$$

This taxation procedure is analogous to that for immediate fixed annuities. Unlike immediate fixed annuities, however, poor fund performance can render actual annual benefit payments less than the tax-excludable amount. For example, suppose the tax-excludable amount were $6,000, but poor fund performance made the sum of actual benefit payments for the year only $4,000. (This is an extreme example, but it makes the arithmetic tractable.)

The $2,000 nontaxable return of principal is not lost to the annuitant but rather distributed evenly across the remaining term of the annuity.[6] For example, if the $4,000 of benefit payments occurred in the 8th year of a 10-year annuity, the $2,000 shortfall would be spread evenly over the remaining two years, $1,000 in each year. This $1,000 additional annual exclusion added to the $6,000 original annual exclusion makes the new annual exclusion $7,000 for the final two years.

Recalculation of Tax-Excludable Amount

Original Annual Exclusion	$6,000
Actual 8th Year Benefit	− 4,000
Shortfall	$2,000
Remaining Years of Payments	÷ 2
Additional Annual Exclusion	$1,000
Original Annual Exclusion	$6,000
Additional Annual Exclusion	+ 1,000
New Annual Exclusion	$7,000

An annuitant may elect to aggregate the lost tax-excludable amounts for the prior year or years for which he has not already done so. For a fixed-period payout, he then divides this by the number of years remaining in the fixed period, as in the preceding example. For a life-contingent payout, the annuitant divides this by his life expectancy according to IRS annuity tables for his attained age as of the tax year in which he makes the election. The result of this division is added to the originally determined (or last-determined, if done previously) excludable amount.

Figure 10.1 illustrates the annuity income and the nontaxable portion for a male age 65 who elects a single life only annuity with a $100,000 premium. It assumes his initial annual benefit is $8,000. It further assumes 20 years is the expected number of years of annuity payments according to IRS

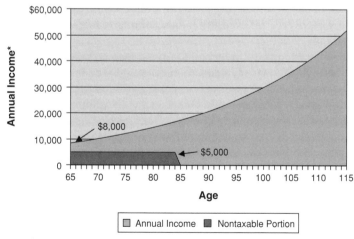

FIGURE 10.1   Annuity Income
*Assumes 5% AIR and 9% subaccount performance.

tax tables. This results in a $5,000 nontaxable return of principal in each of the first 20 years.

If a lifetime annuity option contains a guarantee such as a refund feature (e.g., unit refund, installment refund) or a certain period—which could result in a lump sum or continuing periodic payments going to the beneficiary on death of the annuitant—then the investment in the contract is reduced, reducing the nontaxable portion of each annuity benefit payment.

The present value of the refund or certain period guarantee—as determined by IRS annuity tables—is subtracted from the investment in the contract. The remainder is the *adjusted* investment in the contract, which is used to determine the tax-excludable portion of each annuity payment in the same way as for a straight life annuity.

If an annuitant dies before receiving all payments for an annuity payable only for a fixed period of time—where no payment depends on continuing survival—his beneficiary will exclude the same portion of each annuity payment as the annuitant.[7]

If an annuitant with a straight life annuity dies before recovering her investment in the contract, a deduction may be taken on her final tax return in the amount of the unrecovered investment.[8]

If an annuitant dies before receiving the full amount guaranteed under a refund or a period certain feature attached to a life annuity, one or more payments are due to the beneficiary. The beneficiary will have no taxable income unless the total amount that the beneficiary receives plus the amount received tax free by the annuitant (the tax-excludable portions of each annuity payment) exceeds the investment in the contract;[9] that is, all amounts the beneficiary receives are tax exempt until the investment in the contract has been recovered tax free. After this point, any further payments to the beneficiary are taxable.

The owner of an annuity contract cannot avoid income taxes by assigning the right to receive annuity payments to another individual while retaining ownership of the contract. A basic tax principle attributes "fruit" (annuity payments) to the "tree" (contract) on which it grows. Without transferring ownership of the underlying annuity contract itself, gifting or gratuitously assigning the income stream to someone else will not shift taxability of the income away from the contract owner. Annuity payments are taxable to the owner even if paid to a third party.

The taxable portion of IVA benefits is assessed ordinary income tax rates, regardless of whether the underlying investments produced some appreciation that otherwise would have been taxed at (lower) long-term capital gains rates. Because at the time of this writing all income from IVAs is taxed at ordinary income rates, retirees may consider applying tax-deferred account money, such as from 401(k) plans, to purchase their IVAs. This money is already going to be taxed at ordinary income rates (with Roth IRAs [individual retirement accounts] being an exception). These tax-deferred accounts constitute the buckets of money many retirees have mentally earmarked to provide retirement income.

Money kept outside of annuities to provide liquidity may be better invested in taxable accounts where it can enjoy lower tax rates on long-term capital gains and stock dividends.

Insurers do not charge annuity contract owners anything for tax deferral on the capital gains, dividends, and interest generated by the subaccounts contract owners have chosen, the performance of which governs their income payments. The tax deferral on any buildup in reserves is achieved simply by virtue of federal income tax law construction as defined in the Internal Revenue Code. Even if excellent performance of stock and bond subaccounts drives reserves way up to cover magnificently higher-than-expected future annuity benefit payments, such gains are not taxable currently but rather only piecewise as future annuity benefit payments occur.

USE OF IMMEDIATE ANNUITIES TO AVOID 10% PENALTY TAX ON PREMATURE DISTRIBUTIONS

In order to encourage long-term private-sector retirement savings, Congress grants favorable tax treatment to *deferred* annuity contracts by providing for deferral of taxation on inside buildup until distributions are actually taken. In order to discourage use of deferred annuity contracts as short-term tax-deferred investments, Internal Revenue Code Section 72(q) imposes a 10% penalty tax on certain "premature" distributions. A distribution from a deferred annuity contract to a taxpayer who is younger than age 59½ is generally considered premature.

To the extent any portion of a deferred annuity distribution payment is includable in taxable income, an additional 10% tax is imposed on premature distributions. There are specific exemptions from the 10% tax, including death or disability of the taxpayer. One important exemption is that the tax does not apply to any payment that is part of a series of substantially equal periodic payments made no less frequently than annually for the life or life expectancy of the taxpayer or the joint lives or joint life expectancies of the taxpayer and his designated beneficiary.

Distributions from deferred annuity contracts made on or after the date on which a taxpayer becomes age 59½ are also exempt. Thus, one way to receive penalty-tax-free distributions from a deferred annuity contract before age 59½ is to annuitize the contract by electing a single life or a joint life immediate annuity.

ESTATE TAXATION

When the owner-annuitant of a straight life annuity dies, no further annuity payments are due, and there is no property interest remaining at his death to be included in his gross estate. If the annuity option was such that further payments are due—as possible with unit refund, installment refund, life with period certain, fixed-period, or joint and survivor options—tax implications turn on whether the remaining benefit is payable to the decedent's estate or to a named beneficiary.

Sometimes a beneficiary is named in the immediate annuity application, but the owner-annuitant outlives the beneficiary. If no other primary or contingent beneficiaries exist or are surviving at the owner-annuitant's death, annuity contract language may prescribe that the residual value be paid to the owner's estate. Annuity contract language may further prescribe that if the annuity option were such that the additional payments were to occur in a continuing periodic series and if no beneficiaries should exist, the residual value equal to the discounted value of the remaining periodic payments may be paid to the owner's estate in a lump sum. This facilitates estate settlement.

If any remaining immediate annuity value after the owner's death is payable to his estate, the value of the postdeath payment(s) is includable in his gross estate as a property interest owned by him at the time of his death.[10]

If payments due under the annuity after the owner's death are payable to a named beneficiary, a "premium payment" test determines inclusion in the gross estate.[11] The postdeath residual value of the annuity is includable in the owner's gross estate in proportion to the percentage of the annuity premium the owner paid. If the owner paid the entire premium, the residual value is fully includable. If the owner furnished only part of the premium, the owner's gross estate includes only a proportional share. For example, in a joint and survivor annuity, if the deceased annuitant purchased the contract, the full value of the survivor's annuity is included in the decedent's gross estate. If the survivor purchased the contract, none of the value of the survivor's annuity is included in the deceased annuitant's estate. If both contributed equally to the purchase price, 50% of the value of the survivor's annuity is included in the decedent's estate. Where community funds of a husband and wife are used to purchase a joint and survivor annuity, 50% of the value of the survivor's annuity is includable in the gross estate of the spouse who dies first.

Deferred variable annuities—those that have not been converted into an *immediate* variable annuity—may not be good vehicles for passing wealth to the next generation. The oft-cited maxim, "Annuities are meant to be spent," is valid; that is, deferred annuities are well suited as a source of retirement income by conversion to an immediate annuity. They are less well suited as a wealth-transfer vehicle.

It is important to note, though, that use of an IVA to generate income for the whole of life may allow individuals to safely set other money aside as a legacy for their heirs and/or to purchase efficient wealth-transfer vehicles. Absent use of an IVA, individuals may instead be forced to continually draw down accumulated savings—perhaps to zero—even if they live parsimoniously since there is uncertainty as to how much will be needed to sustain quality of life during retirement; and only the residual amount of money, if any, will be available for a less efficient bequest than could have resulted.

If an individual absolutely wants to bequeath assets, an IVA purchase may facilitate this by providing the individual with lifetime income, thereby safely allowing him to apply part of his assets to satisfy his wealth-transfer objective, such as through the purchase of life insurance. The simplified decision matrix in Table 10.1 illustrates the outcomes of two possible actions, namely, (1) buy an IVA and (2) do not buy an IVA, and two possible events, namely, (1) live long and (2) do not live long. If the individual does not live long, there are residual assets available for a bequest; either the individual bought an IVA and the residual assets were available for bequest, or the individual did not buy an IVA and all assets were available for bequest. If the individual lives long and buys an IVA, the IVA may provide sufficient income, leaving residual assets available for a bequest (possibly including the benefit of a life insurance policy purchased simultaneously with the IVA). If the individual lives long and does not buy an IVA, exhaustion of assets may occur, leaving zero assets for a bequest. Thus, of the two possible actions, not buying an IVA is the only action that may result in no bequest. Ironically, individuals sometimes avoid IVA purchase on the grounds that their objective is to provide a bequest.

If your situation is such that corporate pensions, Social Security, and other sources provide higher retirement income than you expected and your deferred annuity is no longer necessary to generate even more retirement income by conversion to an immediate annuity, you may wish to consult a financial advisor. Your advisor may suggest estate planning approaches to help you achieve efficient wealth transfer if that is now your objective since your retirement income needs are adequately met. For example, your deferred

TABLE 10.1 IVA Purchase Decision Matrix for Individuals with Bequest Objective

	Buy IVA	Do Not Buy IVA
Live Long	Bequest	No Bequest
Do Not Live Long	Bequest	Bequest

annuity might be converted into an immediate annuity with benefit payments serving as life insurance policy premiums. Future estate tax law and your particular circumstances will govern whether life insurance is appropriate and, if so, in what amount.

GIFT TAXATION

If a person purchases an annuity contract where the proceeds are payable to a beneficiary other than himself or his estate and he has no power to change the beneficiary or to otherwise derive economic benefit for himself or his estate, he has made a gift of the annuity contract. Similarly, if he absolutely assigns an annuity contract or relinquishes through assignment every power he retained in a previously issued contract, he has made a gift. If he pays the premium for an annuity contract in which he has no ownership rights, he had made a gift equal to the premium.

The purchase of a joint and survivor annuity results in a taxable gift if the designation of the beneficiary of the survivor payments is irrevocable. For example, if a donor purchases a joint and 100% to survivor annuity covering himself and his sister, the gift tax value is the cost of the joint and 100% to survivor annuity less the cost of a single life annuity covering the donor. If the joint and 100% to survivor immediate variable annuity with first monthly benefit of $1,000 has a premium of $150,000 and if a single life annuity with the identical first monthly benefit covering the donor's life has a premium of $100,000, the value of the gift is $50,000.

If an immediate annuity is purchased by a donor on his own life and immediately given to another, the gift value is the premium. If an immediate annuity is purchased by a donor on his own life and given to another person at a later date, gift tax value is the single premium the insurer would charge for an annuity with identical benefits based on the annuitant's attained age at time of the gift.

When a life annuity with a refund feature is purchased and the beneficiary to receive payments under the refund feature is irrevocably designated, a gift has been made. This is true even though the beneficiary will receive nothing if the annuitant survives beyond the point where any refund is due. The gift is contingent on the annuitant's death within a specific period. Gift tax value is the present value of the contingent right to receive any refund payments due on the annuitant's death, whether as a lump sum or in continuing installments.

There is an annual exclusion of $10,000 (indexed) for gifts to each donee. The exclusion is $20,000 (indexed) if a donor makes a gift to a third party with the consent of his spouse.

Gifts related to annuity contracts qualify for the annual exclusion if they are gifts of "present interests." The annual exclusion is not available for gifts of "future interests."

A "future interest" is created when restrictions are placed on the recipient's right to receive benefits. The gift involving the naming of an irrevocable beneficiary under a refund annuity mentioned three paragraphs earlier is an example of a gift of "future interest," since annuitant death within a specified period is a restriction on the beneficiary's right to receive benefits. Because this is a gift of "future interest," it does not qualify for the annual gift-tax exclusion. A gift is not of "future interest" solely because contractual benefits become payable at some future time.

PREMIUM TAX

Some U.S. states and territories assess a premium tax on immediate variable annuities, although this is now a minority of states. The tax is equal to a specific percentage—usually 2% or less—of the premium. The tax rate may differ depending on whether the immediate variable annuity is sold in the "tax-qualified" market (e.g., IRAs) or "non-tax-qualified" market.

Premium tax is assessed on insurers by states on a state-specific basis; that is, insurers owe premium tax to a state equal to total immediate annuity premiums collected times the appropriate tax rate. Insurers may pass this tax through to immediate annuity purchasers on a state-specific basis; that is, they factor exactly the premium tax caused by that sale into the process that converts a single premium associated with a particular sale into a series of annuity units payable on each future payment date.

Other insurers simply factor into the process the average state premium tax across all states in which they conduct business and assess this average on every sale. Obviously, immediate variable annuity purchasers who live in states without a premium tax benefit slightly by purchasing an immediate annuity from insurers who assess the tax on a state-specific basis, while purchasers living in states with a relatively high premium tax benefit slightly by purchasing an immediate annuity from insurers who assess the tax on an average basis.

State premium tax may be due based on state of residency or the state in which the business is transacted, depending on state tax code language. Because state premium tax is such a small percentage and because there are so many factors to consider in purchasing an immediate variable annuity—subaccounts available, investment managers, fees, customer service, conversion factors, AIRs available, technical support, allowable frequency of subaccount reallocation, knowledge and experience and proximity of financial adviser—one should not base an IVA purchase decision on how an insurer assesses state premium tax.

If an IVA purchaser lives in a U.S. state or territory that has a premium tax, however, the purchaser should clarify for himself or herself whether an annuity option with a refund feature applies to the gross premium or to the premium net of premium tax. For example, if a $300,000 single premium is applied to purchase a "unit refund" variable annuity option in a state with a 2% premium tax, one should inquire whether the insurer's promise is to ensure that the annuitant via periodic annuity benefit payments and the beneficiary via a lump sum on the annuitant's death jointly and cumulatively receive the value of annuity units purchased by $300,000 or $294,000; that is, if investment experience exactly matched the AIR at all times and annuity income remained level, which of these two amounts does the insurer guarantee?

DAC TAX

Internal Revenue Code Section 848 applies to non-tax-qualified annuity purchases, including immediate variable annuity purchases, the equivalent of a federal premium tax. This is the so-called DAC (Deferred Acquisition Cost) tax, which took effect October 1, 1990, as a result of the Revenue Reconciliation Act of 1990.

The DAC tax, when it applies, is not assessed directly against the gross premium like state premium tax. Rather, DAC tax is assessed indirectly, yet still with the end result of retirement income lower than it would be absent the DAC tax. Insurers might factor it into the conversion rates (as a front-end load) or into the mortality and expense (M&E) charge (spreading its impact over the life of the annuity payout). While insurers may use different conversion factors for business subject to the DAC tax, it is more common to use one set of conversion factors or one M&E charge that assumes that a specific percentage of IVA business written is subject to the tax.

When an annuity is sold, an insurer incurs acquisition expenses, such as paying the salesperson a commission, paying the wholesaler who trains salespeople about the product, issuing the purchaser a contract, processing the premium payment, calculating benefit amounts, and setting up policyholder records listing the owner(s), annuitant(s) and beneficiary(ies), addresses, tax identification numbers, date(s) of birth, type of annuity option, state of residence, agent of record, and so on.

Rather than allowing an insurer to recognize these acquisition expenses at time of sale, IRS rules spread insurer recognition of these expenses over approximately 10 years under the thinking that the insurer will derive revenue over a course of future years as a result of incurring these acquisition expenses, so such spreading better pairs revenue with expenses.

The exact wording of IRC Section 848 is:

In the case of an insurance company—
(1) specified policy acquisition expenses for any taxable year shall be capitalized, and
(2) such expenses shall be allowed as a deduction ratably over the 120-month period beginning with the first month in the second half of such taxable year.

The Internal Revenue Code requires insurers to capitalize 1.75% of the non-tax-qualified immediate variable annuity premium. Amortization occurs over a 120-month period. Insurers recognize 5% of the capitalized amount in the first year, 10% in each of the next nine years, and 5% in the subsequent year. Recognition of acquisition costs is not immediate but deferred, resulting in the terminology "Deferred Acquisition Cost."

In the example shown in Table 10.2, it is assumed that an insurer issues IVA business uniformly throughout the calendar year. As a result, a midyear

TABLE 10.2 IVA Policy Acquisition Expense Recognition Pattern under Internal Revenue Code Section 848 (DAC Tax)

Single Premium: $1,000,000 Capitalization Rate: 1.75% Amount Capitalized: $17,500		
Time	DAC Amortization	DAC Outstanding
0.0		$17,500
0.5	$ 875	16,625
1.5	1,750	14,875
2.5	1,750	13,125
3.5	1,750	11,375
4.5	1,750	9,625
5.5	1,750	7,875
6.5	1,750	6,125
7.5	1,750	4,375
8.5	1,750	2,625
9.5	1,750	875
10.5	875	0
Total	$17,500	

(July 1) average policy issue date is assumed. Thus, July 1 will be Time 0, December 31 will be Time 0.5, December 31 of the following year will be Time 1.5, and so on.

The example shown in Table 10.2 assumes a $1,000,000 single premium. Because tax law requires that insurers capitalize 1.75% of non-tax-qualified annuity premiums, the amount capitalized is $17,500. The insurer recognizes as a DAC amortization expense $875 in the first policy year, $1,750 in each of policy years 2 through 10, and $875 in policy year 11.

Relative to the pre–DAC-tax environment, this speeds up federal income tax payments by insurers. Insurers pay the same cumulative amount of tax over the life of the policy. They just pay it sooner as a result of the DAC tax. Thus, while the so-called DAC tax is not really a tax *per se* but rather merely accelerates the timing of federal income tax payments, it has the equivalent effect of a tax.

The Revenue Reconciliation Act of 1990 affected the timing of federal tax obligations of annuity writers but not the cumulative amounts. The cost to insurers is the interest lost that would have been earned on these funds had the timing of their payment not been accelerated. As illustrated in the preceding example, a portion of expenses once used to offset revenue are no longer permitted to be recognized in the year incurred. Rather, they are required to be capitalized as a deferred acquisition cost (DAC) asset and amortized back into expenses on a straight-line basis over a 10-year period.

This extra tax is directly allocable to specific contracts. For example, it *is* allocable to new non-tax-qualified immediate variable annuities; it *is not* allocable to annuities associated with funding of tax-qualified pension plans, is not allocable to annuities received under an internal exchange program where a new contract replaces an old contract with similar characteristics, and is not allocable to premiums returned under a "free look" provision.

In other words, the amount to be capitalized is 1.75% of the "net premium" as defined in IRC Section 803(b), which is, in general, premiums received minus those returned under a "free look" provision. In the year of capitalization, one-half year of amortization is allowed. As a result, amortization will span 11 tax years.

The extra tax is fully defined at time of premium payment. The financial impact depends on the insurer's time value of money and its federal income tax rates over the amortization period.

To quantify the impact of the DAC tax, assume an insurer requires a 15% after-tax return on the capital it allocates to projects, typically insurance products (including annuities, which are technically insurance products).

Further assume a 35% corporate federal income tax rate and a fiscal year that is the calendar year.

Previously, insurers recognized no gain or loss at point of sale of an IVA. For example, if they incurred acquisition expenses equal to 5% of the gross premium to put the business on the books, they based the annuity payments on the remaining 95%. Thus, they had assets equal to 95% of the gross premium and a liability (the "reserve") to pay future annuity benefits also equal to 95% of the gross premium. Therefore, there was no taxable gain at point of sale. Rather, earnings and, hence, tax liability would materialize over the life of the immediate annuity policy to the extent revenue (such as mortality and expense risk charges) exceeded expenses (such as calculating benefit payments, printing and mailing monthly benefit checks and annual customer tax statements, and providing a customer service call center).

With the imposition of the DAC tax, an insurer in the preceding example situation ($1,000,000 premium and 5% acquisition expenses) no longer begins with $950,000 in assets and $950,000 in reserve liability. Rather, the insurer begins with $967,500 in assets, which consist of the $950,000 net premium and $17,500 of DAC asset.

The result is immediate recognition for federal income tax purposes of a $17,500 gain. The insurer gets to amortize $875 in that first calendar year and shows a $16,625 gain as a result of the DAC tax. This produces a tax bill of $16,625 × 35%, or $5,818.75.

The insurer's tax liability is reduced in each of the next nine years by $1,750 × 35%, or $612.50, and in the final year by $875 × 35%, or $306.25. Table 10.3 shows the additional tax paid in the year of policy issue and the reduced tax paid in subsequent years.

If, in the absence of DAC tax, the insurer could have deployed the amount of DAC tax paid in projects returning 15% after tax, then the present value (PV) of forgone earnings attributable to the "early" payment of federal income tax (FIT) can be found by discounting the "DAC Tax" column in Table 10.3 by 15%. The result is $2,630.08, or roughly 0.26% of the $1,000,000 premium.[12] The present value of the forgone use of these funds as a percentage of annuity premiums is about 0.26%.

The cash flow stream comprised of the extra tax paid in the first year and reduced taxes paid in the subsequent 10 years is discounted at a 15% interest rate—15% is assumed since had the funds not been remitted to the federal government, they might have earned 5% after tax on their own and served as the necessary surplus to support the safe issuance of further annuity business that could generate an additional 10% after tax, making the opportunity cost of not having these funds 15%.

TABLE 10.3 Present Value Impact of DAC Tax

Time	DAC Tax	Present Value of DAC Tax @ 15% as of Time 0.0
0.5	$5,818.75	$5,426.01
1.5	−612.50	−496.66
2.5	−612.50	−431.88
3.5	−612.50	−375.55
4.5	−612.50	−326.56
5.5	−612.50	−283.97
6.5	−612.50	−246.93
7.5	−612.50	−214.72
8.5	−612.50	−186.71
9.5	−612.50	−162.36
10.5	−306.25	−70.59
	0.00	$2,630.08

$$\frac{\$2,630.08}{\$1,000,000.00} = 0.002630 = \text{Present Value of Forgone Use of Funds as Percent of Premium}$$

$$\frac{0.002630}{1 - 0.35} = 0.004046 = \text{Front-End Load Necessary to Offset DAC Tax}$$

An equivalent way to quantify the impact of the DAC tax is to look at it on an accumulated value basis. The second column in Table 10.4 shows the cumulative FIT prepayment resulting from the DAC tax. The third column shows what this could earn at 15% interest, accumulated to the end of the 10.5-year period, the point at which the capitalized policy acquisition expenses have been fully allowed as a deduction.

For example, the Time 8.5 value of $918.75 could have earned 15%, or $137.81, over the next one-year period. Accumulating $137.81 for one year at 15% brings the Time 10.5 value to $158.48.

Note that $11,410.31 discounted 10.5 years at 15% equals $2,630.08, verifying the result obtained in Table 10.3.

TABLE 10.4 Accumulated Value Impact of DAC Tax

Time	Cumulative FIT Paid "Prematurely" Relative to Pre–DAC-Tax Era	15% Return on Prior Column Accumulated to Time 10.5 @ 15%
0.5	$5,818.75	$ 3,070.45
1.5	5,206.25	2,388.91
2.5	4,593.75	1,832.92
3.5	3,981.25	1,381.33
4.5	3,368.75	1,016.36
5.5	2,756.25	723.10
6.5	2,143.75	489.06
7.5	1,531.25	303.76
8.5	918.75	158.48
9.5	306.25	45.94
10.5	0.00	0.00
Total		$11,410.31

An insurer would need to assess a front-end charge on the immediate variable annuity equal to 0.2630%/(1 − 35% FIT rate), or 0.4046%, to fully negate the impact of the DAC tax; that is, by assessing a front-end load of 0.4046% pretax, the insurer collects an extra 0.2630% after tax, placing the insurer in a similar financial position to what existed prior to the imposition of the DAC tax. The end result is a reduction in immediate variable annuity benefits since this extra loading decreases the net premium on which benefits (i.e., the number of annuity units the value of which is payable each period) are based. For example, an annuitant with an initial $50,000 annual benefit might receive $202 less in the first year and $202 as adjusted for subaccount performance less in all future years.

If an insurer desires to fully offset the DAC tax effect in the preceding scenario, the insurer could either assess a one-time, front-end load of, say, 0.41% when calculating the number of annuity units to be paid on each benefit date or increment the M&E&A charge by a smaller amount sufficient to produce an equivalent present value effect. Again, the insurer's time value of money (here assumed 15%), FIT rate (here assumed 35%), and degree of precision in calculating DAC tax impact (here taxes are assumed payable only at year-end when, in fact, they are payable with greater frequency) all govern the exact number, but the illustration gives a very good order of magnitude.

Annuity writers may offer two sets of conversion factors: (1) a higher set for tax-qualified IVA business and (2) a lower set for non-tax-qualified IVA business subject to DAC tax. This approach allows the annuity writer to be as competitive as possible in the tax-qualified marketplace, where individuals may be more likely to have mentally earmarked exchanging their accumulated assets for lifetime retirement income.

Alternatively, annuity writers can use one set of conversion factors, blending the tax-qualified and non-tax-qualified rates in some assumed proportions. This approach effectively subsidizes non-tax-qualified business by tax-qualified business but offers simplicity.

Note that there is no connection between the acquisition cost an insurer issuing an immediate variable annuity actually incurs and the 1.75% of premium rate at which the IRC requires capitalization.

While state premium tax and federal DAC tax introduce "friction" into the system in the sense that these items reduce annuity benefits otherwise available to consumers, to the extent that state premium tax goes to fund state departments of insurance whose triennial examinations of insurers reveal potential problems, early detection can spare healthier insurers state guaranty fund assessments. This helps insurers who properly price their products and properly manage their business from effectively burdening their future customers with surcharges to cover errors or misfortunes of less healthy insurers.

In terms of public policy, taxes are often assessed on undesirable activities (e.g., tobacco, alcohol) or, with the hope of lessening consumption, on natural resources (e.g., oil, gasoline). To the extent taxes are passed through to end consumers, the supply curve shifts left ($S^1 \rightarrow S^2$), the demand curve is unchanged (D), and the result is that the new market-clearing equilibrium point is associated with a reduced quantity of the good or service taxed ($Q_1 \rightarrow Q_2$). (See Figure 10.2.) Thus, the imposition of the DAC tax

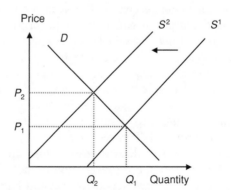

FIGURE 10.2 Higher Taxation Effect on Price and Quantity

may serve to deter use of non-tax-qualified annuities. Higher taxation has a price-increasing and a quantity-decreasing effect for products like IVAs that exhibit elasticity of demand—those products for which consumers are relatively responsive to price changes, which give rise to considerable changes in the quantity purchased.

Certain tax policies encumber greater self-reliance through use of private-sector retirement income products, thereby increasing reliance on governmental assistance programs. On the flip side, tax incentives could be offered to encourage greater self-reliance, a topic to which we now turn.

TAX INCENTIVES

At the time of this writing, there is a federal legislative movement to increase the incentive for private-sector retirement savings and financial security through introduction of tax policy that would reduce taxes on either non-tax-qualified or all immediate annuities. A variety of programs with names such as the Lifetime Annuity Proposal (LAP) have been introduced for consideration.

The idea is to reduce the tax rate for immediate annuities to something lower than the ordinary income tax rate. While capital gains occurring inside the annuity could be taxed at capital gains rates and bond interest could be taxed at ordinary income rates, in the interest of administrative simplicity, the notion is to apply a single tax rate somewhere between the lower capital gains rate and the higher ordinary income rate. To qualify for the more favorable income tax treatment, the annuity option elected would need to be sufficiently long, such as a single life or joint life annuity.

Other federal proposals to provide incentive for Americans to consider immediate annuities to help ensure that their income lasts as long as they do include not taxing the first few thousand dollars per year of income derived from lifetime annuities or only taxing one-half of income derived from lifetime annuities up to an annual limit such as $20,000.

Proposals regarding partial Social Security privatization emerge that include use of immediate annuities. For example, 2% of the Federal Insurance Contributions Act (FICA) withholding tax could be directed to private individual accounts rather than to the Social Security trust fund. Such accounts might require mandatory conversion to immediate annuities, or "annuitization."

Social Security privatization, full or partial, is a complex, political, emotionally charged issue. For example, if common stock investments are permitted, a major government-sponsored program could effectively determine which corporations have access to large amounts of capital and which corporations are denied such access. To remedy this, asset diversification rules may be such as to require the use of index funds. As another example, if demographics result in a large number of the "baby boom" generation reaching retirement age and liquidating such accounts rather than accumulating savings in such accounts, this constant selling of common shares could result in downward pressure on the price of such shares. This phenomenon may be muted by several factors:

■ *Such sales will happen gradually.* The "baby boom" generation spans almost two decades. Once any particular individual commences distributions, his or her liquidation period may also span several decades

■ *Well-to-do individuals may liquidate little during retirement.* The wealthiest 10% of U.S. households own 88% of the individual equities held by households.[13] These wealthy baby boomers are likely to live off of their dividend income. They may leave their financial assets to future generations rather than liquidate them.

■ *Market participants extend beyond baby boomers.* The baby boom generation represents roughly only one quarter of the U.S. population. Subsequent generations are more likely to be purchasing (demanding) equities and bidding up their price as the baby boom generation is selling (supplying) equities, driving down their price. With their newfound wealth, international investors in rapidly developing countries could create a rising demand for U.S. securities, bidding up their price. Foundations and endowments unaffected by aging temper any "price meltdown" scenario.

■ *Multiple factors affect equity prices.* Normal factors that drive equity markets—corporate earnings, interest rates, investor sentiment, tax environment, technological innovation, and political events—will likely continue to have a more profound collective effect on equity prices than one oversized demographic group aging its way through the financial markets over multiple decades.

Allowable underwriting classifications—age, sex, health, race, tobacco use, and other characteristics for which genuine mortality differences exist—would need to be determined. There is no question that genuine mortality differences exist due to these and other characteristics. The question rather is whether it is politically expedient to recognize such risks. Using one single unisex, uniage conversion factor for everyone is likely too broad. Using all the underwriting classifications just mentioned that would promote the fairest economic value of income benefits in relation to premium applied is likely too narrow. Subpopulations of the U.S. population will likely have different viewpoints depending on whether inclusion of a specific underwriting classification is to their benefit or detriment.

Government-sponsored social (poverty) programs exist—and have a cost to taxpayers—for those who become destitute. Tax policy that encourages self-reliance through providing for one's own lifetime income reduces the number who become destitute and require government support. The cost/benefit question turns on the relative balance between government revenue forgone due to tax incentives designed to encourage individuals to provide for themselves in old age and additional government expenses incurred in the way of poverty programs for elderly who fail to provide for themselves.

Just as the imposition of the DAC tax may serve to reduce the use of non-tax-qualified immediate annuities, passage of the LAP or similar legislation may serve to increase their use.

Political factors involved in such legislation involve weighing concerns about inadequate national retirement savings and security (including Social Security) against reduced tax revenues attributable to incentives to further use of immediate annuities as a personal—and national—risk-reduction device. Such tax incentives may not be as costly as first appears, since while wealth doesn't significantly decline around age 65, income does. Therefore, any tax revenue reduction may be from ordinary income tax rates associated with the lower income tax brackets frequently found in retirement to something like the capital gains tax rates.

Annuity trade associations, including the National Association for Variable Annuities[14] (NAVA) and the Committee of Annuity Insurers, and the American Council of Life Insurers (ACLI) are part of the coalition to advocate tax incentives encouraging economic self-reliance through the use of immediate annuities.

The likelihood of living in poverty escalates with age for both men and women. See Figures 10.3 and 10.4.[15] An income annuity is one instrument

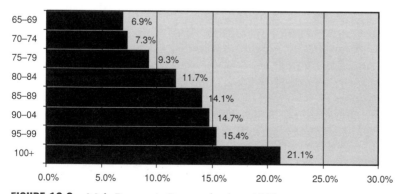

FIGURE 10.3 Male Percent in Poverty by Age: 1989
Source: U.S. Census Bureau.

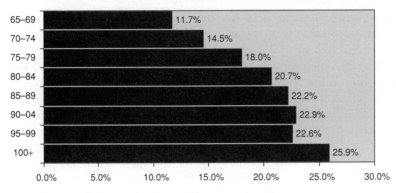

FIGURE 10.4   Female Percent in Poverty by Age: 1989
Source: U.S. Census Bureau.

to combat individuals outliving their means to sustain themselves. Tax incentives to encourage greater use of income annuities represent one class of devices to prolong individual economic self-reliance.

CHAPTER 11

Services and Fees

Be silent as to services you have rendered, but speak of favours you have received.
　　　　　　　　　—Seneca, *Roman dramatist and philosopher*

SERVICE FEATURES

Immediate variable annuities (IVAs) may offer some or all of the following service features:

- Ability to reallocate among subaccounts the performance of which govern retirement income benefits.
- Customer service representative access.
- Internet service center and/or automated voice response (telephony) service (e.g., to access daily annuity unit values for each subaccount).
- Direct deposit of retirement income benefits.
- On-line prospectuses and Statements of Additional Information (SAI).
- Periodic (e.g., quarterly) customer statements of account,[1] showing the subaccounts that currently determine benefit payments, the number of annuity units paid on each payment date for each subaccount, benefit payments made during the most recent reporting period, reallocations of subaccounts that determine benefit payments made during the most recent reporting period, annuity payout option information (e.g., time remaining in certain period), and so on.

If one purchases an IVA from a highly rated insurer, which has a low mortality and expense (M&E) charge, invests in low-cost index subaccounts where the underlying funds are managed by a reputable investment manager, adequately diversifies across asset classes collectively appropriate for the annuitant's risk tolerance, and can obtain automatic portfolio rebalancing to maintain the desired investment allocation, then increased freedom from anxiety about longevity-related financial concerns can result. Such a program can reasonably and safely be placed on "autopilot," a factor of high value to retirees who, by virtue of interest or health, choose not to serve in an ongoing capacity as their own chief investment officer and pension plan administrator.

Annuity writers require massive computer code to store and process all the information and transactional activity required for policy issue, deposits, partial withdrawals, full surrenders, transfers, account values, reserving, tax calculations, and so forth. Variable annuities are significantly more complex than fixed annuities. Some insurance systems are "home grown," with code written and maintained internally. Many insurers use vendor-provided software, sometimes further customized to their specific needs. For example, insurers can purchase repetitive payment system software modules to calculate and pay immediate variable annuity benefits.

PRODUCT FEES AND CHARGES

Federal securities laws govern many characteristics of IVA products, such as registration with the Securities and Exchange Commission (SEC). An early standard governing variable annuity contracts required each charge to be specified as to purpose and use and to comply with numerical limits. The National Securities Markets Improvements Act of 1996 added a new rule to The Investment Company Act of 1940 dealing with variable annuity fees and charges. The most pertinent portion of the rule—found in Section 26.f.2.—states:

> It shall be unlawful for any registered separate account funding variable insurance contracts, or for the sponsoring insurance company of such account, to sell any such contract unless the fees and charges deducted under the contract, in the aggregate, are reasonable in relation to the services rendered, the expenses expected to be incurred, and the risks assumed by the insurance company, and . . . the insurance company so represents in the registration statement for the contract.

There is no definitive test as to what does or does not constitute a "reasonable" level of fees and charges. A number of factors are germane to such an assessment. These factors include whether each of the individual charges complies with specific limits imposed by the prior regulatory regime; the benefits conferred on contract owners;[2] whether the charges are within the range of industry practice;[3] reasonable profit for the issuing company; industry trends; and the requirements of state laws, rules, and regulations, such as applicable nonforfeiture and valuation laws.

Immediate variable annuity products typically have an M&E risk charge that is expressed as a percentage of the reserve, for example, 1.25%. They also typically have an administrative (A) charge expressed as a percentage of the reserve, for example, 0.15%. Sometimes these are jointly referenced as the "M&E&A charge." Immediate variable annuities sometimes have an annual fee of a flat dollar amount, such as $35. These charges flow to the insurance company administering the program and absorbing the risks.

Unless an insurer has a current level of charges and a guaranteed level of charges above which it can never go, the M&E risk charge can never be raised once the contract is issued. This remains true even if mortality experience or expense experience proves unfavorable to the insurer.

Section 50.6(a)(1) of New York State Insurance Department Regulation 47 states:

> *Mortality and Expense Guarantees—Contracts and certificates must contain a statement that neither expenses actually incurred, other than taxes on the investment return, nor mortality actually experienced, shall adversely affect the dollar amount of variable annuity payments after such payments have commenced.*

The M&E&A charges are at the IVA product level. At the level of the underlying investment funds, there are investment management expenses that flow to the investment management company, for example, 0.70% for a domestic common stock fund. There may also be 12b-1 fee distribution expenses, for example, 0.25%.

Fees that are asset-based (e.g., based on assets equal to the level of immediate annuity reserve for a contract), such as investment management fees, 12b-1 fees, and M&E&A fees, are less visible to contract owners than a flat dollar charge. While asset-based fees are entirely visible in terms of being disclosed in the annuity contract and prospectus, they are much less visible than a flat dollar charge, such as $35 per contract per year. This is because while asset-based fees tend to represent the difference between gross investment performance and the net return that annuitants experience—where the net return through interplay with the AIR determines periodic annuity benefits—such fees do not appear on any statements sent to contract owners. In contrast, a flat dollar annual fee (e.g., $35) may appear on contract owner statements.

As a result, a contract owner might complain about a small, visible flat dollar fee (e.g., $35 per year) while being oblivious to a larger asset-based charge (e.g., a 1.25% M&E risk charge on a $100,000 reserve, which comes to $1,250 that year). In fairness, certain expenses tend to be the same regardless of the size of the IVA contract (e.g., it costs the same for the insurer to print and mail 12 annuity benefit checks and one tax statement per year regardless of contract size), and such expenses may be most precisely offset by a flat dollar charge.

Insurers sometimes view small flat dollar amount annual fees—such as $35 per year—as a "nuisance" in that they may result in relatively large customer annoyance even though they are a relatively small fraction of revenue. They are more important for small-sized annuity contracts to cover annual expenses unrelated to contract size. As a result, an insurer may assess the flat dollar annual fee on small-sized contracts to help cover servicing expenses but may waive the fee for contracts above a certain threshold size (e.g., $50,000).

Because immediate annuities are liquidation products, the underlying reserve starts at the net premium (or some amount close to it) and grades to zero over time. As a result, asset-based charges provide higher amounts of revenue to the insurer in the early years and lower amounts in later years. In addition to absorbing mortality risk and administering benefits, insurers have a host of responsibilities requiring funding.

Because IVA writers tend to incur expenses that are heavier at the front end (issuing a contract, processing a premium, calculating initial benefit, setting up contract owner records, calculating initial reserves) and at the back end (calculating and paying death benefit claims if due, determining which beneficiaries survived the annuitant and whether governmental tax authorities may have a claim against their death benefit before payment), their revenue may not match up precisely with their expenses on a year-by-year basis but is projected to prove adequate over the life of a block of business.

The National Securities Markets Improvements Act of 1996 modified The Investment Company Act of 1940 whereby Section 26.f.3. states that *"the fees and charges deducted under the contract shall include all fees and charges imposed for any purpose and in any manner."* As a result, total charges must be examined for purposes of the reasonableness of fees and charges test: M&E risk charge, administrative charge, annual fee, investment management charge, 12b-1 fee, and so on.

This is appropriate since some product-level charges could be low due to effective subsidization of the product by investment advisory fees. For example, if Insurance Company A has an investment department that invests annuity premiums received and operates at cost, an investment management fee in excess of the cost of investment management may allow for lower product-level expenses; that is, any basis points of profit generated from investment management of the underlying funds could serve to reduce the number of basis points of product-level expenses needed to achieve the same profit target.

In contrast, if Insurance Company B outsources underlying investment fund management and the full investment advisory fee flows to this external manager to provide for both actual cost of investment management and profit, product-level expenses will need to be higher to generate comparable profit. Since consumers must buy the IVA as a package and cannot buy the "insurance wrapper" component from one company and the "investment management" component from another company, it makes sense that the totality of IVA expenses is considered in any demonstration of reasonableness of fees and charges.

Any investigation with regard to the factor "Is the profit for the issuing company reasonable?" in relation to an assessment of whether fees and charges in a variable product are reasonable raises interesting questions in itself. For example, "Should an efficient company be made to have a more competitive product, or can it simply have a more profitable product?" If two companies offer an identical product with identical fees and charges and if one company is small and/or run inefficiently so as to produce losses while the other is extremely large having reached critical mass and/or is run extremely efficiently so as to produce substantial profits, can profits really be viewed as a legitimate factor in the determination of reasonableness with regard to fees and charges?

It is interesting that a literal reading of The National Securities Markets Improvements Act of 1996 suggests that variable annuity fees and charges that are unreasonably *low* in relation to the services rendered, the expenses expected to be incurred, and the risks assumed by the insurance company equally violate the Investment Company Act of 1940.

A prospective end consumer of IVA products can, as a starting point, gauge his or her purchase decision on a single measure: the initial dollar amount of annuity benefit for a given single premium. Intercompany comparisons need to reflect the same assumed investment rate (AIR). The initial amount of annuity benefit alone, however, is not conclusory as to best product value. A second numeric measure, the total of product fees (M&E&A charge) and investment management fees, needs to be compared. A company with the highest initial annuity benefit may not provide the best value if high product-related fees and charges retard future net subaccount performance, thereby making it smaller relative to the AIR and dampening the annuity unit value progression and the steepness of the (hopefully upward sloping) curve of future benefit payments.

As will be described in Chapter 12, financial advisers play an important role in the distribution of IVA products. Because of the importance of decisions relating to the deployment of one's lifetime accumulation of retirement savings, even do-it-yourselfers tend to value advice of financial counsel. As a result, the form and magnitude of initial and ongoing financial adviser compensation associated with an IVA sale meaningfully influences product distribution.

Initial and ongoing advice of financial counsel frequently is packaged within the product price. For end consumers using financial advisers operating under a fee-for-service rather than a commission revenue structure, to make adequate comparisons, such consumers need to add together IVA product price and advisory fees.

INSURER PERSPECTIVE: VARIABLE INCOME ANNUITY EXPENSES

Insurers incur a variety of expenses in providing services associated with an immediate variable annuity business, which must be covered by the product fees and charges just mentioned. Such expenses include but are not limited to:

Product Development
- Design.
- Pricing.
- Underwriting standards.

Policy Issue
- Contract preparation and issuance.
- Setting up and maintaining policyholder records.

Product Management/Operations
- Calculating and paying periodic annuity benefits.
- Calculating and paying death benefits to beneficiaries.
- Calculating and mailing annual tax statements to annuity contract owners.
- Auditing (e.g., periodically verifying continued survival of annuitants).
- Electronic commission feeds to financial advisers.

Customer Service
- Access to customer service consultants via 800 toll-free access line.
- 24 hour/365 day access to annuity unit value information via Internet and automated phone system.
- Automatic subaccount reallocation service.
- Quarterly customer statements.
- Customer newsletters and other customer communications.

Sales Representative Access
- Availability of face-to-face communication with licensed financial adviser.

Marketing

- Creation, production, and distribution of print and electronic media to inform contract owners and prospective contract owners of product benefits.
- Computer illustration systems.

Wholesaling

- Financial adviser training and support, initial and ongoing.

Securities Law

- Prospectus and registration statement creation, filing, and maintenance.
- Statement of Additional Information creation, filing, and maintenance.
- Semiannual and annual reports on separate accounts.

State Compliance

- Contract and application creation and filing, complying with state regulations.
- Preparation and filing of actuarial memoranda.
- Compliance with state valuation laws.
- Review of changing state regulations and introduction of resultant procedural changes.
- State insurance department examinations.

Market Conduct

- Compliance with SEC, National Association of Securities Dealers (NASD), and state advertising regulations.
- Ongoing financial adviser training regarding sales practice and market conduct issues.
- Optional: Insurance Marketplace Standards Association (IMSA) certification.

Financial Reporting

- Statutory, generally accepted accounting principles (GAAP), and tax reporting.
- Audits by independent public accountants.

Information Systems

- Purchase and maintenance of hardware and software necessary to track customer transactions, pay benefits, produce customer account statements, generate tax statements, generate financial reports, calculate reserves, and produce subaccount performance reports.

Human Resources

■ Hiring and training of personnel to provide services (customer service, legal, information systems, actuarial, sales, marketing, financial reporting, product development, product management, valuation, etc.) that benefit IVA contract owners.
■ Continuing education of such personnel.

Capital Raising and Allocation

■ Raising of capital with which to fund operations, initially and ongoing.
■ Maintenance of capital allocation to IVA business (e.g., required risk-based capital).

Valuation

■ Valuation of IVA reserve liabilities.

Such expenses (as well as federal income taxes and profit) tend to be covered through M&E&A charge revenue, although the investment advisory agreement regarding the management of the underlying investment funds may also generate revenue for the insurer. The mortality risk an insurer assumes is that annuitants may live longer than expected and that it will need to pay more in annuity benefits than expected. This could happen by random chance, by a healthier-than-average collection of individuals purchasing that company's product, by financial advisers directing sales of certain annuity options to one insurer and sales of other annuity options to other insurers because of some pricing anomaly, because of heart disease or cancer cures, because of increased transplant utilization, because of discovering how the human body can reproduce any degenerating organ from some of its own primal cells, and so on. Regardless of how adverse actual mortality experience gets relative to what the insurer assumed, the M&E charge cannot be raised—even if everyone becomes a Methuselah.

Similarly, the M&E charge cannot be raised even if actual expenses exceed those assumed. This could occur if the corporate income tax rate were increased, if states or the federal government mandated more frequent or more comprehensive periodic reporting either to policyholders or regulators or both, if postage rates increased, and so on.

In reality, the M&E charges cover not just these risks but may also partially or wholly cover financial adviser sales compensation as well as all the expenses in the preceding bulleted lists. Traditionally, front-end expense loads cover front-end expense items such as sales commissions, wholesaler allowances, and policy setup, whereas M&E&A charges cover ongoing expense items. As one example, front-end sales compensation may be primarily covered by a front-end load whereas ongoing asset-based sales compensation may be covered by M&E&A charges. To the extent any front-end compensation exceeds front-end loading, the excess may be recovered over time through the M&E&A charges.

The SEC, which regulates securities including variable annuities, previously had a "desk drawer" (i.e., noncodified) rule capping the M&E risk charge at 1.25% annually. An administrative expense charge could also be assessed provided this was a nonprofit element; that is, an insurer would need to be able to demonstrate actual expenses at least as high as the annual administrative charge, which typically ran 0.10% to 0.15%. (When these administrative expense charges started, the terminology shifted from "M&E" charge to "M&E&A" charge.) Annual policy fees of $25 to $40 were also common for variable annuities, although this charge sometimes dropped off at the point at which a deferred variable annuity was converted into an immediate variable annuity.

In the 1990s, the SEC changed its approach to a "reasonableness of fees and charges" requirement. Each insurer needs to create a document supporting the contention that its variable annuity fees and charges are reasonable in light of the benefits offered and risks assumed. Actual wording from Section 26.f of the Investment Company Act of 1940 regarding reasonableness of fees and charges appears earlier in this chapter.

Annuity writers hope that the combination of product fees and charges and sales volume is sufficient to generate revenue to cover expenses and to produce a profit. The immediate annuity expense information in Tables 11.1 and 11.2 comes from a Society of Actuaries intercompany[4] study of expenses

TABLE 11.1 Acquisition Expense for Individual Annuities (2002)

Product Type	Number of Companies	Per Policy Issued	Percent of First-Year Premium	Commissions (% of Premium)	
				First-Year/ Single	Renewal Commission
Immediate Fixed	27	$194.69	1.1%	3.0%	n/a
Immediate Variable	5	647.75	1.8	5.7	n/a

TABLE 11.2 Nonacquisition Expense for Individual Annuities (2002)

Product Type	Number of Companies	Per Policy in Force	Premium Tax
Immediate Fixed	27	$167.03[5]	0.28%
Immediate Variable	5	280.41	0.19

for individual annuity business, based on Year 2002 data. Because of variations in expense allocations used by companies, the limited number and variety of sizes (i.e., small, medium, large) of companies that contributed data to this category and because results by distribution channel may differ from aggregate results, these results should be viewed cautiously. The study nonetheless suggests a rough order of magnitude of up-front (acquisition) and ongoing (nonacquisition) expenses associated with immediate annuities.

CHAPTER 12

Product Distribution

"Would you tell me which way I ought to go from here?"
asked Alice.
    "That depends a good deal on where you want to get," said
the Cat.
    "I really don't care where," replied Alice.
    "Then it doesn't much matter which way you go," said
the Cat.

        —Lewis Carroll, *Alice's Adventures in Wonderland*

FINANCIAL ADVISERS

Because it often involves large sums of money, because one's standard of living during retirement years is at stake, and because of the irrevocable nature of an immediate variable annuity (IVA) election, many prospects may desire the assistance of a financial adviser who is knowledgeable about available annuity options, assumed investment rates (AIRs), subaccounts, taxation, and related matters. It is important to consider one's overall asset portfolio to determine what percentage, if any, should be applied to an IVA. Liquidity needs and pension income, for example, will have a bearing.

Do-it-yourselfers may feel comfortable researching IVAs and purchasing one directly without financial adviser assistance. To date, however, Internet-based direct-to-consumer variable annuity sales have been minimal, in part because of consumer desire to receive expert counsel on the immensely important decision as to how to liquidate one's retirement assets optimally to sustain oneself for the whole of life.

A fairly complex, irrevocable decision regarding one's retirement assets generally warrants some degree of hand-holding that is absent in an Internet sale or a sale over an 800 toll-free telephone line or at least is less prevalent than in a face-to-face meeting between prospect and financial adviser. Prospects understand they are at a point in their lives where they may not wish to return to work—or may be physically unable to return to work—to produce more retirement assets if they make mistakes during the liquidation phase.

Either way, the individual at the selling end of the transaction must have a valid insurance license in each state in which he or she does business and be a National Association of Securities Dealers (NASD) Series 6 registered representative. The latter requires passing an examination on annuity mechanics and compliance, a background check, continuing education requirements, and affiliation with a broker/dealer.

Because immediate variable annuities are relatively complex (as compared to simpler retirement savings vehicles like stocks, bonds, mutual funds, or certificates of deposit), because there may be more decisions to make when buying an annuity than when buying these other products, because more education may be required of financial advisers selling variable annuities due to dual insurance and securities licensing requirements, and because the selling process may take longer due to the higher level of financial counseling necessary relative to faster transaction-oriented sales of simpler products, financial advisers appropriately look to be compensated at a level commensurate with the time and service they provide.

Financial advisers may set proper client expectations. Both hearing and reading salient IVA points—benefits fluctuating, illiquidity, an income that can't be outlived—may improve client understanding and expectations regarding future product performance. Videos that clients can access—whether in a direct-to-consumer sale or in a financial adviser–assisted sale—may similarly set appropriate client expectations and enliven the subject.

The gravity of the decisions being made is profound. We're talking about making optimal decisions regarding a client's lifetime retirement savings. This contrasts sharply with temporary, revocable decisions such as the choice of money market fund to house assets for a few months while accumulating money for a new car. Especially those conscientious individuals who did an exemplary job of saving for decades toward retirement now ask, much like Alice in Wonderland, "Would you tell me which way I ought to go from here?"

There was a time when financial advisers had an ossified bias against clients converting a single premium into a series of lifetime income benefits, called "annuitization." Financial advisers correctly understood that annuitants who died early in the program forfeited the reserve held to cover their liability to the insurance company. Some financial advisers, however, erroneously believed that the insurer enjoyed a windfall, rather than recognizing that reserves released by deceased annuitants are a natural consequence of program construction and are generally redeployed to sustain longer-surviving annuitants.

Some advisers believed that purchasing an IVA put these client assets "beyond their reach." Some believed the purchase of an IVA would represent "the last commission earned on this money," since it was thereafter inaccessible and couldn't be repositioned into other financial products later. Such perceptions—often fallacious—and their associated negative connotations were so deeply ingrained in certain brokers' psyches that their recalcitrance to explore the realities of IVAs could not be overcome.

Actually, IVAs were doing exactly the opposite of what these advisers thought. A number of IVAs pay the financial advisers ongoing "trail commissions" that are a percentage of the reserve held by the insurer.[1] Effectively, the sale of a lifetime IVA by a financial adviser to a client may now produce an annuity of trail commissions for the financial adviser equally long to the lifetime annuity benefits to the client. Financial advisers may offer ongoing client support during the retirement income phase in the way of asset allocation or rebalancing decisions; review of new subaccounts made available for investment; guidance on income tax or estate tax questions; advice on whether to exercise certain optional features regarding liquidity or fund performance that may now be available during the retirement income phase; and so on.

IVAs may actually tie clients more closely to their financial advisers. While it may be quite easy for a client to move a portfolio of individual stocks and bonds from one adviser to another, IVAs are not as easily transportable. For example, if a client moves to a new geographic location, his new financial adviser may not be licensed with the insurance company underwriting the IVA product, making that adviser ineligible to be named "broker of record" unless and until she is so licensed.

There is a slight trend today toward the other end of the spectrum. Some financial advisers believe that the highest and best use of annuities is to provide lifetime income that offers an opportunity to keep pace with inflation, where owners control the allocation of their investment, and where financial advisers receive ongoing compensation for counsel they provide during the all-important retirement income phase. In other words, some advisers believe that annuities are best used for "annuitization," and that deferred annuities may be costlier than some accumulation phase savings alternatives.

A financial adviser might receive a front-end commission, an ongoing trail commission, or both from the sale of an IVA. Once the present value of annuity payments is known, an expense factor (often called a "loading" factor) is added when an insurer derives its conversion factors, or initial payout rate per $1,000 of net premium (i.e., gross premium less state premium tax, if applicable). This is the main approach to fund the front-end IVA expenses an insurer incurs, such as financial adviser commissions, wholesaler compensation, application processing, contract preparation and issue, and policyholder record set-up.

Ongoing trail commissions may be a percentage of the reserve an insurer holds and are therefore referenced as "asset-based" commissions, in contrast to a front-end "premium-based" commission. A portion of the mortality and expense (M&E) risk charge may serve to fund ongoing trail commissions to financial advisers.

Alternatively, ongoing trail commissions may be a percentage of the annuity benefits the annuitant receives. Because the trail commission is paid on a lower base amount—the annuity benefit rather than the reserve—the percentage commission is higher. The annuity benefit may be calculated in the normal way, with the bulk of it going to the annuitant and a small percentage to the financial adviser. Under such a construction, no portion of the M&E charge may be needed to fund ongoing trail commissions to financial advisers.

Trail commissions based on the reserve start high and reduce over time. They form a pattern of commissions similar to what the financial adviser receives if the client takes comparable withdrawals from a retail mutual fund to generate retirement income. In contrast, trail commissions based on annuity benefits may form a more level or even increasing pattern over time. Figures 12.1 and 12.2 illustrate the general pattern of trail commissions as a percentage of reserves and as a percentage of annuity benefits, respectively.

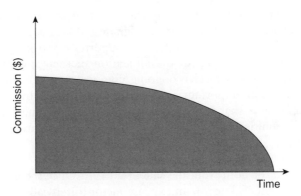

FIGURE 12.1   Reserve-Based Trail Commission Pattern

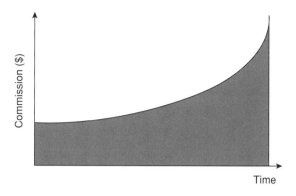

FIGURE 12.2 Annuity-Benefit-Based Trail
Commission Pattern

If any front-end load built into the payout rates per $1,000 of net pre-
mium is inadequate to compensate financial advisers at the point of sale for
counseling annuitants about their important up-front decisions (e.g., annuity option, AIR, subaccount characteristics), any shortfall may be recovered
over time through a portion of the M&E charge; that is, the present value
of some portion of the M&E charge may serve to cover up-front IVA
expenses. If this approach is used, insurers can pay higher commissions on
longer-term payouts—those that deplete the reserve on which the insurer
assesses the asset charge less rapidly.

To the extent that part of the acquisition expense is not covered by
front-end loading factors but will be recovered over time through a portion
of the M&E charge, a deferred acquisition cost (DAC) asset may be set up
under generally accepted accounting principles (GAAP), with M&E risk
charge revenue being paired over time with the expense of writing down the
DAC asset.

Financial advisers may prefer a blend of front-end commission and trail
commission. Because they exert more effort and spend more time educating
and counseling clients at the point of sale, they look to receive some up-
front compensation for this work. Because they may provide postsale ongoing reviews, counseling, and administrative support in the nature of asset
reallocation, explanations of taxation, or death claim processing, they look
to receive ongoing trail compensation.

Because reserve-based trail compensation may continue only so long as
the annuitant (or last survivor in a multilife status) survives, financial advisers may prefer some up-front compensation, rather than exclusively trail
compensation, lest the annuitant die shortly after contract issue and the

financial adviser be subject to mortality risk of the client. Joint life annuities with lengthy certain periods and low AIRs deplete the reserve most slowly, so such annuity options provide the highest expected present value of trail compensation to financial advisers.

To some extent, annuity options with slow reserve depletion align the interests of financial advisers with the interests of insurers. To the extent that the insurer owns one or more investment managers represented in the IVA or receives revenue from such investment managers in proportion to the IVA assets it manages, a slower depletion of assets under management generates a higher and longer revenue stream for the insurer. By the same token, lengthy certain periods may not be in the best interest of annuitants, since these decrease retirement income relative to straight life annuities. They also reduce the possibility for the insurer to experience mortality gains.

As with the sale of virtually any financial product, there are competing tensions and factors whereby a financial adviser must strike a balance between adequate compensation for himself or herself and value for clients.

Financial advisers offering immediate variable annuities must be insurance licensed in the appropriate jurisdiction, whether that be state of residence or state of transaction. Financial advisers must also be NASD Series 6 registered, as defined earlier.

It is important to note that the customers of the insurance company writing the immediate variable annuity are the financial advisers. The customers of the financial advisers are the end consumers. Because these insurance company products don't generally reach the end consumer without a financial adviser serving as intermediary, insurers are cautious about ever stepping in between a financial adviser and his or her client, lest the trust of that financial adviser be breached and this distribution avenue lost.

With the advent of *deferred* variable annuities, contract owners could convert their accumulated account value at some future point into a series of variable retirement income benefits. Early on, this was seen as just one of many transactions related to the product, much like transferring from one subaccount to another or changing an address.

Because a financial adviser could apply the account value accumulated in Company A's deferred annuity contract to the purchase of Company B's immediate annuity contract (fixed or variable), annuitization of a deferred annuity contract became a commissionable event. This was a necessary defensive measure to promote asset retention.

Depending on the compensation arrangement associated with the deferred variable annuity sale, a financial adviser may also be compensated again on those same dollars in the same annuity product when conversion to retirement income commences. In some instances, a certain period of time must elapse from the deferred annuity sale in order for the annuitization to be commissionable.

Terms and conditions of compensation to a securities firm for selling the IVA product of a specific insurer are spelled out in a "selling group agreement." The securities firm receives the "gross dealer concession" (GDC). The securities firm, in turn, has agreements with its financial advisers describing the formulas by which some portion of the GDC will be passed through to them, for example, a percentage based on their overall sales production. The selling group agreement describes trail compensation, if any, as well as up-front compensation. In addition to the GDC, the selling group agreement may also describe terms and conditions of incentive arrangements offered by the insurer to the securities firm to sell more of its products, for example, additional monetary incentives, sometimes known as sales volume allowances, for achieving certain annual sales thresholds.

DISTRIBUTION CHAIN

Variable annuities, including immediate annuities, tend to have a fairly long distribution chain, as seen in Figure 12.3. For example, a publicly traded company generates earnings, some of which are paid out as dividends and some of which are retained and may result in capital appreciation. This stock is part of a variable insurance series fund run by an investment management company, which extracts a fee. The insurance series fund is the underlying investment vehicle for a particular subaccount of a variable annuity product. The insurance company extracts a charge for developing and administering the product and assuming risks associated with the product, such as mortality risk for an immediate variable annuity. A wholesaling organization may call on affiliated and unaffiliated brokerage firms to obtain approvals from the "gatekeepers" for product distribution within their national or regional systems. Once approved, trained wholesalers call on brokerage offices to present the variable annuity product to brokers and to provide literature, software, and general support. Financial advisers affili-

FIGURE 12.3   Distribution Chain

ated with the brokerage firm, in turn, present the variable annuity product to their clients, the ultimate consumers, as appropriate.

Because each element in the distribution chain must be compensated for the value-added services provided, the totality of related expenses must be kept in mind. These represent the difference between the total return (dividends plus capital appreciation) provided by the stock on the left end of Figure 12.3 and the consumer on the right end.

As a result, scale is important to insurers to achieve unit costs at the level assumed in product pricing or better—a level acceptable to end consumers while still providing sufficient compensation to achieve enthusiasm for the product among wholesalers, broker/dealers, and financial advisers. Lacking such cost control can diminish insurance company shareholder value even if actual mortality and underlying fund performance compare favorably with product pricing assumptions. (Important, high-level information regarding price setting by an annuity company follows in the next section.)

Alternative variable annuity product distribution methods have been tried. "Direct" sales include those via the Internet and via an 800 toll-free telephone line. Due to the importance of an individual's retirement savings program and the complexity of products and regulations, experience has shown that financial adviser involvement is almost universally desired. Sales results reflect this.

IVA PRICING OPTIMIZATION PROCESS

Only variable costs (not fixed costs) should be considered in determining whether to manufacture an IVA product and, if so, in determining the optimal price for this product.[2] That is, classical microeconomic theory tells us nonmarginal costs have no impact in setting the optimal price level. To see this, consider:

$$\text{Total Profit} = P \times Q - ME \times Q - NME$$

where

P = price per unit
Q = quantity expected to be sold
ME = marginal expense per unit sold
NME = nonmarginal expenses

If we assume quantity sold is related to price by the function $Q = f(P)$, then

$$\text{Total Profit} = P \times f(P) - ME \times f(P) - NME$$

To maximize total profit, we take the first derivative with respect to P and set the result equal to zero:

$$f(P) + f'(P) \times (P - ME) = 0 \qquad (12.1)$$

Equation 12.1 can be solved for the price P that yields the greatest total expected profit. Note that the NME term is absent in equation 12.1 and therefore is unrelated to the determination of optimal price.

While admittedly optimization equation 12.1 oversimplifies—because marginal expenses may not be a smooth, continuous function of quantity produced but rather may include step functions with points of discontinuity—the concept that NME are irrelevant to optimal pricing decisions remains valid.

NME, commonly called "allocated overhead," can be deducted from the financial results of all actions under consideration to arrive at the total result. Because NME are a uniform amount across all possible actions in the decision set, an identical amount is subtracted from the financial result of each possible action, leaving their ordinal ranking unchanged—as expected, since NME are irrelevant to the decision.

IVA product pricing is an optimization process to select a price that maximizes total profit, illustrated by the point at the apex of the profit curve in Figure 12.4. Selecting a higher price increases profit per unit sold but decreases total profit. Selecting a lower price increases sales, but the marginal profit per unit is reduced, making total profit less than optimally achievable.

Total projected profitability can be determined only after evaluations of sales production levels are offered (generally by the marketing executive) for various prices assigned a given IVA product construction (generally by the actuarial executive). While the law of demand pervades the optimal

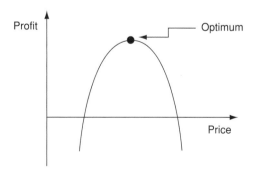

FIGURE 12.4 Profit as a Function of Price

decision-making analysis, IVA education—for financial advisers and consumers—can shift the IVA demand curve. Congress's tax and retirement policy-making actions—both those affecting IVAs and those affecting financial instruments that are (imperfect) substitutes for IVAs—can also shift the IVA demand curve.

If one tries to allocate nonmarginal expenses to a particular action, such as developing an IVA product with specific characteristics, this exaggerates the cost of that action, which results in an inaccurate comparison of the value of that course of action to other courses of action, including no action. Insurance companies semi-arbitrarily allocating overhead to the IVA or any other product line (e.g., by assets, premiums, employee head count, etc.) and then using pricing paradigms that distort the optimum result remained part of insurance and annuity pricing for a long time—and at some companies remain today. Postulated historical reasons for this include (1) that during the 1900s dividend determination in participating life insurance was more important than premium setting and *NME* had to be allocated to units of insurance among the various sets of policyholders in order to determine dividends and (2) for regulated insurance prices, regulators may use a "cost-plus" pricing algorithm, where they allow a price that covers the cost of insurance sold plus a "reasonable" profit.

WHOLESALERS

Because financial adviser–assisted IVA sales outpace direct-to-customer sales and because financial advisers have such a large number of product manufacturers from which to choose, *which* immediate variable annuity products are sold in the marketplace is highly dependent on the effectiveness of wholesalers to persuade financial adviser retailers to sell their product.

Deferred variable annuity accumulation product offerings increased from a few dozen in 1980 to many hundreds by 2000. Immediate variable annuity liquidation product offerings may also become voluminous, with wholesaler effectiveness, subaccount performance, and level of product fees and charges being important sales factors. Customer service quality—measured by performance metrics including average speed of answer, longest wait time, and percentage of calls abandoned—is also important. Independent firms rank annuity company service quality.

Different distribution channels have different characteristics. Studies often divide the channels into (1) national wirehouses, (2) regional broker/dealers, (3) independent financial planners, (4) insurance, and (5) financial institutions (e.g., banks). Financial advisers of a large national wirehouse office in a major metropolitan location may have substantial computer support, numerous external wholesalers paying them personal visits and vying for their attention, company-provided insurance benefits, and a large base of peers with whom they interact daily. In contrast, a one-person independent financial adviser with an office in a remote location has none of these things, and internal wholesalers providing both proactive and responsive support via phone is a more viable approach for such an adviser. Clearly, insurance companies and wholesaling organizations must recognize the disparate needs of each channel to appeal to it most effectively, for example, via a ratio of external wholesalers to internal wholesalers that is optimal for that channel, which may differ from the commonly used one-to-one ratio.

Wholesaling organizations typically run several "campaigns" or "road shows" per year around a theme, which might be a new subaccount introduction, a new product feature, the asset allocation benefits of using a specific collection of subaccounts, or particular sales concepts. Because financial advisers may offer a very broad array of products (stocks, bonds, mutual funds, certificates of deposit, life insurance, fixed and variable annuities), it is challenging to stay current, especially in an era of increasing product complexity. Wholesaling organizations may provide support to financial advisers via campaigns dealing with methods for generating retirement income from accumulated assets. Immediate variable annuities are one potential tool in the financial adviser's product arsenal, which can be used for part—but not all—of a client's retirement plan.

Dedicated wholesalers concentrate their attention specifically on one product area, such as variable annuities. *Generalist* wholesalers provide support for a range of products, for example, mutual funds, annuities, life insurance, and 401(k) plan products. Historically, insurance companies have achieved superior variable annuity sales using *dedicated* variable annuity wholesalers and have usually seen variable annuity sales attenuate with any shift toward a *generalist* wholesaling model. This is an expected result. Mutual funds are easier to sell than variable annuities and are more uniformly understood by financial advisers. Variable annuities are more complex, require more wholesaler time to explain, and typically represent a smaller percentage of a generalist wholesaler's income than do mutual funds. As a result, it is only natural that wholesalers gravitate toward the easier and more economically rewarding mutual fund sales and away from variable annuity sales. Some companies have tried the generalist approach, then returned to a dedicated annuity wholesaling force.

While the dedicated wholesaling model tends to produce superior sales results, a generalist model may offer a greater chance for a wholesaling organization to pay only one "access toll" or "financial participation" fee to gain access to a securities firm distribution system, to appear on its "preferred product" or "preferred vendor" list, or to sponsor or get podium time at its sales award conventions, rather than having to pay one such toll per product line—one for variable annuities, one for variable life insurance, and so on. Whether one wholesaling organization is used—comprised either of generalists or specialists—or whether multiple unaffiliated wholesaling organizations are used—such as a different one for each product line or even a different one for different product brands within a single product line—it may be beneficial for the insurance company manufacturing the products to provide a coordinated distribution effort as perceived by its customers (which are the securities firms and their financial advisers), for example, coordinating financial adviser visit schedules, promotional campaigns, shared sales concepts, and so on.

It is clearly less expensive to send one generalist wholesaler to provide support to a financial adviser than two or more dedicated wholesalers. Yet dedicated wholesalers, because of their narrower focus, tend to have deeper expertise. Some financial advisory firms desire to have expert wholesalers coming through their offices and prefer dedicated wholesalers, while other advisory firms desire generalist wholesalers to minimize the time their advisers spend with wholesalers to allow more face time with clients.

Some wholesaling organizations hire fewer but only senior, highly experienced wholesalers and pay them more handsomely. The "halo effect" of their greater expertise may carry over to the financial services company they represent. Other wholesaling organizations recruit and employ an entire army of younger, less experienced wholesalers, pay them less, but thereby achieve greater financial adviser "coverage"—the number of face-to-face meeting circuits or call rotations completed with advisers per year. Increased contact frequency may outweigh inexperience, since it may be preferable to have a marginally skilled individual making contact with a financial adviser to promote an immediate variable annuity product than to have no one at all.

Both approaches have pros and cons yet might share comparable overall cost. The primary productivity measure, dollar volume of annual sales *per wholesaler,* will tend to be superior under the first organizational approach (experience). Wholesaling organizations using the second approach (quantity) may experience greater turnover as the newly minted wholesalers who are most successful may gravitate toward wholesaling organizations using the first model. A natural tendency under the second approach is to attempt to retain the previously inexperienced but now highly experienced and successful wholesalers by creating a tiered compensation structure.

An insurance company may be denied access to a national or regional securities firm if the company doesn't have enough variable annuity wholesalers to visit each of that firm's offices with sufficient regularity to train their financial advisers; provide them with sales ideas, sales literature, applications, proposal systems, and phone numbers to call for support; help them resolve problems; and update them on product enhancements. It is easier for a securities firm to deal with a small, carefully selected handful of annuity writing companies—and their particular forms, procedures, systems, call centers, products, wholesalers, compensation structures, and other unique characteristics—than it is to grant every annuity writer entrée into their system.

At the other extreme, it is possible to have too many wholesalers, where the expense of a large wholesaling force becomes overly detrimental to the earnings of the insurance company manufacturing the immediate variable annuity product. At that point, the incremental expense of one additional wholesaler destroys shareholder value (i.e., the return on capital relative to the insurer's cost of capital) rather than increases it.

Wholesaling organizations are typically paid from a "wholesaling allowance" built into product pricing, normally a percentage of new business written. Insurers may pay wholesaling organizations a higher percentage allowance in early, formative years—either formative years of the wholesaling organization itself or formative years of a newly introduced annuity product—when a smaller sales volume using the standard allowance may provide insufficient revenue. Insurers temporarily may also pay a higher percentage allowance so that special promotional offerings to draw attention to newly introduced products may be run.

Each distribution channel may demonstrate different growth rates for different financial products. The product portfolio the wholesaling organization needs to promote and the revenue it derives from each will therefore influence which channel it chooses as its primary target and which as its secondary target. Because of the disparate needs of the various channels and the finite resources of any product manufacturer (e.g., to pay any "financial participation" tolls to securities firm gatekeepers to gain or maintain shelf space), it is unreasonable to expect to target every conceivable distribution channel. This results in an effort too diffuse to outperform competitors who focus virtually exclusively on a specific channel and its needs.

Deeper penetration of financial advisers in fewer securities firms may produce better sales results than wider penetration of an equal number of advisers spread across more securities firms. This enhances the number of times per year an external wholesaler can meet face-to-face with financial advisers in his or her territory. As wholesaling is very much a "relationship management" business, this is quite important. While redistricting of sales territories to reduce their size logically might be expected to reduce a wholesaler's annual compensation, in some cases the effect is just the opposite. Precisely because of the primacy of relationship management to wholesaling success, stability in the way of continuity of personnel is a hugely important factor.

Because of the ability of insurers to "reverse engineer" and to quickly replicate new products or product features of competitors—at least those products and features without patent protection—product-led advantages are ephemeral, making the manufacturing vendor-to-distributor relationships more important. Because existing wholesaler relationships with financial advisers may be well entrenched, it can prove difficult to unseat these. Similarly, financial advisers and their firms may have well-entrenched relationships with and existing knowledge about their current array of products and need a compelling reason to learn a new product that is merely comparable to something with which they are already familiar.

Because of the product, regulatory, sales illustration, and sales story differences between deferred variable annuities focused on accumulation and immediate variable annuities focused on liquidation, *dedicated IVA wholesalers* may be expected to be increasingly in vogue. Because the IVA market represents such a considerable untapped or undertapped opportunity for many financial services companies with trillions of retirement savings dollars at stake, the expectation is that a larger portion of the annuity company universe will have not only dedicated IVA wholesalers but also dedicated retirement income divisions.

Thus, a variety of factors enters into the wholesaling organizational model, but it is primarily driven by what is wanted by the customers—the "gatekeepers" of product shelf space at securities firms and the financial advisers of the various securities firms.

SAMPLE IVA WHOLESALING STORY

For retirement *accumulation* products, mutual fund wholesalers often feel they have an advantage over deferred variable annuity wholesalers in that they sometimes espouse mutual funds as lower-cost investment vehicles that—in the non-tax-qualified market—provide the more favorable tax treatment (i.e., lower) for capital gains and stock dividends.

For retirement *distribution* products, variable annuity wholesalers may feel they have the more compelling story and a distinct competitive advantage. As an example, consider the following comparison for a female, age 65, applying $500,000 to the purchase of (1) a mutual fund and (2) an IVA. Assume both are invested identically. Table 12.1 reveals the amount of mutual fund income achievable where there is a 1%, 5%, 10%, 25%, 50%, and 71% chance of outliving the income the deposit is capable of generating and compares this to a pure lifetime annuity.

TABLE 12.1 Pretax Monthly Income Funded by $500,000 Investment (female, age 65)

Mutual Fund		IVA—Life Annuity	
Probability of Outliving Income	Initial Income	Probability of Outliving Income	Initial Income
1%	$2,050	0%	$3,275
5	2,157	0	3,275
10	2,237	0	3,275
25	2,417	0	3,275
50	2,739	0	3,275
71	3,275	0	3,275

The data in Table 12.1 is predicated on these assumptions:

- Annuity 2000 Basic Mortality Table.
- 8% investment performance.
- 4% AIR.
- Monthly annuity-due IVA benefits are projected, then mutual fund distributions are set equal to a percentage of IVA benefits so that the mutual fund balance is exhausted when 99%, 95%, 90%, 75%, 50%, and 29% of females originally age 65 have died.

Data in the shaded row in Table 12.1 appear graphically in Figure 12.5.

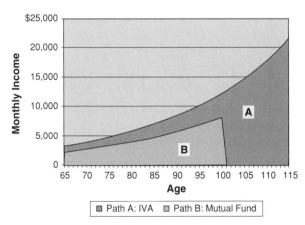

FIGURE 12.5 IVA vs. Mutual Fund Income Comparison ($500,000, Female, Age 65)
Note: Mutual fund income equals 65.86% of IVA income for all months until mutual fund assets are exhausted.

The choice becomes:

1. Path A and illiquidity.
2. Path B and liquidity.

Remember that other assets are kept outside the IVA for liquidity needs. To give up *more than one-third* of potential income and still risk running out of money (Path B) is a very high price to pay to maintain liquidity on 100% of one's assets. The extent of retirement income forgone by using a mutual fund rather than an annuity is revealed in the right-hand column of Table 12.2. The age at which retirement income runs out by using a mutual fund—even taking this lower income—is revealed in the second and third columns of Table 12.2.

Again, data in the shaded row in Table 12.2 appear as Path B of Figure 12.5. It is important to note that the reduction in retirement income by using a mutual fund rather than an annuity occurs not just in the first year but in all years. For example, for the shaded row in Table 12.2, the annuitant gives up over $35,000 of income just during the single year of age 90, where the annuity provides $102,744 and the mutual fund provides $67,665.

This is an *incredibly* compelling story. The choices for this female age 65 are:

1. IVA: Receive monthly income guaranteed to last a lifetime.
2. Mutual Fund: Receive only two thirds as much monthly income and run out of money 5% to 10% of the time.

TABLE 12.2 IVA vs. Mutual Fund Income Comparison ($500,000 premium, female, age 65)

Probability of Outliving Income	Age Mutual Fund Balance Is Exhausted Years	Months	Mutual Fund Initial Monthly Income	Mutual Fund Income as a Percentage of Annuity Income
1%	105	5	$2,050	63%
5	100	11	2,157	66
10	98	3	2,237	68
25	93	7	2,417	74
50	88	0	2,739	84
71	82	6	3,275	100

Even if the female age 65 is willing to accept a 50/50 chance of running out of money by using a mutual fund for retirement income, she still receives less income than with the annuity.

If she is willing to accept a 71% chance of running out of money by using a mutual fund for retirement income, even then she receives only the *same* amount as with an annuity—and exhausts her savings by age $82\frac{1}{2}$.

Through analyses like that just given, wholesalers and financial advisers can demonstrate that IVAs provide real value to investors who want the assurance of lifetime income.

UNBUNDLING

"Unbundling" is the term associated with the product design approach of offering a stripped-down base IVA product that prospects can then build up and customize to their individual preferences by judicious selection of additional optional features. Examples of additional optional features will be described in Chapter 18, Product Development Trends.

At the opposite end of the product design spectrum is the "bundled" approach of offering several fully built IVA products that each come with a prepackaged feature collection.

Although it might seem to be a minor distinction, the marketing decision to use a totally unbundled approach, a partially unbundled approach, or a fully bundled approach has pronounced impacts.

While it might seem that when it comes to choices "more is better," such may not always be the case. Prospective IVA purchasers may already view the product as complex. They may need to be educated about how and why income benefits fluctuate, why certain decisions affecting liquidity are irrevocable, what elements of control they may still exercise after purchase, who the investment managers are, and what factors they should consider about insurance carriers providing the mortality risk and expense risk guarantees, for example, claims-paying rating and service quality. Consumers have to make decisions about annuity payout option, subaccount allocation, benefit frequency, and perhaps about beneficiary, automatic portfolio rebalancing, and electronic account statements. If they are then asked to understand and make decisions about numerous additional optional features, they may simply become overwhelmed with the complexity of the financial instrument and abandon the purchase altogether. Overchoice kills the sale.

Consumers then don't feel comfortable placing a meaningful portion of their retirement savings into something that they thought they understood but that now involves a host of new features foreign to them. Because each of these optional features carries a cost that may serve to reduce their retirement income and because—since they have never retired before—the value of each feature relative to its cost is challenging to ascertain, they have an increasing level of discomfort about whether they are making the right decisions with perhaps much of their life savings.

As a result, numerous optional features that are well intended to address traditional impediments to IVA sales—such as access to funds beyond the regularly scheduled retirement income benefits—or to distinguish one insurer's product offering in the marketplace can introduce sufficient incremental complexity so as to cause an actual *reduction* in sales. This can happen because the sales process now becomes so drawn out because it takes so long to explain the unbundled offering that the client simply abandons the product; financial advisers who are more transaction oriented than planning oriented may equally find the sales process long and abandon the product. This can also happen because at some point it becomes too difficult for financial advisers or their clients—or both—to understand. Complexity is the enemy of growth.

Recall that most financial advisers sell a broad array of securities and insurance products. If IVA sales are a low-frequency event for them, they will allocate less time to staying current on them, especially if they find them unduly complicated.

Clearly, easy-to-understand sales literature and illustrations for the consumer and training and support for financial advisers are paramount to IVA sales success. Additionally, certain longstanding cultural mindsets at some securities firms against immediate annuity usage—predating trail commissions on IVAs, ability to exercise control by reallocation among subaccounts, and other advances—simultaneously need to be overcome.

Media articles tend to advocate an unbundled approach, feeling that more choices and greater degrees of personal customization are universally in the consumer's interest. For more financially sophisticated purchasers or for those willing and able to educate themselves sufficiently on IVA concepts, this might be. For prospects who would have benefited from an IVA but abandoned their purchase because of the number of choices they had to make and enter retirement without the combination of longevity insurance and potential inflation protection, the unbundled approach was detrimental.

Certain optional features can interact with certain other optional features to offset the insurer's risks or to exacerbate the insurer's risks. Unbundling can therefore introduce increased complexity into pricing and asset/liability management as well as administration, as each conceivable combination needs to be considered.

Increased complexity from unbundling can lengthen the time needed for a financial adviser to close the sale, if full disclosure regarding all available options is made. While generally considered a negative, such viewpoint may differ by distribution channel and by financial advisers within a channel.

A financial adviser operating in a fee-based capacity may find the opportunity to explain one or two optional features to her client a chance to demonstrate her depth of expertise, further solidifying the belief in the client's mind that he is correct in paying for advice. For example, an independent, fee-based financial planner may be in this category. A financial adviser operating in a product commission-based capacity who is more transaction oriented and less planning oriented may view anything that extends the time to close a sale negatively.

There's no one right answer to the distribution issue of unbundling. Partial unbundling with mostly prepackaged option sets where the client can make one or two customization decisions beyond those required of a traditional IVA may be a safe middle ground.

IVA ILLUSTRATIONS

Customized hypothetical illustrations can be produced showing how immediate variable annuity benefit payments would have looked historically had a certain annuity option, a certain starting date, and a certain combination of subaccounts been chosen by a person of a specific age and sex. These are sometimes called "mountain charts" because of their shape, although this terminology was first used with asset accumulation charts—which grow higher and faster since the periodic liquidations are absent. Graphical depictions of these payout streams are especially valuable in that they visually exhibit not only the trend of payment levels but also the level of payment volatility that particular subaccount collections historically experienced.

Such historical IVA hypothetical illustration software can be created even if annuity unit values for certain subaccounts didn't yet exist, as long as the subaccount did; that is, while insurers start tracking *accumulation* unit values immediately on availability of a deferred annuity subaccount, sometimes they don't start calculating and tracking *annuity* unit values until the first person elects an immediate variable annuity payout based wholly or partially on that subaccount. (Insurers use various terminology for the event whereby a deferred annuity contract owner exchanges his or her accumulated account value for a series of annuity benefit payments, including "annuitizing," "going on-benefit," or "purchasing an immediate variable annuity." Technically, the first two events are associated with maintaining the existing combination deferred and immediate annuity contract, while the last involves the issuance of a new contract.) Annuity unit values can always be derived from accumulation unit values, making historical IVA hypothetical illustrations possible back to subaccount inception—even if annuity unit values weren't actually calculated that early.

Automated IVA quotation systems facilitate sales. A financial adviser enters data on the annuitant(s) into quotation software. It calculates and prints initial benefit amounts for all annuity options and AIRs selected, and it provides a concise description of each annuity option of interest. Such customized comparisons increase the ease with which financial advisers can close an IVA sale because prospective clients can see exactly the trade-offs between the various annuity options available to them.

If the IVA prospect currently owns a deferred variable annuity with the same insurer the proceeds of which will be applied to IVA purchase, all necessary data to generate a historical illustration—client age, sex, state of residence, current account value—can be electronically downloaded, saving the financial adviser from the need to input this information. If the IVA prospect wishes to purchase, all client and account data on the IVA application can be preprinted in the same electronic manner, leaving only signatures to be completed manually.

Variable-payout paper rate books may also be available for manual quotes in case a financial adviser doesn't happen to have access to a computer while on a sales call. For combination fixed and variable immediate annuities, proposal software can also show the amount of the first payment if a client elects a payout that is $X\%$ fixed and $(100 - X)\%$ variable.

"Jet issue" or "instant issue" may at some point also become commonplace: Instead of the insurance company receiving the application, transferring the data onto new records, assembling a paper contract appropriate for use in the state of purchase, and mailing it to the financial adviser some time later for ultimate delivery to the client, the client will walk away from the financial adviser's office with point-of-purchase contract in hand. A central underwriting, pricing, and policy issue system is at the front of the process, with data feeds to the insurer's annuity benefit disbursement system (often a treasurer's function), to the insurer's reserve calculation system (a valuation actuary's function), to a tax statement system, and to other systems where such data are required.

BUYER DEMOGRAPHICS

People aged 65 and older will have an estimated $10.1 trillion in savings in 2012.[3] There are an estimated 76 million individuals classified as belonging to the baby boomer generation. Both in terms of aggregation of wealth and sheer volume of retirees, the retirement income market is staggeringly large.

A 2005 survey of 1,022 owners of *nonqualified* (NQ) annuity contracts (deferred *and* immediate, fixed *and* variable) was performed by the Gallup

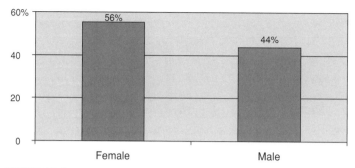

FIGURE 12.6   Gender of NQ Annuity Owners

Organization and commissioned by the Committee of Annuity Insurers. Variable and fixed annuity owners were surveyed in relative proportion to total variable and fixed annuity ownership nationally. The survey reveals the following demographic characteristics.[4]

Gender

- Annuity owners are slightly more likely to be female than male (56% vs. 44%). See Figure 12.6.

Type of Annuity—Fixed or Variable

- Females are more likely than males to own *fixed* annuities (54% vs. 47%).
- Males are more likely than females to own *variable* annuities (53% vs. 46%). (See Figure 12.7.)
- In total, NQ annuity owners are almost equally likely to own variable annuities (49%) than fixed (51%).

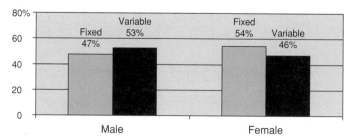

FIGURE 12.7   Fixed vs. Variable NQ Annuity Ownership by Gender

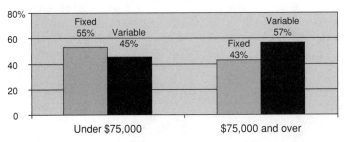

FIGURE 12.8   Type of Annuity by Household Income

- Households with lower incomes are more likely to own *fixed* annuities (74% of households with income under $20,000).
- Households with higher incomes are more likely to own *variable* annuities (57% of households with income of $75,000 and over). (See Figure 12.8.)

Marital Status

- Majority of annuity owners are married (60%).
- Next largest group is widowed (22%). (See Figure 12.9.)

Education

- Annuity owners have diverse educational backgrounds. (See Figure 12.10).

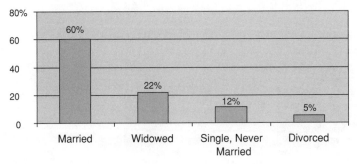

FIGURE 12.9   Marital Status of NQ Annuity Owners

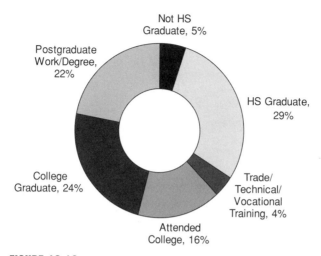

FIGURE 12.10   Education Level of NQ Annuity Owners

Occupation

■ Occupations (former occupations for retirees) of annuity owners vary widely, with business owner/company officer/professional being the largest category (42%). (See Figure 12.11.)

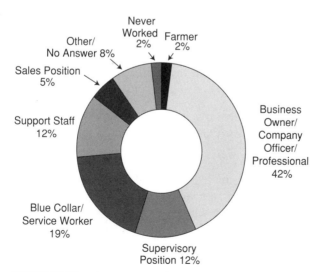

FIGURE 12.11   Occupation of NQ Annuity Owners

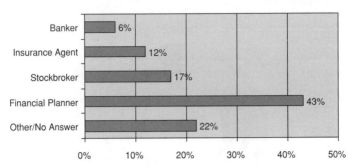

FIGURE 12.12 Who NQ Annuity Owners Talked to When Making Purchase Decision

Sources of Annuity Information

A 2001 survey of 1,005 owners of NQ annuity contracts performed by The Gallup Organization and commissioned by the Committee of Annuity Insurers revealed the following data on sources of annuity information:

- Annuity owners reported talking to a variety of people when making their annuity purchase decision, with the most frequently mentioned groups being financial planners (43%), stockbrokers (17%), insurance agents (12%), and bankers (6%). (See Figure 12.12.)
- Variable annuity owners are more likely to talk to a financial planner (50%) than are owners of fixed annuity contracts (29%).

Owner Demographics

An American Council of Life Insurers (ACLI) survey[5] of 460 immediate annuity owners in 2002 revealed the profile of immediate annuity owners shown in Table 12.3.

- Most immediate annuity owners are currently older and retired. More than half (52%), however, say they purchased their immediate annuity *before* retiring.
- Immediate annuity owners are relatively evenly divided between married (44%) and single or widowed (56%).
- Middle-income status characterizes immediate annuity owners surveyed, with 64% reporting annual household income of less than $50,000.
- While annual income from immediate annuities may appear modest with 70% reporting annual annuity income under $10,000, this makes an important contribution to financial security given that 64% reported annual income from all sources under $50,000.

TABLE 12.3 Characteristics of Immediate
Annuity Owners

Age	Percentage
Younger than 60	9%
60–69	18
70–79	42
80 and older	31

Employment Status	
Retired	80%
Employed	15
Not employed	5

Marital Status	
Married	44%
Widowed	41
Single	15

Annual Income*	
Under $25,000	22%
$25,000–$49,999	42
$50,000–$99,999	30
$100,000 and above	6

Annual Annuity Income†	
Under $5,000	41%
$5,000–$9,999	29
$10,000–$19,999	17
$20,000 and above	13

Annuity Purchase Date	
Before retirement	52%
After retirement	48

*Twenty-four percent of survey participants
did not report their annual income.
†Fifteen percent of survey participants did
not report an annual annuity income level.

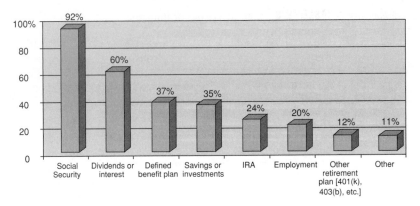

FIGURE 12.13 Immediate Annuity Owners with Income from Other Sources
Source: ACLI Survey of Immediate Annuity Owners.

- Most owners report receiving Social Security income (92%) and 60% receive dividends or interest. (See Figure 12.13.) The 63% without defined benefit pension income have effectively created their own through their immediate annuity.
- The most common source of funds for purchasing an immediate annuity was non-tax-qualified savings (54%)—those that are separate from a retirement plan at work (26%) such as a 401(k) or those in an individual retirement account (24%). (See Figure 12.14.)

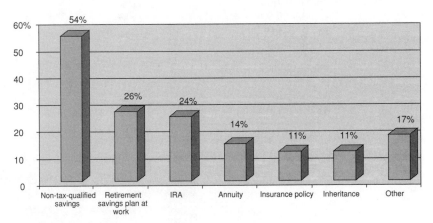

FIGURE 12.14 Funding Sources Used for Immediate Annuity Purchase
Source: ACLI Survey of Immediate Annuity Owners.

Immediate Annuity Features

- More than half of owners (58%) report that their household owns multiple immediate annuities. (See Table 12.4.) These may be in a spouse's name or purchased at different times.
- Exclusively fixed payouts constitute 72% of immediate annuities, exclusively variable payouts constitute 19%, and combination fixed and variable payouts constitute 9%. (See Table 12.4.)
- Nearly three-quarters of owners have an immediate annuity with a lifetime payout period (71%). (See Table 12.4.)
- Among lifetime annuity owners, 76% have elected a certain period, cash/unit refund, or installment refund feature, while 24% elected a straight life annuity that maximizes income payments.
- Among married owners of lifetime immediate annuities, 63% chose an option that covers both spouses.

Motivations for Ownership

- Most owners bought their immediate annuity (46%) because it provides regular monthly retirement income. (See Figure 12.15.)

TABLE 12.4   Features of Immediate
Annuities Owned

Annuities per Household	
One	42%
Two	26
Three or more	32
Type of Annuity	
Fixed	72%
Variable	19
Both	9
Benefit Payment Period	
Lifetime	59%
Term certain	29
Both	12

Source: ACLI Survey of Immediate
Annuity Owners.

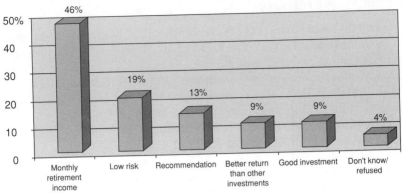

FIGURE 12.15   Most Important Reason for Immediate Annuity Purchase
Source: ACLI Survey of Immediate Annuity Owners.

- When owners first considered an immediate annuity purchase, the source of information they sought most often was a life insurance agent (57%), followed by financial planners (42%) and stockbrokers/advisers (41%). Life insurance agents were the most influential (37%) in convincing prospects to purchase an immediate annuity. (See Table 12.5.)
- Stability of the insurance company was the most important factor in deciding which annuity to purchase (81%). Company brand name, product features, and amount of benefit payments were also rated very important by at least one-half of owners. (See Figure 12.16.)

TABLE 12.5   Information Sources for Immediate Annuity Purchase

	Source Used	Most Convincing Source*
Life insurance agent	57%	37%
Financial planner	42	16
Stockbroker/adviser	41	16
Spouse	34	7
Family or friends	29	7
Accountant or attorney	16	4
Benefits representative at work	8	3

Source: ACLI Survey of Immediate Annuity Owners.
*Ten percent of respondents did not answer this question.

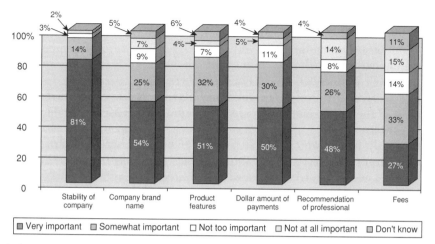

FIGURE 12.16 Importance of Selected Factors in Deciding Which
Annuity to Purchase
Source: ACLI Survey of Immediate Annuity Owners.

Owner Satisfaction

- Owners are quite satisfied with their immediate annuity: 22% rate it as
  one of the best financial decisions they ever made, with another 60%
  rating it a good financial decision. (See Table 12.6.)

Annuity Characteristics

The ACLI Survey of Immediate Annuity Owners examined the importance
of specific annuity characteristics:

- About three-quarters of owners think predictable monthly income is a
  very important benefit (76%), while 19% think it is somewhat important.

TABLE 12.6 Owner Satisfaction with Immediate Annuity

One of best financial decisions ever made	22%
Good financial decision	60
Fair financial decision	14
Poor financial decision	2
One of worst financial decisions ever made	2

Source: ACLI Survey of Immediate Annuity Owners.

- Among those with a lifetime annuity, the fact that payments will continue as long as they live is very important to 86% and somewhat important to another 9%.
- Among those with a *fixed* immediate annuity, 73% think the stability of their payments is a very important benefit.
- Few owners are very concerned they may be unable to sell their annuity if they want money for something else (14%); 13% are somewhat concerned.
- Nearly one-quarter of fixed annuity owners are very concerned that inflation will decrease the value of their payments over time (22%), while another third are somewhat concerned (31%).

Individuals between the ages of 55 and 71 are the primary target market for IVAs. Some individuals elect early retirement by age 55. The most common IVA issue age is 65. In tax-qualified markets, mandatory required minimum distributions commence by age 70½.

Immediate annuity issue ages of 62, 65, and 71 tend to occur with higher frequency than other ages, likely because these represent, respectively, the earliest age for reduced Social Security benefit availability, the long-accepted "normal" retirement age, and what had previously been a mandatory retirement age and is now an age at which distributions are required by the Internal Revenue Code for many savings plans.

Because mortality tables are constructed on—among other alternatives—age-last-birthday, age-nearest-birthday, and age-next-birthday bases, insurance companies may operate using one or the other of these as their classification basis for payout-rate setting. Any studies of immediate variable annuitant characteristics should recognize that data could be premised on any of these (or even other) bases.

Males and females in both upscale and downscale net worth categories are included in this primary target market, although below some point, assets are too few for an IVA to be of much help, and above some point, assets may be so large that living off interest and dividends alone may be satisfactory. Still, to the extent that high net worth is coupled with above-average longevity, an IVA could prove a prudent investment, as demonstrated in Chapter 8 of this book, Rate of Return.

Sources of funds for IVA premiums include:

- Money in deferred fixed or variable annuities.
- Death benefit proceeds of a life insurance or deferred annuity policy where the beneficiary may be better served by a lifetime income stream than by a lump sum,[6] for example, when the beneficiary might imprudently manage a lump sum due to disability, character, or lack of knowledge.

- Maturing endowment contracts.
- Maturing certificates of deposit.

Clearly, for an insurance company offering deferred annuities, its best prospects—and the ones likely already generating the bulk of its IVA sales—are its existing deferred annuity contract owners. These individuals already have familiarity with the insurer and a relationship with a financial adviser representing the insurer. These individuals may also have some knowledge of what an IVA can do. It's the typical situation where it is easier to keep an existing customer—albeit in a product geared for his or her next life phase—than it is to find a new one.

While many other entities have need for regular, periodic payments—such as state lotteries, magazine sweepstakes, and plaintiffs who receive "structured settlement" damage awards—these tend to rely on immediate *fixed* annuities.

The Gallup Organization study cited earlier shows male NQ annuity ownership (deferred and immediate combined) slightly exceeds that for females. If just NQ *immediate* annuities are considered, one might surmise that female ownership will outnumber male ownership as sales escalate because, at the ages they are most frequently purchased, females outnumber males in the population. Females, however, are slightly less inclined than males to own NQ *variable* annuities.

Geographically, the IVA target market is dispersed primarily in relation to where individuals in the 55–71 age group tend to reside, since the majority of—but clearly not all—IVA prospects tend to work with financial advisers and these financial advisers tend to be local representatives. About 7% of all deferred variable annuity sales emanate from New York, which may suggest a comparable level for immediate variable annuity sales. Looking forward, the areas that will grow and decline for IVA prospects are those areas where retirees tend to locate themselves and not to locate themselves.

In Year 2003, the top states for *annuity premium receipts* (of all types of annuities) were California (10.8%), New York (8.9%), Florida (7.1%), Texas (5.8%), and Pennsylvania (5.1%). In Year 2003, top states for *annuity benefit payments* (of all types of benefits) were New York (9.7%), California (9.4%), Connecticut (8.5%), Florida (5.7%), and Pennsylvania (5.5%).[7]

Life-contingent payout options may tend to grow faster than non-life-contingent options because increased consumer education about the protective purpose of IVAs will tend to favor the former and because the Tax Reform Act of 1986 made non-life-contingent annuities generally less attractive before age 59½.

When studying types of payout options elected, it is important to recognize that life-contingent options tend to run a long time, whereas designated period non-life-contingent options may run a short time, such as for five years. As a result, if one looks at the distribution of annuity options for all in-force business as of a single point in time, such a study will be biased, being overly skewed toward life-contingent payout options since some of the non-life-contingent options will have run their course. As a result, one may choose to study the distribution of annuity options for all newly written business, whether in-force or terminated, covering any number of years.

While the distribution of annuity options elected will necessarily hinge on the range of annuity options offered, historically "life with 10 years certain" has generally been the most widely elected option. "Life with 20 years certain" is often the next most widely elected option. This is true despite the fact that every additional year of certain period elected reduces the annuity payout—since no benefits of survivorship accrue—and thereby diminishes the capacity of the financial instrument to perform one of its chief objectives: maximizing retirement income.

Again, immediate annuities are intended to serve the purposes of safeguarding against financial risks associated with longevity and of potentially maintaining or improving the retiree's standard of living by providing maximal retirement income. If wealth transfer to the next generation is also a need, there are more optimal and tax-efficient instruments to achieve that goal. Clearly, psychological benefits weigh heavily in annuity option election.

Depending on the reason for any study of IVA buyer demographics (age, sex, geographic location) or preferences (annuity options, subaccounts, AIRs), one can conduct the study based either on (1) number of contracts or (2) written premium.

There is mild seasonality to IVA sales. December and January tend to exhibit higher sales, perhaps due to year-end tax planning, year-end retirements, individuals entering the calendar year in which they first need to take distributions from tax-qualified retirement savings plans, and financial advisers working extra hard in December to achieve sales goals for the year or extra hard in January to get their year off to a good start. In contrast, May and August through October tend to exhibit lower sales.

Annual IVA benefit amounts vary substantially due to premium size, age, annuity option, and subaccount performance. To eliminate the need to make very small annuity benefit payments, some insurers require a less frequent payment mode (e.g., quarterly instead of monthly) if the first annuity benefit would be below a certain minimum amount (e.g., $50). A sufficiently high minimum acceptable premium amount may preclude such low benefit dollar amounts from occurring. Because insurers incur certain administrative expenses (e.g., prospectus updates and mailing, benefit calculations and disbursements, annual tax statement preparation and mailing) regardless of contract size, IVA contracts below a threshold premium amount will produce insufficient revenue to offset those expenses and are therefore generally forbidden through establishment of the minimum acceptable premium.

When interest rates are high, initial annuity benefits under an immediate variable annuity are lower than under an immediate fixed annuity. The combination of higher initial income and 100% certainty regarding future benefit amounts may simply be too much to entice very conservative investors to consider an IVA. Such near-term factors often unduly influence the decision-making process, being granted too much weight, whereas after several decades of inflation take their toll on purchasing power, annuitants realize in hindsight that they should have given greater consideration to at least a partially variable payout.

When interest rates are low, prospective immediate annuity buyers who might ordinarily have elected an immediate fixed annuity may give greater consideration to the purchase of an immediate variable annuity. Variable payouts typically start at lower benefit levels due to the use of a 3%, 4%, or 5% assumed investment rate in their construction. Over time, provided investment returns exceed the AIR, variable payouts climb and at some crossover point exceed the immediate fixed annuity benefit level. See Figure 12.17.

When interest rates on fixed-income instruments (like bonds and mortgages) that serve as the investments underlying an immediate fixed annuity—less the spread the insurer requires for expenses and profit—are low, initial variable payouts may be the same as or even higher than initial fixed payouts. In other words, the effective interest rate the insurer credits to the underlying reserve—the pool of assets not yet paid out in immediate fixed annuity benefits—may be the same as or lower than the AIR that affects the underlying reserve that determines the initial variable annuity benefit. This may sway prospects who are on the cusp of electing a variable payout over a fixed payout to actually make that decision.

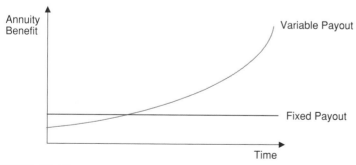

FIGURE 12.17 Typical Relationship between Variable Payout and Fixed Payout

TABLE 12.7   Immediate Annuities, Year 2000

	Policies/ Certificates (units)	Reserves		New Considerations	
		Combined Accounts (millions)	Percent Distribution	Combined Accounts (millions)	Percent Distribution
Individual Immediate Annuities					
Qualified	1,008,606	$ 41,152	36.4	$ 702	10.5
Nonqualified	1,179,303	71,852	63.6	5,992	89.5
Total	2,187,909	113,004	100.0	6,694	100.0
Group Immediate Annuities					
Qualified	4,276,434	$182,749	95.8	$20,143	84.7
Nonqualified	167,137	8,019	4.2	3,637	15.3
Total	4,443,571	190,768	100.0	23,780	100.0
Total Immediate Annuities					
Qualified	5,285,040	$223,901	73.7	$20,845	68.4
Nonqualified	1,346,440	79,871	26.3	9,629	31.6
Total	6,631,480	303,772	100.0	30,474	100.0

Source: American Council of Life Insurers.

As of Year 2000, almost $304 billion of immediate annuity (fixed and variable) reserves existed (see Table 12.7), while there were more than $30 billion of new immediate annuity considerations (fixed and variable).

As of Year 2000, about one-sixth of all annuity reserves were attributable to immediate annuities (fixed and variable), while new immediate annuity considerations (fixed and variable) were one-tenth of all annuity considerations. See Table 12.8.

TABLE 12.8   Immediate and Deferred Annuities, Year 2000

	Policies/ Certificates (units)	Reserves		New Considerations	
		Combined Accounts (millions)	Percent Distribution	Combined Accounts (millions)	Percent Distribution
Immediate	6,631,481	$ 303,771	16.7	$ 30,474	10.0
Deferred	66,126,506	1,515,908	83.3	273,344	90.0
Total	72,757,987	1,819,680	100.0	303,818	100.0

Source: American Council of Life Insurers.

Of the $304 billion of immediate annuity reserves in Year 2000, over $98 billion, or about one-third, were variable (see Table 12.9). Immediate variable annuity reserves per policy or certificate were $91,626, while immediate fixed annuity reserves per policy or certificate were $36,997.

Of new immediate annuity considerations in Year 2000, 18.6% were directed to IVAs (see Table 12.9). Year 2000 was a very difficult year of stock performance, which can negatively influence IVA purchases.

IRA assets totaled $2.47 trillion, and defined contribution retirement plan assets totaled $2.40 trillion in 1999.

A 2002 report by the ACLI placed assets in private-sector defined contribution plans, such as 401(k), 403(b), and 457 plans, at $3 trillion, of which over $2 trillion was in 401(k) plans. The same report placed individual retirement account (IRA) assets at $2.5 trillion.

Forecasts predict that 64% of men's retirement wealth and 55% of women's will come from defined contribution plans and IRAs at age 65 for the oldest "baby boomers," those born in 1946. For the youngest baby boomers, those born in 1964, 74% is forecast for men and 63% for women at age 65.[8]

True individual single-premium immediate variable annuity sales plus annuitizations of variable deferred annuity contracts by insurers proactively marketing deferred variable annuity payout provisions produced about $1 billion of premium in 2002 and $800 million of premium in 2003.[9] The average size of a true IVA sale was $114,000 while the average size of an annuitization by insurers proactively marketing these was $112,000 in 2003.[10]

Single-premium fixed immediate annuity sales and fixed annuitizations of deferred annuity contracts collectively with IVA sales and variable annuitizations comprise the totality of the individual immediate annuity market. It should be noted that in addition to providing individual retirement income, fixed immediate annuity sales also occur in conjunction with structured settlements, state lotteries, and funding periodic life insurance premiums.

In an effort to cater to the needs of prospective IVA customers, insurers or their marketing companies will accommodate the special needs of this class of investors. For example, larger font sizes may be used for printing IVA sales literature. Sales literature, applications, contracts, prospectuses, Statements of Additional Information (SAI), and Internet web sites may be printed in multiple languages, particularly Spanish in recognition of the growing Spanish-speaking population in the United States. Model portfolios (e.g., three portfolios) comprised of a specific collection of subaccounts in specific proportions ranging from conservative to moderate to aggressive may be offered to ease the number of decisions necessary at point of sale.

TABLE 12.9 Immediate Annuities by Type, Year 2000

	Policies/ Certificates (units)	Reserves				New Considerations	
		General Account (millions)	Separate Account (millions)	Combined Accounts (millions)	Percent Distribution	Combined Accounts (millions)	Percent Distribution
Variable	1,074,073	$ 44,510	$53,903	$ 98,413	32.4	$ 5,671	18.6
Fixed	5,492,610	193,134	10,074	203,208	66.9	24,802	81.4
Other	64,797	19	2,131	2,150	0.7	1	0.0
Total	6,631,481	237,664	66,107	303,771	100.0	30,474	100.0

Source: American Council of Life Insurers.

Age Distribution by State

Table 12.10 shows the number of people aged 55 through 79 by state according to the U.S. Census Bureau as of July 1, 2002. This distribution may serve as an approximation for how domestic prospective IVA purchasers are distributed geographically. While more refined data sorting to include economic factors such as net worth will certainly improve the picture of the target market, Table 12.10 provides a start. The data shown are

TABLE 12.10   U.S. Population Age 55–79 by State

State	Population Age 55–79	% of Total	State	Population Age 55–79	% of Total
Alabama	875,694	1.7%	Montana	181,869	0.3%
Alaska	87,854	0.2	Nebraska	313,335	0.6
Arizona	1,013,070	1.9	Nevada	405,099	0.8
Arkansas	547,638	1.0	New Hampshire	232,995	0.4
California	5,570,004	10.7	New Jersey	1,627,729	3.1
Colorado	713,207	1.4	New Mexico	340,343	0.7
Connecticut	659,628	1.3	New York	3,585,923	6.9
Delaware	156,689	0.3	North Carolina	1,532,416	2.9
District of Columbia	102,809	0.2	North Dakota	121,024	0.2
Florida	3,776,988	7.2	Ohio	2,166,678	4.1
Georgia	1,338,499	2.6	Oklahoma	678,653	1.3
Hawaii	242,116	0.5	Oregon	654,961	1.3
Idaho	229,279	0.4	Pennsylvania	2,554,801	4.9
Illinois	2,188,423	4.2	Rhode Island	203,674	0.4
Indiana	1,113,147	2.1	South Carolina	790,295	1.5
Iowa	571,224	1.1	South Dakota	141,491	0.3
Kansas	483,376	0.9	Tennessee	1,111,740	2.1
Kentucky	790,552	1.5	Texas	3,410,331	6.5
Louisiana	794,224	1.5	Utah	303,379	0.6
Maine	270,648	0.5	Vermont	120,535	0.2
Maryland	967,546	1.9	Virginia	1,298,408	2.5
Massachusetts	1,203,448	2.3	Washington	1,038,265	2.0
Michigan	1,826,785	3.5	West Virginia	402,761	0.8
Minnesota	863,634	1.7	Wisconsin	994,186	1.9
Mississippi	515,403	1.0	Wyoming	94,242	0.2
Missouri	1,089,317	2.1	Total	52,296,335	100.0

Source: U.S. Census Bureau; population estimates as of July 1, 2002.
Shading indicates top 10 states.

for males and females combined. The top 10 states are highlighted, which collectively represent 54% of the national population aged 55 through 79.

Percentage distribution information contained in the table also appears in the U.S. map in Figure 12.18.

THREE-LEGGED STOOL

Retirement income security is often described as a "three-legged stool," with the three legs being

1. Social Security.
2. Company pension.
3. Personal savings.

Social Security may provide only a small portion of income needed during retirement. Today, company pensions are less frequently of the defined benefit variety, which pay a definitely determinable guaranteed monthly income as long as the retiree lives, and instead are more frequently of the defined contribution variety, in which the retiree has an account balance that he or she must make last through retirement.

FIGURE 12.18   Top Ten States of Prospective IVA Purchasers by Population

The Employee Benefit Research Institute indicates that in 1974 56% of retirement income came from guaranteed sources. Cerulli Associates projects that by 2030 that will drop to 24%.[11]

This puts more weight on the personal savings leg. Immediate annuities (variable, fixed, or combination) are the only products within the personal savings leg that ensure lifetime income. As was shown earlier, some systematic withdrawal programs may claim to offer lifetime income, but the payments are not actually life-contingent and are comprised only of principal and appreciation, lacking the survivorship credits that accompany IVAs.

Variable income annuities can be used with defined benefit pension plans[12] and defined contribution pension plans. Conceptually, they could be used as part of Social Security. Thus, while today they can be part of the company pension leg, the important distinction is that for those individuals who don't have adequate lifetime retirement income through the other two legs and need supplementation by the personal savings leg, immediate annuities are uniquely able to provide this.

LOOKING TO THE FUTURE

By 2010, one-quarter of all Americans—75.1 million people—will be age 55 or older. By 2050, one-third of all Americans will be age 55 or older. In the next two decades, 43 million baby boomer households consisting of 76 million people will move into retirement. As of 1999, over $4.5 trillion of U.S. retirement assets were in private defined contribution plans and individual retirement accounts. Also as of 1999, combined mutual fund, retirement plan (including defined benefit plans), and certificate of deposit (CD) assets were $19.5 trillion.

In 1999, 34.5 million Americans were age 65 or older. By 2030, this segment will more than double to 70.3 million people.

Demographics strongly suggest that both absolute and relative use of financial products dealing with the payout phase will increase. The point in their lives at which individuals will start some systematic liquidation of their accumulated retirement savings may depend more on affordability than on age, especially as fewer workers are covered by a defined benefit pension plan that heretofore played a pronounced role due to its definition of "normal retirement age" that governed benefit determination.

It will become increasingly clear to more individuals—especially as they see firsthand some friends, relatives, neighbors, or former co-workers exhaust their savings—that affirmative steps must be taken to minimize the chance of the same outcome for themselves. Two likely consequences are (1) greater recognition that common stock assets and their potential higher returns play an important role in retirement, and (2) mortality credits will become increasingly appreciated as a device to extend retirement income beyond what savings and appreciation alone allow.

The first consequence produces greater use of asset classes with variable rather than fixed returns. The second consequence produces greater use of immediate annuities. The combined effect may well be greater use of immediate variable annuities.

IVAs will be especially important for women due to their greater longevity and due to the fact that they constitute a larger target market than men. In 2000, 47% of women age 60 and over were widows.

A chief concern of the baby boomer generation is outliving their money. Whether this is caused by insufficient savings, extended longevity, or large healthcare expenses, *immediate variable annuities can provide income superior to that of an identically invested asset portfolio outside an IVA.* A reasonably expected result is that an increased number and percentage of prospective IVA purchasers will come to this same conclusion and act on it—hopefully before they dissipate their assets and recognize this optimizing solution only in hindsight.

Some of those who say, "I'd rather be destitute in my old age than risk forfeiting some of my hard-earned savings by purchasing an IVA," will certainly make the former event a self-fulfilling prophecy! Heuristic devices such as "electronic wholesaling," where basic IVA concepts may be discovered by both financial advisers and prospective purchasers in an educational, entertaining way (i.e., via "edutainment"), may play an important role in the ascendancy of this important financial instrument.

While far from uniformly dispersed, there will be an increased concentration of wealth among prospective retirees, guaranteeing sufficient assets to serve as a source of future IVA premiums. Baby boomers will inherit trillions of dollars from their parents in the largest intergenerational wealth transfer in history.

In addition to consumer education, greater use of immediate annuities as a preferred from of distribution from defined contribution pension plans will require greater offering of them. Only 27% of 401(k) plan participants had access to an immediate annuity as an allowable distribution option as part of their plan as of 1997.[13]

While higher mortality previously suppressed motivation to purchase immediate annuities, the cumulative effect of ongoing mortality improvement expands purchase motivation. From the insurer perspective, as greater use is made of immediate variable annuities and as the product category matures, insurers can expect increased product complexity, greater distribution channel diversity, compressed product life cycles, and an increased risk profile.

COMPARISON INDEXES AND DISCLOSURE

Currently, there is no standard comparison index for IVAs. As we look to the future, it seems inevitable that one or more standardized ranking processes for comparing IVAs will emerge. As it is unlikely that any single comparative index or other comparison method can adequately account for all factors affecting a prospective buyer's purchase decision, any product comparison system likely should be accompanied by disclosure language. The disclosure language might state the factors that are given emphasis by the comparative index (e.g., M&E&A charge) and mention that additional factors that relate to an individual's specific situation (e.g., proximity to adviser, preference for insurer with high claims-paying ratings or excellent customer service reputation) are excluded from index values. Such an index and disclosure language could be stand-alone or part of a "buyer's guide."

Such an index would need to recognize differences in initial payout per $1,000 of gross premium applied—for product comparisons with identical AIR. This would account for the effect of any front-end load and for differences in mortality assumptions. (Certainly, IVA products premised on group mortality would yield a different range of index values than IVA products premised on individual mortality, but at least theoretically the same index could be used for both.)

The index would need to recognize the magnitude of product expenses—M&E&A charge, investment management expenses, 12b-1 fees, annual fees, and so on. The index would need to be designed so as to deal with product comparisons having different AIRs.

The index would recognize the effects of floor benefits or ceiling benefits (both to be described later in Chapter 18).

The index would likely compare identical annuity payout options[14]—single life only, life and 10 years certain, and so on. There would likely be separate index values for several selected issue ages, for example, age 60, 65, 70, and 80. Index values could be sex distinct. Because the purpose of an index is to offer prospects a simple and *general* guide as to "value," having too many index values defeats the purpose.

Because of the cost of compliance with index and disclosure regulations, which are ultimately borne by the annuitant, one may and should question any such statutorily imposed *mandatory* requirement, especially in the absence of any abuses requiring correction.[15] Even if the National Association of Insurance Commissioners (NAIC) created a model regulation, there could still be state-by-state variations, raising compliance costs.

Independent institutions can—and likely will when volume warrants—produce comparative indexes. Competitive forces so resulting might improve index construction faster than a regulatory approach would.

An index could be calculated based on a set of prescribed subaccount performance scenarios. Annuity companies offering very high floor guarantees may prefer scenarios that include periods of large negative returns, where their floor guarantees would illustrate well.

Comparison methods could be "event specific," reflecting a particular set of circumstances. Comparison methods could be "average representations," reflecting the weighted average value of a variety of circumstances.

The mere presence of comparative indexes may spawn product designs that produce the most attractive index values possible—whether by improving the product or merely by rearranging an equivalent package to "game the system." Shoppers may have a single numerical index value that may be given weight in their purchase decision. Of course, the totality of factors should be considered. For example, one IVA that produces a slightly better index value than another due to a slightly lower cost structure may be no bargain if certain subaccount asset classes the prospect wishes to use are absent or if the investment manager has a lengthy track record of underperformance.

It would be a misconception to believe that a comparative index illustrates "true cost," "true performance," or "true relative value" of a particular IVA. Such a characterization is invalid. Since an infinite number of future scenarios are possible, it would be an error to ascribe to any one index number based on one or a few prescribed scenarios and calculated a priori the label "true cost" or "true performance." At time of IVA policy issue, such measures cannot be determined by *any* method. For example, actual subaccount performance and, for life-contingent IVAs, length of survival will influence the measure of value ultimately received.

A year-by-year "ledger statement" of projected annuity benefits—clearly labeled as hypothetical and for index calculation purposes only—could add robustness to information conveyed by any single numerical index value. Inappropriately perceived, it could equally add confusion, distorted expectations, and even claims that projected benefits were inadequately explained and mistaken at point of sale as guarantees (i.e., misrepresentation).

An ideal comparison index might have as a criterion that it reflects the levels of benefits at all durations in the specified period being measured as opposed to, say, merely comparing Year 20 projected benefits under the prescribed scenario(s). An ideal index would likely recognize the time value of money, although it is unlikely that the particular time value of money (or vector of values) assigned necessarily applies to a particular individual.

Clearly, an ideal index would be capable of being understood by both financial adviser and prospective IVA consumer and would be acceptable to the consumer, being viewed as helpful in the decision process. An exact understanding of index construction is unnecessary; the Consumer Price Index, the Dow Jones Industrial Average Index, and other indexes convey accepted meanings even absent specific knowledge of calculation methodology.

Other nuances exist. For example, a product might have a subaccount that invests in an underlying fund with a *current* 0.25% 12b-1 charge for which the board of managers of that underlying fund approved a lifetime *maximum* 0.30% 12b-1 charge. A participating IVA may use more conservative mortality than a nonparticipating IVA, but it would provide additional experience-based, nonguaranteed benefits attributable to actual mortality more favorable than the conservatively assumed mortality. IVA products with a prepackaged set of ancillary benefits included should be compared to "plain vanilla IVA" base products with optional ancillary benefits on as similar a basis as possible, lest uncompetitiveness is argued to stem from inclusion of a particular ancillary benefit—which may or may not be true. If health underwriting standards result in multiple classes of annuitants, then comparisons likely should be based on similar class definitions (recognizing that such definitions may not be precisely identical between companies). Not to identify a "standard," however, renders any comparisons meaningless.

Annuitants may allocate to, say, three different subaccounts with three different investment management fees in unequal proportions. How to recognize this in the index would need to be determined, noting that not all IVAs offer directly comparable subaccounts. One approach would be to take a weighted average cost of all subaccounts, with weights based on relative reserve levels of all IVA owners participating in each subaccount.

Giving an IVA buyer full assistance with the purchase decision via a simplified single index measure is an infeasible task. No index by itself can convey the particular IVA product and particular annuity payout option that best meets the needs of the individual purchaser. Nonetheless, an (imperfect) index may be constructed for use as a general tool in guiding buyers toward products of greater relative value.

Chapter 8, Rate of Return, in this book suggests a starting point for index construction. For example, a method that solves for the level, annually effective compound interest rate that equates gross premium with a projected benefit stream given a prescribed investment return pattern on the assets underlying an IVA subaccount (from which investment management fees and 12b-1 fees at the underlying fund level and M&E&A charges at the product level must be deducted to arrive at *net* performance) over a specified period could be used.

UNCERTAINTY

Uncertainty is one notion that may play an integral role in framing longevity risk in such a way as to make individuals more receptive to IVAs. Prospective retirees, recent retirees, or those adopting a phased retirement approach are plagued by uncertainty because of the wide distribution of possible outcomes they face. They might live only a few years and be just fine financially. They might live a long time, exhaust all their financial resources, and live in poverty. The point is that they face uncertainty. As long as individuals do not know the length of their future lifetime, they will *always* lack the requisite information to convert uncertainty into certainty.

Immediate annuities convert *uncertainty* into *certainty*. Insurance companies are one institution that developed to convert uncertainty into certainty. This allows individuals to better plan their lives, and society is advanced. Insurance, including longevity insurance, removes anxiety about losses beyond the individual's financial means to sustain. Uncertainty about economic affairs can weigh heavily on a person's psyche.

For example, a 60-year-old female may experience a very wide distribution of future outcomes. She may require retirement income for 1 year or for 50 years. Figure 12.19 illustrates the enormous uncertainty she faces regarding the length of the future lifetime over which she requires retirement income. At some age, she may well outlive the ability of her assets to sustain her, especially when one considers that even at 4% inflation, when she is age 100, goods and services will cost 480% of what they do at age 60.

Decision making under uncertainty involves the decision maker's attitude toward uncertainty. Consider a situation where a contest winner can

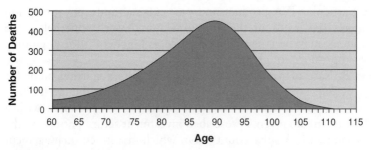

FIGURE 12.19 Distribution of Age at Death
(for group of 10,000 60-year-old females)
Source: Annuity 2000 Basic Mortality Table.

elect either (1) $50,000 with certainty or (2) the chance to win either $100,000 with probability ½ or $0 with probability ½. In electing a choice, the decision maker is expressing a preference with respect to the two probability distributions affecting payoffs.

Both choices have the same expected value of $50,000. The variance of choice (2) is larger than the variance of choice (1). Those choosing (2) may be called *risk loving* while those choosing (1) may be called *risk averse*. Each choice expresses a different mind-set toward risk and uncertainty. A *risk averse* individual prefers the expected value with certainty to the game. A *risk loving* individual prefers the game to receiving with certainty the expected value of the game. A *risk neutral* individual is indifferent.

As will be described in a section on utility theory in Chapter 16, if one probability distribution is preferred to another, then the first is assigned a higher utility number. A decision maker chooses to maximize his *expected utility*, the sum of the utilities of each possible outcome multiplied by the probability each occurs.

A risk averse individual is willing to pay someone else to replace the distribution of all possible outcomes with an alternative that offers the expected value of all outcomes. For example, a risk averse individual offered only choice (2)—where he is forced to play a game to determine the outcome—would be willing to pay, say, $5,000 to someone who would play the game for him and would instead give him the $50,000 expected value of the game with certainty.

Risk aversion implies a willingness to pay for insurance that will reduce uncertainty. *Variance* measures the dispersion of outcomes about the expected value. The risk averse individual is therefore willing to pay something for insurance that enables him to *reduce* the variance of outcomes.

This willingness to pay to reduce uncertainty provides incentive to produce something to accomplish this. The economic system responds to this demand of risk averse individuals by supplying insurance—hence, the creation of insurance institutions.

In contrast, the risk loving individual will actually pay something to *increase* the dispersion of outcomes, provided the expected value remains unchanged. The economic system responds to this demand of risk loving individuals by supplying casinos.

That risk averse decision makers will pay to replace a distribution of outcomes that results in uncertainty with the expected value of that distribution that results in certainty explains the demand side of insurance. The insurance company converts an uncertain financial situation for the immediate annuity customer into one in which a lifetime of retirement income benefits is guaranteed.

What explains the supply side of insurance? Insurance companies are presumably owned by risk averse stock holders. Why are they willing to assume the full range of the distribution of outcomes? The supply side of insurance is driven by the law of large numbers:

Suppose that $X_1, X_2, \ldots, X_k, \ldots$ is a sequence of independent, identically distributed random variables, each with mean μ and variance σ^2. Define the new sequence of $\bar{X}_i$ values by

$$\bar{X}_n = \frac{1}{n} \sum_{i=1}^{n} X_i = \frac{X_1 + X_2 + \cdots + X_n}{n}, \quad n = 1, 2, 3, \ldots$$

Then, $\lim_{n \to \infty} P(|\bar{X}_n - \mu| > \varepsilon) = 0$, for any $\varepsilon > 0$.

In other words, as the random sample of size n from a population gets arbitrarily large (i.e., as n goes to infinity), the probability that the sample mean $\bar{X}$ will differ from the population mean μ goes to zero.

Figure 12.20 visually illustrates the law of large numbers. When n equals 1, $\bar{x}$ simply equals x_1, the first and only observation. Because it is any observation from the entire population, the curve shown for $n = 1$ is simply the probability distribution of the random variable.

As n gets bigger, the probability distribution concentrates more around the expected value $E(X)$. Taken to the extreme, as n goes to infinity, the probability distribution of $\bar{X}$ effectively collapses to $E(X)$ itself. For a very large sample, the sample average $\bar{x}$ is effectively known with certainty.

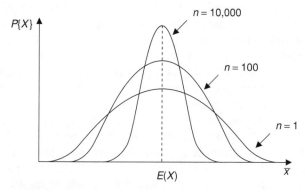

FIGURE 12.20   Law of Large Numbers

Think about the random variable defined by the average number of heads in n tosses of a fair coin. With only four tosses, one can imagine getting only one head and arriving at a sample mean $\bar{x}$ of ¼, deviating from the population mean μ of ½ by 50%. It is more challenging (but possible) to imagine 1,000 tosses and getting only 250 heads, again arriving at a sample mean $\bar{x}$ of ¼, again deviating from the population mean μ of ½ by 50%. Intuitively, we sense that dispersion about the mean narrows with progressively more tosses.

When an insurance company sells immediate annuities, it draws a sample of size equal to the number of contracts it sells from the population of actual and prospective immediate annuitants of the same class (e.g., nonunderwritten, voluntarily elected, individual annuitants). As the insurance company gets more customers sharing the same underlying probability distribution of annuity payouts (i.e., sharing the same underlying mortality distribution) and as long as independence is preserved, the series of annuity payouts the company will make to its annuitants becomes progressively more certain, even though the payouts to any one individual remain uncertain.

Because the law of large numbers requires independent, identically distributed random variables, insurance companies may identify risk classes to stratify individuals whose distributions differ markedly from the "standard" distribution. As aggregators of hazard risk (here the mortality-based hazard of longevity), insurers layer the aggregate loss distributions (here the periodic immediate annuity claim payments) into insurance "tranches" that partition different risk classes (here mortality risk as evaluated by underwriters). Such IVA underwriting is the subject of Chapter 13.

In summary, longevity insurance is feasible when:

- There exist risk averse individuals.
- Insurance companies can use the law of large numbers to translate uncertainty for individuals into certainty for a group.
- The probability distribution (i.e., mortality rates) for individuals is roughly the same for all class members (i.e., homogeneity of risk).
- Independence of risks exists.
- The probability distribution can be reasonably accurately determined by the insurance company.

If these conditions exist, immediate annuity contracts can convert a world of uncertainty into one of certainty. Framing longevity risk in terms of converting uncertainty to certainty and thereby giving individuals greater *control* over their financial destiny may be paramount in achieving greater use of immediate annuity instruments.

With immediate variable annuities, individuals can convert uncertainty as to lifetime income into certainty and thereby *control* their financial future. Individuals can *control* the asset classes in which their retirement savings are invested, both initially and subsequently. Individuals can *control* the major guidelines under which the funds invest by voting through proxy statements. Individuals can *control* who receives any residual assets after their deaths through beneficiary designations.

Yet historically and ironically, "loss of control" is a phrase sometimes heard as an *objection* to purchasing an IVA. Individuals are so used to being in the asset accumulation phase of their lives where they favor 100% access to 100% of their assets 100% of the time that this gains great psychological stature. It may take counseling to recognize that at this phase of their lives, lifetime income may outweigh perfect liquidity—at least for part of their assets.

CHAPTER 13

Individual Immediate Variable Annuity Underwriting

We should manage our fortunes as we do our health—enjoy it when good, be patient when it is bad, and never apply violent remedies except in an extreme necessity.
—Francois de La Rouchefoucauld

STANDARD LIFE UNDERWRITING

A large number of factors impact the level of variable annuity benefits that can be provided for a given premium. For example, individuals purchasing an immediate variable annuity (IVA) likely consider themselves in average or better-than-average health. This alone suggests that individual annuitant mortality will be superior to (i.e., lower than) general population mortality.

A host of stratification factors—age, gender, health status, wealth, geographic location, hobbies (e.g., private aircraft pilots)—affects individual annuitant mortality rates. For example, intercompany mortality experience under individual immediate annuities clearly shows that actual to expected annuitant mortality ratios are substantially lower for contracts providing higher annual income than for contracts providing lower annual income. Mortality rates are one element in pricing immediate variable annuities.

The process of subdividing a population into groups for purposes of insurance ratemaking is called "underwriting," and those who perform this process are called "underwriters." The historical derivation is from sixteenth-century London coffeehouses, involving the writing of names underneath a description of cargo and vessel by those who were willing to provide insurance that the ship's cargo would safely reach its destination.[1] Much as a prism refracts light waves so as to produce a spectrum of colors in order of their wavelengths, the underwriting process partitions annuity or insurance applicants into classes in order of the degree of risk they pose relative to the hazard insured against.

Immediate annuity underwriting today is generally limited to age and gender. The resulting large groupings facilitate sales, since fewer questions need to be asked on the application and no time or money related to medical evaluations needs to be spent.

Insurers go to great lengths to simplify IVA sales, sacrificing much individual equity for the sake of simplicity. Underwriting results in costs for data collection and evaluation, additional processing time that delays contract issue, and increased "not taken" rates as prospective annuitants shop insurance companies for their best underwriting deal. A lengthy underwriting-and-issue process is a competitive disadvantage.

When an IVA application and premium are received in an insurer's home office, annuity operations personnel processing new business must verify the age(s) and sex(es) of the annuitant(s). Birth certificates and numerous other documents may serve as acceptable documentation.

Minimum premium sizes are required, since below some threshold, the insurer's administrative expenses overwhelm revenue derived from the mortality and expense (M&E) risk charge, asset management, and other sources. Maximum acceptable premiums are often established—either formally or as a matter of administrative practice—to ensure a spread of mortality risk among a large number of lives and to avoid undue mortality risk concentration in one life or a handful of lives.

Sometimes maximum premiums are established as the limit "without home office approval." Larger premiums may be accepted on a case-by-case basis, for example, where the vast majority of the premium goes toward a lengthy, non-life-contingent certain period followed by a deferred lifetime annuity that begins at a very advanced age, to which only a small portion of the premium is applied. If the jumbo immediate annuity happens to be part variable and part fixed, requiring prior home office approval also serves to alert the fixed-income investment staff to invest the portion of this large premium designated to cover the fixed annuity appropriately to cover the projected annuity benefits plus expenses plus taxes associated with the transaction.

SUBSTANDARD LIFE UNDERWRITING

The next likeliest form of immediate annuity underwriting beyond the age and gender bases in use today is health underwriting (as opposed to occupation, avocation, financial underwriting, geographic location, etc.). This is especially prominent in "structured settlement" annuities that compensate a plaintiff who suffered economic harm at the hands of the defendant and where restitution to make the injured party economically whole is better achieved via an annuity than a lump sum, for example, a baby injured by an obstetrician in the birthing process or a worker injured on the job, thus reducing future earning capacity. Recipients often prefer a structured settlement to a lump sum, since if the latter is then applied to the purchase of an immediate annuity, a portion of each payment is taxable gain, whereas the entirety of the structured settlement benefit stream is deemed nontaxable as it is presumably structured to make the injured party economically whole and therefore no part represents a gain. Such medically underwritten products are called "impaired life annuities" or "substandard annuities." A minimal number of insurers today offer immediate annuity underwriting. Life insurance companies with affiliated property/casualty insurance companies are likely candidates to offer medically underwritten structured settlement immediate annuities that result from claims settlements of the property/casualty company.

As greater levels of sales are achieved, increasing degrees of underwriting will likely result. Marketplace opportunity virtually assures the forthcoming of a large number of underwriting classes replacing the uniclass environment today, as such classes will be necessary to capture into immediate annuity products the retirement savings assets of individuals with impaired health. Greater competition will spawn the desire to offer better pricing, for example, higher periodic benefits for the same premium to those with impaired health relative to those in excellent health. In contrast to the dominant U.S. practice of assuming everyone is a self-selected healthy risk and recognizing only age and gender in pricing, the United Kingdom has an active substandard annuity market for less healthy individuals.

While some underwriting factors provide opportunity for anti-selection (e.g., a nonsmoker smoking for some minimal period of time to qualify for more favorable "smoker's" annuity payout rates), other factors (e.g., education, income) are less amenable to manipulation. Unlike life insurance, where insureds benefit by demonstrating good health (or possibly concealing poor health), annuitants benefit by demonstrating poor health and engagement in risky behaviors with high accidental death rates. Will prospects who claim to imbibe alcohol excessively, use illicit drugs, or engage in skydiving, hang gliding, cliff diving, or airplane acrobatics (including wing-walking) promise to do so in the future?! Basing substandard ratings only on specific major health impairments typically of a permanent nature—such as heart disease—seems a reasonable approach. Conditions more within the control of an annuitant would not be ratable.

Immediate annuities currently include no contestability provisions allowing for denial of or adjustment to claims after issue. Without this, answers may not be reliable if health underwriting or other types of under-writing are introduced. For example, if an insurer granted a very high con-version factor because of a life-threatening medical condition that was later found never to have actually existed, it will want to possess a corrective mechanism. Right now, a contestability provision in an immediate variable annuity would be outside of mainstream annuity offerings.

Greater volumes of sales will also warrant the incursion of greater expense by insurers of having medical directors or medical underwriters on staff to aid in the determination of appropriate benefit adjustments for dif-ferent types of medical impairments. This may be done with "age rate-ups." For example, a 65-year-old with a specific collection of medical impairments may be "rated up" five years and treated like a 70-year-old for immediate variable annuity purposes, qualifying him for higher levels of periodic income.

Some annuity companies limit the degree to which they will apply a rat-ing to a life-contingent annuity. One approach is to make an allowance for 50% of the extra mortality that would be provided based on life insurance policy underwriting, the effect of which may be limited to a maximum of five years of "age rate-up." At very advanced issue ages, no annuity "age rate-ups" are usually allowed.

Other annuity companies may make substantial age rate-ups—even many decades of age—when they feel this is warranted. Substandard annu-ity underwriting is some art, some science. The corollary can be a relatively wide range of prices for a given impaired-life annuity shopped across a number of companies.

Substandard life insurance underwriting methodology can be applied to substandard immediate annuity underwriting. To evaluate the mortality risk presented by an IVA applicant with some measure of impaired health, an annuity company establishes the underwriting criteria to consider. A "debit system" is then used whereby each criterion is assigned a range of debits that depends on how greatly it influences mortality. This formulaic approach produces a total number of debits that suggests a pricing basis for the IVA. This may be a specific number of years of "age rate-up." It may be a multiple of and/or addition to standard mortality rates that are then employed in the usual fashion to arrive at the actuarial present value of the annuity and therefore the purchase price.

One must ask the question, "If initial benefit determination of an indi-vidual immediate annuitant pool is based on projected mortality experience for all lives in that pool—some very healthy, some less healthy—and if an insurer begins to offer higher initial benefits (substandard annuities) to those with medical impairment, is not the result that the remaining subset of 'stan-dard' (healthier) annuitants will exhibit lower mortality than the mortality table premised on aggregate mortality predicts?" If those who qualify for substandard rates truly represent only incremental IVA purchases that would not be made in the absence of such a rating, then the addition of substandard annuitants might not affect the overall pricing integrity.

If such substandard lives would have purchased an IVA at standard rates, then there would need to be adjustments. For example, a third class, that of "super-select" (extra-healthy) lives, might need to be created, lives that receive lower initial annuity benefits than the "standard" and "substandard" lives do. This is not a commercially viable approach. Those whose constitution makes them more impervious to disease will not accept being penalized for excellent health. Rather, if substandard rates are to be offered, then super-select and standard life annuity payout rates would need to be predicated on one combined mortality table with lower q_x values than if only one set of rates were used for everyone. Of course, to the extent that less healthy lives purchase IVAs on a more favorable basis from competing insurers that offer substandard rates, this may leave IVA writers without such rating classes selling to the remaining healthier-than-average IVA prospect population.

Life-contingent immediate annuities should not be issued to individuals in extremely poor health where longevity risk is such a very low probability event as to make the sale unsuitable. In the interest of good public relations, insurance companies may have administrative practices, procedures, or rules whereby they return the full premium if the annuitant dies before receiving any benefits, even if there is no contractual obligation to do so. For the same reason, insurers might require that any annuitant age 90 or over elect some form of refund or guarantee feature with his or her life annuity; that is, a straight "life only" annuity is not available above a certain age.

Greater emphasis will also be placed on the collection of individual immediate variable annuitant mortality experience data—including standardized impairment codes defining the nature of medical conditions—for lives with health impairments. This will improve the ability to provide the appropriate relationship between premiums paid and retirement income benefits received. While this has long been the case for life insurance, such data is today scant for immediate annuities. Such studies will likely be industry-wide so as to more quickly provide statistically meaningful information. Reinsurers of annuitant mortality will be especially well positioned to glean the benefit of large volumes of such data from multiple direct writers and will potentially develop automated impaired-life annuity underwriting systems for their client companies.

The competitive nature of U.S. variable annuity business may preclude some insurers from participating in intercompany annuitant mortality studies, simply due to associated expenses. The paucity of annuitant mortality data at advanced ages may argue for collaborative studies. Similarly, there is a dearth of mortality data on immediate annuities written on a substandard basis for which a pooling of data would be mutually beneficial.

Cost/benefit analyses may then be performed that suggest a point beyond which the benefit of gathering additional medical data to perform substandard underwriting is outweighed by the incremental cost. Some battery of tests has strong "predictive value" about the IVA applicant's mortality. For example, underwriting requirement testing protocols such as examination of blood and urine specimens profoundly influence mortality results that insurers experience. "Underwriting packages" are the combination of assessment tools used and may include nonmedical items, such as a credit check. Further testing beyond some point adds weaker predictive data, adds expense, and delays the ultimate underwriting decision.

As with life insurance, underwriting requirements may vary with contract size. A *nonmedical* insurance application requires no examination, although medical history information is gathered, often in the application itself. A *paramedical* examination is performed by a nonphysician health care professional, such as a nurse. A *medical* insurance application involves applicant examination by a licensed physician. The notion of issuing a policy quickly due to less underwriting based on point-of-sale information gathering goes by the name "simplified issue," which is akin to nonmedical insurance.

The underwriting decision set for life insurance includes a rating classification that finds the applicant uninsurable, in which case no contract is issued. In contrast, the underwriting decision set for immediate annuities includes only rating classifications that still result in a contract being issued. The only question is where on the price-to-benefit ratio spectrum the applicant should be placed. No applicant is deemed "too healthy" to qualify for an immediate annuity. While primarily but not exclusively "bionic man" science fiction today, migration toward engineered replacement parts (e.g., mechanical hearts) for humans could challenge the notion of being "too healthy" to qualify for an immediate annuity.

Underwritten life insurance—in contrast to "guaranteed issue"—uses "select" and "ultimate" mortality rates. The underwriting process "selects" out candidates with superior risk profiles and issues life insurance to them at "preferred" rates. Over time, as the years elapse since the underwriting evaluation occurs, "select" mortality grades into "ultimate" mortality, the latter representing mortality for the aggregation of lives both previously screened as "preferred" and those screened as "standard."

It is possible that over time and with collection of sufficient medically underwritten individual annuitant mortality experience, "select" and "ultimate" annuity mortality rates might evolve. In contrast to life insurance, "select" status would be associated with higher q_x values than "standard" would. These would grade over a number of years into "ultimate" mortality rates, again comprised of aggregate mortality rates of individuals previously classified as "select" and those classified as "standard." With the passage of time, those who previously were "standard" risks may have developed health problems, while those previously diagnosed as "select" with meaningful medical impairments might have had them resolved or might not have deteriorated further, bringing the mortality of the two groups closer together.

The ratio $q_{[x]}/q_{[x-t]+t}$ indicates the impact of underwriting. For a select period of s years, where t is less than s, it compares mortality of a newly selected life with that of a life selected t years earlier. Similarly, when t is greater than or equal to s, the ratio $q_{[x]}/q_x$ compares mortality of a newly selected life with that of annuitants rated either select or standard t years earlier; that is, it compares select period mortality with ultimate period mortality for the same attained age.

Insurance ratemaking is predicated on a group of "homogeneous exposure units." These can be automobile drivers of the same gender and age group, life insureds with comparable health status, or annuitants. The higher the level of homogeneity, the more tightly one should be able to predict experience of the group.

To gain a sense for the magnitude to which "impaired life" mortality influences annuity benefits available for a single premium, Table 13.1 shows how initial monthly benefits vary when mortality rates are increased relatively by 25%, 50%, and 100%. Benefits shown are for a $100,000 premium under a straight life annuity for males of selected issue ages using a 5% assumed investment rate (AIR). For example, a healthy male aged 65 might receive an initial monthly benefit of $710, while one with a medical impairment associated with twice normal mortality might receive an initial benefit of $877.

TABLE 13.1 Initial Monthly Life Only Annuity Benefit

	Male Aged...		
Relative Increase in q_x	65	75	85
0%	$710	$ 970	$1,485
25	755	1,066	1,702
50	798	1,159	1,919
100	877	1,337	2,355

Based on $100,000 premium, Annuity 2000 Basic Table mortality; no expenses, first payment in one month.

Table 13.2 shows information similar to that in Table 13.1 but in terms of the percentage increase in benefits when medical impairment is associated with 25%, 50%, or 100% higher mortality relative to the standard basis.

Because the percentage increases in IVA benefits for annuitants in substandard health can be so large—as Table 13.2 indicates—insurers prefer to operate on a relatively scientific basis; that is, they may feel uncomfortable managing the mortality risk associated with immediate annuities for medically impaired lives on an approximate basis.

If insurance codes do not provide a lower reserve standard for substandard annuities, their issuance creates surplus strain (i.e., application of an insurer's "free surplus" toward IVA reserves) that must be recognized in pricing, partially offsetting some of the higher initial benefit.

While a limited degree of substandard immediate annuities—those where impaired-life mortality affects the payout rates—are offered today, they still represent a niche market, as opposed to a mainstream market. Because variable annuities are such a complex business, the industry today is dominated by large companies that tend to cover their commensurately large expenses by writing high volumes of mainstream products and that have trepidation over entry into niche markets.

Substandard immediate annuity market growth may also be tempered because potential customers with impaired health tend less to consider a lifetime annuity, since they feel they may survive shorter than the average person. Because their health impairment, not unexpected longevity, is their primary concern, life annuities may not cross many prospects' minds, as they may focus their finite resources more on long-term care or medical insurance.

Insurance companies that do not offer IVAs underwritten on a substandard basis may still be able to compete for a prospect's business using non-life-contingent annuity options, where mortality rates and substandard underwriting will not be elements factored into pricing the annuity.

TABLE 13.2 Increase in Initial Annuity Benefit

	Male Aged ...		
Relative Increase in q_x	65	75	85
0%	0%	0%	0%
25	6	10	15
50	12	19	29
100	24	38	59

Note that for substandard life-contingent annuities with *n*-year certain periods, while annuity benefits will be paid for *n* years regardless of the survival or nonsurvival of the annuitant, the substandard mortality rates during the first *n* years still play a role. This is because all life-contingent annuity benefits after the *n*-year certain period are discounted through the certain period by using substandard mortality rates to derive the present value of the annuity and therefore the number of annuity units payable per period.

Impaired risk annuity underwriting was originally available only in the structured settlement (litigation) annuity market but is now available in the nonlitigation annuity market from about a dozen domestic insurers. National Association of Insurance Commissioners (NAIC) Actuarial Guideline IX-C, approved in March 2001, applies to nonstructured settlement substandard annuities. It allows insurers to hold reserves more reflective of the true substandard mortality risk. Forcing insurers to hold standard reserves results in overcharging substandard risk annuitants due to the extra cost of capital associated with the higher reserve. The new guideline may result in more insurers entering the impaired risk annuity market, with greater competition and lower reserve requirements driving better products and lower consumer prices.

NAIC Actuarial Guideline IX-C requires (1) a medical opinion and (2) at least a 25% reduction in the expectation of life in order for substandard reserves to be held in lieu of larger, standard reserves. A modification to this guideline that permits some degree of substandard reserves for conditions (such as a modest degree of hypertension or obesity) that don't meet the preceding two criteria may develop to permit finer underwriting gradations, enhancing premium-to-benefit equity among annuitants. For example, a proposal was made to require an independent medical assessment that supports at least a 15% reduction in life expectancy rather than 25%. The rationale behind having a percentage requirement is to avoid an adverse impact on the sufficiency of annuity reserving, permitting only those policies issued to truly substandard risk annuitants to be covered by the guideline.

The current province of impaired risk annuity underwriting is the immediate fixed annuity market. Extension to the immediate variable annuity market is a reasonable expectation.

To lend perspective, while much has been mentioned here about mortality assumptions, it is the subaccount investment returns that will likely be the primary determinants of profitability for insurance companies writing IVAs.

CHAPTER 14

Legal Issues

Law is the crystallization of the habit and thought of society.
—Woodrow Wilson

It is in justice that the ordering of society is centered.
—Aristotle

UNISEX RATES

"Payout rates" and "conversion factors" are terms used to describe the translation of a single premium into a periodic retirement income benefit amount. Recall that for immediate variable annuities (IVAs), the amount of the first benefit payment is known with certainty for any given single premium once a specific annuity option and assumed investment rate (AIR) are chosen. Future benefit amounts fluctuate with the performance of the sub-account(s) chosen by the contract owner.

For individuals who saved up for retirement using a deferred variable annuity contract as their savings vehicle, there are usually guaranteed fixed and variable annuity payout rates shown in the back of their deferred annuity contract. States typically require that contract owners receive the higher of (1) the benefit associated with such guaranteed rates or (2) rates currently available to new customers of the same class at the time the accumulated value is converted into a periodic income stream.

A formula is used to provide such a conversion of a single premium into a periodic retirement income amount. From the *gross premium* applied may be deducted items such as state premium tax and a flat dollar amount fee to help defray expenses associated with performing the calculations and setting up policyholder records on check disbursement, tax reporting, reserve calculation, customer service, and other systems. The result is the *net premium*.

This is typically divided by 1,000 and then multiplied by the "payout rate per $1,000 of net premium" appropriate for the individual's age, sex, type of annuity option, and benefit frequency. For example, a $100,000 net premium would be divided by 1,000 to arrive at 100; 100 would then be multiplied by the proper payout rate per $1,000 of net premium, such as $6.50. The result, $650, determines the first benefit amount.

That $650 is then divided by the annuity unit value. Suppose it is $2.00. The result is 325. The annuitant will receive the value of 325 annuity units on each future payment date.

Federal law requires *unisex* payout rates for certain employer-sponsored employee benefit plans; that is, similarly situated males and females—those of the same age, with the same accumulated value, and having elected the same form of annuity option—must receive equal retirement income benefits. By contrast, for individuals outside such plans, *sex-distinct* payout rates are used.

Unisex rates can be any percentage blend of the separate male and female payout rates that would otherwise be used.[1] In markets where employees have no access to a lump sum alternative to an annuity and cannot roll their accumulated values to an individual retirement account (IRA) outside the umbrella of the employer's tax-qualified pension program, a unisex rate might be based on the same male/female percentage blend as exists in that employer's employee population, such as 50% male/50% female.

In cases where a male employee has the option to roll his accumulated value into an IRA outside the umbrella of the employer's tax-qualified pension program, the unisex rate might be set equal to the female payout rate; that is, it assumes a 100% female/0% male blend. This may be prudent because a male employee would be better off performing a rollover of his tax-qualified pension program account into an IRA, removing it from the requirement of being subject to unisex rates and allowing him to qualify for the higher sex-distinct male payout rates.

For unisex joint annuity payout options involving two lives, an assumption must also be made regarding the male/female proportion of the second life.

Unisex payout rates may be required to apply to all immediate annuities—not just those in an employer's tax-qualified pension program—in states that have legislated unisex requirements. For example, Montana Code Annotated Section 49-2-309 stipulates:

49-2-309. Discrimination in insurance and retirement plans. (1) It is an unlawful discriminatory practice for a financial institution or person to discriminate solely on the basis of sex or marital status in the issuance or operation of any type of insurance policy, plan, or coverage or in any pension or retirement plan, program, or coverage, including discrimination in regard to rates or premiums and payments or benefits.

Montana law prohibits the use of sex as a rating factor for pensions and all lines of insurance for all policies sold and benefit programs formed after October 1, 1985. In effect, state government dictates acceptable underwriting classifications rather than insurance company actuaries and underwriters.

Genuine mortality rate differences exist between males and females. (Mortality rate differences even exist between females in tropical regions and females in arctic regions, who, through evolutionary adaptation, have slightly different genetic structures.) Recognizing these differences results in less expensive life insurance for females, who tend to live longer, pay premiums longer, and have their death claims deferred further into the future. Recognizing these differences results in higher annuity benefits for males, who tend to survive for shorter periods than females of the same age and therefore receive fewer annuity benefit payments.

Not every female who begins an immediate annuity program at age x lives longer than every male who begins an immediate annuity program at age x. As a group, however, this is currently true. There is no question but that empirical evidence shows that humans with two "X" chromosomes (females) tend to draw a longer series of immediate annuity benefits than humans with one "X" and one "Y" chromosome (males), and therefore there must be a difference in the amount of each benefit payment if each is to derive the same present value of benefits for the same premium.

Some tried to argue for equal benefits for females and males for equal premiums on "overlap theory"[2] grounds. The contention was that a high percentage of male annuitant deaths could be matched by female annuitant deaths for a group initially consisting of half men and half women of the same age. The argument was that there was a significant overlap in deaths. This line of reasoning, however, failed to recognize the time value of money—more male deaths unmatched by female deaths occurred in the earlier years of the annuity program, while more female deaths unmatched by male deaths occurred in the later years.

It is important to recall that risk classification is a method for evaluating average claims experience for a particular group, not for predicting the experience of any single individual within the group. Indeed, as was shown earlier, the reason immediate variable annuities so satisfactorily fulfill their objective of transferring longevity risk away from an individual retiree who can't absorb it to a large pool of annuitants who can is precisely because the experience of the group is highly predictable whereas the experience of any one individual is not.

Risk classification, a fundamental insurance principle, is a procedure for differentiating among individuals, the purpose of which is to assure that each insured contributes in proportion to his or her expected benefits. If one person is allowed to pay less than his or her share, it necessitates overcharging others to keep the fund solvent.

Fair discrimination has an important role in the world of insurance and annuities. Equity is provided not only by charging equal premiums for equal risks but also by requiring that unequal classes not be treated equally.

Legislators may choose to establish regulations requiring unisex treatment of males and females for *insurance* purposes (auto, home, life, annuities, etc.). The greater one's leaning toward egalitarianism—the identical treatment for all—the higher the propensity to legislate against classifications based on degree of risk posed. The result is that where genuine underwriting differences exist and must be suppressed, one group ends up subsidizing the other.

The point at issue in the unisex mortality debate is not whether the present value of annuities genuinely differs by sex—it does. The question rather is whether it is socially desirable to recognize the difference, which is a matter of opinion. Hence the debate, since, as Mark Twain put it, "in all matters of opinion, our adversaries are insane."[3]

Said another way, there is empirical evidence that male mortality rates exceed female mortality rates. When placed in mathematical equations describing present values of life annuities, these present values are different. Political capriciousness determines whether the difference is recognized. Albert Einstein's statement regarding permanence versus evanescence has relevance: "Yes, we have to divide up our time like that, between our politics and our equations. But to me our equations are far more important, for politics are only a matter of present concern. A mathematical equation stands forever." Political and other knowledge grows increasingly perishable.

Title VII of the Civil Rights Act of 1964, as amended by the Equal Employment Opportunity Act of 1972, prohibits discrimination in employment practices on the basis of race, color, religion, sex, or national origin. Litigation focusing on the prohibition against discrimination in employment brought pensions and employee benefits under attack.

The U.S. Supreme Court has decided cases involving sex-distinct mortality in pension plans:

- In *Marie Manhart v. Los Angeles Department of Water and Power* (1978), the U.S. Supreme Court said a contributory defined benefit pension plan requiring women to contribute more than men because they could expect to receive retirement benefits for a longer period than men violates Section 703(a)(1) of Title VII of the Civil Rights Act of 1964.
- In *Arizona Governing Committee for Tax Deferred Annuity and Deferred Compensation Plans v. Nathalie Norris* (1983), the Supreme Court said that lifetime annuity purchase rates that were different for men and women in a voluntary deferred compensation plan constitutes discrimination on the basis of sex in violation of Title VII.

As a result of the *Norris* decision, all retirement benefits derived from contributions made after August 1, 1983, must be calculated without regard to sex. The Court, however, said the *Norris* decision "will in no way preclude any insurance company from offering annuity benefits that are calculated on the basis of sex-segregated actuarial tables." It is only the practice of offering sex-distinct annuity benefits to employees *by an employer* that is prohibited.

While social insurance programs like Social Security can demand unisex rates and compel payment of premiums that force one group to subsidize another, in the private sector people cannot be forced to buy something they deem to be at an unfair price.

If male mortality improvement factors exceed female mortality improvement factors sufficiently long, male mortality rates will progressively metamorphose into female mortality rates. Should this convergence occur, unisex annuity payout rates and sex-distinct annuity payout rates will be identical (or nearly so), vanquishing the often emotionally charged debate as to whether it is socially desirable to ignore mortality differences and resultant economic present value of annuity differences between males and females in retail annuities, annuities associated with employer-sponsored plans, and government-sponsored annuities.

SEPARATE ACCOUNT INSULATION

For many forms of insurance and for fixed annuities, the assets backing these insurance and annuity obligations are housed in the insurer's general account. Insurers may segment the general account into a number of asset portfolios. For example, assets backing a collection of insurance or fixed annuity policies with similar characteristics may be grouped into one general account asset portfolio segment with its own statement of investment policy. This helps insurers do a better job of asset/liability management, making it easier for them to model how a specific collection of assets might perform vis-à-vis a specific collection of liabilities the assets are intended to support.

This segmenting makes it easier to model and manage the business. It also helps show via internal financial reporting by general account segment how specific products are performing and, when necessary, provides clues as to corrective action management may wish to take. It also helps track actual emerging experience versus actuarial assumptions.

Such general account asset segmentation, however, is purely for internal management purposes. It is still the case that all general account assets of an insurer support all general account liabilities of the insurer. For example, if an insurer offers both fixed annuity and disability income products and has adequate assets in its fixed annuity segment of the general account but its disability income insurance claims exceed the assets in its disability income insurance segment, the insurer could become insolvent. In such a case, its fixed annuity customers are affected because the insurer experienced excessive claims in an unrelated product line.

Conservative statutory reserve requirements, the required holding of surplus in excess of reserves, and required regulatory notifications ("alarm bells") when surplus is drawn down to certain levels are some of the safeguards to protect insurance company policyholders before an insolvency would occur. The existence of state guaranty associations is a safeguard to protect insurance company general account policyholders after insolvency occurs. Protection afforded insureds by state guaranty fund laws usually extends only to licensed insurers. The National Organization of Life & Health Guaranty Associations (NOLHGA) seeks to coordinate various state guaranty association approaches and attempts to provide a degree of uniformity. While such safeguards exist, the point is that all general account assets support all general account liabilities.

As another safeguard, state insurance law imposes restrictions on investments in the general account. For example, these help provide diversification and liquidity.

For variable annuities, an insurer establishes a separate account. A separate account is distinct and apart from the general account. A separate account can have one or more subaccounts, such as a common stock subaccount, a bond subaccount, and a money market subaccount.

Variable annuity contract owners allocate their deposit among the subaccounts of the separate account. The assets of the subaccounts at the variable annuity contract level are then invested in underlying investment funds. The underlying funds—which can be managed by investment managers internal or external to the insurance company—increase in value by dividends, interest, and realized and unrealized capital gains; and they decrease by realized and unrealized capital losses, investment expenses, and taxes.

On each active trading day, the underlying fund is valued (typically only once daily). The valuation is reported by the investment management company to the insurer writing the variable annuity. Accounting is then performed at the subaccount level, which reflects expenses at the variable annuity contract level, such as the mortality and expense (M&E) risk charge. The end result is "accumulation unit values" for deferred annuity contracts and "annuity unit values" for immediate annuity contracts. The former determine the deferred annuity account value. The latter determine the size of immediate annuity retirement income checks (or electronic transfers).

Because with a variable annuity, investment risk is borne by the contract owner and not by the insurer, general account investment restrictions are inapplicable. For example, while the general account cannot be 100% invested in common stock, the separate account can. Investment objectives and policies are spelled out in the prospectuses for the funds underlying each variable annuity subaccount.

An insurer establishes a separate account to allow variable annuities to operate as desired, free from the investment constraints imposed on the general account. Separate accounts, while necessary to allow the desired functioning of variable annuity products, also provide the highly desirable protective benefit of insulation from general account liabilities; that is, if properly provided for in separate account agreements, assets supporting an insurance company's variable annuity products are insulated from adverse events associated with the insurer's general account products. Such assets are also insulated from adverse events associated with products of any other separate accounts the insurer may have. For example, Section 4240(a)(12) of New York Insurance Law states in part:

> *If and to the extent so provided in the applicable agreements, the assets in a separate account shall not be chargeable with liabilities arising out of any other business of the insurer.*

Section 4240(a)(8) of New York Insurance Law requires insurers to maintain assets in the separate account at least equal to the value needed to support deferred variable annuities plus the value needed to support immediate variable annuities associated with the separate account:

> *Unless otherwise provided in approvals given by the superintendent and under such conditions as he may prescribe, the insurer shall maintain in each separate account assets with a value at least equal to the amounts accumulated in accordance with the terms of the applicable agreements with respect to such separate account and the reserves for annuities in the course of payment that vary with the investment experience of such separate account.*

In actual practice, alarm bells tend to go off before an insurer gets too deeply into trouble. If needed, state insurance regulators can step in and control the company to protect the interests of policyholders, after which it may be turned over to one or more healthy insurers.

Any given state may not have an actual track record for how it would handle an insurance company insolvency. While an insurer operates in a healthy fashion (or is at least solvent), separate account contract owners are insulated from liabilities associated with general account business. In the event of an insolvency, however, might not a state insurance commissioner try to attach any of the insurer's assets, including separate account assets that are technically owned by the insurer?

While some state statutes are silent on this issue, a few make it indisputably clear that variable annuity contract owners have first claim on assets of an insulated separate account in the event of insurer insolvency. For example, Section 7435(b) of New York Insurance Law, dealing with priority of distribution of claims of the estate of a life insurance company, states:

> *Every claim under a separate account agreement providing, in effect, that the assets in the separate account shall not be chargeable with liabilities arising out of any other business of the insurer shall be satisfied out of the assets in the separate account equal to the reserves maintained in such account for such agreement and, to the extent, if any, not fully discharged thereby, shall be treated as a class four claim against the estate of the life insurance company.*

Section 7435(c)(1) goes further by specifically excluding from the estate of the insurance company insulated separate account assets:

> *"The estate of the life insurance company" shall mean the general assets of such company less any assets held in separate accounts that, pursuant to section four thousand two hundred forty of this chapter, are not chargeable with liabilities arising out of any other business of the insurer.*

TONTINES

Around 1653, Lorenza Tonti, a banker, introduced the tontine system in France to raise funds for the government.[4] A *tontine* is a financial arrangement whereby a group of participants makes contributions that provide a form of life annuity. The annuity amount increases each year for the survivors, who claim payouts that would have gone to those who died. The final survivor receives the entire remaining fund.

Tontines are generally outlawed today as contrary to public interest, since they effectively create *moral hazard*—a situation where members have financial incentive to encourage the demise of other members—although incremental gain to one survivor by one death may be minor for a large group. Tontines may be more in the nature of a contest than a reasonable economic program to help participants cope with longevity risk.

In 1869, Equitable Life Assurance Society implemented a life insurance tontine plan where dividends—instead of being paid annually to policyholders—were placed in a separate deferred dividend fund.[5] If the life insurance policyholder survived and kept his policy in force for 10, 15, or 20 years, he would receive a proportionate share of the fund. The more deaths and lapses that occurred prior to the fund distribution date, the bigger each survivor's share.

Because the fundamental purpose of life insurance is to pay policy proceeds on death, often to cover the risk of dying before one has fulfilled certain financial obligations, forfeitures of the annual dividends by those who died early to those who survived the target period were deemed inappropriate. Insurance (including annuity) nonforfeiture laws that restrict the extent of transfers of value between generations of policyholders were imposed.

In contrast, with immediate annuities, forfeiture of value by those who die early to provide sufficient funds for those who survive to advanced years is integral to the construction, success, and solvency of the program. As a result, immediate annuities tend to be exempt from state nonforfeiture law requirements.[6]

NONFORFEITURE LAWS

The Standard Nonforfeiture Law for Deferred Annuities, as adopted by the states either verbatim or with changes, states that no annuity contract shall be delivered or issued for delivery in the state unless the contract contains in substance specified provisions or corresponding provisions that in the opinion of the state insurance commissioner are at least as favorable to the contract owner. Nonforfeiture law defines minimum values of any paid-up annuity, cash surrender, or death benefits available under the annuity.

Nonforfeiture laws typically exempt immediate annuities, variable annuities, any deferred annuity contract after annuity payments have commenced, and other situations for which nonforfeiture safeguards are usually unnecessary. Thus, standard nonforfeiture laws and state variations thereof typically do not apply to traditional immediate variable annuities.

VARIABLE ANNUITY CONTRACT

Before an immediate variable annuity contract can be sold in any state, it must be filed with—and in most states approved by—the state insurance department. A System for Electronic Rate and Form Filing (SERFF) has been implemented and used by some states to speed the policy form approval process. Annuity contracts generally must meet an ease of readability requirement known as a Flesch score, based on number of syllables per word and number of words per sentence.

The National Association of Insurance Commissioners (NAIC) works to promote some degree of uniformity of state regulation by adopting model regulations that are passed by the state legislatures either verbatim or with some modification. The NAIC adopted a model variable annuity regulation, but state variable annuity laws and regulations contain numerous deviations. There is a lengthy list of contract-related filing requirements, which often include:

- Actual contract form.
- Full insurance company name and address and two officer signatures on first page.
- "Right to examine" provision on cover page (also known as "free look").
- Form identification number.
- Caption of type of coverage provided (e.g., immediate variable annuity contract).
- Indication of participating or nonparticipating contract (whether contract owner participates in divisible surplus of company).
- Clear statement that benefits are variable and will decrease or increase to reflect investment experience.
- Specifications page, including date annuity payments are scheduled to begin.
- Description of availability of contract assignments.
- Provision for describing terms and conditions for naming or changing beneficiaries.
- Provision stating what constitutes entire contract between insurer and contract holder (e.g., whether application form is part of entire contract).
- Incontestability provision.
- Misstatement of age or sex provision (New York Insurance Law Section 3219(a)(5) limits interest—charged or credited—due to misstatement of age or sex to 6% per annum).
- Description of mortality table and assumed interest rates used in calculating annuity payments.
- Description of how annuity payments after the first are determined.
- Ownership provision, including terms and conditions for designating or changing ownership.
- Explanation of available separate account(s) and subaccount(s).
- Explanation of allocation to subaccounts and any restrictions on transfers.
- If applicable, a statement guaranteeing that expense and mortality results shall not adversely affect the dollar amount of annuity benefits.
- AIR shall not exceed 5%, except with approval of state insurance commissioner.
- If benefit levels may be affected by future mortality results, the mortality factor shall be determined from the Annuity Mortality Table for 1949, Ultimate, or another mortality table if approved by the commissioner.

If an insurer doesn't offer a true single premium IVA contract, its equivalent may be synthetically created by purchasing a deferred variable annuity contract and immediately "annuitizing" it, generally by completing a "notification to effect annuity payments" form. Certain provisions that are active during the preannuitization accumulation phase typically become inactive in the postannuitization liquidation phase. These include surrender charges, waiver of surrender charges for specified events, annual fees, guaranteed minimum death benefits, and partial withdrawal and full surrender provisions. A new face page to the deferred variable annuity contract or an amendment form can be used to negate provisions that become inapplicable in the postannuitization phase if deferred annuity contract language does not already do so. Drafting and filing a true single premium immediate variable annuity (SPIVA) contract and prospectus is the preferable approach, to give purchasers a more tersely worded contract and prospectus free of language about extraneous provisions.

Insurance companies try to improve their "speed to market" by filing "master policy forms" with state insurance departments. These are constructed to be as broad as possible to eliminate the need to file future products or at least to minimize the effort. For example, as much information as possible is bracketed in state policy form filings, where the bracket indicates a variable value, which may be constrained to fall within specific limits. A host of pages dealing with optional riders, some subset of which may be used in future product offerings, is included in master policy form filings.

Immediate variable annuity contracts, like all insurance contracts, are *contracts of adhesion,*[7] where the written contract language is unilaterally drafted by the insurance company, giving an applicant no choice as to terminology. Even though there are two parties to the contract, one party drafted the contract language in its entirety, and the other party merely has the opportunity to accept it or reject it. As a result, courts typically construe ambiguities in favor of the contract owner, who had no hand in drafting any language.[8]

While the law of contracts is an expansive field unto itself, there are several other important points related to variable income annuity contracts:

- The agreement of the parties is the contract. The written annuity policy is not the contract but merely physical evidence of a contract. Interpretation of these written statements has as its objective discovery of what the parties intended the agreement to be.
- Words in the written annuity policy are given the meaning an ordinary layman would expect, although technical annuity terms are given their technical meaning unless the context indicates otherwise.
- The written annuity policy language is to be considered as a whole. If one part is ambiguous, an interpretation that is consistent with the rest of the document will carry greater weight than an interpretation that makes some other provision nonsensical.

IVA CONTRACT PROVISIONS

Free Look

State insurance regulations require a "free look" privilege, whereby immediate variable annuity purchasers can return the contract for a refund within the free look period. This period varies by state but typically runs from 10 to 30 days.

So as not to suffer investment losses in states mandating return of the exact premium unadjusted by market movement, IVA writers may place the net premium in a money market subaccount during the free look period. After this, they allocate it to the subaccounts selected on the application by the owner.

Transfers among Subaccounts

Excessive reallocations (transfers) among subaccounts, the performance of which determine retirement income, can disrupt portfolio management strategy and increase portfolio expenses, thereby driving down returns and reducing retirement income of all annuitants invested or partially invested in the subaccount. For example, excessive reallocation may force a common stock portfolio manager to hold a larger cash position than would otherwise be the case, possibly driving down portfolio return; it also increases commission and other expenses associated with trading securities.

As a result, the IVA contract may limit the number of reallocations permitted, such as to 6 or 12 per year. To control costs, some insurers allow a higher number of reallocations when done without human intervention, such as via Internet or telephony self-servicing.

Another device used to mitigate the effect of excessive reallocations among subaccounts on other annuitants is for the funds underlying the subaccounts to impose a short-term redemption fee. For example, to the extent an interest in the fund has been held less than 60 days, the fund might impose a 1% short-term trading fee. This fee is retained by the underlying fund, not the insurer. The impact is to reduce variable annuity income of short-term traders. For example, if you were 100% allocated to a subaccount whose underlying fund charged a 1% short-term trading fee and you reallocated 100% to a different subaccount within the 60-day period, all future benefit payments would be 1% less than they otherwise would have been because you now have only 99% as many assets working for you. To the extent that you were only partially allocated to that subaccount, the impact would be less.

IVA Contract Parties

Owner The owner is the person who owns the IVA contract and can exercise the privileges contained therein, such as the free look, reallocating among subaccounts, and excess withdrawals to the extent the contract offers a liquidity privilege.

Annuitant An annuitant is a person to whom annuity payments are made and, for life-contingent annuity options, a person on whose survival annuity payments are contingent.

Beneficiary A beneficiary is a person who may receive certain benefits under the contract when there is no longer a living annuitant or joint annuitant. There may be primary beneficiaries and contingent beneficiaries.

Premium Tax

Some states charge a premium tax that is a percentage of the premium. Smaller subdivisions of a state—counties or parishes—may also charge a premium tax. Technically, these taxes are assessed against the insurer. As a matter of practice, the insurer then typically assesses an identical charge to IVA applicants. In most cases, an amount equal to the premium tax is deducted from the gross premium to arrive at a net premium. Annuity benefit payments are calculated based on the net premium. In some cases, the insurer may instead determine an "average" state premium tax on all IVA business it writes—taking into account both states with and without premium taxes—and build this into its annuity conversion factors applicable to everyone.

IVA CONTRACT ADMINISTRATION

Proof of Age

An annuitant's driver's license, passport, or birth certificate are documents customarily acceptable as proof of date of birth and gender. Sometimes two such documents are required. If post-issue the date of birth and/or the gender of one or more annuitants are found to be other than that on the application and on which payments were based, contract language typically prescribes the corrective action to be taken. For example, if an annuitant were older than stated on the application, the insurer might make up underpayments to the annuitant in one lump sum. If an annuitant were younger than stated on the application, the insurer might (1) reduce future annuity benefits in such a way as to set them at the level where they should be now if the correct age had been used at inception and withhold benefit payments until the amount of overpayments has been recovered or (2) reduce future annuity benefits in such a way as to reflect both the correct age at inception and past overpayments, without interrupting the payment stream.

Death Claims

Insurers periodically need to ascertain the continuing survival of annuitants. If annuity benefit checks are used, endorsements suggest continuing survival. In the case of direct deposit of annuity payments, the possibility is higher that benefit payments may persist for some time after the annuitant's death.

Contract language typically reserves for the insurer the right to require annuitants periodically to prove their continuing survival, such as by signing and dating a form. Insurers might only exercise this right for a small subset of annuitants, perhaps those at the most advanced ages.

To the extent annuity payments are made after the annuitant's death when no further payments are due, the estate is obligated to return excess payments to the insurer.

Frozen bank accounts, checking annuitant Social Security numbers against Social Security death benefit claims, and forms verifying continued survival are some indicators of annuitant death or survival. Organizations exist to which such verification work may be subcontracted.

In the case of a joint and 100% to survivor annuity where the joint annuitants share a bank account, the first death may go unreported to the insurer. This is because the account may remain open and the surviving annuitant sees no need to notify the insurer since the benefit level doesn't change. As a result, the insurer holds a higher reserve than it should, since it still holds the higher reserve for a joint life annuity whereas it should now hold a lower reserve for what has become a single life annuity. This underreporting of deaths also affects the insurer's mortality experience studies, resulting in lower actual-to-expected (A/E) ratios than truly exist.

Before lump-sum death benefits can be released to beneficiaries—such as under a unit refund annuity option—a variety of processing events must be performed, for example, checking which potential recipients are alive (if there are no survivors among the class of primary beneficiaries, the class of contingent beneficiaries will be examined) and checking to ensure that payment can be released to the named recipient(s) (in some cases funds are to be paid to governmental entities to cover unpaid back taxes).

If death benefit payments go unclaimed because the recipient(s) cannot be located, after a statutorily specified period of time, such payments *escheat;* that is, such property reverts to the state in the absence of legal claimants.

SUITABILITY QUESTIONNAIRE

To ensure that prospective IVA purchasers understand the nature of the contract for which they are applying, some insurers ask them to complete a "suitability assessment questionnaire" along with the application form. For example, they may ask whether the applicant understands:

- The irrevocable nature of the purchase decision.
- That part of one's retirement savings should be retained outside of the annuity in readily accessible form for emergencies (e.g., medical expenses, home repairs).
- That the product will generate periodic income and is not a savings or accumulation-type product.
- That income payments may increase or decrease based on investment performance.
- That specific annuity options must be elected if income is to be provided for more than one person.
- That if a single (or joint) life annuity option is elected with no certain period or refund feature, payments cease upon death of the annuitant (or last surviving annuitant) with no additional payments made to any beneficiaries.

COMPLIANCE COSTS

It may appear that a cornucopia of laws, rules, and regulations exist affecting IVAs and an abundance of regulatory entities exist promulgating them. Because IVAs are regulated both as securities and as insurance, this is correct. To sell an IVA nationally, an insurer must simultaneously comply with rules of the Securities and Exchange Commission (SEC), National Association of Securities Dealers (NASD), the Internal Revenue Service (IRS), the Department of Labor (DOL), 50 state insurance departments, and 50 sets of state insurance laws and regulations. The last situation may change if insurers have the option of a single federal charter.

Many such rules in some form are absolutely necessary. For example, one needs to know how IVAs are taxed. To the extent politicians pile on rules—especially ones that don't improve the investment outcomes of immediate variable annuitants—one ramification is that increased compliance costs tilt the playing field in favor of large, established insurance companies and investment management companies.

MARKET CONDUCT

Internal practices, procedures, and standardized guidelines can help minimize or prevent certain market conduct events that lead to federal or state regulatory compliance violations and ultimately legal actions. Because immediate variable annuities and other insurance products are intangible, their sale depends in large part on an emotional attribute: trust.

Market conduct scandals or other public relations debacles undermine the ability of insurers to sell their products, even if alleged perpetrators are subsequently exculpated. As such, it is in their own best economic self-interest to police themselves and the rest of their industry to guard against abusive market practices. Well-publicized illegal, unethical, or abusive behaviors of even a few individuals within the insurance industry or sales personnel licensed to distribute its products convince some consumers that the vilification these groups occasionally experience is warranted.

Insurers can voluntarily obtain certification and periodic recertification by the Insurance Marketplace Standards Association (IMSA), based on examination of a wide range of processes and procedures across the insurance company enterprise. The first step is an internal self-assessment and completion of a questionnaire. The second step to IMSA qualification is an assessment by an approved independent external assessor, such as an accounting, actuarial, or legal firm.

The IMSA Mission Statement is: "To strengthen trust and confidence in the life insurance industry by requiring member companies to demonstrate commitment to high, ethical marketplace standards."

The National Association of Insurance Commissioners Market Conduct Examiners Handbook also defines requirements that may help insurers in internal operational assessments.

Producer appointment and licensing and termination, policy form filing, record retention, sales and marketing practices, underwriting and rating practices, policyholder services, claim payments, complaint handling, regulatory compliance, internal and external policy replacements, suitability of products sold, and anti-fraud programs are some of the categories investigated in market conduct assessments.

Promoting fidelity and quashing activities inimical to contract owner interests are the objectives of preventative policies to ensure appropriate market conduct in the sale and management of variable income annuities. Public relations damage from adjudicating a violation once it occurs can be vastly more harmful than the economic damage of such a single incident.

INTELLECTUAL PROPERTY

Intellectual property rights are evolving under U.S. and international patent law. New ideas related to financial services product, feature, or service offerings are finding a greater degree of receptivity to protections afforded in the nature of intellectual property rights. For example, "systems and apparatus" to administer a new immediate variable annuity product feature may be granted patent protection by the U.S. Patent and Trademark Office. Due to the competitive nature of the domestic variable annuity market, advantages created by new products or services are transient absent patent protection as competing insurers operate at a frenetic pace to match or beat new product, feature, and service offers.

An insurer that files a patent application and that makes known that it has a "patent pending" on a new product or feature may create a "chilling effect" on potential imitators. This is especially true for its largest competitors who write meaningful amounts of business of a similar nature, since usurpation of the patent(s) can subject the violator to treble damages.

35 U.S.C. 284 DAMAGES—PATENT LAWS

Upon finding for the claimant the court shall award the claimant damages adequate to compensate for the infringement but in no event less than a reasonable royalty for the use made of the invention by the infringer, together with interest and costs as fixed by the court.

When the damages are not found by a jury, the court shall assess them. In either event the court may increase the damages up to three times the amount found or assessed. Increased damages under this paragraph shall not apply to provisional rights under section 154(d) of this title.

The court may receive expert testimony as an aid to the determination of damages or of what royalty would be reasonable under the circumstances.

If a patent is granted, the insurer may capitalize by exclusively offering the unique product, feature, or service; or the insurer may selectively sell licensing rights to others. To date, intellectual property rights to retirement income management concepts have not resulted in any one company attracting retirement distribution assets in monolithic proportions.

PARTIAL ANNUITIZATION

In 1998, the Tax Court ruled in *Dona Conway v. Commissioner* that a *partial* exchange of a *deferred* annuity from one insurance carrier to another is permitted under Internal Revenue Code Section 1035, at least for the specific set of facts and circumstances existent in the case before the court. It was previously clear that a *full* exchange was permissible.

If a deferred annuity contract owner can perform a *partial* tax-free exchange of a deferred annuity contract, then this helps define tax treatment for *partial* annuitizations of a deferred annuity contract, since this is equivalent to a partial exchange followed by a full annuitization.

To the extent further developments in this area promote the ease with which *part* of a deferred annuity contract may be applied toward an immediate variable annuity (i.e., without having to take constructive receipt of the deferred annuity, pay tax on any gain, and apply part of the remainder to an immediate variable annuity purchase), this flexibility should result in more frequent use of immediate variable annuities as part of an individual's total retirement income program.

PRIVACY

When immediate annuity underwriting is involved, there is greater access by insurers to information about prospective annuitants. This raises privacy issues that accompany underwriting for any form of financial products, including health insurance and life insurance. Privacy information safeguards exist.

A futuristic glimpse suggests that as genetic screening becomes more widely available, individuals may have a much better picture of the kinds of health problems to which they may be predisposed and at what ages this may happen. As a result, such knowledge improves one's ability to select against insurance companies to the extent equal disclosure of such information is forbidden to them or hidden from them.

The emotionally charged maelstrom of medical information privacy may be less of an issue for immediate annuity writers, where it is to the contract owner's benefit to disclose such information, than it is for life insurance writers, where it is to the contract owner's benefit to conceal such information. Nonetheless, if an individual learns she has a 90% predisposition toward a certain debilitating, life-shortening disease, she may elect not to purchase an immediate annuity in the first place.

To the extent annuity writers have access to sufficient information about their annuitant pool to establish payout rates predicated on anticipated mortality experience truly representative of that pool, not only can fair pricing and program solvency continue to be achieved, but it can even be enhanced as additional prospective annuitant information allows for refinements in the way of finer gradations in pricing. To the extent annuity writers are denied access to such information, the arrangement works less well, and conservatism in pricing and reserving may be introduced to cover the uncertainties associated with concealed data.

Any legislation governing the use of genetic information in underwriting must consider and balance societal concerns for privacy with economic concerns for financial security program cost, anti-selection, inequitable subsidization of one health class by another, and solvency.

STATUS OF IMMEDIATE ANNUITIES IN CREDITOR ATTACHMENT AND ASSISTANCE PROGRAM QUALIFICATION

If an individual with assets insufficient to pay his debts enters into an immediate annuity contract with an insurer and irrevocably assigns benefit payments to, say, a relative for the express purpose of trying to place such assets beyond the reach of creditor attachment, such assignment may be "in fraud of creditors." The rights of creditors are superior to those of the assignee if the assignment is voidable because of being in fraud of the creditor's rights. The timing of purchase of the immediate annuity contract relative to the establishment of indebtedness accompanied by insufficient assets is one key factor in adjudicating such a matter. The facts and circumstances specific to the situation must be considered.

Qualification for certain governmental and other assistance programs may be conditioned on personal assets or net worth being below a specific dollar threshold. An individual can purchase an immediate annuity, thereby reducing a person's liquid assets—although generating for himself an income stream the present value of which is equivalent (or nearly so) to the premium applied. To the extent the action of the annuity purchase reduces a person's assets—as defined by the assistance program—to a level that permits program qualification, the purchaser may have either made a prudent economic decision or "gamed the system," depending on one's perspective. Whether assets used to purchase an immediate annuity are included in or excluded from any such calculation depends on the facts and circumstances specific to the situation.

CHAPTER 15

Securities Law

Security: one of the most insecure things in the world.
                                        —Anonymous

FEDERAL SECURITIES LAW

Because variable annuities have elements of insurance and elements of investment, they fall under dual regulation, with insurance elements primarily regulated at the state level and investment elements primarily regulated at the federal level. As an insurance product, variable annuities—being effectively a long series of endowments—are subject to state insurance laws and state insurance department regulations. For tax purposes, variable annuity markets are created by and their income tax treatment defined by sections of the federal Internal Revenue Code (IRC), with regulation by the Internal Revenue Service (IRS). Department of Labor (DOL) regulations can sometimes apply. The written agreement between annuity company and annuity owner is a contract, governed by contract law. Hence, legal statutes and regulations—the interpretations of which are revealed and sculpted through case law—permeate the variable annuity landscape.

Variable annuity contracts and the insurance companies that issue them are also subject to federal securities law, with regulation by the Securities and Exchange Commission (SEC). *Securities* are written evidence of ownership or creditorship. For example, a stock certificate is written evidence of an ownership interest. Like stocks and bonds, variable annuities, because of their investment component, are considered securities. One enters into a securities arrangement with an expectation of, but not a guarantee of, gain.

Following the Great Depression, securities laws were developed and enhanced to restore public confidence in U.S. financial markets. Variable annuities are subject to provisions of the Securities Act of 1933 and the

Securities Exchange Act of 1934, acts largely concerned with prevention of fraud in the issuance and trading of securities. Variable annuities are also subject to the Investment Company Act of 1940, which grants the Securities and Exchange Commission (SEC) regulatory power over sales of insurance products with a substantial equity component, such as variable annuities.

Variable annuities registered with the SEC are sold with the benefit of a prospectus. The prospectus describes in detail information about the variable annuity product itself and the underlying investment funds. For example, it discloses information about product expenses and investment fund objectives and management.

A variable annuity is regulated as a security; its underlying investment funds are regulated as open-end investment companies and its salespeople as securities broker-dealers. Variable annuities registered with the SEC can only be sold by individuals registered with the National Association of Securities Dealers (NASD).

A 1959 landmark Supreme Court decision, *SEC v. VALIC* (Variable Annuity Life Insurance Company), ruled that variable annuities were subject to these federal securities regulations. As a result, insurance companies temporarily stopped issuing variable annuities until they could come into compliance with federal securities acts. Variable annuity issuance resumed once the handful of insurance companies then issuing variable annuities achieved the necessary securities registration status.

Securities Act of 1933

The 1933 Act is primarily concerned with investor protection and secondarily with promotion of efficiency, competition, and capital formation. Investor protection is achieved by requiring securities to be registered with the SEC and through specific information required to be shown in the registration statement and in a prospectus, including disclosures about the issuer and the issuer's financial condition. The Securities Act of 1933 provides a right of recovery for securities purchasers harmed by false or misleading statements.

Insurance companies offering a variable annuity must file a registration statement with the SEC before sales of these securities begin. Civil liability is imposed on officers, directors, and others who sign an untrue or misleading registration statement. Potential liability extends to accountants, actuaries, lawyers, and others who prepare or certify to any part of the registration statement on which the signatories rely. Criminal penalties are imposed for any fraudulent scheme or transaction that would deceive the purchaser.

Prospective variable annuity purchasers must receive a prospectus, which is included in the registration statement. The prospectus contains information important to a prospective purchaser in making an informed decision. Name and location of the business issuing the variable annuity, a recent balance sheet and income statement of the issuer, the specific purpose to which funds raised will be applied, the price of shares to be offered, the name and location of the underwriter, commissions paid by the issuer to the underwriters for sales of the security, and noncommission expenses associated with the security offering are among the required disclosures.

Securities Exchange Act of 1934

In contrast to the 1933 Act, which deals primarily with new issues of securities, the 1934 Act focuses on the subsequent trading (i.e., purchase or sale) of existing securities commonly conducted on securities exchanges and over-the-counter markets. The 1934 Act focuses on maintaining a fair securities marketplace, free of deception and manipulation.

Under the 1934 Act, *brokers* (any people engaged in the business of effecting transactions in securities for the account of *others*) and *dealers* (any people engaged in the business of buying and selling securities for such people's *own accounts*) must file a registration with the SEC and have that registration granted before it is lawful to engage in interstate commerce involving the purchase or the sale of a security. The insurance company or sales company it hires to distribute its variable annuity must typically register as a broker-dealer.

Registered broker-dealers cannot purchase or sell any security until that broker or dealer and all associated persons of that broker or dealer meet operational capability standards (e.g., training, experience, competence) that the SEC deems necessary or appropriate for the public interest or for the protection of investors. The 1934 Act allows the SEC to cooperate with registered securities associations in devising and administering tests that cover bookkeeping, accounting, internal control over cash and securities, supervision of employees, maintenance of records, and other appropriate matters.

"Associated person" in the preceding paragraph means any partner, officer, director, or branch manager of a broker or dealer; any person directly or indirectly controlling, controlled by, or under common control with such broker or dealer; or any employee of such broker or dealer, excepting any person associated with a broker or dealer whose functions are solely clerical or ministerial.

The 1934 Act requires sales agents, home office customer service personnel, and any other associated person to pass one or more examinations on the securities business. These examinations differ by the type of securities offered.

The NASD, established in 1939, is a registered securities association with which all broker-dealers must now register. The NASD administers examinations for people associated with variable annuity sales. The NASD Series 6 examination is for registered representatives engaged in variable annuity and/or mutual fund sales. The NASD Series 26 examination is for registered principals, who supervise registered representatives.

The 1934 Act also regulates annual reports to shareholders, shareholder proxies, misleading statements, recordkeeping, and financial reporting requirements. It requires an issuer of registered securities to file periodic financial reports and other reports (e.g., director and officer trading activity in corporation shares) with the SEC and with the exchanges on which it is listed.

Investment Company Act of 1940

The 1940 Act deals with "investment companies," meaning any issuer that holds itself out as being engaged primarily in the business of investing, reinvesting, or trading in securities. While insurance companies themselves receive an exemption from being included under this definition, for purposes of variable annuities, they establish separate accounts, which are investment companies. As a result, the 1940 Act plays an important role in securities regulation of variable annuities.

The 1940 Act deals with classification of investment companies (management company, face-amount certificate company, unit investment trust), subclassification (open-end, closed-end, diversified, nondiversified), registration, investment policy, boards of directors, accounting, financial reports, and a host of operational and managerial topics.

A "diversified company" is a management company where at least 75% of the value of its total assets is represented by cash and cash items (including receivables), government securities, securities of other investment companies, and other securities where the value in respect of any one issuer is limited to an amount not greater than 5% of the value of the total assets of such management company and to not more than 10% of the outstanding voting securities of such issuer.

Registering an investment company with the SEC requires filing information regarding classification and subclassification, policies regarding borrowing money, issuing senior securities, investment concentration, use of real estate and commodities, making loans, portfolio turnover, investment policies that are changeable only by shareholder vote, other fundamental investment policies, and names and addresses of affiliated persons registering the investment company.

The 1940 Act makes sure that at least 40% of an investment management company's board of directors are outsiders. Directors of an investment management company must be elected to that office by holders of the outstanding voting securities. No registered investment company shall have a board of directors where more than 60% are "interested persons."

"Interested persons" include officers, employees, 5% owners, investment advisers or principal underwriters for the investment management company, recent legal counsel, and immediate family members, among others.

Investment advisers must have a written contract with the registered investment company approved by a majority of voting shares. Similarly, a principal underwriter for a registered open-end investment company must have a written contract—known as the principal underwriting agreement—with the company, approved annually by the board of directors or a majority of voting shares.

The 1940 Act deals with acceptable levels of variable annuity contract fees and charges. Section 26.f. states, in part:

1. *Limitation on sales. It shall be unlawful for any registered separate account funding variable insurance contracts, or for the sponsoring insurance company of such account, to sell any such contract—*

   A. *unless the fees and charges deducted under the contract, in the aggregate, are reasonable in relation to the services rendered, the expenses expected to be incurred, and the risks assumed by the insurance company, and, beginning on the earlier of August 1, 1997, or the earliest effective date of any registration statement or amendment thereto for such contract following the date of enactment of this subsection, the insurance company so represents in the registration statement for the contract.*

Insurance companies are exempt from portions of the 1940 Act incompatible with variable annuities. For example, Rule 22e-1 states that a registered separate account during the annuity payout period shall be exempt from the Section 22(e) provisions prohibiting the suspension of redemption rights of a redeemable security; that is, the normal requirement that a security be redeemable at any time is waived for an immediate variable annuity—but only for life-contingent annuity options. The exact wording is:

Rule 22e-1 — Exemption from Section 22(e) of the Act During Annuity Payment Period of Variable Annuity Contracts Participating in Certain Registered Separate Accounts

a. *A registered separate account shall, during the annuity payment period of variable annuity contracts participating in such account, be exempt from the provisions of section 22(e) of the Act prohibiting the suspension of the right of redemption or postponement of the date of payment or satisfaction upon redemption of any redeemable security, with respect to such contracts under which payments are being made based upon life contingencies.*

Note that one implication of this wording is that non-life-contingent (e.g., designated period) immediate variable annuity options must be redeemable upon request at any time as there is no exemption from the right of redemption requirement.

Investment Advisors Act of 1940

The Investment Advisors Act of 1940 defines *investment advisor* as "any person who, for compensation, engages in the business of advising others, either directly or through publications or writings, as to the value of securities or as to the advisability of investing in, purchasing, or selling securities, or who, for compensation and as part of a regular business, issues or promulgates analyses or reports concerning securities." There are exceptions for banks, for lawyers whose performance of such services is incidental to the practice of their profession, for publishers of newspapers and financial publications, and for select others.

With limited exceptions, this act requires investment advisers to file a registration form containing the adviser's name, business form, location, education, past business affiliations, balance sheet, scope of authority with respect to client funds, and basis of compensation. The act grants the SEC authority to penalize advisers engaging in misconduct, including censure, limiting activities, suspension, barring people from being associated with an investment adviser, dollar penalties, and disgorgement, including reasonable interest.

The act requires investment advisers to make and retain specific records and to establish policies to prevent use of material, nonpublic information. In short, this act seeks to ensure that only reputable investment advisers hold a valid registration by weeding out disreputable candidates through the application process and to grant the SEC authority to deal appropriately with advisers alleged to engage in misconduct.

STATE SECURITIES LAW

Long before the 1933, 1934, and 1940 federal securities acts following the Great Depression, states adopted "blue-sky" laws to protect the public against phony sales of stocks of companies with investment merit having "no more basis than so many feet of 'blue sky.'"[1] The purpose of most state securities statutes (blue-sky laws) is to assure that the true financial condition of a corporation issuing stock to the investing public is revealed.

State securities laws vary. Some state securities laws merely prohibit fraud in the sale of securities. Other state statutes regulate the activities of brokers and securities dealers and require their registration. Other statutes require registration of securities, with some requiring approval by a state official before the security can be offered for sale. While the Securities Act of 1933 allows concurrent jurisdiction by state agencies and the SEC, some states with registration statutes exempt securities that have been registered with the SEC.

New York's Martin Act of 1921 defines the "willful and knowing" commission of an illegal act as *fraud*. The 1996 National Securities Markets Improvement Act affirmed the right of states to bring enforcement actions in these situations.

Virtually all states exempt variable annuities from their blue-sky laws. The Texas Securities Act Section 4.A. defines *securities* and then states:

> [T]his definition shall not apply to any insurance policy, endowment policy, annuity contract, optional annuity contract, or any contract or agreement in relation to and in consequence of any such policy or contract, issued by an insurance company subject to the supervision or control of the Texas Department of Insurance when the form of such policy or contract has been duly filed with the Department as now or hereafter required by law.

ORGANIZATIONAL STRUCTURES OF VARIABLE ANNUITY ISSUERS

Classification of Investment Companies

Section 4 of the Investment Company Act of 1940 (U.S. Code Title 15, Chapter 2D, Subchapter I, Section 80a-4) divides investment companies into three principal classes:

1. *Face-amount certificate company* means an investment company that is engaged or proposes to engage in the business of issuing face-amount certificates of the installment type or that has been engaged in such business and has any such certificate outstanding.
2. *Unit investment trust* means an investment company that (1) is organized under a trust indenture, contract of custodianship or agency, or similar instrument; (2) does not have a board of directors; and (3) issues only redeemable securities, each of which represents an undivided interest in a unit of specified securities, but does not include a voting trust.
3. *Management company* means any investment company other than a face-amount certificate company or a unit investment trust.

Classification of Organizational Structures of Separate Accounts Underlying Variable Annuities

The three investment company classifications may be helpful as we examine three different organizational structures that exist for separate accounts underlying variable annuities. Each structure has its own advantages and disadvantages.

1. *Separate Account as an Open-End, Diversified Management Investment Company*   The insurance company establishes a separate account. The separate account assets are segregated from general account assets of the insurer and from assets of other separate accounts. The separate account is registered as an investment company under the Investment Company Act of 1940.

   The insurance company registers as an investment adviser. As is required, a written investment advisory contract exists between the investment adviser and the registered separate account.

   The separate account issues units of interest in itself to variable annuity contract owners. The variable annuity contract owners elect a board to manage the separate account. The 1940 Act defines the percentage of directors on the board who must be outsiders and not "interested persons" who have some affiliation.

   An insurer offering multiple variable annuity products with different underlying asset pools may establish multiple separate accounts. These are commonly labeled alphabetically—Separate Account A, Separate Account B, and so on.

   This approach is characterized by limited flexibility. Contract owner approval is required for most changes to the separate account.

   This is perhaps the simplest, most straightforward approach. It was used early on, when variable annuities had only one underlying investment, that being a common stock fund. As it was likely the first such fund of an insurer, these are often labeled Separate Account A, Fund A, and so on.

2. *Separate Account as a Unit Investment Trust, Investing in One or More Open-End Diversified Management Investment Companies*   A unit investment trust (UIT) is a special type of investment company regulated by the Investment Company Act of 1940. An insurance company desirous of issuing variable annuity contracts may organize a separate account as a unit investment trust.

   The UIT invests in securities of one or more open-end investment companies (funds). (*Open-end* means the investment company is currently offering for sale or has outstanding redeemable securities of which it is the issuer.) These funds, registered under the 1940 Act, may be organized by the insurance company or by an unaffiliated company. Originally, insurers tended to have just a small number of funds, each of which it organized itself. With time, the notion of multiple fund managers—some affiliated with the insurer, some unaffiliated—came into vogue for use in the same separate account. The number of funds per separate account also grew from low single digits to as high as many dozens.

These open-end investment companies in which the UIT invests are the stock funds, bond funds, money market funds, and other actively or passively managed funds of investments. Control of the investments (purchases, sales, portfolio composition, and cash levels) rests here at the fund level, not in the UIT.

These funds are truly mutual funds under the law, typically corporations or trusts. These mutual funds, however, are not the publicly available retail mutual funds. Rather, they are funds available to variable annuity (and variable life insurance) contract owners.

In 1981, Treasury Department regulation 81-225 stipulated that investment in publicly available mutual funds—available to people other than variable annuity contract owners—would result in annuity contracts losing their tax-favored status. The Tax Reform Act of 1984 codified the prohibition against use of publicly available mutual funds for variable annuity contracts. The prohibitions might reflect concern regarding possible different investment motivations among public shareholders and variable annuity separate account shareholders. There may also have been concern with permitting a state insurance regulatory authority to affect the operations of a publicly available mutual fund.

IRS Revenue Ruling 81-225, dealing with "investor control" restrictions, articulates the IRS's long-standing position that the owner of a variable annuity contract—not the insurer issuing the contract—is (1) to be treated for tax purposes as the owner of the underlying assets supporting the contract and (2) subject to current taxation on those underlying assets *if* he or she exercises too much control over the assets by directing how they are to be invested.

IRS Revenue Ruling 2003-91 provides a "safe harbor" for variable annuity designs to fall within acceptable investor control restrictions. It recognizes that at least 20 investment subaccount options can be offered under a variable annuity contract without causing the contract owner to be treated as the owner of the underlying assets, whereas the largest number of investment subaccount options in a variable annuity contract previously recognized by the IRS was four (Private Letter Ruling 9433030). Revenue Ruling 2003-91 acknowledges that at least one investment subaccount reallocation per month is allowable without violating investor control restrictions. It recognizes that "sector funds" limited to one industry or one geographical region are permissible. Unofficially, IRS staff members have periodically articulated that *at some point* investor control restrictions do limit the number of permissible investment subaccounts, the frequency of subaccount reallocations, and the level of specificity with which investment objectives are defined.

These mutual funds, in which the separate account organized as a UIT invests, can elect to qualify under IRC Subchapter M, which says that if the mutual funds (1) distribute all realized capital gains and dividend income to the separate account in the form of dividends and (2) meet diversification requirements, then they are not taxed on this income.

The UIT approach offers insurers greater flexibility and control than the first approach, where the separate account is organized as an open-end, diversified management investment company. The UIT is the shareholder of the underlying mutual funds in which it invests.

The UIT approach, where the separate account is organized as a UIT investing in open-end investment companies (non–publicly available mutual funds), is attractive to insurance companies offering multimanager variable annuities.

3. *Separate Account as a Unit Investment Trust, Investing in One or More Series Open-End, Diversified Management Investment Companies*   Here again, the insurance company looking to offer a variable annuity organizes a separate account as a unit investment trust. This time, the UIT purchases shares of a *single* mutual fund. This mutual fund issues different classes of shares where each class is associated with a distinct asset portfolio, such as a common stock portfolio, a bond portfolio, or a money market portfolio.

Unlike the UIT that invests in multiple mutual funds, here only a single investment advisory agreement is needed. This might be the case for a single-manager variable annuity.

To the extent that the UIT purchases shares of several such mutual funds (series), there are still efficiencies achieved. For example, if the UIT purchases shares of three mutual funds each of which issues five classes of shares representing distinct asset portfolios, the end result is 15 distinct asset portfolios, yet only three investment advisory agreements.

ADMINISTRATIVE IMPACTS

Securities law stipulates[2] that transactions must be processed effective as of the date paperwork is received in good order. If the request is received before the close of stock exchanges, the transaction must be processed (assuming daily valuation) at unit values calculated as of the close of business that day.

Net asset values associated with each underlying investment fund must be calculated by each investment management company and transmitted to the insurer. The insurer, in turn, calculates accumulation unit values and annuity unit values. These values are entered into the insurer's administrative computer system, which processes requested transactions typically during an overnight cycle.

It is imperative that both net asset values of the underlying funds and unit values at the annuity product level are correctly calculated. Otherwise, there is substantial rework in reversing all transactions originally processed incorrectly and then reprocessed correctly. This can result in unnecessary financial losses or gains to the insurance company issuing the annuity—primarily because units are purchased or sold as of the transaction date, and buying or selling units at a later date to correct a misprocessing situation can produce losses or gains, and secondarily because of the additional administrative expense of reversals and reprocessing.

Because annuities are a thin-margin, high-volume business, such misprocessing gains and losses can add noticeable volatility to earnings—an undesirable result. Such reprocessing and ensuing delays can also cause administrative systems to be temporarily unavailable for customer service personnel to respond to inquiries or to annuity customers to verify data or perform transactions online or via automated telephony systems. Incorrect unit values may also shake customer confidence in the annuity company.

Investment advisory indemnification agreements often place the onus for any adverse financial impact that the insurance company may experience as a result of incorrect net asset value calculations by the investment management company or its designee on the investment management company.

In addition to gains and losses attributable to incorrect calculations of unit values affecting all clients, gains and losses that only affect certain individual clients can also occur, such as those due to errors in selling the right number of units to raise the cash to make a monthly IVA benefit disbursement, errors as to which subaccounts have units sold from them, errors in calculating numbers of annuity units per subaccount following an asset reallocation by the contract owner, and so on. Effective audit procedures help curb such gains and losses, for example, by categorizing the reason for every gain and loss in excess of a prescribed variance and by implementing corrective training, documentation, balancing, systems, or other measures.

CHAPTER 16

Forms of Insurance and Insurers

Annual income twenty pounds, annual expenditure nineteen six, result happiness. Annual income twenty pounds, annual expenditure twenty pounds ought and six, result misery.

—Charles Dickens
David Copperfield

INSURANCE VERSUS GAMBLING

Both insurance and gambling are premised on the laws of probability, redistributing wealth based on the occurrence of random events. There is, however, a very important definitional distinction:

- *Gambling* is the assumption of risk one does not otherwise have.
- *Insurance* is the transfer of risk one has to another party.

When one places a $100 bet on red at the roulette wheel of a casino, one assumes the risk that he did not otherwise have of losing $100. This is gambling.

When one purchases an immediate variable annuity (IVA), one transfers the risk he already had of living too long and outliving his accumulated assets to an insurer. This is insurance.

The modus operandi of the gambler is speculation. The modus operandi of the insured is hedging an existing risk.

Insurance and gambling are incongruous concepts. As such, their legal regulation is quite different. Annuities are regulated under state *insurance* laws. Insurance, including annuities, has historically been deemed to be a "public good" or "in the public interest"; as such, its use has been historically encouraged by tax law incentives.

As a financial security system, longevity insurance reduces adverse financial consequences resulting from an uncertain length of future lifetime, as measured by the elapsed time until death random variable. Failure to use insurance and to transfer risks that one cannot safely absorb to another entity that, through pooling, can absorb the risks results in increased dependency on governmental safety net programs by that class of individuals on whom those risks befall.

UTILITY THEORY

People insure their $35,000 car and their $200,000 house rather than self-absorb these risks. They value being reimbursed for damage to these items more than they value the dollar amount of the insurance premium they must pay to enter into such an agreement. In economics parlance, their utility of potential reimbursement for damage that may or may not occur exceeds their utility of the dollar amount of insurance premium forgone. As a result, they pay the premium.

This degree of risk aversion is actually necessary for an insurance program to succeed. People must be willing to pay something more than the expected value of their loss, where *expected value* is the probability of a claim times the amount of the claim, summed over all possible claim amounts. If they weren't willing, then an entity that tried to run an insurance program would receive less in total premiums than it paid in claims and could not continue to exist.

The body of knowledge that provides insights into decision making in the face of uncertainty is called *utility theory*. Because of its relevance to longevity insurance, a brief overview follows.

One solution to the problem of decision making in the face of uncertainty is to base decisions on a single value, the expected value (in dollars) of the random monetary outcomes resulting from the distribution of possible outcomes of economic projects. Under this approach, a decision maker would be indifferent to choosing between assuming a random loss X and paying an amount $E[X]$ (the expected value of the loss) to be relieved of the possible loss.

The expected value approach to decision making is too simplified. Clearly, other factors, such as the distribution of possible outcomes and the wealth of the decision maker, play important roles in influencing decisions. For example, suppose an individual has a net worth of $100,000. Faced with a potential maximum loss of $1,000, not of grave concern to the decision maker, he might be unwilling to pay more than the expected value of the loss to buy insurance. However, faced with a catastrophic potential maximum loss of $200,000 (e.g., his $200,000 home with a sizable mortgage), which exceeds his net worth, the decision maker might be willing to pay more than the expected value of the loss to buy insurance.

That the decision maker would pay more than the expected value of the loss for a large potential loss suggests the expected value approach is inadequate to model decision-making behavior. A different approach is to assume that the value or *utility* a particular decision maker places on wealth of amount x can be specified in the form of a *utility function* $u(x)$.

A sample utility of wealth function appears in Figure 16.1. Since "more wealth is better," *ceteris paribus*, $u(x)$ is an increasing function. With each equal increment in wealth beyond some point, however, the associated utility is smaller. Economists refer to this as "decreasing marginal utility." This implies that $u(x)$ is concave downward beyond some point.

If the utility of wealth function is continuous (as seems reasonable), students of calculus would say that its increasing property means $u'(x)$ is greater than 0, and its concave downward property means $u''(x)$ is less than 0; that is, its first derivative is positive, and its second derivative is negative.

The principal entity in a competitive economy is the consumer. Production, distribution, and exchange are designed to satisfy consumer wants, which are expressed as demands for goods and services in the marketplace. Utility factors into consumer preferences in that utility indicates a measure of net satisfaction that a consumer receives from an action such as consuming a commodity—the difference between pleasure enjoyed and pain suffered as a consequence of the action.

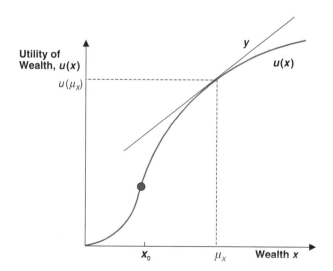

FIGURE 16.1 Utility of Wealth Function

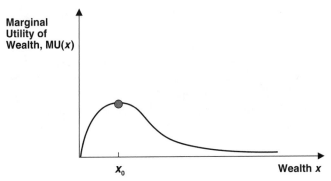

FIGURE 16.2   Marginal Utility (MU) of Wealth Function

We can define *marginal utility* as the increase in satisfaction a consumer obtains from consuming an additional unit of a commodity. The *law of diminishing marginal utility* states that after sufficient units of a commodity have been consumed, a consumer experiences diminishing marginal utility from additional units consumed.

The law of diminishing marginal utility is illustrated in Figure 16.2. The marginal utility at any level of wealth x is simply the slope of the utility curve $u(x)$. The $u(x)$ curve has an inflection point, indicated by the dot in Figure 16.1, where marginal utility is at a maximum, indicated by the corresponding dot in Figure 16.2. There is diminishing marginal utility of wealth beyond this point.

The rationale for the law of diminishing marginal utility is clear. An individual with only a few units of a commodity, including money, will apply them to his or her most vital needs. As more units are obtained, the needs to which they are applied are progressively less important to the individual and thus yield less and less increase in utility. An individual with only a small amount of wealth will apply this to food, water, clothing, and shelter—the most basic physiological needs as expressed by psychologist Abraham Maslow's hierarchy of needs. If enormous wealth is available, it may be applied to activities well beyond those necessary for human survival, for example, art collections or a new yacht. In short, an extra dollar is worth more to a poor person than it is to a rich person.

While *marginal utility* diminishes, note that *total utility* rises as wealth rises, indicating greater satisfaction to the consumer: We assume *nonsatiation,* the absence of a "bliss point" beyond which a consumer is completely satisfied and would pass up another helping of wealth.

Let w be the decision maker's current wealth measured in dollars. Let Y be the random variable representing the present value of annuity benefits. There exists some certain dollar amount p such that the decision maker will be indifferent between (1) paying that certain amount p to the insurer and having the insurer assume longevity risk through continuing claim payments (annuity benefits) as long as the annuitant is alive and (2) assuming the risk himself.

$$u(w - p) = E[u(w - Y)]$$

The left side of the equation represents the decision maker's utility of wealth net of paying a known amount p for protection against longevity risk. The right side represents the decision maker's expected utility of wealth net of self-funding an unknown number of payouts having a present value denoted by the random variable Y. As we will see momentarily, if p is greater than or equal to the IVA premium set by an annuity company, the opportunity for a mutually advantageous transaction exists.

One hears of *risk-averse* individuals and *risk-loving* individuals. What this means quantitatively and its implications for longevity insurance appear in the following shaded box.

RISK AVERSION

Let $E[X] = \mu_X$ be the expected value of wealth. In Figure 16.1, consider the tangent line, $y = u(\mu_X) + u'(\mu_X)(x - \mu_X)$ at the point $(\mu_X, u(\mu_X))$.

Because the wealth utility function is strictly concave downward beyond some minimal wealth level x_0, the graph of $u(x)$ is below the tangent line; that is, for all $x \geq x_0$,

$$u(x) \leq u(\mu_X) + u'(\mu_X)(x - \mu_X)$$

If we replace the singular numeric value x by the random variable X and take expected values on both sides of the inequality, we have

$$E[u(X)] \leq u(\mu_X)$$

If we apply this inequality to the aforementioned IVA decision maker, we have

$$u(w - p) = E[u(w - Y)] \leq u(w - \mu_Y)$$

Because the utility of wealth function is an increasing function, we know that the inequality

$$u(w - p) \leq u(w - \mu_Y)$$

implies that

$$w - p \leq w - \mu_Y$$

This tells us that $p \geq \mu_Y$, with $p > \mu_Y$ unless Y is a constant.

What This Tells Us

If the utility of wealth function $u(x)$ is increasing and concave downward, the decision maker will pay an amount p greater than the expected loss $E[Y] = \mu_Y$ for longevity (or any other) insurance. Such a decision maker is said to be *risk averse*. If p, the amount the decision maker is willing to pay for protection against undue longevity, is at least equal to the premium set by an annuity company, the opportunity for a mutually advantageous IVA policy exists.

While utility theory assumes that a decision maker's preferences exist and are consistent, it does not require the utility function to be of any specific form. For example, for a risk-averse decision maker where by definition $u'(x) > 0$ and $u''(x) < 0$ are true, the families of exponential, quadratic, fractional power, and logarithmic utility functions (or a spliced combination of them) may apply. For example, an exponential utility function and its first and second derivatives are:

$$u(x) = -e^{-\lambda x}, \lambda > 0$$
$$u'(x) = \lambda e^{-\lambda x} > 0$$
$$u''(x) = -\lambda^2 e^{-\lambda x} < 0$$

Insurers, as well as insureds, have their own utility functions. An annuity policy or an insurance policy that increases the utility of both parties—or at least does not decrease the utility of either party—is a feasible contract.

The independent variable horizontal axis in Figure 16.1 measures wealth in *dollars*. The dependent variable vertical axis measures utility. No unit of measurement was named; if one is desired, it can be called *utils*.

Rank ordering by utility of different decisions lets the highest-utility decision be made regardless of scale. For example, if $u(x)$ is a utility function and $\tilde{u}(x) = m \cdot u(x) + c$ with slope $m > 0$ is a linear transformation, then $E[u(X)] > E[u(Y)]$ is equivalent to $E[\tilde{u}(X)] > E[\tilde{u}(Y)]$. In words, preferences are preserved when a utility function is modified by an increasing linear transformation.

The point is that decision making is premised on the utility of dollars rather than simply on the expected value in dollars of the distribution of outcomes that might result from a decision. In fact, market research into variable income annuity prospects is an effort to learn about their utility functions (that is, risk preferences).

Utility theory provides a conceptual framework for the proposition that financial security systems like variable income annuities will increase total welfare. In economics phraseology, one economic state is *Pareto-superior*[1] to another if it increases the welfare (personal utility) of at least one party without reducing the utility of any other.[2] Said another way, if no one prefers economic State A to State B and at least one person prefers B to A, then B is said to be *Pareto-superior* to A.

Given a set of states of the economy {A, B, C, ...}, if there exists a state X in that set with the property that no other state in the set is *Pareto-superior* to X, then X is said to be a *Pareto-optimal* state. Said another way, a state of the economy X is said to be *Pareto-optimal* relative to some set of states if it belongs to the set and if no state in the set is *Pareto-superior* to X.

For an individual who requires $50,000 per year in living expenses, the risk of living 15 years longer than expected and longer than one had managed assets to sustain oneself is $750,000. If a person feels compelled to purchase automobile collision insurance to protect against a $35,000 loss, logically the compulsion to protect oneself against a loss more than 20 times this magnitude should be clear.

Yet, for a number of reasons, purchase of longevity insurance hasn't historically been as strong as would be expected. The psychological issue of the irrevocable nature of the election, some financial advisers' aversion to placing client assets beyond the ability to reposition them in other products later, and similar factors are responsible.

People buy insurance to guard against their greatest financial risks. They self-insure against smaller financial risks, for example, avoiding those multiyear warranties on small appliances for an additional premium. Yet how much greater is the financial risk of living too long relative to other financial risks they face? Automobile insurance and homeowner's insurance are purchased, yet they safeguard against risks that pale in comparative magnitude to the much more potentially financially devastating consequences of going uninsured and living too long.

Longevity is a risk that becomes more apparent at time of retirement. Throughout life, individual investors face the risk that their bonds might default, that interest rates might rise causing their bond holdings to fall in value, that their stocks might depreciate, or that high inflation might reduce their purchasing power. Default risk, interest rate risk, asset depreciation risk, inflation risk, and similar investment risks exist and are apparent throughout the accumulation period of one's retirement account assets and continue throughout the liquidation phase. The one new concern—or at least the one that rises to the forefront as individuals reach normal retirement ages—is longevity risk, the inexorable need to make one's assets last as long as he does.

Exactly as one pays an insurance premium for indemnification against the risks of fire or storms to one's home, one may choose to pay an insurance premium for indemnification against the risks of living too long and outliving one's accumulated assets. The decision to apply a premium to the purchase of longevity insurance is not picayune, especially for the 60-year-old who had sufficient assets to cover him to age 80 but was so "unfortunate" as to live a long, healthy life, surviving to 100.

One can think of "economic death" as an inability to provide for one's economic needs or outliving one's financial productivity. Economic death results from illness, disabling injury, or old age. Individuals frequently own health insurance and disability insurance to guard against the first two causes of economic death. A lifetime annuity safeguards against economic death from the third cause.

Voluntary business contracts and transactions are likely to provide a *Pareto-superior* economic state between the contracting parties (although third parties not a part of the contracting set may sometimes be adversely affected by what are called *externalities*). For a set comprised of individual annuitants and an insurer offering immediate variable annuities, all parties enjoy a *Pareto-superior* economic state. The utility of the longevity risk transfer achieved by each individual annuitant exceeds his or her utility of retaining the lump-sum premium and possibly running out of money. The utility of the prospect for an uncertain but potentially higher rate of return from offering and administering the IVA program—even in the face of subjecting the capital necessary to run such a program to adverse mortality experience, regulatory risk, and other risks—exceeds the insurer's utility of a known but potentially lower rate of return by simply investing a like amount of capital in risk-free, fixed-income instruments without engaging in any IVA program.

Utility is closely related to happiness. In economic theory, utility is a "joyousness yardstick" for the satisfaction people derive from decisions they make and goods and services they consume. Economics assumes people try to achieve as much utility as possible.

There is a high (but less than perfect) correlation between per capita income of countries and the happiness ranking of their citizens as reflected in surveys. Thus, the financial element of a person's decisions is a heavily weighted factor in his or her own personal utility set, but other factors enter into utility; that is, not all utility is monetary.

While all individual annuitants may be in comparable health at inception, some will die before receiving in annuity benefits an amount equal to their annuity premium. Yet the benefits of relief from anxiety over outliving one's assets, professional investment management at a point in their lives where they may no longer desire to perform or be capable of performing this function themselves, and similar benefits collectively result in greater utility than retaining the premium and retaining the longevity risk.

PRIVATE INSURANCE VERSUS SOCIAL INSURANCE

As mentioned earlier, every individual immediate variable annuity participant has equal expectation of value when commencing the program; that is, each participant is treated identically to each other immediate annuity pool participant. The amount of periodic income benefit that annuitants derive from their single premium is premised on the same mortality, expense, and other assumptions as other immediate variable annuitants.

Equivalently stated, the premium they pay is based exactly on the degree of longevity risk they transfer to the entity responsible for organizing and maintaining the longevity risk pool and ensuring its long-run solvency. In the United States, the responsible entities are insurance companies. These are currently state-regulated enterprises, although there is movement toward an option of being federally or state chartered.

As is generally the case with private insurance systems, premiums are charged in relation to risks assumed; that is, such systems are premised on *individual equity*. Older entrants into an immediate annuity program receive higher periodic benefits for an identical premium than younger entrants do. Male annuitants receive higher periodic benefits than similarly situated female annuitants do—unless barred by regulation forcing use of unisex rates that, while intended to prohibit inequality, actually mandate inequality by forcing one class of individuals with a lower present value of future claims (males) to subsidize another class of individuals with a higher present value of future claims (females).

To the extent, if any, that the level of periodic income benefits to annuitants are predicated on additional underwriting criteria beyond age and gender—such as health status—such refinements further enhance the level of individual equity, whereby premiums and annuity benefits bear a closer and fairer relationship.

Because mortality differs not only by age and gender but also health impairments, education level, smoker status, alcohol use, geography, avocations, ethnicity, wealth, occupation, marital status, religion, obesity, and a host of other factors,[3] increasingly larger underwriting refinements governing the relationship between premiums and annuity benefits could be used to result in increasingly larger and ever-fairer degrees of individual equity. At some point, however, the benefit of a greater degree of underwriting criteria becomes outweighed by the cost of gathering, processing, and storing the information and establishing an evermore complex array of premium rates.

As is true with life insurance today, a finite set of factors will evolve as the strongest predictors of retirement mortality. It is this class of factors on which workable immediate annuity ratemaking will be premised.

In contrast to private insurance systems predicated on *individual equity,* "social insurance" systems tend to be predicated on *social adequacy.*[4] Social insurance systems concern themselves more with providing a safety net for certain classes of individuals than with maintaining a constant relationship between premiums paid and risks assumed.

The *social norm* of a country will influence the nature of its social insurance systems. Social insurance systems of countries with a social norm emphasizing *individual rights* (e.g., the United States) may lean more toward the *individual equity* end of the spectrum. Systems of countries with a social norm emphasizing *social solidarity* (e.g., the United Kingdom) may lean more toward *social adequacy.*

The federal Old Age Survivors and Disability Insurance (OASDI) program, of which Social Security is a part, is an example of a social insurance program. This program differs from a private insurance system such as for immediate variable annuities in that it (1) is public; (2) is intergenerational, where active workers today support a previous generation of workers now retired; and (3) offers benefits that are not actuarially equivalent to premiums paid but, rather, pays proportionately higher benefits to participants that made smaller contributions to the program.

There are discussions regarding privatization or partial privatization of Social Security. That private insurance systems require premiums that bear a fairly tight actuarial equivalence to claims expected to be paid (such as a lifetime series of monthly retirement income benefits) and social insurance systems by their nature require certain classes of individuals to subsidize others where the relationship of premiums paid to benefits received is not uniform clearly is one of the main challenges in privatization.

Under private individual account arrangements, the cost of longevity is borne by the account owner, who must stretch a finite amount of funds over his or her entire retirement period—and who is welcome, if he or she so chooses, to accomplish this in part via purchase of a lifetime annuity. For government-sponsored, "pay-as-you-go" (i.e., not prefunded) retirement income programs, the cost of longevity is borne primarily by younger generations that are working and paying taxes.

DEFINED BENEFIT PENSION PLANS

Private-sector defined benefit pension plans covering employee groups are yet another form of financial security program involving lifetime annuities. Benefits are based on a formula typically involving salary and years of service, with adjustment for "early retirement" or "late retirement." For defined benefit plans, the *benefit* is definitely determinable. In contrast, for defined contribution plans, the *contribution* is definitely determinable.

The employer sponsoring the defined benefit plan makes periodic contributions to cover benefits earned in the current year and possibly to cover a portion of benefits attributable to past service before the plan was installed for which credit is given. In the United States, the minimum pension contribution for a fiscal year is determined in relation to a "funding standard account." There is also a maximum tax-deductible contribution level.

Prefunding defined benefit plan benefits over the working lifetimes of employees to some degree is required. Optimally, safety would be achieved if prefunding were sufficient to accumulate totally the present value of each employee's lifetime annuity at his point of retirement. In contrast, a "pay-as-you-go" funding arrangement—which is not allowed for U.S. private-sector defined benefit plans—could put employee pension benefits in greater jeopardy if the employer were unable to afford the greater cash outlays as more employees retired and became pensioners.

Proper cost recognition of benefits accruing to employees is necessary. The pattern of cost recognition will depend on assumptions about the rate of return on assets in the pension fund and on mortality, turnover rates, salary increases, retirement ages, new entrants, vesting schedule, and similar factors. The pattern of cost recognition will also depend on the philosophical approach the employer-sponsor wishes to take with regard to funding.

For example, the employer-sponsor may wish to fund each year the present value of benefits earned individual by individual in that year of service (the "normal cost") plus some portion of the present value of accrued benefits less assets (the "amortization of unfunded accrued liability"), the latter possibly attributable to granting credit for past service at time of plan installation, minus amortization of any gain due to actual pension plan experience being more favorable than assumed. Any such arrangement for assigning a pattern of costs to a pension plan is called an *actuarial cost method* or, simply, a *cost method*. The example just described is the "unit credit" cost method.

Because under the "unit credit" method, the "normal cost" could rise more rapidly than salary as one approaches retirement (since there are fewer and fewer years of discounting), the "entry age normal" cost method provides for a "normal cost" each year that is a level percentage of salary. Such an approach may produce a more manageable series of pension expense for the corporate sponsor.

The objective here is not to elucidate cost methods—of which there are several more—but to provide a flavor for how lifetime annuities in defined benefit pension plans differ from lifetime annuities purchased by individuals. In pension plans, the plan sponsor usually provides the funding, with some possibility of cost sharing by employees, in the case of *contributory* defined benefit plans. Because the employer and the pension plan are often ongoing entities, annual employer contribution levels can be adjusted as actual benefit experience emerges.

In contrast, for privately purchased individual lifetime annuities, the insurer must collect adequate premium because there exists no adjustment mechanism after the contract is issued should actual mortality or expense experience deviate from that assumed. (An exception is *participating* annuities, described later.) Because an employer may have a few employees or a few hundred, there may well be material deviations in actual experience from assumed, making the ability for midcourse corrections more important. The Law of Large Numbers may be more closely operable for insurance companies specializing in retirement income with larger annuitant population bases.

Defined benefit pension plans can and do use variable income annuities. For example, a pensioner might be given the choice of a "traditional" pension, with income fixed at a given level, or its actuarial equivalent in the form of a variable income pension where benefits fluctuate based on the performance of investment funds chosen by the pensioner from a defined set. A percentage split of some portion of traditional fixed-income pension and some portion of variable-income pension may be allowed. Defined benefit pension plan language governs.

If the defined benefit pensioner at the point of retirement has no option to take a lump sum but must elect some form of single life or joint life annuity, then group annuitant mortality—with its higher q_x values—will be used, rather than individual annuitant mortality. The self-selection effect of the healthiest individuals electing straight life annuities grading down to the unhealthiest electing a lump sum will be absent or at least reduced.

The point here is not to make the reader an expert in defined benefit plans, but, rather, to foster a better understanding of individual variable income annuities by contrasting these with a close relative.

TYPES OF INSURANCE ORGANIZATIONS

Stock companies, mutual companies, fraternal societies, and nonprofit organizations are the four types of organizations through which insurance transactions are primarily conducted. As one purchases annuity products, it may be beneficial to understand the type of insurer with which one is dealing.

Stock insurance companies (whether publicly traded or privately held) are corporations owned by their stockholders, in whom—at least theoretically—insurance company control is ultimately vested.

Mutual insurance companies are corporations without capital stock. Policyholders ultimately control mutual insurance companies.

Fraternal life insurance societies are mutual organizations. They furnish life insurance to their members in a manner comparable to that of legal reserve life insurance companies. The lodge system characterizes a fraternal life insurance society.

Nonprofit organizations are insurance companies having no individuals with an ownership interest. A board of directors exercises control of these companies.

Mutual companies have historically used conservative assumptions in pricing their products as to mortality, expenses, and investment returns. To the extent that actual experience is more favorable, mutual companies pay policyholders a dividend; that is, guaranteed elements of their products can be set at lower levels and "topped off" by nonguaranteed dividends to the extent real-world performance allows. Philosophically, mutual companies and fraternal benefit societies consider the equitable distribution of surplus to the classes of annuitants that generate it.

Stock companies can similarly offer "participating" policies, where policyholders participate in the experience of the insurer; they also offer nonparticipating products, which require more aggressive pricing than their participating counterparts. If nonparticipating products were priced identically to participating ones, prospects would buy the latter, hoping that the nonguaranteed dividends would then provide a superior return.

Insurance company surplus serves as a backup should reserves prove inadequate. The degree of surplus needed depends on the riskiness or the volatility of returns of the products offered. Because mutual companies only need to provide a return on their surplus sufficient to grow it enough to allow protective support against experience deviations to whatever extent they expect to grow their book of business in the following year—say, 9%—they can target lower returns in product pricing than can stock companies where shareholders may be seeking a higher return on surplus—say, 15%.

Participating immediate annuities reduce or eliminate statutory surplus strain. Because statutory reserves are based on statutory valuation mortality and because something closer to statutory valuation mortality can be used in pricing participating immediate annuities, surplus strain and its associated costs are reduced or eliminated. If mortality is higher than this conservative pricing basis—as is expected—then the surplus so generated is returned to annuitants in the way of a nonguaranteed dividend. A similar arrangement holds true for the expense assumptions used in pricing participating immediate annuities.

There are arguments that stock insurance companies try harder to be more efficient to generate profits for shareholders, whereas mutual company policyholders are buying insurance protection—not looking for profits—and so press less strongly on mutual insurer managements for efficiencies.

Stock companies have the capability to raise capital through the issuance of stock should they desire to fund growth beyond that supportable by their own additions to surplus through retained earnings.

Independent rating agencies like A. M. Best assign claims-paying ratings to insurers. These ratings indicate the relative financial strength of insurers to meet their obligations to contract owners, including annuitants.

Recall, however, that variable annuities are separate account products; that is, assets backing them are outside of the insurance company general account. To the extent that an insurer doesn't layer on to its IVA products fund performance guarantees or other features that can create reliance on the general account, if actual mortality is close to that assumed in pricing, sufficient assets should always exist in the separate account to fund IVA obligations—even if the insurer gets in trouble with its general account products.

IVA COMPANY ORGANIZATIONAL STRUCTURE

While there is no single structural model common to IVA organizations, there are functions that must be performed—either in-house or on an out-sourced basis—if the IVA enterprise is to form and operate on a successful, sustained, regulatory-compliant basis. There is no single best organizational structure model. Rather, there are different choices, each with its own advantages and disadvantages. Depending on the management objective, some structures facilitate innovation, others expense control, and others cross–product line teamwork.

Departmentalization is traditionally performed on a functional, geographic, or product basis. The skeletal organizational structure that follows illustrates a basic functional model and selected activities within a function. It assumes a large, mature business. A small, newly formed operation will omit or combine certain activity areas. While early year losses are likely inevitable, the business must achieve scale sufficient to permit acquisition-expense and maintenance-expense allowables assumed in pricing to be met in real-world experience if target profitability is to result.

Because the first job of any company is to earn a profit, organizational structure decisions must give this factor dominant weight. To ensure that there is one person accountable for profitability and sufficiently powerful to exert expense control and to have the final word on strategic decisions so as to be truly vested with sufficient span of authority to be held accountable for profitability, some insurance companies organize for performance by using a "profit center" structure.

The IVA company or profit center must target a profit level that represents an adequate return on capital deployed, a target (1) at least equal to the cost of capital and (2) commensurate with the level of risk assumed. If returns greater than the cost of capital are achieved, value is created. If returns less than the cost of capital are achieved, value is destroyed. While market share, number of new products, and the like are admirable goals, value creation is the ultimate measure of management accomplishment or lack thereof.

While poor organizational structure may impede IVA company value creation, good organizational structure—one that supports the strategic basis for competition described in Chapter 18—does not by itself provide competitive advantage. Chronic or even too frequent reorganizations can be detrimental, as experienced talent may be lost, position descriptions must be rewritten and reevaluated, and personnel must figure out with whom they are to interact in the most recent structure to get things done.

Skeletal Organizational Structure

Board of Directors

■ Governance.

Executive Officers

■ General Management.

Product Development

- IVA base product and optional features design.
- Pricing.
  - Actuarial assumption setting.
  - Modeling.

In-Force Management

- Experience studies.
- Management and third-party reporting.
- Reinsurance.

Distributor Relationship Management

- Wholesaling and financial adviser training.
- Managing product manufacturer relationships with agency system, brokerage firms, and financial institutions.

Federal Government Relations

- Federal legislative issues affecting IVAs.

State Government Relations

- State legislative issues affecting IVAs.
- Complaint management.
- State filing assistance.

Financial Reporting/Accounting/Auditing

- Accounting (Statutory, GAAP [generally accepted accounting principles], tax).
- Budget.
- Control procedures.
- Annual statement preparation.
- Expense analysis.
- Financial plan.
- Rating agency liaison.
- Tax.
- Unit value calculations.

Investments

- Investment policy statements.
- Investment selection and administration.
- Asset custodian.

Funds Management

- Relationship management with external investment advisers.
- Subaccount performance reporting.

Marketing

- Market research and analysis.
- Marketing material creation, production, and distribution.
  - Product fact sheets.
  - Client brochures.
  - Financial adviser guides.
  - Presentation visuals and scripts.
- Sales illustration systems.
- Advertising.
- Web site management.
  - For clients.
  - For financial advisers.
- Product manuals.
- Wholesaler training.

Communications

- Newsletters.
- Media management.
- Public relations.

Administration/Customer Service

- New business.
  - Application processing.
  - Premium processing.
  - Policy issue.
  - Record setup.
  - Forms and procedures.
- Sales commissions.
- Customer support.
  - Call center staffed with representatives.
  - Automated telephony/interactive voice-response systems.
  - Internet self-service center.
- Claims/death benefits.
- Annuity unit value determination.
- Annuity units redetermination following client reallocations.
- IVA benefit determination.
- Daily buys/sells of units per subaccount.

- Quarterly client statements.
- Audit ongoing annuitant survival.
- Mortality gain/loss administration.
- Training manuals.

Actuarial

- Reserve liability determination.
- Statements of actuarial opinion.
- Actuarial memorandums.
- Target surplus formulas.
- Asset/liability management.

Legal

- Securities registration statements.
- Contract, prospectus, and statement of additional information (SAI) review and updates.
- Agreement drafting and review.
    - Principal underwriting agreement.
    - Fund participation agreement.
    - Selling group agreement.
    - Indemnification agreement.
- Certificates of variable authority.
- Internal legal analysis of statutory and court law.
- Intellectual property protection.
- Court cases (e.g., contested claims).

Underwriting/Medical

- Classification and selection standards.
- Rating decisions on applicants.

Information Systems

- Administrative systems.
    - Transaction processing (premiums, annuity benefits, death benefits).
    - Policyholder records.
    - Reserve systems.
    - Tax systems.
    - Customer-service-consultant work-station information systems.
- Hardware and software management.

Treasurers

- Annuity premium receipts and benefit disbursements.
- Client tax statements.

Human Resources

- Payroll.
- Employee tax withholding and tax statements.
- Employee benefits.
- Position descriptions.
- Compensation evaluation.
- Human resource policies.
- Recruiting.

State Compliance

- Policy form (applications, contracts, riders) drafting and filing.
- State regulation review and compliance.

Sales Compliance

- Suitability policies.
- National Association of Securities Dealers (NASD) advertising and forms compliance.
- Privacy.
- Financial adviser appointment/licensing/contracting.
- Insurance Marketplace Standards Association (IMSA) certification/recertification.

Purchasing

- Business asset procurement and tracking.

The preceding list assumes that the insurance company manufactures the annuity products and provides servicing to both financial advisers and annuity contract owners. It assumes that investment management, wholesaling, and retailing functions are outsourced—if greater integration is desired, affiliated companies can provide these three functions.

CHAPTER 17

IVA Business Value to Annuity Company

*Any business arrangement that is not profitable to the other
person will in the end prove unprofitable for you. The bargain
that yields mutual satisfaction is the only one that is apt to
be repeated.*

—B.C. Forbes

SAMPLE MODEL

A stock annuity company selling immediate variable annuity (IVA) products
does so with the expectation of deriving financial gain from putting at risk
those assets necessary to establish and run the business and absorb the mortality and general business risks. Sophisticated computer models are used to
project various future experience scenarios that may emerge.

A variety of approaches to and methods for product development and
pricing exists. In this chapter, we will demonstrate in greatly simplified form
one approach that looks at multiple profit measures on a statutory accounting basis.

One summary profit measure, "value added margin," equals the present
value of distributable earnings divided by the present value of premiums,
where the present value discounting is done at the insurer's cost of capital.
Distributable earnings on a statutory accounting basis are used because they
represent the "free cash flows" generated by the business that can be paid
out as a dividend. The insurer's "cost of capital" is that weighted average
rate of return expected by the various constituencies (e.g., bond holders,
stock owners) who provide the capital to fund the "starting and running an
IVA business" project. Insurers finance their operations by three mechanisms:
(1) issuing stock, (2) issuing debt, and (3) reinvesting prior earnings.

Because the insurer's financial gain or loss hinges on, among other
things, investment returns, multiple investment scenarios are modeled and

outcomes are ranked to illustrate the range of potential results. The resultant graph of investment returns on the horizontal axis—unitized in terms of percentiles—and financial summary measure on the vertical axis is called a "risk curve." Summary statistics such as mean and standard deviation of the profit measure of interest (e.g., return on assets—ROA, return on equity—ROE, and return on investment—ROI) can be determined. Investment returns may be deterministic or, preferably, generated by a stochastic generator, appropriately parameterized for the nature of the assets modeled.

For example, ROA is a summary profitability measure equal to the present value of profits as a percentage of the present value of reserves. If modeled under a large number of possible investment scenarios, a graph similar to Figure 17.1 might result.

Technically, other variables—such as mortality and expenses (M&E)—should fluctuate in the modeling as well. In practice, because investment return plays such a dominant role, it is allowed to fluctuate while other variables often are assumed constant.

Pricing runs are performed for selected cells, such as for each 5- or 10-year age grouping, in the age spectrum most crucial to the business. Sensitivity tests of summary profitability statistics are performed for key pricing assumptions.

Each insurer may have its own pricing models, methodologies, assumptions, profitability measures, and profitability targets for each. Some insurers may use a vendor-provided pricing model. Some pricing constraints are common to all insurers (e.g., even if summary profit measures are appealing, there can be zero years during the pricing horizon for which the insurer is statutorily insolvent). Other pricing constraints may be unique to an insurer (e.g., even if summary profit measures meet targets, there must be sufficient year-by-year smoothness to the earnings pattern).

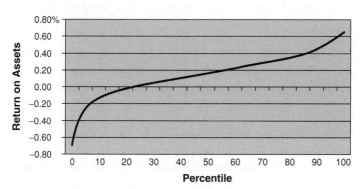

ROM statistics: Mean = 0.13%; standard deviation = 0.29%

FIGURE 17.1 Proposed Product

For simplicity, clarity, and tractability, the following example assumes that net investment returns at the IVA subaccount level are exactly the 5% assumed by the 5% assumed investment rate (AIR) in all years.

The returns in the example assume that the only capital employed is that necessary to support the 10 IVA contracts to Annuilanders. It ignores all development costs (e.g., contract and prospectus drafting and filing, computer system development, actuarial personnel) and overhead expense allocations (e.g., corporate governance).

Although a variety of limiting resources constrain the value of a particular annuity company, a company must ensure that its IVA product produces a projected return on invested capital at least as great as the company's cost of capital. The cost of capital value is often called the "hurdle rate." For a product to be acceptable, the present value of distributable earnings discounted at the hurdle rate must be nonnegative.

Comparison of profit measures between two similar products requires both to be calculated on the same basis; for example, either pretax or aftertax, either inclusive or exclusive of target surplus, same interest rate used for discounting, and same pricing horizon over which profits are measured.

EXAMPLE

Our example will make use of those 10 Annuilanders we met earlier in this book and will develop under these assumptions:

- 10 lives.
- Age 90.
- $105,000 gross single premium per life; $100,000 net single premium per life (i.e., $5,000 front-end load).
- Single life only annuity.
- Annual payments made at end of year, just before one annuitant dies.
- No state premium tax in Annuiland.
- No Internal Revenue Code Section 848 DAC tax (i.e., assume tax-qualified business not subject to deferred acquisition cost [DAC] tax).
- $4,000 gross dealer concession per contract paid to securities firm selling IVA.
- $1,000 wholesaling allowance per contract paid to IVA distribution company.
- $250 expenses at time of issue (e.g., policy preparation and mailing, master record setup, allocating net premium among subaccounts, initial reserve calculation).
- $125 maintenance expenses per year (e.g., issuing benefit checks, tax statements).

- $450 expenses at time of death (e.g., death benefit processing).
- Maintenance expenses and year-of-death terminal expenses increase at 3% annually (e.g., 4% actual inflation − 1% productivity gains = 3% net inflation).
- 34% federal income tax rate.
- 10% cost of capital.[1]
- Risk-based capital (RBC) = 1.75% of statutory reserve.
- Statutory valuation mortality used as pricing mortality.[2]
- 5% AIR.
- 0.75% M&E risk charge.
- 0.50% investment management charge offset by 0.50% investment management expense, as function is subcontracted (and will therefore be omitted from income statement for simplicity; investment returns illustrated will be net of investment management fees).
- RBC earns 6% pretax.
- Ignores "dividend received deduction" (DRD).

The statutory income statement, statutory balance sheet, and profit measures appear in Tables 17.1, 17.2, and 17.3, respectively. Because a front-end load covers distribution company (wholesaling) and securities firm (gross dealer concession) expenses and because pricing mortality is set equal to valuation mortality and all annuitants die perfectly on schedule, assets (premium) provided by customers and appreciation thereon are exactly sufficient at all times to cover reserve liabilities. As a result, pretax earnings (i.e., statutory gains) each year are merely the excess, if any, of M&E revenue over issue, maintenance, and death benefit processing expenses.

Statutory gain is suppressed in the first year by policy issue expenses. Otherwise, there is a uniformly decreasing series of statutory income values. This is because (1) assets continuously decline as 100% of appreciation is paid out each year along with some principal and (2) M&E revenue, which is a percentage of assets, therefore uniformly declines. Expenses also decline, but at a slower rate, producing the series of declining statutory income values. The $1,000,000 of net premium produces $10,979 of cumulative statutory income over the 10-year life of this block of business.

The progression of statutory reserves for our Annuiland example is shown in Figure 17.2. The insurer allocates funds from its own surplus account to provide a cushion against deviations (mortality, investment, expense, and general business risks such as legal actions) more adverse than those contemplated by statutory reserves. An internal target surplus formula, guided by outside rating agency RBC formulas (e.g., the formulas by which A.M. Best, Moody's, and Standard & Poor's arrive at their insurer financial strength ratings), establishes the allocation. For illustration purposes, we assume an allocation equal to 1.75% of statutory reserves.

TABLE 17.1 Statutory Income Statement

	At Issue	Year 1	2	3	4	5	6	7	8	9	10	Total
Revenue												
Gross Premium	1,050,000	0	0	0	0	0	0	0	0	0	0	
Investment Income	0	50,000	41,527	33,727	26,635	20,285	14,716	9,965	6,074	3,085	1,045	
M&E*	0	7,685	6,383	5,184	4,094	3,118	2,262	1,532	934	474	161	
Total	1,050,000	57,685	47,910	38,911	30,729	23,403	16,978	11,496	7,007	3,560	1,206	10,979
Expenses												
Annuity Benefits	0	219,465	197,519	175,572	153,626	131,679	109,733	87,786	65,840	43,893	21,947	
Reserve Increase (EOY†)	1,000,000	−169,465	−155,992	−141,845	−126,991	−111,394	−95,017	−77,821	−59,766	−40,808	−20,901	
Gross Dealer Concession	40,000	0	0	0	0	0	0	0	0	0	0	
Wholesaling Allowance	10,000	0	0	0	0	0	0	0	0	0	0	
Policy Issue	2,500	0	0	0	0	0	0	0	0	0	0	
Maintenance	0	1,250	1,159	1,061	956	844	725	597	461	317	163	
Death Benefit Processing	0	450	464	477	492	506	522	537	553	570	587	
Total	1,052,500	51,700	43,149	35,265	28,083	21,636	15,962	11,099	7,088	3,972	1,795	
Pretax Statutory Gain	−2,500	5,985	4,761	3,646	2,646	1,767	1,016	397	−81	−412	−590	
Federal Income Tax	850	−2,035	−1,619	−1,240	−900	−601	−345	−135	28	140	200	
After-Tax Statutory Gain	−1,650	3,950	3,142	2,406	1,746	1,166	670	262	−53	−272	−389	

*M&E revenue is assumed to be 0.75% of midyear assets, or 0.75% × Beginning-of-year assets × $1.05^{\frac{1}{2}}$.
†EOY = End of year.
6.25% gross return − 0.50% investment management fee = 5.75% return for underlying investment fund.
5.75% return for underlying investment fund − 0.75% M&E charge = 5% return to IVA subaccount.

477

TABLE 17.2 Statutory Balance Sheet

	At Issue	Year 1	2	3	4	5	6	7	8	9	10	Total
Assets	1,000,000	830,535	674,543	532,698	405,707	294,313	199,296	121,475	61,709	20,902	0	
Liabilities (Reserves)	1,000,000	830,535	674,543	532,698	405,707	294,313	199,296	121,475	61,709	20,902	0	
Statutory Surplus	0	0	0	0	0	0	0	0	0	0	0	
Risk-Based Capital												
RBC	17,500	14,534	11,805	9,322	7,100	5,150	3,488	2,126	1,080	366	0	
RBC Increase	17,500	−2,966	−2,730	−2,482	−2,222	−1,949	−1,663	−1,362	−1,046	−714	−366	
Interest on RBC at 6% pretax*	0	1,076	894	726	573	437	317	214	131	66	22	
Federal Income Tax	0	−366	−304	−247	−195	−148	−108	−73	−44	−23	−8	
After-Tax Interest on RBC	0	710	590	479	378	288	209	142	86	44	15	2,941

*Interest on RBC is assumed to be 6% of midyear RBC, or 6% × Beginning-of-year RBC × 1.05$^{1/2}$.

TABLE 17.3 Profit Measures

	At Issue	Year 1	2	3	4	5	6	7	8	9	10	Total
Year-by-Year Profit Measures												
After-Tax Statutory Gain + After-Tax Interest on RBC	-1,650	4,660	3,732	2,885	2,125	1,455	879	404	33	-228	-374	13,920
% Return on Surplus*		16.8%	25.1%	23.9%	22.2%	20.0%	16.7%	11.3%	1.5%	-20.6%	-99.9%	
Distributable Earnings	-19,150	7,626	6,462	5,368	4,347	3,404	2,542	1,766	1,079	486	-9	

Summary Profit Measures

PVDE at 10%	$5,285.22	where
VAM = PVDE/NP	0.53%	
IRR (Statutory ROI)	19.88%	
ROA = PV Profits at 10%/PV Reserves†	0.45%	
Profit Margin = PV Statutory Gain at 10%/NP‡	0.85%	

where PVDE = Present Value of Distributable Earnings
VAM = Value-Added Margin
IRR = Internal Rate of Return
ROA = Return on Assets
NP = Net Premium
ROI = Return on Investment
PV = Present Value

* % Return on Surplus = (After-Tax Statutory Gain + After-Tax Interest on RBC) / Midyear RBC.

† Return on assets (ROA), like other profit measures, can be defined in multiple ways. As defined here, letting "Profits" be A-T Stat Gain + A-T Interest on RBC, the numerator includes investment income from an asset source (i.e., RBC) that is excluded from the denominator. This definition can create decision-making anomalies since a product with more required surplus would produce a higher ROA than an identical product with less required surplus. It is illogical that ROA should improve because a rating agency desires greater surplus held for a product, which would result from this definition. As a result, we can define ROA = PV Profits / PV Assets, where the denominator reflects both asset sources (product assets and RBC) that produce the profits in the numerator. This latter definition lowers ROA from 0.45% to 0.44%. [*Note:* The ROA calculation discounts the 10 end-of-year reserve values at 10% for the denominator; it similarly discounts the 10 end-of-year profit values at 10% for the numerator and then adds the "at issue" profit value to the numerator. Because year-end (terminal) reserves are postpayment of the annual benefit in this example, such a reserve, is lower than the reserve that existed for the entire year; this depresses the denominator, thereby increasing the resultant ROA. A more accurate and more representative ROA measure results from discounting monthly values rather than these annual values.]

‡ Profit margin as defined above excludes investment income generated from RBC in the numerator and excludes RBC assets in the denominator, thereby avoiding the anomaly described in the prior footnote.

479

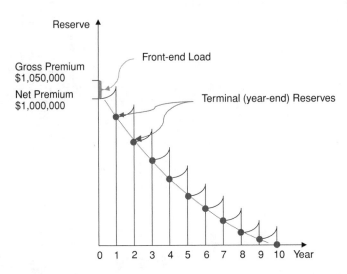

FIGURE 17.2 Total Reserve for Cohort of 10 Annuilanders

There is a capital inflow at inception from the insurer to the IVA product program, with capital outflows in ensuing years. The capital outflows consist of after-tax statutory gain, after-tax interest on surplus, and the freeing up of surplus no longer needed as the amount of surplus required to back an ever-smaller collection of liabilities reduces each year. In effect, the dividends are released (to stakeholders, to other projects) as they emerge.

Interest on allocated surplus cumulatively produces $2,941 over the 10 years. Together with statutory gain of $10,979, after-tax income of $13,920 cumulatively results from the sale of the 10 IVAs—79% is from margin on assets provided by annuity contract owners, while 21% is attributable to funds originating in the insurer's own surplus account.

The ROI that equates the capital inflow with the series of capital outflows on a present value basis is 19.88%. This is the internal rate of return (IRR), the interest rate that if uniformly applied to all capital flows (+ and –) produces a present value of zero.

The ROA, the present value of profits divided by the present value of reserves, is 0.45%.

The profit margin, the present value of statutory gains (discounted at the 10% cost of capital) as a percentage of net premium, is 0.85%.

Of course, it's a given that the IVA product specifications need to be competitive in the universe among which the insurer seeks to compete. For example, a dominant player in the variable annuity industry may decide that its competitive universe consists of the top-10 selling IVAs. To the extent it cannot best every IVA product in terms of every element (e.g., lowest M&E charge, highest sales commissions, broadest array of optional benefits, a singular but overly rich benefit a new entrant is using temporarily to break into the market), it instead defines its competitive universe as the top-10 IVA products and only seeks to compare well to these. The end result is often a mainstream product with broad appeal, rather than one with a "sales hook" that appeals to only a narrow market niche.

The projected financial results, using a method like that illustrated, then need to meet corporate profitability objectives. In the preceding example, there is positive value added, since the IRR (19.88%) exceeds the cost of capital hurdle rate (10%), producing a positive value-added margin (VAM). Whether an insurer would move forward with such a product depends on the competitiveness of the product specifications in the universe selected, corporate profitability objectives, alternative opportunities, alignment with strategic objectives, and available resources.

While the IRR is high, actual dollar income may be low relative to competing opportunities because the capital employed in such a product is low. This is because with an IVA, unlike with an immediate fixed annuity where the insurer bears all investment risk, investment risk is passed through to the annuitant in the way of benefits that fluctuate with subaccount performance relative to the AIR. For the same reason, consumers receive a more competitive product with an IVA than with an immediate fixed annuity, in that the insurer's spread between what is earned on the underlying assets and what is credited to the reserve is narrower for an IVA and wider for an immediate fixed annuity.

What can be said about the results of the preceding model is that the proposed product cannot be ruled out for failing to earn at least the cost of capital. Yet an IVA company may starve on high IRR products because, as just mentioned, they may produce a low magnitude of absolute dollar income. In contrast, the VAM profit measure defined in Table 17.3 gives the company a measure of how many dollars it will pull out of the product above and beyond its cost of capital relative to the net premium it writes. How an insurer defines its profit objective(s) will determine the profit measure(s) on which it will base decisions.

While the previous example illustrates selected concepts associated with IVA pricing, real-world examples differ in the following ways:

- IVAs are generally written at issue ages younger than the age-90 case illustrated, providing a lengthier period than the 10 years shown in the example for annuity writers to earn a margin.
- Mortality rates at more traditional issue ages are significantly less than the 10% quickly grading up to 100% illustrated in the example, producing a slower dissipation of assets.

- Valuation mortality rates are lower (i.e., more conservative) than pricing mortality rates, producing an initial statutory reserve higher than the initial pricing reserve (i.e., net premium), causing the insurer to employ some of its own surplus in addition to the surplus referenced as RBC in the example; it's often the case that as products require more insurer capital, they produce a higher absolute dollar amount of earnings (because of the "rent" paid on the extra capital tied up) but lower percentage earnings in relation to capital employed.
- M&E risk charges are higher in order to provide asset-based (more accurately, reserve-based) compensation to financial advisers.
- Stochastic modeling,[3] which looks at the range of likely investment outcomes, is used rather than a single, deterministic, constant return path equal to the 5% AIR.

In reality, annuity companies use pricing models that recognize increment and decrement events (e.g., deaths, expenses, lapses) with much greater frequency than the annual snapshots shown in Table 17.1. More frequent recognition—such as a semimonthly (24 times per year) convention—improves accuracy. This is particularly important due to the relatively Lilliputian margins on which the business operates, where a few basis points matter.

As with any business, financial reporting provides information about how management of an enterprise discharges its stewardship responsibility to owners for use of the enterprise resources entrusted to it. An "earnings by source" analysis sheds light on constituent parts of earnings relative to targets—mortality, expense, interest margin, and so on.

Retirement income/longevity insurance products, like other insurance products, begin with an economic cost that would exist absent any regulatory framework, consisting of a best-estimate price sufficient to pay future benefits, administrative expenses, and profit.

To this, there is a layering on of the cost of the legally required statutory reserve, should it prove higher than the reserve that would otherwise be generated naturally by pricing. Finally, to this, there is a layering on of the cost of surplus allocated to a target level to provide a very high level of protection against insolvency. It is associated rent that must be paid for tying up this additional capital in the form of incremental reserves and allocated surplus—thereby making it unavailable for other investment projects—that results in these cost layers.

Stated another way, when an insurer sells a variable income annuity, it incurs acquisition costs, such as wholesaling allowance, sales commission, related bonuses and benefits, record setup, and policy issuance. Accounting rules and insurance regulations require the company to hold capital to provide for future annuity benefits (i.e., the reserve) and to guard against adverse experience (i.e., risk-based capital). The sum of acquisition costs, reserve, and statutorily required capital may exceed the premium paid by the annuity contract owner. The business, however, may still be profitable. Using realistic mortality rates, the present value of future annuity benefits (PVFB) and the acquisition expenses collectively may still be less than the premium, so the annuity company position is improved by writing the business. It merely must dedicate capital in order to grow.

While annual earnings as a percentage of the reserve in the realm of 0.50% may seem trifling, one must consider the scope of the business. Eight thousand sales per year nationwide at an average size of $125,000 produces $1 billion a year of new premium. Once an annuity company reaches $14 billion in reserves—on a steady-state basis with new incoming premiums adequate to offset outgoing annuity benefits—this produces $70 million of annual after-tax earnings using the 0.50% ratio. At a 14.3 price-to-earnings ratio, our newly created annuity company has a market capitalization of $1 billion!

With 76 million U.S. baby boomers, 8,000 sales per year is a very small fraction of the market—literally one person in ten thousand. Even in Year 2001, the average size IVA premium of $129,000 exceeded the assumption in the example. As a result, the preceding proposition may be quite conservative. While not all baby boomers are yet of an age to be prospective IVA buyers and while not all possess the means to fund an IVA premium equal to the recent average size of $129,000, this discussion still provides insight as to the magnificent scope of this opportunity.

INTERPLAY OF PRICING, RESERVING, AND RISK-BASED CAPITAL

Mortality, expense, and investment factors are possible margin elements. For pricing simplicity, insurers can use their best (i.e., nonconservative, nonliberal) estimate of mortality and look to derive all earnings from the expense charge elements, including investment-related expenses.

If an insurer happened to use mortality and interest assumptions for pricing annuities that were identical to those for "valuing" annuities (i.e., by performing the valuation of liabilities via reserve determination) and if the net premium (after acquisition and issue expenses) exactly matched the time-zero reserve, the insurer would look to introduce a margin between the earned rate on assets and the credited rate on liabilities that would cover ongoing administrative expenses, profit, and taxes.

To get a brief idea how such a process to set the product margin component to provide a targeted return on surplus—where RBC is the only equity employed in the simplified scenario described in the preceding paragraph—works, suppose the insurer decides to allocate an amount of its surplus equal to 3% of the reserve to provide a specific degree (e.g., 96th percentile) of certainty that it can meet its obligations to annuitants and thereby get the claims-paying and credit ratings it desires from major rating agencies (e.g., A. M. Best, Fitch, Moody's, Standard & Poor's, Weiss).[4] For example, if the initial immediate annuity reserve were $100,000, the insurer would set aside another $3,000 in allocated surplus.

An insurer might set the amount of surplus in its internal target surplus formula to guard against any specific contingency (C-1 through C-5 risks) at a specific level, such as the 96th percentile; that is, in 96% of all future economic scenarios that may materialize, capital comprised of assets equal to the reserve and allocated surplus collectively should remain nonnegative, proving adequate to meet claim obligations. Equivalently stated, there is only a 4% probability of ruin specific to any one contingency.

Since all types of contingencies do not befall an insurer simultaneously, aggregate protection tends to exceed the 99% level, with less than a 1% probability of ruin. For example, unexpectedly high mortality improvements (C-2 pricing inadequacy risk), unexpectedly large drops in stock and bond values (C-1 asset depreciation risk), and unexpectedly high expenses due to new regulations or unexpectedly large increases in corporate federal income tax rates (C-4 general business risk) are less than perfectly correlated; so it is unlikely all will befall the insurer simultaneously.[5] As a result, the overall level of the insurer's ability to meet its obligations from the totality of its surplus is higher than the basis on which it sets its surplus level to guard against any one specific category of risk. Said another way, an insurer may allocate surplus at such a level so that there is only a 4% probability of ruin specific to any one contingency. The aggregate resultant protection tends to exceed the 99% level, with less than a 1% probability of ruin.

Further suppose that the corporate federal income tax rate is 34%, that the insurer feels it can earn 6% after-tax on the surplus allocated to further safeguard its ability to meet its obligations to annuitants, and that the insurer targets a 15% after-tax return on the money it ties up for this purpose (a commonly stated goal in insurance company annual reports), which money thereby becomes unavailable for other corporate projects.

The insurer would look to introduce a margin of $[(0.15 - 0.06) / (1 - 0.34)]$ $\times$ 0.03 or 0.41% to achieve its targeted return on allocated surplus. The allocated surplus itself earns 6% after-tax, so the product must have sufficient margin introduced to return the remaining 9% after-tax, or 13.6% pretax. This must be earned on the percentage of the reserve for which allocated surplus is held, or 3%. (The 3% value can be thought of as the "surplus/ reserve" ratio or, for deferred annuities, the "equity/account value" ratio. The 3% is derived by considering the C-1 through C-5 risks, then possibly multiplying by a factor to arrive at a total surplus value in line to achieve desired claims-paying ratings from rating agencies.) It is apparent from the preceding calculation that in a low-interest-rate environment, where something less than 6% after-tax can be earned on allocated surplus, a higher product margin must be introduced if the same total 15% after-tax return is desired.

Of course, in addition to the 0.41% profit margin element, the total margin must also include an expense element to recover administrative expenses. The profit margin element plus the expense recovery element (for both acquisition and ongoing maintenance expenses) plus the default margin element (for immediate fixed annuities but not for immediate variable annuities) produces the total margin or "spread" between "earned" and "credited" rates. For fixed annuities, which often have no annual administrative charge, "spread" can be thought of exactly as the margin between earned and credited rates. For variable annuities, "spread" can be thought of as the sum of the M&E risk charge, the annual administrative charges, if any, and the excess of the investment management charge over actual investment management expense.

The "reserve" is that pot of assets sufficient—together with interest thereon and any future premiums—to meet an insurer's future obligations to policyholders. Depending on its construction, it can be a best-estimate reserve (e.g., 50% chance of adequacy to pay off obligations) or it can be a conservative reserve (e.g., 85% chance of adequacy to pay off obligations).

When surplus is allocated to increase the level of assurance that the combination of reserve and allocated surplus can meet the insurer's obligations to annuitants, this may raise the chance of adequacy to pay off annuitant obligations to, say, 99%. Again, while each surplus factor on its own may be protective only to, say, 95% or 96% adequacy, the collective probability of adequacy of all factors may be something like 99%. This is because of the lower likelihood that all relevant factors will go wrong simultaneously.

There are five types of contingencies against which a surplus formula typically guards, not all of which happen to pertain to variable income annuities:

C-1 risk ("C" stands for "Contingency" while "1" represents the first type of contingency) deals with "asset depreciation"—the risk that assets may have depreciated values (e.g., bonds in default, stocks with depressed prices) at the time they're needed to pay policyholder benefits.

C-2 risk is pricing inadequacy risk (e.g., that actual mortality may be other than expected).

C-3 risk is interest rate risk—the risk that interest rates may rise causing market values of fixed-income securities to fall at the time they're needed to fulfill their safeguarding mission; or the risk that interest rates may fall to levels unable to support contractually guaranteed minimum rates, where the situation may be exacerbated for the insurer if contract owners hold the right to dump in unlimited additional deposits to earn such guaranteed minimum rates that are higher than supportable and higher than rates available elsewhere.

C-4 risk is general business risk—a catchall basket meant to handle things like regulatory changes and tax changes.

C-5 risk has been added more recently to address foreign exchange risk for insurers and reinsurers doing business in multiple countries with multiple currencies.

An insurer may create its own internal target surplus formula that shows surplus factors for each of the C-1 to C-5 risks based on its own scientific analysis that would protect the insurer to the degree desired. It may then adjust the end result to arrive at a level of total surplus (e.g., a desired multiple of the National Association of Insurance Commissioners Action Level) appropriate to garner desired claims-paying and credit-agency ratings. The surcharge—the difference between the internally determined scientific basis to be protective to the desired level and that total surplus actually held—may be allocated to business lines in proportion to the scientifically determined basis or on some other basis that would favor some business lines at the expense of others (i.e., that might allocate less "redundant" or "cosmetic" surplus to product lines the insurer wishes to favor for competitive reasons— "favor" because it has less "rent" to pay on allocated surplus due to the smaller amount allocated to it, which allows it to have a lower profit margin element factored into pricing, which allows it to meet its target profit objective [e.g., 15% after-tax return] at a lower price to the end customer).

To the extent "redundant" or "cosmetic" surplus in excess of that scientifically determined as necessary to safeguard against risks to a targeted level is tied up to achieve desired claims-paying or credit agency ratings and because the cost of this excess is factored into the product price, customers are effectively "buying" additional security that their retirement benefit will be received.

Because the amount of allocated surplus so determined by formula is held in the form of assets most of which hold the possibility to become impaired, these assets themselves pose their own C-1 risk, and thus an insurer must hold "surplus on surplus." (This typically stops with one iteration; that is, the insurer doesn't hold "surplus on surplus on surplus.")

While mathematical models can be constructed to incorporate the interplay of the various factors impacting pricing and to target specific profit objectives, it is clear that actual IVA business value to an insurer will depend on real-world experience that emerges post-issue. Because of the long-tailed nature of variable income annuity liabilities, those responsible for pricing and product design may have moved on (to other operations, to other companies, to retirement, or to "the great beyond") before having a chance to witness the fit of eventual experience with their assumptions for it.

IMMEDIATE ANNUITY VALUE CREATION

Value *for the consumer* is created via immediate annuities by virtue of the ability to genuinely transfer mortality risk to the insurer, thereby achieving greater utility of wealth. Immediate annuities address the consumer's challenge of generating progressively increasing retirement income from a progressively decreasing asset base through the mechanism of survivorship credits, which are unavailable from any other asset class. Immediate annuities produce lifetime income levels superior to all identically invested alternatives because, while alternatives rely solely on the two components of principal and appreciation to generate income, immediate annuities add the third component of survivorship credits.

The simple algebra of survivorship credits quickly reveals their strength. Chapter 9, Reserves and Risk-Based Capital, shows that the progression from time t to time $t + 1$ of the reserve liability for an annuitant age x involves accumulating for interest and survivorship and then deducting the year-end benefit B:

$$V_{t+1} = V_t \frac{(1+i)}{p_x} - B$$

The corresponding progression of an identically invested nonannuity account, where A_t denotes account value at time t, is:

$$A_{t+1} = A_t (1 + i) - B$$

The annual increment in value of the asset base supporting the annuity, $(1 + i)/p_x - 1$, exceeds the annual increment in value of the asset base supporting the nonannuity account, i:

$$(1 + i)/p_x - 1 > i$$

This value creation is illustrated in Chapter 8, Rate of Return, where it is made evident that, beyond a crossover point, annuitants enjoy a cumulative lifetime rate of return superior to that provided by the invested assets underlying their annuity. In fact, the longer their lifetime, the more the cumulative lifetime rate of return from the annuity outperforms the return of the underlying assets. Perhaps this knowledge in itself might spawn longevity-encouraging incentive effects.

Value *for the insurer* is created via immediate annuities—at least in this chapter—by means of compensation from consumers for assuming mortality and expense risks and for creating and administering a longevity insurance program. Risk curves of various profitability measures illustrate the potential range of "value" ultimately realizable.[6] This traditional perspective (even held by insurance companies themselves) of insurers solely as aggregators of hazard risk (with the mortality hazard here being longevity) is longstanding. This age-old viewpoint is that insurance is strictly an underwriting activity involving diversifiable risks and possessing a singular profit driver, namely, underwriting gain or loss; for example, will mortality be such that ongoing immediate annuity claims (e.g., monthly benefits) result in annuity present values that are more than, the same as, or less than the net premiums collected?

Due to competition or a belief that the financial markets will reward companies more handsomely for holding a well-managed collection of both diversifiable and nondiversifiable risks than for holding only diversifiable risks, some annuity writers are embedding increased levels of nondiversifiable risks in their product offerings. This risk profile shift transforms insurers into broader financial institutions, where enterprise risk management that focuses on the full mix of assets and liabilities—well beyond underwriting guidelines and claims handling practices—becomes more critical.

Identifying the types of risk (recognition); understanding risks (qualitative evaluation), sometimes with the help of dynamic risk modeling (quantitative evaluation); establishing policies and practices for addressing individual and collective risks (mitigation); and performing ongoing observation of the risks (monitoring) become more important as the nondiversifiable risk set expands. Risk management approaches that include avoidance, minimization, and transfer are evaluated. Analytical studies using risk management tools (e.g., derivatives) having various levels of efficacy (e.g., helpful but imperfect equity market hedging) serve as compasses for navigating a course of action.

The future evolution of value creation for insurance companies—including annuity writers—may shift the emphasis away from underwriting. For example, as the insurance securitization market develops, insurers might decide to focus on risk aggregation and policy servicing activities, while transferring underwriting risks and investment risks to the capital markets. This wider collection of risks assumed and wider collection of options for handling such risks allow annuity writers to concentrate their resources on business value creation activities where they believe they have a competitive advantage.

Product development is the heart of immediate annuity business value creation for the insurer. Product features and pricing determine the competitive position of the offering in the marketplace. Product structure determines in large part the nature and magnitude of the risks that the insurer assumes. It may well be the case that the insurer derives zero revenue from investment, legal, or tax advice and derives all or the vast majority of its revenue from its insurance product offerings. Thus, we now turn our attention to the topic of product development—and some of the resultant product management activities it creates, including the management of nondiversifiable risks, the transfer of investment risk via the derivatives market, and the transfer of underwriting risk to the capital markets through securitization—in Chapter 18.

CHAPTER 18

Product Development Trends

If we knew what it was we were doing, it would not be called research, would it?

—Albert Einstein

PRODUCT VARIATIONS

Immediate variable annuities—the basic product—are designed to fulfill their core function of guaranteeing lifetime income to annuitants, where that income depends on the investment elections made by the contract owners and on the performance of those investments.

Within labyrinthine constraints imposed by the Securities and Exchange Commission (SEC), the National Association of Securities Dealers (NASD), the Internal Revenue Service (IRS), the Department of Labor, state insurance departments, financial advisers, insurance company stockholders, annuity consumers, marketplace competition, and other constituencies and forces, immediate variable annuity (IVA) product developers seek to weave salable and profitable solutions that simultaneously satisfy all laws, regulations, and requirements of affected parties.

Regardless of bells and whistles, payout floors, liquidity periods, bonuses, or other distractive accoutrement used to draw attention to a specific product offering, it is imperative to remember that foremost in a consumer's decision-making process should be the consideration of how well the IVA product offering can be expected to achieve its basic mission. Satisfactory conversion rates, prudent investment management, low cost, and financial strength of the insurer over many decades are important assessment factors.

Product features that are only peripheral to the core mission of an IVA should not be given undue attention. Sometimes such peripheral benefits receive greater emphasis in the sales process than the overall purchase decision warrants simply because this one peripheral feature is the "hook" the insurance company hopes to use to differentiate its otherwise similar IVA

489

HARVARD BUSINESS REVIEW, OCT. 2001

"HENDERSON, YOU'VE GOT THE FOLKS UPSTAIRS PRETTY EXCITED
OVER THIS PROJECT."

product offering from the many comparable offerings in the marketplace. Claims that a peripheral feature makes a specific IVA product state-of-the-art should be critically reviewed, especially if it will result in a lifetime of additional expense.

To the extent that core product designs are commoditized, marketers can be indefatigable in overemphasizing slight differences that are only tangential to the primary reasons for owning an IVA. As Will Rogers put it, "Advertising is the art of convincing people to spend money they don't have for something they don't need." As a result, IVAs may be festooned with ancillary benefits that should each be critically reviewed.

When a person purchases a basic immediate variable annuity, he or she achieves important benefits:

- Lifetime income; transfer of longevity risk; freedom from anxiety about outliving assets.
- Potential for increasing income; inflation hedge.
- Asset diversification; professional money management; freedom from serving as one's own chief investment officer at a time in life where one may not desire to perform or may be incapable of performing this function.
- Ability to customize investment mix that determines the level of income.
- Tax deferral (income tax becomes due only as benefit payments are received by the annuitant rather than when capital gains, dividends, and interest occur in the underlying investment fund).

- Freedom from serving as one's own pension administrator at a time in life where one may not desire to perform or may be incapable of performing this function; tax-qualified minimum distribution requirements are met by a properly established IVA.

To the extent that extra features at additional expense are elected that drive down retirement income, one must question whether these features are appropriate because they run counter to the main product objective: maximizing lifetime retirement income. To the extent that long-term care (LTC) insurance provisions, accessibility to funds beyond regularly scheduled annuity payments, guaranteed levels of income regardless of how subaccounts perform, or additional features peripheral to the main mission of the product are available, a prospective IVA purchaser needs to determine (1) if these are worth the reduction in retirement income and (2) whether the same need (e.g., LTC insurance) can be more effectively procured through an independent product specifically designed to meet that need.

As will be seen, greater levels of flexibility, accessibility, and options embedded in IVA product designs may actually detract from the ability of an IVA to accomplish its core mission of providing maximum lifetime income at least cost.

The riskier the additional promises and guarantees layered onto the basic product (e.g., effectively guaranteeing some level of subaccount performance by guaranteeing some income level regardless of subaccount performance), the greater is the need for analysis of whether the offering insurer is likely to be able to live up to these over a span of many decades and through the periodic economic downturns that inevitably occur.

Variable subaccount performance guarantees and liquidity are two areas receiving attention in the evolution of immediate variable annuity product design.

PAYOUT FLOOR GUARANTEES

Product variations exist as insurers attempt to differentiate their product offerings from those of competitors, seeking to remain in the vanguard of retirement income product innovation. This can be done by providing additional guarantees to annuitants, such as stipulating that no future variable benefit payment will be less than, say, 80% of the initial payment.[1] (A variation of this theme is to reduce the initial benefit payment below that determined under the conventional approach and then to guarantee that no future benefit payment will be less than, say, 90% or 100% of the initial one.)

It would be more comforting if there were some level of income below which that monthly check in the mailbox were guaranteed not to fall. Such a "guaranteed floor payment," or guaranteed payout annuity floor (GPAF) as it is generically called in insurance industry nomenclature, guarantees variable fund performance in some fashion.[2] It may require the contract owner[3] to adhere to one or more specific asset allocations, perhaps with periodic forced rebalancing. Otherwise, annuitants have an incentive to shoot for the moon by electing the most aggressive investment posture they can, knowing a safety net exists in the way of a floor guarantee. The high volatility of returns of such aggressive investments increases the probability that any such floor may be penetrated.

The risk of "excessive claims" associated with such a floor guarantee may be fully borne by the insurer, which factors some level of charge into pricing for absorption of this risk. Yet such a risk is not necessarily an insurable event. Unlike life insurance, where pooling of ever-larger numbers of insured lives tends to reduce variation from mean death benefit claim costs by the insured population "dying too soon," and unlike immediate annuities, where pooling of ever-larger numbers of annuitants tends to reduce variation from expected annuity benefit payments as a result of the annuitant population "living too long," equity market risk is *nondiversifiable* in the sense that when the stock market goes down for one it goes down for all. Pooling greater and greater numbers of individuals exposed to the same equity market risk does nothing toward mitigation of that risk. This is why GPAF reinsurance is not as readily available as, say, life reinsurance.

When people say, "Insurance companies are in the business of assuming risk," they are not precisely correct. Insurance companies—at least historically—are in the business of *spreading* risk. As was shown in the first chapters of this book, immediate annuities allow people who individually can't manage longevity risk well to *spread* that risk among many similarly situated people who collectively can manage longevity risk well. The Law of Large Numbers tells us that spreading of longevity risk across ever greater numbers of annuitants improves risk management capability. A more precise statement of the historical function of insurance companies would be to say, "Insurance companies are in the business of *spreading diversifiable risk* and are not in the business of *assuming nondiversifiable risk*."

Indeed, spreading diversifiable risk is the crux of the annuity business and is what separates insurers from other asset accumulators. Mortality risk spreading—and the vastly improved longevity management it provides to individuals—is the value proposition unique to annuities.

Mortality risk ideally involves *independent* risk units, whereby pooling greater numbers leads to risk reduction. Financial risks, such as guaranteeing that annuity benefits tied to a major stock index will not fall below a prescribed level, are perfectly or highly *correlated,* so the pooling mechanism will not reduce risk. If an annuity writer issues more such IVA contracts, its exposure to stock market risk is *increased.* Pooling does not reduce risk.

"Risk" is synonymous with exposing oneself to a course involving uncertain danger. Public perception of risk is often askew, as people's behavioral decisions frequently overweight their subjective, memory-based, judgmental biases and underweight objective, statistical evidence. That human decision making in the face of risk is so quirky may be attributable in part to evolution causing human brains to retain the more primitive, reactive area—the one that evolved in an earlier era when reacting to a tangible, current, predator-filled environment was vastly more important than planning for an uncertain future. Even today, humans tend to place greater weight on the present and discount future events even if the latter are highly projectable and cataclysmic.

The part of the brain dealing with calculations, probabilities, and logic is operative and must collaborate with and reconcile differences with experience-based emotional biases when compromising to make decisions in the face of uncertainty. *Behavioral economics* draws on psychology and other social sciences to explore economic decision making; for example, different schedules of reinforcement yield different behavioral responses. Behavioral economics studies specific annuity-buying decisions that arise from behavioral drivers associated with risk aversion. For example, individuals are often conditioned for the first 65 years of life to equate safety with principal preservation; therefore, their innate risk aversion is associated with loss of principal and their decision making responds accordingly. Around age 65, if six and a half decades of conditioning can be overcome so that individuals shift to equate safety with adequate inflation-adjusted lifetime income— recognizing that they could spend down every last penny yet never have lost principal in any investment so that principal preservation is no longer perceived as the primary threat—their innate risk aversion may become associated with loss of adequate income and their decision making will respond accordingly, favoring financial instruments that address this newly perceived primary threat in the strongest manner.

The more recent interdisciplinary field of *neuroeconomics* includes the relationship between biology and economic decision making, it uses brain-imaging technology such as magnetic resonance imaging (MRI) to determine which brain regions become active during economic decision making, and it measures brain chemicals such as those released by the pleasurable stimulus of monetary rewards. Early research suggests that individuals whose logic and cognitive reasoning predominate over their emotions— such as people with brain lesions that suppress their emotional centers— may excel in the ability to act in their own best economic self-interest with less interference from emotional reactions.

Until the seventeenth century, good luck or misfortune were often attributed to the capriciousness of the gods. Probability measurement then began to replace fate, allowing risk analysis and risk management to evolve.

Regardless of why human behavior sometimes causes us to act contrary to our own best economic self-interest, a description of financial risk will help us understand the subject more precisely in general and will serve as a prerequisite to a fuller understanding of risks associated with guaranteed payout annuity floors in particular. The following "lesson" describes the nature of financial risk with some rigor.

A Brief Lesson on Financial Risk

Definition 1: An *experiment* is any operation whose outcome cannot be predicted with certainty.

Definition 2: The *sample space S* of an experiment is the set of all possible outcomes of the experiment.

Definition 3: A *random variable X* is a real-valued function of the elements of a sample space S.

Notation: A lowercase x will stand for the particular values the random variable X may assume.

Definition 4: The *probability function* for X is the probability that the random variable X assumes the value x and is denoted by $p_X(x) = P\{X = x\}$; that is, if we repeatedly perform the experiment, $p_X(x)$ is the relative proportion of the time we would observe the random variable X taking on the numerical value x.

Experiment: Investor 1 invests $1,000 in a particular stock market index for one year. Let the random variable X be the dollar value of the investment at the end of the year, having possible outcomes of $800, $1,000, or $1,200 with the probabilities

$$p_X(x) = 0.3, \quad x = \$\ \ 800$$
$$= 0.1, \quad x = \$1,000$$
$$= 0.6, \quad x = \$1,200$$

The sample space $S = \{x : x = \$800, \$1,000, \$1,200\}$.

Definition 5: The *expected value* of X, called the *mean* or *average*, is denoted by $\mu_X = E[X]$, where $E[X] = \sum_S x\, p_X(x)$; that is, to find the mean, we multiply the values x that the random variable X may assume by the likelihood each occurs and add the results.

In the preceding experiment,

$$\mu_X = E[X] = \sum_S x \, p_X(x)$$

$$= (\$800)(0.3) + (\$1,000)(0.1) + (\$1,200)(0.6)$$

$$= \$1,060$$

If we think of the x axis in Figure 18.1 as a wooden plank and the bars as weights, then μ_X represents the point at which a pencil placed vertically would balance the plank.

The mean of a random variable gives a measure of the middle of the probability distribution. To glean information about the variability of the random variable, we look at its *variance*.

Definition 6: The *variance* of a random variable X, denoted by σ_X^2, is defined as

$$\sigma_X^2 = E[(X - \mu_X)^2]$$

Definition 7: The *standard deviation* of a random variable X, denoted by σ_X, is the positive square root of the variance, defined as

$$\sigma_X = \sqrt{\sigma_x^2}$$

The variance is the average of the square of the distance between the random variable X and its mean μ_X. If X varies little, its value will be close to its mean, so this average squared distance will be small. If X varies greatly, then its value will differ from its mean by a large amount, so this average squared distance will be large.

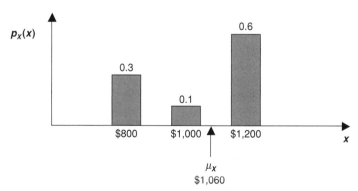

FIGURE 18.1   Expected Value of Random Variable X

In the experiment, the variance is

$$\sigma_X^2 = E[(X - \mu_X)^2]$$
$$= \sum_S (x - 1{,}060)^2 \, p_X(x)$$
$$= (800 - 1{,}060)^2 (0.3) + (1{,}000 - 1{,}060)^2 (0.1) + (1{,}200 - 1{,}060)^2 (0.6)$$
$$= 32{,}400$$

and the standard deviation is

$$\sigma_X = \sqrt{\sigma_X^2}$$
$$= \sqrt{32{,}400}$$
$$= 180$$

Now suppose that Investor 2, also with \$1,000, similarly places his investment that again promises to pay out the value of \$1,000 at the end of one year adjusted for performance of the same particular stock index having the same probabilities of return. Let the random variable Y be the dollar value of his investment at the end of the year.

Let the random variable Z denote the combination of X and Y; that is, $Z = X + Y$. Then

$$\mu_Z = E[Z] = E[X + Y] = E[X] + E[Y] = \mu_X + \mu_Y$$

Since X and Y are *identically distributed* (i.e., have the same probability distribution function),

$$\mu_X = \mu_Y$$

Therefore,

$$\mu_Z = \mu_X + \mu_Y = 2\,\mu_X$$

The variance of the random variable Z is given by

$$\sigma_Z^2 = E[(Z - \mu_Z)^2] = E[(X + Y - 2\mu_X)^2]$$
$$= E[X^2 + 2XY + Y^2 - 4X\mu_X - 4Y\mu_X + 4\mu_X^2]$$
$$= E[X^2] + 2E[XY] + E[Y^2] - 4\mu_X E[X] - 4\mu_X E[Y] + 4\mu_X^2$$
$$= E[X^2] + 2E[XY] + E[Y^2] - 4\mu_X^2$$
$$= E[X^2] - \mu_X^2 + E[Y^2] - \mu_Y^2 + 2E[XY] - 2\mu_X \mu_Y \tag{18.1}$$
$$= \sigma_X^2 + \sigma_Y^2 + 2\{E[XY] - \mu_X \mu_Y\} \tag{18.2}$$
$$= \sigma_X^2 + \sigma_Y^2 + 2\sigma_{XY} \tag{18.3}$$

Thus, the variance of the random variable Z equals the variance of X plus the variance of Y plus twice the *covariance* of X and Y.

Definition 8: The *covariance* of X and Y is defined as

$$\sigma_{XY} = E[(X - \mu_X)(Y - \mu_Y)]$$

A simpler formula for the covariance σ_{XY} is derived as follows and is what allows us to move from equation (18.2) to equation (18.3):

$$
\begin{aligned}
\sigma_{XY} &= E[(X - \mu_X)(Y - \mu_Y)] \\
&= E[XY - \mu_X Y - X\mu_Y + \mu_X \mu_Y] \\
&= E[XY] - \mu_X E[Y] - \mu_Y E[X] + \mu_X \mu_Y \\
&= E[XY] - \mu_X \mu_Y
\end{aligned}
$$

Similarly, a simpler formula for the variance of X, σ_X^2, is derived and shows the equivalency of equations (18.1) and (18.2):

$$
\begin{aligned}
\sigma_X^2 &= E[(X - \mu_X)^2] = E[X^2 - 2X\mu_X + \mu_X^2] \\
&= E[X^2] - 2\mu_X E[X] + \mu_X^2 \\
&= E[X^2] - \mu_X^2
\end{aligned}
$$

The covariance measures how X and Y vary together. Because σ_{XY} equals $E[(X - \mu_X)(Y - \mu_Y)]$, if X is larger than its mean μ_X when Y is larger than its mean μ_Y, then the covariance σ_{XY} will be positive. If $X - \mu_X$ and $Y - \mu_Y$ tend to have opposite signs, then σ_{XY} will be negative. If $X - \mu_X$ is positive as often as it is negative when $Y - \mu_Y$ is positive or negative, then $\sigma_{XY} = 0$ would be an expected result.[4]

The magnitude of σ_{XY} is relatively meaningless without knowledge of σ_X^2 and σ_Y^2, since the covariance σ_{XY} could be high simply because X and Y might be highly variable, which tends to increase σ_{XY}. To normalize this effect, the *correlation coefficient* ρ_{XY} in Definition 9 measures covariability relative to the individual variances of X and Y. While not proven here, $-1 \leq \rho_{XY} \leq 1$.

Definition 9: *Correlation* between random variables X and Y is defined as

$$\rho_{XY} = \frac{\sigma_{XY}}{\sigma_X \sigma_Y}$$

Returning to the two similarly situated investors, we know that for the random variable $Z = X + Y$,

$$\sigma_Z^2 = \sigma_X^2 + \sigma_Y^2 + 2\sigma_{XY}$$

Now

$$\sigma_{XY} = E[XY] - \mu_X\mu_Y$$
$$= \sum_S xy\, p_{XY}(x,y) - \mu_X\mu_Y \text{ (where } p_{XY}(x,y) = P\{X=x, Y=y\})$$
$$= (800)(800)(0.3) + (1,000)(1,000)(0.1) + (1,200)(1,200)(0.6) - (1,060)(1,060)$$
$$= 32,400$$

So

$$\sigma_Z^2 = 32,400 + 32,400 + (2)(32,400)$$
$$= 129,600$$

and

$$\sigma_Z = 360$$

Thus, the variance $\sigma_Z^2 = 129,600$ for two investors subject to exactly the same risk is more than the sum of the two variances for each of them, $\sigma_X^2 + \sigma_Y^2 = 64,800$. This is because the stock market index fell for both of them, remained constant for both of them, or increased for both of them.

As would be expected, the correlation between random variables X and Y is unity:

$$\rho_{XY} = \frac{\sigma_{XY}}{\sigma_X\sigma_Y} = \frac{32,400}{(180)(180)} = 1$$

Summary: Assume that we have two random variables X and Y. Risk relates to the uncertainty of the outcome. A common measure of this uncertainty is the variance of the outcome distribution. Assume that the variances are denoted by σ_X^2 and σ_Y^2. If we create a linear combination $Z = X + Y$, then the variance is

$$\sigma_Z^2 = \sigma_X^2 + \sigma_Y^2 + 2\sigma_{XY}$$

To the extent X is above its mean μ_X when Y is above its mean μ_Y, the covariance term μ_{XY} is positive, making the variance of the sum Z higher than the sum of the individual variances of X and Y. For example, when two investors are exposed to the same stock market risk, this occurs. The result of combining similar risks is therefore proven to be risk increasing rather than risk reducing.

While this result may have been intuitively obvious, the preceding example offers a framework for evaluation. For example, if Investor 2 had invested in a *foreign* stock index while Investor 1 invested in a *domestic* stock index, the combined risk as measured by the variance σ_Z^2 would likely be less than when both invested in the same domestic stock index. If Investor 2 had invested in a *bond* index, σ_Z^2 might be even less.

If Investor 2 had invested in an asset that had a negative correlation with the first asset (i.e., due to a negative covariance), such as a stock index put option or perhaps a commodity index, that would actually be risk reducing rather than risk increasing. Using a stock index put option that is highly negatively correlated with the stock index is an example of a *hedging* technique.

If a random variable U is the number of deaths in the next one-year period for 1,000 65-year-old females and if V is the number of deaths in the same one-year period for another 1,000 65-year-old females, then—if the deaths in the first group are truly *independent* of the deaths in the second group (as would be expected other than for an epidemic or a concentration of lives in one geographic area hit with a natural disaster)—the covariance σ_W^2 where $W = U + V$ would be zero.

Carrying this one step further, suppose that $X_1, X_2, \ldots, X_n$ are *independent, identically distributed* random variables, each with mean μ and variance σ^2. Let $\bar{X}$ be the arithmetic average of these n random variables:

$$\bar{X} = \frac{1}{n}\sum_{i=1}^{n} X_i = \frac{1}{n}(X_1 + X_2 + \cdots + X_n)$$

Then it can be shown that

$$\mu_{\bar{X}} = \sum_{i=1}^{n} \frac{1}{n}\mu = \mu$$

and

$$\sigma_{\bar{X}}^2 = \sum_{i=1}^{n}\left(\frac{1}{n}\right)^2 \sigma^2 = \frac{\sigma^2}{n}$$

The expected value of $\bar{X}$ is μ, the same as the expected value of each of the individual random variables X_i. Importantly, however, the variance of $\bar{X}$, $\sigma_{\bar{X}}^2$, is $\frac{\sigma^2}{n}$, which is $\frac{1}{n}$ times the variance σ^2 of each of the individual random variables X_i; that is, $\bar{X}$ is substantially less variable than the original random variables X_i.

Because $\sigma_{\bar{X}}^2 = \frac{\sigma^2}{n}$, this variance tends to zero as n tends to infinity. If we combine a large number of similar independent (i.e., uncorrelated) risk units, the variance—and therefore the standard deviation—tends to zero. The implication is that the risk faced by the owner of an individual risk unit (such as an insurer writing one IVA) can be diversified away by combining this risk with a large number of uncorrelated risks (such as the insurer writing many IVA contracts). Indeed, that σ^2/n tends to zero with large n is an important element in the proof of the Law of Large Numbers, described earlier.

The salient point is that if an insurance company writes more immediate annuities, the mortality risk as defined by the uncertainty of mortality rates as measured by their variance does not increase. The independent nature of the individual risk units causes the covariance to be zero. The *total* variance of the sum $W = U + V$ is just the sum of the individual variances. The random variable that is the arithmetic average has a lower variance than that of the individual random variables. IVA mortality risk reduction is achieved via the operation of the Law of Large Numbers.

When the risk units are not independent but there is a strong positive covariance—such as when all investors are subject to identical stock market risk—the total variance of the sum $Z = X + Y$ is larger than the sum of the individual variances. Guaranteeing a floor on IVA benefits is tantamount to guaranteeing performance of a particular asset portfolio (which may include stocks), resulting in just such a situation. Asset-performance risk reduction is not achievable by writing more IVA business. Rather, risk reduction is achievable via *hedging*, by pairing with a negatively correlated security.

Note: While not proven here, the following results for a random variable X, where k is a constant, hold and were used in some of the preceding equations:

- $E[k] = k$
- $E[kX] = kE[X]$
- $E[X + Y] = E[X] + E[Y]$

Also, here we investigated and offered a numerical example of a *discrete* random variable X, so-called because the range of values it may assume is a discrete set of real numbers. There is a *continuous* random variable analogue, where the range of values that a random variable X may assume is an interval or a union of intervals on the real number line and where the probability of the random variable equaling any single numerical value in the range is zero. The latter may be important when observing random variables whose values vary continuously with time.

While we investigated *mean* and *variance*, additional parameters of the probability distribution of a random variable are of interest. Define μ_k equal to $E[(X - \mu_X)^k]$ where k is a positive integer. This is called the *central moment of order k* or the *moment of order k about the mean*. For $k = 2$, we have

$$\mu_2 = E[(X - \mu_X)^2] = \sigma_X^2 = \text{variance of } X$$

When evaluating financial risk, one may be interested in how asymmetric the probability distribution is. One measure of asymmetry is

$$Coefficient\ of\ skewness = \frac{\mu_3}{\mu_2^{3/2}}$$

A random variable X is *symmetric* about a point α if $P\{X \geq \alpha + x\}$ equals $P\{X \leq \alpha - x\}$ for all x. If X is symmetric with α as the center of symmetry, then $E[X] = \alpha$. If in the earlier stock market index example, we let

$$
\begin{aligned}
p_X(x) &= 0.2, & x &= \$\ \ 800 \\
&= 0.6, & x &= \$1,000 \\
&= 0.2, & x &= \$1,200
\end{aligned}
$$

then X is symmetric about $\$1,000$.

Kurtosis is a parameter that describes the shape of the probability function of a random variable. This measure conveys information about the "peakedness" of a probability distribution around the mean and about the fatness of the tails of the distribution. The parameter is defined as

$$
\text{Kurtosis} = \frac{\mu_4}{\mu_2^2}
$$

When evaluating financial risk, one may be interested in more information than the variance (or the standard deviation) parameter alone provides. For example, a probability function that is higher and more peaked at the center might lead us to believe that it has a lower variance. Yet that same probability function may have fatter tails, suggesting that it has a higher variance. The combination of a more acute peak about the mean and fatter tails of the distribution may yield offsetting effects on the variance, resulting in a variance identical to that of a random variable whose probability distribution has a lower and more rounded peak about the mean and thinner tails. A high kurtosis means relatively more of the variance is due to infrequent but extreme deviations and relatively less is due to frequent but modest deviations.[5] In this sense, kurtosis is sometimes said to measure the volatility of volatility. Kurtosis may provide important information should those extreme deviations represent wide swings in monetary values.

Effectively, when an insurer offers a GPAF, it is offering a lengthy series of complex put options. For simplicity, assume the annuitant elects a 100% allocation to a domestic stock fund. The insurer guarantees that an annuitant will only absorb reduced benefit payments to a certain level. Below that level, the annuitant is immune to any fund performance shortfall; that is, the annuitant is treated the same as though no further investment losses resulted.

This is what a put option achieves. The writer (seller) of a put option accepts a premium from the buyer. The buyer is guaranteed that he is immunized against any losses beyond a certain level. These are absorbed by the writer, who, if the underlying instrument falls below a specified level (the "strike price") as of a specified time, is legally required by the terms of the option contract to make up any shortfall.

An insurer could restore itself to a risk-neutral position by purchasing put options to offset those it has sold or granted to annuitants. (This characteristic makes it clear that the insurer has offered embedded put options to immediate variable annuitants via such a floor guarantee product design since buying offsetting options restores risk neutrality.)

Such a "guaranteed payout annuity floor" is one form of a larger class of variable annuity guaranteed living benefits (VAGLBs) that insurers writing variable annuities offer. (Variable annuities previously contained "death benefits" payable to beneficiaries of annuity owners; hence the designation "living benefit" that provides something extra for surviving annuity owners themselves.) Financial Accounting Standard #133 (FAS #133), "Accounting for Derivatives," covers this type of benefit.

Note that even if the insurance series funds underlying the variable annuity subaccounts have a zero return or even small positive returns, the floor guarantee can still be triggered. This is because benefit payments decline whenever subaccount performance is lower than the assumed investment rate (AIR), for example, 5%. To the extent an insurer raises its mortality and expense (M&E) risk charge to cover this floor guarantee, that actually makes a triggering of the floor guarantee more likely because the underlying funds must perform even better just to offset the additional charge.

Risks associated with offering such a floor guarantee can be partially transferred to the annuitant, depending on product construction. For example, future benefit payments could be reduced to the extent necessary (but never lower than the floor) to cover any shortfalls that had previously arisen due to poor fund performance. Effectively, this has the annuitant "borrowing from himself" in the sense that he is really receiving an "advance" against future benefit payments to make up the shortfall.

The benefit check for a period where there would be a shortfall would be increased by the "advance" to the floor level. The difference between the floor benefit and what the annuitant would have received slightly reduces all future benefit payments. Effectively, the advance in the amount of the shortfall becomes a "negative premium" that reduces all future benefits by the same amount as the benefits that a positive net premium of equivalent size could purchase at the annuitant's attained age.

The insurer still must make up the current period shortfall from its own assets but it has reduced a liability—the present value of future annuity benefits exclusive of the floor benefit guarantee—by a like amount. The cost of such a product construction to the insurer is less than one where the insurer alone funds 100% of any shortfalls because once benefit payments again equal or exceed the floor level, the insurer is paying a lower number of annuity units per payment than the original number. Because any advance serves as a negative premium that reduces the number of annuity units the value of which is payable per benefit period, it may take longer for the benefit level to climb back up to the floor.

Another design approach would be to provide the floor benefit guarantee only for a specific period of time, for example, 5 or 10 years. Historically, a well-diversified investment mix has been such that after an extended period of years, average annual returns tend to be positive. It is short-term volatility that is more of a problem. If the AIR selected is sufficiently low and if asset class performance is somewhat in line with historical averages, the probability that income payments fall below the floor tends to decrease with time. To the extent the historical mean return of the collection of subaccounts used exceeds the AIR, this may result in an upward drift in income, periodically accelerated or tempered by volatility.

Nonetheless, to guarantee program solvency, the insurer issuing the IVA may be on the hook to provide any additional funds needed as a result of the floor benefit guarantee—additional funds that are never needed with a "traditional" IVA.

The most common floor benefit approaches today call on the insurer to make up all shortfalls whenever benefit payments would otherwise have fallen below the floor level, with no advances by the annuitant against future benefit payments.

Such an approach to payout floors—and to other embedded option guarantees—increases reliance by annuitants on the financial strength and claims-paying ability of the issuing insurer, possibly for many decades into the future. With a traditional IVA, if mortality experience were close to historic norms or at least within any deviations from historic norms for which the insurer's immediate annuity pricing provided, there would always be adequate funds in the pool with no need for an annuitant to expect anything beyond administration from the insurer.

With inclusion of floor benefits, annuitants now must count on the insurer's ability to chip in additional funds when needed—perhaps for many decades into the future. Such a design concept changes the nature of a variable annuity from being one of the least risky products from an insurance company's perspective, because previously investment risk was borne by annuitants in the form of fluctuating benefits, to one of the most risky, because the insurer now guarantees subaccount performance above a certain level—something over which it has little or no control.

The insurer has some devices to mitigate the risk. It can impose asset allocation requirements that call for diversification among asset classes, especially ones that have low or negative correlations in performance. It can eliminate nondiversified subaccounts like sector funds from any program offering floor benefits.

Regardless of approach, an insurer offering such a floor benefit is offering something of increased value. There is a price tag associated with such a benefit to be borne by the insurer, by the annuitant, or by both.

Reinsuring the floor benefit guarantee with one or more other insurance companies for a price might be possible, although the nondiversifiable nature of the guarantee makes this approach less viable. Purchasing financial instruments to offset the fund performance guarantees the insurer has effectively embedded in its product is another approach.

A "derivative" is one financial instrument that derives its value from the performance of another. A "put option" is one type of derivative. We next turn our attention to financial *options,* since these shed light on the quantitative nature of the floor benefit provided to annuitants (the liabilities) and on the comparable financial instruments (the assets) that if purchased help the insurer move to a more risk-neutral position.

AN INTRODUCTORY LESSON ON OPTIONS

An *option* is the right—but not the obligation—to buy or to sell a particular *underlying security* at a certain price for a limited period of time. A *call option* gives the owner the right to buy the underlying security. A *put option* gives the owner the right to sell the underlying security. The price at which the underlying security may be bought or sold is called the *exercise price* or *strike price*. The end of the limited period of time that a stock option affords its holder the right to buy or to sell is the *expiration date.*

Four characteristics uniquely describe an option contract:

1. Type (put or call).
2. Name of underlying security.
3. Expiration date.
4. Strike price.

For example, an "ABC June 50 call" is an option to buy (a call) 100 shares (typically) of ABC Corporation common stock (the underlying security) for $50 per share (strike price) before its June expiration date. Listed option exchanges have standardized the *terms* of option contracts, which include all four of the descriptive specifications.

An option is a security by itself. It is a *derivative* security. Because the option is linked to an underlying security, its value at any time *derives* from, among other things, the fluctuating price of the underlying security.

Call Options

A call option is said to be *in-the-money* if the price of the underlying security is above the strike price of the option. For example, if ABC stock is trading at $53 per share, the "ABC June 50 call" option is in-the-money. This is because the call option holder has the right to buy ABC stock, currently trading in the open market at $53 per share, for $50 per share.

Conversely, a call option is said to be *out-of-the-money* if the underlying security is trading below the strike price of the option. For example, if ABC stock is trading at $47 per share, the "ABC June 50 call" option is out-of-the-money.

The *intrinsic value* of a call option is the amount by which the price of the underlying security exceeds the strike price. If ABC stock is currently trading at $53, the "ABC June 50 call" option has an intrinsic value of $3 per share.

For an out-of-the-money call option, one where the underlying security trades below the strike price of the option, the intrinsic value is zero. If ABC stock trades at $47 per share, the intrinsic value of an "ABC June 50 call" option is zero.

The price for which an option sells is called the *premium*. The premium is composed of two elements, *intrinsic value* and *time value*:

$$\text{Option Premium} = \text{Intrinsic Value} + \text{Time Value}$$

For example, suppose ABC common stock is trading at $53 and the "ABC June 50 call" option sells for $5. The total price of the option, the *option premium*, is $5. The amount the option is in-the-money, its intrinsic value, is $3 ($53 – $50). The time value is $2 ($5 – $3).

If the option is out-of-the-money, then its intrinsic value is zero. The option premium then consists solely of *time value*.

If an option trades for exactly its intrinsic value, the option is said to be trading *at parity* with the underlying security. For example, if ABC common stock is trading at $53 and the "ABC June 50 call" option sells for $3, the call option is at parity. If ABC common stock is trading at $53 and the "ABC June 50 call" option sells for $4, the call option is said to be one point over parity.

An option is a "wasting asset" in that the time value (also known as time value premium or time premium) decays over time, approaching zero as the expiration date nears. The pattern over which time value declines is known as time value premium decay. An option may expire worthless, in which case the option seller simply pockets the premium.

An *opening transaction* is the initial transaction, which can be a buy or a sell of an option. An opening transaction increases a position in the customer's account. A *closing transaction* reduces a position in the customer's account. It is possible to have the opening transaction be a buy of an option and the closing transaction be a sell. It is equally permissible for the opening transaction to be the sell of an option and the closing transaction the buy.

Open interest is the number of opening transactions for which no related closing transaction has yet occurred. Every opening transaction adds to the open interest by the number of option contracts involved, for example, 10 "ABC June 50 call" options. Every closing transaction decreases the open interest. Open interest is an indicator of liquidity of the option. A large open interest suggests little difficulty in making large trades.

A person who buys an option as the opening transaction is the *holder*. A person who sells an option as the opening transaction is the *writer*. The holder is said to be *long* the option contract. The writer is said to be *short* the option contract.

Unlike earlier times when there was a direct link between the writer of an option and the buyer of an option, this is no longer true in the listed option market. Today, the Options Clearing Corporation issues all options using standardized contracts. This allows for the secondary markets that now exist.

The owner (or holder) of an option may sell the option in a listed option market before expiration. The owner may invoke her right to *exercise* the option before expiration,[6] in which case the underlying security is traded at the exercise price. Whenever a holder exercises an option, someone who sold such an option (an option writer) is assigned the obligation to fulfill the terms of the option contract. If a call holder exercises the right to buy the underlying security at the strike price, a call writer is assigned the obligation to sell.

Put Options

A put option gives its holder the right—but not the obligation—to sell (put) shares of the underlying security to the writer at the exercise price before the expiration date.

For example, an "ABC June 50 put" is an option to sell (a put) 100 shares (typically) of ABC Corporation common stock (the underlying security) for $50 per share (strike price) before its June expiration date.

A put option is said to be *in-the-money* if the price of the underlying security is below the strike price of the option. For example, if ABC stock is trading at $46 per share, the "ABC June 50 put" option is in-the-money. This is because the put option holder has the right to sell ABC stock, currently trading in the open market at $46 per share, for $50 per share.

Conversely, a put option is said to be *out-of-the-money* if the underlying security is trading above the strike price of the option. For example, if

ABC stock is trading at $54 per share, the "ABC June 50 put" option is out-of-the-money.

The *intrinsic value* of a put option is the amount by which the strike price exceeds the price of the underlying security. If ABC stock is currently trading at $46, the "ABC June 50 put" option has an intrinsic value of $4 per share.

For an out-of-the-money put option, one where the underlying security trades above the strike price of the option, the intrinsic value is zero. If ABC stock trades at $54 per share, the intrinsic value of an "ABC June 50 put" option is zero.

Again, the price for which an option sells is called the *premium*, composed of the two elements *intrinsic value* and *time value:*

$$\text{Option Premium} = \text{Intrinsic Value} + \text{Time Value}$$

For example, suppose ABC common stock is trading at $46 and the "ABC June 50 put" option sells for $5. The total price of the option, the *option premium*, is $5. The amount the option is in-the-money, its intrinsic value, is $4 ($50 − $46). The time value is $1 ($5 − $4).

If the option is out-of-the-money, then its intrinsic value is zero. The option premium then consists entirely of *time value*.

The buyer of the option pays the seller the premium. If the financial instrument underlying the put option never falls below the "strike price," the seller simply pockets the premium and nothing further happens. This is because if the owner of the put option actually owns the underlying security (the 100 shares of ABC stock), she could sell it in the open market for more than the strike price, so there is no reason to "put" the underlying security to the put option seller for only the strike price.

Option Price

Factors influencing the price of an option include:

1. Price of the underlying security.
2. Strike price of the option.
3. Time remaining until option expiration.
4. Volatility of the underlying security.
5. Current risk-free interest rate (e.g., for Treasury bills).
6. Dividend rate, if the underlying security is a stock.

The first four factors tend to determine in major part the price of an option.

Call Option Price Curve

The call option price curve in Figure 18.2 graphically portrays the price of a stock option relative to (i.e., as a function of) various prices of the underlying security.

The horizontal axis shows the price of the underlying security, here ABC common stock. The vertical axis shows the price of the option, here the "ABC June 50 call" option.

The solid black "hockey stick" line that runs along the horizontal axis until it reaches the strike price and then bends upward at a 45 degree angle represents *intrinsic value*. When the call option is out-of-the-money or the underlying security price is equal to the option strike price, intrinsic value is zero. As the price of ABC common stock increases above the strike price, the intrinsic value goes up dollar for dollar. Since a call is typically worth at least its intrinsic value, this solid black line indicates the lower bound for the worth of the call option.

A call option with time left before the expiration date typically has some time value in addition to its intrinsic value. As a result, the price of the option generally exceeds its intrinsic value. The call option price curve with some time remaining until expiration resembles the curved line in Figure 18.2. The difference between the option price and the intrinsic value at any point on the curve is the time value.

Time value is greatest when the stock price is at the option strike price. When the stock price is far below or far above the option strike price, the option value asymptotically approaches its intrinsic value. The result is a concave upward option value curve.

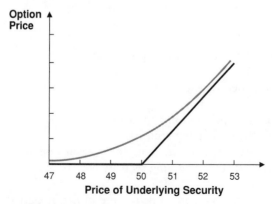

FIGURE 18.2   Call Option Price Curve

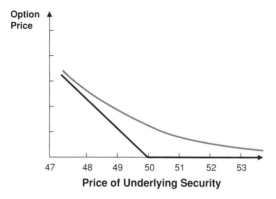

FIGURE 18.3   Put Option Price Curve

Put Option Price Curve

The put option price curve in Figure 18.3 graphically portrays the price of an option relative to various prices of the underlying security.

The horizontal axis shows the price of the underlying security, here ABC common stock. The vertical axis shows the price of the option, here the "ABC June 50 put" option.

The solid black line that bends at the strike price again represents intrinsic value. When the put option is out-of-the-money or the underlying security price is equal to the option strike price, intrinsic value is zero. As the price of ABC common stock decreases below the strike price, the intrinsic value goes up dollar for dollar. Since a put is typically worth at least its intrinsic value, this solid black line indicates the lower bound for the worth of the put option.

A put option with time left before expiration usually has some time value in addition to intrinsic value. As a result, the price of the option generally exceeds its intrinsic value. The put option price curve with some time remaining until expiration resembles the curved line in Figure 18.3. The difference between the option price and the intrinsic value at any point on the curve is the time value.

Again, time value is greatest when the stock price is at the option strike price. When the stock price is far below or far above the option strike price, the option value asymptotically approaches its intrinsic value.

Time to Expiration

Figure 18.4 illustrates the effect of the time left until the option expiration date on the price of the option. As the expiration date gets closer and closer,

FIGURE 18.4   Time to Expiration Affects Option Value

the option price curve draws nearer and nearer to the intrinsic value line. At the option expiration date—when no time and, hence, no time value remain—option price equals intrinsic value.

Maximum Option Value

While the black intrinsic value line in Figure 18.5 represents the *minimum* value of the option, the dotted line represents the *maximum* value of the

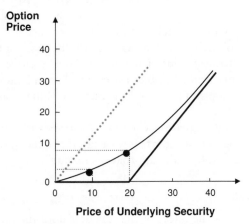

FIGURE 18.5   Maximum Option Value

option. (Note here that the scale on both axes is identical.) This is because the option cannot be worth more than the stock. For example, if the stock trades at $20 per share, no investor would pay $25 for a call option granting him the right to buy the stock at $20. He could just buy the stock for $20 right now.

Also, because the option value curve is concave upward and because it lies below the dotted 45 degree line, we observe that the option will be more volatile than the stock. This is because a given percentage change in the stock price (the "run" across the horizontal axis) produces a larger percentage change in the option price (the "rise" up the vertical axis).

Think of it this way: If the curve were instead a straight line with slope ¼, then a 100% increase in relative stock price (e.g., from $10 to $20) would always produce a 100% increase in relative option price (e.g., from $2.50 to $5). But because the curve is concave upward, the slope is always increasing as the stock price increases. So if the slope were ¼ when the stock price is $10, then it might be ⅜ when the stock price is $20. As a result, a 100% increase in relative stock price (from $10 to $20) produces a 200% increase in relative option price (from $2.50 to $7.50).

The two points on the option price curve in Figure 18.5 illustrate this example. (This assumes time to expiration is held constant; that is, the move in stock price didn't take so long that the option curve shifted materially downward.)

Time Value Premium Decay

The rate of decay of the time value component of option price is not linear (see Figure 18.6). The portion of the option price attributable to time value

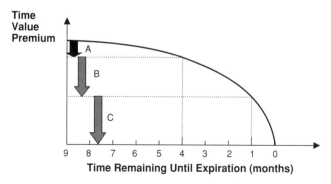

FIGURE 18.6   Time Value Premium Decay (assumes stock price remains constant)

decays more rapidly as it nears the option expiration date. Note the relatively small time value premium decay between nine months to expiration and four months to expiration (arrow A), the relatively larger (per unit of time) decay between four months and one month (arrow B), and the even larger decay during the final month to expiration (arrow C).

Volatility

The more volatile the price of the underlying security, the higher is the price of the option. This is reasonable, since if the underlying security can rise in price a great deal in a short time, buyers of call options are willing to pay a greater price for those options.

Risk-Free Interest Rate

The rate on short-term risk-free instruments such as U.S. Treasury bills plays a minor role in option price determination. Higher interest rates imply higher option prices. Lower risk-free interest rates imply lower option prices.

Dividend Rate

If the underlying security happens to be a stock that pays dividends, this will have a minor impact on option price. Barring all other factors, stock price will decrease by the amount of the dividend to be paid as the stock crosses the point where it is traded inclusive of the upcoming dividend to where it is traded exclusive of the dividend. The bigger the dividend, the bigger is the drop in stock price, all other factors held constant.

As a result, call option premiums will be lower on dividend-paying stocks. The larger the dividend, the lower is the price of the call option.

Totality of Influences Determines Option Price

The six option price factors listed earlier are those that tend to be found in option pricing formulas. Factors more challenging to quantify—such as investor sentiment—also influence actual marketplace option prices, even if they are absent in option prices based on "theoretically correct" mathematical option pricing formulas. Strong bull or bear markets can have a pronounced impact on investor emotions, which may cause option prices—at least temporarily—to deviate from prices more objectively determined by these six factors.

It is important to remember that it is the entire interplay among factors that results in the option price. For example, even though a rise in stock price might suggest that a call option value should have increased, the passage of time may result in a more-than-offsetting time value premium decay. The call option price may have declined even though the price of the underlying security went up.

Sale of an Uncovered Put

There are numerous option strategies involving purchases and sales of call options, put options, and combinations of both.[7] Because of its importance in immediate variable annuity payout floors, one such strategy—the sale of an uncovered put option—is briefly described here. "Uncovered" or "naked" simply means that the seller of the put option does not own the underlying security.

The writer (seller) of a put option obligates himself to buy the underlying security at the strike price. For example, the writer of an "ABC June 50 put" option obligates himself to buy 100 shares of ABC common stock at $50 per share if a holder (buyer) of that same option exercises his right to sell the stock at the strike price and the writer happens to be the one assigned the obligation to fulfill the terms of the option contract.

The writer receives the put option premium. If ABC stock stays at or above $50 per share, the option holder will not exercise the option since if he can sell ABC stock in the open market at a higher price, he will not choose to exercise the option and sell the stock for only $50 per share. In this instance—or in any instance in which the put writer is not assigned the obligation to fulfill the terms of the option contract—the maximum profit the put writer can realize equals the option premium initially received.

The option writer has a large downside risk, since ABC stock could fall well below $50 per share. Theoretically, it could go to $0 per share.

For example, suppose ABC stock is at $50 per share and a nine-month put option with a strike price of $50 trades for $4. The option writer sells one put option, representing 100 shares, and receives the $400 premium (100 shares × $4). This is his maximum potential profit. (We will ignore commissions and taxes.)

The profit graph in Figure 18.7 for writing an uncovered put option shows the stock price at expiration as the abscissa (horizontal axis coordinate) and the profit or loss from the sale of the put option at expiration as the ordinate (vertical axis coordinate). Selected points on that graph appear in Table 18.1.

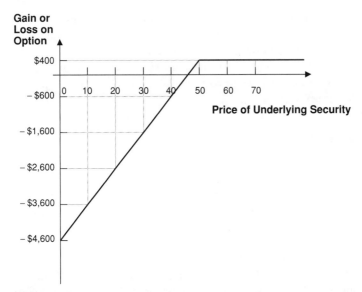

FIGURE 18.7 Payoff Diagram at Expiration for Sale of Uncovered Put Option

The put option writer is likely bullish or neutral on the underlying stock. If the stock moves up or stays the same, the put option writer will make a profit equal to the option premium. If the stock moves down slightly (staying above $46), the put option writer will still make a profit, albeit a smaller one. If the stock moves down to $46, the break-even point, the put writer

TABLE 18.1 Profit from Sale of Uncovered Put Option

ABC Stock Price at Expiration	Put Option Price at Expiration	Put Sale Profit or Loss
0	50	−4,600
10	40	−3,600
20	30	−2,600
30	20	−1,600
40	10	−600
50	0	+400
60	0	+400
70	0	+400

realizes neither a profit nor a loss. If the stock moves down substantially, the put option writer is exposed to large losses.

Pricing of Options

Since the quantifiable factors that affect the price of an option—underlying security price, strike price, time to expiration, volatility, risk-free interest rate, and dividend rate—are known, it is logical to ask whether a mathematical formula can be derived to ascertain the "correct" or "fair" value of the option. The answer is "yes."

While behavioral factors such as investor sentiment may cause actual marketplace prices for options to differ from such mathematically determined fair values, such objectively derived values provide a consistent basis against which to compare actual market prices—a comparison that in itself may be informational as an indicator of market sentiment.

The foundation for option pricing—and indeed for modern corporate finance itself—begins with a 1958 paper by Franco Modigliani and Merton H. Miller.[8] They were exemplars, who first declared the absence of arbitrage opportunity in equilibrium. The principle: If two or more apparently different financial instruments produce the same cash flows in all states of nature, then they must have identical present values. While Modigliani and Miller's work deduced that in a frictionless framework the value of a firm does not depend on capital structure,[9] it was their absence-of-arbitrage-opportunity approach that set the stage for Fischer Black and Myron Scholes to apply the notion to option pricing.

Fischer Black of the University of Chicago and Myron Scholes of the Massachusetts Institute of Technology describe a clever approach to option valuation in their seminal paper published in 1973 in the *Journal of Political Economy* titled "The Pricing of Options and Corporate Liabilities." Their work was superior to that of predecessors in that their formula is complete, being a closed form solution involving no arbitrary parameters. The underlying premise for their research is described in the first two sentences of the abstract of the paper: "If options are correctly priced in the market, it should not be possible to make sure profits by creating portfolios of long and short positions in options and their underlying stocks. Using this principle, a theoretical valuation formula for options is derived."[10]

It is possible to create a "hedged" position that consists of a long position in the stock and a short position in the option. The value of the hedged position will *not* depend on the price of the stock. Because of this, the return on the hedged position is certain. Call this certain rate of return *r*.

It is also true that the risk in the hedged position is zero. Since (1) the return on a riskless position is the risk-free rate of return and (2) the return on the hedged position is certain and riskless, the expected return on the fully hedged position, r, must be the short-term risk-free rate.

If the return were not the short-term risk-free rate, speculators would seek to profit by borrowing large amounts of money to create such riskless hedged positions, which would in the process force returns down to the short-term risk-free rate.

Armed with this approach, one can derive a mathematical formula for the value of an option. Such a derivation follows. While the mathematics of the formula is technical, the rationale underlying formula development is straightforward. This digression to provide the reader with a basic understanding of options and their characteristics will greatly aid comprehension of their role in immediate variable annuity product development.

Derivation of the Black-Scholes Option Formula[11]

Let $w(x, t)$ be the value of the option as a function of the stock price x and time t. The number of options that must be sold short against one share of stock long is $1/w_1(x,t)$. The subscript refers to the partial derivative of $w(x,t)$ with respect to its first argument.

For example, suppose that in Figure 18.8 the stock price starts at $10, so that the option price starts at $2. Assume the slope of the tangent line at

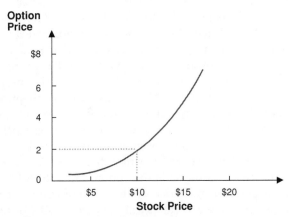

FIGURE 18.8 Relation between Option Value and Stock Price

that point is ¼. This means the hedged position is created by buying one share of stock and selling four options short. One share of stock costs $10, and the sale of four options brings in $8; so the equity in the position is $2.

For the moment, let's assume we fail to adjust the number of options creating the hedge as the stock price changes because this will illustrate an important point. Suppose the stock goes from $10 to $15 and the four options go from a total of $8 to $13.50. When the stock goes up $5, the equity decreases from $2 to $1.50. (We own one share of stock at $15, and we're short four options totaling $13.50, creating equity of $1.50.)

Suppose the stock goes down from $10 to $5 and the four options go from a total of $8 to $3.50. When the stock goes down $5, the equity decreases from $2 to $1.50. (We own one share of stock at $5, and we're short four options totaling $3.50, creating equity of $1.50.)

The equity goes from $2 to $1.50 when the stock changes by $5 in either direction. That is, there is a $0.50 decline in equity for a $5 change in stock price in either direction.

This illustrates a point made earlier: The value of the hedged position will *not* depend on the price of the stock. The value of the hedged position is the same with the stock at $5 or at $15.

If we adjust the hedge continuously so that we're short the right number of options $1/w_1(x,t)$ regardless of where the stock price x is, then the risk in the hedged position is zero. (Such a portfolio the value of which is insensitive to changes in stock price is called "delta neutral.") Equity in the fully hedged position is *invariant* with respect to stock price.

Since the hedged position consists of one share of stock at price x long and $1/w_1$ options short, the value of equity in the position is

$$x - w/w_1 \qquad (18.4)$$

The change in equity value over a short interval Δt is

$$\Delta x - \Delta w/w_1 \qquad (18.5)$$

If the short position is changed continuously, then Δw, which is $w(x + \Delta x, t + \Delta t) - w(x,t)$, can be expanded using stochastic calculus as follows:

$$\Delta w = w_1 \Delta x + \tfrac{1}{2} w_{11} v^2 x^2 \Delta t + w_2 \Delta t \qquad (18.6)$$

where v^2 is the variance rate of the return on the stock, which is the limit—as the size of the measurement interval goes to zero—of the variance of the return over that interval divided by the length of the interval.

Substituting equation (18.6) into equation (18.5), the change in equity value of the hedged position is:

$$- (\tfrac{1}{2}w_{11}v^2x^2 + w_2)\, \Delta t / w_1 \tag{18.7}$$

Since the return on equity in the hedged position is certain, it must equal the rate of return r times the elapsed time Δt. Thus, the change in the value of the equity given by equation (18.7) must equal the value of the equity given by equation (18.4) times $r\Delta t$:

$$- (\tfrac{1}{2}w_{11}v^2x^2 + w_2)\, \Delta t / w_1 = (x - w/w_1)\, r\, \Delta t \tag{18.8}$$

Simplifying and rearranging, we arrive at the following differential equation for the value of the option:

$$w_2 = rw - rxw_1 - \tfrac{1}{2}v^2x^2w_{11} \tag{18.9}$$

If t^* is the expiration date of the option and c is the strike price, we know

$$w(x,t^*) = x - c, \qquad \text{where } x \geq c$$

and

$$w(x,t^*) = 0, \qquad \text{where } x < c \tag{BC 1}$$

Only one formula satisfies differential equation (18.9) subject to boundary condition (BC 1). Therefore, it must be the option valuation formula.

To solve differential equation (18.9), we make the following substitution relating a new function y to the existing function w:

$$w(x,t) = e^{r(t - t^*)}\, y\, \{(2/v^2)\,(r - \tfrac{1}{2}v^2)\, [\ln x/c - (r - \tfrac{1}{2}v^2)(t - t^*)]$$
$$- (2/v^2)(r - \tfrac{1}{2}v^2)^2\,(t - t^*)\} \tag{18.10}$$

Making this substitution, the differential equation becomes

$$y_2 = y_{11} \tag{18.11}$$

and the boundary condition becomes

$$y(u,0) = 0, \qquad \text{where } u < 0 \tag{BC 2}$$

and

$$y(u,0) = c\left[e^{u(\tfrac{1}{2}v^2)/(r - \tfrac{1}{2}v^2)} - 1 \right], \qquad \text{where } u \geq 0$$

This differential equation is the heat-transfer equation of physics, the solution of which is

$$y(u,s) = 1/\sqrt{2\pi} \int_{-u/\sqrt{2}s}^{\infty} c \left[e^{\left(u+q\sqrt{2}s\right)\left(\frac{1}{2}v^2\right)\left(r-\frac{1}{2}v^2\right)} - 1 \right] e^{-q^2/2} dq \qquad (18.12)$$

Substituting from equation (18.12) into equation (18.10) and simplifying produces

$$w(x,t) = xN(d_1) - ce^{r(t-t^*)}N(d_2) \qquad (18.13)$$

where $\quad d_1 = \dfrac{\ln x / c + (r + \frac{1}{2}v^2)(t^* - t)}{v\sqrt{t^* - t}}$

$$d_2 = \dfrac{\ln x / c + (r - \frac{1}{2}v^2)(t^* - t)}{v\sqrt{t^* - t}}$$

and N is the cumulative normal density function.

Recall from the beginning of this derivation of the Black-Scholes formula that when $w(x,t)$ is the value of the option as a function of stock price x and time t, the number of options that must be sold short against one share of stock to create a hedged position is $1/w_1(x,t)$. From equation (18.13), we see that $w_1(x,t) = N(d_1)$. Because the delta of a call option reflects the sensitivity (partial derivative) of the call option price w with respect to the underlying stock price x, the delta of the call option, $w_1(x, t)$, equals $N(d_1)$.

Black and Scholes state the conditions underlying their derivation of the option formula, which include that the short-term interest rate is constant, the variance rate of return on the stock is constant, distribution of stock price is lognormal, the stock pays no dividends, there are no transaction costs, and the option can only be exercised at maturity. They also show an alternative derivation of the same formula.

A normal distribution (bell-shaped curve) for stock prices would be inappropriate, since that would allow for negative stock prices. A lognormal distribution allows stock prices in the interval $(0, \infty)$.

Black and Scholes performed empirical studies comparing actual call option prices to those predicted by the formula. They found that option buyers pay prices higher than predicted by the formula; but they also found that option writers receive prices in line with those predicted by the formula, suggesting that option market transaction costs are effectively borne by option buyers.

Other option valuation formulas followed this important one. Some use empirical distributions rather than the lognormal distribution, since Black-Scholes model critics claim the lognormal distribution tends to overprice in-the-money calls and underprice out-of-the-money calls.

Because stock volatility tends to change over time, because basing volatility on an *annual* standard deviation encompasses too long a period of time, and because the option pricing model is so sensitive to volatility, accurately computing volatility is important. One can therefore adopt a different approach: Assume the actual market price of an option is the "fair" price. Let this be a fixed value in the Black-Scholes equation, and solve for *volatility* as the unknown variable. The result is termed *implied volatility*.

Once the *implied volatility* has been calculated, it can be used in the Black-Scholes model or in other option pricing models as the volatility value. The theoretical value of each option (e.g., different strike prices, expiration dates) can be calculated and compared to actual option price. The difference is the amount by which the option is overpriced or underpriced compared to other options on the same stock.

Black and Scholes explain that "since almost all corporate liabilities can be viewed as a combination of options, the formula and the analysis that led to it are also applicable to corporate liabilities such as common stock, corporate bonds, and warrants."

If the prices of a default-free bond and the securities underlying a derivative are known and if a combination of them replicates the payoffs provided by the derivative, then the market price of the derivative should be the same as the price of the combination of the default-free bond and underlying securities. This fundamental technique is known as the "no-arbitrage" pricing concept, where *arbitrage* is defined as the possibility of making a trading gain with no chance of loss. The "law of one price" says that the price of the derivative must equal the price of the replicating basket of securities.

By owning stock and selling an appropriate number of call options against that stock—adjusted continuously as the stock price moves—a risk-free position can be established. The return on this hedged portfolio must equal the risk-free rate of return, otherwise an arbitrage opportunity would exist. Using stochastic calculus and differential equations, a formula is derived mathematically proving what the theoretical value of the options must be.

Following the development of the model for pricing European call options on assets that do not pay dividends by Fischer Black and Myron Scholes in 1973, numerous advancements in option pricing models occurred.

One particularly noteworthy development was proposed in 1979 by John C. Cox, Stephen A. Ross, and Mark Rubinstein, where a discrete-time binomial model values options, relying on the fundamental economic principles of option pricing by arbitrage methods, similar to the celebrated Black-Scholes model.[12] The method proposed by Cox, Ross, and Rubinstein became popular due to its simplicity and ease of implementation. This model inspired further development of and greater use of lattice (tree) methods for valuing derivatives.

The foregoing background in options is helpful in understanding the nature of the risks that insurance companies assume when they embed options, such as guaranteed payout annuity floors, in immediate variable annuities.

For example, if an insurer guarantees that at no time during the first five years after IVA contract issue will payments be less than 85% of the initial payment, then it has clearly issued a series of options to the contract owner—assuming that the insurer is truly on the hook for this promise and that any shortfalls in payments that would otherwise occur are not simply advanced from the annuitant's own future benefit payments, thereby reducing them.

Rather than a single stock being the underlying security, the pool of assets collectively contained in the subaccounts chosen to determine annuity benefit payment levels represents the underlying security. If only a single subaccount representing a stock index fund were used, this would greatly facilitate hedging. Typically, however, several subaccounts—perhaps none of which are index funds—representing multiple asset classes are used. The ability to reallocate among subaccounts on an ad hoc basis further challenges implementation of an effective hedging program. Reallocation among subaccounts through a regular program of rebalancing improves the situation somewhat, since the relative proportions of assets for each asset class are more determinable.

Insurers offering a GPAF benefit could require use of one or more "model asset portfolios" as a qualifying eligibility condition for GPAF benefit participation. The constituency of the model portfolios would be what stochastic modeling demonstrates will minimize the frequency and the severity of claims, based on the means, volatilities, and correlations of asset classes employed and recognizing the regularly scheduled benefit disbursements from the asset portfolio. (For insurers offering variable annuity (VA) "living benefits" during the accumulation phase as well as the liquidation phase, to the extent the optimal model asset portfolios differ when funds are simply left to accumulate versus when they are regularly piecewise liquidated, insurers may wish to devise some middle-ground model portfolios so that the same model portfolios can be used in both instances, to simplify the marketing story.)

Alternatively, a stand-alone subaccount invested in a similar mixture of assets could be used for those annuitants desirous of a GPAF benefit. This could be a new subaccount, or it could be a "fund of funds" subaccount that simply invests in specific proportions in other available funds already within the product.

While the insurer has issued an option, it (at least today) is unable to purchase an offsetting option and thereby place itself in a risk-neutral position. As a result, while a "fair" price of the option can be calculated, the actual "claim" an insurer may need to pay could greatly exceed the price of the option. Recall the earlier example involving the sale of a put option where $400 in option premium was collected but losses of several thousand dollars were possible.

As a result, it would be dangerous for an insurer to presume that if it collects the fair price of the options it embeds in its IVA products over a sufficiently long time that "premiums" and "claims" will be in balance. It is not acceptable for any insurer to be "temporarily insolvent," anticipating that it will make up the difference in the future through VA living benefit premium collections during better fund performance times. The insurer must stay solvent at all points in time.

Large early claims could well exceed premiums, so additional security in the nature of reserves and risk-based capital is necessary. Again, the tying up of this capital now unavailable for other corporate projects will require payment of "rent," to be paid from IVA product charges.

Writers of VA "living benefits" need to be able to handle the low-frequency, high-severity fund performance events. Equivalently stated, the writers need to focus particularly strongly on the variance of fund performance returns and not just the averages.

Extreme value theory[13] is concerned with extreme events such as the low-frequency, high-severity claims against insurance companies that can result from VA living benefits, including GPAFs. When one looks at the range of financial results across the domain of feasible economic scenarios, the tails of such distributions can reflect highly severe monetary claims levels. Unless some form of stop-loss protection is put in place, significantly large claims and possibly ultimate ruin of the insurers can result.

A brief, highly generalized look at the *surplus process*, which is one aspect of the field of risk theory, follows. The connection with GPAF benefits is clear: An extreme event resulting in ongoing large claims—in this case, the payment of variable income annuity benefits at a floor level higher than would be payable absent such floor for an extended period of time—can draw down surplus and potentially lead to insurance company ruin.

Surplus Process

Individual risk models consider claims produced by an individual policy. Summing over all such policies in the portfolio under observation produces aggregate claims.

Collective risk models consider a random process that generates claims for the portfolio of policies under observation. The focus is on the process governing the whole portfolio rather than on the individual policies that comprise it. The surplus process, therefore, falls within the purview of collective risk models.

The classic surplus model includes an aggregate claims process for a portfolio of insurance contracts given by

$$S(t) = \sum_{i=1}^{N} Y_i$$

where $t \geq 0$

$\{Y_i\}$ denotes independent, identically distributed random variables with cumulative distribution function F_Y that represent claim amounts

$E[Y_i] = \mu$

$N = N(t)$ is the number of claims produced by the portfolio of policies within a given time period $t \geq 0$

Thus, Y_1 denotes the amount of the first claim, Y_2 the amount of the second claim, and so forth; $S(t)$ represents aggregate claims produced by the portfolio up to time t; and $N(t)$ represents the number of claims up to time t.

Individual claim amounts $Y_1, Y_2, \ldots, Y_N$ are random variables. They measure the severity of claims. A common distribution for these individual claim amounts (e.g., normal, gamma) is assumed. Similarly, a distribution for the number of claims N (e.g., Poisson, negative binomial) must be selected for modeling. (When a Poisson distribution is chosen for N, then S has a compound Poisson distribution. When a negative binomial distribution is chosen for N, then S has a compound negative binomial distribution.)

Define *surplus* of an insurer as the excess of an initial fund plus premium collected over claims paid. Note that this is an expedient mathematical definition but not an accounting definition of surplus. Let $U(t)$ denote the surplus of the insurer at time $t \geq 0$.

Assume premiums are received continuously at a constant rate $c = (1 + \theta) \cdot E[Y_i] = (1 + \theta) \mu$, with $c > 0$. The insurer wishes to collect a premium greater than the expected claim to allow for some degree of claim deviation from expectations. In addition to the expected claim amount

$E[Y_i]$, it charges an extra amount $\theta \cdot E[Y_i]$, called the *security loading*; θ is called the *relative security loading*. By such a uniform loading procedure, each individual policyholder pays a premium bearing the same proportion to his expected claim.

Let u represent the initial surplus at time 0. The *surplus process* that tracks the variations in the amount of surplus of an insurer over time can be defined as

$$U(t) = u + ct - S(t) \tag{18.14}$$

for $t \geq 0$. Should surplus $U(t)$ become negative, the point at which this first happens is referred to as *ruin* having occurred.

Define $T = \min \{t: t \geq 0 \text{ and } U(t) < 0\}$ as the time when ruin occurs, understanding that it may never occur.

Let the probability of ruin ψ, which is a function of the initial surplus u, be defined over a finite time horizon (which is of most interest to insurers) by

$$\psi(u) = P\{T \leq t\}$$

for $0 < t < \infty$. Similarly, let the probability of ruin over an infinite time horizon be defined by

$$\psi(u) = P\{T \leq \infty\}$$

One measure of the riskiness of the portfolio of policies is ψ; $U(t)$, showing the degree to which surplus is negative at the time of ruin, is also of interest.

As might be intuitively expected, it is the case that ultimate ruin is certain—$\psi(u) = 1$—when θ tends to 0 and when θ is less than 0. When the relative security loading is inadequate to handle deviations, ruin at some point occurs.

Other aspects of the surplus process are of interest. For example, insurers are interested in the probability that surplus will ever fall below the initial level u. Also of interest are the probabilities of how far below the initial level surplus will fall the first time this occurs.

One other measure of riskiness of the portfolio of policies is the *stop-loss premium*. Consider an insurance policy where claim payments do not start until the loss exceeds a deductible amount d. Assume all losses above the deductible amount are paid under the terms of the policy.

If loss is a random variable denoted by X, then the insurance claim payable is defined by

$$I_d(x) = 0, \qquad \text{for } x \le d$$

and

$$I_d(x) = x - d, \qquad \text{for } x > d$$

"Stop-loss" coverage or "excess of loss" coverage are names given to this type of policy. "Stop-loss" coverage applies to a collection of insurance risks (aggregate claims), while "excess of loss" coverage applies to individual claims. Letting $f(x)$ represent the probability density function[14] associated with the random variable X, expected claims are given by

$$\text{Expected Claims} = \int_d^\infty (x - d)\, f(x)\, dx$$

Define *maximal aggregate loss* L (that is, the maximal excess of aggregate claims paid over premiums received) as

$$L = \max_{t \ge 0} \{S(t) - ct\}$$

Because at time $t = 0$, we have $S(t) - ct = 0$, it is true that $L \ge 0$.

To derive the distribution function of the random variable L, we look at the complement of the probability of ruin, $1 - \psi(u)$. Note that for $u \ge 0$:

$$\begin{aligned}
1 - \psi(u) &= P\{U(t) \ge 0 \text{ for all } t\} \\
&= P\{u + ct - S(t) \ge 0 \text{ for all } t\} \\
&= P\{S(t) - ct \le u \text{ for all } t\} \\
&= P\{L \le u\}, \text{ for } u \ge 0
\end{aligned}$$

As a result, we see that $1 - \psi(u)$ represents the distribution function[15] F_L of the maximal aggregate loss L.

Note that the highly generalized mathematical model for surplus $U(t)$ shown in equation (18.14) is simplified. For example, it ignores interest (which would serve to increase surplus) and ignores expenses and dividends (which would serve to decrease surplus). Nonetheless, it still facilitates a conceptual understanding of surplus variation, an element of high interest to insurers offering variable annuity living benefits. These insurers must manage the impact of variable annuity living benefits on surplus variation by product design, derivative procurement, or other means.

Attachment of a GPAF changes the nature of an immediate variable annuity from the perspective of the insurer from a low-risk venture, where results of investment experience are passed through to annuitants in the form of fluctuating benefits, to a high-risk venture, where the insurer guarantees investment results at some level.

Black and Scholes noted that, barring friction in the system (such as transaction expenses), a risk-free investment should provide a risk-free rate of return, such as that available on default-free U.S. Treasuries (since the U.S. government always has the power to tax to raise the revenue to pay its debt). By owning common stock and by selling options that together with the stock create a risk-free portfolio that by definition must provide the risk-free rate of return, Black and Scholes were able to determine what the price of those options must be.

While the mathematics of their proof requires stochastic calculus and differential equations, the important point is that a credible option pricing methodology emerged. This provides insurance company actuaries developing products with embedded options such as immediate variable annuities with floor guarantees with a tool to price intelligently. This provides regulators establishing reserve and risk-based capital requirements for such products with a conceptual framework for setting these levels. (Similar requirements exist in the options market, where, for example, the writer of a naked call option must meet a margin requirement to ensure enough collateral to cover the eventuality of buying stock in the open market and immediately selling it at a lower strike price if assigned the obligation to sell.)

Too high a price, and the product feature is commercially unviable. Too low a reserve or risk-based capital requirement, and retirement benefits contractually promised to annuitants are at risk.

Still somewhat in its infancy, GPAF benefits pose certain issues:

- **Guarantees Inclusive of Contract Owners' Investment Timing Behavior** Reallocations among subaccounts by IVA contract owners can produce poor investment results attributable to poor market timing, triggering GPAF "claims"—even if subaccount investment experience might otherwise have been adequate to avoid any claims had the contract owner stuck to one specific mix of subaccounts.
- **Guarantees Inclusive of Contract Owners' Investment Risk Behavior** If GPAF benefits are present, they provide a safety net, allowing contract owners to shoot for the moon in subaccount selection—with large allocations to volatile, ultra-aggressive equity subaccounts—if no asset allocation requirements exist to qualify for GPAF benefit participation.
- **Effective Hedging Unavailability** The insurer may find an inability to lay off GPAF risk via hedging these lengthy (multidecade) contingent complex options with variable notional amounts spanning multiple asset

classes, perhaps none of which are index funds (which results in "basis risk"). Some equity subaccount investment objectives are sufficiently broad so as to allow the investment manager to shift from one style box to another, resulting in "style drift," which may reduce the effectiveness of any hedge. Because of the long-term nature of variable income annuities, lack of effective hedging and/or mispricing may lead to huge losses.

Suppose an immediate variable annuitant allocated 100% of her premium to a single common stock subaccount intended to mimic the Standard & Poor's (S&P) 500 index. If the subaccount performed too far below the AIR, the floor benefit level might be pierced and the insurer forced to make up the difference. Put options on the S&P 500 index are available. An insurer could purchase options with the right strike prices and thereby lay off its risk.

While derivative markets provide some opportunity for insurers to more safely offer floor benefit guarantees, any such transfer of risk currently is incomplete. "Basis risk" exists when investments in the stock fund underlying the variable annuity subaccount differ from the index tied to the derivative chosen to help hedge it.

Since these options expire within a reasonably short time period (e.g., one year) relative to the possibly multidecade duration of an immediate annuity payout, the insurer would need to buy a rolling series of such put options to protect itself against loss. Because option prices fluctuate due to a number of factors, including degree of market volatility, there is no guarantee that an insurer could purchase such an extended series of options for a price within its option budget.

Because annuity unit values of bond subaccounts can decrease as interest rates rise or as credit quality (real or perceived) of the bond issuers deteriorates, immediate variable annuity benefits can also decline due to bond subaccount performance. Immediate variable annuity floor benefit guarantee programs for which an insurer desires hedging also need to consider bonds (e.g., put options tied to interest rates).

Basis risk, multidecade period, fluctuating notional amounts, and multiple asset classes, the relative proportion of which can change at any time through customer reallocation, are some of the factors leading to effective hedging unavailability; that is, no perfect option is commercially available for an insurer to purchase to offset the complex option granted the policyholder. Such hedge imperfections that can result in a net liability much higher than projected are sometimes called "holes in the hedge."

■ **Risk-Increasing Transformation of Issuing Entity** A company offering GPAF benefits effectively transforms itself from an insurance company (which assumes diversifiable risks) into a derivatives dealer (which assumes nondiversifiable risks). If a common stock subaccount tanks for one annuitant, it tanks for all annuitants, resulting in greater concentration of risk with more and more annuitants.

■ **Hedging Expertise Required** Insurance companies that offer a GPAF benefit have written derivatives and are concerned with managing the risk in their portfolio of derivatives. This is analogous to hedging interest rate risk on their fixed annuity business through *immunization* concepts, such as the early ideas put forth by Redington.[16] Such a program to manage GPAF and other written derivatives is labeled "dynamic hedging," since the portfolio used to hedge the written derivatives is rebalanced in a dynamic way. Insurers need to have or procure expertise in managing the book of derivatives they write.

The pricing model used to accomplish the GPAF hedging has output values (prices) that are sensitive to the input values (assumptions). These sensitivities are called *risk statistics* (or in options jargon, "the Greeks"). The sensitivities are partial derivatives of the option price function with respect to price of the underlying asset, time, interest rate, and volatility. They include:

  ❑ Delta (Δ)—Sensitivity of derivative price to change in price of the underlying asset; hedging delta attempts to limit exposure to market movement.
  ❑ Gamma (Γ)—Sensitivity of delta to change in price of the underlying asset; hedging gamma attempts to limit exposure to market movement.
  ❑ Theta (Θ)—Sensitivity of derivative price with respect to time to expiration (time decay); hedging theta attempts to limit exposure as it changes with time.
  ❑ Rho (P)—Sensitivity to change in interest rate; hedging rho attempts to limit exposure to interest rate risk.
  ❑ Vega[17]—Sensitivity to change in volatility; hedging vega attempts to limit exposure to changes in volatility.

Delta hedging is first-order hedging. It is comparable to duration hedging against interest rate movement for fixed-income securities. Delta hedging may approximately protect against the changing value of the GPAF liability for small changes in the underlying index. If there are large changes in the underlying index between hedge adjustment dates, a delta-only hedge may prove inadequate because the delta of the liability may have changed significantly. An asset portfolio (underlying assets and derivative hedge instruments) with a delta that changes in parallel with the delta of the liability eliminates this mistracking. Such an asset portfolio is called *gamma-matched*. A delta- and gamma-matched portfolio provides a better hedge than a delta-only hedge, although gamma matching is more expensive than delta hedging.

- **Effective Reinsurance Unavailability** Precisely because the GPAF risk is nondiversifiable, reinsurers cannot offer effective risk relief by piling on ever-greater concentrations of the same nondiversifiable risk through higher sales volumes any better than a direct writer can, making reinsurance an inadequate source of risk relief.
- **Increased Earnings Volatility** In the absence of laying off such risk in the derivatives market, through reinsurance, or otherwise, the insurer may expect to experience greater earnings volatility. Many annuitants will simultaneously incur GPAF claims in down economic scenarios, while many annuitants will simultaneously incur zero GPAF claims in up scenarios. Furthermore, the same down economic scenarios that cause GPAF claim expense to increase also cause M&E risk charge revenue and asset management revenue to decrease, making multiple components of earnings go south in unison.

It is precisely because of the shape of the uncovered put option payoff diagram (Figure 18.7) that the risk curve for a variable income annuity with a GPAF feature drops off so precipitously in the left tail of the distribution, similar to that in the sample risk curve graph shown earlier (Figure 17.1). While investment variation (primary factor), mortality variation (secondary factor), and expense variation (tertiary factor) contribute to the general shape of the risk curve, an unhedged or underhedged GPAF benefit causes the change in shape at the left end.

This drop can be truncated to the extent that the risk is laid off on a derivative counterparty or reinsurer and that the counterparty is able to successfully meet its financial obligation, which may be quite large in dollar magnitude and become payable at a time of high economic stress. Payment for the hedge raises the left end of the risk curve by transferring the risk of large claims to a counterparty and downshifts the central and right portions of the risk curve due to sacrificing some potential profit to buy the hedge.

To the extent that IVA contract owners reallocate from stock funds to money market and bond funds during periods of negative stock market returns triggering GPAF claims and reserve increases, the insurance company will experience a decline in its dividends-received deduction associated with separate account stock funds, further reducing its profitability.

To the extent that negative equity market performance makes annuitants so skittish that they retreat to money market and bond funds, annuitants may exacerbate the insurer's earnings volatility woes by failing to be in the stock subaccounts when the equity market turns positive, missing out on part of the recovery. This is part of the investment-timing behavior risk mentioned earlier.

- **Derivative Counterparty Risk** Because of the specialized nature of the immediate variable annuity obligation, a standardized derivative offering where the Options Clearing Corporation is the counterparty is unlikely. Rather, the insurer will likely need to find a different counterparty or counterparties (such as an investment bank), whose expected creditworthiness over the life of the derivative contract is acceptable. After all, hedging involves risk transfer. After the hedging stops, the risk comes to rest in someone's portfolio.

- **Model Risk** The complex nature of the GPAF feature results in pricing and risk management models that may poorly mimic real-world experience. Volatility and correlation assumptions must be made, which are quantities that are not stable but fluctuate—sometimes widely—over time. Historic correlations can break down in high-economic-stress scenarios. The model must make IVA contract owner behavioral assumptions.

- **Fluctuating Benefit Cost** The changing volatilities of asset classes change the option premium for the identical benefit, so the worth of the GPAF feature to an annuitant—and the hedging cost of the GPAF feature to the insurer—will vary over time, even if the benefit definition stays constant.

- **Positive Investment Performance Might Still Trigger Claims** Even positive investment returns can trigger a GPAF claim, since any investment return below the AIR reduces the annuity benefit level. The higher the AIR, the greater is the propensity for annuity benefit payments to fall. For the same price, an insurer might offer a higher percentage floor guarantee on a 3% AIR and a lower percentage floor guarantee on a 5% AIR.

- **High Expenses, Including GPAF Premiums Themselves, Increase Claim Risk** To the extent GPAF expenses reduce net investment performance, a high GPAF premium can itself trigger GPAF claims that otherwise might have been avoided.

- **Above a Threshold, Higher GPAF Premiums Provide Zero Additional Protection** Higher GPAF premiums do not necessarily safeguard an insurer better. Once the guaranteed floor benefit level has been pierced, any GPAF premiums collected further serve to reduce the annuity benefits and are thus effectively paid right out as part of the claims. Of course, if the higher GPAF premiums are used to purchase hedging instruments, such incremental claims attributable to these higher premiums are paid by the hedging instrument counterparty.

- **Choice of Offering Higher Initial Benefit with Lower Percentage Floor versus Lower Initial Benefit with Higher Percentage Floor** Rather than starting IVA benefits at their normal level and guaranteeing, say, a floor benefit equal to 85% of the initial annuity benefit, an insurer could start the annuity benefit at 85% of the normal level and declare a 100% floor guarantee—and be in a safer, though not necessarily more marketable, position. Such an approach differs more than semantically; it differs economically. Some might label such an approach deceitful, since part of the guarantee is effectively retracted through annuity payout rates lower than would otherwise apply. There are opportunities for misrepresentation.

- **Permanency** The GPAF could be permanent or temporary. Because returns of a well-diversified asset portfolio over a longer period tend to be more predictable, whereas returns over a short period (such as shortly after IVA contract issue) may be more volatile, the need for a GPAF may be perceived as greater during the early years. Thus, while a permanent guarantee is more comforting, a temporary GPAF guarantee may cover a period of great concern to prospective IVA purchasers. While any few years of income—including the first few years—may be volatile, over a retirement horizon "mean reversion" of asset performance may cause up periods and down periods to counterbalance.

- **Temporary Benefit with Optional Extensions** If the GPAF is temporary, a floor guarantee equal to $X\%$ (e.g., 90%) of the initial benefit could be granted for Y years (e.g., $Y = 3$). One-year extensions might be available for purchase at time of issue, up to some maximum number of years. The floor could be constant or could grade down slightly (e.g., 2.5% per year) with time. As an example, the annuitant might elect a three-year 90% floor guarantee and purchase two one-year extensions, the first at 87.5% and the second at 85%.

  This gives the annuitant five years to figure out how much income he needs during retirement, which may differ from income needs in working years, and to make any necessary adjustments either inside or outside the immediate variable annuity. During these five years, "training wheels" are placed on his income to keep it from falling too far from the initial level. After five years (or some sufficiently long period), a well-diversified portfolio spread over multiple asset classes may perform sufficiently well so as to obviate the need for (and the expense of) a floor.

  To aid perspective, the ability for upside income growth potential over a multidecade retirement horizon may be more important than downside protection offered by an annuity benefit floor. Even at only 3.5% annual inflation, Figure 18.9 illustrates the dollar amounts of annual income necessary to maintain a constant level of purchasing power. Thus, one may desire that the opportunity for upside income growth be impeded by additional expenses associated with floor benefit guarantees to the minimum extent tolerable by the annuitant.

- **Static versus Dynamic Floor** The GPAF level could change over time rather than remain one static value forever. Annuitants can adapt to

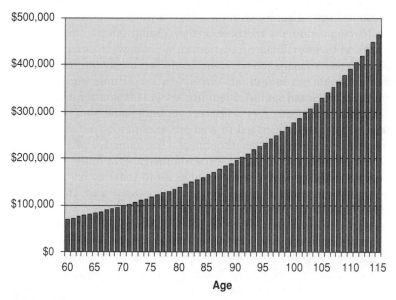

FIGURE 18.9 $70,000 Annual Pretax Income Inflated at 3.5%

some gradual degree of change in annuity benefits but are maladaptive to large, abrupt changes.

■ **Ratcheting Benefit** Although more expensive, it is theoretically possible to offer a GPAF benefit construction such that annuity benefit levels "ratchet"; that is, once a benefit level has been achieved, all future benefits must be equal to or greater than this new level. This type of benefit also goes by the name "high-water mark."

■ **Laws of Finance Must Hold** There is no investment magic or alchemy whereby a risky asset portfolio (e.g., common stock fund) can simultaneously be transmuted into an asset that poses no downside risk (i.e., is risk-free) and that still maintains all of the upside potential. By definition, it would be unreasonable to assume that one could be perpetually offered the arbitrage opportunity of being guaranteed more than the risk-free rate of return while holding a riskless asset.

For example, one should not expect to receive 100% equity market appreciation with zero downside risk. Even in a frictionless environment, the best result is 100% equity market participation less the cost of put options offering downside protection. The annuity environment is far from frictionless, with gross dealer concessions; issue and maintenance expenses; deferred acquisition cost (DAC), premium, and

federal income taxes; administration costs (systems, client statements, tax reporting); investment expenses; regulatory filings; and so on.
- **Floors, Ceilings, Collars, and Corridors** If an annuitant were willing to forgo annuity benefits above some high level, that could serve to reduce GPAF benefit cost. Effectively, a "collar" or "corridor"—static or moving—could be placed around annuity benefits, which would then have both a "ceiling" and a "floor." Call options could be sold with strike prices where the annuity benefit hits the ceiling, and these premiums could be applied to purchase put options with strike prices where the annuity benefit hits the floor. "No cost" collars could exist, where the higher the floor, the lower the ceiling. "Positive cost" collars could be purchased with progressively higher charges whereby the ceiling is raised, including up to the point of elimination.

"Corridor" benefits may offer practical consumer value, since investors can likely tolerate some oscillation in retirement income as long as that oscillation—even if heavy—is confined to a range, preferably an upward sloping "corridor," where the slope equals or exceeds that of the long-run inflation rate for goods and services traditionally purchased by seniors. There could be a variety of shapes of corridors, where the slope of the ceiling and the slope of the floor could be parallel or nonparallel. The floors and ceilings could start at specific values and then progress over time in some predetermined or formula-driven fashion, such as in an arithmetic or a geometric progression.

This "floor and ceiling" or "collar" or "corridor" approach could feature a "corridor" that resembles the upward sloping—as opposed to horizontal—tube with time on the x axis and benefit amount on the y axis in Figure 18.10. The lower the AIR, the more positively sloping

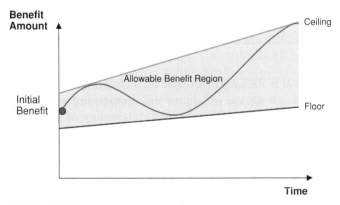

FIGURE 18.10 Corridor Approach

the tube can be. The tube floor and ceiling could be lines or curves. The floor and ceiling barriers could prove "reflecting," "absorbing," or "temporarily absorbing," with transitions to future states dependent on subaccount performance. Certainly a floor alone is easier to sell than a corridor, but a floor also carries a higher expense that serves as a drain on every annuity payment—a drain that in some cases is unnecessary.

■ **Discrete, Continuous, or Combination Funding of Benefit** Clearly, there is a cost to the downside protection. As a result, less than 100% of the upside gain otherwise achievable is realized when this protection is in place. Charges to the IVA contract owner for a GPAF benefit can occur up front as a percentage of premium, can be ongoing as an asset-based charge against the reserve, or can be some combination.

■ **Accounting** Financial Accounting Standard #133 (FAS 133), issued by the Financial Accounting Standards Board, addresses the issue of *Accounting for Derivatives,* such as immediate variable annuity floor guarantees. This is expected to bring some sunlight to GAAP (generally accepted accounting principles) accounting statements regarding the financial impacts attributable to the liabilities that insurers assume by writing VA "living benefits" and to the assets or reinsurance they may purchase (if any) to lay off such risks. This financial standard took effect January 1, 2003, for companies whose fiscal year is the calendar year.

During the payout phase of a variable payout annuity, would a provision that guarantees a minimum level of periodic payments require separate accounting as an embedded derivative under Standard 133? FASB staff authored implementation guidance on this question, stating that accounting treatment depends on the type of annuity option. For a non-life-contingent period certain annuity option, the guaranteed minimum periodic payments are an embedded derivative that is required to be separated under Standard 133. This conclusion is based on the assessment that the guaranteed payout floor is not closely related to the host variable payout annuity contract.

In contrast, a strictly life-contingent annuity option with no certain period and no withdrawal features is not subject to the requirements of Standard 133. For a lifetime annuity with a certain period, the contract is bifurcated, with the embedded derivative related only to the guaranteed minimum payouts during the certain period requiring separate accounting.

■ **Reserving and Risk-Based Capital Requirements** While emerging, future refinements may occur. Sufficiently large requirements could result in hefty charges inside IVA products, which otherwise might be significantly less due to the pass-through nature of investment risk (asset depreciation C-1 risk) associated with traditional IVAs.

Regulators are developing reserve and risk-based capital require-ments for these types of benefits to safeguard the interests of annui-tants. Independent rating agencies, such as A. M. Best, Fitch, Moody's, and Standard & Poor's, also have an interest in frequency and severity of claims that can arise from any insurance or annuity offering and in ways in which an insurer controls such risks as they make financial strength and claims-paying rating determinations about insurers.

In 2002, the National Association of Insurance Commissioners (NAIC) adopted Actuarial Guideline 39, which provides an interpreta-tion of the model standard valuation law for variable annuities with guaranteed living benefits. There is a related practice note explaining its applications.

At the time of this writing, the American Academy of Actuaries has committees that are focusing on *nonformulaic* statutory reserve standards and risk-based capital (RBC) requirements for variable annuity living benefits such as a GPAF. Product development spawns innovations unanticipated by existing regulations. Historically, in such instances, how regulatory formulas might apply to a novel product design was unclear until the regulatory framework caught up and synchronized.

An approach under consideration is to migrate away from hard-coded formulas and toward concept positions with which insurers' own stochastic testing (with scenario-generating models calibrated using his-torical returns) and certifications must comply. This *principles-based* approach, rather than *rules-based* or *factor-based* approaches, may make regulatory examiners' auditing work more challenging since it is easier to monitor compliance with a rule than with a principle; but it provides earlier and clearer guidance as to the level of reserves and RBC a novel combination of benefits within a product offering should require. Actuarial opinions and memorandums may lend transparency for regulators. Replacing numerical rules with statements of principles or objectives has its own issues; for example, unlike a rule, a principle does not convey precisely when you cross the line. A principle, however, is a constant reminder of the rule makers' intent.

Statutory reserves are calculated under the Commissioners' Annu-ity Reserve Valuation Method (CARVM), where each possible benefit stream is considered and the CARVM reserve is the present value of benefits using the benefit stream that produces the greatest present value. A proposed reserving guideline applied to GPAFs would set the GPAF reserve equal to the difference of the reserve calculated including the effect of the GPAF in the universe of benefit streams and the reserve excluding the GPAF. (The former is the "integrated reserve," which equals the greatest present value of future integrated benefit streams, which include all variable annuity "guaranteed living benefits" under the contract.) Clearly, the reserve inclusive of the GPAF will be higher since in addition to the "base benefit stream" it will contain a series of positive "net amounts at risk" (NAR) in some scenarios, where NAR equals the actual income payment less the income payment that would have been made in the absence of the guarantee.

While there is a meaningful relationship between reserves and RBC, it is noteworthy that reserves are regulated by the states while RBC requirements are set by the NAIC.

Introducing stochastic reserve valuation techniques within financial planning and projection models that are themselves stochastic creates so-called "stochastic on stochastic" modeling. Because this multiplies systems design complexity, computationally efficient techniques are evolving to improve tractability, making it possible to run thousands of stochastically generated economic scenarios. This is particularly important as financial management systems shift from periodic, after-the-fact, point-in-time measures of value to a real-time basis.

- **Interested Parties** Rating agencies, state regulators, and insurance company boards of directors have a keen interest in the effects on the aggregate risk profile, NAIC RBC ratios, and rating-agency capital-adequacy ratios of an insurer attributable to variable annuity living benefits, including GPAF fund performance guarantees.

- **Competitive Forces** To grow sales, to increase market share, to attract attention as a new entrant into a market dominated by large and established players, and/or to simply place enormous bets with stockholder money, some variable annuity writers periodically issue—either intentionally and cavalierly or unknowingly—product design, commission, and guaranteed benefit combinations that are imprudent and unsustainable. Especially given the complex nature of GPAF benefits, select IVA writers may disrupt this area of the annuity marketplace with rich guarantees, low charges, and/or lack of investment restrictions. While product offerings far outside the mainstream typically result in abrupt withdrawal at some point (occasionally due to insurance company failure), until that occurs, the marketplace may experience distortion relative to products and features that can be offered on a sustainable basis.

A guaranteed payout annuity floor addresses the fundamental human emotions of fear (through protection against large market drops) and need for assurance (via knowing at point of sale a minimum level of retirement income). A GPAF therefore has a strong emotional "hook."

It is important to note that alternative devices exist to satisfy similar cravings:

- **Immediate Fixed Annuities with Increasing Benefits** An immediate fixed annuity can be purchased where benefits increase on a predetermined basis each year (e.g., 2% to 6%). Benefit payments can increase by the same dollar amount each year (linear increase) or by the same percentage each year (geometric increase).
- **Combination Fixed and Variable Immediate Annuities** An immediate fixed annuity (level or increasing benefits) provides a baseline income floor that can never be penetrated. The immediate variable annuity— used in conjunction—offers an opportunity for growth. The relative mix of the fixed and variable components produces an income floor anywhere from 0% to 100% of the initial annuity payment.

  Judicious allocation of a single premium to a combination of fixed and variable immediate annuities allows the contract owner to fine-tune his or her desired balance of income stability (since the fixed annuity income component doesn't fluctuate), death benefit (through allocations to cash refund or modified cash refund options), and growth (via the variable annuity income component), all while being assured of lifetime income.

  With a portion of retirement assets in an immediate fixed annuity, where the annuitant is assured a baseline level of income, such assurance may allow the annuitant to be more aggressive with both immediate variable annuity asset allocation and nonannuity assets. The annuitant may potentially reap higher rewards for which, in the absence of the immediate fixed annuity, he or she would not have felt comfortable striving.

  Freedom from financial worry and the contentment with adequate lifetime income provided by the combination of annuities may be conducive to longevity!
- **Asset Allocation** Some subaccount allocations produce lower volatility than others. Diversifying across asset classes with correlations less than unity, leaning more heavily on shorter-term bond subaccounts that are less price sensitive to interest rate movement, and similar steps can reduce income volatility for those whose level of aversion to income fluctuation is high.
- **IVA Hedged Subaccounts** A particular subaccount can be constructed to offer equity market participation with limited downside risk. These "protected equity" subaccounts may operate in any of a number of fashions. For example, they could invest in an underlying stock index,

such as the S&P 500, and then buy put options at an appropriate strike level and maturity. Or they could operate like an equity-indexed annuity and buy a portfolio of zero-coupon bonds to mature at some future date to guarantee a minimum return plus buy stock index call options at an appropriate strike level and maturity to provide the benefit of upward movement in the stock index. IVA contract owners could then allocate whatever percentage they wish to such a subaccount.

As previously mentioned, the standard approach to a GPAF presumes that the full and immediate burden to make up any shortfalls in periodic retirement income—when a payment normally calculated would penetrate the floor—resides entirely with the insurance company. Variations of the GPAF concept can be devised where the annuity owner shares in this risk, which should result in lower cost for the feature. For example, recall the previously mentioned approach whereby when an annuity benefit payment as normally calculated falls beneath the guaranteed floor benefit level, the shortfall could be made up by advancing a small part of every future benefit payment and taking the shortfall from the reserve. A slightly smaller number of annuity units is thereafter payable on each future payment date, yet the dollar amount of the benefit floor stays constant.

If subaccount performance improves and future benefit payments—as normally calculated and reflecting the now smaller number of annuity units per payment—are above the floor and stay above the floor, it is possible that all benefit shortfalls are simply provided via partial advances of the annuitant's future benefit stream. If subaccount performance remains poor for a prolonged period and benefits normally calculated remain below the floor, the insurer clearly incurs GPAF claims for which it must provide the funding. In advance of this occurring, the insurer builds a reserve to prepare for this contingency.

Because of the risk-sharing and cost-sharing nature of this approach between insurer and annuitant, such a GPAF feature construction carries a lower expense than one where the insurer bears 100% of the brunt of any shortfalls. This approach is a form of "stop-loss coinsurance," in which the initial claims are effectively handled through self-insurance and claims beyond a certain level revert to the responsibility of the insurance company.

Another variation could simply be to not allow benefit payments to rise above the floor until the cumulative shortfall has been replenished by withholding from payment any portion of a future benefit that is above the floor. Such withholding would raise the number of annuity units per payment. Once the number of annuity units per payment is restored to the initial level, withholding ceases.

Yet another variation on this approach involves a temporary benefit "ceiling." When annuity benefit payments rise above the temporary ceiling, the reserve could be replenished by paying out only the ceiling benefit and adding the excess back into the reserve. The benefit could be structured so that the ceiling only kicks in until the original number of annuity units per payment—previously reduced by floor benefit payments—is fully restored. Thereafter, the program is equivalent to one where benefit floor payments and benefit ceiling payments never occurred.

Of course, there are additional variations limited only by one's imagination, such as handling *all* floor benefit claims on a coinsurance basis (where the annuitant pays a copayment equal to 50% of each benefit shortfall in the way of an advance and a concomitant reduction in number of annuity units per future payment and the insurer picks up the remaining 50%).

Such variant approaches to a GPAF feature need to consider legal and tax implications. For example, if the number of annuity units is higher for benefits before the floor is first penetrated and lower thereafter, is the "substantially equal payments" requirement in the tax definition of an immediate annuity still met?

A prospective annuitant considering some form of GPAF election (or any of the non-GPAF alternatives) needs to strike a balance. Too rich a GPAF benefit may unnecessarily reduce all future retirement income benefits. Most retirees can adapt to some degree of variation in benefit amount, especially if temporary. Retirees may be more concerned with catastrophic loss and construct a less expensive program geared to safeguard against that.

However designed, a GPAF needs to be able to be explained with an "elevator story," one simple enough to be conveyed in a 30-second conversation. It must be clear, memorable, and sufficiently compelling to pique the interest of financial advisers and to attract the interest of their clients.

GPAF Hedging Example

As a GPAF hedging example, consider a newly purchased IVA by a female age 65 with an initial annual benefit of $10,000 where each of the five subsequent benefits is guaranteed to be at least 85% of the initial one. That is, annual benefits paid one, two, three, four, and five years after purchase are guaranteed to equal or exceed $8,500 regardless of subaccount performance (see Figure 18.11).

Assume the following:

- Initial annuity unit value $UV_0 = 1.000$.
- Value of 10,000 annuity units payable per benefit.

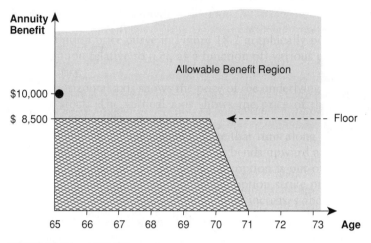

FIGURE 18.11   GPAF Example

- 5% AIR.
- 1.00% M&E charge.
- 0.50% investment management expense.
- 100% allocation to an index subaccount (e.g., Dow Jones Wilshire 5000 Index) for which put options are available.
- Initial index value = 100.

The floor benefit triggers should the annuity unit value fall below 0.850. Since the total of investment and M&E charges is 1.50%, this implies that gross investment performance (GIP) of the underlying fund assets in the first year must be at least –9.25%:

$$\frac{1+\text{Actual Subaccount Performance}}{1+\text{AIR}} = \frac{1+(\text{GIP}-.0150)}{1+.05} \geq 0.850$$

$$.985 + \text{GIP} \geq (0.850)(1.05)$$

$$\text{GIP} \geq .8925 - .985$$

$$\text{GIP} \geq -.0925$$

That is, if the value of the index one year later—on the valuation date used to determine the second annual benefit payment—is 90.75 or higher, the floor benefit will not trigger.

To fully hedge the annuity benefit payable one year after contract purchase, the insurer could buy a one-year put option on the index with a strike level of 90.75. The usual factors governing option prices—volatility, risk-free rate, time to expiration, index level, option strike level—determine the price the insurer pays for the option.

Note that for a 3% AIR the option strike level would be 89.05, meaning the price would be lower than for a 5% AIR since the put option is further out-of-the-money. Thus, an insurer can charge a lower price for the same floor benefit for a 3% AIR than for a 5% AIR.

For the annuity benefit two years out, again the annuity unit value must be at least 0.850 to avoid a floor benefit trigger; that is, $UV_2 \geq 0.850$. Now

$$UV_2 = UV_0 \times \frac{1+(GIP_1 - .0150)}{1+.05} \times \frac{1+(GIP_2 - .0150)}{1+.05}$$

Setting $GIP_1 = GIP_2$ and simply calling this GIP, we see that $UV_2 \geq 0.850$ implies

$$1.000 \times \frac{1+(GIP - .0150)}{1.05} \times \frac{1+(GIP - .0150)}{1.05} \geq 0.850$$

$$[1 + (GIP - .0150)]^2 \geq 0.850(1.05)^2$$

$$.985 + GIP \geq \sqrt{.937125}$$

$$GIP \geq -0.0169$$

For a 5% AIR annuity, the gross investment performance of the underlying index cannot fall below a geometric mean of −1.69% per year for the first two years. Thus, the strike level of the two-year put option is 96.64.

This should come as no surprise. With a 5% AIR and 1.50% of expenses, the underlying fund must perform at 6.50% annually just for annuity benefits to remain level. At −1.69% gross investment performance, the annuity unit value one year out is about 92.2% of the original. The annuity unit value two years out is about 92.2% of that one year out. The cumulative result is an annuity unit value that is 85% of the original one.

The same procedure follows for the next three annual benefits with a floor guarantee. Table 18.2 shows the minimum geometric average annual returns necessary to avoid a GPAF claim involving a level 85% floor for five years. Table 18.2 also shows the put option strike levels for hedging the GPAF benefit where the initial value of the index underlying the single subaccount elected is 100.

Note that for this flat GPAF equal to 85% of the initial benefit, the insurer must purchase in-the-money options for the benefit three years out where a 4% or 5% AIR is elected. The insurer must purchase in-the-money options for the benefits four years out and thereafter under the 3%, 4%, or

TABLE 18.2   GPAF Hedge: Put Option Strike Levels

Guaranteed Payout Annuity Floor
Annual Annuity-Due Benefits
Floor = 85% of Initial Benefit
GPAF Term Spans Five Annual Benefits Subsequent to Initial Benefit
Initial Underlying Index Value = 100

	3% AIR		4% AIR		5%AIR	
Benefit Year	Put Option Strike Level	Minimum Average Annual Return to Avoid Claim	Put Option Strike Level	Minimum Average Annual Return to Avoid Claim	Put Option Strike Level	Minimum Average Annual Return to Avoid Claim
0						
1	89.05	−10.95%	89.90	−10.10%	90.75	−9.25%
2	93.05	−3.54	94.83	−2.62	96.64	−1.69
3	97.23	−0.93	100.05	0.02	102.92	0.96
4	101.61	0.40	105.55	1.36	109.61	2.32
5	106.18	1.21	111.35	2.17	116.73	3.14

5% AIRs. To control risk and to reign in GPAF benefit price, an insurer might offer a lower floor (e.g., 75% or 80%), might require use of a 3% or 3.5% AIR, or might require as a GPAF benefit eligibility condition the use of one or more permissible collections of subaccounts that reduce volatility of returns—although such collections can only afford to trade off a certain amount of expected rate of return for reduced volatility because the gross investment performance of the underlying investment funds must exceed the AIR by at least the amount of investment management fees plus mortality and expense and administrative (M&E&A) charges just for IVA benefits to remain level.

At least for life-contingent annuity options—where fewer recipients are alive each year—total notional amounts the insurer must purchase decline. Recall that an IVA is a series of pure endowments. The notional amount of the put option hedge for any specific IVA benefit payment relates to this single endowment, not to the entire reserve. If the annuitant in this example elects a life only annuity with a 5% AIR and if $q_{65} = .01$ for female annuitants, then a one-year put option with a notional amount of $10,000 and a strike level of 90.75 must be purchased at contract inception for 99% of similarly situated annuitants if the GPAF hedge is to be complete and precise.

Because we assume an initial index value of 100, a $10,000 notional amount is analogous to 100 shares of a single stock at $100 per share. If we assume a 0% AIR and no investment management or M&E&A charges, then we would purchase a one-year put option on 100 shares with a strike level of 85. If after one year the stock is at 80, then our 100 shares of stock are worth $8,000 and the put counterparty owes us 100 × ($85 − $80) = $500 for a total annuity floor benefit of $8,500. Even though the initial reserve at contract inception might be on the order of $136,000, in this example it is only the five annuity benefits after the one paid immediately that must be hedged, resulting in a notional amount less than the full reserve.

In the real world, the hedging opportunity is less precise. The contract owner may allocate to stock subaccounts other than stock index subaccounts, resulting in basis risk. The contract owner may invest in bond subaccounts, REIT subaccounts, and specialty subaccounts—and may periodically change the asset allocation either directly or through automatic rebalancing. Funding for the options generally arrives over the life of the annuity payout rather than up front. Long-dated options may not be commercially available. Options purchased for existing annuitants in the future may be more expensive because volatility increases or because— due to a drop in the market—the options are already deeply in-the-money at time of purchase. GPAF benefits that "ratchet up" rather than remain level require more complex options. Still, partial hedging may be preferable to no hedging— known as "going naked"—on the part of the insurer offering GPAF benefits.

Because the total return of a common stock subaccount will reflect dividends as well as realized and unrealized capital gains, a stock index used to hedge common stock subaccount performance should be one constructed so as to reflect values inclusive of dividends.

The modeling of prices that an asset—such as the underlying stock index in our GPAF example—might assume over time is clearly important to an understanding of risks (from the insurer's perspective) and of benefits (from the annuitant's perspective) associated with a GPAF offering. The model where asset prices have a *lognormal distribution* is one of the most omnipresent models in finance. Because asset values typically can—at least theoretically—go infinitely high but are bounded by zero on the lower end, the lognormal probability distribution shares this characteristic.

A random variable X has a lognormal distribution if its natural logarithm, $Y = \ln (X)$, has a normal distribution. The probability density function (PDF) $f_X(x)$ for such a continuous random variable X with a mean of 10 and a standard deviation of 5 appears in Figure 18.12.

The lognormal distribution is skewed to the right (i.e., positively skewed). The PDF starts at zero, increases to its mode, and decreases thereafter.

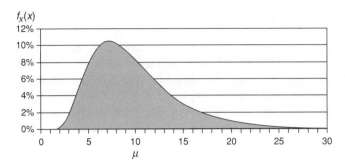

FIGURE 18.12   Probability Density Function for Lognormal Distribution with Mean of 10 and Standard Deviation of 5

We can consider a stochastic process representing an asset value over time. Figure 18.12 might represent the probability density function of the prices that a specific asset takes on at the end of a single-period observation. We can obtain the probability that the asset price will fall between any two values by integrating this function between those values. Since definite integrals give the area between the function being integrated and the horizontal axis, the probability that the asset price random variable X resides between points a and b is the area under $f_X(x)$ between the definite limits a and b.

The class of *regime-switching* lognormal models, which often fit monthly return series of major stock market indexes better than the traditional lognormal model, has enjoyed a recent surge in popularity. The thinking behind regime-switching models is that a stock market may occasionally switch from a low-volatility state to a high-volatility state, perhaps triggered by a political or economic shock that increases short-term uncertainty.

The regime-switching lognormal process captures this stochastic variability in the volatility parameter by assuming that volatility takes on one of k values and switches between these values randomly. As a result, a regime-switching lognormal process more accurately captures more extreme price movements than does the traditional lognormal model.[18]

LIQUIDITY

Liquidity or *accessibility* relate to the fact that traditional immediate variable annuities call for irrevocable relinquishment of access to the single premium at time of sale. Traditionally, purchasers exchange a lump-sum premium for a series of future periodic retirement benefits where the variable income annuity contract describes the exact specifications of the arrange-ment. No access to principal exists.[19] This may be the primary characteris-tic accounting for the dearth of actual IVA usage relative to potential usage.

Contract owner access to payments beyond the contractually promised series of retirement income benefits has historically not been permitted so as to keep annuitants who find themselves in ill health from withdrawing excess funds from the pool, leaving it inadequate to provide benefits to the longest-surviving members of the pool; that is, in the interest of solvency, restrictions against withdrawing extra funds from the pool are imposed to prevent mortality anti-selection.

Monies that retirees need to cover large, one-time expenses (such as pur-chase of a second home, a recreational vehicle, or exotic travel) should be in-vested separately and not be applied to the purchase of an immediate annuity. Prospective purchasers must be made aware that an immediate annuity is illiquid and, like any investment tool, should be used only to the extent it fills a need.

Yet prospective purchasers are more apt to buy an IVA if it offers acces-sibility to some degree of funds beyond normal retirement income benefits. Certainly, the integrity of the fund to fulfill its obligation to pay benefits to the longest-lived annuitants in the pool is of primary concern when consid-ering ways to improve accessibility to funds.

Some insurers offer product variations that provide some degree of access to funds beyond the normal annuity benefit payments. Theoretically, if an insurer offers full access to the purchase price (adjusted for value changes due to market movement) less annuity benefits paid out during some introductory period of time, say the first two years of the contract, it should make an adjustment to pricing. Since annuitants who find themselves in unexpectedly poor health or become terminally ill during this period would withdraw all remaining value, no discounting for survivorship should be employed in pricing for these years. This is because there would be no reserve released by deceased annuitants to be reallocated among surviving annuitants. As a result, the annuity would be slightly more costly, requiring a higher premium for the same benefits or reduced benefits for the same pre-mium. Effectively, in this situation, the annuitant is taking systematic with-drawals for two years and deferring true annuitization two years.

The longer the liquidity period, the smaller annuity payments will be. Taken to the extreme, if you continue extending liquidity for progressively more years, say up to age 115, you will have invented . . . the retail mutual fund! At that point, annuity benefits will have fallen all the way down to what a retail mutual fund could provide.

It will almost certainly be the case that an annuitant will not be entitled to forfeitures of others in the annuitant pool unless they're entitled to his or her forfeiture. One will likely never receive the benefits of survivorship that prop up one's income level without entering into a life-contingent transaction oneself.

Recall that immediate variable annuity benefit payments consist of principal, appreciation, and a survivorship element attributable to forfeitures of deceased annuitants being spread across surviving annuitants. In the preceding example of full liquidity in the first two years, there would be no survivorship element, reducing the initial annuity benefit payment and, therefore, all future benefit payments, which differ from the initial one only due to subaccount performance.

One method to deal with the liquidity issue is to require underwriting evidence of good health by those who wish to withdraw excess funds. If an annuitant in excellent health wanted to make a withdrawal equal to part of the reserve associated with his liability or opt out of the program completely by a withdrawal equal to the total reserve, such a withdrawal could be allowed without jeopardizing the program for others. This is because an individual in excellent health who wishes to withdraw funds for other than health-related reasons does not pose the mortality anti-selection risk that occurs if unhealthy lives were permitted to withdraw funds on learning of information such as terminal illness. In the latter case, their pending death is about to result in the release of their reserve and its redistribution among remaining annuitants. In the case of a medically proven healthy life, it is not necessarily the case that a near-term death and its related reserve reallocation would occur—the situation where forced continued inclusion in the annuitant pool is necessary to maintain the financial integrity of the program. Of course, death by accidental means might still occur shortly for a medically healthy life. Because this medically proven healthy annuitant received the benefit of discounting for both "natural" and "accidental" deaths when his initial benefit level was established, this theoretically might argue for release of less than the full reserve should the annuitant wish to withdraw the maximum funds possible; that is, that portion of the reserve associated with "accidental" deaths should be retained rather than released to the annuitant.

This back-end underwriting approach to liquidity is administratively more complex than a traditional IVA. Such a program requires reliable health screens to verify that people who want to withdraw from the program are in good health, eliminating mortality anti-selection. "Good health" may be difficult to demonstrate at advanced ages. There exists a financial incentive to hide health problems.

There are safe and legitimate ways to enhance accessibility. To the extent certain annuity benefits are guaranteed to be made regardless of the survival or nonsurvival of the annuitant, the discounted value of such benefits can be paid in a lump sum without injury to fund solvency. For example, for a "life with 10 years certain" annuity option, no survivorship element is factored into pricing for the first 10 years of payments. If an annuitant 3 years into this annuity had an emergency need for additional funds (e.g., extraordinarily high surgical expenses), the entire "present value" or "commuted value" of the remaining 7 years of "certain period" annuity benefits could be paid without upsetting program solvency. Benefits would then cease for 7 years. If the annuitant were still alive at the end of the original 10-year period, benefit payments would recommence and be payable for life.

If only a part of the present value of remaining certain period payments were taken, reduced periodic annuity benefits could be paid for the remainder of the certain period without affecting IVA program solvency. They would jump after the certain period if the annuitant were still alive and would pay the value of the same number of annuity units as originally scheduled. Since an immediate variable annuity is a security, the conditions under which such "commutation privileges" are allowed would need to be defined in the prospectus.

Immediate variable annuities are by their very nature market-value adjusting daily via the unit value process. They are therefore amenable to paying a commuted value. In contrast, commuted values associated with immediate fixed annuities could only be safely allowed when a market-value adjustment formula is used.

When there is a payment of a commuted value, the insurer forgoes the margin it was expecting to earn on this business for the remainder of the period over which benefits otherwise would have been paid. One way around this is to capture the present value of the margins to which the insurer would have been entitled but for commutation in the commutation formula.

One insurer offers a program that "seamlessly integrates" a systematic withdrawal program and a true immediate variable annuitization: At inception, the insurer calculates that level of benefit payments the annuitant can receive for a specific liquidity period—where a visible account value exists just as it would for a typical deferred variable annuity contract from which systematic withdrawal payments are being taken—such that at the end of the liquidity period and the commencement of the true annuitization period, there is no discontinuity in the level of benefit payments. The progression of benefit payments just before and just after the crossover point from the systematic withdrawal program into the true annuitization program is "smooth," depending on the relation of subaccount performance to the AIR, just like any other two sequential benefit payments. While there is liquidity during the "access period," as would be expected, the initial benefit payment is lower than would exist for a true immediate variable annuity taken right from the start, since no survivorship element exists during the "access period" that would boost payments to the same level as a true immediate variable annuity.

Another conceptual approach could be the offering of liquidity for some predetermined period over which regularly scheduled withdrawals fully exhaust the account, where either a portion of each withdrawal or an ongoing additional asset charge is retained by the insurer to continue to provide lifetime annuity benefits once the end of the predetermined period is reached and the individual has watched his or her account value gradually decline to zero. Such a product construction may provide a clearer perception to the contract owner that he or she is deriving value from the transaction because, even though the owner watched the account value dwindle to zero, he or she is still receiving lifetime income.

Short predetermined liquidity periods would not be commercially viable, since too large a "longevity insurance premium" extraction (either as a percentage of each withdrawal or as an asset charge) would have to be taken to fund the deferred life annuity. Some funding for the deferred life annuity would come from extractions assessed against contract owners who died or who opted out of the program (e.g., by terminating the feature or by withdrawing all account value) prior to the end of the liquidity period.

Variations on this theme that may be commercially viable include having lengthy liquidity periods, having a liquidity period that stops sometime before the account value runs down to zero, having the annuity after the liquidity period be for something shorter than a lifetime, or making an adjustment in the annuity benefit level so that it is sustainable for a lifetime.

As IVA product developers invent new approaches to enhance liquidity, whether the new design qualifies under tax law for the more favorable immediate annuity treatment needs to be kept in mind. For example, how much access to funds via lump-sum withdrawals in excess of traditional IVA benefits is permissible before the contract fails to qualify as an immediate annuity for income tax purposes under the definition in Internal Revenue Code Section 72(u)(4)?

Recall that in the non-tax-qualified market, distributions from an immediate annuity are treated as part nontaxable return of principal until cost basis is fully recovered. Individuals may request private letter rulings (PLRs) from the IRS as to the tax treatment of a new design if there is any question.

If accessibility were such that the contract were treated as a deferred annuity rather than as an immediate annuity, early distributions might be fully taxable because appreciation is deemed to be withdrawn first, followed by nontaxable return of principal.[20,21]

A future development that might enhance liquidity of immediate variable annuities is for third parties to exchange a lump sum for some or all future annuity benefits, whether non-life-contingent or life-contingent. For example, a single sum could be exchanged for the right to receive 50% of monthly annuity benefits for the next three years. An individual selling pieces of an IVA income stream is akin to an investment firm selling specific tranches of a mortgage pool: both carve up their income stream in creative ways for resale and both involve the sale of securities and would be so regulated.

The third-party investor providing the annuity contract owner/annuitant with the lump sum would need to consider the mortality risk involved if payments partially or wholly spanned a life-contingent period of the annuity payout. To the extent that the IVA offered reallocation among subaccounts, the third-party investor might have limited authorization to modify the risk profile of the investment portfolio to his or her liking. To the extent that the IVA offered index subaccounts, the third-party investor could sculpt the risk profile through judicious derivative purchases. The third-party investor could still do this even if the IVA didn't offer index subaccounts, although there would be some "basis risk"—the "sloppiness" attributable to the fact that the securities underlying a subaccount don't exactly match the basket of securities underlying the derivative instrument.

Numerous issues are associated with development of such a secondary immediate annuities market. For example, annuity contracts are generally nonassignable according to contract and prospectus language. In the individual retirement account (IRA) market, loans made using IRA assets as collateral disqualify the IRA from favorable tax deferral; the exchange of a series of future cash flows for a lump sum today may be identical whether the transaction is structural as a sale or a loan. For life-contingent annuity benefits, annuitants would need to share their medical records with third-party investors to evaluate the purchase price the investors should offer. In the non-tax-qualified market, issues surrounding continuation of favorable immediate annuity tax treatment are involved, since the benefit stream differs from the traditional immediate annuity payment stream envisioned at issue.

"Viatical settlement" companies emerged to offer life insureds with terminal diseases a discounted value for their life insurance policies—more than the current cash value of their policies but a fraction of their face amount—creating a secondary market for life insurance policies. "Senior settlement" companies emerged to offer life insureds even without health impairment a discounted value for their life insurance policies, where the senior's original insurance need is now absent (e.g., a retiree who purchased life insurance decades ago to protect a young family then dependent on his income but who no longer has dependents).

Such life insurance settlements create ethical concerns regarding "insurable interest." What happens when unrelated third-party investors who put up the money grow impatient because the insured is living too long and deferring the death claim payment the investors have coming?

Insurable interest issues are absent where a third party offers a lump-sum payment now in exchange for some degree of future immediate annuity payments. Such third-party investors are better off with continuing annuitant survival. If the annuity benefits are life-contingent, continuing annuitant survival keeps annuity benefits flowing to the third-party investor. If the payments are non-life-contingent, continuing annuitant survival keeps a third-party investor's customer around to possibly repeat the experience at a future date.

When such financial instruments can be traded in the open market to have greater liquidity, the lines distinguishing annuity contracts, insurance contracts, and other asset types blur. An investor looks at the projected series of cash flows and arrives at a purchase price he's willing to pay in exchange for it, taking into account likelihood of payment, alternative investment opportunities, and related factors.

The occasional need to trade future income for current cash creates a mutually beneficial opportunity for third-party investors to develop secondary markets in immediate annuity policies. Annuitants receive cash because they need to cover, for example, unexpectedly high medical expenses or because an unanticipated inheritance or windfall terminates their need for ongoing annuity income. Third-party investors receive a rate of return they find satisfactory for the risks undertaken.

Another future scenario would be for insurance companies to adjust their product offerings and practices to reduce or eliminate the need for secondary market development by replication of secondary market benefits themselves. Statutes granting insurers the flexibility to achieve this result would need enactment.

Insurers, by virtue of their immediate variable annuity technical expertise, might be well positioned to price, administer, and gauge associated risks. Immediate variable annuity owners might take comfort in limiting the sharing of their medical information with insurance companies well versed in privacy rules rather than with third-party investors.

Effectively, this is a special case of health underwriting mentioned earlier, where it was stated that annuitants in excellent health could withdraw funds without jeopardizing solvency of the entire program, since they were less likely (i.e., ignoring accidental death) to generate forfeitures needed to sustain the program and were more likely long-lived annuitants who stood to benefit from the forfeitures of those who predeceased them. Here the notion is that even those in subpar health could withdraw *some* degree of funds—an amount less than the full reserve. The difference between the full reserve and the smaller present value of future benefits attributable to the higher mortality rates that would be associated with their condition would need to remain in the overall annuity program fund for solvency.

While achievable, such a program adds expense (e.g., annuity company medical directors to evaluate data, medical examinations to evaluate annuitant health) and complexity. There is additional concern that prospective IVA purchasers may have a misperception that the instrument they are about to buy carries a high degree of liquidity; whereas for those who find themselves terminally ill, it will offer virtually zero liquidity; and for those in impaired health, the liquidity value could be significantly less than their original premium less annuity benefits already paid—even if investment performance is good.

As a result, perhaps the better approach is to educate prospects as to why illiquidity is one characteristic of an IVA program, a characteristic likely outweighed by transfer of longevity risk, by freedom from anxiety about outliving one's assets, by freedom to control one's asset allocation, by favorable tax treatment, by freedom from serving as one's personal pension administrator (including performing annual IRS required minimum distribution calculations), and by other positive characteristics.

Comments about IVA premiums "going behind the wall" of the insurance company or "into the proverbial black hole" carry negative connotations that may sway IVA prospects away from their purchase, without understanding that this is to their benefit in that it ensures the necessary ownership titling of those assets so that value transfer to the prospect from those annuitants who predecease the prospect will occur—unimpeded by any need for the insurer to establish a legal claim on those assets later. (A group of otherwise unaffiliated people who happened to own shares of the same mutual fund theoretically could form their own annuitant pool and retain ownership of their accounts if they each agreed (1) that they would only withdraw monthly a varying dollar amount someone knowledgeable calculated to keep the program solvent and (2) that they would on their death turn over any residual account balance to the annuitant pool.)

Reverse mortgages are already available where a house-rich, cash-poor client's entire home is exchanged for a series of annuity benefits, with the annuitant continuing to live in the house until death. If psychologically a person can exchange his or her entire house for a series of annuity benefits, how much easier it should be to exchange but a portion of one's paper assets for such a series of annuity benefits, especially where the income stream is customizable at issue (e.g., AIR selection) and post-issue (e.g., asset reallocation). Such a reverse mortgage arrangement has illiquidity comparable to an IVA.

Mathematics deals with "existence" and "uniqueness" of solutions. It may be proven for a specific problem that a solution cannot exist or that it can—even if we don't yet know what it is. If it exists, it may be shown to be a unique solution, or it may be shown to be one of an entire family of solutions.

While no such level of rigorous proof is here offered, it does appear that the existence of an approach to liquidity that doesn't reduce annuity benefits may be limited to one that is a function of health status at the attained age. Available liquidity without impacting fund solvency would range from zero liquidity for an annuitant so unhealthy as certainly to die before receiving the next annuity benefit to liquidity in the amount of the full reserve for an annuitant so perfectly healthy as to be most likely the longest-lived annuitant in the pool and who otherwise—but for withdrawing from the pool—would eventually have received benefits stemming from the forfeitures of every other annuitant in the pool.

There is emotional attachment to lump sums and their associated liquidity. For example, 401(k) plan participants, given the choice of a lump sum or an annuity, often take a lump sum. The irony is that once they have the lump sum—and have paid income taxes associated with its distribution to them—they realize that what they need is an income stream.

Clearly, emotions associated with liquidity influence decisions regarding the positioning of retirement assets. The rational approach, of course, is first to evaluate your needs during retirement and then to position your assets to support those needs. To the extent one has liquidity needs, assets need to be positioned in liquid financial instruments. To the extent one has the need to safeguard against longevity risk, assets need to be positioned in less liquid or illiquid financial instruments that sacrifice liquidity to improve the ability to provide longevity protection.

For instance, recall the earlier example where full IVA liquidity is offered for the first few years. This causes there to be no discounting for survivorship in those years, which produces lower retirement income for the same premium. Increasing liquidity decreases retirement income in all years. Each financial instrument should be used to the extent it fills a specific need. One class of financial instruments (e.g., IVAs) should not be rendered ineffective or less effective by trying to fill a need (e.g., liquidity) already met by another class of asset.

Apprehension about entering into an illiquid transaction can be partially quelled by reminding prospects that an IVA represents only *part* of their retirement assets and that, for this part to work for them to its maximal capability, illiquidity is requisite. The reality is that a more economically optimal, more protective result can be achieved if individuals don't demand 100% liquidity on 100% of their assets 100% of the time.

Just as individuals shouldn't put all their assets in life insurance to guard against dying too soon, individuals shouldn't put all their assets in an immediate variable annuity to guard against living too long; but there is a place for both. IVAs meet a need; and, like any financial instrument, only as much should be allocated to this product as is necessary to satisfy the need.

INCOME STABILIZATION

Immediate variable annuity benefits typically fluctuate with each payment. Since the most common benefit frequency mode is monthly, annuitants are subject to some degree of "mailbox shock" with each monthly payment.

To overcome this fluctuation and to help annuitants with family budgeting, some insurers offer immediate variable annuities with monthly benefit payments for which the level of those benefit payments changes only annually or semiannually based on investment performance. This "income stabilizer" feature needs to be accounted for in product pricing since the underlying investments really do fluctuate in value and the conventional approach calls for benefit payments that fluctuate monthly as well.

One method by which an insurer can handle this design is to treat the immediate variable annuity as though it had annual benefit payments, withdraw the appropriate annual amount, pay one-twelfth of it immediately, and put the remainder in a money market subaccount from which the other 11 monthly benefit payments will be made that year. Such an approach creates no additional risk or cost.

Another method is to pay a stable benefit for a 6- or 12-month period while tracking the benefits that would have been paid under the traditional approach. At the end of the current stability period, the cumulative overage or underage can be applied to the reserve. A new number of annuity units payable per benefit can be determined based on that fundable by the newly adjusted reserve. The process repeats at equal intervals.

However achieved, remedying income fluctuation through stabilizing benefits for a period poses substantially less risk—possibly even no risk—to an insurer than the offering of a minimum guaranteed level of income might. Prospective IVA purchasers should feel comfortable that an income stabilization feature of this nature and magnitude does not pose undue risk to the long-run viability of the insurance company.

Future developments in the realm of income stabilization might include some form of averaging technique—defined in the IVA contract and prospectus—where some multiperiod rolling average of fair market value of subaccounts is used to determine annuity benefit payments. Such averaging or smoothing techniques retard the abruptness with which annuity benefit payments can change. For example, using a 24-month average, a new monthly data point would be added and the oldest monthly data point would drop from the calculation, whereby 96% of the determination of the benefit payment remains stable and 4% is attributable to performance of the most recent period. This alleviates annuitant concern over benefit reductions that are "too far, too fast."

The IVA contract owner might have full subaccount investment discretion or might need to meet certain rules to qualify for eligibility to participate in such an income stabilization arrangement. Gains or losses in an averaging account that tracks stabilized annuity payments relative to traditional annuity payments would carry over with reallocations among subaccounts that determine annuity income.

Income stabilization for an investor/retiree may be more easily achieved through a combination of an IVA and other assets. This hybrid approach allows an IVA owner to supplement shortfalls in current IVA income relative to the investor's target income by making withdrawals from, say, a retail mutual fund. Similarly, to the extent current IVA income exceeds the investor's target income, the excess may be contributed to the retail mutual fund to replenish it.

OTHER PRODUCT DEVELOPMENT POSSIBILITIES

Insurers may look to carry over some practices from their deferred variable annuity product offerings into their IVA offerings. These might include:

- **Joint "Rights of Accumulation"**   Under this concept, holdings by individuals or by households of financial products manufactured by the insurer or its affiliates (e.g., mutual funds, variable annuities) are aggregated in value to determine the degree to which preferential treatment on the next product purchase will be offered, for example, in the way of a bonus or a reduced front-end load.
- **Bonuses**   The single premium may be "grossed up" or "bonused" by a certain percentage for IVA purchases made with account values of the same insurer's deferred variable annuities that have been in force for longer than some predetermined holding period in the way of a "loyalty bonus." Alternatively, the bonus may depend on premium size. To the extent that the bonus is covered by higher product charges—which are relatively less visible due to being embedded in the annuity unit value calculations and therefore do not hit customer account statements in the way of an explicit dollar charge—the bonus is more illusory than real.
- **Tiered Rates**   Larger premiums may qualify for preferential treatment. For example, the asset management fees that affect the annuity unit values might be lower above some premium threshold. If some expenses that are flat or relatively flat regardless of premium size—such as the cost to calculate periodic income benefits, to disburse benefits, to issue tax statements, to issue semiannual and annual reports, and to calculate reserves—are covered in pricing by a percent of assets charge (e.g., in the unit value calculation), then very high premiums pay substantially more than their share. As a result, they may receive relief via a lower M&E&A charge.

Securities firms and clearing firms will likely seek some degree of IVA product standardization so that they can transact this business more efficiently. This "commoditization" may put greater emphasis on payout rate comparisons per $1,000 of premium, although investment managers available within the product may still be a major differentiating factor.

COMMENTS ON PRODUCT VARIATIONS

It has been said "the insurance industry is always in the grip of its dumbest competitor!" By this is meant that insurers who stretch on product design, pricing, inclusion of ultrarich or highly volatile embedded options, commissions, sales promotions and the like in order to differentiate themselves and to win market share on an unsound basis temporarily steal sales from those companies with financially sound practices. Yet it is the continuing, healthy, well-run, and well-disciplined companies that often must make up the shortfalls of the radical companies through guaranty fund assessments, while the radical companies and the previously rationally managed companies drawn into their vortex of illogic merely fade into oblivion.

As a result, insurers have self-interest in appropriate regulatory oversight and periodic examination of the books and practices of all insurers by auditors and regulatory authorities. Quick detection of irrational pricing and imprudent risk taking is important, as are effective early warning systems.

Competition forces product innovation. By definition, product innovation tends to run ahead of a precisely defined regulatory framework for such products, since the regulations never envisioned them. As a result, insurers need to assess how existing regulations or anticipated regulations will apply to their specific product situation and cannot simply wait for regulation to catch up. Thus, there can be a lag between when an unsound offering is made and when clearly defined rules for valuing the liabilities or for holding adequate capital exist under which it becomes objectively determinable whether an offering is sound.

Insurers can enhance their profitability to the extent that they can design products whose psychologically *perceived value* exceeds their *actual value*. Greater degrees of product complexity make it increasingly challenging for consumers—or even their financial advisers—to ascertain measures of value on an absolute basis, although if comparable product offerings exist, they can at least ascertain measures of value on a relative basis.

Stock insurance companies are in business to maximize profit for the enterprise. They are not the United Way. As a result, they look to sell what the public wants to buy and what financial advisers find most salable. IVA products may therefore be loaded up with features offering higher psychological appeal, even if the product design is less economically beneficial in meeting a retiree's desire for lifelong, inflation-protected income. For example, an IVA product design may offer a payout option featuring:

- *Liquidity*—a full or partial withdrawal of a visible account value any time during the first five years (subject to a surrender charge of 5% grading down to 1%).
- *Death benefit*—current account balance in years 1 through 5; in years 6 through 15, the present value of future annuity benefits through year 15 (or continuing payments to the beneficiary through year 15).
- *Floor benefit*—all annuity benefits guaranteed to be at least 80% of the initial benefit.
- *Income stability*—monthly annuity income, with the benefit level changing annually based on subaccount performance relative to the AIR.
- *Guarantee of 15 years of annuity benefits*—annuity benefits payable for life, with a further guarantee that benefits will be paid for at least 15 years to the annuitant, if surviving, or to the beneficiary.

All these factors give the product psychological appeal. It is often important to offer such features if only as a defensive measure to keep competitors from selling against your company by pointing out their absence.

Because of full liquidity during the first 5 years, the annuity benefits are lower than they otherwise would be because there is (or should be) no discounting the deferred lifetime annuity that starts 15 years out for survivorship during those 5 years, since those who find themselves terminally ill will remove all their funds, forfeiting nothing to longer-lived annuitants.

Because of the 15-year certain period, annuity benefits are lower than they otherwise would be. The deferred lifetime annuity that starts 15 years out can, however, reflect discounting for survivorship in years 6 through 15 since there is no liquidity in this interval.

The floor benefit may come at an extra annual price of 0.85% of the underlying reserve. For example, on a $300,000 reserve, this would reduce annual income by about $2,550.

The liquidity, certain period, and floor benefit features each add some form of guarantee that serves to reduce retirement income in the majority of scenarios, defeating to varying degrees the main reason for owning an IVA. This may be because humans often are what some have termed "pathologically risk averse."

An insurer offering such a prepackaged combination of benefits may also offer lower-cost annuity options. It is incumbent on the financial adviser to aid his or her investor client in the determination of trade-offs between more comprehensive, higher-cost options and less-inclusive, lower-cost options that maximize initial retirement income. For example, the aforementioned product design containing the features described by the five bullet points effectively decomposes into a 5-year systematic withdrawal followed by a 10-year designated period annuity followed by a life annuity in order to possess a period of liquidity, a period containing a death benefit and guaranteed annuity benefits regardless of survival, and a period where a lifetime of annuity income is guaranteed. While psychologically appealing, a financial adviser should contrast such a prepackaged arrangement with other less expensive alternative options—even a straight life annuity at the low-cost, high-income end of the spectrum—to ensure that the client is aware of the economic trade-offs.

In addition to joint rights of accumulation, bonuses, and tiered rates, future IVA product offerings may contain:

- Ability to change AIR.
- Ability to structure a benefit based on different AIRs in different years.
- Ability to change benefit frequency.
- Ability to change liquidity period and/or switch to alternative liquidity options defined differently.
- More complex definitions of floor guarantees; for example, nonlevel floors, temporary floors, choice of floor level, floors with deductibles or copays, floor and ceiling combinations.
- Additional death benefits beyond those in traditional certain period, unit refund, and installment refund options.
- Benefits that adjust via mortality experience participation and expense experience participation, as well as investment experience participation.
- Variety of income stability or income smoothing options; for example, income can only change by $X\%$ per period (month, quarter, half year, year), regardless of subaccount performance—much like an adjustable rate mortgage (ARM)—possibly subject to a lifetime floor, ceiling, or corridor cap.
- Mortality credits spread among survivors in other than a uniform fashion; for example, by formula that grants proportionately more to the oldest or to those who have participated in the program the longest.
- Medical underwriting and other underwriting; for example, avocation, geographic region, credit history, education, wealth.
- Benefit payments in multiple currencies.

Product design is limited only by imagination and regulation—and even regulation can be adjusted if a compelling case is made. Of course, "more is better" only if it improves an individual's ability to achieve his or her objectives. For example, the ability to change benefit frequency may be of little value to anyone. The ability to increase the death benefit or to increase liquidity almost certainly is to the detriment of the main objective: maximizing lifetime retirement income.

STOCHASTIC MODELING OF MORTALITY

Variable income annuity companies have long recognized the stochastic nature of investment risks inherent in this longevity insurance financial security program. Companies may run a large number of hypothetical future investment scenarios when establishing IVA product pricing, reserving policy, and internal target surplus formulas.

There has been considerably less focus on the stochastic modeling of mortality risk associated with IVAs. This is because for immediate annuities issued at traditional retirement ages, the investment return assumption has a significantly more pronounced impact than does the mortality assumption.

This is easily understood. To arrive at the present value of a future series of projected annuity benefit payments, they are discounted for interest and survivorship. The AIR might be on the order of 5%. Even at age 70, the chance of a female annuitant dying before reaching age 71 is only about 1% (per the Annuity 2000 Basic Table).

A life-contingent payment of $100 one year out in such a situation is $100 \times 0.99/1.05$, or $94.29. Discounting for mortality (i.e., survivorship) alone would result in a present value of $99.00. Discounting for investment return alone would result in a present value of $95.24.

Thus, it is clear why the focus of stochastic modeling of fluctuation phenomena primarily resides with the investment return element, since it has the more dramatic effect. Yet actual mortality experience will exhibit some degree of dispersion about the mean values heretofore often used as a static pricing assumption. Stochastic mortality modeling techniques will be increasingly used to gain further insight into the economics of longevity insurance offered through IVA products.

LIFE ANNUITY MORTALITY RISK SECURITIZATION

It has been mentioned that life-contingent annuity writers can sculpt their risk profile by also selling life insurance and achieving some measure of "natural immunization"—playing the risk of living too long in one product against the risk of living too short in the other. It has also been mentioned that annuity writers have other tools with which to sculpt their risk profile. For example, if they have assumed liabilities with embedded options, such as by selling variable income annuities with a floor benefit (GPAF) feature, they can assume assets in the way of complex put options that (partially and imperfectly) mitigate this investment performance risk. In a similar vein, tools are beginning to evolve with which annuity writers—and their reinsurers—can sculpt their mortality risk profile.

Mortality bonds and swaps with embedded mortality options are potentially useful instruments in the management of mortality risks via securitization. In 2003, the first mortality bond was traded on *pure mortality risk*. This contrasts with earlier securitizations associated with annuity and life insurance business where future cash flows were sold in exchange for an up-front payment, just like any other asset-backed securitization (e.g., credit card receivables).

The first mortality bond was based on a multicountry mortality index and hedged life insurance, which concerns itself with "too many" deaths. The bond pays interest commensurate with the risk assumed. If the mortality index is too high, principal is reduced. If the mortality index is excessively high, principal is exhausted. This principle is akin to catastrophe bonds—sometimes called "cat bonds"—used in conjunction with property/casualty insurance.

Writers of life-contingent immediate annuities—fixed or variable—as well as reinsurers and pension plans focus on the opposite concern of "too few" deaths. As a result, the structure of a mortality bond counterpart to handle this type of risk is immediately discernable.

As mentioned in the immediately preceding section, mortality is a dynamic rather than a static process. As a result, mere extrapolation of past trends may not accurately predict the future. For example, mortality improvement factors may be other than postulated. Mortality risk management—in the way of guarding against the economic ramifications of excessive longevity for life-contingent immediate annuity writers—thus becomes an indispensable function of operational management.

If demand for life-contingent annuities increases, either through increased private-sector awareness of their benefits or through governmental actions such as tax incentives or Social Security reform, securitization through mortality bonds may be a means for insurers and reinsurers to increase capacity to write such business as additional capital is brought to the annuity industry. Longevity insurance risk—to whatever degree the insurer desires, the terms of the financial instrument specify, and the competitive marketplace and regulatory landscape allow—is passed to bondholders.

One argument proposed as to why investors might prefer to hold mortality bonds over conventional bonds of identical investment quality is because of their low covariance with other holdings of the investor. If mortality bonds are assumedly uncorrelated or lowly correlated with conventional bond markets, then substituting mortality bonds into the investment portfolio for conventional bonds of the same quality offers identical expected returns with lower overall volatility, improving the investor's portfolio characteristics (i.e., left-shifting the "efficient frontier").

Unlike conventional bonds, where default risk is tied to general economic conditions, industry conditions, and management decisions, default risk in mortality bonds is tied exclusively to mortality experience, that is, excessive mortality (for life insurance) or light mortality (for annuities). Other than by coincidence, default experience of conventional bonds is likely unassociated in timing with that of mortality bonds.

Figure 18.13 portrays the workings of a mortality securitization. The annuity company buys reinsurance from a special purpose vehicle (SPV). The SPV issues bonds to investors. The SPV invests both the reinsurance premium and the bond sale proceeds in default-free securities, allowing it to pay the reinsurance benefits due the annuity company and the bond payments due the investors with certainty, according to the terms of the reinsurance agreement and the terms of the bond contract, respectively.

The reinsurance agreement and the bond contract convey mortality risk precisely from the annuity company to the investors. The SPV assumes no mortality risk but, rather, functions to hold the capital until experience dictates its distribution.

Theoretically—and perhaps someday practically—a "mortality swap" could be used in lieu of or in addition to mortality bonds. How this would work is more easily first conceived in terms of immediate fixed annuities.

Suppose an insurer must pay \$10,000 annually at the beginning of the year to each of 100 annuitants now aged x if then alive; that is, $l_x = 100$. The insurer pays \$10,000 $\cdot$ l_x, or \$1,000,000, right now. In future years, the insurer has a total obligation to annuitants equal to \$10,000 $\cdot$ l_{x+t}.

The annuity-writing insurer and a swap counterparty agree on a set of duration-based factors F_t such that in year t the insurer pays to the counterparty a fixed amount equal to \$10,000 $\cdot$ F_t and receives from the counterparty \$10,000 $\cdot$ l_{x+t}. The insurer desires to pay a fixed, known-in-advance series of payments and receive a floating or variable, unknown-in-advance series of payments.

Only *net* payments are actually made. If more annuitants survive than expected, then the insurer receives \$10,000 $\cdot$ $(l_{x+t} - F_t)$. While the insurer

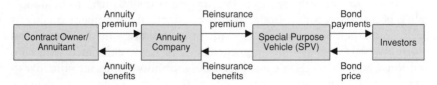

FIGURE 18.13 Mortality Bond Cash Flow Diagram

owes more in aggregate to annuitants than expected, this is offset by positive cash flow generated from the swap. If fewer annuitants survive than expected, the insurer makes a payment to the swap counterparty. Either way, the insurer via the swap has transformed a series of future annuity benefit cash flows unknown in amount for a series of fixed future cash flows.

Whether an initial exchange of cash, if any, is required to initiate the swap depends on how the series of F_t values compares with the series of values of the expected number of survivors $E[l_{x+t}]$ from the initial group of 100 annuitants. Any year-by-year differences between F_t and $E[l_{x+t}]$ are discounted at the appropriate rate based on current bond market yields to determine the magnitude of any up-front exchange of cash to initiate the swap. For example, if the counterparty's opinion is that the insurer's l_{x+t} values are too high, the counterparty may simply agree to let $F_t = l_{x+t}$ for all durations, in which case zero cash changes hands at swap inception.

Both mortality bonds and mortality swaps function to hedge cash flows of an annuity company. To what degree securitization of pure mortality risk occurs remains to be seen. More and larger securitization transactions spawned by increased demand for immediate annuities and mortality hedging thereof will likely drive down securitization transaction expenses. Given that life-contingent annuities can span multiple decades, effective hedge instruments need to be appropriately long but needn't run to the end of the mortality table. For example, hedging immediate annuities for 25 years for a group of 70-year-olds provides meaningful (although incomplete) longevity risk protection for an annuity company.

Investment management (e.g., mutual fund) companies related to insurance companies would love to manage the potentially enormous volume of life-contingent annuity assets available in the decades ahead. Their sister insurance companies, however, heretofore often had reservations about collecting those assets in equally large volume given the risk associated with revolutionary, life-prolonging, technical innovations.

While such large mutual fund companies with small insurance company affiliates were comfortable managing assets associated with non-life-contingent annuities and the non-life-contingent portion of life annuities with certain periods or refund features, some were sufficiently skittish so as to desire to reinsure all immediate annuity mortality risk. Life annuity mortality risk securitization offers a new avenue to lay off this risk.

PROPRIETARY PRODUCTS

To gain access to a securities firm's network of financial advisers, an insurance company manufacturing a variable annuity is sometimes asked or required to create a special product version that includes investment funds managed by an investment company owned by the securities firm. Such an arrangement is frequently known as "plug 'n' play." Effectively, the securities firm tells the insurer, "If you 'plug' one or several of our investment funds into your variable annuity product offering or product suite, you can 'play' in our system."

The base product of an insurer pursuing this approach is often referred to as a "common chassis," into which one or more funds managed by the investment operation of the securities firm looking to sell the variable annuity are plugged.

Depending on its size and the power of the securities firm's ability to distribute variable annuity products, such an arrangement and the additional expenses associated with it (relative to simply selling a standard product offering of the insurer) may or may not warrant proprietary product development.

To the extent there are multiple annuity company manufacturers—which securities firms may view as simply product vendors from which they are free to choose—securities firms may determine which variable annuities are the most successful selling products in the industry and then demand customization for their firm to include their funds.

If securities firms have an affiliated life insurance company in their corporate family, an additional demand may be to coinsure the IVA product. While this forces the original insurance company to give up some portion of its potential profit, it has the desirable effect of aligning the interests of the original writer and the coinsurer. For example, if the sales area of the securities firm presses for higher sales compensation than is supportable by the product, their own insurance affiliate may be more influential about keeping this in check. This is because the reinsurer "follows the fortunes" of the original writing insurer, due to their comparable risk taking.

An annuity company creating a proprietary product for a broker/dealer will want to investigate the partnership history of the broker/dealer. Some broker/dealers truly value genuine, long-term partnerships and adopt a philosophy that the partnership needs to be a win-win proposition—mutually beneficial, where both parties must prosper in any actions taken affecting the product. Other broker/dealers solicit multiple partners, play them off against each other, and hire consultants every few years to bring in a new partner whose price of entry is to offer a better deal than existing partners, forcing one or more out. This cycle repeats with the end result being that the broker/dealer controlling distribution wins and the annuity companies lose, since they are forced to match a higher deal than that to which they originally agreed or are forced out completely before having a chance to recover proprietary product development costs.

ANNUITY WRITERS' STRATEGIC BASES OF COMPETITION

Insurers need to determine the basis on which they wish to compete: product, price, or service. They can strive to be *product innovators*, which can be a costly approach in terms of research-and-development (R&D) expenditures; divining how regulations that never envisioned such product construction should apply; training regulators, wholesalers, customer service representatives, and financial advisers; conducting focus groups; and not knowing in advance whether their concepts are truly marketable. A challenge is to develop products and features differentiable from existing offerings while at the same time being sufficiently mainstream so as to gain the level of market share targeted.

Annuity writers can strive to compete on the basis of *operational efficiency*. They provide mainstream products the acceptability of which has already been proven in the marketplace and do so at low cost, focusing on being operationally efficient. They may be "fast followers" when it comes to adding products and features, waiting until others have spent the R&D money and trained financial advisers on new concepts.

Annuity writers may choose a *customer intimacy* value discipline. They may have plain-vanilla product offerings and average prices, yet they look to distinguish themselves by getting closer to their customers than their competitors do. They may offer "tiered" or "concierge" services for their best customers, well beyond what competitors offer and even well beyond the somewhat higher than average standard they use for their own other customers. They may offer the longest hours of access to human customer service representatives, may have the fastest customer service response time (e.g., in answering phones, in resolving problems), may have the most informative and customer-friendly account statements, may have the best customer newsletter, may have the most customer-friendly web site, and so on. Those attributes may apply more to direct-to-consumer companies looking to sell over a toll-free 800 phone number or the Internet.

Many annuity manufacturers view the financial adviser as their customer. A customer intimacy value discipline in the world of financial adviser-assisted annuity sales may entail high-quality wholesaling, offering negotiated discounts on office products that financial advisers frequently use in their businesses, offering not only product support but also coaching in running their business operations, providing new sales ideas daily or weekly, and offering special sections of web sites with a library of concepts that financial advisers may reference or use as a tutorial.

Annuity writers internally monitor "key value drivers," which may include fund performance versus benchmarks, expense levels, wholesaler productivity, premium growth, average premium size, patent applications and grants, customer service survey rankings, number of new financial advisers selling the insurer's IVA, number of justifiable written complaints, percentage of financial advisers at targeted securities firms selling the insurer's IVA, percentage of contract owners electing lower-cost electronic account statements and prospectuses, distribution breadth, and a host of other factors. Key value drivers may be monitored on a real-time "performance dashboard" that offers a snapshot glimpse of financial metrics, such as embedded value measures, in addition to the factors just listed.

The point is that the drivers of value measured and monitored depend on the value discipline that the annuity writer has selected as the primary basis on which it will compete. Given finite resources, it cannot hope to achieve execution of *all* value disciplines in a fashion superior to its competitors, especially those competitors that are allocating their resources to be superb in just their one chosen value discipline.

In the United States, the competitive environment for insurance companies is intense. By way of comparison, at the time of this writing, bank return on equity (ROE) values are in the 15% range, whereas insurance company ROE values are in the 12% range, with banks consequently enjoying higher price-to-earnings (P/E) ratios. While the two industries differ—the insurance business being a long-term business with long-term liabilities and not principally transaction oriented, whereas the banking business is a short-term business with short-term liabilities and heavily transaction oriented—the point is that such a comparison indicates the relatively thin margins on annuity business. Domestic annuity business is currently a low-margin, high-volume business, akin to "picking up dimes with a bulldozer."

CHAPTER 19

Conclusion

The logical way of reaching a conclusion is by following a train of thought.

—Anonymous

Immediate variable annuities (IVAs) meet a very real need. While government-sponsored Social Security and corporate-sponsored defined benefit pension plans also provide lifetime income, there's no other individual financial product in the world that provides insurance against living too long and offers a higher level of income with a lower probability of outliving it when the underlying assets are identically invested than an immediate annuity. Immediate variable annuities can guarantee *inexhaustible* income for a lifetime, and their variable nature gives the annuitant the prospect of having that income sustain or increase in purchasing power.

The supremacy of variable income annuities over alternative retirement income vehicles can be mathematically demonstrated and need not reside with purely emotion-based arguments. Persuasion of prospective IVA purchasers can and does rely on emotional factors that supplement logic-based factors. For example, the potential to keep up with or to outpace inflation, the ability to control the allocation of investments that govern one's income, and the guarantee of a complete lifetime of income have strong emotional appeal.

Although this volume contains mathematical formulas to facilitate a relatively full understanding of the subject,[1] end consumers who enjoy its benefits needn't fully understand all the esoteric intricacies any more than they need to understand their automobile or television set to enjoy those benefits. For end users, variable income annuities need not be "rocket science." Rather, retirees need to understand that (1) the income they'll need to sustain their standard of living for the whole of life likely looks like the curve in Figure 19.1 and (2) they should therefore structure their assets in such a manner as to produce income having a similar pattern at the maximum level safely achievable.

For example, suppose a new retiree selects an investment mix (e.g., X% stock, 100% minus X% bond) that based on historic norms might be expected to generate a 7% return net of investment management fees and mortality and expense (M&E) risk charges. Suppose the retiree assumes a 4% inflation rate. He or she may want to consider a 3% assumed investment rate (AIR). While there's no guarantee that annuity benefits will increase annually at approximately 4% [(1 + 0.07 return) ÷ (1 + 0.03 AIR) ≈ (1 + 0.04 benefit increase)] to offset assumed 4% inflation, one may wish to consider selecting an AIR that synchronizes with investment mix and inflation assumption.

Immediate variable annuities can be used in conjunction with immediate fixed annuities. The fixed annuity may provide a guaranteed baseline level of income with the variable annuity offering the opportunity for increasing income.

One should avoid overemphasis on near-term factors, where 100% assurance of income level provided by immediate fixed annuities may color one's decision-making process to an undue degree. For example, if an individual can receive $55,000 of annual immediate fixed annuity income at age 60 and has $50,000 of annual expenses, it may be shortsighted to enter into

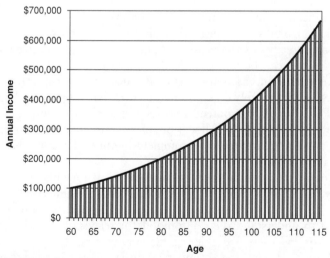

FIGURE 19.1 Retirement Income Pattern Needed to Sustain Purchasing Power (under constant 3.5% inflation rate)

such an arrangement. Recall the earlier inflation chart (Figure 1.3) showing that at 4% inflation, annual expenses will be $109,556 in 20 years and $162,170 in 30 years. That $55,000 guaranteed annual income may seem like less of a good idea further into retirement.[2] Over the long run of retirement, immediate variable annuities may be seen as the optimal instrument.

Immediate inflation-indexed annuities, where the benefit level is tied to an appropriate Consumer Price Index (CPI), may offer a good means for the benefit level to keep pace with inflation—at least as long as the goods and services desired by the annuitant match up reasonably well with the basket of goods and services comprising the price index used for immediate annuity benefit adjustment.[3] Insurers have historically been reluctant to offer such a CPI-adjusted immediate annuity because (1) the rates of future inflation and therefore the projected liabilities are unknown at time of issue, leading to the possibility that future benefit levels might be significantly higher than assumed in pricing if conventional immediate fixed annuity investment approaches are used and (2) alternative investment approaches that allow better asset-liability management of CPI-adjusted immediate annuities are in their infancy.[4] Several U.S. insurers now offer CPI-adjusted immediate annuities, with some placing an annual cap (of about 10%) on benefit increases. CPI-adjusted immediate annuity benefits may decrease if the CPI decreases, although some product versions stipulate that at no time will the annuity benefit be less than the initial benefit.

Immediate variable annuities can be used in conjunction with mutual funds or other investments to customize the desired level of income stability. For example, to the extent the immediate variable annuity produces less income than desired for a period, withdrawals from more liquid assets can be taken. To the extent the IVA produces more income than needed for a period, liquid assets can be replenished.

Owning an immediate annuity in addition to a conventional portfolio of stocks, bonds, mutual funds, certificates of deposit, and cash substantially reduces the odds you'll have inadequate income to sustain your standard of living. A hybrid approach featuring some percentage of a conventional portfolio for liquidity and featuring some percentage of immediate annuities for longevity insurance will provide the optimal balance for many retirees. These financial tools allow one to be the master of unknown longevity rather than its victim.

Some classes of individuals—particularly those who survive to advanced ages—are going to have inadequate income to sustain your standard of living. This is a looming social problem. Absent longevity insurance, longevity pauperizes retirees. With longevity insurance in place, an antidissipation mechanism safeguards against pauperization; accumulated retirement wealth cannot be dissipated in a premature way.

It will become increasingly difficult to ask the progressively smaller working population to give up a greater portion of its output for the progressively larger elderly population. Governments of industrialized nations will no longer be able to afford the fiscal burdens of social insurance pensions they did in the past. A minimal pension system may be replaced by welfare programs to ensure provision of basic necessities.

Individuals have, to date, more heavily relied on the so-called "three-legged stool" of Social Security, employer pension, and personal savings to carry them financially through retirement years. The first two legs of this traditional three-legged stool of retirement security are gradually being filed down. Employer-sponsored defined benefit pension plans that provided monthly lifetime income based on a formula involving final average salary and years of service are diminishing in number. Defined contribution plans that provide retirement savings accounts are increasing in importance, but they leave participants with the risk of applying their accumulated savings in such a way as to carry them through retirement. One idea for tax-qualified defined contribution plans is to require employees to examine all distribution options and to certify their choices before receiving their benefits because employees presented with an option of a large lump sum may not perceive an actuarially equivalent annuity as equivalent.

To the extent that individuals use personal savings and defined contribution retirement plan account values to carry them through retirement, they have typically counted on principal plus investment credits to achieve this. Due to longer periods in retirement, market depreciation, inadequate retirement savings, and other factors, it will be increasingly important in the future to rely on principal plus investment credits *plus* mortality credits to sustain retirees financially for a lifetime. Because immediate annuities offer retirement income predicated on the combination of three items—principal, investment credits, and mortality credits—rather than on only the first two, applying $200,000 to an immediate annuity will generate an income stream that is larger than the one the $200,000 could generate identically invested outside the annuity. In that sense, retirement security may be enhanced even though liquidity is relinquished.

At more advanced ages, annual "mortality credits" tend to have a more pronounced influence than "investment credits" on retirement income; that is, credit for survivorship exceeds credit for investment earnings. For example, at an age where 10% of the annuitant population dies (around age 89 for males), because the projected benefit was multiplied by 0.9 in pricing to reflect that only 90% of the group would survive to receive the annuity payment the following year, the benefit is divided by 0.9 going the other direction, where reserves accumulate. This causes the credit for survivorship to be

$(1 / 0.9) - 1 = 1.111 - 1 = 0.111$, or 11.1%, that year. Investment earnings might also be positive but could well be below 11.1%, causing "mortality credits" to have a bigger impact on annuity benefits that year than "investment credits."

This is why monthly benefits for the same premium increase so much at higher issue ages. It also explains why the rate of return in the Annuiland example was so high. Mortality credits greatly added to the 5% investment credits.

The dichotomy of desiring complete protection from longevity risk and complete access to all of one's assets all of the time will increasingly be resolved in favor of the former. As people see relatives, neighbors, and friends deplete assets—making the risk real to them—longevity risk protection begins to carry more value than complete asset accessibility. Much as a pebble dropped in a pool creates a wave that extends in an ever-widening circle, communication and circumstances will spread appreciation for the ability of variable income annuities to provide longevity risk protection superior to alternatives. Like automobile and sailboat racing, those who seize the lead by adeptly navigating this turn—retiree/investors and insurers alike—will experience victory. Mastering a deep change requires understanding, passion, and creativity. Cultural desires for instant gratification (e.g., fast food) and something for nothing (e.g., lotteries) impede the long-range outlook and the perspective on trade-offs necessary to achieve a longevity risk protection objective.

It will require a paradigm shift—the moment when a new worldview replaces an old one—for retirees to perceive that immediate variable annuities are exactly what can provide them with *control* over their financial destiny. A 60-year-old female doesn't know if she'll need her retirement savings to sustain her for one year or for one half century. As Figure 19.2 illustrates, the length of her future lifetime is so uncertain that the likelihood

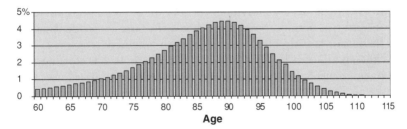

FIGURE 19.2 Percentage of Deaths by Age for 60-Year-Old Females. *Source:* Annuity 2000 Basic Table.

she'll die in any one particular future year never even reaches 4.5%. As Figure 19.2 also illustrates, the likelihood that a 60-year-old female will die at age 70, thereby requiring income for 10 years, equals the likelihood that she will die at age 102, thereby requiring income for 42 years. Absent an immediate annuity, the wide variance in the number of years for which she must plan a series of withdrawals to sustain her makes her program very susceptible to suboptimization: She either plans too short and exhausts her income or plans too long and lives on lesser income than was necessary. Either way, she unnecessarily exposes herself to longevity risk. Clearly, due to the wide dispersion of future years she might live—anywhere from 0 years to 55 years—setting up a withdrawal program to sustain her for a period equal to her 26-year life expectancy—that is, to age 86—is dangerous, as over half of 60-year-old females will survive beyond that point. As such, whether she admits it consciously or not, unless she has amassed massive assets, absent use of an immediate annuity her financial destiny is beyond her control.

There is a lag—a gestation period—between invention and widespread commercial application. While the application of an invention may be obvious to the inventor, the target audience may require persuasion. Change can be challenging to sell. An invention may be ahead of its time. An invention may solve a problem that people don't know they have. All these statements may be true for the invention of the IVA.

It is inconceivable that rational individuals—once made aware of a mechanism to ensure lifetime income on a basis having characteristics superior to alternatives—will let their situation degenerate to the more primitive conditions of the past whereby they are reduced to going it alone, hoping longevity doesn't decimate their income, and knowing that if it does they will be reduced to living at a subsistence level on the government dole. While it takes learning for individuals to understand IVA benefits and to overcome certain psychological hurdles related to IVA purchases, it is hardly likely that any approach could be more dangerous than the system currently in vogue, where individuals believe they should go it alone—with no mortality risk pooling—and hope that luck, fate, or accident will spare them financial hardship often associated with longevity.

While an IVA is a better solution to a problem that is starting to have weaker but easier-to-sell solutions, its ascendancy in importance and use will escalate in speed as better tools evolve to illustrate the value of an IVA as measured against competing alternatives. This process of enlightenment will accelerate as more baby boomers, with their attractive retirement assets, reach the systematic liquidation phase of their economic lives.

Demographics and increased consumer awareness of the benefits of immediate variable annuities bode well for the future of this product. Given the trillions of dollars of retirement savings assets, the U.S. age distribution, and exclusive franchise rights, with appropriate education and favorable tax law conducive to self-reliance over governmental dependency, income annuities may usher in the Golden Age of the insurance industry—as banking and mutual fund industry retirement assets migrate to some degree to annuity vehicles that optimize their distribution and thereby maximize economic quality of life in retirement.

The immediate annuity industry will prosper by serving a fundamental need of the population: enhanced financial security. Immediate annuity growth will arise from an intrinsic human need for income security. While tax incentives may be implemented to encourage greater economic self-reliance through immediate annuities, because immediate annuities fulfill a genuine human need, their growth is assured independent of tax structure—progressive, flat, or regressive. While tax law may affect the *rate* of growth of their usage, immediate annuity existence and growth are driven by the control they bring to a retiree over his or her financial destiny, not by tax law.

A high proportion of wealth of currently retired households is "preannuitized"; that is, if one reflects on one's personal balance sheet an asset equal to the present value of defined benefit pension plan income and another asset equal to the present value of Social Security income, it is seen that a high proportion of wealth is preannuitized. As a result, currently retired households (appropriately) seek to keep much of their remaining assets liquid. In contrast, younger cohorts will likely have smaller proportions of preannuitized wealth—as defined contribution plan account balances replace defined benefit pension plan lifetime incomes and as the richness of Social Security benefits subsides. An expected result is progressively increasing demand for annuitization as successively younger cohorts age.

While securities and tax laws may vary by country, the underlying variable income annuity concepts and mechanics apply equally well around the world. The United States might lead in variable income annuity product development advancements for the near-term simply because domestic demographics favor greatly escalated use, but one would expect the global spread of these instruments. Such spread won't be isotropic but rather will naturally occur faster in countries with the insurance, investment, and legal frameworks advanced enough to accommodate variable income annuities.

> "...*with all thy getting, get understanding.*"
> —Solomon, *Proverbs 4:7*

TABLE 19.1   The Future of Immediate Variable Annuities: Factors Favoring
IVA Growth

- Reduced availability of defined benefit pensions.
- Increased use of defined contribution retirement savings plans, where participants desiring lifetime income elect an IVA.
- Uncertainty over Social Security benefit levels, as relatively fewer workers must support relatively more retirees.
- U.S. demographics of baby-boomer cohort transitioning into retirement— enormous target market.
- Longer lives lead to increased awareness of risk of outliving one's assets.
- Desire for retirement income inflation protection.
- Large pool of assets in deferred variable annuities that can annuitize in the same product.
- Inadequate retirement savings prompts the need for supplementation by survivorship credits.
- Tax deferral.
- Ability to reallocate and rebalance investment subaccounts without taxation.
- Ability to meet IRS required minimum distribution (RMD) rules without the need to calculate the RMD every year.
- Possibility of improved tax treatment for immediate annuities to encourage greater economic self-reliance and to deal with the issue of inadequate retirement savings by encouraging seniors to stretch their assets through election of lifetime income annuity options.

Regional mortality rate and mortality improvement factor differences must be recognized.

Factors favoring IVA growth appear in Table 19.1. Factors restricting IVA growth, along with ways to overcome these restricting factors, appear in Table 19.2.

Just as people don't want to learn at three minutes to midnight that the master plan they expected to execute at the stroke of twelve is flawed, they similarly don't want to learn at age 90 (as they just ran out of money) that they should have purchased an immediate variable annuity at some earlier point. Here's hoping that information gleaned from the pages of this book may help you make an informed decision as to whether and to what extent an immediate variable annuity may be right for you.

Sometimes a broad array of new information can seem to be merely a sequence of haphazardly associated images like those seen in dreams—what physiologists call phantasmagoria. This volume will have accomplished its mission if it helped crystallize the cornucopia of topics surrounding variable income annuities into a more cohesive whole for you.

TABLE 19.2   The Future of Immediate Variable Annuities: Factors Restricting IVA Growth

Restricting Factor	Ways to Overcome Restricting Factor
• Illiquidity.	• Educate consumers: —Why illiquidity is key to success of IVA program. —That liquidity reduces retirement income, and maximizing retirement income is a primary objective. —That liquidity features can be added, but most serve to cancel survivorship credits during liquidity period and reduce every annuity benefit payment. —That the premium is "spent" on longevity insurance, as opposed to "invested" in a fund. —To fund liquidity needs separately.
• Lack of guaranteed income level.	• Educate consumers that due to pattern of future income needs, potential for upside income increases are more important than downside income guarantees. • IVA guaranteed minimum floor benefit, although additional cost of this guarantee decreases every annuity benefit payment. • Create guaranteed, baseline income level through immediate fixed annuity, preferably one that increases benefits $X\%$ per year.
• Income fluctuation.	• Income stabilization feature. • Asset allocation selections that produce more stable IVA income.
• Perception of loss of control.	• Educate consumers that while they do not have access to additional withdrawals beyond regularly scheduled annuity benefits, they retain elements of control, including: —Ability to control their assets while living, via investment allocation. —Ability to control their assets after death, via naming beneficiaries to receive any proceeds due after death. —Ability to vote proxy statements regarding management policies of investment funds.
• Financial advisers' perception that front-end commission on IVA sale is last commission they'll ever receive on this pool of dollars.	• Trail commissions for financial advisers that run for lifetime of annuity payout, based on percentage of IVA reserve or benefits.

Having accumulated savings to sustain oneself during retirement years, understanding the potential of a variable income annuity to safeguard against longevity risk enhances one's knowledge base for making informed decisions that can improve quality of life. Even King Solomon two millennia ago acknowledged the value of understanding.

Some view the underlying mathematics to this topic as having a special elegance, like Bertrand Russell, who said, "Mathematics, rightly viewed, possesses not only truth, but supreme beauty—a beauty cold and austere, like that of sculpture."[5] Others may see mathematics merely as a tool to accomplish the desired application: creation of a sound system to enhance quality of life during its final decades on this side of eternity.

I hope the grand adventure of understanding the elegance of a variable income annuity-based financial security system has been a pleasurable one for you. As a Spanish proverb goes, "The pleasures of the senses pass quickly, but those of the mind are ever with us, even to the end of our journey."

Appendixes

A Annuity 2000 Basic Mortality Table[1]

B Annuity 2000 Mortality Table[2]

C Single Premium for Single Life Only Annuity-Immediate of $1 per Year Annuity 2000 Basic Table and Annuity 2000 Mortality Table

D Annuity 2000 Basic Table Complete Expectation of Life, $\mathring{e}_x$

E Annuity 2000 Mortality Table Complete Expectation of Life, $\mathring{e}_x$

F Projection Scale G Mortality Improvement Factors[3]

G Annuity 2000 Mortality Tables—Male Commutation Columns D, N, S, at 3%, 4%, 5%, 6%

H Annuity 2000 Mortality Tables—Female Commutation Columns D, N, S, at 3%, 4%, 5%, 6%

I Annuity 2000 Mortality Tables—Male Commutation Columns C, M, R, at 3%, 4%, 5%, 6%

J Annuity 2000 Mortality Tables—Female Commutation Columns C, M, R, at 3%, 4%, 5%, 6%

K Annuity 2000 Mortality Table—Male Mortality Functions L_x, T_x, Y_x

L Annuity 2000 Mortality Table—Female Mortality Functions L_x, T_x, Y_x

M n-Year Fixed-Period Annuity-Due Present Values $\ddot{a}_{\overline{n}|}^{(m)}$ at 3%, 4%, 5%, 6% AIR

N n-Year Fixed-Period Annuity-Immediate Present Values $a_{\overline{n}|}^{(m)}$ at 3%, 4%, 5%, 6% AIR

O Benefits Conferred on Immediate Variable Annuity Contract Owners

P Proof of the Law of Large Numbers

Q Derivation of Final Benefit Payment of Fixed-Period Annuity for $n + f$ Years

R 1971 Individual Annuity Mortality Table[4]

S 1983 Table a[5]

575

APPENDIX A

Annuity 2000 Basic Mortality Table

Age Nearest Birthday (x)	1,000 q_x		Age Nearest Birthday (x)	1,000 q_x		Age Nearest Birthday (x)	1,000 q_x	
	Male	Female*		Male	Female*		Male	Female*
5	0.324	0.189	45	1.948	1.043	85	81.326	63.907
6	0.301	0.156	46	2.198	1.148	86	88.863	71.815
7	0.286	0.131	47	2.463	1.267	87	96.958	80.682
8	0.328	0.131	48	2.740	1.400	88	105.631	90.557
9	0.362	0.134	49	3.028	1.548	89	114.858	101.307
10	0.390	0.140	50	3.330	1.710	90	124.612	112.759
11	0.413	0.148	51	3.647	1.888	91	134.861	124.733
12	0.431	0.158	52	3.980	2.079	92	145.575	137.054
13	0.446	0.170	53	4.331	2.286	93	156.727	149.552
14	0.458	0.183	54	4.698	2.507	94	168.290	162.079
15	0.470	0.197	55	5.077	2.746	95	180.245	174.492
16	0.481	0.212	56	5.465	3.003	96	192.565	186.647
17	0.495	0.228	57	5.861	3.280	97	205.229	198.403
18	0.510	0.244	58	6.265	3.578	98	218.683	210.337
19	0.528	0.260	59	6.694	3.907	99	233.371	233.027
20	0.549	0.277	60	7.170	4.277	100	249.741	237.051
21	0.573	0.294	61	7.714	4.699	101	268.237	252.985
22	0.599	0.312	62	8.348	5.181	102	289.305	271.406
23	0.627	0.330	63	9.093	5.732	103	313.391	292.893
24	0.657	0.349	64	9.968	6.347	104	340.940	318.023
25	0.686	0.367	65	10.993	7.017	105	372.398	347.373
26	0.714	0.385	66	12.188	7.734	106	408.210	381.520
27	0.738	0.403	67	13.572	8.491	107	448.823	421.042
28	0.758	0.419	68	15.160	9.288	108	494.681	466.516
29	0.774	0.435	69	16.946	10.163	109	546.231	518.520
30	0.784	0.450	70	18.920	11.165	110	603.917	577.631
31	0.789	0.463	71	21.071	12.339	111	668.186	644.427
32	0.789	0.476	72	23.388	13.734	112	739.483	719.484
33	0.790	0.488	73	25.871	15.391	113	818.254	803.380
34	0.791	0.500	74	28.552	17.326	114	904.945	896.693
35	0.792	0.515	75	31.477	19.551	115	1000.000	1000.000
36	0.794	0.534	76	34.686	22.075			
37	0.823	0.558	77	38.225	24.910			
38	0.872	0.590	78	42.132	28.074			
39	0.945	0.630	79	46.427	31.612			
40	1.043	0.677	80	51.128	35.580			
41	1.168	0.732	81	56.250	40.030			
42	1.322	0.796	82	61.809	45.017			
43	1.505	0.868	83	67.826	50.600			
44	1.715	0.950	84	74.322	56.865			

*Based on 50% of Female Improvement Scale G.

APPENDIX B
Annuity 2000 Mortality Table

Age Nearest Birthday (x)	1,000 q_x		Age Nearest Birthday (x)	1,000 q_x		Age Nearest Birthday (x)	1,000 q_x	
	Male	Female*		Male	Female*		Male	Female*
5	0.291	0.171	45	1.752	0.939	85	73.275	57.913
6	0.270	0.141	46	1.974	1.035	86	80.076	65.119
7	0.257	0.118	47	2.211	1.141	87	97.370	73.136
8	0.294	0.118	48	2.460	1.261	88	95.169	81.991
9	0.325	0.121	49	2.721	1.393	89	103.455	91.577
10	0.350	0.126	50	2.994	1.538	90	112.208	101.758
11	0.371	0.133	51	3.279	1.695	91	121.402	112.395
12	0.388	0.142	52	3.576	1.864	92	131.017	123.349
13	0.402	0.152	53	3.884	2.047	93	141.030	134.486
14	0.414	0.164	54	4.203	2.244	94	151.422	145.689
15	0.425	0.177	55	4.534	2.457	95	162.179	156.846
16	0.437	0.190	56	4.876	2.689	96	173.279	167.841
17	0.449	0.204	57	5.228	2.942	97	184.706	178.563
18	0.463	0.219	58	5.593	3.218	98	196.946	189.604
19	0.480	0.234	59	5.988	3.523	99	210.484	210.557
20	0.499	0.250	60	6.428	3.863	100	225.806	215.013
21	0.519	0.265	61	6.933	4.242	101	243.398	230.565
22	0.542	0.281	62	7.520	4.668	102	263.745	248.805
23	0.566	0.298	63	8.207	5.144	103	287.334	270.326
24	0.592	0.314	64	9.008	5.671	104	314.649	295.719
25	0.616	0.331	65	9.940	6.250	105	346.177	325.576
26	0.639	0.347	66	11.016	6.878	106	382.403	360.491
27	0.659	0.362	67	12.251	7.555	107	423.813	401.054
28	0.675	0.376	68	13.657	8.287	108	470.893	447.860
29	0.687	0.389	69	15.233	9.102	109	524.128	501.498
30	0.694	0.402	70	16.979	10.034	110	584.004	562.563
31	0.699	0.414	71	18.891	11.117	111	651.007	631.645
32	0.700	0.425	72	20.967	12.386	112	725.622	709.338
33	0.701	0.436	73	23.209	13.871	113	808.336	796.233
34	0.702	0.449	74	25.644	15.592	114	899.633	892.923
35	0.704	0.463	75	28.304	17.564	115	1000.000	1000.000
36	0.719	0.481	76	31.220	19.805			
37	0.749	0.504	77	34.425	22.328			
38	0.796	0.532	78	37.948	25.158			
39	0.864	0.567	79	41.812	28.341			
40	0.953	0.609	80	46.037	31.933			
41	1.065	0.658	81	50.643	35.985			
42	1.201	0.715	82	55.651	40.552			
43	1.362	0.781	83	61.080	45.690			
44	1.547	0.855	84	66.948	51.456			

*Based on 50% of Female Improvement Scale G.

APPENDIX C

Single Premium for Single Life Only Annuity-Immediate of $1 per Year
Annuity 2000 Basic Table

Age Nearest Birthday	3% AIR		5% AIR		7% AIR	
	Male	Female	Male	Female	Male	Female
60	15.750	17.224	12.700	13.683	10.518	11.196
65	13.640	15.127	11.278	12.336	9.527	10.299
70	11.467	12.892	9.720	10.798	8.378	9.211
75	9.370	10.553	8.135	9.077	7.153	7.916
80	7.412	8.267	6.581	7.293	5.900	6.500
85	5.688	6.179	5.154	5.579	4.702	5.073
90	4.259	4.461	3.928	4.105	3.640	3.798
95	3.134	3.243	2.935	3.031	2.757	2.843

Annuity 2000 Mortality Table

Age Nearest Birthday	3% AIR		5% AIR		7% AIR	
	Male	Female	Male	Female	Male	Female
60	16.204	17.624	12.991	13.929	10.712	11.354
65	14.116	15.554	11.603	12.617	9.756	10.491
70	11.957	13.332	10.075	11.107	8.643	9.434
75	9.849	11.001	8.501	9.411	7.439	8.171
80	7.868	8.701	6.946	7.635	6.197	6.774
85	6.104	6.584	5.502	5.913	4.996	5.353
90	4.627	4.835	4.247	4.429	3.919	4.079
95	3.439	3.564	3.208	3.318	3.004	3.101

APPENDIX D

Annuity 2000 Basic Table Complete Expectation of Life, $\overset{\circ}{e}_x$

Age	Male	Female*	Age	Male	Female*	Age	Male	Female*
5	75.42	79.63	45	36.86	40.47	85	7.19	7.82
6	74.45	78.65	46	35.93	39.51	86	6.79	7.32
7	73.47	77.66	47	35.00	38.55	87	6.40	6.85
8	72.49	76.67	48	34.09	37.60	88	6.03	6.41
9	71.51	75.68	49	33.18	36.65	89	5.69	6.00
10	70.54	74.69	50	32.28	35.71	90	5.36	5.62
11	69.57	73.70	51	31.39	34.77	91	5.05	5.27
12	68.60	72.71	52	30.50	33.84	92	4.76	4.94
13	67.62	71.72	53	29.62	32.90	93	4.49	4.65
14	66.65	70.73	54	28.75	31.98	94	4.23	4.38
15	65.68	69.75	55	27.88	31.06	95	3.98	4.13
16	64.72	68.76	56	27.02	30.14	96	3.75	3.90
17	63.75	67.77	57	26.17	29.23	97	3.52	3.68
18	62.78	66.79	58	25.32	28.33	98	3.30	3.46
19	61.81	65.81	59	24.47	27.43	99	3.09	3.25
20	60.84	64.82	60	23.64	26.53	100	2.88	3.04
21	59.87	63.84	61	22.80	25.64	101	2.67	2.84
22	58.91	62.86	62	21.98	24.76	102	2.46	2.63
23	57.94	61.88	63	21.16	23.89	103	2.26	2.42
24	56.98	60.90	64	20.35	23.02	104	2.07	2.21
25	56.02	59.92	65	19.55	22.17	105	1.88	2.01
26	55.06	58.94	66	18.76	21.32	106	1.70	1.82
27	54.09	57.96	67	17.98	20.48	107	1.53	1.63
28	53.13	56.99	68	17.22	19.65	108	1.36	1.45
29	52.17	56.01	69	16.48	18.83	109	1.21	1.28
30	51.21	55.04	70	15.76	18.02	110	1.07	1.12
31	50.25	54.06	71	15.05	17.22	111	0.94	0.98
32	49.29	53.08	72	14.36	16.43	112	0.81	0.84
33	48.33	52.11	73	13.70	15.65	113	0.70	0.72
34	47.37	51.14	74	13.05	14.89	114	0.60	0.60
35	46.41	50.16	75	12.41	14.14	115	0.50	0.50
36	45.44	49.19	76	11.80	13.41			
37	44.48	48.21	77	11.21	12.70			
38	43.51	47.24	78	10.63	12.02			
39	42.55	46.27	79	10.08	11.35			
40	41.59	45.30	80	9.55	10.70			
41	40.63	44.33	81	9.03	10.08			
42	39.68	43.36	82	8.54	9.48			
43	38.73	42.39	83	8.07	8.90			
44	37.79	41.43	84	7.62	8.35			

*Based on 50% of Female Improvement Scale G.

APPENDIX E

Annuity 2000 Mortality Table Complete Expectation of Life, $\mathring{e}_x$

Age	Male	Female*	Age	Male	Female*	Age	Male	Female*
5	76.62	80.68	45	37.94	41.44	85	7.75	8.37
6	75.64	79.69	46	37.01	40.48	86	7.33	7.85
7	74.67	78.70	47	36.08	39.52	87	6.92	7.37
8	73.68	77.71	48	35.16	38.57	88	6.53	6.91
9	72.71	76.72	49	34.24	37.61	89	6.17	6.48
10	71.73	75.73	50	33.34	36.67	90	5.82	6.08
11	70.75	74.74	51	32.43	35.72	91	5.50	5.72
12	69.78	73.75	52	31.54	34.78	92	5.19	5.38
13	68.81	72.76	53	30.65	33.84	93	4.89	5.06
14	67.83	71.77	54	29.77	32.91	94	4.61	4.77
15	66.86	70.78	55	28.89	31.99	95	4.35	4.50
16	65.89	69.79	56	28.02	31.06	96	4.09	4.24
17	64.92	68.81	57	27.16	30.15	97	3.84	4.00
18	63.95	67.82	58	26.30	29.23	98	3.60	3.76
19	62.98	66.83	59	25.44	28.33	99	3.36	3.52
20	62.01	65.85	60	24.59	27.42	100	3.13	3.29
21	61.04	64.87	61	23.75	26.53	101	2.89	3.05
22	60.07	63.88	62	22.91	25.64	102	2.66	2.81
23	59.10	62.90	63	22.08	24.76	103	2.44	2.58
24	58.14	61.92	64	21.26	23.88	104	2.22	2.35
25	57.17	60.94	65	20.45	23.02	105	2.01	2.12
26	56.20	59.96	66	19.65	22.16	106	1.81	1.91
27	55.24	58.98	67	18.86	21.31	107	1.61	1.70
28	54.28	58.00	68	18.09	20.47	108	1.43	1.51
29	53.31	57.02	69	17.33	19.63	109	1.27	1.33
30	52.35	56.04	70	16.59	18.81	110	1.11	1.16
31	51.38	55.07	71	15.87	17.99	111	0.96	1.00
32	50.42	54.09	72	15.17	17.19	112	0.83	0.86
33	49.46	53.11	73	14.48	16.40	113	0.71	0.73
34	48.49	52.14	74	13.81	15.62	114	0.60	0.61
35	47.52	51.16	75	13.16	14.86	115	0.50	0.50
36	46.56	50.18	76	12.53	14.12			
37	45.59	49.21	77	11.92	13.40			
38	44.62	48.23	78	11.33	12.69			
39	43.66	47.26	79	10.75	12.01			
40	42.70	46.28	80	10.20	11.34			
41	41.74	45.31	81	9.67	10.70			
42	40.78	44.34	82	9.16	10.08			
43	39.83	43.37	83	8.67	9.48			
44	38.88	42.40	84	8.20	8.91			

*Based on 50% of Female Improvement Scale G.

APPENDIX F
Projection Scale G
Mortality Improvement Factors

Age	Males	Females
5–9	1.50%	1.50%
10–14	0.25	1.00
15–19	0.20	0.50
20–24	0.10	0.50
25–29	0.10	0.75
30–34	0.75	1.25
35–39	1.00	2.25
40–44	2.00	2.25
45–49	1.75	2.00
50–54	1.75	2.00
55–59	1.50	1.75
60–64	1.50	1.75
65–69	1.50	1.75
70–74	1.25	1.75
75–79	1.25	1.50
80–84	1.25	1.50
85–89	1.25	1.50
90–94	1.00	1.25

APPENDIX G.1

Annuity 2000 Mortality Table—Male Commutation Columns at 3%

Age Nearest Birthday x	$1,000\,q_x$	l_x	d_x	v^x	D_x	N_x	$N_x^{(12)}$	S_x
5	0.291	10,000.0000	2.9100	0.862609	8,626.0878	262,016.8299	258,063.2063	6,675,506.5189
6	0.270	9,997.0900	2.6992	0.837484	8,372.4055	253,390.7421	249,553.3896	6,413,489.6890
7	0.257	9,994.3908	2.5686	0.813092	8,126.3543	245,018.3366	241,293.7575	6,160,098.9469
8	0.294	9,991.8222	2.9376	0.789409	7,887.6367	236,891.9823	233,276.8154	5,915,080.6104
9	0.325	9,988.8846	3.2464	0.766417	7,655.6483	229,004.3455	225,495.5067	5,678,188.6281
10	0.350	9,985.6382	3.4950	0.744094	7,430.2527	221,348.6972	217,943.1648	5,449,184.2825
11	0.371	9,982.1433	3.7034	0.722421	7,211.3127	213,918.4446	210,613.2596	5,227,835.5853
12	0.388	9,978.4399	3.8716	0.701380	6,998.6770	206,707.1319	203,499.4049	5,013,917.1407
13	0.402	9,974.5683	4.0098	0.680951	6,792.1956	199,708.4549	196,595.3653	4,807,210.0088
14	0.414	9,970.5585	4.1278	0.661118	6,591.7137	192,916.2593	189,895.0572	4,607,501.5539
15	0.425	9,966.4307	4.2357	0.641862	6,397.0726	186,324.5455	183,392.5539	4,414,585.2946
16	0.437	9,962.1949	4.3535	0.623167	6,208.1105	179,927.4729	177,082.0889	4,228,260.7491
17	0.449	9,957.8415	4.4711	0.605016	6,024.6578	173,719.3624	170,958.0609	4,048,333.2761
18	0.463	9,953.3704	4.6084	0.587395	5,846.5561	167,694.7046	165,015.0330	3,874,613.9137
19	0.480	9,948.7620	4.7754	0.570286	5,673.6399	161,848.1485	159,247.7302	3,706,919.2092
20	0.499	9,943.9866	4.9620	0.553676	5,505.7443	156,174.5085	153,651.0424	3,545,071.0607
21	0.519	9,939.0245	5.1584	0.537549	5,342.7154	150,668.7643	148,220.0197	3,388,896.5522
22	0.542	9,933.8662	5.3842	0.521893	5,184.4103	145,326.0488	142,949.8608	3,238,227.7879
23	0.566	9,928.4820	5.6195	0.506692	5,030.6799	140,141.6386	137,835.9103	3,092,901.7391
24	0.592	9,922.8625	5.8743	0.491934	4,881.3908	135,110.9587	132,873.6545	2,952,760.1005

Annuity 2000 Mortality Table—Male Commutation Columns at 3% *(Continued)*

Age Nearest Birthday x	$1,000\,q_x$	l_x	d_x	v^x	D_x	N_x	$N_x^{(12)}$	S_x
25	0.616	9,916.9882	6.1089	0.477606	4,736.4088	130,229.5678	128,058.7138	2,817,649.1419
26	0.639	9,910.8793	6.3331	0.463695	4,595.6225	125,493.1591	123,386.8321	2,687,419.5740
27	0.659	9,904.5462	6.5271	0.450189	4,458.9183	120,897.5366	118,853.8657	2,561,926.4150
28	0.675	9,898.0191	6.6812	0.437077	4,326.1941	116,438.6183	114,455.7793	2,441,028.8784
29	0.687	9,891.3380	6.7953	0.424346	4,197.3533	112,112.4242	110,188.6373	2,324,590.2601
30	0.694	9,884.5426	6.8599	0.411987	4,072.3007	107,915.0709	106,048.5997	2,212,477.8359
31	0.699	9,877.6828	6.9045	0.399987	3,950.9461	103,842.7702	102,031.9199	2,104,562.7650
32	0.700	9,870.7783	6.9095	0.388337	3,833.1888	99,891.8241	98,134.9459	2,000,719.9948
33	0.701	9,863.8687	6.9146	0.377026	3,718.9374	96,058.6353	94,354.1223	1,900,828.1707
34	0.702	9,856.9541	6.9196	0.366045	3,608.0878	92,339.6979	90,685.9910	1,804,769.5354
35	0.704	9,850.0346	6.9344	0.355383	3,500.5388	88,731.6101	87,127.1965	1,712,429.8375
36	0.719	9,843.1001	7.0772	0.345032	3,396.1887	85,231.0714	83,674.4849	1,623,698.2274
37	0.749	9,836.0230	7.3672	0.334983	3,294.8999	81,834.8827	80,324.7202	1,538,467.1560
38	0.796	9,828.6558	7.8236	0.325226	3,196.5359	78,539.9828	77,074.9039	1,456,632.2733
39	0.864	9,820.8322	8.4852	0.315754	3,100.9626	75,343.4469	73,922.1724	1,378,092.2905
40	0.953	9,812.3470	9.3512	0.306557	3,008.0421	72,242.4843	70,863.7984	1,302,748.8436
41	1.065	9,802.9958	10.4402	0.297628	2,917.6460	69,234.4423	67,897.1878	1,230,506.3593
42	1.201	9,792.5556	11.7609	0.288959	2,829.6493	66,316.7962	65,019.8736	1,161,271.9170
43	1.362	9,780.7947	13.3214	0.280543	2,743.9329	63,487.1469	62,229.5110	1,094,955.1208
44	1.547	9,767.4733	15.1103	0.272372	2,660.3841	60,743.2141	59,523.8714	1,031,467.9739

APPENDIX G.1

Annuity 2000 Mortality Table—Male Commutation Columns at 3% *(Continued)*

Age Nearest Birthday x	$1,000\,q_x$	l_x	d_x	v^x	D_x	N_x	$N_x^{(12)}$	S_x
45	1.752	9,752.3630	17.0861	0.264439	2,578.9015	58,082.8300	56,900.8335	970,724.7598
46	1.974	9,735.2769	19.2174	0.256737	2,499.4012	55,503.9285	54,358.3696	912,641.9298
47	2.211	9,716.0594	21.4822	0.249259	2,421.8130	53,004.5273	51,894.5297	857,138.0013
48	2.460	9,694.5772	23.8487	0.241999	2,346.0761	50,582.7143	49,507.4295	804,133.4740
49	2.721	9,670.7286	26.3141	0.234950	2,272.1405	48,236.6383	47,195.2405	753,550.7597
50	2.994	9,644.4145	28.8754	0.228107	2,199.9592	45,964.4978	44,956.1831	705,314.1214
51	3.279	9,615.5391	31.5294	0.221463	2,129.4879	43,764.5385	42,788.5232	659,349.6236
52	3.576	9,584.0098	34.2724	0.215013	2,060.6848	41,635.0506	40,690.5701	615,585.0851
53	3.884	9,549.7374	37.0912	0.208750	1,993.5105	39,574.3658	38,660.6735	573,950.0345
54	4.203	9,512.6462	39.9817	0.202670	1,927.9298	37,580.8554	36,697.2209	534,375.6687
55	4.534	9,472.6645	42.9491	0.196767	1,863.9094	35,652.9256	34,798.6338	496,794.8133
56	4.876	9,429.7155	45.9793	0.191036	1,801.4160	33,789.0162	32,963.3672	461,141.8877
57	5.228	9,383.7362	49.0582	0.185472	1,740.4197	31,987.6002	31,189.9079	427,352.8715
58	5.593	9,334.6780	52.2089	0.180070	1,680.8939	30,247.1806	29,476.7709	395,365.2713
59	5.988	9,282.4692	55.5834	0.174825	1,622.8084	28,566.2866	27,822.4994	365,118.0907
60	6.428	9,226.8857	59.3104	0.169733	1,566.1078	26,943.4782	26,225.6788	336,551.8040
61	6.933	9,167.5753	63.5588	0.164789	1,510.7193	25,377.3704	24,684.9574	309,608.3258
62	7.520	9,104.0165	68.4622	0.159990	1,456.5490	23,866.6511	23,199.0661	284,230.9555
63	8.207	9,035.5543	74.1548	0.155330	1,403.4910	22,410.1020	21,766.8353	260,364.3044
64	9.008	8,961.3995	80.7243	0.150806	1,351.4297	21,006.6110	20,387.2057	237,954.2023

Age Nearest Birthday x	$1,000\,q_x$	l_x	d_x	v^x	D_x	N_x	$N_x^{(12)}$	S_x
65	9.940	8,880.6752	88.2739	0.146413	1,300.2486	19,655.1813	19,059.2341	216,947.5913
66	11.016	8,792.4013	96.8571	0.142149	1,249.8292	18,354.9327	17,782.0944	197,292.4100
67	12.251	8,695.5442	106.5291	0.138009	1,200.0593	17,105.1035	16,555.0763	178,937.4773
68	13.657	8,589.0151	117.3002	0.133989	1,150.8324	15,905.0442	15,377.5794	161,832.3737
69	15.233	8,471.7149	129.0496	0.130086	1,102.0539	14,754.2118	14,249.1038	145,927.3295
70	16.979	8,342.6653	141.6501	0.126297	1,053.6566	13,652.1579	13,169.2320	131,173.1177
71	18.891	8,201.0152	154.9254	0.122619	1,005.5986	12,598.5013	12,137.6020	117,520.9598
72	20.967	8,046.0898	168.7024	0.119047	957.8659	11,592.9027	11,153.8809	104,922.4585
73	23.209	7,877.3874	182.8263	0.115580	910.4682	10,635.0368	10,217.7389	93,329.5558
74	25.644	7,694.5612	197.3193	0.112214	863.4342	9,724.5686	9,328.8279	82,694.5189
75	28.304	7,497.2418	212.2019	0.108945	816.7886	8,861.1344	8,486.7730	72,969.9503
76	31.220	7,285.0399	227.4389	0.105772	770.5536	8,044.3458	7,691.1754	64,108.8159
77	34.425	7,057.6010	242.9579	0.102691	724.7543	7,273.7922	6,941.6132	56,064.4700
78	37.948	6,814.6430	258.6021	0.099700	679.4220	6,549.0379	6,237.6362	48,790.6778
79	41.812	6,556.0410	274.1212	0.096796	634.6012	5,869.6160	5,578.7571	42,241.6399
80	46.037	6,281.9198	289.2007	0.093977	590.3566	5,235.0147	4,964.4346	36,372.0239
81	50.643	5,992.7190	303.4893	0.091240	546.7751	4,644.6582	4,394.0529	31,137.0091
82	55.651	5,689.2298	316.6113	0.088582	503.9658	4,097.8831	3,866.8988	26,492.3510
83	61.080	5,372.6184	328.1595	0.086002	462.0578	3,593.9173	3,382.1408	22,394.4679
84	66.948	5,044.4589	337.7164	0.083497	421.1994	3,131.8595	2,938.8097	18,800.5506

APPENDIX 6.1

Annuity 2000 Mortality Table—Male Commutation Columns at 3% *(Continued)*

Age Nearest Birthday x	$1,000\,q_x$	l_x	d_x	v^x	D_x	N_x	$N_x^{(12)}$	S_x
85	73.275	4,706.7425	344.8866	0.081065	381.5543	2,710.6601	2,535.7810	15,668.6911
86	80.076	4,361.8559	349.2800	0.078704	343.2970	2,329.1058	2,171.7613	12,958.0310
87	97.370	4,012.5759	350.5788	0.076412	306.6089	1,985.8088	1,845.2797	10,628.9252
88	95.169	3,661.9972	348.5086	0.074186	271.6703	1,679.1999	1,554.6844	8,643.1164
89	103.455	3,313.4886	342.7970	0.072026	238.6561	1,407.5296	1,298.1456	6,963.9165
90	112.208	2,970.6916	333.3354	0.069928	207.7339	1,168.8735	1,073.6622	5,556.3869
91	121.402	2,637.3562	320.1803	0.067891	179.0529	961.1396	879.0737	4,387.5133
92	131.017	2,317.1759	303.5894	0.065914	152.7335	782.0868	712.0839	3,426.3737
93	141.030	2,013.5865	283.9761	0.063994	128.8571	629.3532	570.2937	2,644.2869
94	151.422	1,729.6104	261.9011	0.062130	107.4606	500.4961	451.2434	2,014.9337
95	162.179	1,467.7093	238.0316	0.060320	88.5327	393.0356	352.4581	1,514.4376
96	173.279	1,229.6777	213.0773	0.058563	72.0141	304.5029	271.4964	1,121.4020
97	184.706	1,016.6004	187.7722	0.056858	57.8015	232.4887	205.9963	816.8992
98	196.946	828.8282	163.2344	0.055202	45.7527	174.6872	153.7172	584.4104
99	210.484	665.5938	140.0968	0.053594	35.6717	128.9345	112.5850	409.7233
100	225.806	525.4969	118.6604	0.052033	27.3431	93.2628	80.7305	280.7888
101	243.398	406.8366	99.0232	0.050517	20.5523	65.9197	56.4999	187.5260
102	263.745	307.8134	81.1842	0.049046	15.0970	45.3674	38.4479	121.6063
103	287.334	226.6291	65.1183	0.047617	10.7915	30.2704	25.3243	76.2389
104	314.649	161.5109	50.8192	0.046231	7.4667	19.4789	16.0567	45.9685

APPENDIX 6.1

Annuity 2000 Mortality Table—Male Commutation Columns at 3% *(Continued)*

Age Nearest Birthday x	$1{,}000\,q_x$	l_x	d_x	v^x	D_x	N_x	$N_x^{(12)}$	S_x
105	346.177	110.6916	38.3189	0.044884	4.9683	12.0122	9.7350	26.4896
106	382.403	72.3727	27.6756	0.043577	3.1538	7.0439	5.5984	14.4774
107	423.813	44.6972	18.9432	0.042307	1.8910	3.8901	3.0234	7.4335
108	470.893	25.7539	12.1273	0.041075	1.0578	1.9991	1.5143	3.5434
109	524.128	13.6266	7.1421	0.039879	0.5434	0.9413	0.6922	1.5443
110	584.004	6.4845	3.7870	0.038717	0.2511	0.3978	0.2828	0.6031
111	651.007	2.6975	1.7561	0.037590	0.1014	0.1468	0.1003	0.2052
112	725.622	0.9414	0.6831	0.036495	0.0344	0.0454	0.0296	0.0584
113	808.336	0.2583	0.2088	0.035432	0.0092	0.0110	0.0068	0.0131
114	899.633	0.0495	0.0445	0.034400	0.0017	0.0019	0.0011	0.0020
115	1000.000	0.0050	0.0050	0.033398	0.0002	0.0002	0.0001	0.0002

APPENDIX G.2

Annuity 2000 Mortality Table—Male Commutation Columns at 4%

Age Nearest Birthday x	$1,000\,q_x$	l_x	d_x	v^x	D_x	N_x	$N_x^{(12)}$	S_x
5	0.291	10,000,000.0000	2.9100	0.821927	8,219.2711	200,636.9223	196,869.7564	4,391,091.3682
6	0.270	9,997,090.0900	2.6992	0.790315	7,900.8454	192,417.6513	188,796.4304	4,190,454.4458
7	0.257	9,994,390.8	2.5686	0.759918	7,594.9156	184,516.8058	181,035.8029	3,998,036.7946
8	0.294	9,991,822.2	2.9376	0.730690	7,300.9266	176,921.8902	173,575.6322	3,813,519.9887
9	0.325	9,988,884.6	3.2464	0.702587	7,018.0578	169,620.9636	166,404.3538	3,636,598.0985
10	0.350	9,985,638.2	3.4950	0.675564	6,745.9394	162,602.9058	159,511.0169	3,466,977.1349
11	0.371	9,982,143.3	3.7034	0.649581	6,484.2099	155,856.9664	152,885.0368	3,304,374.2291
12	0.388	9,978,439.9	3.8716	0.624597	6,232.5041	149,372.7564	146,516.1921	3,148,517.2628
13	0.402	9,974,568.3	4.0098	0.600574	5,990.4672	143,140.2523	140,394.6215	2,999,144.5063
14	0.414	9,970,558.5	4.1278	0.577475	5,757.7491	137,149.7851	134,510.8168	2,856,004.2540
15	0.425	9,966,430.7	4.2357	0.555265	5,534.0052	131,392.0360	128,855.6170	2,718,854.4689
16	0.437	9,962,194.9	4.3535	0.533908	5,318.8973	125,858.0308	123,420.2029	2,587,462.4329
17	0.449	9,957,841.5	4.4711	0.513373	5,112.0894	120,539.1335	118,196.0925	2,461,604.4020
18	0.463	9,953,370.4	4.6084	0.493628	4,913.2635	115,427.0441	113,175.1317	2,341,065.2685
19	0.480	9,948,762.0	4.7754	0.474642	4,722.1045	110,513.7806	108,349.4827	2,225,638.2244
20	0.499	9,943,986.6	4.9620	0.456387	4,538.3057	105,791.6761	103,711.6193	2,115,124.4438
21	0.519	9,939,024.5	5.1584	0.438834	4,361.5779	101,253.3704	99,254.3139	2,009,332.7677
22	0.542	9,933,866.2	5.3842	0.421955	4,191.6483	96,891.7925	94,970.6203	1,908,079.3973
23	0.566	9,928,482.0	5.6195	0.405726	4,028.2466	92,700.1442	90,853.8645	1,811,187.6048
24	0.592	9,922,862.5	5.8743	0.390121	3,871.1217	88,671.8976	86,897.6334	1,718,487.4606

APPENDIX G.2

Annuity 2000 Mortality Table—Male Commutation Columns at 4% *(Continued)*

Age Nearest Birthday x	$1,000\, q_x$	l_x	d_x	v^x	D_x	N_x	$N_x^{(12)}$	S_x
25	0.616	9,916.9882	6.1089	0.375117	3,720.0289	84,800.7758	83,095.7626	1,629,815.5630
26	0.639	9,910.8793	6.3331	0.360689	3,574.7475	81,080.7469	79,442.3210	1,545,014.7872
27	0.659	9,904.5462	6.5271	0.346817	3,435.0608	77,505.9995	75,931.5966	1,463,934.0403
28	0.675	9,898.0191	6.6812	0.333477	3,300.7664	74,070.9387	72,558.0875	1,386,428.0408
29	0.687	9,891.3380	6.7953	0.320651	3,171.6715	70,770.1723	69,316.4895	1,312,357.1021
30	0.694	9,884.5426	6.8599	0.308319	3,047.5890	67,598.5008	66,201.6892	1,241,586.9298
31	0.699	9,877.6828	6.9045	0.296460	2,928.3404	64,550.9118	63,208.7558	1,173,988.4290
32	0.700	9,870.7783	6.9095	0.285058	2,813.7437	61,622.5714	60,332.9389	1,109,437.5172
33	0.701	9,863.8687	6.9146	0.274094	2,703.6289	58,808.8277	57,569.6644	1,047,814.9458
34	0.702	9,856.9541	6.9196	0.263552	2,597.8209	56,105.1987	54,914.5309	989,006.1181
35	0.704	9,850.0346	6.9344	0.253415	2,496.1511	53,507.3779	52,363.3086	932,900.9194
36	0.719	9,843.1001	7.0772	0.243669	2,398.4556	51,011.2267	49,911.9346	879,393.5415
37	0.749	9,836.0230	7.3672	0.234297	2,304.5492	48,612.7711	47,556.5194	828,382.3147
38	0.796	9,828.6558	7.8236	0.225285	2,214.2529	46,308.2219	45,293.3560	779,769.5436
39	0.864	9,820.8322	8.4852	0.216621	2,127.3946	44,093.9690	43,118.9131	733,461.3217
40	0.953	9,812.3470	9.3512	0.208289	2,043.8044	41,966.5744	41,029.8307	689,367.3527
41	1.065	9,802.9958	10.4402	0.200278	1,963.3237	39,922.7700	39,022.9133	647,400.7783
42	1.201	9,792.5556	11.7609	0.192575	1,885.8007	37,959.4463	37,095.1210	607,478.0083
43	1.362	9,780.7947	13.3214	0.185168	1,811.0922	36,073.6456	35,243.5617	569,518.5620
44	1.547	9,767.4733	15.1103	0.178046	1,739.0630	34,262.5534	33,465.4829	533,444.9164

APPENDIX G.2

Annuity 2000 Mortality Table—Male Commutation Columns at 4% (Continued)

Age Nearest Birthday x	$1,000\,q_x$	l_x	d_x	v^x	D_x	N_x	$N_x^{(12)}$	S_x
45	1.752	9,752.3630	17.0861	0.171198	1,669.5891	32,523.4905	31,758.2621	499,182.3630
46	1.974	9,735.2769	19.2174	0.164614	1,602.5615	30,853.9014	30,119.3941	466,658.8725
47	2.211	9,716.0594	21.4822	0.158283	1,537.8827	29,251.3399	28,546.4770	435,804.9711
48	2.460	9,694.5772	23.8487	0.152195	1,475.4639	27,713.4572	27,037.2029	406,553.6312
49	2.721	9,670.7286	26.3141	0.146341	1,415.2253	26,237.9933	25,589.3484	378,840.1740
50	2.994	9,644.4145	28.8754	0.140713	1,357.0908	24,822.7681	24,200.7681	352,602.1807
51	3.279	9,615.5391	31.5294	0.135301	1,300.9881	23,465.6773	22,869.3910	327,779.4126
52	3.576	9,584.0098	34.2724	0.130097	1,246.8483	22,164.6891	21,593.2170	304,313.7354
53	3.884	9,549.7374	37.0912	0.125093	1,194.6053	20,917.8409	20,370.3134	282,149.0462
54	4.203	9,512.6462	39.9817	0.120282	1,144.1976	19,723.2355	19,198.8117	261,231.2054
55	4.534	9,472.6645	42.9491	0.115656	1,095.5659	18,579.0380	18,076.9036	241,507.9698
56	4.876	9,429.7155	45.9793	0.111207	1,048.6525	17,483.4721	17,002.8397	222,928.9318
57	5.228	9,383.7362	49.0582	0.106930	1,003.4031	16,434.8196	15,974.9265	205,445.4598
58	5.593	9,334.6780	52.2089	0.102817	959.7667	15,431.4165	14,991.5234	189,010.6401
59	5.988	9,282.4692	55.5834	0.098863	917.6911	14,471.6498	14,051.0414	173,579.2237
60	6.428	9,226.8857	59.3104	0.095060	877.1115	13,553.9588	13,151.9494	159,107.5738
61	6.933	9,167.5753	63.5588	0.091404	837.9552	12,676.8473	12,292.7845	145,553.6151
62	7.520	9,104.0165	68.4622	0.087889	800.1400	11,838.8921	11,472.1613	132,876.7677
63	8.207	9,035.5543	74.1548	0.084508	763.5798	11,038.7521	10,688.7780	121,037.8756
64	9.008	8,961.3995	80.7243	0.081258	728.1857	10,275.1723	9,941.4205	109,999.1235

APPENDIX 6.2

Annuity 2000 Mortality Table—Male Commutation Columns at 4% (Continued)

Age Nearest Birthday x	$1,000\,q_x$	l_x	d_x	v^x	D_x	N_x	$N_x^{(12)}$	S_x
65	9.940	8,880.6752	88.2739	0.078133	693.8713	9,546.9866	9,228.9623	99,723.9512
66	11.016	8,792.4013	96.8571	0.075128	660.5521	8,853.1153	8,550.3623	90,176.9646
67	12.251	8,695.5442	106.5291	0.072238	628.1495	8,192.5632	7,904.6613	81,323.8492
68	13.657	8,589.0151	117.3002	0.069460	596.5904	7,564.4137	7,290.9764	73,131.2860
69	15.233	8,471.7149	129.0496	0.066788	565.8104	6,967.8232	6,708.4934	65,566.8724
70	16.979	8,342.6653	141.6501	0.064219	535.7610	6,402.0128	6,156.4557	58,599.0492
71	18.891	8,201.0152	154.9254	0.061749	506.4080	5,866.2519	5,634.1482	52,197.0364
72	20.967	8,046.0898	168.7024	0.059374	477.7321	5,359.8439	5,140.8833	46,330.7845
73	23.209	7,877.3874	182.8263	0.057091	449.7265	4,882.1118	4,675.9871	40,970.9406
74	25.644	7,694.5612	197.3193	0.054895	422.3930	4,432.3853	4,238.7885	36,088.8289
75	28.304	7,497.2418	212.2019	0.052784	395.7319	4,009.9923	3,828.6151	31,656.4436
76	31.220	7,285.0399	227.4389	0.050754	369.7415	3,614.2604	3,444.7955	27,646.4513
77	34.425	7,057.6010	242.9579	0.048801	344.4213	3,244.5189	3,086.6592	24,032.1909
78	37.948	6,814.6430	258.6021	0.046924	319.7736	2,900.0976	2,753.5347	20,787.6720
79	41.812	6,556.0410	274.1212	0.045120	295.8066	2,580.3240	2,444.7460	17,887.5744
80	46.037	6,281.9198	289.2007	0.043384	272.5369	2,284.5174	2,159.6047	15,307.2504
81	50.643	5,992.7190	303.4893	0.041716	249.9905	2,011.9805	1,897.4016	13,022.7330
82	55.651	5,689.2298	316.6113	0.040111	228.2021	1,761.9901	1,657.3975	11,010.7525
83	61.080	5,372.6184	328.1595	0.038569	207.2139	1,533.7880	1,438.8149	9,248.7624
84	66.948	5,044.4589	337.7164	0.037085	187.0743	1,326.5741	1,240.8317	7,714.9744

APPENDIX G.2

Annuity 2000 Mortality Table—Male Commutation Columns at 4% (Continued)

Age Nearest Birthday x	$1{,}000\,q_x$	l_x	d_x	v^x	D_x	N_x	$N_x^{(12)}$	S_x
85	73.275	4,706.7425	344.8866	0.035659	167.8366	1,139.4998	1,062.5747	6,388.4003
86	80.076	4,361.8559	349.2800	0.034287	149.5561	971.6632	903.1167	5,248.9005
87	97.370	4,012.5759	350.5788	0.032969	132.2887	822.1071	761.4748	4,277.2372
88	95.169	3,661.9972	348.5086	0.031701	116.0871	689.8184	636.6118	3,455.1301
89	103.455	3,313.4886	342.7970	0.030481	100.9993	573.7313	527.4400	2,765.3116
90	112.208	2,970.6916	333.3354	0.029309	87.0677	472.7320	432.8260	2,191.5803
91	121.402	2,637.3562	320.1803	0.028182	74.3250	385.6643	351.5987	1,718.8483
92	131.017	2,317.1759	303.5894	0.027098	62.7902	311.3393	282.5605	1,333.1840
93	141.030	2,013.5865	283.9761	0.026056	52.4650	248.5491	224.5027	1,021.8447
94	151.422	1,729.6104	261.9011	0.025053	43.3326	196.0841	176.2234	773.2955
95	162.179	1,467.7093	238.0316	0.024090	35.3568	152.7516	136.5464	577.2114
96	173.279	1,229.6777	213.0773	0.023163	28.4833	117.3948	104.3399	424.4599
97	184.706	1,016.6004	187.7722	0.022272	22.6421	88.9114	78.5338	307.0651
98	196.946	828.8282	163.2344	0.021416	17.7500	66.2694	58.1340	218.1536
99	210.484	665.5938	140.0968	0.020592	13.7059	48.5194	42.2375	151.8843
100	225.806	525.4969	118.6604	0.019800	10.4049	34.8135	30.0446	103.3649
101	243.398	406.8366	99.0232	0.019039	7.7456	24.4086	20.8586	68.5514
102	263.745	307.8134	81.1842	0.018306	5.6349	16.6631	14.0804	44.1428
103	287.334	226.6291	65.1183	0.017602	3.9892	11.0281	9.1998	27.4797
104	314.649	161.5109	50.8192	0.016925	2.7336	7.0390	5.7861	16.4516

APPENDIX G.2

Annuity 2000 Mortality Table—Male Commutation Columns at 4% *(Continued)*

Age Nearest Birthday x	$1,000\,q_x$	l_x	d_x	v^x	D_x	N_x	$N_x^{(12)}$	S_x
105	346.177	110.6916	38.3189	0.016274	1.8014	4.3054	3.4797	9.4126
106	382.403	72.3727	27.6756	0.015648	1.1325	2.5040	1.9849	5.1072
107	423.813	44.6972	18.9432	0.015046	0.6725	1.3715	1.0632	2.6032
108	470.893	25.7539	12.1273	0.014468	0.3726	0.6989	0.5282	1.2318
109	524.128	13.6266	7.1421	0.013911	0.1896	0.3263	0.2394	0.5328
110	584.004	6.4845	3.7870	0.013376	0.0867	0.1368	0.0970	0.2065
111	651.007	2.6975	1.7561	0.012862	0.0347	0.0500	0.0341	0.0697
112	725.622	0.9414	0.6831	0.012367	0.0116	0.0153	0.0100	0.0197
113	808.336	0.2583	0.2088	0.011891	0.0031	0.0037	0.0023	0.0044
114	899.633	0.0495	0.0445	0.011434	0.0006	0.0006	0.0004	0.0007
115	1000.000	0.0050	0.0050	0.010994	0.0001	0.0001	0.0000	0.0001

APPENDIX G.3

Annuity 2000 Mortality Table—Male Commutation Columns at 5%

Age Nearest Birthday x	$1,000\, q_x$	l_x	d_x	v^x	D_x	N_x	$N_x^{(12)}$	S_x
5	0.291	10,000.0000	2.9100	0.783526	7,835.2617	158,894.9993	155,303.8377	3,013,053.5293
6	0.270	9,997.0900	2.6992	0.746215	7,459.9825	151,059.7376	147,640.5790	2,854,158.5300
7	0.257	9,994.3908	2.5686	0.710681	7,102.8269	143,599.7551	140,344.2928	2,703,098.7924
8	0.294	9,991.8222	2.9376	0.676839	6,762.8586	136,496.9282	133,397.2847	2,559,499.0373
9	0.325	9,988.8846	3.2464	0.644609	6,438.9241	129,734.0696	126,782.8961	2,423,002.1091
10	0.350	9,985.6382	3.4950	0.613913	6,130.3157	123,295.1455	120,485.4175	2,293,268.0395
11	0.371	9,982.1433	3.7034	0.584679	5,836.3524	117,164.8298	114,489.8350	2,169,972.8940
12	0.388	9,978.4399	3.8716	0.556837	5,556.3687	111,328.4774	108,781.8084	2,052,808.0642
13	0.402	9,974.5683	4.0098	0.530321	5,289.7265	105,772.1087	103,347.6507	1,941,479.5868
14	0.414	9,970.5585	4.1278	0.505068	5,035.8096	100,482.3822	98,174.3028	1,835,707.4781
15	0.425	9,966.4307	4.2357	0.481017	4,794.0236	95,446.5726	93,249.3118	1,735,225.0959
16	0.437	9,962.1949	4.3535	0.458112	4,563.7963	90,652.5491	88,560.8091	1,639,778.5233
17	0.449	9,957.8415	4.4711	0.436297	4,344.5732	86,088.7528	84,097.4900	1,549,125.9742
18	0.463	9,953.3704	4.6084	0.415521	4,135.8310	81,744.1795	79,848.5903	1,463,037.2214
19	0.480	9,948.7620	4.7754	0.395734	3,937.0629	77,608.3485	75,803.8614	1,381,293.0419
20	0.499	9,943.9866	4.9620	0.376889	3,747.7840	73,671.2856	71,953.5513	1,303,684.6933
21	0.519	9,939.0245	5.1584	0.358942	3,567.5370	69,923.5016	68,288.3805	1,230,013.4077
22	0.542	9,933.8662	5.3842	0.341850	3,395.8909	66,355.9647	64,799.5147	1,160,089.9061
23	0.566	9,928.4820	5.6195	0.325571	3,232.4289	62,960.0738	61,478.5439	1,093,733.9414
24	0.592	9,922.8625	5.8743	0.310068	3,076.7612	59,727.6450	58,317.4627	1,030,773.8676

APPENDIX 6.3
Annuity 2000 Mortality Table—Male Commutation Columns at 5% (Continued)

Age Nearest Birthday x	$1{,}000\,q_x$	l_x	d_x	v^x	D_x	N_x	$N_x^{(12)}$	S_x
25	0.616	9,916.9882	6.1089	0.295303	2,928.5141	56,650.8837	55,308.6481	971,046.2227
26	0.639	9,910.8793	6.3331	0.281241	2,787.3430	53,722.3696	52,444.8374	914,395.3389
27	0.659	9,904.5462	6.5271	0.267848	2,652.9161	50,935.0266	49,719.1068	860,672.9693
28	0.675	9,898.0191	6.6812	0.255094	2,524.9217	48,282.1106	47,124.8548	809,737.9427
29	0.687	9,891.3380	6.7953	0.242946	2,403.0642	45,757.1889	44,655.7845	761,455.8321
30	0.694	9,884.5426	6.8599	0.231377	2,287.0603	43,354.1247	42,305.8888	715,698.6432
31	0.699	9,877.6828	6.9045	0.220359	2,176.6410	41,067.0645	40,069.4373	672,344.5185
32	0.700	9,870.7783	6.9095	0.209866	2,071.5424	38,890.4235	37,940.9665	631,277.4540
33	0.701	9,863.8687	6.9146	0.199873	1,971.5165	36,818.8811	35,915.2693	592,387.0306
34	0.702	9,856.9541	6.9196	0.190355	1,876.3185	34,847.3646	33,987.3853	555,568.1495
35	0.704	9,850.0346	6.9344	0.181290	1,785.7156	32,971.0460	32,152.5931	520,720.7849
36	0.719	9,843.1001	7.0772	0.172657	1,699.4842	31,185.3305	30,406.4002	487,749.7389
37	0.749	9,836.0230	7.3672	0.164436	1,617.3927	29,485.8463	28,744.5413	456,564.4084
38	0.796	9,828.6558	7.8236	0.156605	1,539.2202	27,868.4536	27,162.9777	427,078.5621
39	0.864	9,820.8322	8.4852	0.149148	1,464.7571	26,329.2334	25,657.8863	399,210.1086
40	0.953	9,812.3470	9.3512	0.142046	1,393.8015	24,864.4762	24,225.6505	372,880.8752
41	1.065	9,802.9958	10.4402	0.135282	1,326.1650	23,470.6747	22,862.8491	348,016.3990
42	1.201	9,792.5556	11.7609	0.128840	1,261.6692	22,144.5097	21,566.2447	324,545.7243
43	1.362	9,780.7947	13.3214	0.122704	1,200.1466	20,882.8406	20,332.7734	302,401.2145
44	1.547	9,767.4733	15.1103	0.116861	1,141.4400	19,682.6940	19,159.5340	281,518.3740

APPENDIX 6.3

Annuity 2000 Mortality Table—Male Commutation Columns at 5% (Continued)

Age Nearest Birthday x	$1,000\,q_x$	l_x	d_x	v^x	D_x	N_x	$N_x^{(12)}$	S_x
45	1.752	9,752.3630	17.0861	0.111297	1,085.4040	18,541.2540	18,043.7772	261,835.6799
46	1.974	9,735.2769	19.2174	0.105997	1,031.9070	17,455.8501	16,982.8927	243,294.4259
47	2.211	9,716.0594	21.4822	0.100949	980.8286	16,423.9431	15,974.3967	225,838.5758
48	2.460	9,694.5772	23.8487	0.096142	932.0571	15,443.1145	15,015.9217	209,414.6327
49	2.721	9,670.7286	26.3141	0.091564	885.4898	14,511.0574	14,105.2080	193,971.5182
50	2.994	9,644.4145	28.8754	0.087204	841.0289	13,625.5677	13,240.0961	179,460.4607
51	3.279	9,615.5391	31.5294	0.083051	798.5818	12,784.5388	12,418.5222	165,834.8930
52	3.576	9,584.0098	34.2724	0.079096	758.0602	11,985.9570	11,638.5128	153,050.3542
53	3.884	9,549.7374	37.0912	0.075330	719.3804	11,227.8968	10,898.1808	141,064.3972
54	4.203	9,512.6462	39.9817	0.071743	682.4631	10,508.5165	10,195.7209	129,836.5004
55	4.534	9,472.6645	42.9491	0.068326	647.2331	9,826.0533	9,529.4048	119,327.9839
56	4.876	9,429.7155	45.9793	0.065073	613.6176	9,178.8203	8,897.5788	109,501.9306
57	5.228	9,383.7362	49.0582	0.061974	581.5482	8,565.2026	8,298.6597	100,323.1103
58	5.593	9,334.6780	52.2089	0.059023	550.9599	7,983.6544	7,731.1311	91,757.9077
59	5.988	9,282.4692	55.5834	0.056212	521.7889	7,432.6945	7,193.5412	83,774.2533
60	6.428	9,226.8857	59.3104	0.053536	493.9662	6,910.9055	6,684.5044	76,341.5589
61	6.933	9,167.5753	63.5588	0.050986	467.4199	6,416.9394	6,202.7052	69,430.6533
62	7.520	9,104.0165	68.4622	0.048558	442.0755	5,949.5194	5,746.9015	63,013.7140
63	8.207	9,035.5543	74.1548	0.046246	417.8582	5,507.4439	5,315.9255	57,064.1946
64	9.008	8,961.3995	80.7243	0.044044	394.6942	5,089.5856	4,908.6841	51,556.7507

Annuity 2000 Mortality Table—Male Commutation Columns at 5% (Continued)

Age Nearest Birthday x	1,000 q_x	l_x	d_x	v^x	D_x	N_x	$N_x^{(12)}$	S_x
65	9.940	8,880.6752	88.2739	0.041946	372.5131	4,694.8915	4,524.1563	46,467.1651
66	11.016	8,792.4013	96.8571	0.039949	351.2479	4,322.3784	4,161.3897	41,772.2736
67	12.251	8,695.5442	106.5291	0.038047	330.8367	3,971.1305	3,819.4970	37,449.8952
68	13.657	8,589.0151	117.3002	0.036235	311.2225	3,640.2937	3,497.6501	33,478.7647
69	15.233	8,471.7149	129.0496	0.034509	292.3544	3,329.0712	3,195.0754	29,838.4710
70	16.979	8,342.6653	141.6501	0.032866	274.1914	3,036.7167	2,911.0457	26,509.3998
71	18.891	8,201.0152	154.9254	0.031301	256.7009	2,762.5253	2,644.8707	23,472.6831
72	20.967	8,046.0898	168.7024	0.029811	239.8586	2,505.8244	2,395.8892	20,710.1578
73	23.209	7,877.3874	182.8263	0.028391	223.6472	2,265.9658	2,163.4608	18,204.3334
74	25.644	7,694.5612	197.3193	0.027039	208.0538	2,042.3186	1,946.9606	15,938.3676
75	28.304	7,497.2418	212.2019	0.025752	193.0652	1,834.2648	1,745.7766	13,896.0489
76	31.220	7,285.0399	227.4389	0.024525	178.6674	1,641.1996	1,559.3104	12,061.7841
77	34.425	7,057.6010	242.9579	0.023357	164.8470	1,462.5322	1,386.9773	10,420.5846
78	37.948	6,814.6430	258.6021	0.022245	151.5925	1,297.6852	1,228.2053	8,958.0524
79	41.812	6,556.0410	274.1212	0.021186	138.8951	1,146.0927	1,082.4324	7,660.3672
80	46.037	6,281.9198	289.2007	0.020177	126.7501	1,007.1975	949.1037	6,514.2745
81	50.643	5,992.7190	303.4893	0.019216	115.1571	880.4474	827.6671	5,507.0770
82	55.651	5,689.2298	316.6113	0.018301	104.1192	765.2903	717.5690	4,626.6296
83	61.080	5,372.6184	328.1595	0.017430	93.6428	661.1711	618.2515	3,861.3393
84	66.948	5,044.4589	337.7164	0.016600	83.7362	567.5283	529.1492	3,200.1682

APPENDIX 6.3

Annuity 2000 Mortality Table—Male Commutation Columns at 5% *(Continued)*

Age Nearest Birthday x	1,000 q_x	l_x	d_x	v^x	D_x	N_x	$N_x^{(12)}$	S_x
85	73.275	4,706.7425	344.8866	0.015809	74.4098	483.7921	449.6876	2,632.6399
86	80.076	4,361.8559	349.2800	0.015056	65.6737	409.3823	379.2818	2,148.8478
87	97.370	4,012.5759	350.5788	0.014339	57.5379	343.7086	317.3370	1,739.4655
88	95.169	3,661.9972	348.5086	0.013657	50.0103	286.1706	263.2492	1,395.7569
89	103.455	3,313.4886	342.7970	0.013006	43.0961	236.1603	216.4079	1,109.5863
90	112.208	2,970.6916	333.3354	0.012387	36.7977	193.0642	176.1986	873.4259
91	121.402	2,637.3562	320.1803	0.011797	31.1130	156.2665	142.0064	680.3617
92	131.017	2,317.1759	303.5894	0.011235	26.0342	125.1535	113.2212	524.0952
93	141.030	2,013.5865	283.9761	0.010700	21.5459	99.1193	89.2441	398.9417
94	151.422	1,729.6104	261.9011	0.010191	17.6260	77.5734	69.4948	299.8224
95	162.179	1,467.7093	238.0316	0.009705	14.2448	59.9474	53.4185	222.2490
96	173.279	1,229.6777	213.0773	0.009243	11.3663	45.7026	40.4930	162.3016
97	184.706	1,016.6004	187.7722	0.008803	8.9493	34.3363	30.2345	116.5990
98	196.946	828.8282	163.2344	0.008384	6.9489	25.3870	22.2021	82.2628
99	210.484	665.5938	140.0968	0.007985	5.3146	18.4381	16.0023	56.8758
100	225.806	525.4969	118.6604	0.007604	3.9961	13.1236	11.2920	38.4376
101	243.398	406.8366	99.0232	0.007242	2.9465	9.1274	7.7770	25.3141
102	263.745	307.8134	81.1842	0.006897	2.1231	6.1810	5.2079	16.1866
103	287.334	226.6291	65.1183	0.006569	1.4887	4.0578	3.3755	10.0057
104	314.649	161.5109	50.8192	0.006256	1.0104	2.5691	2.1060	5.9478

APPENDIX G.3

Annuity 2000 Mortality Table—Male Commutation Columns at 5% (*Continued*)

Age Nearest Birthday x	$1,000\ q_x$	l_x	d_x	v^x	D_x	N_x	$N_x^{(12)}$	S_x
105	346.177	110.6916	38.3189	0.005958	0.6595	1.5586	1.2563	3.3788
106	382.403	72.3727	27.6756	0.005675	0.4107	0.8991	0.7109	1.8201
107	423.813	44.6972	18.9432	0.005404	0.2416	0.4884	0.3777	0.9210
108	470.893	25.7539	12.1273	0.005147	0.1326	0.2469	0.1861	0.4326
109	524.128	13.6266	7.1421	0.004902	0.0668	0.1143	0.0837	0.1857
110	584.004	6.4845	3.7870	0.004668	0.0303	0.0475	0.0336	0.0714
111	651.007	2.6975	1.7561	0.004446	0.0120	0.0172	0.0117	0.0239
112	725.622	0.9414	0.6831	0.004234	0.0040	0.0052	0.0034	0.0067
113	808.336	0.2583	0.2088	0.004033	0.0010	0.0013	0.0008	0.0015
114	899.633	0.0495	0.0445	0.003841	0.0002	0.0002	0.0001	0.0002
115	1000.000	0.0050	0.0050	0.003658	0.0000	0.0000	0.0000	0.0000

APPENDIX G.4

Annuity 2000 Mortality Table—Male Commutation Columns at 6%

Age Nearest Birthday x	$1,000\, q_x$	l_x	d_x	v^x	D_x	N_x	$N_x^{(12)}$	S_x
5	0.291	10,000.0000	2.9100	0.747258	7,472.5817	129,301.4332	125,876.5000	2,147,052.8154
6	0.270	9,997.0900	2.6992	0.704961	7,047.5540	121,828.8515	118,598.7226	2,017,751.3822
7	0.257	9,994.3908	2.5686	0.665057	6,646.8407	114,781.2975	111,734.8289	1,895,922.5307
8	0.294	9,991.8222	2.9376	0.627412	6,268.9929	108,134.4569	105,261.1685	1,781,141.2331
9	0.325	9,988.8846	3.2464	0.591898	5,912.4055	101,865.4640	99,155.6115	1,673,006.7763
10	0.350	9,985.6382	3.4950	0.558395	5,575.9282	95,953.0585	93,397.4247	1,571,141.3123
11	0.371	9,982.1433	3.7034	0.526788	5,258.4686	90,377.1303	87,966.9989	1,475,188.2538
12	0.388	9,978.4399	3.8716	0.496969	4,958.9789	85,118.6617	82,845.7964	1,384,811.1235
13	0.402	9,974.5683	4.0098	0.468839	4,676.4668	80,159.6828	78,016.3022	1,299,692.4618
14	0.414	9,970.5585	4.1278	0.442301	4,409.9876	75,483.2160	73,461.9716	1,219,532.7790
15	0.425	9,966.4307	4.2357	0.417265	4,158.6433	71,073.2283	69,167.1835	1,144,049.5630
16	0.437	9,962.1949	4.3535	0.393646	3,921.5810	66,914.5850	65,117.1937	1,072,976.3347
17	0.449	9,957.8415	4.4711	0.371364	3,697.9880	62,993.0040	61,298.0929	1,006,061.7497
18	0.463	9,953.3704	4.6084	0.350344	3,487.1015	59,295.0160	57,696.7612	943,068.7456
19	0.480	9,948.7620	4.7754	0.330513	3,288.1953	55,807.9145	54,300.8250	883,773.7296
20	0.499	9,943.9866	4.9620	0.311805	3,100.5820	52,519.7192	51,098.6191	827,965.8151
21	0.519	9,939.0245	5.1584	0.294155	2,923.6178	49,419.1372	48,079.1457	775,446.0959
22	0.542	9,933.8662	5.3842	0.277505	2,756.6985	46,495.5194	45,232.0326	726,026.9587
23	0.566	9,928.4820	5.6195	0.261797	2,599.2494	43,738.8210	42,547.4983	679,531.4392
24	0.592	9,922.8625	5.8743	0.246979	2,450.7342	41,139.5716	40,016.3184	635,792.6183

Annuity 2000 Mortality Table—Male Commutation Columns at 6% *(Continued)*

Age Nearest Birthday x	$1,000\,q_x$	l_x	d_x	v^x	D_x	N_x	$N_x^{(12)}$	S_x
25	0.616	9,916.9882	6.1089	0.232999	2,310.6447	38,688.8374	37,629.7919	594,653.0467
26	0.639	9,910.8793	6.3331	0.219810	2,178.5107	36,378.1927	35,379.7087	555,964.2094
27	0.659	9,904.5462	6.5271	0.207368	2,053.8855	34,199.6821	33,258.3179	519,586.0167
28	0.675	9,898.0191	6.6812	0.195630	1,936.3509	32,145.7966	31,258.3024	485,386.3346
29	0.687	9,891.3380	6.7953	0.184557	1,825.5131	30,209.4457	29,372.7522	453,240.5380
30	0.694	9,884.5426	6.8599	0.174110	1,720.9990	28,383.9326	27,595.1414	423,031.0923
31	0.699	9,877.6828	6.9045	0.164255	1,622.4572	26,662.9336	25,919.3074	394,647.1597
32	0.700	9,870.7783	6.9095	0.154957	1,529.5501	25,040.4764	24,339.4326	367,984.2261
33	0.701	9,863.8687	6.9146	0.146186	1,441.9617	23,510.9263	22,850.0272	342,943.7497
34	0.702	9,856.9541	6.9196	0.137912	1,359.3876	22,068.9646	21,445.9119	319,432.8235
35	0.704	9,850.0346	6.9344	0.130105	1,281.5409	20,709.5769	20,122.2040	297,363.8589
36	0.719	9,843.1001	7.0772	0.122741	1,208.1497	19,428.0360	18,874.3007	276,654.2820
37	0.749	9,836.0230	7.3672	0.115793	1,138.9444	18,219.8863	17,697.8701	257,226.2459
38	0.796	9,828.6558	7.8236	0.109239	1,073.6711	17,080.9419	16,588.8427	239,006.3596
39	0.864	9,820.8322	8.4852	0.103056	1,012.0910	16,007.2709	15,543.3959	221,925.4177
40	0.953	9,812.3470	9.3512	0.097222	953.9778	14,995.1799	14,557.9401	205,918.1468
41	1.065	9,802.9958	10.4402	0.091719	899.1214	14,041.2021	13,629.1048	190,922.9669
42	1.201	9,792.5556	11.7609	0.086527	847.3244	13,142.0807	12,753.7237	176,881.7648
43	1.362	9,780.7947	13.3214	0.081630	798.4026	12,294.7563	11,928.8218	163,739.6841
44	1.547	9,767.4733	15.1103	0.077009	752.1841	11,496.3537	11,151.6026	151,444.9278

APPENDIX 6.4

Annuity 2000 Mortality Table—Male Commutation Columns at 6% (Continued)

Age Nearest Birthday x	$1,000\,q_x$	l_x	d_x	v^x	D_x	N_x	$N_x^{(12)}$	S_x
45	1.752	9,752.3630	17.0861	0.072650	708.5099	10,744.1696	10,419.4359	139,948.5741
46	1.974	9,735.2769	19.2174	0.068538	667.2345	10,035.6597	9,729.8439	129,204.4046
47	2.211	9,716.0594	21.4822	0.064658	628.2240	9,368.4252	9,080.4892	119,168.7449
48	2.460	9,694.5772	23.8487	0.060998	591.3537	8,740.2012	8,469.1641	109,800.3197
49	2.721	9,670.7286	26.3141	0.057546	556.5085	8,148.8475	7,893.7811	101,060.1185
50	2.994	9,644.4145	28.8754	0.054288	523.5795	7,592.3390	7,352.3651	92,911.2711
51	3.279	9,615.5391	31.5294	0.051215	492.4640	7,068.7595	6,843.0468	85,318.9321
52	3.576	9,584.0098	34.2724	0.048316	463.0653	6,576.2955	6,364.0572	78,250.1726
53	3.884	9,549.7374	37.0912	0.045582	435.2919	6,113.2302	5,913.7214	71,673.8771
54	4.203	9,512.6462	39.9817	0.043001	409.0577	5,677.9383	5,490.4535	65,560.6469
55	4.534	9,472.6645	42.9491	0.040567	384.2816	5,268.8805	5,092.7515	59,882.7087
56	4.876	9,429.7155	45.9793	0.038271	360.8861	4,884.5990	4,719.1928	54,613.8281
57	5.228	9,383.7362	49.0582	0.036105	338.7985	4,523.7129	4,368.4302	49,729.2292
58	5.593	9,334.6780	52.2089	0.034061	317.9502	4,184.9144	4,039.1872	45,205.5163
59	5.988	9,282.4692	55.5834	0.032133	298.2754	3,866.9641	3,730.2546	41,020.6019
60	6.428	9,226.8857	59.3104	0.030314	279.7069	3,568.6887	3,440.4897	37,153.6378
61	6.933	9,167.5753	63.5588	0.028598	262.1783	3,288.9818	3,168.8167	33,584.9491
62	7.520	9,104.0165	68.4622	0.026980	245.6232	3,026.8035	2,914.2262	30,295.9673
63	8.207	9,035.5543	74.1548	0.025453	229.9775	2,781.1803	2,675.7740	27,269.1638
64	9.008	8,961.3995	80.7243	0.024012	215.1793	2,551.2028	2,452.5790	24,487.9835

APPENDIX G.4

Annuity 2000 Mortality Table—Male Commutation Columns at 6% *(Continued)*

Age Nearest Birthday x	$1,000\,q_x$	l_x	d_x	v^x	D_x	N_x	$N_x^{(12)}$	S_x
65	9.940	8,880.6752	88.2739	0.022653	201.1707	2,336.0236	2,243.8203	21,936.7806
66	11.016	8,792.4013	96.8571	0.021370	187.8972	2,134.8528	2,048.7333	19,600.7571
67	12.251	8,695.5442	106.5291	0.020161	175.3088	1,946.9556	1,866.6057	17,465.9042
68	13.657	8,589.0151	117.3002	0.019020	163.3596	1,771.6468	1,696.7736	15,518.9486
69	15.233	8,471.7149	129.0496	0.017943	152.0081	1,608.2872	1,538.6169	13,747.3018
70	16.979	8,342.6653	141.6501	0.016927	141.2194	1,456.2792	1,391.5536	12,139.0146
71	18.891	8,201.0152	154.9254	0.015969	130.9638	1,315.0598	1,255.0347	10,682.7355
72	20.967	8,046.0898	168.7024	0.015065	121.2167	1,184.0960	1,128.5384	9,367.6757
73	23.209	7,877.3874	182.8263	0.014213	111.9577	1,062.8793	1,011.5653	8,183.5796
74	25.644	7,694.5612	197.3193	0.013408	103.1691	950.9216	903.6357	7,120.7003
75	28.304	7,497.2418	212.2019	0.012649	94.8335	847.7524	804.2871	6,169.7788
76	31.220	7,285.0399	227.4389	0.011933	86.9333	752.9190	713.0745	5,322.0264
77	34.425	7,057.6010	242.9579	0.011258	79.4521	665.9857	629.5701	4,569.1074
78	37.948	6,814.6430	258.6021	0.010620	72.3745	586.5335	553.3619	3,903.1217
79	41.812	6,556.0410	274.1212	0.010019	65.6868	514.1590	484.0526	3,316.5882
80	46.037	6,281.9198	289.2007	0.009452	59.3777	448.4722	421.2574	2,802.4292
81	50.643	5,992.7190	303.4893	0.008917	53.4378	389.0945	364.6022	2,353.9570
82	55.651	5,689.2298	316.6113	0.008412	47.8600	335.6567	313.7209	1,964.8624
83	61.080	5,372.6184	328.1595	0.007936	42.6382	287.7967	268.2542	1,629.2057
84	66.948	5,044.4589	337.7164	0.007487	37.7678	245.1585	227.8482	1,341.4090

APPENDIX G.4

Annuity 2000 Mortality Table—Male Commutation Columns at 6% *(Continued)*

Age Nearest Birthday x	$1,000 \, q_x$	l_x	d_x	v^x	D_x	N_x	$N_x^{(12)}$	S_x
85	73.275	4,706.7425	344.8866	0.007063	33.2447	207.3907	192.1535	1,096.2505
86	80.076	4,361.8559	349.2800	0.006663	29.0648	174.1460	160.8247	888.8598
87	97.370	4,012.5759	350.5788	0.006286	25.2239	145.0812	133.5203	714.7138
88	95.169	3,661.9972	348.5086	0.005930	21.7171	119.8573	109.9036	569.6326
89	103.455	3,313.4886	342.7970	0.005595	18.5380	98.1402	89.6436	449.7753
90	112.208	2,970.6916	333.3354	0.005278	15.6794	79.6022	72.4158	351.6351
91	121.402	2,637.3562	320.1803	0.004979	13.1321	63.9228	57.9039	272.0329
92	131.017	2,317.1759	303.5894	0.004697	10.8848	50.7906	45.8018	208.1102
93	141.030	2,013.5865	283.9761	0.004432	8.9233	39.9059	35.8160	157.3196
94	151.422	1,729.6104	261.9011	0.004181	7.2310	30.9826	27.6684	117.4137
95	162.179	1,467.7093	238.0316	0.003944	5.7887	23.7516	21.0984	86.4311
96	173.279	1,229.6777	213.0773	0.003721	4.5754	17.9629	15.8658	62.6795
97	184.706	1,016.6004	187.7722	0.003510	3.5685	13.3875	11.7519	44.7167
98	196.946	828.8282	163.2344	0.003312	2.7447	9.8190	8.5610	31.3292
99	210.484	665.5938	140.0968	0.003124	2.0794	7.0743	6.1213	21.5102
100	225.806	525.4969	118.6604	0.002947	1.5488	4.9950	4.2851	14.4358
101	243.398	406.8366	99.0232	0.002780	1.1312	3.4462	2.9278	9.4408
102	263.745	307.8134	81.1842	0.002623	0.8074	2.3151	1.9450	5.9946
103	287.334	226.6291	65.1183	0.002475	0.5608	1.5077	1.2506	3.6795
104	314.649	161.5109	50.8192	0.002334	0.3770	0.9469	0.7740	2.1719

APPENDIX G.4

Annuity 2000 Mortality Table—Male Commutation Columns at 6% *(Continued)*

Age Nearest Birthday x	$1{,}000\,q_x$	l_x	d_x	v^x	D_x	N_x	$N_x^{(12)}$	S_x
105	346.177	110.6916	38.3189	0.002202	0.2438	0.5698	0.4581	1.2250
106	382.403	72.3727	27.6756	0.002078	0.1504	0.3260	0.2571	0.6552
107	423.813	44.6972	18.9432	0.001960	0.0876	0.1757	0.1355	0.3291
108	470.893	25.7539	12.1273	0.001849	0.0476	0.0881	0.0662	0.1535
109	524.128	13.6266	7.1421	0.001744	0.0238	0.0404	0.0295	0.0654
110	584.004	6.4845	3.7870	0.001646	0.0107	0.0167	0.0118	0.0250
111	651.007	2.6975	1.7561	0.001553	0.0042	0.0060	0.0041	0.0083
112	725.622	0.9414	0.6831	0.001465	0.0014	0.0018	0.0012	0.0023
113	808.336	0.2583	0.2088	0.001382	0.0004	0.0004	0.0003	0.0005
114	899.633	0.0495	0.0445	0.001304	0.0001	0.0001	0.0000	0.0001
115	1000.000	0.0050	0.0050	0.001230	0.0000	0.0000	0.0000	0.0000

APPENDIX H.1

Annuity 2000 Mortality Table—Female Commutation Columns at 3%

Age Nearest Birthday x	$1,000\,q_x$	l_x	d_x	v^x	D_x	N_x	$N_x^{(12)}$	S_x
5	0.171	10,000.0000	1.7100	0.862609	8,626.0878	266,674.1367	262,720.5131	6,972,666.9810
6	0.141	9,998.2900	1.4098	0.837484	8,373.4105	258,048.0489	254,210.2357	6,705,992.8443
7	0.118	9,996.8802	1.1796	0.813092	8,128.3785	249,674.6384	245,949.1316	6,447,944.7955
8	0.118	9,995.7006	1.1795	0.789409	7,890.6984	241,546.2599	237,929.6898	6,198,270.1571
9	0.121	9,994.5211	1.2093	0.766417	7,659.9682	233,655.5616	230,144.7428	5,956,723.8971
10	0.126	9,993.3118	1.2592	0.744094	7,435.9625	225,995.5934	222,587.4439	5,723,068.3356
11	0.133	9,992.0526	1.3289	0.722421	7,218.4714	218,559.6309	215,251.1648	5,497,072.7422
12	0.142	9,990.7237	1.4187	0.701380	7,007.2926	211,341.1595	208,129.4837	5,278,513.1114
13	0.152	9,989.3050	1.5184	0.680951	6,802.2306	204,333.8669	201,216.1778	5,067,171.9519
14	0.164	9,987.7866	1.6380	0.661118	6,603.1036	197,531.6363	194,505.2138	4,862,838.0850
15	0.177	9,986.1486	1.7675	0.641862	6,409.7288	190,928.5327	187,990.7403	4,665,306.4488
16	0.190	9,984.3811	1.8970	0.623167	6,221.9362	184,518.8039	181,667.0831	4,474,377.9161
17	0.204	9,982.4840	2.0364	0.605016	6,039.5670	178,296.8677	175,528.7328	4,289,859.1122
18	0.219	9,980.4476	2.1857	0.587395	5,862.4611	172,257.3007	169,570.3393	4,111,562.2445
19	0.234	9,978.2619	2.3349	0.570286	5,690.4633	166,394.8396	163,786.7105	3,939,304.9439
20	0.250	9,975.9270	2.4940	0.553676	5,523.4289	160,704.3762	158,172.8046	3,772,910.1043
21	0.265	9,973.4330	2.6430	0.537549	5,361.2117	155,180.9473	152,723.7253	3,612,205.7281
22	0.281	9,970.7900	2.8018	0.521893	5,203.6806	149,819.7356	147,434.7154	3,457,024.7808
23	0.298	9,967.9883	2.9705	0.506692	5,050.6974	144,616.0551	142,301.1521	3,307,205.0452
24	0.314	9,965.0178	3.1290	0.491934	4,902.1284	139,565.3577	137,318.5488	3,162,588.9901

APPENDIX H.1

Annuity 2000 Mortality Table—Female Commutation Columns at 3% (*Continued*)

Age Nearest Birthday x	$1,000\,q_x$	l_x	d_x	v^x	D_x	N_x	$N_x^{(12)}$	S_x
25	0.331	9,961.8888	3.2974	0.477606	4,757.8536	134,663.2292	132,482.5464	3,023,023.6324
26	0.347	9,958.5914	3.4556	0.463695	4,617.7463	129,905.3757	127,788.9086	2,888,360.4031
27	0.362	9,955.1358	3.6038	0.450189	4,481.6932	125,287.6294	123,233.5200	2,758,455.0275
28	0.376	9,951.5320	3.7418	0.437077	4,349.5833	120,805.9362	118,812.3772	2,633,167.3981
29	0.389	9,947.7902	3.8697	0.424346	4,221.3086	116,456.3529	114,521.5865	2,512,361.4619
30	0.402	9,943.9205	3.9975	0.411987	4,096.7636	112,235.0443	110,357.3610	2,395,905.1090
31	0.414	9,939.9231	4.1151	0.399987	3,975.8415	108,138.2807	106,316.0200	2,283,670.0647
32	0.425	9,935.8080	4.2227	0.388337	3,858.4422	104,162.4393	102,393.9866	2,175,531.7840
33	0.436	9,931.5852	4.3302	0.377026	3,744.4683	100,303.9971	98,587.7824	2,071,369.3447
34	0.449	9,927.2551	4.4573	0.366045	3,633.8211	96,559.5288	94,894.0274	1,971,065.3477
35	0.463	9,922.7977	4.5943	0.355383	3,526.3976	92,925.7077	91,309.4421	1,874,505.8189
36	0.481	9,918.2035	4.7707	0.345032	3,422.1018	89,399.3101	87,830.8468	1,781,580.1112
37	0.504	9,913.4328	4.9964	0.334983	3,320.8308	85,977.2083	84,455.1608	1,692,180.8011
38	0.532	9,908.4364	5.2713	0.325226	3,222.4827	82,656.3775	81,179.4062	1,606,203.5928
39	0.567	9,903.1652	5.6151	0.315754	3,126.9595	79,433.8948	78,000.7050	1,523,547.2154
40	0.609	9,897.5501	6.0276	0.306557	3,034.1617	76,306.9353	74,916.2779	1,444,113.3206
41	0.658	9,891.5225	6.5086	0.297628	2,943.9941	73,272.7736	71,923.4430	1,367,806.3853
42	0.715	9,885.0138	7.0678	0.288959	2,856.3659	70,328.7796	69,019.6118	1,294,533.6116
43	0.781	9,877.9460	7.7147	0.280543	2,771.1880	67,472.4136	66,202.2858	1,224,204.8321
44	0.855	9,870.2314	8.4390	0.272372	2,688.3725	64,701.2257	63,469.0549	1,156,732.4184

APPENDIX H.1

Annuity 2000 Mortality Table—Female Commutation Columns at 3% *(Continued)*

Age Nearest Birthday x	$1,000\,q_x$	l_x	d_x	v^x	D_x	N_x	$N_x^{(12)}$	S_x
45	0.939	9,861.7923	9.2602	0.264439	2,607.8388	62,012.8531	60,817.5937	1,092,031.1928
46	1.035	9,852.5321	10.1974	0.256737	2,529.5049	59,405.0144	58,245.6580	1,030,018.3396
47	1.141	9,842.3347	11.2301	0.249259	2,453.2882	56,875.5095	55,751.0857	970,613.3253
48	1.261	9,831.1046	12.3970	0.241999	2,379.1155	54,422.2213	53,331.7933	913,737.8158
49	1.393	9,818.7076	13.6775	0.234950	2,306.9082	52,043.1057	50,985.7728	859,315.5945
50	1.538	9,805.0301	15.0801	0.228107	2,236.5968	49,736.1975	48,711.0907	807,272.4888
51	1.695	9,789.9500	16.5940	0.221463	2,168.1135	47,499.6007	46,505.8820	757,536.2913
52	1.864	9,773.3560	18.2175	0.215013	2,101.3966	45,331.4872	44,368.3471	710,036.6905
53	2.047	9,755.1385	19.9688	0.208750	2,036.3880	43,230.0906	42,296.7461	664,705.2033
54	2.244	9,735.1697	21.8457	0.202670	1,973.0287	41,193.7026	40,289.3978	621,475.1127
55	2.457	9,713.3240	23.8656	0.196767	1,911.2633	39,220.6739	38,344.6782	580,281.4102
56	2.689	9,689.4584	26.0550	0.191036	1,851.0362	37,309.4106	36,461.0190	541,060.7363
57	2.942	9,663.4034	28.4297	0.185472	1,792.2901	35,458.3744	34,636.9081	503,751.3256
58	3.218	9,634.9737	31.0053	0.180070	1,734.9681	33,666.0843	32,870.8906	468,292.9512
59	3.523	9,603.9683	33.8348	0.174825	1,679.0146	31,931.1162	31,161.5679	434,626.8669
60	3.863	9,570.1336	36.9694	0.169733	1,624.3683	30,252.1016	29,507.5995	402,695.7507
61	4.242	9,533.1641	40.4397	0.164789	1,570.9645	28,627.7333	27,907.7079	372,443.6491
62	4.668	9,492.7245	44.3120	0.159990	1,518.7383	27,056.7688	26,360.6804	343,815.9158
63	5.144	9,448.4124	48.6026	0.155330	1,467.6202	25,538.0305	24,865.3713	316,759.1470
64	5.671	9,399.8098	53.3063	0.150806	1,417.5444	24,070.4103	23,420.7024	291,221.1165

APPENDIX H.1

Annuity 2000 Mortality Table—Female Commutation Columns at 3% *(Continued)*

Age Nearest Birthday x	$1,000\,q_x$	l_x	d_x	v^x	D_x	N_x	$N_x^{(12)}$	S_x
65	6.250	9,346.5035	58.4156	0.146413	1,368.4520	22,652.8659	22,025.6587	267,150.7061
66	6.878	9,288.0878	63.8835	0.142149	1,320.2905	21,284.4139	20,679.2808	244,497.8403
67	7.555	9,224.2043	69.6889	0.138009	1,273.0189	19,964.1234	19,380.6564	223,213.4264
68	8.287	9,154.5155	75.8635	0.133989	1,226.6032	18,691.1045	18,128.9114	203,249.3030
69	9.102	9,078.6520	82.6339	0.130086	1,181.0081	17,464.5013	16,923.2060	184,558.1985
70	10.034	8,996.0181	90.2660	0.126297	1,136.1733	16,283.4933	15,762.7471	167,093.6972
71	11.117	8,905.7521	99.0052	0.122619	1,092.0126	15,147.3199	14,646.8141	150,810.2039
72	12.386	8,806.7468	109.0804	0.119047	1,048.4201	14,055.3073	13,574.7815	135,662.8840
73	13.871	8,697.6665	120.6453	0.115580	1,005.2761	13,006.8872	12,546.1357	121,607.5767
74	15.592	8,577.0211	133.7329	0.112214	962.4581	12,001.6112	11,560.4845	108,600.6894
75	17.564	8,443.2882	148.2979	0.108945	919.8558	11,039.1530	10,617.5524	96,599.0783
76	19.805	8,294.9903	164.2823	0.105772	877.3781	10,119.2972	9,717.1656	85,559.9252
77	22.328	8,130.7080	181.5424	0.102691	834.9531	9,241.9191	8,859.2322	75,440.6280
78	25.158	7,949.1656	199.9851	0.099700	792.5342	8,406.9660	8,043.7212	66,198.7090
79	28.341	7,749.1805	219.6195	0.096796	750.0928	7,614.4318	7,270.6392	57,791.7430
80	31.933	7,529.5609	240.4415	0.093977	707.6063	6,864.3389	6,540.0194	50,177.3112
81	35.985	7,289.1195	262.2990	0.091240	665.0585	6,156.7327	5,851.9142	43,312.9722
82	40.552	7,026.8205	284.9516	0.088582	622.4528	5,491.6741	5,206.3833	37,156.2396
83	45.690	6,741.8689	308.0360	0.086002	579.8166	4,869.2213	4,603.4720	31,664.5654
84	51.456	6,433.8329	331.0593	0.083497	537.2085	4,289.4047	4,043.1841	26,795.3441

609

APPENDIX H.1

Annuity 2000 Mortality Table—Female Commutation Columns at 3% *(Continued)*

Age Nearest Birthday x	$1,000\, q_x$	l_x	d_x	v^x	D_x	N_x	$N_x^{(12)}$	S_x
85	57.913	6,102.7736	353.4299	0.081065	494.7242	3,752.1962	3,525.4476	22,505.9394
86	65.119	5,749.3437	374.3915	0.078704	452.4983	3,257.4720	3,050.0769	18,753.7432
87	73.136	5,374.9522	393.1025	0.076412	410.7107	2,804.9737	2,616.7313	15,496.2712
88	81.991	4,981.8497	408.4668	0.074186	369.5854	2,394.2630	2,224.8696	12,691.2975
89	91.577	4,573.3828	418.8167	0.072026	329.4007	2,024.6775	1,873.7022	10,297.0345
90	101.758	4,154.5661	422.7603	0.069928	290.5196	1,695.2768	1,562.1220	8,272.3570
91	112.395	3,731.8058	419.4363	0.067891	253.3562	1,404.7572	1,288.6356	6,577.0802
92	123.349	3,312.3695	408.5775	0.065914	218.3303	1,151.4010	1,051.3329	5,172.3230
93	134.486	2,903.7920	390.5194	0.063994	185.8248	933.0706	847.9009	4,020.9221
94	145.689	2,513.2726	366.1562	0.062130	156.1495	747.2458	675.6773	3,087.8515
95	156.846	2,147.1165	336.7666	0.060320	129.5148	591.0964	531.7355	2,340.6056
96	167.841	1,810.3498	303.8509	0.058563	106.0203	461.5816	412.9890	1,749.5092
97	178.563	1,506.4989	269.0050	0.056858	85.6560	355.5613	316.3023	1,287.9276
98	189.604	1,237.4939	234.6338	0.055202	68.3117	269.9053	238.5958	932.3663
99	210.557	1,002.8601	202.1335	0.053594	53.7471	201.5936	176.9595	662.4610
100	215.013	800.7267	172.1666	0.052033	41.6641	147.8465	128.7505	460.8674
101	230.565	628.5600	144.9239	0.050517	31.7532	106.1824	91.6289	313.0209
102	248.805	483.6361	120.3311	0.049046	23.7204	74.4292	63.5574	206.8385
103	270.326	363.3050	98.2108	0.047617	17.2996	50.7089	42.7799	132.4092
104	295.719	265.0942	78.3934	0.046231	12.2554	33.4092	27.7921	81.7004

APPENDIX H.1

Annuity 2000 Mortality Table—Female Commutation Columns at 3% (Continued)

Age Nearest Birthday x	$1,000\,q_x$	l_x	d_x	v^x	D_x	N_x	$N_x^{(12)}$	S_x
105	325.576	186.7008	60.7853	0.044884	8.3799	21.1538	17.3130	48.2912
106	360.491	125.9155	45.3914	0.043577	5.4870	12.7739	10.2590	27.1374
107	401.054	80.5241	32.2945	0.042307	3.4068	7.2869	5.7255	14.3635
108	447.860	48.2296	21.6001	0.041075	1.9810	3.8801	2.9722	7.0766
109	501.498	26.6295	13.3546	0.039879	1.0620	1.8991	1.4124	3.1964
110	562.563	13.2749	7.4679	0.038717	0.5140	0.8371	0.6016	1.2973
111	631.645	5.8069	3.6679	0.037590	0.2183	0.3232	0.2231	0.4602
112	709.338	2.1390	1.5173	0.036495	0.0781	0.1049	0.0691	0.1370
113	796.233	0.6217	0.4950	0.035432	0.0220	0.0268	0.0167	0.0321
114	892.923	0.1267	0.1131	0.034400	0.0044	0.0048	0.0028	0.0053
115	1000.000	0.0136	0.0136	0.033398	0.0005	0.0005	0.0002	0.0005

APPENDIX H.2

Annuity 2000 Mortality Table—Female Commutation Columns at 4%

Age Nearest Birthday x	$1,000\,q_x$	l_x	d_x	v^x	D_x	N_x	$N_x^{(12)}$	S_x
5	0.171	10,000.0000	1.7100	0.821927	8,219.2711	203,108.1075	199,340.9416	4,537,548.6559
6	0.141	9,998.2900	1.4098	0.790315	7,901.7938	194,888.8364	191,267.1809	4,334,440.5484
7	0.118	9,996.8802	1.1796	0.759918	7,596.8074	186,987.0426	183,505.1726	4,139,551.7120
8	0.118	9,995.7006	1.1795	0.730690	7,303.7605	179,390.2352	176,042.6783	3,952,564.6694
9	0.121	9,994.5211	1.2093	0.702587	7,022.0180	172,086.4747	168,868.0498	3,773,174.4342
10	0.126	9,993.3118	1.2592	0.675564	6,751.1234	165,064.4567	161,970.1919	3,601,087.9595
11	0.133	9,992.0526	1.3289	0.649581	6,490.6469	158,313.3334	155,338.4536	3,436,023.5027
12	0.142	9,990.7237	1.4187	0.624597	6,240.1765	151,822.6865	148,962.6056	3,277,710.1694
13	0.152	9,989.3050	1.5184	0.600574	5,999.3177	145,582.5100	142,832.8227	3,125,887.4828
14	0.164	9,987.7866	1.6380	0.577475	5,767.6979	139,583.1923	136,939.6641	2,980,304.9729
15	0.177	9,986.1486	1.7675	0.555265	5,544.9539	133,815.4944	131,274.0572	2,840,721.7806
16	0.190	9,984.3811	1.8970	0.533908	5,330.7427	128,270.5405	125,827.2834	2,706,906.2862
17	0.204	9,982.4840	2.0364	0.513373	5,124.7402	122,939.7978	120,590.9585	2,578,635.7457
18	0.219	9,980.4476	2.1857	0.493628	4,926.6296	117,815.0576	115,557.0190	2,455,695.9479
19	0.234	9,978.2619	2.3349	0.474642	4,736.1064	112,888.4280	110,717.7125	2,337,880.8903
20	0.250	9,975.9270	2.4940	0.456387	4,552.8829	108,152.3216	106,065.5836	2,224,992.4623
21	0.265	9,973.4330	2.6430	0.438834	4,376.6775	103,599.4387	101,593.4615	2,116,840.1408
22	0.281	9,970.7900	2.8018	0.421955	4,207.2286	99,222.7612	97,294.4481	2,013,240.7021
23	0.298	9,967.9883	2.9705	0.405726	4,044.2753	95,015.5326	93,161.9064	1,914,017.9409
24	0.314	9,965.0178	3.1290	0.390121	3,887.5674	90,971.2573	89,189.4555	1,819,002.4083

APPENDIX H.2
Annuity 2000 Mortality Table—Female Commutation Columns at 4% *(Continued)*

Age Nearest Birthday x	$1,000\,q_x$	l_x	d_x	v^x	D_x	N_x	$N_x^{(12)}$	S_x
25	0.331	9,961.8888	3.2974	0.375117	3,736.8719	87,083.6899	85,370.9569	1,728,031.1510
26	0.347	9,958.5914	3.4556	0.360689	3,591.9567	83,346.8180	81,700.5045	1,640,947.4611
27	0.362	9,955.1358	3.6038	0.346817	3,452.6060	79,754.8613	78,172.4169	1,557,600.6431
28	0.376	9,951.5320	3.7418	0.333477	3,318.6117	76,302.2553	74,781.2249	1,477,845.7818
29	0.389	9,947.7902	3.8697	0.320651	3,189.7730	72,983.6435	71,521.6642	1,401,543.5266
30	0.402	9,943.9205	3.9975	0.308319	3,065.8963	69,793.8705	68,388.6680	1,328,559.8830
31	0.414	9,939.9231	4.1151	0.296460	2,946.7922	66,727.9742	65,377.3611	1,258,766.0125
32	0.425	9,935.8080	4.2227	0.285058	2,832.2809	63,781.1820	62,483.0533	1,192,038.0383
33	0.436	9,931.5852	4.3302	0.274094	2,722.1896	60,948.9011	59,701.2308	1,128,256.8563
34	0.449	9,927.2551	4.4573	0.263552	2,616.3488	58,226.7114	57,027.5516	1,067,307.9552
35	0.463	9,922.7977	4.5943	0.253415	2,514.5905	55,610.3626	54,457.8420	1,009,081.2437
36	0.481	9,918.2035	4.7707	0.243669	2,416.7560	53,095.7722	51,988.0924	953,470.8811
37	0.504	9,913.4328	4.9964	0.234297	2,322.6861	50,679.0162	49,614.4518	900,375.1089
38	0.532	9,908.4364	5.2713	0.225285	2,232.2264	48,356.3302	47,333.2264	849,696.0927
39	0.567	9,903.1652	5.6151	0.216621	2,145.2296	46,124.1038	45,140.8735	801,339.7626
40	0.609	9,897.5501	6.0276	0.208289	2,061.5512	43,978.8741	43,033.9965	755,215.6588
41	0.658	9,891.5225	6.5086	0.200278	1,981.0536	41,917.3229	41,009.3400	711,236.7846
42	0.715	9,885.0138	7.0678	0.192575	1,903.6058	39,936.2693	39,063.7833	669,319.4617
43	0.781	9,877.9460	7.7147	0.185168	1,829.0815	38,032.6634	37,194.3344	629,383.1925
44	0.855	9,870.2314	8.4390	0.178046	1,757.3587	36,203.5819	35,398.1259	591,350.5290

APPENDIX H.2

Annuity 2000 Mortality Table—Female Commutation Columns at 4% (Continued)

Age Nearest Birthday x	$1,000\,q_x$	l_x	d_x	v^x	D_x	N_x	$N_x^{(12)}$	S_x
45	0.939	9,861.7923	9.2602	0.171198	1,688.3232	34,446.2233	33,672.4085	555,146.9471
46	1.035	9,852.5321	10.1974	0.164614	1,621.8633	32,757.9001	32,014.5461	520,700.7239
47	1.141	9,842.3347	11.2301	0.158283	1,557.8699	31,136.0368	30,422.0131	487,942.8238
48	1.261	9,831.1046	12.3970	0.152195	1,496.2427	29,578.1669	28,892.3890	456,806.7870
49	1.393	9,818.7076	13.6775	0.146341	1,436.8807	28,081.9242	27,423.3539	427,228.6201
50	1.538	9,805.0301	15.0801	0.140713	1,379.6914	26,645.0436	26,012.6850	399,146.6959
51	1.695	9,789.9500	16.5940	0.135301	1,324.5860	25,265.3521	24,658.2502	372,501.6524
52	1.864	9,773.3560	18.2175	0.130097	1,271.4816	23,940.7661	23,358.0037	347,236.3003
53	2.047	9,755.1385	19.9688	0.125093	1,220.2996	22,669.2845	22,109.9805	323,295.5342
54	2.244	9,735.1697	21.8457	0.120282	1,170.9631	21,448.9849	20,912.2935	300,626.2497
55	2.457	9,713.3240	23.8656	0.115656	1,123.3995	20,278.0218	19,763.1304	279,177.2647
56	2.689	9,689.4584	26.0550	0.111207	1,077.5378	19,154.6224	18,660.7509	258,899.2429
57	2.942	9,663.4034	28.4297	0.106930	1,033.3079	18,077.0846	17,603.4851	239,744.6205
58	3.218	9,634.9737	31.0053	0.102817	990.6423	17,043.7767	16,589.7323	221,667.5359
59	3.523	9,603.9683	33.8348	0.098863	949.4754	16,053.1344	15,617.9582	204,623.7593
60	3.863	9,570.1336	36.9694	0.095060	909.7407	15,103.6590	14,686.6945	188,570.6249
61	4.242	9,533.1641	40.4397	0.091404	871.3715	14,193.9183	13,794.5397	173,466.9658
62	4.668	9,492.7245	44.3120	0.087889	834.3031	13,322.5467	12,940.1578	159,273.0476
63	5.144	9,448.4124	48.6026	0.084508	798.4697	12,488.2437	12,122.2784	145,950.5008
64	5.671	9,399.8098	53.3063	0.081258	763.8100	11,689.7739	11,339.6943	133,462.2571

Annuity 2000 Mortality Table—Female Commutation Columns at 4% (*Continued*)

Age Nearest Birthday x	$1,000\,q_x$	l_x	d_x	v^x	D_x	N_x	$N_x^{(12)}$	S_x
65	6.250	9,346.5035	58.4156	0.078133	730.2677	10,925.9639	10,591.2579	121,772.4832
66	6.878	9,288.0878	63.8835	0.075128	697.7919	10,195.6962	9,875.8749	110,846.5193
67	7.555	9,224.2043	69.6889	0.072238	666.3389	9,497.9043	9,192.4989	100,650.8231
68	8.287	9,154.5155	75.8635	0.069460	635.8699	8,831.5654	8,540.1250	91,152.9188
69	9.102	9,078.6520	82.6339	0.066788	606.3466	8,195.6954	7,917.7866	82,321.3535
70	10.034	8,996.0181	90.2660	0.064219	577.7189	7,589.3488	7,324.5610	74,125.6580
71	11.117	8,905.7521	99.0052	0.061749	549.9251	7,011.6299	6,759.5809	66,536.3092
72	12.386	8,806.7468	109.0804	0.059374	522.8957	6,461.7049	6,222.0443	59,524.6793
73	13.871	8,697.6665	120.6453	0.057091	496.5569	5,938.8091	5,711.2206	53,062.9745
74	15.592	8,577.0211	133.7329	0.054895	470.8357	5,442.2523	5,226.4526	47,124.1653
75	17.564	8,443.2882	148.2979	0.052784	445.6677	4,971.4166	4,767.1522	41,681.9130
76	19.805	8,294.9903	164.2823	0.050754	421.0000	4,525.7489	4,332.7906	36,710.4964
77	22.328	8,130.7080	181.5424	0.048801	396.7905	4,104.7489	3,922.8866	32,184.7475
78	25.158	7,949.1656	199.9851	0.046924	373.0105	3,707.9584	3,536.9953	28,079.9986
79	28.341	7,749.1805	219.6195	0.045120	349.6407	3,334.9479	3,174.6959	24,372.0402
80	31.933	7,529.5609	240.4415	0.043384	326.6649	2,985.3072	2,835.5858	21,037.0923
81	35.985	7,289.1195	262.2990	0.041716	304.0707	2,658.6423	2,519.2765	18,051.7851
82	40.552	7,026.8205	284.9516	0.040111	281.8545	2,354.5716	2,225.3882	15,393.1429
83	45.690	6,741.8689	308.0360	0.038569	260.0238	2,072.7170	1,953.5394	13,038.5713
84	51.456	6,433.8329	331.0593	0.037085	238.5994	1,812.6932	1,703.3352	10,965.8543

Age Nearest Birthday x	$1,000\,q_x$	l_x	d_x	v^x	D_x	N_x	$N_x^{(12)}$	S_x
85	57.913	6,102.7736	353.4299	0.035659	217.6173	1,574.0938	1,474.3526	9,153.1611
86	65.119	5,749.3437	374.3915	0.034287	197.1293	1,356.4765	1,266.1256	7,579.0672
87	73.136	5,374.9522	393.1025	0.032969	177.2042	1,159.3473	1,078.1287	6,222.5907
88	81.991	4,981.8497	408.4668	0.031701	157.9271	982.1431	909.7598	5,063.2434
89	91.577	4,573.3828	418.8167	0.030481	139.4024	824.2159	760.3231	4,081.1003
90	101.758	4,154.5661	422.7603	0.029309	121.7657	684.8135	629.0042	3,256.8844
91	112.395	3,731.8058	419.4363	0.028182	105.1684	563.0477	514.8456	2,572.0709
92	123.349	3,312.3695	408.5775	0.027098	89.7577	457.8794	416.7404	2,009.0232
93	134.486	2,903.7920	390.5194	0.026056	75.6598	368.1217	333.4443	1,551.1438
94	145.689	2,513.2726	366.1562	0.025053	62.9659	292.4619	263.6025	1,183.0221
95	156.846	2,147.1165	336.7666	0.024090	51.7236	229.4960	205.7894	890.5602
96	167.841	1,810.3498	303.8509	0.023163	41.9336	177.7724	158.5529	661.0642
97	178.563	1,506.4989	269.0050	0.022272	33.5533	135.8389	120.4603	483.2918
98	189.604	1,237.4939	234.6338	0.021416	26.5018	102.2856	90.1389	347.4529
99	210.557	1,002.8601	202.1335	0.020592	20.6509	75.7838	66.3187	245.1673
100	215.013	800.7267	172.1666	0.019800	15.8544	55.1328	47.8662	169.3836
101	230.565	628.5600	144.9239	0.019039	11.9668	39.2784	33.7936	114.2507
102	248.805	483.6361	120.3311	0.018306	8.8536	27.3116	23.2537	74.9723
103	270.326	363.3050	98.2108	0.017602	6.3950	18.4580	15.5270	47.6608
104	295.719	265.0942	78.3934	0.016925	4.4868	12.0630	10.0066	29.2028

APPENDIX H.2

Annuity 2000 Mortality Table—Female Commutation Columns at 4% (*Continued*)

Age Nearest Birthday x	$1{,}000\,q_x$	l_x	d_x	v^x	D_x	N_x	$N_x^{(12)}$	S_x
105	325.576	186.7008	60.7853	0.016274	3.0384	7.5763	6.1837	17.1397
106	360.491	125.9155	45.3914	0.015648	1.9704	4.5379	3.6348	9.5635
107	401.054	80.5241	32.2945	0.015046	1.2116	2.5675	2.0122	5.0256
108	447.860	48.2296	21.6001	0.014468	0.6978	1.3559	1.0361	2.4581
109	501.498	26.6295	13.3546	0.013911	0.3704	0.6581	0.4884	1.1022
110	562.563	13.2749	7.4679	0.013376	0.1776	0.2877	0.2063	0.4440
111	631.645	5.8069	3.6679	0.012862	0.0747	0.1101	0.0759	0.1563
112	709.338	2.1390	1.5173	0.012367	0.0265	0.0354	0.0233	0.0462
113	796.233	0.6217	0.4950	0.011891	0.0074	0.0090	0.0056	0.0107
114	892.923	0.1267	0.1131	0.011434	0.0014	0.0016	0.0009	0.0017
115	1000.000	0.0136	0.0136	0.010994	0.0001	0.0001	0.0001	0.0001

APPENDIX H.3

Annuity 2000 Mortality Table—Female Commutation Columns at 5%

Age Nearest Birthday x	$1{,}000\,q_x$	l_x	d_x	v^x	D_x	N_x	$N_x^{(12)}$	S_x
5	0.171	10,000.0000	1.7100	0.783526	7,835.2617	160,276.6131	156,685.4515	3,087,893.2577
6	0.141	9,998.2900	1.4098	0.746215	7,460.8779	152,441.3515	149,021.7824	2,927,616.6445
7	0.118	9,996.8802	1.1796	0.710681	7,104.5961	144,980.4735	141,724.2003	2,775,175.2931
8	0.118	9,995.7006	1.1795	0.676839	6,765.4836	137,875.8774	134,775.0307	2,630,194.8195
9	0.121	9,994.5211	1.2093	0.644609	6,442.5574	131,110.3938	128,157.5549	2,492,318.9422
10	0.126	9,993.3118	1.2592	0.613913	6,135.0265	124,667.8363	121,855.9492	2,361,208.5484
11	0.133	9,992.0526	1.3289	0.584679	5,842.1462	118,532.8098	115,855.1594	2,236,540.7121
12	0.142	9,990.7237	1.4187	0.556837	5,563.2088	112,690.6636	110,140.8595	2,118,007.9023
13	0.152	9,989.3050	1.5184	0.530321	5,297.5417	107,127.4548	104,699.4148	2,005,317.2387
14	0.164	9,987.7866	1.6380	0.505068	5,044.5109	101,829.9131	99,517.8455	1,898,189.7839
15	0.177	9,986.1486	1.7675	0.481017	4,803.5082	96,785.4021	94,583.7942	1,796,359.8709
16	0.190	9,984.3811	1.8970	0.458112	4,573.9600	91,981.8939	89,885.4956	1,699,574.4687
17	0.204	9,982.4840	2.0364	0.436297	4,355.3247	87,407.9339	85,411.7434	1,607,592.5749
18	0.219	9,980.4476	2.1857	0.415521	4,147.0821	83,052.6092	81,151.8632	1,520,184.6410
19	0.234	9,978.2619	2.3349	0.395734	3,948.7371	78,905.5270	77,095.6892	1,437,132.0318
20	0.250	9,975.9270	2.4940	0.376889	3,759.8220	74,956.7900	73,233.5382	1,358,226.5048
21	0.265	9,973.4330	2.6430	0.358942	3,579.8876	71,196.9680	69,556.1862	1,283,269.7148
22	0.281	9,970.7900	2.8018	0.341850	3,408.5133	67,617.0804	66,054.8451	1,212,072.7468
23	0.298	9,967.9883	2.9705	0.325571	3,245.2910	64,208.5671	62,721.1421	1,144,455.6665
24	0.314	9,965.0178	3.1290	0.310068	3,089.8322	60,963.2761	59,547.1030	1,080,247.0994

Annuity 2000 Mortality Table—Female Commutation Columns at 5% (Continued)

Age Nearest Birthday x	$1,000\,q_x$	l_x	d_x	v^x	D_x	N_x	$N_x^{(12)}$	S_x
25	0.331	9,961.8888	3.2974	0.295303	2,941.7734	57,873.4439	56,525.1311	1,019,283.8233
26	0.347	9,958.5914	3.4556	0.281241	2,800.7616	54,931.6705	53,647.9881	961,410.3794
27	0.362	9,955.1358	3.6038	0.267848	2,666.4664	52,130.9090	50,908.7785	906,478.7089
28	0.376	9,951.5320	3.7418	0.255094	2,538.5725	49,464.4426	48,300.9302	854,347.7999
29	0.389	9,947.7902	3.8697	0.242946	2,416.7790	46,925.8701	45,818.1797	804,883.3573
30	0.402	9,943.9205	3.9975	0.231377	2,300.7990	44,509.0910	43,454.5582	757,957.4873
31	0.414	9,939.9231	4.1151	0.220359	2,190.3562	42,208.2921	41,204.3788	713,448.3962
32	0.425	9,935.8080	4.2227	0.209866	2,085.1899	40,017.9359	39,062.2238	671,240.1041
33	0.436	9,931.5852	4.3302	0.199873	1,985.0512	37,932.7459	37,022.9308	631,222.1683
34	0.449	9,927.2551	4.4573	0.190355	1,889.7006	35,947.6948	35,081.5820	593,289.4223
35	0.463	9,922.7977	4.5943	0.181290	1,798.9068	34,057.9941	33,233.4952	557,341.7276
36	0.481	9,918.2035	4.7707	0.172657	1,712.4514	32,259.0873	31,474.2137	523,283.7335
37	0.504	9,913.4328	4.9964	0.164436	1,630.1216	30,546.6359	29,799.4968	491,024.6462
38	0.532	9,908.4364	5.2713	0.156605	1,551.7143	28,916.5143	28,205.3119	460,478.0103
39	0.567	9,903.1652	5.6151	0.149148	1,477.0369	27,364.8000	26,687.8247	431,561.4960
40	0.609	9,897.5501	6.0276	0.142046	1,405.9043	25,887.7631	25,243.3903	404,196.6959
41	0.658	9,891.5225	6.5086	0.135282	1,338.1410	24,481.8588	23,868.5442	378,308.9329
42	0.715	9,885.0138	7.0678	0.128840	1,273.5814	23,143.7178	22,559.9930	353,827.0741
43	0.781	9,877.9460	7.7147	0.122704	1,212.0675	21,870.1364	21,314.6055	330,683.3562
44	0.855	9,870.2314	8.4390	0.116861	1,153.4484	20,658.0689	20,129.4051	308,813.2199

APPENDIX H.3

Annuity 2000 Mortality Table—Female Commutation Columns at 5% *(Continued)*

Age Nearest Birthday x	$1,000\,q_x$	l_x	d_x	v^x	D_x	N_x	$N_x^{(12)}$	S_x
45	0.939	9,861.7923	9.2602	0.111297	1,097.5831	19,504.6205	19,001.5616	288,155.1510
46	1.035	9,852.5321	10.1974	0.105997	1,044.3356	18,407.0375	17,928.3836	268,650.5304
47	1.141	9,842.3347	11.2301	0.100949	993.5760	17,362.7018	16,907.3128	250,243.4930
48	1.261	9,831.1046	12.3970	0.096142	945.1831	16,369.1259	15,935.9169	232,880.7912
49	1.393	9,818.7076	13.6775	0.091564	899.0393	15,423.9427	15,011.8830	216,511.6653
50	1.538	9,805.0301	15.0801	0.087204	855.0352	14,524.9034	14,133.0123	201,087.7226
51	1.695	9,789.9500	16.5940	0.083051	813.0668	13,669.8683	13,297.2126	186,562.8192
52	1.864	9,773.3560	18.2175	0.079096	773.0368	12,856.8015	12,502.4929	172,892.9509
53	2.047	9,755.1385	19.9688	0.075330	734.8532	12,083.7647	11,746.9570	160,036.1494
54	2.244	9,735.1697	21.8457	0.071743	698.4276	11,348.9115	11,028.7988	147,952.3848
55	2.457	9,713.3240	23.8656	0.068326	663.6765	10,650.4839	10,346.2988	136,603.4733
56	2.689	9,689.4584	26.0550	0.065073	630.5198	9,986.8074	9,697.8192	125,952.9894
57	2.942	9,663.4034	28.4297	0.061974	598.8804	9,356.2876	9,081.8008	115,966.1820
58	3.218	9,634.9737	31.0053	0.059023	568.6842	8,757.4072	8,496.7603	106,609.8944
59	3.523	9,603.9683	33.8348	0.056212	539.8611	8,188.7230	7,941.2866	97,852.4872
60	3.863	9,570.1336	36.9694	0.053536	512.3421	7,648.8618	7,414.0384	89,663.7642
61	4.242	9,533.1641	40.4397	0.050986	486.0599	7,136.5197	6,913.7423	82,014.9023
62	4.668	9,492.7245	44.3120	0.048558	460.9505	6,650.4598	6,439.1908	74,878.3826
63	5.144	9,448.4124	48.6026	0.046246	436.9513	6,189.5093	5,989.2399	68,227.9228
64	5.671	9,399.8098	53.3063	0.044044	414.0034	5,752.5580	5,562.8064	62,038.4135

620

APPENDIX H.3

Annuity 2000 Mortality Table—Female Commutation Columns at 5% *(Continued)*

Age Nearest Birthday x	$1,000\,q_x$	l_x	d_x	v^x	D_x	N_x	$N_x^{(12)}$	S_x
65	6.250	9,346.5035	58.4156	0.041946	392.0530	5,338.5546	5,158.8636	56,285.8555
66	6.878	9,288.0878	63.8835	0.039949	371.0501	4,946.5016	4,776.4370	50,947.3010
67	7.555	9,224.2043	69.6889	0.038047	350.9505	4,575.4515	4,414.5992	46,000.7994
68	8.287	9,154.5155	75.8635	0.036235	331.7134	4,224.5010	4,072.4657	41,425.3479
69	9.102	9,078.6520	82.6339	0.034509	313.2995	3,892.7876	3,749.1920	37,200.8469
70	10.034	8,996.0181	90.2660	0.032866	295.6646	3,579.4881	3,443.9751	33,308.0593
71	11.117	8,905.7521	99.0052	0.031301	278.7599	3,283.8234	3,156.0584	29,728.5712
72	12.386	8,806.7468	109.0804	0.029811	262.5343	3,005.0635	2,884.7353	26,444.7478
73	13.871	8,697.6665	120.6453	0.028391	246.9357	2,742.5292	2,629.3503	23,439.6843
74	15.592	8,577.0211	133.7329	0.027039	231.9147	2,495.5935	2,389.2992	20,697.1551
75	17.564	8,443.2882	148.2979	0.025752	217.4274	2,263.6788	2,164.0246	18,201.5616
76	19.805	8,294.9903	164.2823	0.024525	203.4366	2,046.2514	1,953.0096	15,937.8829
77	22.328	8,130.7080	181.5424	0.023357	189.9120	1,842.8148	1,755.7718	13,891.6315
78	25.158	7,949.1656	199.9851	0.022245	176.8301	1,652.9028	1,571.8557	12,048.8167
79	28.341	7,749.1805	219.6195	0.021186	164.1728	1,476.0727	1,400.8268	10,395.9139
80	31.933	7,529.5609	240.4415	0.020177	151.9238	1,311.8999	1,242.2682	8,919.8412
81	35.985	7,289.1195	262.2990	0.019216	140.0689	1,159.9761	1,095.7779	7,607.9413
82	40.552	7,026.8205	284.9516	0.018301	128.5986	1,019.9072	960.9662	6,447.9651
83	45.690	6,741.8689	308.0360	0.017430	117.5083	891.3086	837.4506	5,428.0579
84	51.456	6,433.8329	331.0593	0.016600	106.7994	773.8003	724.8506	4,536.7493

APPENDIX H.3

Annuity 2000 Mortality Table—Female Commutation Columns at 5% *(Continued)*

Age Nearest Birthday x	$1,000\,q_x$	l_x	d_x	v^x	D_x	N_x	$N_x^{(12)}$	S_x
85	57.913	6,102.7736	353.4299	0.015809	96.4799	667.0009	622.7810	3,762.9490
86	65.119	5,749.3437	374.3915	0.015056	86.5642	570.5210	530.8458	3,095.9481
87	73.136	5,374.9522	393.1025	0.014339	77.0736	483.9568	448.6314	2,525.4271
88	81.991	4,981.8497	408.4668	0.013657	68.0350	406.8832	375.7005	2,041.4703
89	91.577	4,573.3828	418.8167	0.013006	59.4826	338.8482	311.5854	1,634.5871
90	101.758	4,154.5661	422.7603	0.012387	51.4622	279.3656	255.7788	1,295.7389
91	112.395	3,731.8058	419.4363	0.011797	44.0243	227.9034	207.7255	1,016.3732
92	123.349	3,312.3695	408.5775	0.011235	37.2154	183.8790	166.8219	788.4699
93	134.486	2,903.7920	390.5194	0.010700	31.0714	146.6636	132.4225	604.5908
94	145.689	2,513.2726	366.1562	0.010191	25.6121	115.5922	103.8533	457.9273
95	156.846	2,147.1165	336.7666	0.009705	20.8388	89.9801	80.4290	342.3351
96	167.841	1,810.3498	303.8509	0.009243	16.7336	69.1413	61.4717	252.3550
97	178.563	1,506.4989	269.0050	0.008803	13.2619	52.4077	46.3293	183.2137
98	189.604	1,237.4939	234.6338	0.008384	10.3751	39.1457	34.3905	130.8060
99	210.557	1,002.8601	202.1335	0.007985	8.0076	28.7707	25.1005	91.6603
100	215.013	800.7267	172.1666	0.007604	6.0891	20.7631	17.9723	62.8896
101	230.565	628.5600	144.9239	0.007242	4.5523	14.6740	12.5875	42.1265
102	248.805	483.6361	120.3311	0.006897	3.3359	10.1217	8.5928	27.4525
103	270.326	363.3050	98.2108	0.006569	2.3866	6.7858	5.6920	17.3308
104	295.719	265.0942	78.3934	0.006256	1.6585	4.3993	3.6391	10.5449

APPENDIX H.3

Annuity 2000 Mortality Table—Female Commutation Columns at 5% *(Continued)*

Age Nearest Birthday x	$1,000\, q_x$	l_x	d_x	v^x	D_x	N_x	$N_x^{(12)}$	S_x
105	325.576	186.7008	60.7853	0.005958	1.1124	2.7408	2.2309	6.1456
106	360.491	125.9155	45.3914	0.005675	0.7145	1.6284	1.3009	3.4049
107	401.054	80.5241	32.2945	0.005404	0.4352	0.9138	0.7144	1.7765
108	447.860	48.2296	21.6001	0.005147	0.2482	0.4787	0.3649	0.8626
109	501.498	26.6295	13.3546	0.004902	0.1305	0.2304	0.1706	0.3840
110	562.563	13.2749	7.4679	0.004668	0.0620	0.0999	0.0715	0.1535
111	631.645	5.8069	3.6679	0.004446	0.0258	0.0379	0.0261	0.0537
112	709.338	2.1390	1.5173	0.004234	0.0091	0.0121	0.0079	0.0157
113	796.233	0.6217	0.4950	0.004033	0.0025	0.0030	0.0019	0.0036
114	892.923	0.1267	0.1131	0.003841	0.0005	0.0005	0.0003	0.0006
115	1000.000	0.0136	0.0136	0.003658	0.0000	0.0000	0.0000	0.0000

Annuity 2000 Mortality Table—Female Commutation Columns at 6%

Age Nearest Birthday x	$1,000\,q_x$	l_x	d_x	v^x	D_x	N_x	$N_x^{(12)}$	S_x
5	0.171	10,000.0000	1.7100	0.747258	7,472.5817	130,118.0966	126,693.1633	2,186,847.9529
6	0.141	9,998.2900	1.4098	0.704961	7,048.3999	122,645.5148	119,414.9982	2,056,729.8563
7	0.118	9,996.8802	1.1796	0.665057	6,648.4963	115,597.1149	112,549.8874	1,934,084.3415
8	0.118	9,995.7006	1.1795	0.627412	6,271.4262	108,948.6186	106,074.2149	1,818,487.2266
9	0.121	9,994.5211	1.2093	0.591898	5,915.7417	102,677.1924	99,965.8108	1,709,538.6080
10	0.126	9,993.3118	1.2592	0.558395	5,580.2131	96,761.4507	94,203.8530	1,606,861.4156
11	0.133	9,992.0526	1.3289	0.526788	5,263.6887	91,181.2376	88,768.7136	1,510,099.9650
12	0.142	9,990.7237	1.4187	0.496969	4,965.0836	85,917.5489	83,641.8856	1,418,918.7274
13	0.152	9,989.3050	1.5184	0.468839	4,683.3760	80,952.4653	78,805.9180	1,333,001.1785
14	0.164	9,987.7866	1.6380	0.442301	4,417.6077	76,269.0893	74,244.3525	1,252,048.7132
15	0.177	9,986.1486	1.7675	0.417265	4,166.8709	71,851.4817	69,941.6658	1,175,779.6239
16	0.190	9,984.3811	1.8970	0.393646	3,930.3145	67,684.6108	65,883.2166	1,103,928.1422
17	0.204	9,982.4840	2.0364	0.371364	3,707.1394	63,754.2962	62,055.1907	1,036,243.5315
18	0.219	9,980.4476	2.1857	0.350344	3,496.5879	60,047.1569	58,444.5541	972,489.2352
19	0.234	9,978.2619	2.3349	0.330513	3,297.9454	56,550.5690	55,039.0107	912,442.0783
20	0.250	9,975.9270	2.4940	0.311805	3,110.5412	53,252.6236	51,826.9589	855,891.5093
21	0.265	9,973.4330	2.6430	0.294155	2,933.7392	50,142.0824	48,797.4520	802,638.8857
22	0.281	9,970.7900	2.8018	0.277505	2,766.9451	47,208.3432	45,940.1601	752,496.8033
23	0.298	9,967.9883	2.9705	0.261797	2,609.5920	44,441.3982	43,245.3352	705,288.4600
24	0.314	9,965.0178	3.1290	0.246979	2,461.1456	41,831.8062	40,703.7811	660,847.0619

APPENDIX H.4
Annuity 2000 Mortality Table—Female Commutation Columns at 6% *(Continued)*

Age Nearest Birthday x	$1{,}000\,q_x$	l_x	d_x	v^x	D_x	N_x	$N_x^{(12)}$	S_x
25	0.331	9,961.8888	3.2974	0.232999	2,321.1064	39,370.6605	38,306.8201	619,015.2557
26	0.347	9,958.5914	3.4556	0.219810	2,188.9983	37,049.5541	36,046.2632	579,644.5952
27	0.362	9,955.1358	3.6038	0.207368	2,064.3761	34,860.5558	33,914.3834	542,595.0411
28	0.376	9,951.5320	3.7418	0.195630	1,946.8196	32,796.1797	31,903.8874	507,734.4853
29	0.389	9,947.7902	3.8697	0.184557	1,835.9317	30,849.3601	30,007.8914	474,938.3056
30	0.402	9,943.9205	3.9975	0.174110	1,731.3373	29,013.4284	28,219.8988	444,088.9455
31	0.414	9,939.9231	4.1151	0.164255	1,632.6805	27,282.0911	26,533.7792	415,075.5171
32	0.425	9,935.8080	4.2227	0.154957	1,539.6269	25,649.4106	24,943.7482	387,793.4261
33	0.436	9,931.5852	4.3302	0.146186	1,451.8609	24,109.7836	23,444.3474	362,144.0155
34	0.449	9,927.2551	4.4573	0.137912	1,369.0829	22,657.9227	22,030.4264	338,034.2319
35	0.463	9,922.7977	4.5943	0.130105	1,291.0078	21,288.8398	20,697.1279	315,376.3091
36	0.481	9,918.2035	4.7707	0.122741	1,217.3680	19,997.8320	19,439.8717	294,087.4694
37	0.504	9,913.4328	4.9964	0.115793	1,147.9079	18,780.4640	18,254.3396	274,089.6374
38	0.532	9,908.4364	5.2713	0.109239	1,082.3862	17,632.5561	17,136.4624	255,309.1734
39	0.567	9,903.1652	5.6151	0.103056	1,020.5758	16,550.1699	16,082.4060	237,676.6172
40	0.609	9,897.5501	6.0276	0.097222	962.2615	15,529.5941	15,088.5576	221,126.4473
41	0.658	9,891.5225	6.5086	0.091719	907.2410	14,567.3326	14,151.5138	205,596.8532
42	0.715	9,885.0138	7.0678	0.086527	855.3246	13,660.0916	13,268.0679	191,029.5206
43	0.781	9,877.9460	7.7147	0.081630	806.3330	12,804.7671	12,435.1978	177,369.4290
44	0.855	9,870.2314	8.4390	0.077009	760.0974	11,998.4341	11,650.0561	164,564.6619

625

APPENDIX H.4

Annuity 2000 Mortality Table—Female Commutation Columns at 6% *(Continued)*

Age Nearest Birthday x	$1{,}000\,q_x$	l_x	d_x	v^x	D_x	N_x	$N_x^{(12)}$	S_x
45	0.939	9,861.7923	9.2602	0.072650	716.4599	11,238.3366	10,909.9592	152,566.2278
46	1.035	9,852.5321	10.1974	0.068538	675.2709	10,521.8767	10,212.3775	141,327.8912
47	1.141	9,842.3347	11.2301	0.064658	636.3887	9,846.6058	9,554.9276	130,806.0145
48	1.261	9,831.1046	12.3970	0.060998	599.6817	9,210.2170	8,935.3629	120,959.4088
49	1.393	9,818.7076	13.6775	0.057546	565.0240	8,610.5354	8,351.5660	111,749.1917
50	1.538	9,805.0301	15.0801	0.054288	532.2990	8,045.5113	7,801.5409	103,138.6563
51	1.695	9,789.9500	16.5940	0.051215	501.3966	7,513.2123	7,283.4055	95,093.1450
52	1.864	9,773.3560	18.2175	0.048316	472.2139	7,011.8157	6,795.3844	87,579.9327
53	2.047	9,755.1385	19.9688	0.045582	444.6544	6,539.6019	6,335.8020	80,568.1170
54	2.244	9,735.1697	21.8457	0.043001	418.6266	6,094.9475	5,903.0770	74,028.5151
55	2.457	9,713.3240	23.8656	0.040567	394.0445	5,676.3209	5,495.7172	67,933.5676
56	2.689	9,689.4584	26.0550	0.038271	370.8267	5,282.2764	5,112.3141	62,257.2467
57	2.942	9,663.4034	28.4297	0.036105	348.8958	4,911.4497	4,751.5391	56,974.9703
58	3.218	9,634.9737	31.0053	0.034061	328.1787	4,562.5538	4,412.1386	52,063.5206
59	3.523	9,603.9683	33.8348	0.032133	308.6062	4,234.3751	4,092.9306	47,500.9668
60	3.863	9,570.1336	36.9694	0.030314	290.1123	3,925.7689	3,792.8008	43,266.5917
61	4.242	9,533.1641	40.4397	0.028598	272.6335	3,635.6567	3,510.6996	39,340.8227
62	4.668	9,492.7245	44.3120	0.026980	256.1104	3,363.0231	3,245.6392	35,705.1661
63	5.144	9,448.4124	48.6026	0.025453	240.4857	3,106.9127	2,996.6901	32,342.1429
64	5.671	9,399.8098	53.3063	0.024012	225.7063	2,866.4270	2,762.9783	29,235.2302

Annuity 2000 Mortality Table—Female Commutation Columns at 6% (*Continued*)

Age Nearest Birthday x	$1,000\, q_x$	l_x	d_x	v^x	D_x	N_x	$N_x^{(12)}$	S_x
65	6.250	9,346.5035	58.4156	0.022653	211.7229	2,640.7207	2,543.6810	26,368.8032
66	6.878	9,288.0878	63.8835	0.021370	198.4903	2,428.9977	2,338.0230	23,728.0826
67	7.555	9,224.2043	69.6889	0.020161	185.9670	2,230.5075	2,145.2726	21,299.0848
68	8.287	9,154.5155	75.8635	0.019020	174.1151	2,044.5404	1,964.7377	19,068.5774
69	9.102	9,078.6520	82.6339	0.017943	162.8983	1,870.4253	1,795.7636	17,024.0369
70	10.034	8,996.0181	90.2660	0.016927	152.2789	1,707.5270	1,637.7325	15,153.6116
71	11.117	8,905.7521	99.0052	0.015969	142.2179	1,555.2481	1,490.0649	13,446.0846
72	12.386	8,806.7468	109.0804	0.015065	132.6763	1,413.0302	1,352.2202	11,890.8366
73	13.871	8,697.6665	120.6453	0.014213	123.6160	1,280.3539	1,223.6966	10,477.8064
74	15.592	8,577.0211	133.7329	0.013408	115.0012	1,156.7380	1,104.0291	9,197.4525
75	17.564	8,443.2882	148.2979	0.012649	106.8001	1,041.7367	992.7867	8,040.7145
76	19.805	8,294.9903	164.2823	0.011933	98.9852	934.9366	889.5684	6,998.9778
77	22.328	8,130.7080	181.5424	0.011258	91.5328	835.9515	793.9989	6,064.0411
78	25.158	7,949.1656	199.9851	0.010620	84.4236	744.4187	705.7245	5,228.0897
79	28.341	7,749.1805	219.6195	0.010019	77.6412	659.9950	624.4095	4,483.6710
80	31.933	7,529.5609	240.4415	0.009452	71.1706	582.3538	549.7339	3,823.6760
81	35.985	7,289.1195	262.2990	0.008917	64.9980	511.1832	481.3925	3,241.3222
82	40.552	7,026.8205	284.9516	0.008412	59.1123	446.1852	419.0921	2,730.1390
83	45.690	6,741.8689	308.0360	0.007936	53.5049	387.0729	362.5498	2,283.9538
84	51.456	6,433.8329	331.0593	0.007487	48.1700	333.5680	311.4901	1,896.8809

APPENDIX H.4

Annuity 2000 Mortality Table—Female Commutation Columns at 6% *(Continued)*

Age Nearest Birthday x	1,000 q_x	l_x	d_x	v^x	D_x	N_x	$N_x^{(12)}$	S_x
85	57.913	6,102.7736	353.4299	0.007063	43.1051	285.3980	265.6415	1,563.3128
86	65.119	5,749.3437	374.3915	0.006663	38.3102	242.2929	224.7341	1,277.9149
87	73.136	5,374.9522	393.1025	0.006286	33.7881	203.9827	188.4965	1,035.6220
88	81.991	4,981.8497	408.4668	0.005930	29.5444	170.1946	156.6534	831.6393
89	91.577	4,573.3828	418.8167	0.005595	25.5868	140.6502	128.9230	661.4447
90	101.758	4,154.5661	422.7603	0.005278	21.9279	115.0634	105.0131	520.7945
91	112.395	3,731.8058	419.4363	0.004979	18.5817	93.1355	84.6189	405.7310
92	123.349	3,312.3695	408.5775	0.004697	15.5596	74.5538	67.4223	312.5955
93	134.486	2,903.7920	390.5194	0.004432	12.8683	58.9942	53.0962	238.0417
94	145.689	2,513.2726	366.1562	0.004181	10.5072	46.1259	41.3101	179.0475
95	156.846	2,147.1165	336.7666	0.003944	8.4683	35.6187	31.7374	132.9216
96	167.841	1,810.3498	303.8509	0.003721	6.7360	27.1504	24.0630	97.3029
97	178.563	1,506.4989	269.0050	0.003510	5.2881	20.4144	17.9907	70.1525
98	189.604	1,237.4939	234.6338	0.003312	4.0980	15.1263	13.2481	49.7381
99	210.557	1,002.8601	202.1335	0.003124	3.1330	11.0283	9.5924	34.6119
100	215.013	800.7267	172.1666	0.002947	2.3599	7.8953	6.8137	23.5835
101	230.565	628.5600	144.9239	0.002780	1.7476	5.5354	4.7344	15.6882
102	248.805	483.6361	120.3311	0.002623	1.2686	3.7878	3.2063	10.1528
103	270.326	363.3050	98.2108	0.002475	0.8990	2.5192	2.1071	6.3650
104	295.719	265.0942	78.3934	0.002334	0.6189	1.6202	1.3365	3.8459

Annuity 2000 Mortality Table—Female Commutation Columns at 6% (*Continued*)

Age Nearest Birthday x	$1,000\,q_x$	l_x	d_x	v^x	D_x	N_x	$N_x^{(12)}$	S_x
105	325.576	186.7008	60.7853	0.002202	0.4112	1.0013	0.8128	2.2257
106	360.491	125.9155	45.3914	0.002078	0.2616	0.5901	0.4702	1.2244
107	401.054	80.5241	32.2945	0.001960	0.1578	0.3285	0.2562	0.6343
108	447.860	48.2296	21.6001	0.001849	0.0892	0.1707	0.1298	0.3058
109	501.498	26.6295	13.3546	0.001744	0.0465	0.0815	0.0602	0.1351
110	562.563	13.2749	7.4679	0.001646	0.0218	0.0350	0.0250	0.0536
111	631.645	5.8069	3.6679	0.001553	0.0090	0.0132	0.0091	0.0186
112	709.338	2.1390	1.5173	0.001465	0.0031	0.0042	0.0027	0.0054
113	796.233	0.6217	0.4950	0.001382	0.0009	0.0010	0.0006	0.0012
114	892.923	0.1267	0.1131	0.001304	0.0002	0.0002	0.0001	0.0002
115	1000.000	0.0136	0.0136	0.001230	0.0000	0.0000	0.0000	0.0000

APPENDIX I.1

Annuity 2000 Mortality Table—Male Commutation Columns at 3%

Age Nearest Birthday x	$1,000\, q_x$	l_x	d_x	v^{x+1}	C_x	M_x	R_x
5	0.291	10,000.0000	2.9100	0.837484	2.4371	1,021.0717	69,612.8668
6	0.270	9,997.0900	2.6992	0.813092	2.1947	1,018.6346	68,591.7952
7	0.257	9,994.3908	2.5686	0.789409	2.0276	1,016.4399	67,573.1606
8	0.294	9,991.8222	2.9376	0.766417	2.2514	1,014.4122	66,556.7207
9	0.325	9,988.8846	3.2464	0.744094	2.4156	1,012.1608	65,542.3085
10	0.350	9,985.6382	3.4950	0.722421	2.5248	1,009.7452	64,530.1477
11	0.371	9,982.1433	3.7034	0.701380	2.5975	1,007.2203	63,520.4025
12	0.388	9,978.4399	3.8716	0.680951	2.6364	1,004.6229	62,513.1822
13	0.402	9,974.5683	4.0098	0.661118	2.6509	1,001.9865	61,508.5593
14	0.414	9,970.5585	4.1278	0.641862	2.6495	999.3355	60,506.5728
15	0.425	9,966.4307	4.2357	0.623167	2.6396	996.6861	59,507.2373
16	0.437	9,962.1949	4.3535	0.605016	2.6339	994.0465	58,510.5512
17	0.449	9,957.8415	4.4711	0.587395	2.6263	991.4126	57,516.5047
18	0.463	9,953.3704	4.6084	0.570286	2.6281	988.7863	56,525.0921
19	0.480	9,948.7620	4.7754	0.553676	2.6440	986.1582	55,536.3059
20	0.499	9,943.9866	4.9620	0.537549	2.6673	983.5141	54,550.1477
21	0.519	9,939.0245	5.1584	0.521893	2.6921	980.8468	53,566.6336
22	0.542	9,933.8662	5.3842	0.506692	2.7281	978.1547	52,585.7868
23	0.566	9,928.4820	5.6195	0.491934	2.7644	975.4266	51,607.6321
24	0.592	9,922.8625	5.8743	0.477606	2.8056	972.6622	50,632.2055

APPENDIX I.1

Annuity 2000 Mortality Table–Male Commutation Columns at 3% *(Continued)*

Age Nearest Birthday x	$1,000\,q_x$	l_x	d_x	v^{x+1}	C_x	M_x	R_x
25	0.616	9,916.9882	6.1089	0.463695	2.8326	969.8565	49,659.5433
26	0.639	9,910.8793	6.3331	0.450189	2.8511	967.0239	48,689.6868
27	0.659	9,904.5462	6.5271	0.437077	2.8528	964.1728	47,722.6629
28	0.675	9,898.0191	6.6812	0.424346	2.8351	961.3200	46,758.4901
29	0.687	9,891.3380	6.7953	0.411987	2.7996	958.4848	45,797.1701
30	0.694	9,884.5426	6.8599	0.399987	2.7439	955.6853	44,838.6853
31	0.699	9,877.6828	6.9045	0.388337	2.6813	952.9414	43,883.0000
32	0.700	9,870.7783	6.9095	0.377026	2.6051	950.2601	42,930.0586
33	0.701	9,863.8687	6.9146	0.366045	2.5310	947.6550	41,979.7985
34	0.702	9,856.9541	6.9196	0.355383	2.4591	945.1240	41,032.1435
35	0.704	9,850.0346	6.9344	0.345032	2.3926	942.6649	40,087.0195
36	0.719	9,843.1001	7.0772	0.334983	2.3707	940.2723	39,144.3546
37	0.749	9,836.0230	7.3672	0.325226	2.3960	937.9016	38,204.0823
38	0.796	9,828.6558	7.8236	0.315754	2.4703	935.5056	37,266.1807
39	0.864	9,820.8322	8.4852	0.306557	2.6012	933.0352	36,330.6752
40	0.953	9,812.3470	9.3512	0.297628	2.7832	930.4340	35,397.6400
41	1.065	9,802.9958	10.4402	0.288959	3.0168	927.6509	34,467.2059
42	1.201	9,792.5556	11.7609	0.280543	3.2994	924.6341	33,539.5551
43	1.362	9,780.7947	13.3214	0.272372	3.6284	921.3346	32,614.9210
44	1.547	9,767.4733	15.1103	0.264439	3.9957	917.7063	31,693.5864

APPENDIX I.1

Annuity 2000 Mortality Table—Male Commutation Columns at 3% (*Continued*)

Age Nearest Birthday x	$1,000\, q_x$	l_x	d_x	v^{x+1}	C_x	M_x	R_x
45	1.752	9,752.3630	17.0861	0.256737	4.3866	913.7105	30,775.8801
46	1.974	9,735.2769	19.2174	0.249259	4.7901	909.3239	29,862.1696
47	2.211	9,716.0594	21.4822	0.241999	5.1987	904.5338	28,952.8457
48	2.460	9,694.5772	23.8487	0.234950	5.6032	899.3351	28,048.3120
49	2.721	9,670.7286	26.3141	0.228107	6.0024	893.7318	27,148.9769
50	2.994	9,644.4145	28.8754	0.221463	6.3948	887.7294	26,255.2450
51	3.279	9,615.5391	31.5294	0.215013	6.7792	881.3346	25,367.5156
52	3.576	9,584.0098	34.2724	0.208750	7.1544	874.5554	24,486.1810
53	3.884	9,549.7374	37.0912	0.202670	7.5173	867.4010	23,611.6256
54	4.203	9,512.6462	39.9817	0.196767	7.8671	859.8837	22,744.2246
55	4.534	9,472.6645	42.9491	0.191036	8.2048	852.0166	21,884.3409
56	4.876	9,429.7155	45.9793	0.185472	8.5279	843.8118	21,032.3243
57	5.228	9,383.7362	49.0582	0.180070	8.8339	835.2840	20,188.5124
58	5.593	9,644.4145	53.9412	0.174825	9.4303	826.4501	19,353.2285
59	5.988	9,590.4733	57.4278	0.169733	9.7474	817.0198	18,526.7784
60	6.428	9,533.0456	61.2784	0.164789	10.0980	807.2724	17,709.7586
61	6.933	9,471.7671	65.6678	0.159990	10.5062	797.1744	16,902.4862
62	7.520	9,406.0994	70.7339	0.155330	10.9871	786.6682	16,105.3119
63	8.207	9,335.3655	76.6153	0.150806	11.5540	775.6811	15,318.6437
64	9.008	9,258.7502	83.4028	0.146413	12.2113	764.1271	14,542.9626

APPENDIX I.1

Annuity 2000 Mortality Table—Male Commutation Columns at 3% *(Continued)*

Age Nearest Birthday x	$1,000\ q_x$	l_x	d_x	v^{x+1}	C_x	M_x	R_x
65	9.940	9,175.3473	91.2030	0.142149	12.9644	751.9158	13,778.8355
66	11.016	9,084.1444	100.0709	0.138009	13.8106	738.9514	13,026.9197
67	12.251	8,984.0735	110.0639	0.133989	14.7473	725.1408	12,287.9683
68	13.657	8,874.0096	121.1923	0.130086	15.7655	710.3934	11,562.8275
69	15.233	8,752.8172	133.3317	0.126297	16.8394	694.6280	10,852.4341
70	16.979	8,619.4856	146.3502	0.122619	17.9453	677.7885	10,157.8061
71	18.891	8,473.1353	160.0660	0.119047	19.0554	659.8432	9,480.0175
72	20.967	8,313.0693	174.3001	0.115580	20.1456	640.7878	8,820.1743
73	23.209	8,138.7692	188.8927	0.112214	21.1963	620.6422	8,179.3865
74	25.644	7,949.8765	203.8666	0.108945	22.2103	599.4459	7,558.7443
75	28.304	7,746.0099	219.2431	0.105772	23.1898	577.2356	6,959.2984
76	31.220	7,526.7668	234.9857	0.102691	24.1310	554.0458	6,382.0628
77	34.425	7,291.7811	251.0196	0.099700	25.0267	529.9148	5,828.0170
78	37.948	7,040.7616	267.1828	0.096796	25.8623	504.8881	5,298.1022
79	41.812	6,773.5788	283.2169	0.093977	26.6159	479.0258	4,793.2141
80	46.037	6,490.3619	298.7968	0.091240	27.2622	452.4099	4,314.1883
81	50.643	6,191.5651	313.5594	0.088582	27.7759	425.1477	3,861.7785
82	55.651	5,878.0057	327.1169	0.086002	28.1328	397.3718	3,436.6308
83	61.080	5,550.8888	339.0483	0.083497	28.3097	369.2390	3,039.2590
84	66.948	5,211.8405	348.9223	0.081065	28.2855	340.9293	2,670.0200

APPENDIX I.1

Annuity 2000 Mortality Table—Male Commutation Columns at 3% (Continued)

Age Nearest Birthday x	$1,000\,q_x$	l_x	d_x	v^{x+1}	C_x	M_x	R_x
85	73.275	4,862.9182	356.3303	0.078704	28.0447	312.6438	2,329.0907
86	80.076	4,506.5879	360.8695	0.076412	27.5748	284.5990	2,016.4469
87	97.370	4,145.7183	362.2114	0.074186	26.8712	257.0243	1,731.8479
88	95.169	3,783.5069	360.0726	0.072026	25.9344	230.1531	1,474.8236
89	103.455	3,423.4343	354.1714	0.069928	24.7664	204.2187	1,244.6705
90	112.208	3,069.2629	344.3959	0.067891	23.3814	179.4522	1,040.4518
91	121.402	2,724.8671	330.8043	0.065914	21.8045	156.0709	860.9995
92	131.017	2,394.0628	313.6629	0.063994	20.0725	134.2663	704.9287
93	141.030	2,080.3999	293.3988	0.062130	18.2288	114.1938	570.6624
94	151.422	1,787.0011	270.5913	0.060320	16.3222	95.9650	456.4685
95	162.179	1,516.4098	245.9298	0.058563	14.4025	79.6428	360.5035
96	173.279	1,270.4800	220.1475	0.056858	12.5171	65.2404	280.8607
97	184.706	1,050.3325	194.0027	0.055202	10.7093	52.7233	215.6203
98	196.946	856.3298	168.6507	0.053594	9.0386	42.0140	162.8971
99	210.484	687.6790	144.7454	0.052033	7.5315	32.9754	120.8831
100	225.806	542.9336	122.5977	0.050517	6.1933	25.4439	87.9077
101	243.398	420.3359	102.3089	0.049046	5.0178	19.2505	62.4638
102	263.745	318.0270	83.8780	0.047617	3.9941	14.2327	43.2133
103	287.334	234.1490	67.2790	0.046231	3.1103	10.2387	28.9806
104	314.649	166.8700	52.5055	0.044884	2.3567	7.1283	18.7419

APPENDIX I.1

Annuity 2000 Mortality Table—Male Commutation Columns at 3% (*Continued*)

Age Nearest Birthday x	$1,000\, q_x$	l_x	d_x	v^{x+1}	C_x	M_x	R_x
105	346.177	114.3645	39.5904	0.043577	1.7252	4.7717	11.6136
106	382.403	74.7742	28.5939	0.042307	1.2097	3.0464	6.8420
107	423.813	46.1803	19.5718	0.041075	0.8039	1.8367	3.7955
108	470.893	26.6085	12.5298	0.039879	0.4997	1.0328	1.9588
109	524.128	14.0787	7.3791	0.038717	0.2857	0.5331	0.9260
110	584.004	6.6997	3.9126	0.037590	0.1471	0.2474	0.3929
111	651.007	2.7870	1.8144	0.036495	0.0662	0.1003	0.1455
112	725.622	0.9727	0.7058	0.035432	0.0250	0.0341	0.0451
113	808.336	0.2669	0.2157	0.034400	0.0074	0.0091	0.0110
114	899.633	0.0512	0.0460	0.033398	0.0015	0.0017	0.0019
115	1000.000	0.0051	0.0051	0.032425	0.0002	0.0002	0.0002

APPENDIX I.2

Annuity 2000 Mortality Table—Male Commutation Columns at 4%

Age Nearest Birthday x	$1,000\,q_x$	l_x	d_x	v^{x+1}	C_x	M_x	R_x
5	0.291	10,000.0000	2.9100	0.790315	2.2998	514.6190	32,663.7021
6	0.270	9,997.0900	2.6992	0.759918	2.0512	512.3192	32,149.0831
7	0.257	9,994.3908	2.5686	0.730690	1.8768	510.2680	31,636.7638
8	0.294	9,991.8222	2.9376	0.702587	2.0639	508.3912	31,126.4958
9	0.325	9,988.8846	3.2464	0.675564	2.1931	506.3273	30,618.1046
10	0.350	9,985.6382	3.4950	0.649581	2.2703	504.1341	30,111.7773
11	0.371	9,982.1433	3.7034	0.624597	2.3131	501.8639	29,607.6432
12	0.388	9,978.4399	3.8716	0.600574	2.3252	499.5508	29,105.7793
13	0.402	9,974.5683	4.0098	0.577475	2.3155	497.2256	28,606.2285
14	0.414	9,970.5585	4.1278	0.555265	2.2920	494.9100	28,109.0030
15	0.425	9,966.4307	4.2357	0.533908	2.2615	492.6180	27,614.0929
16	0.437	9,962.1949	4.3535	0.513373	2.2350	490.3565	27,121.4750
17	0.449	9,957.8415	4.4711	0.493628	2.2070	488.1215	26,631.1185
18	0.463	9,953.3704	4.6084	0.474642	2.1873	485.9145	26,142.9969
19	0.480	9,948.7620	4.7754	0.456387	2.1794	483.7271	25,657.0824
20	0.499	9,943.9866	4.9620	0.438834	2.1775	481.5477	25,173.3553
21	0.519	9,939.0245	5.1584	0.421955	2.1766	479.3702	24,691.8076
22	0.542	9,933.8662	5.3842	0.405726	2.1845	477.1936	24,212.4374
23	0.566	9,928.4820	5.6195	0.390121	2.1923	475.0091	23,735.2438
24	0.592	9,922.8625	5.8743	0.375117	2.2036	472.8168	23,260.2347

APPENDIX I.2

Annuity 2000 Mortality Table—Male Commutation Columns at 4% (*Continued*)

Age Nearest Birthday x	$1,000\,q_x$	l_x	d_x	v^{x+1}	C_x	M_x	R_x
25	0.616	9,916.9882	6.1089	0.360689	2.2034	470.6132	22,787.4179
26	0.639	9,910.8793	6.3331	0.346817	2.1964	468.4098	22,316.8046
27	0.659	9,904.5462	6.5271	0.333477	2.1766	466.2134	21,848.3948
28	0.675	9,898.0191	6.6812	0.320651	2.1423	464.0368	21,382.1813
29	0.687	9,891.3380	6.7953	0.308319	2.0951	461.8945	20,918.1445
30	0.694	9,884.5426	6.8599	0.296460	2.0337	459.7993	20,456.2501
31	0.699	9,877.6828	6.9045	0.285058	1.9682	457.7657	19,996.4507
32	0.700	9,870.7783	6.9095	0.274094	1.8939	455.7975	19,538.6850
33	0.701	9,863.8687	6.9146	0.263552	1.8223	453.9036	19,082.8876
34	0.702	9,856.9541	6.9196	0.253415	1.7535	452.0813	18,628.9840
35	0.704	9,850.0346	6.9344	0.243669	1.6897	450.3277	18,176.9027
36	0.719	9,843.1001	7.0772	0.234297	1.6582	448.6380	17,726.5750
37	0.749	9,836.0230	7.3672	0.225285	1.6597	446.9799	17,277.9369
38	0.796	9,828.6558	7.8236	0.216621	1.6948	445.3202	16,830.9570
39	0.864	9,820.8322	8.4852	0.208289	1.7674	443.6254	16,385.6369
40	0.953	9,812.3470	9.3512	0.200278	1.8728	441.8580	15,942.0115
41	1.065	9,802.9958	10.4402	0.192575	2.0105	439.9852	15,500.1535
42	1.201	9,792.5556	11.7609	0.185168	2.1777	437.9747	15,060.1683
43	1.362	9,780.7947	13.3214	0.178046	2.3718	435.7969	14,622.1936
44	1.547	9,767.4733	15.1103	0.171198	2.5869	433.4251	14,186.3967

APPENDIX I.2

Annuity 2000 Mortality Table—Male Commutation Columns at 4% *(Continued)*

Age Nearest Birthday x	1,000 q_x	l_x	d_x	v^{x+1}	C_x	M_x	R_x
45	1.752	9,752.3630	17.0861	0.164614	2.8126	430.8382	13,752.9716
46	1.974	9,735.2769	19.2174	0.158283	3.0418	428.0256	13,322.1333
47	2.211	9,716.0594	21.4822	0.152195	3.2695	424.9838	12,894.1077
48	2.460	9,694.5772	23.8487	0.146341	3.4900	421.7144	12,469.1239
49	2.721	9,670.7286	26.3141	0.140713	3.7027	418.2243	12,047.4095
50	2.994	9,644.4145	28.8754	0.135301	3.9069	414.5216	11,629.1852
51	3.279	9,615.5391	31.5294	0.130097	4.1019	410.6148	11,214.6636
52	3.576	9,584.0098	34.2724	0.125093	4.2872	406.5129	10,804.0488
53	3.884	9,549.7374	37.0912	0.120282	4.4614	402.2256	10,397.5359
54	4.203	9,512.6462	39.9817	0.115656	4.6241	397.7643	9,995.3103
55	4.534	9,472.6645	42.9491	0.111207	4.7762	393.1402	9,597.5460
56	4.876	9,429.7155	45.9793	0.106930	4.9166	388.3639	9,204.4059
57	5.228	9,383.7362	49.0582	0.102817	5.0440	383.4473	8,816.0420
58	5.593	9,644.4145	53.9412	0.098863	5.3328	378.4033	8,432.5946
59	5.988	9,590.4733	57.4278	0.095060	5.4591	373.0705	8,054.1913
60	6.428	9,533.0456	61.2784	0.091404	5.6011	367.6114	7,681.1208
61	6.933	9,471.7671	65.6678	0.087889	5.7715	362.0103	7,313.5094
62	7.520	9,406.0994	70.7339	0.084508	5.9776	356.2389	6,951.4990
63	8.207	9,335.3655	76.6153	0.081258	6.2256	350.2613	6,595.2602
64	9.008	9,258.7502	83.4028	0.078133	6.5165	344.0357	6,244.9989

Annuity 2000 Mortality Table—Male Commutation Columns at 4% *(Continued)*

Age Nearest Birthday x	$1{,}000\,q_x$	l_x	d_x	v^{x+1}	C_x	M_x	R_x
65	9.940	9,175.3473	91.2030	0.075128	6.8519	337.5192	5,900.9632
66	11.016	9,084.1444	100.0709	0.072238	7.2289	330.6673	5,563.4441
67	12.251	8,984.0735	110.0639	0.069460	7.6450	323.4384	5,232.7768
68	13.657	8,874.0096	121.1923	0.066788	8.0942	315.7934	4,909.3384
69	15.233	8,752.8172	133.3317	0.064219	8.5625	307.6991	4,593.5450
70	16.979	8,619.4856	146.3502	0.061749	9.0370	299.1367	4,285.8459
71	18.891	8,473.1353	160.0660	0.059374	9.5038	290.0996	3,986.7092
72	20.967	8,313.0693	174.3001	0.057091	9.9509	280.5958	3,696.6096
73	23.209	8,138.7692	188.8927	0.054895	10.3693	270.6449	3,416.0138
74	25.644	7,949.8765	203.8666	0.052784	10.7608	260.2756	3,145.3690
75	28.304	7,746.0099	219.2431	0.050754	11.1274	249.5148	2,885.0934
76	31.220	7,526.7668	234.9857	0.048801	11.4676	238.3874	2,635.5786
77	34.425	7,291.7811	251.0196	0.046924	11.7790	226.9198	2,397.1912
78	37.948	7,040.7616	267.1828	0.045120	12.0552	215.1408	2,170.2714
79	41.812	6,773.5788	283.2169	0.043384	12.2872	203.0856	1,955.1306
80	46.037	6,490.3619	298.7968	0.041716	12.4645	190.7984	1,752.0450
81	50.643	6,191.5651	313.5594	0.040111	12.5773	178.3339	1,561.2466
82	55.651	5,878.0057	327.1169	0.038569	12.6164	165.7566	1,382.9127
83	61.080	5,550.8888	339.0483	0.037085	12.5736	153.1402	1,217.1561
84	66.948	5,211.8405	348.9223	0.035659	12.4421	140.5666	1,064.0159

APPENDIX I.2

Annuity 2000 Mortality Table—Male Commutation Columns at 4% (Continued)

Age Nearest Birthday x	1,000 q_x	l_x	d_x	v^{x+1}	C_x	M_x	R_x
85	73.275	4,862.9182	356.3303	0.034287	12.2176	128.1245	923.4493
86	80.076	4,506.5879	360.8695	0.032969	11.8973	115.9069	795.3248
87	97.370	4,145.7183	362.2114	0.031701	11.4823	104.0095	679.4180
88	95.169	3,783.5069	360.0726	0.030481	10.9755	92.5272	575.4084
89	103.455	3,423.4343	354.1714	0.029309	10.3804	81.5518	482.8812
90	112.208	3,069.2629	344.3959	0.028182	9.7056	71.1714	401.3294
91	121.402	2,724.8671	330.8043	0.027098	8.9640	61.4658	330.1580
92	131.017	2,394.0628	313.6629	0.026056	8.1726	52.5017	268.6922
93	141.030	2,080.3999	293.3988	0.025053	7.3506	44.3291	216.1905
94	151.422	1,787.0011	270.5913	0.024090	6.5185	36.9785	171.8614
95	162.179	1,516.4098	245.9298	0.023163	5.6965	30.4600	134.8830
96	173.279	1,270.4800	220.1475	0.022272	4.9032	24.7634	104.4230
97	184.706	1,050.3325	194.0027	0.021416	4.1547	19.8602	79.6596
98	196.946	856.3298	168.6507	0.020592	3.4729	15.7055	59.7993
99	210.484	687.6790	144.7454	0.019800	2.8660	12.2327	44.0938
100	225.806	542.9336	122.5977	0.019039	2.3341	9.3667	31.8611
101	243.398	420.3359	102.3089	0.018306	1.8729	7.0326	22.4944
102	263.745	318.0270	83.8780	0.017602	1.4764	5.1597	15.4618
103	287.334	234.1490	67.2790	0.016925	1.1387	3.6833	10.3021
104	314.649	166.8700	52.5055	0.016274	0.8545	2.5446	6.6188

APPENDIX I.2

Annuity 2000 Mortality Table—Male Commutation Columns at 4% *(Continued)*

Age Nearest Birthday x	1,000 q_x	l_x	d_x	v^{x+1}	C_x	M_x	R_x
105	346.177	114.3645	39.5904	0.015648	0.6195	1.6901	4.0742
106	382.403	74.7742	28.5939	0.015046	0.4302	1.0706	2.3841
107	423.813	46.1803	19.5718	0.014468	0.2832	0.6403	1.3135
108	470.893	26.6085	12.5298	0.013911	0.1743	0.3572	0.6732
109	524.128	14.0787	7.3791	0.013376	0.0987	0.1829	0.3160
110	584.004	6.6997	3.9126	0.012862	0.0503	0.0842	0.1331
111	651.007	2.7870	1.8144	0.012367	0.0224	0.0339	0.0489
112	725.622	0.9727	0.7058	0.011891	0.0084	0.0114	0.0151
113	808.336	0.2669	0.2157	0.011434	0.0025	0.0030	0.0036
114	899.633	0.0512	0.0460	0.010994	0.0005	0.0006	0.0006
115	1000.000	0.0051	0.0051	0.010571	0.0001	0.0001	0.0001

APPENDIX I.3

Annuity 2000 Mortality Table—Male Commutation Columns at 5%

Age Nearest Birthday x	$1,000\, q_x$	l_x	d_x	v^{x+1}	C_x	M_x	R_x
5	0.291	10,000.0000	2.9100	0.746215	2.1715	274.5000	15,836.5299
6	0.270	9,997.0900	2.6992	0.710681	1.9183	272.3285	15,562.0299
7	0.257	9,994.3908	2.5686	0.676839	1.7385	270.4103	15,289.7013
8	0.294	9,991.8222	2.9376	0.644609	1.8936	268.6718	15,019.2911
9	0.325	9,988.8846	3.2464	0.613913	1.9930	266.7782	14,750.6193
10	0.350	9,985.6382	3.4950	0.584679	2.0434	264.7852	14,483.8412
11	0.371	9,982.1433	3.7034	0.556837	2.0622	262.7417	14,219.0560
12	0.388	9,978.4399	3.8716	0.530321	2.0532	260.6795	13,956.3143
13	0.402	9,974.5683	4.0098	0.505068	2.0252	258.6263	13,695.6348
14	0.414	9,970.5585	4.1278	0.481017	1.9855	256.6011	13,437.0084
15	0.425	9,966.4307	4.2357	0.458112	1.9404	254.6156	13,180.4073
16	0.437	9,962.1949	4.3535	0.436297	1.8994	252.6751	12,925.7918
17	0.449	9,957.8415	4.4711	0.415521	1.8578	250.7757	12,673.1166
18	0.463	9,953.3704	4.6084	0.395734	1.8237	248.9179	12,422.3409
19	0.480	9,948.7620	4.7754	0.376889	1.7998	247.0942	12,173.4230
20	0.499	9,943.9866	4.9620	0.358942	1.7811	245.2944	11,926.3288
21	0.519	9,939.0245	5.1584	0.341850	1.7634	243.5133	11,681.0344
22	0.542	9,933.8662	5.3842	0.325571	1.7529	241.7499	11,437.5211
23	0.566	9,928.4820	5.6195	0.310068	1.7424	239.9970	11,195.7712
24	0.592	9,922.8625	5.8743	0.295303	1.7347	238.2546	10,955.7742

APPENDIX I.3

Annuity 2000 Mortality Table—Male Commutation Columns at 5% (Continued)

Age Nearest Birthday x	$1,000\, q_x$	l_x	d_x	v^{x+1}	C_x	M_x	R_x
25	0.616	9,916.9882	6.1089	0.281241	1.7181	236.5199	10,717.5196
26	0.639	9,910.8793	6.3331	0.267848	1.6963	234.8018	10,480.9998
27	0.659	9,904.5462	6.5271	0.255094	1.6650	233.1055	10,246.1980
28	0.675	9,898.0191	6.6812	0.242946	1.6232	231.4405	10,013.0925
29	0.687	9,891.3380	6.7953	0.231377	1.5723	229.8173	9,781.6520
30	0.694	9,884.5426	6.8599	0.220359	1.5116	228.2450	9,551.8347
31	0.699	9,877.6828	6.9045	0.209866	1.4490	226.7334	9,323.5897
32	0.700	9,870.7783	6.9095	0.199873	1.3810	225.2844	9,096.8563
33	0.701	9,863.8687	6.9146	0.190355	1.3162	223.9033	8,871.5719
34	0.702	9,856.9541	6.9196	0.181290	1.2545	222.5871	8,647.6686
35	0.704	9,850.0346	6.9344	0.172657	1.1973	221.3327	8,425.0815
36	0.719	9,843.1001	7.0772	0.164436	1.1637	220.1354	8,203.7488
37	0.749	9,836.0230	7.3672	0.156605	1.1537	218.9716	7,983.6135
38	0.796	9,828.6558	7.8236	0.149148	1.1669	217.8179	7,764.6418
39	0.864	9,820.8322	8.4852	0.142046	1.2053	216.6510	7,546.8239
40	0.953	9,812.3470	9.3512	0.135282	1.2650	215.4457	7,330.1729
41	1.065	9,802.9958	10.4402	0.128840	1.3451	214.1807	7,114.7272
42	1.201	9,792.5556	11.7609	0.122704	1.4431	212.8356	6,900.5465
43	1.362	9,780.7947	13.3214	0.116861	1.5568	211.3925	6,687.7109
44	1.547	9,767.4733	15.1103	0.111297	1.6817	209.8357	6,476.3184

APPENDIX I.3

Annuity 2000 Mortality Table—Male Commutation Columns at 5% (Continued)

Age Nearest Birthday x	$1,000\,q_x$	l_x	d_x	v^{x+1}	C_x	M_x	R_x
45	1.752	9,752.3630	17.0861	0.105997	1.8111	208.1540	6,266.4827
46	1.974	9,735.2769	19.2174	0.100949	1.9400	206.3429	6,058.3287
47	2.211	9,716.0594	21.4822	0.096142	2.0653	204.4029	5,851.9858
48	2.460	9,694.5772	23.8487	0.091564	2.1837	202.3376	5,647.5829
49	2.721	9,670.7286	26.3141	0.087204	2.2947	200.1539	5,445.2453
50	2.994	9,644.4145	28.8754	0.083051	2.3981	197.8592	5,245.0914
51	3.279	9,615.5391	31.5294	0.079096	2.4939	195.4611	5,047.2321
52	3.576	9,584.0098	34.2724	0.075330	2.5817	192.9672	4,851.7710
53	3.884	9,549.7374	37.0912	0.071743	2.6610	190.3855	4,658.8038
54	4.203	9,512.6462	39.9817	0.068326	2.7318	187.7245	4,468.4183
55	4.534	9,472.6645	42.9491	0.065073	2.7948	184.9927	4,280.6938
56	4.876	9,429.7155	45.9793	0.061974	2.8495	182.1979	4,095.7012
57	5.228	9,383.7362	49.0582	0.059023	2.8956	179.3483	3,913.5033
58	5.593	9,644.4145	53.9412	0.056212	3.0322	176.4528	3,734.1550
59	5.988	9,590.4733	57.4278	0.053536	3.0744	173.4206	3,557.7022
60	6.428	9,533.0456	61.2784	0.050986	3.1244	170.3462	3,384.2816
61	6.933	9,471.7671	65.6678	0.048558	3.1887	167.2218	3,213.9354
62	7.520	9,406.0994	70.7339	0.046246	3.2712	164.0331	3,046.7135
63	8.207	9,335.3655	76.6153	0.044044	3.3744	160.7620	2,882.6804
64	9.008	9,258.7502	83.4028	0.041946	3.4985	157.3875	2,721.9184

APPENDIX I.3

Annuity 2000 Mortality Table—Male Commutation Columns at 5% *(Continued)*

Age Nearest Birthday x	$1,000\,q_x$	l_x	d_x	v^{x+1}	C_x	M_x	R_x
65	9.940	9,175.3473	91.2030	0.039949	3.6435	153.8891	2,564.5309
66	11.016	9,084.1444	100.0709	0.038047	3.8074	150.2456	2,410.6418
67	12.251	8,984.0735	110.0639	0.036235	3.9882	146.4382	2,260.3962
68	13.657	8,874.0096	121.1923	0.034509	4.1823	142.4501	2,113.9579
69	15.233	8,752.8172	133.3317	0.032866	4.3821	138.2678	1,971.5078
70	16.979	8,619.4856	146.3502	0.031301	4.5809	133.8857	1,833.2400
71	18.891	8,473.1353	160.0660	0.029811	4.7717	129.3048	1,699.3543
72	20.967	8,313.0693	174.3001	0.028391	4.9486	124.5331	1,570.0496
73	23.209	8,138.7692	188.8927	0.027039	5.1075	119.5846	1,445.5165
74	25.644	7,949.8765	203.8666	0.025752	5.2499	114.4771	1,325.9319
75	28.304	7,746.0099	219.2431	0.024525	5.3770	109.2272	1,211.4548
76	31.220	7,526.7668	234.9857	0.023357	5.4886	103.8502	1,102.2276
77	34.425	7,291.7811	251.0196	0.022245	5.5840	98.3616	998.3774
78	37.948	7,040.7616	267.1828	0.021186	5.6605	92.7776	900.0159
79	41.812	6,773.5788	283.2169	0.020177	5.7145	87.1171	807.2383
80	46.037	6,490.3619	298.7968	0.019216	5.7417	81.4027	720.1211
81	50.643	6,191.5651	313.5594	0.018301	5.7385	75.6609	638.7185
82	55.651	5,878.0057	327.1169	0.017430	5.7015	69.9224	563.0576
83	61.080	5,550.8888	339.0483	0.016600	5.6281	64.2209	493.1351
84	66.948	5,211.8405	348.9223	0.015809	5.5162	58.5928	428.9142

APPENDIX I.3

Annuity 2000 Mortality Table—Male Commutation Columns at 5% (*Continued*)

Age Nearest Birthday x	$1,000\,q_x$	l_x	d_x	v^{x+1}	C_x	M_x	R_x
85	73.275	4,862.9182	356.3303	0.015056	5.3650	53.0767	370.3214
86	80.076	4,506.5879	360.8695	0.014339	5.1747	47.7116	317.2447
87	97.370	4,145.7183	362.2114	0.013657	4.9466	42.5370	269.5331
88	95.169	3,783.5069	360.0726	0.013006	4.6832	37.5904	226.9962
89	103.455	3,423.4343	354.1714	0.012387	4.3871	32.9072	189.4058
90	112.208	3,069.2629	344.3959	0.011797	4.0629	28.5201	156.4986
91	121.402	2,724.8671	330.8043	0.011235	3.7167	24.4572	127.9785
92	131.017	2,394.0628	313.6629	0.010700	3.3563	20.7406	103.5212
93	141.030	2,080.3999	293.3988	0.010191	2.9900	17.3843	82.7807
94	151.422	1,787.0011	270.5913	0.009705	2.6262	14.3943	65.3964
95	162.179	1,516.4098	245.9298	0.009243	2.2732	11.7681	51.0021
96	173.279	1,270.4800	220.1475	0.008803	1.9380	9.4949	39.2339
97	184.706	1,050.3325	194.0027	0.008384	1.6265	7.5569	29.7390
98	196.946	856.3298	168.6507	0.007985	1.3466	5.9304	22.1821
99	210.484	687.6790	144.7454	0.007604	1.1007	4.5838	16.2517
100	225.806	542.9336	122.5977	0.007242	0.8879	3.4831	11.6679
101	243.398	420.3359	102.3089	0.006897	0.7057	2.5952	8.1849
102	263.745	318.0270	83.8780	0.006569	0.5510	1.8895	5.5897
103	287.334	234.1490	67.2790	0.006256	0.4209	1.3385	3.7002
104	314.649	166.8700	52.5055	0.005958	0.3128	0.9176	2.3617

Annuity 2000 Mortality Table—Male Commutation Columns at 5% *(Continued)*

Age Nearest Birthday x	$1{,}000\,q_x$	l_x	d_x	v^{x+1}	C_x	M_x	R_x
105	346.177	114.3645	39.5904	0.005675	0.2247	0.6047	1.4441
106	382.403	74.7742	28.5939	0.005404	0.1545	0.3801	0.8394
107	423.813	46.1803	19.5718	0.005147	0.1007	0.2255	0.4593
108	470.893	26.6085	12.5298	0.004902	0.0614	0.1248	0.2338
109	524.128	14.0787	7.3791	0.004668	0.0344	0.0634	0.1090
110	584.004	6.6997	3.9126	0.004446	0.0174	0.0289	0.0456
111	651.007	2.7870	1.8144	0.004234	0.0077	0.0115	0.0166
112	725.622	0.9727	0.7058	0.004033	0.0028	0.0039	0.0051
113	808.336	0.2669	0.2157	0.003841	0.0008	0.0010	0.0012
114	899.633	0.0512	0.0460	0.003658	0.0002	0.0002	0.0002
115	1000.000	0.0051	0.0051	0.003484	0.0000	0.0000	0.0000

APPENDIX I.4

Annuity 2000 Mortality Table—Male Commutation Columns at 6%

Age Nearest Birthday x	$1,000\,q_x$	l_x	d_x	v^{x+1}	C_x	M_x	R_x
5	0.291	10,000.0000	2.9100	0.704961	2.0514	156.3226	7,966.6656
6	0.270	9,997.0900	2.6992	0.665057	1.7951	154.2712	7,810.3429
7	0.257	9,994.3908	2.5686	0.627412	1.6115	152.4761	7,656.0718
8	0.294	9,991.8222	2.9376	0.591898	1.7388	150.8645	7,503.5957
9	0.325	9,988.8846	3.2464	0.558395	1.8128	149.1258	7,352.7312
10	0.350	9,985.6382	3.4950	0.526788	1.8411	147.3130	7,203.6054
11	0.371	9,982.1433	3.7034	0.496969	1.8405	145.4719	7,056.2924
12	0.388	9,978.4399	3.8716	0.468839	1.8152	143.6314	6,910.8205
13	0.402	9,974.5683	4.0098	0.442301	1.7735	141.8162	6,767.1891
14	0.414	9,970.5585	4.1278	0.417265	1.7224	140.0427	6,625.3729
15	0.425	9,966.4307	4.2357	0.393646	1.6674	138.3203	6,485.3302
16	0.437	9,962.1949	4.3535	0.371364	1.6167	136.6529	6,347.0098
17	0.449	9,957.8415	4.4711	0.350344	1.5664	135.0362	6,210.3569
18	0.463	9,953.3704	4.6084	0.330513	1.5231	133.4698	6,075.3207
19	0.480	9,948.7620	4.7754	0.311805	1.4890	131.9467	5,941.8509
20	0.499	9,943.9866	4.9620	0.294155	1.4596	130.4577	5,809.9042
21	0.519	9,939.0245	5.1584	0.277505	1.4315	128.9981	5,679.4465
22	0.542	9,933.8662	5.3842	0.261797	1.4096	127.5666	5,550.4485
23	0.566	9,928.4820	5.6195	0.246979	1.3879	126.1570	5,422.8819
24	0.592	9,922.8625	5.8743	0.232999	1.3687	124.7691	5,296.7249

APPENDIX I.4

Annuity 2000 Mortality Table—Male Commutation Columns at 6% *(Continued)*

Age Nearest Birthday x	$1,000\,q_x$	l_x	d_x	v^{x+1}	C_x	M_x	R_x
25	0.616	9,916.9882	6.1089	0.219810	1.3428	123.4004	5,171.9557
26	0.639	9,910.8793	6.3331	0.207368	1.3133	122.0576	5,048.5553
27	0.659	9,904.5462	6.5271	0.195630	1.2769	120.7444	4,926.4977
28	0.675	9,898.0191	6.6812	0.184557	1.2331	119.4675	4,805.7533
29	0.687	9,891.3380	6.7953	0.174110	1.1831	118.2344	4,686.2859
30	0.694	9,884.5426	6.8599	0.164255	1.1268	117.0513	4,568.0515
31	0.699	9,877.6828	6.9045	0.154957	1.0699	115.9245	4,451.0002
32	0.700	9,870.7783	6.9095	0.146186	1.0101	114.8546	4,335.0757
33	0.701	9,863.8687	6.9146	0.137912	0.9536	113.8445	4,220.2211
34	0.702	9,856.9541	6.9196	0.130105	0.9003	112.8909	4,106.3766
35	0.704	9,850.0346	6.9344	0.122741	0.8511	111.9906	3,993.4857
36	0.719	9,843.1001	7.0772	0.115793	0.8195	111.1395	3,881.4950
37	0.749	9,836.0230	7.3672	0.109239	0.8048	110.3200	3,770.3555
38	0.796	9,828.6558	7.8236	0.103056	0.8063	109.5152	3,660.0355
39	0.864	9,820.8322	8.4852	0.097222	0.8249	108.7090	3,550.5203
40	0.953	9,812.3470	9.3512	0.091719	0.8577	107.8840	3,441.8113
41	1.065	9,802.9958	10.4402	0.086527	0.9034	107.0263	3,333.9273
42	1.201	9,792.5556	11.7609	0.081630	0.9600	106.1230	3,226.9009
43	1.362	9,780.7947	13.3214	0.077009	1.0259	105.1629	3,120.7780
44	1.547	9,767.4733	15.1103	0.072650	1.0978	104.1371	3,015.6150

APPENDIX I.4

Annuity 2000 Mortality Table—Male Commutation Columns at 6% (*Continued*)

Age Nearest Birthday x	1,000 q_x	l_x	d_x	v^{x+1}	C_x	M_x	R_x
45	1.752	9,752.3630	17.0861	0.068538	1.1710	103.0393	2,911.4780
46	1.974	9,735.2769	19.2174	0.064658	1.2426	101.8683	2,808.4387
47	2.211	9,716.0594	21.4822	0.060998	1.3104	100.6257	2,706.5704
48	2.460	9,694.5772	23.8487	0.057546	1.3724	99.3153	2,605.9447
49	2.721	9,670.7286	26.3141	0.054288	1.4285	97.9429	2,506.6294
50	2.994	9,644.4145	28.8754	0.051215	1.4789	96.5144	2,408.6865
51	3.279	9,615.5391	31.5294	0.048316	1.5234	95.0355	2,312.1721
52	3.576	9,584.0098	34.2724	0.045582	1.5622	93.5121	2,217.1366
53	3.884	9,549.7374	37.0912	0.043001	1.5950	91.9499	2,123.6245
54	4.203	9,512.6462	39.9817	0.040567	1.6220	90.3550	2,031.6745
55	4.534	9,472.6645	42.9491	0.038271	1.6437	88.7330	1,941.3196
56	4.876	9,429.7155	45.9793	0.036105	1.6601	87.0893	1,852.5865
57	5.228	9,383.7362	49.0582	0.034061	1.6710	85.4292	1,765.4972
58	5.593	9,644.4145	53.9412	0.032133	1.7333	83.7582	1,680.0680
59	5.988	9,590.4733	57.4278	0.030314	1.7409	82.0249	1,596.3098
60	6.428	9,533.0456	61.2784	0.028598	1.7525	80.2841	1,514.2848
61	6.933	9,471.7671	65.6678	0.026980	1.7717	78.5316	1,434.0008
62	7.520	9,406.0994	70.7339	0.025453	1.8004	76.7599	1,355.4692
63	8.207	9,335.3655	76.6153	0.024012	1.8397	74.9595	1,278.7093
64	9.008	9,258.7502	83.4028	0.022653	1.8893	73.1199	1,203.7498

Annuity 2000 Mortality Table—Male Commutation Columns at 6% (Continued)

Age Nearest Birthday x	$1,000\,q_x$	l_x	d_x	v^{x+1}	C_x	M_x	R_x
65	9.940	9,175.3473	91.2030	0.021370	1.9490	71.2306	1,130.6299
66	11.016	9,084.1444	100.0709	0.020161	2.0175	69.2815	1,059.3993
67	12.251	8,984.0735	110.0639	0.019020	2.0934	67.2640	990.1178
68	13.657	8,874.0096	121.1923	0.017943	2.1746	65.1707	922.8538
69	15.233	8,752.8172	133.3317	0.016927	2.2570	62.9961	857.6831
70	16.979	8,619.4856	146.3502	0.015969	2.3371	60.7391	794.6870
71	18.891	8,473.1353	160.0660	0.015065	2.4114	58.4020	733.9479
72	20.967	8,313.0693	174.3001	0.014213	2.4772	55.9906	675.5458
73	23.209	8,138.7692	188.8927	0.013408	2.5327	53.5134	619.5552
74	25.644	7,949.8765	203.8666	0.012649	2.5787	50.9807	566.0419
75	28.304	7,746.0099	219.2431	0.011933	2.6163	48.4019	515.0612
76	31.220	7,526.7668	234.9857	0.011258	2.6454	45.7857	466.6592
77	34.425	7,291.7811	251.0196	0.010620	2.6659	43.1403	420.8736
78	37.948	7,040.7616	267.1828	0.010019	2.6770	40.4744	377.7333
79	41.812	6,773.5788	283.2169	0.009452	2.6770	37.7974	337.2589
80	46.037	6,490.3619	298.7968	0.008917	2.6644	35.1204	299.4615
81	50.643	6,191.5651	313.5594	0.008412	2.6378	32.4560	264.3412
82	55.651	5,878.0057	327.1169	0.007936	2.5961	29.8182	231.8852
83	61.080	5,550.8888	339.0483	0.007487	2.5385	27.2221	202.0670
84	66.948	5,211.8405	348.9223	0.007063	2.4645	24.6837	174.8449

APPENDIX I.4

Annuity 2000 Mortality Table—Male Commutation Columns at 6% (*Continued*)

Age Nearest Birthday x	$1,000\,q_x$	l_x	d_x	v^{x+1}	C_x	M_x	R_x
85	73.275	4,862.9182	356.3303	0.006663	2.3744	22.2191	150.1613
86	80.076	4,506.5879	360.8695	0.006286	2.2685	19.8448	127.9421
87	97.370	4,145.7183	362.2114	0.005930	2.1481	17.5763	108.0974
88	95.169	3,783.5069	360.0726	0.005595	2.0145	15.4282	90.5211
89	103.455	3,423.4343	354.1714	0.005278	1.8693	13.4137	75.0929
90	112.208	3,069.2629	344.3959	0.004979	1.7148	11.5444	61.6792
91	121.402	2,724.8671	330.8043	0.004697	1.5539	9.8295	50.1348
92	131.017	2,394.0628	313.6629	0.004432	1.3900	8.2756	40.3052
93	141.030	2,080.3999	293.3988	0.004181	1.2266	6.8856	32.0296
94	151.422	1,787.0011	270.5913	0.003944	1.0672	5.6590	25.1440
95	162.179	1,516.4098	245.9298	0.003721	0.9151	4.5918	19.4850
96	173.279	1,270.4800	220.1475	0.003510	0.7728	3.6767	14.8933
97	184.706	1,050.3325	194.0027	0.003312	0.6424	2.9039	11.2166
98	196.946	856.3298	168.6507	0.003124	0.5269	2.2615	8.3126
99	210.484	687.6790	144.7454	0.002947	0.4266	1.7346	6.0511
100	225.806	542.9336	122.5977	0.002780	0.3409	1.3080	4.3165
101	243.398	420.3359	102.3089	0.002623	0.2684	0.9672	3.0085
102	263.745	318.0270	83.8780	0.002475	0.2076	0.6988	2.0413
103	287.334	234.1490	67.2790	0.002334	0.1571	0.4912	1.3425
104	314.649	166.8700	52.5055	0.002202	0.1156	0.3342	0.8513

Annuity 2000 Mortality Table—Male Commutation Columns at 6% *(Continued)*

Age Nearest Birthday x	$1,000\, q_x$	l_x	d_x	v^{x+1}	C_x	M_x	R_x
105	346.177	114.3645	39.5904	0.002078	0.0823	0.2185	0.5171
106	382.403	74.7742	28.5939	0.001960	0.0560	0.1363	0.2985
107	423.813	46.1803	19.5718	0.001849	0.0362	0.0802	0.1622
108	470.893	26.6085	12.5298	0.001744	0.0219	0.0441	0.0820
109	524.128	14.0787	7.3791	0.001646	0.0121	0.0222	0.0380
110	584.004	6.6997	3.9126	0.001553	0.0061	0.0101	0.0158
111	651.007	2.7870	1.8144	0.001465	0.0027	0.0040	0.0057
112	725.622	0.9727	0.7058	0.001382	0.0010	0.0013	0.0017
113	808.336	0.2669	0.2157	0.001304	0.0003	0.0003	0.0004
114	899.633	0.0512	0.0460	0.001230	0.0001	0.0001	0.0001
115	1000.000	0.0051	0.0051	0.001160	0.0000	0.0000	0.0000

APPENDIX J.1

Annuity 2000 Mortality Table—Female Commutation Columns at 3%

Age Nearest Birthday x	$1,000\ q_x$	l_x	d_x	v^{x+1}	C_x	M_x	R_x
5	0.171	10,000.0000	1.7100	0.837484	1.4321	872.1951	64,645.9170
6	0.141	9,998.2900	1.4098	0.813092	1.1463	870.7630	63,773.7219
7	0.118	9,996.8802	1.1796	0.789409	0.9312	869.6168	62,902.9589
8	0.118	9,995.7006	1.1795	0.766417	0.9040	868.6855	62,033.3421
9	0.121	9,994.5211	1.2093	0.744094	0.8999	867.7816	61,164.6566
10	0.126	9,993.3118	1.2592	0.722421	0.9096	866.8817	60,296.8750
11	0.133	9,992.0526	1.3289	0.701380	0.9321	865.9721	59,429.9933
12	0.142	9,990.7237	1.4187	0.680951	0.9661	865.0400	58,564.0213
13	0.152	9,989.3050	1.5184	0.661118	1.0038	864.0739	57,698.9813
14	0.164	9,987.7866	1.6380	0.641862	1.0514	863.0701	56,834.9074
15	0.177	9,986.1486	1.7675	0.623167	1.1015	862.0187	55,971.8373
16	0.190	9,984.3811	1.8970	0.605016	1.1477	860.9172	55,109.8186
17	0.204	9,982.4840	2.0364	0.587395	1.1962	859.7695	54,248.9013
18	0.219	9,980.4476	2.1857	0.570286	1.2465	858.5733	53,389.1318
19	0.234	9,978.2619	2.3349	0.553676	1.2928	857.3268	52,530.5585
20	0.250	9,975.9270	2.4940	0.537549	1.3406	856.0341	51,673.2317
21	0.265	9,973.4330	2.6430	0.521893	1.3793	854.6934	50,817.1976
22	0.281	9,970.7900	2.8018	0.506692	1.4196	853.3141	49,962.5042
23	0.298	9,967.9883	2.9705	0.491934	1.4613	851.8944	49,109.1901
24	0.314	9,965.0178	3.1290	0.477606	1.4944	850.4332	48,257.2957

APPENDIX J.1

Annuity 2000 Mortality Table—Female Commutation Columns at 3% *(Continued)*

Age Nearest Birthday x	1,000 q_x	l_x	d_x	v^{x+1}	C_x	M_x	R_x
25	0.331	9,961.8888	3.2974	0.463695	1.5290	848.9387	47,406.8626
26	0.347	9,958.5914	3.4556	0.450189	1.5557	847.4097	46,557.9238
27	0.362	9,955.1358	3.6038	0.437077	1.5751	845.8541	45,710.5141
28	0.376	9,951.5320	3.7418	0.424346	1.5878	844.2789	44,864.6600
29	0.389	9,947.7902	3.8697	0.411987	1.5943	842.6911	44,020.3811
30	0.402	9,943.9205	3.9975	0.399987	1.5989	841.0969	43,177.6900
31	0.414	9,939.9231	4.1151	0.388337	1.5981	839.4979	42,336.5931
32	0.425	9,935.8080	4.2227	0.377026	1.5921	837.8999	41,497.0952
33	0.436	9,931.5852	4.3302	0.366045	1.5850	836.3078	40,659.1953
34	0.449	9,927.2551	4.4573	0.355383	1.5841	834.7228	39,822.8875
35	0.463	9,922.7977	4.5943	0.345032	1.5852	833.1387	38,988.1647
36	0.481	9,918.2035	4.7707	0.334983	1.5981	831.5535	38,155.0260
37	0.504	9,913.4328	4.9964	0.325226	1.6250	829.9554	37,323.4725
38	0.532	9,908.4364	5.2713	0.315754	1.6644	828.3305	36,493.5170
39	0.567	9,903.1652	5.6151	0.306557	1.7213	826.6661	35,665.1866
40	0.609	9,897.5501	6.0276	0.297628	1.7940	824.9447	34,838.5205
41	0.658	9,891.5225	6.5086	0.288959	1.8807	823.1507	34,013.5758
42	0.715	9,885.0138	7.0678	0.280543	1.9828	821.2700	33,190.4250
43	0.781	9,877.9460	7.7147	0.272372	2.1013	819.2872	32,369.1550
44	0.855	9,870.2314	8.4390	0.264439	2.2316	817.1859	31,549.8678

APPENDIX J.1

Annuity 2000 Mortality Table—Female Commutation Columns at 3% *(Continued)*

Age Nearest Birthday x	$1{,}000\,q_x$	l_x	d_x	v^{x+1}	C_x	M_x	R_x
45	0.939	9,861.7923	9.2602	0.256737	2.3774	814.9543	30,732.6819
46	1.035	9,852.5321	10.1974	0.249259	2.5418	812.5769	29,917.7276
47	1.141	9,842.3347	11.2301	0.241999	2.7177	810.0351	29,105.1507
48	1.261	9,831.1046	12.3970	0.234950	2.9127	807.3174	28,295.1156
49	1.393	9,818.7076	13.6775	0.228107	3.1199	804.4047	27,487.7982
50	1.538	9,805.0301	15.0801	0.221463	3.3397	801.2848	26,683.3934
51	1.695	9,789.9500	16.5940	0.215013	3.5679	797.9451	25,882.1086
52	1.864	9,773.3560	18.2175	0.208750	3.8029	794.3772	25,084.1635
53	2.047	9,755.1385	19.9688	0.202670	4.0471	790.5743	24,289.7863
54	2.244	9,735.1697	21.8457	0.196767	4.2985	786.5272	23,499.2120
55	2.457	9,713.3240	23.8656	0.191036	4.5592	782.2287	22,712.6847
56	2.689	9,689.4584	26.0550	0.185472	4.8325	777.6695	21,930.4560
57	2.942	9,663.4034	28.4297	0.180070	5.1193	772.8370	21,152.7865
58	3.218	9,805.0301	31.5526	0.174825	5.5162	767.7177	20,379.9495
59	3.523	9,773.4776	34.4320	0.169733	5.8442	762.2015	19,612.2318
60	3.863	9,739.0456	37.6219	0.164789	6.1997	756.3573	18,850.0303
61	4.242	9,701.4237	41.1534	0.159990	6.5841	750.1576	18,093.6730
62	4.668	9,660.2702	45.0941	0.155330	7.0045	743.5735	17,343.5154
63	5.144	9,615.1761	49.4605	0.150806	7.4589	736.5690	16,599.9420
64	5.671	9,565.7156	54.2472	0.146413	7.9425	729.1101	15,863.3730

Annuity 2000 Mortality Table—Female Commutation Columns at 3% (Continued)

Age Nearest Birthday x	$1{,}000\,q_x$	l_x	d_x	v^{x+1}	C_x	M_x	R_x
65	6.250	9,511.4684	59.4467	0.142149	8.4503	721.1676	15,134.2629
66	6.878	9,452.0218	65.0110	0.138009	8.9721	712.7173	14,413.0954
67	7.555	9,387.0108	70.9189	0.133989	9.5023	703.7452	13,700.3781
68	8.287	9,316.0919	77.2025	0.130086	10.0430	694.2429	12,996.6328
69	9.102	9,238.8894	84.0924	0.126297	10.6206	684.1999	12,302.3900
70	10.034	9,154.7971	91.8592	0.122619	11.2637	673.5793	11,618.1901
71	11.117	9,062.9378	100.7527	0.119047	11.9943	662.3156	10,944.6108
72	12.386	8,962.1852	111.0056	0.115580	12.8300	650.3212	10,282.2952
73	13.871	8,851.1795	122.7747	0.112214	13.7770	637.4912	9,631.9740
74	15.592	8,728.4048	136.0933	0.108945	14.8267	623.7142	8,994.4828
75	17.564	8,592.3115	150.9154	0.105772	15.9626	608.8875	8,370.7685
76	19.805	8,441.3962	167.1819	0.102691	17.1681	592.9249	7,761.8810
77	22.328	8,274.2143	184.7467	0.099700	18.4193	575.7568	7,168.9561
78	25.158	8,089.4677	203.5148	0.096796	19.6995	557.3375	6,593.1994
79	28.341	7,885.9528	223.4958	0.093977	21.0035	537.6380	6,035.8619
80	31.933	7,662.4570	244.6852	0.091240	22.3251	516.6345	5,498.2239
81	35.985	7,417.7718	266.9285	0.088582	23.6452	494.3094	4,981.5895
82	40.552	7,150.8433	289.9810	0.086002	24.9390	470.6642	4,487.2800
83	45.690	6,860.8623	313.4728	0.083497	26.1742	445.7252	4,016.6158
84	51.456	6,547.3895	336.9025	0.081065	27.3112	419.5510	3,570.8906

APPENDIX J.1

Annuity 2000 Mortality Table—Female Commutation Columns at 3% (*Continued*)

Age Nearest Birthday x	$1,000\, q_x$	l_x	d_x	v^{x+1}	C_x	M_x	R_x
85	57.913	6,210.4870	359.6679	0.078704	28.3074	392.2399	3,151.3396
86	65.119	5,850.8191	380.9995	0.076412	29.1129	363.9324	2,759.0997
87	73.136	5,469.8196	400.0407	0.074186	29.6776	334.8195	2,395.1673
88	81.991	5,069.7789	415.6762	0.072026	29.9393	305.1419	2,060.3478
89	91.577	4,654.1026	426.2088	0.069928	29.8038	275.2026	1,755.2058
90	101.758	4,227.8939	430.2220	0.067891	29.2082	245.3988	1,480.0032
91	112.395	3,797.6718	426.8393	0.065914	28.1345	216.1905	1,234.6045
92	123.349	3,370.8325	415.7888	0.063994	26.6079	188.0560	1,018.4139
93	134.486	2,955.0437	397.4120	0.062130	24.6912	161.4481	830.3579
94	145.689	2,557.6317	372.6188	0.060320	22.4765	136.7569	668.9099
95	156.846	2,185.0129	342.7105	0.058563	20.0703	114.2804	532.1530
96	167.841	1,842.3024	309.2139	0.056858	17.5812	94.2101	417.8725
97	178.563	1,533.0885	273.7529	0.055202	15.1116	76.6289	323.6624
98	189.604	1,259.3356	238.7751	0.053594	12.7969	61.5173	247.0335
99	210.557	1,020.5605	205.7011	0.052033	10.7032	48.7205	185.5162
100	215.013	814.8594	175.2054	0.050517	8.8509	38.0172	136.7957
101	230.565	639.6541	147.4818	0.049046	7.2334	29.1663	98.7785
102	248.805	492.1722	122.4549	0.047617	5.8310	21.9329	69.6122
103	270.326	369.7173	99.9442	0.046231	4.6205	16.1020	47.6792
104	295.719	269.7731	79.7770	0.044884	3.5807	11.4815	31.5773

Annuity 2000 Mortality Table—Female Commutation Columns at 3% (Continued)

Age Nearest Birthday x	1,000 q_x	l_x	d_x	v^{x+1}	C_x	M_x	R_x
105	325.576	189.9961	61.8582	0.043577	2.6956	7.9008	20.0958
106	360.491	128.1379	46.1926	0.042307	1.9543	5.2052	12.1950
107	401.054	81.9453	32.8645	0.041075	1.3499	3.2509	6.9898
108	447.860	49.0808	21.9813	0.039879	0.8766	1.9010	3.7389
109	501.498	27.0995	13.5903	0.038717	0.5262	1.0244	1.8379
110	562.563	13.5092	7.5997	0.037590	0.2857	0.4982	0.8135
111	631.645	5.9094	3.7326	0.036495	0.1362	0.2126	0.3152
112	709.338	2.1768	1.5441	0.035432	0.0547	0.0763	0.1027
113	796.233	0.6327	0.5038	0.034400	0.0173	0.0216	0.0264
114	892.923	0.1289	0.1151	0.033398	0.0038	0.0043	0.0047
115	1000.000	0.0138	0.0138	0.032425	0.0004	0.0004	0.0004

APPENDIX J.2

Annuity 2000 Mortality Table—Female Commutation Columns at 4%

Age Nearest Birthday x	$1,000\, q_x$	l_x	d_x	v^{x+1}	C_x	M_x	R_x
5	0.171	10,000.0000	1.7100	0.790315	1.3514	413.3355	29,050.8285
6	0.141	9,998.2900	1.4098	0.759918	1.0713	411.9840	28,637.4930
7	0.118	9,996.8802	1.1796	0.730690	0.8619	410.9127	28,225.5089
8	0.118	9,995.7006	1.1795	0.702587	0.8287	410.0508	27,814.5962
9	0.121	9,994.5211	1.2093	0.675564	0.8170	409.2221	27,404.5454
10	0.126	9,993.3118	1.2592	0.649581	0.8179	408.4051	26,995.3233
11	0.133	9,992.0526	1.3289	0.624597	0.8301	407.5872	26,586.9181
12	0.142	9,990.7237	1.4187	0.600574	0.8520	406.7571	26,179.3310
13	0.152	9,989.3050	1.5184	0.577475	0.8768	405.9051	25,772.5738
14	0.164	9,987.7866	1.6380	0.555265	0.9095	405.0283	25,366.6687
15	0.177	9,986.1486	1.7675	0.533908	0.9437	404.1188	24,961.6404
16	0.190	9,984.3811	1.8970	0.513373	0.9739	403.1751	24,557.5216
17	0.204	9,982.4840	2.0364	0.493628	1.0052	402.2012	24,154.3466
18	0.219	9,980.4476	2.1857	0.474642	1.0374	401.1959	23,752.1454
19	0.234	9,978.2619	2.3349	0.456387	1.0656	400.1585	23,350.9494
20	0.250	9,975.9270	2.4940	0.438834	1.0944	399.0929	22,950.7909
21	0.265	9,973.4330	2.6430	0.421955	1.1152	397.9984	22,551.6981
22	0.281	9,970.7900	2.8018	0.405726	1.1368	396.8832	22,153.6996
23	0.298	9,967.9883	2.9705	0.390121	1.1588	395.7465	21,756.8164
24	0.314	9,965.0178	3.1290	0.375117	1.1737	394.5876	21,361.0699

APPENDIX J.2
Annuity 2000 Mortality Table—Female Commutation Columns at 4% (Continued)

Age Nearest Birthday x	1,000 q_x	l_x	d_x	v^{x+1}	C_x	M_x	R_x
25	0.331	9,961.8888	3.2974	0.360689	1.1893	393.4139	20,966.4823
26	0.347	9,958.5914	3.4556	0.346817	1.1985	392.2245	20,573.0684
27	0.362	9,955.1358	3.6038	0.333477	1.2018	391.0261	20,180.8439
28	0.376	9,951.5320	3.7418	0.320651	1.1998	389.8243	19,789.8178
29	0.389	9,947.7902	3.8697	0.308319	1.1931	388.6245	19,399.9935
30	0.402	9,943.9205	3.9975	0.296460	1.1851	387.4314	19,011.3690
31	0.414	9,939.9231	4.1151	0.285058	1.1730	386.2463	18,623.9376
32	0.425	9,935.8080	4.2227	0.274094	1.1574	385.0733	18,237.6913
33	0.436	9,931.5852	4.3302	0.263552	1.1412	383.9158	17,852.6180
34	0.449	9,927.2551	4.4573	0.253415	1.1296	382.7746	17,468.7022
35	0.463	9,922.7977	4.5943	0.243669	1.1195	381.6451	17,085.9275
36	0.481	9,918.2035	4.7707	0.234297	1.1177	380.5256	16,704.2825
37	0.504	9,913.4328	4.9964	0.225285	1.1256	379.4078	16,323.7569
38	0.532	9,908.4364	5.2713	0.216621	1.1419	378.2822	15,944.3491
39	0.567	9,903.1652	5.6151	0.208289	1.1696	377.1404	15,566.0668
40	0.609	9,897.5501	6.0276	0.200278	1.2072	375.9708	15,188.9265
41	0.658	9,891.5225	6.5086	0.192575	1.2534	374.7636	14,812.9557
42	0.715	9,885.0138	7.0678	0.185168	1.3087	373.5102	14,438.1921
43	0.781	9,877.9460	7.7147	0.178046	1.3736	372.2015	14,064.6819
44	0.855	9,870.2314	8.4390	0.171198	1.4448	370.8279	13,692.4804

APPENDIX J.2

Annuity 2000 Mortality Table—Female Commutation Columns at 4% *(Continued)*

Age Nearest Birthday x	$1,000\,q_x$	l_x	d_x	v^{x+1}	C_x	M_x	R_x
45	0.939	9,861.7923	9.2602	0.164614	1.5244	369.3831	13,321.6525
46	1.035	9,852.5321	10.1974	0.158283	1.6141	367.8588	12,952.2694
47	1.141	9,842.3347	11.2301	0.152195	1.7092	366.2447	12,584.4106
48	1.261	9,831.1046	12.3970	0.146341	1.8142	364.5356	12,218.1659
49	1.393	9,818.7076	13.6775	0.140713	1.9246	362.7214	11,853.6303
50	1.538	9,805.0301	15.0801	0.135301	2.0404	360.7968	11,490.9090
51	1.695	9,789.9500	16.5940	0.130097	2.1588	358.7564	11,130.1122
52	1.864	9,773.3560	18.2175	0.125093	2.2789	356.5976	10,771.3558
53	2.047	9,755.1385	19.9688	0.120282	2.4019	354.3187	10,414.7582
54	2.244	9,735.1697	21.8457	0.115656	2.5266	351.9168	10,060.4395
55	2.457	9,713.3240	23.8656	0.111207	2.6540	349.3903	9,708.5226
56	2.689	9,689.4584	26.0550	0.106930	2.7861	346.7362	9,359.1324
57	2.942	9,663.4034	28.4297	0.102817	2.9231	343.9502	9,012.3961
58	3.218	9,805.0301	31.5526	0.098863	3.1194	341.0271	8,668.4460
59	3.523	9,773.4776	34.4320	0.095060	3.2731	337.9077	8,327.4189
60	3.863	9,739.0456	37.6219	0.091404	3.4388	334.6346	7,989.5111
61	4.242	9,701.4237	41.1534	0.087889	3.6169	331.1958	7,654.8765
62	4.668	9,660.2702	45.0941	0.084508	3.8108	327.5789	7,323.6807
63	5.144	9,615.1761	49.4605	0.081258	4.0191	323.7680	6,996.1018
64	5.671	9,565.7156	54.2472	0.078133	4.2385	319.7490	6,672.3338

Annuity 2000 Mortality Table—Female Commutation Columns at 4% *(Continued)*

Age Nearest Birthday x	$1,000\ q_x$	l_x	d_x	v^{x+1}	C_x	M_x	R_x
65	6.250	9,511.4684	59.4467	0.075128	4.4661	315.5105	6,352.5848
66	6.878	9,452.0218	65.0110	0.072238	4.6963	311.0444	6,037.0743
67	7.555	9,387.0108	70.9189	0.069460	4.9260	306.3482	5,726.0299
68	8.287	9,316.0919	77.2025	0.066788	5.1562	301.4221	5,419.6817
69	9.102	9,238.8894	84.0924	0.064219	5.4004	296.2659	5,118.2596
70	10.034	9,154.7971	91.8592	0.061749	5.6723	290.8656	4,821.9936
71	11.117	9,062.9378	100.7527	0.059374	5.9821	285.1933	4,531.1281
72	12.386	8,962.1852	111.0056	0.057091	6.3374	279.2112	4,245.9347
73	13.871	8,851.1795	122.7747	0.054895	6.7397	272.8738	3,966.7236
74	15.592	8,728.4048	136.0933	0.052784	7.1835	266.1341	3,693.8498
75	17.564	8,592.3115	150.9154	0.050754	7.6595	258.9506	3,427.7157
76	19.805	8,441.3962	167.1819	0.048801	8.1587	251.2911	3,168.7651
77	22.328	8,274.2143	184.7467	0.046924	8.6691	243.1324	2,917.4741
78	25.158	8,089.4677	203.5148	0.045120	9.1825	234.4632	2,674.3417
79	28.341	7,885.9528	223.4958	0.043384	9.6962	225.2807	2,439.8785
80	31.933	7,662.4570	244.6852	0.041716	10.2072	215.5845	2,214.5978
81	35.985	7,417.7718	266.9285	0.040111	10.7068	205.3773	1,999.0133
82	40.552	7,150.8433	289.9810	0.038569	11.1841	194.6704	1,793.6361
83	45.690	6,860.8623	313.4728	0.037085	11.6252	183.4863	1,598.9657
84	51.456	6,547.3895	336.9025	0.035659	12.0135	171.8611	1,415.4794

APPENDIX J.2

Annuity 2000 Mortality Table—Female Commutation Columns at 4% (Continued)

Age Nearest Birthday x	1,000 q_x	l_x	d_x	v^{x+1}	C_x	M_x	R_x
85	57.913	6,210.4870	359.6679	0.034287	12.3320	159.8476	1,243.6182
86	65.119	5,850.8191	380.9995	0.032969	12.5610	147.5156	1,083.7707
87	73.136	5,469.8196	400.0407	0.031701	12.6815	134.9546	936.2551
88	81.991	5,069.7789	415.6762	0.030481	12.6703	122.2731	801.3005
89	91.577	4,654.1026	426.2088	0.029309	12.4917	109.6028	679.0274
90	101.758	4,227.8939	430.2220	0.028182	12.1244	97.1110	569.4247
91	112.395	3,797.6718	426.8393	0.027098	11.5664	84.9867	472.3136
92	123.349	3,370.8325	415.7888	0.026056	10.8336	73.4203	387.3270
93	134.486	2,955.0437	397.4120	0.025053	9.9565	62.5867	313.9067
94	145.689	2,557.6317	372.6188	0.024090	8.9763	52.6302	251.3199
95	156.846	2,185.0129	342.7105	0.023163	7.9383	43.6539	198.6897
96	167.841	1,842.3024	309.2139	0.022272	6.8869	35.7156	155.0358
97	178.563	1,533.0885	273.7529	0.021416	5.8626	28.8287	119.3202
98	189.604	1,259.3356	238.7751	0.020592	4.9169	22.9661	90.4915
99	210.557	1,020.5605	205.7011	0.019800	4.0729	18.0492	67.5254
100	215.013	814.8594	175.2054	0.019039	3.3356	13.9763	49.4762
101	230.565	639.6541	147.4818	0.018306	2.6998	10.6407	35.4998
102	248.805	492.1722	122.4549	0.017602	2.1555	7.9408	24.8592
103	270.326	369.7173	99.9442	0.016925	1.6916	5.7854	16.9183
104	295.719	269.7731	79.7770	0.016274	1.2983	4.0938	11.1329

APPENDIX J.2

Annuity 2000 Mortality Table—Female Commutation Columns at 4% *(Continued)*

Age Nearest Birthday x	$1,000\,q_x$	l_x	d_x	v^{x+1}	C_x	M_x	R_x
105	325.576	189.9961	61.8582	0.015648	0.9680	2.7955	7.0391
106	360.491	128.1379	46.1926	0.015046	0.6950	1.8275	4.2437
107	401.054	81.9453	32.8645	0.014468	0.4755	1.1325	2.4161
108	447.860	49.0808	21.9813	0.013911	0.3058	0.6570	1.2836
109	501.498	27.0995	13.5903	0.013376	0.1818	0.3512	0.6266
110	562.563	13.5092	7.5997	0.012862	0.0977	0.1694	0.2754
111	631.645	5.9094	3.7326	0.012367	0.0462	0.0717	0.1060
112	709.338	2.1768	1.5441	0.011891	0.0184	0.0255	0.0343
113	796.233	0.6327	0.5038	0.011434	0.0058	0.0072	0.0087
114	892.923	0.1289	0.1151	0.010994	0.0013	0.0014	0.0016
115	1000.000	0.0138	0.0138	0.010571	0.0001	0.0001	0.0001

APPENDIX J.3

Annuity 2000 Mortality Table—Female Commutation Columns at 5%

Age Nearest Birthday x	1,000 q_x	l_x	d_x	v^{x+1}	C_x	M_x	R_x
5	0.171	10,000.0000	1.7100	0.746215	1.2760	205.7189	13,440.9161
6	0.141	9,998.2900	1.4098	0.710681	1.0019	204.4428	13,235.1972
7	0.118	9,996.8802	1.1796	0.676839	0.7984	203.4409	13,030.7544
8	0.118	9,995.7006	1.1795	0.644609	0.7603	202.6425	12,827.3134
9	0.121	9,994.5211	1.2093	0.613913	0.7424	201.8822	12,624.6709
10	0.126	9,993.3118	1.2592	0.584679	0.7362	201.1398	12,422.7887
11	0.133	9,992.0526	1.3289	0.556837	0.7400	200.4036	12,221.6489
12	0.142	9,990.7237	1.4187	0.530321	0.7524	199.6636	12,021.2453
13	0.152	9,989.3050	1.5184	0.505068	0.7669	198.9112	11,821.5818
14	0.164	9,987.7866	1.6380	0.481017	0.7879	198.1443	11,622.6705
15	0.177	9,986.1486	1.7675	0.458112	0.8097	197.3564	11,424.5262
16	0.190	9,984.3811	1.8970	0.436297	0.8277	196.5467	11,227.1698
17	0.204	9,982.4840	2.0364	0.415521	0.8462	195.7190	11,030.6231
18	0.219	9,980.4476	2.1857	0.395734	0.8650	194.8729	10,834.9040
19	0.234	9,978.2619	2.3349	0.376889	0.8800	194.0079	10,640.0312
20	0.250	9,975.9270	2.4940	0.358942	0.8952	193.1279	10,446.0233
21	0.265	9,973.4330	2.6430	0.341850	0.9035	192.2327	10,252.8954
22	0.281	9,970.7900	2.8018	0.325571	0.9122	191.3292	10,060.6627
23	0.298	9,967.9883	2.9705	0.310068	0.9210	190.4170	9,869.3335
24	0.314	9,965.0178	3.1290	0.295303	0.9240	189.4960	9,678.9165

APPENDIX J.3

Annuity 2000 Mortality Table—Female Commutation Columns at 5% *(Continued)*

Age Nearest Birthday x	$1,000\,q_x$	l_x	d_x	v^{x+1}	C_x	M_x	R_x
25	0.331	9,961.8888	3.2974	0.281241	0.9274	188.5720	9,489.4206
26	0.347	9,958.5914	3.4556	0.267848	0.9256	187.6446	9,300.8486
27	0.362	9,955.1358	3.6038	0.255094	0.9193	186.7190	9,113.2040
28	0.376	9,951.5320	3.7418	0.242946	0.9091	185.7997	8,926.4850
29	0.389	9,947.7902	3.8697	0.231377	0.8954	184.8907	8,740.6853
30	0.402	9,943.9205	3.9975	0.220359	0.8809	183.9953	8,555.7946
31	0.414	9,939.9231	4.1151	0.209866	0.8636	183.1144	8,371.7993
32	0.425	9,935.8080	4.2227	0.199873	0.8440	182.2508	8,188.6849
33	0.436	9,931.5852	4.3302	0.190355	0.8243	181.4068	8,006.4341
34	0.449	9,927.2551	4.4573	0.181290	0.8081	180.5825	7,825.0273
35	0.463	9,922.7977	4.5943	0.172657	0.7932	179.7745	7,644.4447
36	0.481	9,918.2035	4.7707	0.164436	0.7845	178.9812	7,464.6703
37	0.504	9,913.4328	4.9964	0.156605	0.7825	178.1968	7,285.6890
38	0.532	9,908.4364	5.2713	0.149148	0.7862	177.4143	7,107.4923
39	0.567	9,903.1652	5.6151	0.142046	0.7976	176.6281	6,930.0780
40	0.609	9,897.5501	6.0276	0.135282	0.8154	175.8305	6,753.4499
41	0.658	9,891.5225	6.5086	0.128840	0.8386	175.0151	6,577.6194
42	0.715	9,885.0138	7.0678	0.122704	0.8672	174.1765	6,402.6043
43	0.781	9,877.9460	7.7147	0.116861	0.9015	173.3093	6,228.4278
44	0.855	9,870.2314	8.4390	0.111297	0.9392	172.4077	6,055.1185

APPENDIX J.3

Annuity 2000 Mortality Table—Female Commutation Columns at 5% *(Continued)*

Age Nearest Birthday x	$1,000\,q_x$	l_x	d_x	v^{x+1}	C_x	M_x	R_x
45	0.939	9,861.7923	9.2602	0.105997	0.9816	171.4685	5,882.7108
46	1.035	9,852.5321	10.1974	0.100949	1.0294	170.4869	5,711.2424
47	1.141	9,842.3347	11.2301	0.096142	1.0797	169.4575	5,540.7554
48	1.261	9,831.1046	12.3970	0.091564	1.1351	168.3778	5,371.2979
49	1.393	9,818.7076	13.6775	0.087204	1.1927	167.2427	5,202.9201
50	1.538	9,805.0301	15.0801	0.083051	1.2524	166.0500	5,035.6774
51	1.695	9,789.9500	16.5940	0.079096	1.3125	164.7976	4,869.6274
52	1.864	9,773.3560	18.2175	0.075330	1.3723	163.4850	4,704.8299
53	2.047	9,755.1385	19.9688	0.071743	1.4326	162.1127	4,541.3448
54	2.244	9,735.1697	21.8457	0.068326	1.4926	160.6801	4,379.2321
55	2.457	9,713.3240	23.8656	0.065073	1.5530	159.1875	4,218.5521
56	2.689	9,689.4584	26.0550	0.061974	1.6147	157.6344	4,059.3646
57	2.942	9,663.4034	28.4297	0.059023	1.6780	156.0197	3,901.7302
58	3.218	9,805.0301	31.5526	0.056212	1.7736	154.3417	3,745.7104
59	3.523	9,773.4776	34.4320	0.053536	1.8433	152.5681	3,591.3687
60	3.863	9,739.0456	37.6219	0.050986	1.9182	150.7247	3,438.8007
61	4.242	9,701.4237	41.1534	0.048558	1.9983	148.8065	3,288.0759
62	4.668	9,660.2702	45.0941	0.046246	2.0854	146.8082	3,139.2694
63	5.144	9,615.1761	49.4605	0.044044	2.1784	144.7228	2,992.4612
64	5.671	9,565.7156	54.2472	0.041946	2.2755	142.5443	2,847.7384

APPENDIX J.3

Annuity 2000 Mortality Table—Female Commutation Columns at 5% *(Continued)*

Age Nearest Birthday x	1,000 q_x	l_x	d_x	v^{x+1}	C_x	M_x	R_x
65	6.250	9,511.4684	59.4467	0.039949	2.3748	140.2689	2,705.1941
66	6.878	9,452.0218	65.0110	0.038047	2.4735	137.8940	2,564.9252
67	7.555	9,387.0108	70.9189	0.036235	2.5697	135.4206	2,427.0312
68	8.287	9,316.0919	77.2025	0.034509	2.6642	132.8508	2,291.6106
69	9.102	9,238.8894	84.0924	0.032866	2.7638	130.1866	2,158.7598
70	10.034	9,154.7971	91.8592	0.031301	2.8753	127.4228	2,028.5732
71	11.117	9,062.9378	100.7527	0.029811	3.0035	124.5475	1,901.1503
72	12.386	8,962.1852	111.0056	0.028391	3.1516	121.5440	1,776.6028
73	13.871	8,851.1795	122.7747	0.027039	3.3197	118.3925	1,655.0588
74	15.592	8,728.4048	136.0933	0.025752	3.5046	115.0728	1,536.6663
75	17.564	8,592.3115	150.9154	0.024525	3.7012	111.5681	1,421.5936
76	19.805	8,441.3962	167.1819	0.023357	3.9049	107.8669	1,310.0254
77	22.328	8,274.2143	184.7467	0.022245	4.1097	103.9620	1,202.1585
78	25.158	8,089.4677	203.5148	0.021186	4.3116	99.8523	1,098.1965
79	28.341	7,885.9528	223.4958	0.020177	4.5095	95.5406	998.3443
80	31.933	7,662.4570	244.6852	0.019216	4.7019	91.0312	902.8036
81	35.985	7,417.7718	266.9285	0.018301	4.8851	86.3293	811.7724
82	40.552	7,150.8433	289.9810	0.017430	5.0543	81.4442	725.4432
83	45.690	6,860.8623	313.4728	0.016600	5.2035	76.3899	643.9990
84	51.456	6,547.3895	336.9025	0.015809	5.3262	71.1864	567.6091

Annuity 2000 Mortality Table—Female Commutation Columns at 5% (*Continued*)

Age Nearest Birthday x	1,000 q_x	l_x	d_x	v^{x+1}	C_x	M_x	R_x
85	57.913	6,210.4870	359.6679	0.015056	5.4153	65.8602	496.4227
86	65.119	5,850.8191	380.9995	0.014339	5.4633	60.4449	430.5625
87	73.136	5,469.8196	400.0407	0.013657	5.4632	54.9816	370.1176
88	81.991	5,069.7789	415.6762	0.013006	5.4064	49.5184	315.1360
89	91.577	4,654.1026	426.2088	0.012387	5.2794	44.1120	265.6176
90	101.758	4,227.8939	430.2220	0.011797	5.0754	38.8326	221.5055
91	112.395	3,797.6718	426.8393	0.011235	4.7957	33.7573	182.6729
92	123.349	3,370.8325	415.7888	0.010700	4.4491	28.9616	148.9156
93	134.486	2,955.0437	397.4120	0.010191	4.0499	24.5126	119.9540
94	145.689	2,557.6317	372.6188	0.009705	3.6164	20.4626	95.4414
95	156.846	2,185.0129	342.7105	0.009243	3.1678	16.8462	74.9788
96	167.841	1,842.3024	309.2139	0.008803	2.7221	13.6784	58.1326
97	178.563	1,533.0885	273.7529	0.008384	2.2951	10.9564	44.4542
98	189.604	1,259.3356	238.7751	0.007985	1.9066	8.6612	33.4979
99	210.557	1,020.5605	205.7011	0.007604	1.5643	6.7547	24.8366
100	215.013	814.8594	175.2054	0.007242	1.2689	5.1904	18.0820
101	230.565	639.6541	147.4818	0.006897	1.0173	3.9215	12.8916
102	248.805	492.1722	122.4549	0.006569	0.8044	2.9043	8.9700
103	270.326	369.7173	99.9442	0.006256	0.6253	2.0999	6.0658
104	295.719	269.7731	79.7770	0.005958	0.4753	1.4746	3.9659

APPENDIX J.3

Annuity 2000 Mortality Table—Female Commutation Columns at 5% (*Continued*)

Age Nearest Birthday x	1,000 q_x	l_x	d_x	v^{x+1}	C_x	M_x	R_x
105	325.576	189.9961	61.8582	0.005675	0.3510	0.9992	2.4914
106	360.491	128.1379	46.1926	0.005404	0.2496	0.6482	1.4921
107	401.054	81.9453	32.8645	0.005147	0.1692	0.3986	0.8439
108	447.860	49.0808	21.9813	0.004902	0.1078	0.2294	0.4453
109	501.498	27.0995	13.5903	0.004668	0.0634	0.1217	0.2159
110	562.563	13.5092	7.5997	0.004446	0.0338	0.0582	0.0942
111	631.645	5.9094	3.7326	0.004234	0.0158	0.0244	0.0360
112	709.338	2.1768	1.5441	0.004033	0.0062	0.0086	0.0116
113	796.233	0.6327	0.5038	0.003841	0.0019	0.0024	0.0029
114	892.923	0.1289	0.1151	0.003658	0.0004	0.0005	0.0005
115	1000.000	0.0138	0.0138	0.003484	0.0000	0.0000	0.0000

APPENDIX J.4

Annuity 2000 Mortality Table—Female Commutation Columns at 6%

Age Nearest Birthday x	$1,000\,q_x$	l_x	d_x	v^{x+1}	C_x	M_x	R_x
5	0.171	10,000.0000	1.7100	0.704961	1.2055	108.6405	6,428.1719
6	0.141	9,998.2900	1.4098	0.665057	0.9376	107.4351	6,319.5313
7	0.118	9,996.8802	1.1796	0.627412	0.7401	106.4975	6,212.0963
8	0.118	9,995.7006	1.1795	0.591898	0.6981	105.7574	6,105.5988
9	0.121	9,994.5211	1.2093	0.558395	0.6753	105.0592	5,999.8414
10	0.126	9,993.3118	1.2592	0.526788	0.6633	104.3840	5,894.7821
11	0.133	9,992.0526	1.3289	0.496969	0.6604	103.7206	5,790.3982
12	0.142	9,990.7237	1.4187	0.468839	0.6651	103.0602	5,686.6775
13	0.152	9,989.3050	1.5184	0.442301	0.6716	102.3951	5,583.6173
14	0.164	9,987.7866	1.6380	0.417265	0.6835	101.7235	5,481.2223
15	0.177	9,986.1486	1.7675	0.393646	0.6958	101.0400	5,379.4988
16	0.190	9,984.3811	1.8970	0.371364	0.7045	100.3442	5,278.4588
17	0.204	9,982.4840	2.0364	0.350344	0.7134	99.6397	5,178.1146
18	0.219	9,980.4476	2.1857	0.330513	0.7224	98.9263	5,078.4748
19	0.234	9,978.2619	2.3349	0.311805	0.7280	98.2039	4,979.5485
20	0.250	9,975.9270	2.4940	0.294155	0.7336	97.4758	4,881.3447
21	0.265	9,973.4330	2.6430	0.277505	0.7334	96.7422	4,783.8688
22	0.281	9,970.7900	2.8018	0.261797	0.7335	96.0088	4,687.1266
23	0.298	9,967.9883	2.9705	0.246979	0.7336	95.2753	4,591.1178
24	0.314	9,965.0178	3.1290	0.232999	0.7291	94.5416	4,495.8425

APPENDIX J.4

Annuity 2000 Mortality Table—Female Commutation Columns at 6% *(Continued)*

Age Nearest Birthday x	$1,000\,q_x$	l_x	d_x	v^{x+1}	C_x	M_x	R_x
25	0.331	9,961.8888	3.2974	0.219810	0.7248	93.8126	4,401.3009
26	0.347	9,958.5914	3.4556	0.207368	0.7166	93.0878	4,307.4883
27	0.362	9,955.1358	3.6038	0.195630	0.7050	92.3712	4,214.4005
28	0.376	9,951.5320	3.7418	0.184557	0.6906	91.6662	4,122.0293
29	0.389	9,947.7902	3.8697	0.174110	0.6738	90.9756	4,030.3631
30	0.402	9,943.9205	3.9975	0.164255	0.6566	90.3019	3,939.3875
31	0.414	9,939.9231	4.1151	0.154957	0.6377	89.6453	3,849.0856
32	0.425	9,935.8080	4.2227	0.146186	0.6173	89.0076	3,759.4404
33	0.436	9,931.5852	4.3302	0.137912	0.5972	88.3903	3,670.4328
34	0.449	9,927.2551	4.4573	0.130105	0.5799	87.7931	3,582.0425
35	0.463	9,922.7977	4.5943	0.122741	0.5639	87.2132	3,494.2493
36	0.481	9,918.2035	4.7707	0.115793	0.5524	86.6493	3,407.0361
37	0.504	9,913.4328	4.9964	0.109239	0.5458	86.0969	3,320.3869
38	0.532	9,908.4364	5.2713	0.103056	0.5432	85.5511	3,234.2900
39	0.567	9,903.1652	5.6151	0.097222	0.5459	85.0079	3,148.7389
40	0.609	9,897.5501	6.0276	0.091719	0.5528	84.4619	3,063.7310
41	0.658	9,891.5225	6.5086	0.086527	0.5632	83.9091	2,979.2691
42	0.715	9,885.0138	7.0678	0.081630	0.5769	83.3459	2,895.3600
43	0.781	9,877.9460	7.7147	0.077009	0.5941	82.7690	2,812.0141
44	0.855	9,870.2314	8.4390	0.072650	0.6131	82.1749	2,729.2451

APPENDIX J.4

Annuity 2000 Mortality Table—Female Commutation Columns at 6% (Continued)

Age Nearest Birthday x	$1,000\,q_x$	l_x	d_x	v^{x+1}	C_x	M_x	R_x
45	0.939	9,861.7923	9.2602	0.068538	0.6347	81.5618	2,647.0702
46	1.035	9,852.5321	10.1974	0.064658	0.6593	80.9271	2,565.5084
47	1.141	9,842.3347	11.2301	0.060998	0.6850	80.2678	2,484.5813
48	1.261	9,831.1046	12.3970	0.057546	0.7134	79.5827	2,404.3136
49	1.393	9,818.7076	13.6775	0.054288	0.7425	78.8693	2,324.7308
50	1.538	9,805.0301	15.0801	0.051215	0.7723	78.1268	2,245.8615
51	1.695	9,789.9500	16.5940	0.048316	0.8018	77.3545	2,167.7347
52	1.864	9,773.3560	18.2175	0.045582	0.8304	76.5527	2,090.3802
53	2.047	9,755.1385	19.9688	0.043001	0.8587	75.7223	2,013.8275
54	2.244	9,735.1697	21.8457	0.040567	0.8862	74.8637	1,938.1051
55	2.457	9,713.3240	23.8656	0.038271	0.9134	73.9774	1,863.2415
56	2.689	9,689.4584	26.0550	0.036105	0.9407	73.0641	1,789.2640
57	2.942	9,663.4034	28.4297	0.034061	0.9684	72.1234	1,716.2000
58	3.218	9,805.0301	31.5526	0.032133	1.0139	71.1550	1,644.0766
59	3.523	9,773.4776	34.4320	0.030314	1.0438	70.1411	1,572.9216
60	3.863	9,739.0456	37.6219	0.028598	1.0759	69.0973	1,502.7805
61	4.242	9,701.4237	41.1534	0.026980	1.1103	68.0214	1,433.6832
62	4.668	9,660.2702	45.0941	0.025453	1.1478	66.9111	1,365.6618
63	5.144	9,615.1761	49.4605	0.024012	1.1876	65.7633	1,298.7507
64	5.671	9,565.7156	54.2472	0.022653	1.2288	64.5757	1,232.9873

APPENDIX J.4

Annuity 2000 Mortality Table—Female Commutation Columns at 6% *(Continued)*

Age Nearest Birthday x	1,000 q_x	l_x	d_x	v^{x+1}	C_x	M_x	R_x
65	6.250	9,511.4684	59.4467	0.021370	1.2704	63.3469	1,168.4116
66	6.878	9,452.0218	65.0110	0.020161	1.3107	62.0765	1,105.0647
67	7.555	9,387.0108	70.9189	0.019020	1.3488	60.7658	1,042.9883
68	8.287	9,316.0919	77.2025	0.017943	1.3852	59.4169	982.2225
69	9.102	9,238.8894	84.0924	0.016927	1.4235	58.0317	922.8055
70	10.034	9,154.7971	91.8592	0.015969	1.4669	56.6082	864.7738
71	11.117	9,062.9378	100.7527	0.015065	1.5179	55.1413	808.1656
72	12.386	8,962.1852	111.0056	0.014213	1.5777	53.6235	753.0243
73	13.871	8,851.1795	122.7747	0.013408	1.6462	52.0458	699.4008
74	15.592	8,728.4048	136.0933	0.012649	1.7215	50.3996	647.3550
75	17.564	8,592.3115	150.9154	0.011933	1.8009	48.6781	596.9554
76	19.805	8,441.3962	167.1819	0.011258	1.8821	46.8773	548.2773
77	22.328	8,274.2143	184.7467	0.010620	1.9621	44.9952	501.4000
78	25.158	8,089.4677	203.5148	0.010019	2.0391	43.0331	456.4048
79	28.341	7,885.9528	223.4958	0.009452	2.1125	40.9940	413.3718
80	31.933	7,662.4570	244.6852	0.008917	2.1819	38.8815	372.3777
81	35.985	7,417.7718	266.9285	0.008412	2.2455	36.6996	333.4962
82	40.552	7,150.8433	289.9810	0.007936	2.3014	34.4541	296.7966
83	45.690	6,860.8623	313.4728	0.007487	2.3470	32.1528	262.3425
84	51.456	6,547.3895	336.9025	0.007063	2.3796	29.8058	230.1898

APPENDIX J.4

Annuity 2000 Mortality Table—Female Commutation Columns at 6% (Continued)

Age Nearest Birthday x	$1,000\, q_x$	l_x	d_x	v^{x+1}	C_x	M_x	R_x
85	57.913	6,210.4870	359.6679	0.006663	2.3966	27.4262	200.3840
86	65.119	5,850.8191	380.9995	0.006286	2.3950	25.0296	172.9578
87	73.136	5,469.8196	400.0407	0.005930	2.3724	22.6345	147.9282
88	81.991	5,069.7789	415.6762	0.005595	2.3256	20.2621	125.2937
89	91.577	4,654.1026	426.2088	0.005278	2.2495	17.9365	105.0316
90	101.758	4,227.8939	430.2220	0.004979	2.1422	15.6870	87.0951
91	112.395	3,797.6718	426.8393	0.004697	2.0050	13.5448	71.4081
92	123.349	3,370.8325	415.7888	0.004432	1.8426	11.5397	57.8633
93	134.486	2,955.0437	397.4120	0.004181	1.6615	9.6972	46.3236
94	145.689	2,557.6317	372.6188	0.003944	1.4696	8.0357	36.6264
95	156.846	2,185.0129	342.7105	0.003721	1.2752	6.5661	28.5907
96	167.841	1,842.3024	309.2139	0.003510	1.0854	5.2909	22.0246
97	178.563	1,533.0885	273.7529	0.003312	0.9065	4.2055	16.7337
98	189.604	1,259.3356	238.7751	0.003124	0.7459	3.2990	12.5282
99	210.557	1,020.5605	205.7011	0.002947	0.6062	2.5530	9.2292
100	215.013	814.8594	175.2054	0.002780	0.4871	1.9468	6.6762
101	230.565	639.6541	147.4818	0.002623	0.3868	1.4596	4.7294
102	248.805	492.1722	122.4549	0.002475	0.3030	1.0728	3.2698
103	270.326	369.7173	99.9442	0.002334	0.2333	0.7698	2.1970
104	295.719	269.7731	79.7770	0.002202	0.1757	0.5365	1.4272

APPENDIX J.4

Annuity 2000 Mortality Table—Female Commutation Columns at 6% *(Continued)*

Age Nearest Birthday x	$1,000\, q_x$	l_x	d_x	v^{x+1}	C_x	M_x	R_x
105	325.576	189.9961	61.8582	0.002078	0.1285	0.3608	0.8908
106	360.491	128.1379	46.1926	0.001960	0.0905	0.2322	0.5300
107	401.054	81.9453	32.8645	0.001849	0.0608	0.1417	0.2978
108	447.860	49.0808	21.9813	0.001744	0.0383	0.0809	0.1561
109	501.498	27.0995	13.5903	0.001646	0.0224	0.0426	0.0751
110	562.563	13.5092	7.5997	0.001553	0.0118	0.0202	0.0326
111	631.645	5.9094	3.7326	0.001465	0.0055	0.0084	0.0124
112	709.338	2.1768	1.5441	0.001382	0.0021	0.0029	0.0039
113	796.233	0.6327	0.5038	0.001304	0.0007	0.0008	0.0010
114	892.923	0.1289	0.1151	0.001230	0.0001	0.0002	0.0002
115	1000.000	0.0138	0.0138	0.001160	0.0000	0.0000	0.0000

APPENDIX K

Annuity 2000 Mortality Table—Male Mortality Functions: L_x, T_x, Y_x

Age Nearest Birthday x	$1,000\ q_x$	l_x	d_x	L_x	T_x	Y_x
5	0.291	10,000.0000	2.9100	9,999	766,227	30,433,567
6	0.270	9,997.0900	2.6992	9,996	756,228	29,672,340
7	0.257	9,994.3908	2.5686	9,993	746,232	28,921,109
8	0.294	9,991.8222	2.9376	9,990	736,239	28,179,873
9	0.325	9,988.8846	3.2464	9,987	726,249	27,448,629
10	0.350	9,985.6382	3.4950	9,984	716,262	26,727,374
11	0.371	9,982.1433	3.7034	9,980	706,278	26,016,104
12	0.388	9,978.4399	3.8716	9,977	696,298	25,314,816
13	0.402	9,974.5683	4.0098	9,973	686,321	24,623,507
14	0.414	9,970.5585	4.1278	9,968	676,348	23,942,172
15	0.425	9,966.4307	4.2357	9,964	666,380	23,270,808
16	0.437	9,962.1949	4.3535	9,960	656,416	22,609,410
17	0.449	9,957.8415	4.4711	9,956	646,456	21,957,975
18	0.463	9,953.3704	4.6084	9,951	636,500	21,316,497
19	0.480	9,948.7620	4.7754	9,946	626,549	20,684,972
20	0.499	9,943.9866	4.9620	9,942	616,603	20,063,396
21	0.519	9,939.0245	5.1584	9,936	606,661	19,451,764
22	0.542	9,933.8662	5.3842	9,931	596,725	18,850,072
23	0.566	9,928.4820	5.6195	9,926	586,793	18,258,312
24	0.592	9,922.8625	5.8743	9,920	576,868	17,676,482

APPENDIX K

Annuity 2000 Mortality Table—Male Mortality Functions: L_x, T_x, Y_x (Continued)

Age Nearest Birthday x	1,000 q_x	l_x	d_x	L_x	T_x	Y_x
25	0.616	9,916.9882	6.1089	9,914	566,948	17,104,574
26	0.639	9,910.8793	6.3331	9,908	557,034	16,542,583
27	0.659	9,904.5462	6.5271	9,901	547,126	15,990,503
28	0.675	9,898.0191	6.6812	9,895	537,225	15,448,327
29	0.687	9,891.3380	6.7953	9,888	527,330	14,916,050
30	0.694	9,884.5426	6.8599	9,881	517,442	14,393,663
31	0.699	9,877.6828	6.9045	9,874	507,561	13,881,162
32	0.700	9,870.7783	6.9095	9,867	497,687	13,378,537
33	0.701	9,863.8687	6.9146	9,860	487,820	12,885,784
34	0.702	9,856.9541	6.9196	9,853	477,959	12,402,895
35	0.704	9,850.0346	6.9344	9,847	468,106	11,929,862
36	0.719	9,843.1001	7.0772	9,840	458,259	11,466,680
37	0.749	9,836.0230	7.3672	9,832	448,420	11,013,340
38	0.796	9,828.6558	7.8236	9,825	438,587	10,569,837
39	0.864	9,820.8322	8.4852	9,817	428,763	10,136,162
40	0.953	9,812.3470	9.3512	9,808	418,946	9,712,307
41	1.065	9,802.9958	10.4402	9,798	409,138	9,298,265
42	1.201	9,792.5556	11.7609	9,787	399,341	8,894,026
43	1.362	9,780.7947	13.3214	9,774	389,554	8,499,579
44	1.547	9,767.4733	15.1103	9,760	379,780	8,114,912

APPENDIX K

Annuity 2000 Mortality Table—Male Mortality Functions: L_x, T_x, Y_x (Continued)

Age Nearest Birthday x	1,000 q_x	l_x	d_x	L_x	T_x	Y_x
45	1.752	9,752.3630	17.0861	9,744	370,020	7,740,012
46	1.974	9,735.2769	19.2174	9,726	360,276	7,374,864
47	2.211	9,716.0594	21.4822	9,705	350,550	7,019,451
48	2.460	9,694.5772	23.8487	9,683	340,845	6,673,753
49	2.721	9,670.7286	26.3141	9,658	331,162	6,337,750
50	2.994	9,644.4145	28.8754	9,630	321,505	6,011,416
51	3.279	9,615.5391	31.5294	9,600	311,875	5,694,726
52	3.576	9,584.0098	34.2724	9,567	302,275	5,387,652
53	3.884	9,549.7374	37.0912	9,531	292,708	5,090,160
54	4.203	9,512.6462	39.9817	9,493	283,177	4,802,217
55	4.534	9,472.6645	42.9491	9,451	273,684	4,523,787
56	4.876	9,429.7155	45.9793	9,407	264,233	4,254,828
57	5.228	9,383.7362	49.0582	9,359	254,826	3,995,298
58	5.593	9,334.6780	52.2089	9,309	245,467	3,745,152
59	5.988	9,282.4692	55.5834	9,255	236,159	3,504,339
60	6.428	9,226.8857	59.3104	9,197	226,904	3,272,807
61	6.933	9,167.5753	63.5588	9,136	217,707	3,050,502
62	7.520	9,104.0165	68.4622	9,070	208,571	2,837,363
63	8.207	9,035.5543	74.1548	8,998	199,501	2,633,327
64	9.008	8,961.3995	80.7243	8,921	190,503	2,438,325

APPENDIX K

Annuity 2000 Mortality Table—Male Mortality Functions: L_x, T_x, Y_x (Continued)

Age Nearest Birthday x	$1,000\, q_x$	l_x	d_x	L_x	T_x	Y_x
65	9.940	8,880.6752	88.2739	8,837	181,582	2,252,283
66	11.016	8,792.4013	96.8571	8,744	172,745	2,075,120
67	12.251	8,695.5442	106.5291	8,642	164,001	1,906,747
68	13.657	8,589.0151	117.3002	8,530	155,359	1,747,067
69	15.233	8,471.7149	129.0496	8,407	146,828	1,595,973
70	16.979	8,342.6653	141.6501	8,272	138,421	1,453,348
71	18.891	8,201.0152	154.9254	8,124	130,149	1,319,063
72	20.967	8,046.0898	168.7024	7,962	122,026	1,192,975
73	23.209	7,877.3874	182.8263	7,786	114,064	1,074,930
74	25.644	7,694.5612	197.3193	7,596	106,278	964,759
75	28.304	7,497.2418	212.2019	7,391	98,682	862,279
76	31.220	7,285.0399	227.4389	7,171	91,291	767,292
77	34.425	7,057.6010	242.9579	6,936	84,120	679,587
78	37.948	6,814.6430	258.6021	6,685	77,184	598,935
79	41.812	6,556.0410	274.1212	6,419	70,498	525,094
80	46.037	6,281.9198	289.2007	6,137	64,079	457,805
81	50.643	5,992.7190	303.4893	5,841	57,942	396,795
82	55.651	5,689.2298	316.6113	5,531	52,101	341,773
83	61.080	5,372.6184	328.1595	5,209	46,570	292,438
84	66.948	5,044.4589	337.7164	4,876	41,362	248,472

APPENDIX K

Annuity 2000 Mortality Table—Male Mortality Functions: L_x, T_x, Y_x (Continued)

Age Nearest Birthday x	1,000 q_x	l_x	d_x	L_x	T_x	Y_x
85	73.275	4,706.7425	344.8866	4,534	36,486	209,548
86	80.076	4,361.8559	349.2800	4,187	31,952	175,329
87	97.370	4,012.5759	350.5788	3,837	27,764	145,471
88	95.169	3,661.9972	348.5086	3,488	23,927	119,625
89	103.455	3,313.4886	342.7970	3,142	20,439	97,442
90	112.208	2,970.6916	333.3354	2,804	17,297	78,574
91	121.402	2,637.3562	320.1803	2,477	14,493	62,678
92	131.017	2,317.1759	303.5894	2,165	12,016	49,424
93	141.030	2,013.5865	283.9761	1,872	9,851	38,490
94	151.422	1,729.6104	261.9011	1,599	7,979	29,575
95	162.179	1,467.7093	238.0316	1,349	6,380	22,396
96	173.279	1,229.6777	213.0773	1,123	5,032	16,689
97	184.706	1,016.6004	187.7722	923	3,909	12,219
98	196.946	828.8282	163.2344	747	2,986	8,772
99	210.484	665.5938	140.0968	596	2,239	6,160
100	225.806	525.4969	118.6604	466	1,643	4,219
101	243.398	406.8366	99.0232	357	1,177	2,809
102	263.745	307.8134	81.1842	267	820	1,811
103	287.334	226.6291	65.1183	194	552	1,125
104	314.649	161.5109	50.8192	136	358	669

APPENDIX K

Annuity 2000 Mortality Table—Male Mortality Functions: L_x, T_x, Y_x (Continued)

Age Nearest Birthday x	1,000 q_x	l_x	d_x	L_x	T_x	Y_x
105	346.177	110.6916	38.3189	92	222	379
106	382.403	72.3727	27.6756	59	131	203
107	423.813	44.6972	18.9432	35	72	101
108	470.893	25.7539	12.1273	20	37	47
109	524.128	13.6266	7.1421	10	17	19
110	584.004	6.4845	3.7870	5	7	7
111	651.007	2.6975	1.7561	2	3	2
112	725.622	0.9414	0.6831	1	1	1
113	808.336	0.2583	0.2088	0	0	0
114	899.633	0.0495	0.0445	0	0	0
115	1000.000	0.0050	0.0050	0	0	0

APPENDIX L

Annuity 2000 Mortality Table—Female Mortality Functions: L_x, T_x, Y_x

Age Nearest Birthday x	$1,000\,q_x$	l_x	d_x	L_x	T_x	Y_x
5	0.171	10,000.0000	1.7100	9,999	806,757	33,378,082
6	0.141	9,998.2900	1.4098	9,998	796,758	32,576,325
7	0.118	9,996.8802	1.1796	9,996	786,760	31,784,565
8	0.118	9,995.7006	1.1795	9,995	776,764	31,002,803
9	0.121	9,994.5211	1.2093	9,994	766,769	30,231,037
10	0.126	9,993.3118	1.2592	9,993	756,775	29,469,265
11	0.133	9,992.0526	1.3289	9,991	746,782	28,717,486
12	0.142	9,990.7237	1.4187	9,990	736,791	27,975,699
13	0.152	9,989.3050	1.5184	9,989	726,801	27,243,903
14	0.164	9,987.7866	1.6380	9,987	716,812	26,522,097
15	0.177	9,986.1486	1.7675	9,985	706,825	25,810,278
16	0.190	9,984.3811	1.8970	9,983	696,840	25,108,445
17	0.204	9,982.4840	2.0364	9,981	686,857	24,416,596
18	0.219	9,980.4476	2.1857	9,979	676,875	23,734,730
19	0.234	9,978.2619	2.3349	9,977	666,896	23,062,845
20	0.250	9,975.9270	2.4940	9,975	656,919	22,400,937
21	0.265	9,973.4330	2.6430	9,972	646,944	21,749,006
22	0.281	9,970.7900	2.8018	9,969	636,972	21,107,048
23	0.298	9,967.9883	2.9705	9,967	627,003	20,475,060
24	0.314	9,965.0178	3.1290	9,963	617,036	19,853,041

684

APPENDIX L

Annuity 2000 Mortality Table—Female Mortality Functions: L_x, T_x, Y_x (Continued)

Age Nearest Birthday x	$1,000 \, q_x$	l_x	d_x	L_x	T_x	Y_x
25	0.331	9,961.8888	3.2974	9,960	607,073	19,240,986
26	0.347	9,958.5914	3.4556	9,957	597,112	18,638,894
27	0.362	9,955.1358	3.6038	9,953	587,156	18,046,760
28	0.376	9,951.5320	3.7418	9,950	577,202	17,464,581
29	0.389	9,947.7902	3.8697	9,946	567,253	16,892,353
30	0.402	9,943.9205	3.9975	9,942	557,307	16,330,074
31	0.414	9,939.9231	4.1151	9,938	547,365	15,777,738
32	0.425	9,935.8080	4.2227	9,934	537,427	15,235,342
33	0.436	9,931.5852	4.3302	9,929	527,493	14,702,882
34	0.449	9,927.2551	4.4573	9,925	517,564	14,180,353
35	0.463	9,922.7977	4.5943	9,921	507,639	13,667,752
36	0.481	9,918.2035	4.7707	9,916	497,718	13,165,073
37	0.504	9,913.4328	4.9964	9,911	487,803	12,672,313
38	0.532	9,908.4364	5.2713	9,906	477,892	12,189,466
39	0.567	9,903.1652	5.6151	9,900	467,986	11,716,527
40	0.609	9,897.5501	6.0276	9,895	458,085	11,253,492
41	0.658	9,891.5225	6.5086	9,888	448,191	10,800,354
42	0.715	9,885.0138	7.0678	9,881	438,303	10,357,107
43	0.781	9,877.9460	7.7147	9,874	428,421	9,923,745
44	0.855	9,870.2314	8.4390	9,866	418,547	9,500,261

APPENDIX L

Annuity 2000 Mortality Table—Female Mortality Functions: L_x, T_x, Y_x (Continued)

Age Nearest Birthday x	$1,000\, q_x$	l_x	d_x	L_x	T_x	Y_x
45	0.939	9,861.7923	9.2602	9,857	408,681	9,086,647
46	1.035	9,852.5321	10.1974	9,847	398,824	8,682,894
47	1.141	9,842.3347	11.2301	9,837	388,976	8,288,994
48	1.261	9,831.1046	12.3970	9,825	379,140	7,904,936
49	1.393	9,818.7076	13.6775	9,812	369,315	7,530,709
50	1.538	9,805.0301	15.0801	9,797	359,503	7,166,300
51	1.695	9,789.9500	16.5940	9,782	349,705	6,811,696
52	1.864	9,773.3560	18.2175	9,764	339,924	6,466,881
53	2.047	9,755.1385	19.9688	9,745	330,160	6,131,840
54	2.244	9,735.1697	21.8457	9,724	320,414	5,806,553
55	2.457	9,713.3240	23.8656	9,701	310,690	5,491,000
56	2.689	9,689.4584	26.0550	9,676	300,989	5,185,161
57	2.942	9,663.4034	28.4297	9,649	291,312	4,889,010
58	3.218	9,634.9737	31.0053	9,619	281,663	4,602,523
59	3.523	9,603.9683	33.8348	9,587	272,044	4,325,669
60	3.863	9,570.1336	36.9694	9,552	262,457	4,058,419
61	4.242	9,533.1641	40.4397	9,513	252,905	3,800,738
62	4.668	9,492.7245	44.3120	9,471	243,392	3,552,590
63	5.144	9,448.4124	48.6026	9,424	233,921	3,313,933
64	5.671	9,399.8098	53.3063	9,373	224,497	3,084,724

APPENDIX L

Annuity 2000 Mortality Table—Female Mortality Functions: L_x, T_x, Y_x (Continued)

Age Nearest Birthday x	$1,000\,q_x$	l_x	d_x	L_x	T_x	Y_x
65	6.250	9,346.5035	58.4156	9,317	215,124	2,864,913
66	6.878	9,288.0878	63.8835	9,256	205,807	2,654,447
67	7.555	9,224.2043	69.6889	9,189	196,551	2,453,269
68	8.287	9,154.5155	75.8635	9,117	187,361	2,261,313
69	9.102	9,078.6520	82.6339	9,037	178,245	2,078,509
70	10.034	8,996.0181	90.2660	8,951	169,207	1,904,783
71	11.117	8,905.7521	99.0052	8,856	160,257	1,740,051
72	12.386	8,806.7468	109.0804	8,752	151,400	1,584,223
73	13.871	8,697.6665	120.6453	8,637	142,648	1,437,199
74	15.592	8,577.0211	133.7329	8,510	134,011	1,298,869
75	17.564	8,443.2882	148.2979	8,369	125,501	1,169,114
76	19.805	8,294.9903	164.2823	8,213	117,131	1,047,797
77	22.328	8,130.7080	181.5424	8,040	108,919	934,772
78	25.158	7,949.1656	199.9851	7,849	100,879	829,874
79	28.341	7,749.1805	219.6195	7,639	93,030	732,920
80	31.933	7,529.5609	240.4415	7,409	85,390	643,710
81	35.985	7,289.1195	262.2990	7,158	77,981	562,024
82	40.552	7,026.8205	284.9516	6,884	70,823	487,622
83	45.690	6,741.8689	308.0360	6,588	63,938	420,242
84	51.456	6,433.8329	331.0593	6,268	57,351	359,597

APPENDIX L

Annuity 2000 Mortality Table—Female Mortality Functions: L_x, T_x, Y_x *(Continued)*

Age Nearest Birthday x	1,000 q_x	l_x	d_x	L_x	T_x	Y_x
85	57.913	6,102.7736	353.4299	5,926	51,082	305,381
86	65.119	5,749.3437	374.3915	5,562	45,156	257,261
87	73.136	5,374.9522	393.1025	5,178	39,594	214,886
88	81.991	4,981.8497	408.4668	4,778	34,416	177,881
89	91.577	4,573.3828	418.8167	4,364	29,638	145,854
90	101.758	4,154.5661	422.7603	3,943	25,274	118,398
91	112.395	3,731.8058	419.4363	3,522	21,331	95,096
92	123.349	3,312.3695	408.5775	3,108	17,809	75,526
93	134.486	2,903.7920	390.5194	2,709	14,701	59,271
94	145.689	2,513.2726	366.1562	2,330	11,992	45,924
95	156.846	2,147.1165	336.7666	1,979	9,662	35,097
96	167.841	1,810.3498	303.8509	1,658	7,683	26,425
97	178.563	1,506.4989	269.0050	1,372	6,025	19,570
98	189.604	1,237.4939	234.6338	1,120	4,653	14,231
99	210.557	1,002.8601	202.1335	902	3,533	10,139
100	215.013	800.7267	172.1666	715	2,631	7,057
101	230.565	628.5600	144.9239	556	1,916	4,783
102	248.805	483.6361	120.3311	423	1,360	3,145
103	270.326	363.3050	98.2108	314	937	1,996
104	295.719	265.0942	78.3934	226	623	1,217

Annuity 2000 Mortality Table—Female Mortality Functions: L_x, T_x, Y_x (*Continued*)

Age Nearest Birthday x	$1,000\,q_x$	l_x	d_x	L_x	T_x	Y_x
105	325.576	186.7008	60.7853	156	397	707
106	360.491	125.9155	45.3914	103	240	389
107	401.054	80.5241	32.2945	64	137	200
108	447.860	48.2296	21.6001	37	73	95
109	501.498	26.6295	13.3546	20	35	41
110	562.563	13.2749	7.4679	10	15	16
111	631.645	5.8069	3.6679	4	6	5
112	709.338	2.1390	1.5173	1	2	1
113	796.233	0.6217	0.4950	0	0	0
114	892.923	0.1267	0.1131	0	0	0
115	1000.000	0.0136	0.0136	0	0	0

APPENDIX M.1

n-Year Fixed-Period Annuity-Due Present Values $\ddot{a}_{\overline{n}|}^{(m)}$ at 3% AIR

$1 per Annum Payable m Times per Year

Years n	Annual $m = 1$ $\ddot{a}_{\overline{n}|}$	Semiannual $m = 2$ $\ddot{a}_{\overline{n}|}^{(2)}$	Quarterly $m = 4$ $\ddot{a}_{\overline{n}|}^{(4)}$	Monthly $m = 12$ $\ddot{a}_{\overline{n}|}^{(12)}$	Continuously $m = \infty$ $\overline{a}_{\overline{n}|}$
1	1.00000	0.99266	0.98901	0.98658	0.98537
2	1.97087	1.95642	1.94921	1.94442	1.94203
3	2.91347	2.89210	2.88145	2.87437	2.87083
4	3.82861	3.80053	3.78654	3.77723	3.77258
5	4.71710	4.68250	4.66526	4.65379	4.64806
6	5.57971	5.53878	5.51839	5.50482	5.49805
7	6.41719	6.37012	6.34667	6.33107	6.32328
8	7.23028	7.17725	7.15083	7.13325	7.12447
9	8.01969	7.96086	7.93156	7.91206	7.90233
10	8.78611	8.72166	8.68955	8.66819	8.65753
11	9.53020	9.46030	9.42547	9.40230	9.39073
12	10.25262	10.17742	10.13995	10.11503	10.10258
13	10.95400	10.87365	10.83362	10.80699	10.79369
14	11.63496	11.54961	11.50709	11.47881	11.46468
15	12.29607	12.20588	12.16094	12.13105	12.11612
16	12.93794	12.84303	12.79575	12.76430	12.74859
17	13.56110	13.46163	13.41207	13.37910	13.36264
18	14.16612	14.06220	14.01044	13.97600	13.95880
19	14.75351	14.64529	14.59138	14.55551	14.53760
20	15.32380	15.21139	15.15540	15.11814	15.09954
21	15.87747	15.76101	15.70299	15.66439	15.64511
22	16.41502	16.29461	16.23463	16.19472	16.17479
23	16.93692	16.81268	16.75079	16.70961	16.68905
24	17.44361	17.31565	17.25191	17.20950	17.18832
25	17.93554	17.80398	17.73844	17.69483	17.67306
26	18.41315	18.27808	18.21079	18.16603	18.14367
27	18.87684	18.73837	18.66939	18.62350	18.60058
28	19.32703	19.18526	19.11464	19.06765	19.04418
29	19.76411	19.61913	19.54691	19.49886	19.47486
30	20.18845	20.04036	19.96659	19.91751	19.89300
31	20.60044	20.44933	20.37405	20.32397	20.29896
32	21.00043	20.84638	20.76964	20.71859	20.69309
33	21.38877	21.23187	21.15371	21.10171	21.07574
34	21.76579	21.60613	21.52659	21.47368	21.44725
35	22.13184	21.96949	21.88862	21.83481	21.80794
36	22.48722	22.32227	22.24009	22.18542	22.15812
37	22.83225	22.66477	22.58134	22.52583	22.49811
38	23.16724	22.99730	22.91264	22.85631	22.82819
39	23.49246	23.32014	23.23429	23.17717	23.14865
40	23.80822	23.63357	23.54657	23.48869	23.45979

APPENDIX M.2

n-Year Fixed-Period Annuity-Due Present Values $\ddot{a}_{\overline{n}|}^{(m)}$ at 4% AIR

$1 per Annum Payable *m* Times per Year

Years n	Annual $m = 1$ $\ddot{a}_{\overline{n}|}$	Semiannual $m = 2$ $\ddot{a}_{\overline{n}|}^{(2)}$	Quarterly $m = 4$ $\ddot{a}_{\overline{n}|}^{(4)}$	Monthly $m = 12$ $\ddot{a}_{\overline{n}|}^{(12)}$	Continuously $m = \infty$ $\overline{a}_{\overline{n}|}$
1	1.00000	0.99029	0.98546	0.98225	0.98064
2	1.96154	1.94249	1.93302	1.92672	1.92357
3	2.88609	2.85807	2.84413	2.83486	2.83023
4	3.77509	3.73844	3.72020	3.70807	3.70202
5	4.62990	4.58494	4.56257	4.54770	4.54028
6	5.45182	5.39889	5.37255	5.35504	5.34629
7	6.24214	6.18153	6.15137	6.13132	6.12131
8	7.00205	6.93407	6.90024	6.87775	6.86652
9	7.73274	7.65766	7.62030	7.59547	7.58307
10	8.43533	8.35343	8.31267	8.28558	8.27205
11	9.11090	9.02243	8.97841	8.94915	8.93454
12	9.76048	9.66571	9.61855	9.58720	9.57155
13	10.38507	10.28424	10.23407	10.20071	10.18406
14	10.98565	10.87898	10.82591	10.79062	10.77300
15	11.56312	11.45085	11.39498	11.35784	11.33930
16	12.11839	12.00072	11.94217	11.90325	11.88382
17	12.65230	12.52945	12.46832	12.42768	12.40739
18	13.16567	13.03783	12.97423	12.93194	12.91083
19	13.65930	13.52667	13.46068	13.41680	13.39490
20	14.13394	13.99670	13.92842	13.88302	13.86036
21	14.59033	14.44866	14.37817	14.33130	14.30791
22	15.02916	14.88323	14.81062	14.76235	14.73825
23	15.45112	15.30109	15.22644	15.17681	15.15204
24	15.85684	15.70288	15.62627	15.57533	15.54991
25	16.24696	16.08921	16.01072	15.95853	15.93248
26	16.62208	16.46069	16.38038	16.32699	16.30034
27	16.98277	16.81787	16.73582	16.68127	16.65404
28	17.32959	17.16132	17.07760	17.02193	16.99415
29	17.66306	17.49156	17.40623	17.34949	17.32117
30	17.98371	17.80910	17.72221	17.66445	17.63561
31	18.29203	18.11442	18.02605	17.96729	17.93796
32	18.58849	18.40801	18.31820	18.25849	18.22869
33	18.87355	18.69030	18.59911	18.53849	18.50823
34	19.14765	18.96173	18.86922	18.80772	18.77701
35	19.41120	19.22272	19.12894	19.06659	19.03547
36	19.66461	19.47368	19.37867	19.31551	19.28398
37	19.90828	19.71498	19.61880	19.55485	19.52293
38	20.14258	19.94700	19.84969	19.78499	19.75269
39	20.36786	20.17010	20.07170	20.00627	19.97361
40	20.58448	20.38462	20.28517	20.21905	20.18604

APPENDIX M.3

n-Year Fixed-Period Annuity-Due Present Values $\ddot{a}_{\overline{n}|}^{(m)}$ at 5% AIR

$1 per Annum Payable m Times per Year

Years n	Annual $m = 1$ $\ddot{a}_{\overline{n}|}$	Semiannual $m = 2$ $\ddot{a}_{\overline{n}|}^{(2)}$	Quarterly $m = 4$ $\ddot{a}_{\overline{n}|}^{(4)}$	Monthly $m = 12$ $\ddot{a}_{\overline{n}|}^{(12)}$	Continuously $m = \infty$ $\overline{a}_{\overline{n}|}$
1	1.00000	0.98795	0.98196	0.97798	0.97600
2	1.95238	1.92885	1.91716	1.90939	1.90552
3	2.85941	2.82495	2.80783	2.79645	2.79078
4	3.72325	3.67838	3.65609	3.64127	3.63388
5	4.54595	4.49117	4.46395	4.44586	4.43683
6	5.32948	5.26526	5.23334	5.21213	5.20155
7	6.07569	6.00248	5.96609	5.94192	5.92986
8	6.78637	6.70460	6.66396	6.63695	6.62348
9	7.46321	7.37328	7.32859	7.29889	7.28407
10	8.10782	8.01012	7.96157	7.92931	7.91321
11	8.72173	8.61664	8.56441	8.52970	8.51239
12	9.30641	9.19427	9.13854	9.10151	9.08303
13	9.86325	9.74440	9.68533	9.64609	9.62650
14	10.39357	10.26833	10.20609	10.16473	10.14409
15	10.89864	10.76731	10.70204	10.65868	10.63704
16	11.37966	11.24253	11.17438	11.12910	11.10651
17	11.83777	11.69512	11.62423	11.57713	11.55363
18	12.27407	12.12616	12.05266	12.00382	11.97945
19	12.68959	12.53668	12.46068	12.41019	12.38500
20	13.08532	12.92764	12.84928	12.79721	12.77123
21	13.46221	13.29999	13.21937	13.16580	13.13908
22	13.82115	13.65461	13.57184	13.51684	13.48940
23	14.16300	13.99234	13.90752	13.85117	13.82305
24	14.48857	14.31399	14.22722	14.16957	14.14080
25	14.79864	14.62032	14.53169	14.47281	14.44343
26	15.09394	14.91206	14.82167	14.76161	14.73164
27	15.37519	15.18991	15.09784	15.03666	15.00613
28	15.64303	15.45454	15.36085	15.29861	15.26755
29	15.89813	15.70656	15.61135	15.54809	15.51652
30	16.14107	15.94657	15.84991	15.78568	15.75364
31	16.37245	16.17516	16.07711	16.01197	15.97946
32	16.59281	16.39287	16.29350	16.22748	16.19453
33	16.80268	16.60021	16.49958	16.43272	16.39936
34	17.00255	16.79767	16.69585	16.62819	16.59443
35	17.19290	16.98573	16.88277	16.81436	16.78022
36	17.37419	17.16484	17.06079	16.99166	16.95716
37	17.54685	17.33541	17.23033	17.16051	17.12567
38	17.71129	17.49787	17.39180	17.32133	17.28616
39	17.86789	17.65259	17.54558	17.47448	17.43901
40	18.01704	17.79994	17.69204	17.62035	17.58458

APPENDIX M.4

n-Year Fixed-Period Annuity-Due Present Values $\ddot{a}_{\overline{n}|}^{(m)}$ at 6% AIR

$1 per Annum Payable m Times per Year

Years n	Annual $m = 1$ $\ddot{a}_{\overline{n}|}$	Semiannual $m = 2$ $\ddot{a}_{\overline{n}|}^{(2)}$	Quarterly $m = 4$ $\ddot{a}_{\overline{n}|}^{(4)}$	Monthly $m = 12$ $\ddot{a}_{\overline{n}|}^{(12)}$	Continuously $m = \infty$ $\overline{a}_{\overline{n}|}$
1	1.00000	0.98564	0.97852	0.97378	0.97142
2	1.94340	1.91549	1.90164	1.89245	1.88786
3	2.83339	2.79271	2.77252	2.75911	2.75242
4	3.67301	3.62028	3.59410	3.57672	3.56805
5	4.46511	4.40100	4.36918	4.34805	4.33751
6	5.21236	5.13753	5.10038	5.07571	5.06341
7	5.91732	5.83237	5.79020	5.76219	5.74823
8	6.58238	6.48788	6.44097	6.40982	6.39428
9	7.20979	7.10628	7.05490	7.02078	7.00376
10	7.80169	7.68968	7.63408	7.59716	7.57875
11	8.36009	8.24006	8.18048	8.14092	8.12118
12	8.88687	8.75929	8.69595	8.65389	8.63292
13	9.38384	9.24912	9.18224	9.13783	9.11568
14	9.85268	9.71123	9.64101	9.59438	9.57113
15	10.29498	10.14718	10.07381	10.02509	10.00079
16	10.71225	10.55845	10.48211	10.43141	10.40613
17	11.10590	10.94645	10.86730	10.81474	10.78853
18	11.47726	11.31248	11.23068	11.17637	11.14928
19	11.82760	11.65779	11.57350	11.51753	11.48961
20	12.15812	11.98356	11.89691	11.83938	11.81068
21	12.46992	12.29089	12.20202	12.14301	12.11357
22	12.76408	12.58082	12.48985	12.42945	12.39932
23	13.04158	12.85434	12.76140	12.69968	12.66890
24	13.30338	13.11238	13.01757	12.95461	12.92321
25	13.55036	13.35581	13.25924	13.19512	13.16313
26	13.78336	13.58547	13.48723	13.42201	13.38947
27	14.00317	13.80212	13.70232	13.63605	13.60300
28	14.21053	14.00651	13.90523	13.83799	13.80444
29	14.40616	14.19933	14.09666	14.02849	13.99448
30	14.59072	14.38124	14.27725	14.20821	14.17377
31	14.76483	14.55285	14.44762	14.37775	14.34290
32	14.92909	14.71475	14.60835	14.53770	14.50246
33	15.08404	14.86748	14.75998	14.68860	14.65299
34	15.23023	15.01157	14.90302	14.83095	14.79500
35	15.36814	15.14750	15.03797	14.96524	14.92897
36	15.49825	15.27574	15.16528	15.09194	15.05536
37	15.62099	15.39672	15.28538	15.21146	15.17459
38	15.73678	15.51085	15.39869	15.32422	15.28707
39	15.84602	15.61852	15.50558	15.43059	15.39319
40	15.94907	15.72009	15.60642	15.53095	15.49330

APPENDIX N.1

n-Year Fixed-Period Annuity-Immediate Present Values $a_{\overline{n}|}^{(m)}$ at 3% AIR

$1 per Annum Payable m Times per Year

Years n	Annual $m = 1$ $a_{\overline{n}|}$	Semiannual $m = 2$ $a_{\overline{n}|}^{(2)}$	Quarterly $m = 4$ $a_{\overline{n}|}^{(4)}$	Monthly $m = 12$ $a_{\overline{n}|}^{(12)}$	Continuously $m = \infty$ $\overline{a}_{\overline{n}|}$
1	0.97087	0.97810	0.98173	0.98415	0.98537
2	1.91347	1.92771	1.93486	1.93964	1.94203
3	2.82861	2.84967	2.86024	2.86730	2.87083
4	3.71710	3.74477	3.75866	3.76794	3.77258
5	4.57971	4.61380	4.63091	4.64234	4.64806
6	5.41719	5.45752	5.47776	5.49128	5.49805
7	6.23028	6.27666	6.29994	6.31549	6.32328
8	7.01969	7.07195	7.09818	7.11570	7.12447
9	7.78611	7.84407	7.87316	7.89260	7.90233
10	8.53020	8.59371	8.62558	8.64687	8.65753
11	9.25262	9.32151	9.35608	9.37917	9.39073
12	9.95400	10.02811	10.06530	10.09014	10.10258
13	10.63496	10.71413	10.75386	10.78041	10.79369
14	11.29607	11.38017	11.42237	11.45057	11.46468
15	11.93794	12.02681	12.07141	12.10121	12.11612
16	12.56110	12.65461	12.70154	12.73290	12.74859
17	13.16612	13.26413	13.31333	13.34619	13.36264
18	13.75351	13.85590	13.90729	13.94161	13.95880
19	14.32380	14.43043	14.48395	14.51970	14.53760
20	14.87747	14.98823	15.04382	15.08095	15.09954
21	15.41502	15.52978	15.58738	15.62585	15.64511
22	15.93692	16.05556	16.11510	16.15488	16.17479
23	16.44361	16.56602	16.62746	16.66850	16.68905
24	16.93554	17.06162	17.12489	17.16716	17.18832
25	17.41315	17.54278	17.60784	17.65130	17.67306
26	17.87684	18.00993	18.07672	18.12134	18.14367
27	18.32703	18.46347	18.53194	18.57768	18.60058
28	18.76411	18.90380	18.97390	19.02074	19.04418
29	19.18845	19.33130	19.40300	19.45089	19.47486
30	19.60044	19.74636	19.81959	19.86851	19.89300
31	20.00043	20.14932	20.22405	20.27397	20.29896
32	20.38877	20.54055	20.61673	20.66761	20.69309
33	20.76579	20.92038	20.99797	21.04980	21.07574
34	21.13184	21.28915	21.36811	21.42085	21.44725
35	21.48722	21.64718	21.72746	21.78109	21.80794
36	21.83225	21.99478	22.07635	22.13084	22.15812
37	22.16724	22.33226	22.41508	22.47041	22.49811
38	22.49246	22.65991	22.74394	22.80008	22.82819
39	22.80822	22.97801	23.06323	23.12015	23.14865
40	23.11477	23.28685	23.37321	23.43090	23.45979

APPENDIX N.2

n-Year Fixed-Period Annuity-Immediate Present Values $a_{\overline{n}|}^{(m)}$ at 4% AIR

$1 per Annum Payable *m* Times per Year

Years n	Annual $m = 1$ $a_{\overline{n}|}$	Semiannual $m = 2$ $a_{\overline{n}|}^{(2)}$	Quarterly $m = 4$ $a_{\overline{n}|}^{(4)}$	Monthly $m = 12$ $a_{\overline{n}|}^{(12)}$	Continuously $m = \infty$ $\overline{a}_{\overline{n}|}$
1	0.96154	0.97106	0.97584	0.97904	0.98064
2	1.88609	1.90477	1.91415	1.92043	1.92357
3	2.77509	2.80257	2.81638	2.82561	2.83023
4	3.62990	3.66584	3.68390	3.69597	3.70202
5	4.45182	4.49590	4.51805	4.53286	4.54028
6	5.24214	5.29404	5.32013	5.33756	5.34629
7	6.00205	6.06149	6.09135	6.11131	6.12131
8	6.73274	6.79941	6.83291	6.85530	6.86652
9	7.43533	7.50896	7.54595	7.57068	7.58307
10	8.11090	8.19121	8.23157	8.25854	8.27205
11	8.76048	8.84722	8.89081	8.91995	8.93454
12	9.38507	9.47800	9.52470	9.55592	9.57155
13	9.98565	10.08453	10.13421	10.16742	10.18406
14	10.56312	10.66772	10.72028	10.75541	10.77300
15	11.11839	11.22848	11.28380	11.32078	11.33930
16	11.65230	11.76768	11.82565	11.86441	11.88382
17	12.16567	12.28613	12.34666	12.38713	12.40739
18	12.65930	12.78465	12.84763	12.88974	12.91083
19	13.13394	13.26399	13.32934	13.37302	13.39490
20	13.59033	13.72490	13.79252	13.83772	13.86036
21	14.02916	14.16808	14.23788	14.28454	14.30791
22	14.45112	14.59421	14.66611	14.71418	14.73825
23	14.85684	15.00395	15.07787	15.12729	15.15204
24	15.24696	15.39794	15.47380	15.52451	15.54991
25	15.62208	15.77677	15.85450	15.90646	15.93248
26	15.98277	16.14103	16.22055	16.27371	16.30034
27	16.32959	16.49128	16.57253	16.62684	16.65404
28	16.66306	16.82806	16.91097	16.96639	16.99415
29	16.98371	17.15189	17.23639	17.29288	17.32117
30	17.29203	17.46326	17.54929	17.60681	17.63561
31	17.58849	17.76265	17.85017	17.90867	17.93796
32	17.87355	18.05053	18.13946	18.19891	18.22869
33	18.14765	18.32734	18.41764	18.47800	18.50823
34	18.41120	18.59350	18.68511	18.74635	18.77701
35	18.66461	18.84943	18.94229	19.00437	19.03547
36	18.90828	19.09551	19.18959	19.25248	19.28398
37	19.14258	19.33213	19.42737	19.49104	19.52293
38	19.36786	19.55964	19.65601	19.72043	19.75269
39	19.58448	19.77841	19.87585	19.94099	19.97361
40	19.79277	19.98876	20.08724	20.15307	20.18604

APPENDIX N.3

n-Year Fixed-Period Annuity-Immediate Present Values $a_{\overline{n}|}^{(m)}$ at 5% AIR
$1 per Annum Payable m Times per Year

Years n	Annual $m = 1$ $a_{\overline{n}|}$	Semiannual $m = 2$ $a_{\overline{n}|}^{(2)}$	Quarterly $m = 4$ $a_{\overline{n}|}^{(4)}$	Monthly $m = 12$ $a_{\overline{n}|}^{(12)}$	Continuously $m = \infty$ $\overline{a}_{\overline{n}|}$
1	0.95238	0.96414	0.97006	0.97401	0.97600
2	1.85941	1.88237	1.89392	1.90165	1.90552
3	2.72325	2.75687	2.77379	2.78511	2.79078
4	3.54595	3.58973	3.61176	3.62650	3.63388
5	4.32948	4.38294	4.40983	4.42782	4.43683
6	5.07569	5.13836	5.16989	5.19099	5.20155
7	5.78637	5.85782	5.89377	5.91781	5.92986
8	6.46321	6.54302	6.58317	6.61002	6.62348
9	7.10782	7.19559	7.23974	7.26927	7.28407
10	7.72173	7.81708	7.86505	7.89713	7.91321
11	8.30641	8.40898	8.46058	8.49509	8.51239
12	8.86325	8.97269	9.02775	9.06458	9.08303
13	9.39357	9.50956	9.56791	9.60695	9.62650
14	9.89864	10.02086	10.08235	10.12349	10.14409
15	10.37966	10.50782	10.57230	10.61543	10.63704
16	10.83777	10.97159	11.03891	11.08395	11.10651
17	11.27407	11.41327	11.48331	11.53015	11.55363
18	11.68959	11.83392	11.90654	11.95511	11.97945
19	12.08532	12.23454	12.30962	12.35984	12.38500
20	12.46221	12.61609	12.69350	12.74529	12.77123
21	12.82115	12.97946	13.05911	13.11238	13.13908
22	13.16300	13.32553	13.40730	13.46200	13.48940
23	13.48857	13.65512	13.73891	13.79496	13.82305
24	13.79864	13.96902	14.05474	14.11208	14.14080
25	14.09394	14.26797	14.35552	14.41409	14.44343
26	14.37519	14.55268	14.64198	14.70171	14.73164
27	14.64303	14.82384	14.91480	14.97565	15.00613
28	14.89813	15.08208	15.17463	15.23654	15.26755
29	15.14107	15.32803	15.42208	15.48500	15.51652
30	15.37245	15.56226	15.65775	15.72163	15.75364
31	15.59281	15.78534	15.88220	15.94700	15.97946
32	15.80268	15.99780	16.09597	16.16163	16.19453
33	16.00255	16.20014	16.29955	16.36604	16.39936
34	16.19290	16.39285	16.49343	16.56072	16.59443
35	16.37419	16.57638	16.67809	16.74613	16.78022
36	16.54685	16.75116	16.85395	16.92271	16.95716
37	16.71129	16.91763	17.02144	17.09088	17.12567
38	16.86789	17.07617	17.18095	17.25104	17.28616
39	17.01704	17.22716	17.33287	17.40358	17.43901
40	17.15909	17.37096	17.47755	17.54885	17.58458

APPENDIX N.4

n-Year Fixed-Period Annuity-Immediate Present Values $a_{\overline{n}|}^{(m)}$ at 6% AIR

$1 per Annum Payable m Times per Year

Years n	Annual $m = 1$ $a_{\overline{n}|}$	Semiannual $m = 2$ $a_{\overline{n}|}^{(2)}$	Quarterly $m = 4$ $a_{\overline{n}|}^{(4)}$	Monthly $m = 12$ $a_{\overline{n}|}^{(12)}$	Continuously $m = \infty$ $\overline{a}_{\overline{n}|}$
1	0.94340	0.95734	0.96436	0.96907	0.97142
2	1.83339	1.86049	1.87414	1.88328	1.88786
3	2.67301	2.71252	2.73242	2.74575	2.75242
4	3.46511	3.51633	3.54212	3.55939	3.56805
5	4.21236	4.27463	4.30599	4.32699	4.33751
6	4.91732	4.99001	5.02662	5.05113	5.06341
7	5.58238	5.66490	5.70646	5.73428	5.74823
8	6.20979	6.30158	6.34782	6.37877	6.39428
9	6.80169	6.90223	6.95287	6.98677	7.00376
10	7.36009	7.46888	7.52368	7.56036	7.57875
11	7.88687	8.00345	8.06218	8.10148	8.12118
12	8.38384	8.50777	8.57019	8.61197	8.63292
13	8.85268	8.98354	9.04945	9.09357	9.11568
14	9.29498	9.43238	9.50158	9.54791	9.57113
15	9.71225	9.85581	9.92812	9.97653	10.00079
16	10.10590	10.25528	10.33052	10.38088	10.40613
17	10.47726	10.63213	10.71014	10.76235	10.78853
18	10.82760	10.98765	11.06827	11.12223	11.14928
19	11.15812	11.32305	11.40613	11.46174	11.48961
20	11.46992	11.63946	11.72486	11.78203	11.81068
21	11.76408	11.93797	12.02556	12.08419	12.11357
22	12.04158	12.21957	12.30923	12.36924	12.39932
23	12.30338	12.48524	12.57684	12.63816	12.66890
24	12.55036	12.73587	12.82931	12.89186	12.92321
25	12.78336	12.97231	13.06749	13.13120	13.16313
26	13.00317	13.19537	13.29219	13.35699	13.38947
27	13.21053	13.40581	13.50416	13.57000	13.60300
28	13.40616	13.60433	13.70414	13.77096	13.80444
29	13.59072	13.79161	13.89280	13.96053	13.99448
30	13.76483	13.96830	14.07078	14.13938	14.17377
31	13.92909	14.13498	14.23869	14.30811	14.34290
32	14.08404	14.29223	14.39709	14.46728	14.50246
33	14.23023	14.44057	14.54652	14.61744	14.65299
34	14.36814	14.58052	14.68750	14.75911	14.79500
35	14.49825	14.71255	14.82050	14.89275	14.92897
36	14.62099	14.83711	14.94597	15.01883	15.05536
37	14.73678	14.95461	15.06433	15.13778	15.17459
38	14.84602	15.06547	15.17600	15.24999	15.28707
39	14.94907	15.17004	15.28135	15.35585	15.39319
40	15.04630	15.26870	15.38073	15.45572	15.49330

Benefits Conferred on Immediate Variable Annuity Contract Owners

Customer Service

Access to customer service representatives (sometimes 24/7).
Toll-free customer service telephone lines.
Automated telephony services.
Internet self-service center.
Automatic asset-reallocation/portfolio-rebalancing services.
Payment processing of incoming premiums and outgoing annuity benefits.
Tax reporting to customers and governmental entities.
Customer statements of account activity.
Contract preparation and issuance.
Customer newsletters and other customer communications.

Sales Representative Access

Availability of face-to-face communication with licensed sales representative.
Financial adviser training, initial and ongoing.
Computer illustrations of products.

Securities Law

Preparation and mailing of annual prospectus updates.
Preparation and mailing of annual and semiannual separate account performance reports.

Guaranty Funds

Insurer assessments to support guaranty funds of other insurers who may become insolvent and with whom annuity customers may also have other business (for fixed component of combination immediate fixed and variable annuity).

State Compliance

Compliance with state valuation laws.
Compliance with state nonforfeiture laws (possible for newer IVAs with liquidity).
Contract and application preparation and filing, complying with state regulations.
Ongoing review of changing state regulations and introduction of resultant procedural changes.

Market Conduct

Compliance with National Association of Securities Dealers (NASD) and state advertising regulations.

Ongoing financial adviser training regarding sales practice/market conduct issues.
Insurance Marketplace Standards Association (IMSA) compliance.

Accounting

Statutory, GAAP (generally accepted accounting principles), and tax reporting.
Auditing.

Data Processing

Purchase and maintenance of data processing hardware and software necessary to track
  customer accounts and transactions.

Human Resources

Hiring and training of personnel to provide services (customer service, legal, data processing, actuarial, sales, marketing, financial reporting, product development, product
  management, valuation, etc.) that benefit contract owners.
Continuing education of such personnel.

Product Development/Product Management

Initial product development, design, and pricing (e.g., annuity payout options offered,
  subaccounts and investment managers available).
Enhancements to existing products.
Management of in-force business.
Underwriting standards determination.

Capital Raising and Allocation

Raising of capital with which to fund operations.
Allocation of capital to business (e.g., required risk-based capital).

Sales and Marketing

Production of sales materials to inform contract owners of product benefits.

Valuation

Valuation of securities.
Valuation of reserve liabilities.

APPENDIX P
Proof of the Law of Large Numbers

Definition 1 $X_1, X_2, \ldots, X_n$ are *identically distributed* discrete random variables if and only if

$$p_{X_i}(x) = p_X(x), \text{ for all } x, i = 1, 2, \ldots, n$$

where $p_X(x)$ signifies the probability of the event that the random variable X assumes the numerical value x; that is, that $X = x$.

Definition 2 X and Y are *independent* discrete random variables if and only if

$$p_{X,Y}(x,y) = p_X(x)p_Y(y), \text{ for all } (x,y)$$

where $p_{X,Y}(x,y)$ signifies the probability of the joint events $X = x$ and $Y = y$ occurring; that is, $p_{X,Y}(x,y)$ equals $P\{X = x, Y = y\}$.

Theorem 1 If X and Y are independent random variables, then $E[G(X)H(Y)] = E[G(X)] \cdot E[H(Y)]$ where G and H are any two functions of a real variable.

Proof

Let R_X denote the range of X, those values of x such that $p_X(x) > 0$: $R_X = \{x : p_X(x) > 0\}$. Let R_Y denote the range of Y, those values of y such that $p_Y(y) > 0$: $R_Y = \{y : p_Y(y) > 0\}$.

$$
\begin{aligned}
E[G(X)H(Y)] &= \sum_{R_X} \sum_{R_Y} G(x)H(y)p_{X,Y}(x,y) \\
&= \sum_{R_X} \sum_{R_Y} G(x)H(y)p_X(x)p_Y(y) \\
&= \left\{ \sum_{R_X} G(x)p_X(x) \right\} \left\{ \sum_{R_Y} H(y)p_Y(y) \right\} \\
&= E[G(x)] \cdot E[H(y)] \qquad \blacksquare
\end{aligned}
$$

In particular, if $G(X) = X$ and $H(Y) = Y$, then $E[XY] = E[X]E[Y] = \mu_X \mu_Y$.

A consequence of Theorem 1 is that if X and Y are independent random variables, then their covariance σ_{XY} is zero because

$$\sigma_{XY} = E[(X - \mu_X)(Y - \mu_Y)]$$
$$= E[XY - \mu_X Y - X\mu_Y + \mu_X \mu_Y]$$
$$= E[XY] - \mu_X E[Y] - \mu_Y E[X] + \mu_X \mu_Y$$
$$= E[XY] - \mu_X \mu_Y$$
$$= E[X]E[Y] - \mu_X \mu_Y$$
$$= \mu_X \mu_Y - \mu_X \mu_Y$$
$$= 0$$

Theorem 2 $X_1, X_2, \ldots, X_n$ are independent random variables with means $\mu_1, \mu_2, \ldots, \mu_n$ and variances $\sigma_1^2, \sigma_2^2, \ldots, \sigma_n^2$. If $Y = \sum_{i=1}^{n} a_i X_i$ where the a_is are arbitrary constants, then $\mu_Y = \sum_{i=1}^{n} a_i \mu_i$ and $\sigma_Y^2 = \sum_{i=1}^{n} a_i^2 \sigma_i^2$.

Proof

$$\mu_Y = E[Y]$$
$$= E\left[\sum_{i=1}^{n} a_i X_i \right]$$
$$= \sum_{i=1}^{n} E[a_i X_i]$$
$$= \sum_{i=1}^{n} a_i E[X_i]$$
$$= \sum_{i=1}^{n} a_i \mu_i$$
$$\sigma_Y^2 = E[(Y - \mu_Y)^2]$$
$$= E\left[\left\{ \sum_{i=1}^{n} a_i X_i - \sum_{i=1}^{n} a_i \mu_i \right\}^2 \right]$$
$$= E\left[\left\{ \sum_{i=1}^{n} a_i (X_i - \mu_i) \right\}^2 \right]$$
$$= E\left[\sum_{i=1}^{n} a_i^2 (X_i - \mu_i)^2 + 2 \sum_i \sum_{\substack{j \\ i < j}} a_i a_j (X_i - \mu_i)(X_j - \mu_j) \right]$$
$$= \sum_{i=1}^{n} a_i^2 E[(X_i - \mu_i)^2] + 2 \sum_i \sum_{\substack{j \\ i < j}} a_i a_j E[(X_i - \mu_i)(X_j - \mu_j)] \qquad \text{(P.1)}$$
$$= \sum_{i=1}^{n} a_i^2 \sigma_i^2 \qquad \blacksquare$$

Every one of the terms of the double sum of cross products in equation P.1 is zero because each is a constant times the covariance of two of the variables in $X_1, X_2, \ldots, X_n$. Each of these covariances is zero because of the independence of $X_1, X_2, \ldots, X_n$, a consequence of Theorem 1 shown earlier.

Example 1   Suppose that $X_1, X_2, \ldots, X_n$ are independent, identically distributed random variables, each with mean μ and variance σ^2. Let $\bar{X}$ represent the arithmetic average of these n random variables; that is,

$$\bar{X} = \frac{1}{n}\sum_{i=1}^{n} X_i$$

$$= \sum_{i=1}^{n} \frac{1}{n} X_i$$

Consequently, $\bar{X}$ is a linear function of $X_1, X_2, \ldots, X_n$ with $a_i = 1/n$ for all i. From Theorem 2,

$$\mu_{\bar{X}} = \sum_{i=1}^{n} \frac{1}{n}\mu = \mu$$

$$\sigma_{\bar{X}}^2 = \sum_{i=1}^{n}\left(\frac{1}{n}\right)^2 \sigma^2 = \frac{\sigma^2}{n}$$

The expected value of $\bar{X}$ is the same as the common expected value of the X_is. The variance of $\bar{X}$ is $1/n$ times the common variance of the X_is. As a result, $\bar{X}$ is significantly less variable than the original X_is.

The probability that a random variable X will be within k standard deviations of its mean μ_X has a lower bound given by the Chebyshev inequality, named after the Russian mathematician Pafnuty Lvovich Chebyshev who derived it in 1867.

Theorem 3 (Chebyshev inequality)   If X is a random variable with mean μ_X and standard deviation σ_X, then

$$P\{|X - \mu_X| < k\sigma_X\} \geq 1 - \frac{1}{k^2}$$

and

$$P\{|X - \mu_X| \geq k\sigma_X\} \leq \frac{1}{k^2}$$

Proof

Assume X is a discrete random variable with probability function $p_X(x)$, mean μ_X, and variance σ_X^2. Let R_X denote the range of X, those values of x such that $p_X(x) > 0$. Define

$$A = \{x : |x - \mu_X| \geq k\sigma_X\}$$

and its complement

$$\bar{A} = \{x : |x - \mu_X| < k\sigma_X\}$$

where k is any constant.

Then

$$\sigma_X^2 = E[(X - \mu_X)^2]$$
$$= \sum_{x \in R_X} (x - \mu_X)^2 p_X(x)$$
$$= \sum_{x \in A \cap R_X} (x - \mu_X)^2 p_X(x) + \sum_{x \in \bar{A} \cap R_X} (x - \mu_X)^2 p_X(x)$$
$$\geq \sum_{x \in A \cap R_X} (x - \mu_X)^2 p_X(x)$$

because $\displaystyle\sum_{x \in \bar{A} \cap R_X} (x - \mu_X)^2 p_x(x) \geq 0$.

For any $x \in A \cap R_X$, by definition $|x - \mu_X| \geq k\sigma_X$ and so $(x - \mu_X)^2 \geq k^2\sigma_X^2$. Therefore,

$$\sum_{x \in A \cap R_X} (x - \mu_X)^2 p_X(x) \geq \sum_{x \in A \cap R_X} k^2\sigma_X^2 p_X(x)$$
$$= k^2\sigma_X^2 \sum_{x \in A \cap R_X} p_X(x)$$

whereby

$$\sigma_X^2 \geq k^2\sigma_X^2 \sum_{x \in A \cap R_X} p_X(x)$$

or equivalently

$$\frac{1}{k^2} \geq \sum_{x \in A \cap R_X} p_X(x)$$

Because the set A comprises all values of x such that $|x - \mu_X| \geq k\sigma_X$ and the range R_X is the set of all values of x such that $p_X(x) > 0$,

$$\sum_{x \in A \cap R_X} p_X(x) = P\{|X - \mu_X| \geq k\sigma_X\}$$

and thus

$$P\{|X - \mu_X| \geq k\sigma_X\} \leq \frac{1}{k^2} \tag{P.2}$$

which is the second Chebyshev inequality. Multiplying inequality P.2 by -1 (which reverses the inequality) and then adding 1 to both sides produces

$$1 - P\{|X - \mu_X| \geq k\sigma_X\} \geq 1 - \frac{1}{k^2}$$

or

$$P\{|X - \mu_X| < k\sigma_X\} \geq 1 - \frac{1}{k^2} \tag{P.3}$$

which is the first Chebyshev inequality. ∎

While this proof only covers the case of discrete random variables, the same reasoning holds for continuous random variables.

No assumption about the distribution (e.g., exponential, normal) of the random variable X is made when proving the Chebyshev inequality, although the assumption is made that μ_X and σ_X^2 exist. Even without such a distributional assumption, we are still able to place a lower bound on the probability that a random variable X is within k standard deviations of its mean.

Example 2 For $k = 1$, 1.5, 2, 3, and 4, the lower bound for the probability that the random variable X is within k standard deviations of its mean as given by Chebyshev inequality P.3 appears in Table P.1. For comparison, Table P.1 also shows the actual probabilities for random variables having (1) an exponential distribution and (2) a normal distribution being within k standard deviations of their means. While for these two distributions the actual probability is higher than the Chebyshev lower bound, the actual probabilities are based on a stronger assumption—it is assumed that we know the exact probability distribution for the random variable X.

Theorem 4 (Law of Large Numbers) Suppose that $X_1, X_2, \ldots, X_k, \ldots$ is a sequence of independent, identically distributed random variables, each

TABLE P.1 Probability a Random Variable Is Within k Standard Deviations of Its Mean

	$P\{|X - \mu_X| < k\sigma_X\}$		
k	Exponential	Normal	Chebyshev Lower Bound
1.0	0.8647	0.6826	0.0000
1.5	0.9179	0.8664	0.5556
2.0	0.9502	0.9546	0.7500
3.0	0.9817	0.9974	0.8889
4.0	0.9933	1.0000	0.9334

with mean μ and variance σ^2. Define a new sequence of random variables $\overline{X}_1, \overline{X}_2, \ldots, \overline{X}_k, \ldots$ by

$$\overline{X}_n = \frac{1}{n}\sum_{i=1}^{n} X_i, \quad n = 1, 2, 3, \ldots .$$

Then for any $\varepsilon > 0$,

$$\lim_{n \to \infty} P\{|\overline{X}_n - \mu| > \varepsilon\} = 0.$$

Proof

Example 1 shows that for any finite n

$$\mu_{\overline{X}_n} = E[\overline{X}_n] = \mu$$

$$\sigma_{\overline{X}_n}^2 = E[(\overline{X}_n - \mu)^2] = \frac{\sigma^2}{n}$$

Chebyshev's inequality asserts that for any $k > 0$

$$P\{|\overline{X}_n - \mu_{\overline{X}_n}| > k\sigma_{\overline{X}_n}\} \le \frac{1}{k^2}$$

It follows that

$$P\left\{|\overline{X}_n - \mu| > \frac{k\sigma}{\sqrt{n}}\right\} \le \frac{1}{k^2}$$

Let $k = \dfrac{\varepsilon \sqrt{n}}{\sigma}$ for any $\varepsilon > 0$. Then

$$P\{\,|\,\bar{X}_n - \mu\,| > \varepsilon\} \le \frac{\sigma^2}{\varepsilon^2 n}$$

Thus,

$$\lim_{n \to \infty} P\{\,|\,\bar{X}_n - \mu\,| > \varepsilon\} \le \lim_{n \to \infty} \frac{\sigma^2}{\varepsilon^2 n} = 0$$

Because all terms in this sequence of probabilities must be nonnegative,

$$\lim_{n \to \infty} P\{\,|\,\bar{X}_n - \mu\,| > \varepsilon\} = 0 \tag{P.4}$$

regardless of how small ε is chosen to be.   ■

Equation P.4 is the classic law of large numbers, also known as the *weak law of large numbers*. The proof just given assumes that the finite variance of each of the random variables X_i is σ^2. When this is the case, the law of large numbers is a trivial consequence of Chebyshev's inequality.

The restriction that the variance must be finite is actually unnecessary. While the proof uses a different approach, the law of large numbers in the case where the variance does not exist holds true as well.

There also exists a *strong law of large numbers*. The weak law of large numbers asserts that the deviation $|\bar{X}_n - \mu|$ is likely to be small for every particular sufficiently large n but does not imply that it remains small for all large n. It can happen that the law of large numbers applies but that the deviation $|\bar{X}_n - \mu|$ continues to fluctuate, and the only conclusion permitted is that large values of this deviation occur infrequently. In contrast, the strong law of large numbers can be roughly interpreted as saying that with an overwhelming probability the deviation $|\bar{X}_n - \mu|$ *remains* small once n exceeds a certain value.

APPENDIX Q
Derivation of Final Benefit Payment of Fixed-Period Annuity for $n + f$ Years

Curtate expectation of life for a life age x, denoted e_x, is defined as

$$e_x = \frac{1}{l_x} \sum_{t=1}^{\infty} l_{x+t} = \sum_{t=1}^{\infty} {}_t p_x$$

The function e_x may be construed as representing the average (mean) future lifetime at age x. Note that it sums only full years of future lifetime; that is, it adds the probability a life age x survives one full year plus the probability a life age x survives two full years, and so on. It is *curtate*—that is, shortened or abbreviated—in that it ignores final fractional years of life, where the life survives part of the year but not the full year.

Because e_x is not generally an integer—other than by coincidence—it can be represented as $e_x = n + f$, where n is a nonnegative integer and f is a fraction, $0 \le f < 1$.

The mathematical proof that $a_{\overline{e_x}|} > a_x$ for any positive rate of interest i includes a statement that the non-life-contingent fixed-period annuity that runs for $n + f$ years produces in theory a final benefit β at the end of $n + f$ years given by

$$\beta = \frac{(1+i)^f - 1}{i}$$

As expected, the final partial payment is 0 if $f = 0$, is 1 if $f = 1$, and increases at intermediate points. We now derive this benefit formula.

Proof

Because we look to compare the present value of a life annuity-immediate providing annual payments of 1 with the present value of a fixed-period annuity providing annual payments of 1 for n years and a smaller final payment at $n + f$ years (see Figure Q.1), we shall consider both annuities to provide discrete (i.e., not continuous) benefits.

The present value of a fixed-period annuity providing annual benefits of 1 at the end of each year is

$$a_{\overline{n}|} = \frac{1 - v^n}{i} \tag{Q.1}$$

This formula was derived in Chapter 6 from first principles by summing the present values of each individual benefit in seriatim fashion; that is, $a_{\overline{n}|} = v + v^2 + v^3 + \cdots + v^n$.

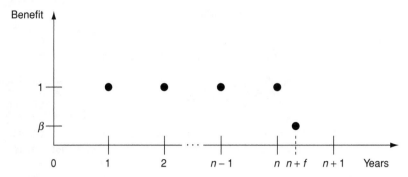

FIGURE Q.1   Fixed-Period Annuity Timeline (annual benefits)

We can, without loss of generality, assume that integers k and m exist such that $f = k/m$, where $k \geq 0$ and $m > 0$. Now let us partition each yearly unit interval on the Figure Q.1 timeline into m equal segments. We seek the benefit amount B that can be paid at the end of each $m$thly segment so as to produce a present value for that year identical to the present value of a single payment of 1 at the end of the year. See Figure Q.2.

The present value (PV) of an n-year fixed-period annuity-immediate paying $m$thly benefits of B is

$$\begin{aligned}
\text{PV} &= B(v^{1/m} + v^{2/m} + \cdots + v^n) \\
&= Bv^{1/m}(1 + v^{1/m} + v^{2/m} + \cdots + v^{n-1/m}) \\
&= Bv^{1/m}\frac{1-v^n}{1-v^{1/m}} \\
&= B\frac{1-v^n}{(1+i)^{1/m}-1}
\end{aligned} \tag{Q.2}$$

Equating the present values in equations Q.1 and Q.2, we find the benefit amount B is

$$B = \frac{(1+i)^{1/m}-1}{i}$$

Thus, from a present value standpoint, a fixed-period annuity with annual end-of-period benefits of 1 is equivalent to a fixed-period annuity with $m$thly end-of-period benefits of B. From a present value standpoint,

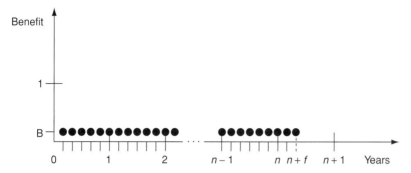

FIGURE Q.2   Fixed-Period Annuity Timeline (*m*thly Benefits)

the annual benefit is interchangeable with the series of *m*thly benefits on any unit subinterval.

With this information, we can extend the series of *m*thly payments that previously spanned *n* years to span *n* + *f* years by adding *k* *m*thly payments of B to the end of the series. The present value of these additional benefits as of commencement of the annuity is

$$PV = v^n \cdot B(v^{1/m} + v^{2/m} + \cdots + v^{k/m})$$

Thus, the total present value of the fixed-period annuity spanning *n* + *f* years is

$$PV = B(v^{1/m} + v^{2/m} + \cdots + v^n + v^{n+1/m} + v^{n+2/m} + \cdots + v^{n+k/m})$$

$$= B \frac{1 - v^{n+k/m}}{(1+i)^{1/m} - 1}$$

$$= \frac{(1+i)^{1/m} - 1}{i} \cdot \frac{1 - v^{n+f}}{(1+i)^{1/m} - 1}$$

$$= \frac{1 - v^{n+f}}{i} \tag{Q.3}$$

The last step is to determine the final partial benefit β payable at time *n* + *f* such that the present value of the annuity comprising annual year-end benefits of 1 for *n* years plus a benefit of β at time *n* + *f* equals the present value of the fixed-period annuity spanning *n* + *f* years shown in equation Q.3:

$$\frac{1 - v^n}{i} + \beta v^{n+f} = \frac{1 - v^{n+f}}{i}$$

whence

$$\beta = \frac{(1+i)^f - 1}{i}$$

Q.E.D. ■

Note that we could simply have given meaning to the symbol $a_{\overline{n+f}|}$ for a positive integer n and $0 \le f < 1$ by applying equation Q.1:

$$a_{\overline{n+f}|} = \frac{1 - v^{n+f}}{i}$$

$$= \frac{1 - v^n + v^n - v^{n+f}}{i}$$

$$= a_{\overline{n}|} + v^{n+f} \cdot \frac{(1+i)^f - 1}{i}$$

Thus, $a_{\overline{n+f}|}$ is the present value of an n-year annuity-immediate of 1 per annum plus a final payment at time $n + f$ of $[(1 + i)^f - 1]/i$.

While this trivial mechanical extension of the annuity-immediate present value formula $a_{\overline{n}|}$ to $a_{\overline{n+f}|}$ arrives at the same conclusion, this is not very satisfying or explanatory. The preceding proof provides a fuller basis for the grounds under which the claim is made that a fixed-period annuity with fractional term $n + f$ produces a final payment of $[(1 + i)^f - 1]/i$ at the end of $n + f$ years.

APPENDIX R
1971 Individual Annuity Mortality Table

	1,000 q_x			1,000 q_x	
Age (x)	Male	Female	Age (x)	Male	Female
5	0.456	0.234	40	1.633	0.938
6	0.424	0.193	41	1.789	1.013
7	0.403	0.162	42	2.000	1.094
8	0.392	0.143	43	2.260	1.186
9	0.389	0.134	44	2.569	1.286
10	0.390	0.132	45	2.922	1.397
11	0.397	0.143	46	3.318	1.519
12	0.405	0.155	47	3.754	1.654
13	0.413	0.167	48	4.228	1.802
14	0.422	0.180	49	4.740	1.967
15	0.433	0.193	50	5.285	2.151
16	0.444	0.205	51	5.860	2.371
17	0.457	0.218	52	6.461	2.641
18	0.471	0.231	53	7.088	2.966
19	0.486	0.245	54	7.740	3.351
20	0.503	0.260	55	8.417	3.791
21	0.522	0.275	56	9.119	4.284
22	0.544	0.292	57	9.850	4.826
23	0.566	0.309	58	10.613	5.409
24	0.591	0.327	59	11.411	6.017
25	0.619	0.347	60	12.249	6.628
26	0.650	0.368	61	13.133	7.219
27	0.684	0.390	62	14.073	7.773
28	0.722	0.414	63	15.083	8.285
29	0.763	0.440	64	16.185	8.775
30	0.809	0.469	65	17.405	9.290
31	0.860	0.499	66	18.767	9.888
32	0.916	0.533	67	20.290	10.622
33	0.978	0.569	68	21.992	11.536
34	1.046	0.608	69	23.890	12.664
35	1.122	0.651	70	26.000	14.029
36	1.204	0.698	71	28.341	15.651
37	1.295	0.750	72	30.933	17.548
38	1.397	0.807	73	33.801	19.742
39	1.509	0.869	74	36.976	22.256

APPENDIX R

1971 Individual Annuity Mortality Table *(Continued)*

	1,000 q_x			1,000 q_x	
Age (x)	Male	Female	Age (x)	Male	Female
75	40.494	25.120	95	283.841	219.896
76	44.393	28.369	96	311.565	231.097
77	48.715	32.050	97	340.214	242.211
78	53.500	36.225	98	369.769	253.823
79	58.787	40.975	99	400.194	266.452
80	64.599	46.386	100	431.413	280.535
81	70.902	52.513	101	463.312	296.449
82	77.668	59.409	102	495.756	314.535
83	84.941	67.160	103	528.599	335.121
84	92.874	75.899	104	561.692	358.537
85	101.689	85.770	105	594.884	385.122
86	111.652	96.898	106	628.022	415.238
87	123.048	109.338	107	660.949	449.274
88	136.123	122.978	108	693.503	487.649
89	151.070	137.508	109	725.521	530.787
90	168.040	152.472	110	756.852	579.040
91	187.147	167.370	111	787.390	632.529
92	208.457	181.776	112	817.125	690.903
93	231.885	195.386	113	846.198	753.081
94	257.146	208.071	114	874.915	817.218
			115	1000.000	1000.000

APPENDIX S
1983 Table *a*

Age (x)	1,000 q_x Male	1,000 q_x Female	Age (x)	1,000 q_x Male	1,000 q_x Female
5	0.377	0.194	40	1.341	0.742
6	0.350	0.160	41	2.492	0.801
7	0.333	0.134	42	2.673	0.867
8	0.352	0.134	43	1.886	0.942
9	0.368	0.136	44	2.129	1.026
10	0.382	0.141	45	2.399	1.122
11	0.394	0.147	46	2.693	1.231
12	0.405	0.155	47	3.009	1.356
13	0.415	0.165	48	3.343	1.499
14	0.425	0.175	49	3.694	1.657
15	0.435	0.188	50	4.057	1.830
16	0.446	0.201	51	4.431	2.016
17	0.458	0.214	52	4.812	2.215
18	0.472	0.229	53	5.198	2.426
19	0.488	0.244	54	5.591	2.650
20	0.505	0.260	55	5.994	2.891
21	0.525	0.276	56	6.409	3.151
22	0.546	0.293	57	6.839	3.432
23	0.570	0.311	58	7.290	3.739
24	0.596	0.330	59	7.782	4.081
25	0.622	0.349	60	8.338	4.467
26	0.650	0.368	61	8.983	4.908
27	0.677	0.387	62	9.740	5.413
28	0.704	0.405	63	10.630	5.990
29	0.731	0.423	64	11.664	6.633
30	0.759	0.441	65	12.851	7.336
31	0.786	0.460	66	14.199	8.090
32	0.814	0.479	67	15.717	8.888
33	0.843	0.499	68	17.414	9.731
34	0.876	0.521	69	19.296	10.653
35	0.917	0.545	70	21.371	11.697
36	0.968	0.574	71	23.647	12.905
37	1.032	0.607	72	26.131	14.319
38	1.114	0.646	73	28.835	15.980
39	1.216	0.691	74	31.794	17.909

APPENDIX S

1983 Table *a (Continued)*

| | 1,000 q_x | | | | 1,000 q_x | |
Age (x)	Male	Female	Age (x)	Male	Female
75	35.046	20.127	95	191.214	174.228
76	38.631	22.654	96	204.721	186.535
77	42.587	25.509	97	219.120	198.646
78	46.951	28.717	98	234.735	211.102
79	51.755	32.328	99	251.889	224.445
80	57.026	36.395	100	270.906	239.215
81	62.791	40.975	101	292.111	255.953
82	69.081	46.121	102	315.826	275.201
83	75.908	51.889	103	342.377	297.500
84	83.230	58.336	104	372.086	323.390
85	90.987	65.518	105	405.278	353.414
86	99.122	73.493	106	442.277	388.111
87	107.577	82.318	107	483.406	428.023
88	116.316	92.017	108	528.989	473.692
89	125.394	102.491	109	579.351	525.658
90	134.887	113.605	110	634.814	584.462
91	144.873	125.227	111	695.704	650.646
92	155.429	137.222	112	762.343	724.750
93	166.629	149.462	113	835.056	807.316
94	178.537	161.834	114	914.167	898.885
			115	1000.000	1000.000

Quotable Wisdom
Regarding Longevity

Nobody loves life like an old man. —Sophocles

Certainly old age has a great sense of calm and freedom; when the passions relax their hold, then, as Sophocles says, you have escaped from the control not of one master, but of many. —Plato

---

Father Time is not always a hard parent, and, though he tarries for none of his children, often lays his hand lightly on those who have used him well. —Charles Dickens

---

I am profoundly grateful to old age, which has increased my eagerness for conversation and taken away that for food and drink. —Cicero

---

Every man desires to live long; but no man would be old. —Jonathan Swift

---

For just as I approve of a young man in whom there is a touch of age, so I approve of the old man in whom there is some of the flavor of youth. He who strives thus to mingle youthfulness and age may grow old in body, but old in spirit he will never be. —Cicero

---

Let us cherish and love old age; for it is full of pleasure, if one knows how to use it. The best morsel is reserved to the last. —Seneca

---

And in the end, it's not the years in your life that count. It's the life in your years. —Abraham Lincoln

Notes

PREFACE

1. Kelvin, Lord, *Popular Lectures and Addresses* (1891–1894).
2. Ruskin, John, *Stones of Venice*, Volume III, *The Fall*.

CHAPTER 1   Retirement Income Basics

1. By permission. From the *Merriam-Webster Online Dictionary* © 2005 by Merriam-Webster, Incorporated (www.Merriam-Webster.com).
2. A lifetime annuity can cover three or more lives as well; covering one or two lives is by far more common.
3. Periodic income benefits can typically be for annual, semiannual, quarterly, or monthly payment frequency modes. For simplicity—and because it is the frequency mode most commonly chosen—throughout this book, we will assume retirement income benefits will be paid monthly.
4. While you *could* choose to just live off your interest under the self-management program and never invade principal, you would have a lower amount of income—and likely a lower standard of living—than if you elected a fixed annuity. A fixed annuity is calculated to safely provide higher monthly income, paying out interest plus some return of principal with each payment, without ever having to fear running out of money. It obviates the need for a retiree to figure out how to systematically spend down principal.
5. To remove the mystery of how an annuity program—whether offered by an insurer or created by members of a community, a church, or any other organization—can safely provide lifetime income, this is briefly described in this opening chapter and fully described later in the book.
6. Actual probabilities of falling in each bin from left to right are: 1/64, 6/64, 15/64, 20/64, 15/64, 6/64, 1/64. Probability literature calls this structure of pins a "binomial lattice," where the probability of a ball falling to the left of the pin is 50%, as is the probability of a ball falling to the right.
7. While any single trial of the game may produce slightly different results, the basic shape the balls form tends to remain the same. The more balls used in the game, the greater the tendency to form a shape closer to a bell-shaped curve. For those conversant in the parlance of probability theory, this improves the approximation of the normal distribution by the binomial distribution.
8. That is, benefits can be level, can form a linear progression, or can form a geometric progression.

9. This is called a "cash refund" annuity when any excess of the single premium applied to purchase the annuity over the cumulative retirement income benefits paid out prior to the annuitant's death is refunded to the beneficiary in a single lump sum. It is called an "installment refund" annuity when any such excess is paid out to the beneficiary in continuing installments equal in dollar amount and payment frequency to what the annuitant was receiving, until the cumulative total of all benefits paid both before and after the annuitant's death equals the premium applied to buy the annuity.

10. This is because if funds in the pool were continually available to annuitants, those annuitants who learned of health impairments suggesting they wouldn't survive much longer would choose to remove their funds from the pool, leaving inadequate funds to pay annuitants who survive to very advanced ages. The technical term for this phenomenon is "mortality anti-selection."

11. These variable subaccounts are invested in special insurance series funds. While analogous to publicly available mutual funds, they are technically not retail mutual funds but rather distinct insurance series funds used in variable annuity and variable life insurance products. Indeed, with limited exceptions, publicly available mutual funds cannot be used in variable annuity products. More on the legal structure of these funds appears later in Chapter 15.

12. Some variable annuity contracts may limit the frequency of investment reallocation. Too frequent reallocations, often performed by so-called "market timers," can negatively impact fund performance due to extra trading commissions, to investment managers holding more low-return cash investments in anticipation of such trades, and so on.

13. While 83% of employers offered traditional defined benefit plans in 1993, only 45% did in 2003, according to Hewitt Associates.

    While 112,000 defined benefit plans existed in 1985, fewer then 30,000 existed in 2004 (PBGC Pension Insurance Data Book 2004, Reference Table S-31).

14. Toffler, Alvin, *Future Shock* (New York: Bantam Books, 1970).

15. An *arithmetic* average simply adds up the annual returns and divides by the number of annual returns. Here, it would add up five returns of –2% and five returns of 18%, arrive at a total of 80%, and divide by 10 to produce an arithmetic average of 8%.

    A *geometric* average finds the product (1 + annual return for Year 1) × (1 + annual return for Year 2) × · · · × (1 + annual return for Year *n*) and takes the *n*th root of that product to arrive at (1 + Geometric Average Return). Here, it would multiply [1+ (–2%)] by itself five times, multiply [1 + 18%] by itself five times, multiply these two results together, arrive at a total of 2.068, and take the tenth root to produce a geometric average of 7.54%.

    Whether we call the average in this example 8% or 7.54% is a matter of definition. Either way, the point is that a static 8% annual rate of return assumption in a world that produces a wide variety of annual rates of return that happens to average the one you assume can still jeopardize your financial program, having you run out of money when a (too simplistic) financial model suggested you'd be fine.

16. *Stochastic* process is synonymous with *random* process, the former term used when a time parameter is introduced. A *determinisitic* model provides a func-

tion giving a value of the item of interest, whereas a *stochastic* model gives a probability distribution.

17. For a purely mathematical treatment of this subject, see "Random Walk and Ruin Problems" (Chapter XIV) in William Feller, *An Introduction to Probability Theory and Its Applications, Volume I,* 3rd ed. (New York: John Wiley & Sons, 1968).

    For a highly technical treatise on this subject as it applies to this very situation, see "Self-Annuitization and Ruin in Retirement" by Moshe Arye Milevsky and Chris Robinson, *North American Actuarial Journal,* (4). © 2000 by the Society of Actuaries. Reprinted with permission. They more precisely define probability of ruin as the probability that the stochastic present value of consumption is greater than initial investable wealth.

CHAPTER 2   Annuity Categorization

1. By permission. From the *Merriam-Webster Online Dictionary* © 2005 by Merriam-Webster, Incorporated (www.Merriam-Webster.com).

2. These are further classified as an *annuity-due* when the first benefit is paid at the start of the payment frequency period and as an *annuity-immediate* when the first benefit is paid at the end of the payment frequency period. For example, if a $300,000 single premium is applied to the purchase of an immediate annuity on January 1, it may provide a first *annuity-due* quarterly benefit payment of $6,000 on January 1 or a first *annuity-immediate* quarterly benefit payment of $6,075 on March 31.

3. Some immediate annuity contracts call for the present value of the remaining non-life-contingent payments to be paid to the annuitant's estate if no beneficiary is named or if all beneficiaries predecease the annuitant.

CHAPTER 3   Immediate Fixed Annuity Mechanics (Non-Life-Contingent)

1. This section is extracted in part from the VARDS Executive Series report, "The Mechanics of Variable Annuitization," by Jeffrey K. Dellinger © 1994. Reprinted with the permission of Morningstar, Inc. VARDS is the Variable Annuity Research and Data Service founded by Rick Carey.

2. The Society of Actuaries (SOA) is a nonprofit professional organization society of about 17,000 members involved in the modeling and management of financial risk and contingent events. The mission of the SOA is to advance actuarial knowledge and to enhance the ability of actuaries to provide expert advice and relevant solutions for financial, business, and societal problems involving uncertain future events. Source: Society of Actuaries.

    For example, actuaries tend to be responsible for the design, implementation, and stewardship of public and private retirement security systems that provide an adequate standard of living after wage-earning years. They are the custodians of financial integrity for immediate annuity policyholders, pension plan participants, and Social Security taxpayers. As architects of financial security systems, actuaries—while few in number, with only six people in a million worldwide being actuaries—have astronomical impact. In the United States, their work is guided by Actuarial Standards of Practice adopted by the Actuarial Standards Board.

"Utilitarianism as a philosophy, and risk aversion as a feature of human psychology, lead to the evolution of financial security systems as a means of reducing the financial consequences of unfavorable events. Actuaries are those with a deep understanding of financial security systems, their reasons for being, their complexity, their mathematics, and the way they work." *Fundamental Concepts of Actuarial Science*, Charles L. Trowbridge, © 1989 by The Actuarial Foundation, pp. 12–13. Reprinted with permission.

3. Fixed-income securities include such instruments as Treasury bills, notes, and bonds; corporate bonds; mortgage loans; asset-backed securities; and mortgage-backed securities. (For more information about fixed-income securities, see *The Fixed Income Securities Handbook*, 6th ed., Frank J. Fabozzi, ed. [New York: McGraw-Hill, 2001].)

4. A 2004 survey by Milliman, Inc., a consulting firm, reveals that insurance companies writing immediate fixed annuity business invest nearly 70% of the premiums in investment-grade public corporate bonds and commercial mortgages. The average investment mix reported by survey participants is:

Asset Type	Percentage
Investment-grade public corporate bonds	54.3%
Commercial mortgages	15.6%
Private placements	9.0%
Commercial mortgage obligations (CMO)	5.1%
Non-investment-grade corporate bonds	5.0%
Asset-backed securities (ABS)	4.5%
Common stocks	0.0%
Other	5.6%

Source: Sue Sell, "Focus on Immediate Annuities," *Product Matters!* Society of Actuaries Product Development Section Newsletter (November 2004). © 2004 by the Society of Actuaries. Reprinted with permission.

5. Reprinted with permission of the National Association of Insurance Commissioners.

6. Early thinking regarding a systematic approach to recognize that the value of insurance company surplus (Surplus = Assets − Liabilities) may change due to interest rate changes affecting assets and liabilities differently may be found in "Discussion of the Preliminary Report of the Committee on Valuation and Related Problems," *Record of the Society of Actuaries* 5(1), pp. 241–284, © 1979 Society of Actuaries. The approach uses first principles of valuation and seeks to derive a provision for interst rate risk, dubbed C_3 risk, since it was the third type of contingency involved in the study. Provision for asset value depreciation (e.g., bond defaults, stock price declines) constituted C_1 risk, while provision for pricing inadequacy (e.g., morbidity or mortality experience deviation attributable to chance variation) constituted C_2 risk. Today, C_4 constitutes general business risk (e.g., regulatory, accounting, managerial) and C_5 constitues foreign exchange risk.

CHAPTER 4   Immediate Variable Annuity Mechanics (Non-Life-Contingent)

1. Copyright © 2005 National Association of Securities Dealers, Inc. (NASD). Reprinted with permission from NASD.
2. Reprinted with permission of the National Association of Insurance Commissioners.
3. Electronic transmission of funds is less expensive for the insurer. While hard-coded checks are more expensive for the insurer to issue, annuitants don't always cash these promptly. During the interim, the insurer benefits from the "float," which is the interest it continues to earn on these funds before they are transferred.
4. Copyright © 2005 The McGraw-Hill Companies, Inc. Standard & Poor's, including its subsidiary corporations ("S&P"), is a division of the McGraw-Hill Companies, Inc.

CHAPTER 5   Annuity Payout Options

1. For example, the present value of each of the three different series of annuity payments shown in Figure 4.6 and Table 4.2 of Chapter 4 (one series each at 3% AIR, 5% AIR, and 7% AIR) at the 12% actual rate of return experienced is $8,107.82. This point will receive elaboration in the concluding section of this chapter, "Value Equivalence of Annuity Options."
2. Other insurers might prefer annuity options such as a single "life only" annuity that instead give them a greater possibility of gains from mortality experience that results in fewer benefit payments than they assumed.
3. Equivalently called and previously also known as an "N Years Certain and Continuous (C&C)" annuity option. It is "continuous" in the sense that payments continue for a lifetime following the N-year certain period. It is not "continuous" in the sense of an annuity with payments made continuously (as opposed to discretely). This latter terminology is used in academic studies of immediate annuities involving continuous mathematical functions rather than discrete mathematical functions, where modal payment frequencies increase from one per year (annual payments) to two per year (semiannual) to four (quarterly) to twelve (monthly) to twenty-four (semimonthly) to twenty-six (biweekly), and ultimately toward their limiting frequency, which is tiny payments made continually.
4. One exception to the prohibition against life insurance in the IRA market is certain life insurance elements considered *de minimis* in nature, such as guaranteed minimum death benefits in *deferred* variable annuities, sometimes used as IRA funding vehicles.
5. Higher benefit frequency increases insurance company administrative expenses, although to the extent these are increasingly electronic (e.g., electronic funds transfer of annuity benefit payments to an annuitant's bank account), the increases are less severe. Some contracts reserve the right for the insurer to reduce benefit frequency if payouts (either in total or from any specific subaccount) fall beneath some minimum level (e.g., $50). There is typically a stagger between the *valuation date* that determines the amount of an immediate

variable annuity benefit payment and the *payment date* on which this amount is transferred to the annuitant. The number of days in between these events is stated in the contract and the prospectus. This gives insurers time to calculate the dollar amount of annuity benefit, sell the appropriate number of units, update records, and issue payment.

6. See Chapter 8 for rate of return examples.

7. Shorter-term cash flows tend to be associated with lower interest rates, while longer-term cash flows tend to be associated with higher interest rates. Theories abound as to why the term structure of interest rates takes on various shapes and cyclically changes. These include that the yield curve simply reflects expected future yields on short-term maturity bonds; that different investor groups have different liquidity preferences (e.g., commercial banks may prefer shorter-maturity assets to pair with demand deposits, while pension funds may have a bias toward longer-maturity assets); and that investors demand greater reward for assuming the greater risks associated with longer-term investing, including greater vulnerability to price declines when interest rates rise and simply greater uncertainty over what financial difficulties the borrower may experience over a longer time horizon.

   The important point is that interest rates tend not to be uniform but rather to increase the further into the future the payments are due. As a result, for their own personal assessment of value, prospective IVA contract owners might choose to discount nearer-term IVA benefits using lower interest rates, which results in higher present values, and to discount longer-term payments at higher interest rates, which results in lower present values.

CHAPTER 6   Annuitant Populations and Annuity Present Values

1. Some insurers may perform immediate annuity underwriting in the sense that they will only accept premiums above a certain minimum amount or below a certain maximum amount. Premiums below some minimum size are too small to be profitable. Premiums above some maximum size may place undue concentration of mortality risk for the insurer on one life or a few lives, potentially causing unacceptably large earnings fluctuations, although this may be ameliorated through reinsurance. One of the underlying tenets of insurance—including longevity insurance offered through immediate annuities—is a relatively homogeneous group of exposure units (see Mehr, Robert I. and Emerson Cammack, *Principles of Insurance*, 6th ed. [Homewood, IL: Richard D. Irwin, Inc. 1976], 34).

2. This mnemonic is found in Chan, Beda, "Geometric Solutions to Stationary Population Problems," *Transactions of the Society of Actuaries* 33:583–616. © 1981 Society of Actuaries.

3. "Pachinko" is a Japanese game of chance where winning is similarly predicated on balls dropping through a lattice of pins into an array of bins.

4. It is important to note that by discounting each future annuity payment at the 5% AIR, we arrive at a smaller present value of the stream of annuity payments than if we didn't discount for interest, that is, if we used a 0% interest rate. Because the level of the initial immediate annuity benefit is determined by divid-

ing the net premium by the present value of the annuity, the end result is a higher first annuity payment than would have been the case had a 0% interest rate been used, that is, if we hadn't discounted for interest. Since the annuitant is given credit for a 5% investment return per year in construction of the first annuity benefit, this is why 5% of investment performance must be "backed out" of the annuity unit value calculation each year. Otherwise, there would be double counting, with the annuitant receiving a higher first annuity benefit because of using a 5% investment return assumption and then again when that 5% investment return actually materializes.

5. The precomputer era shortcut involved "commutation functions" such as D_x and N_x. These are somewhat antiquated in the computer age, some might even say quaintly archaic (having been designed to facilitate calculations in the precomputer era), but admirably serve the purposes of immediate variable annuities since one uniform investment rate (the AIR) is assumed for all durations of the projection. Furthermore, commutation functions simplify formulas. Immediate fixed annuities, in contrast, typically have payments at different durations discounted by different interest rates (i.e., an interest rate vector), with those interest rates typically being based on the shape and height of the Treasury yield curve (plus adjustments for the various asset classes actually used and any options embedded in those assets) at the time a fixed annuity is sold. Financial economics, based on the principle of "no arbitrage," provides a framework for discounting a series of cash flows to arrive at what is today perceived as the appropriate current value.

6. The derivatives $f^{(n)}$ of all orders exist on the radius of convergence $(a - R, a + R)$; that is, the function f is *infinitely differentiable* on the interval $(a - R, a + R)$. The proof is straightforward. While not given here, it can be found in standard calculus textbooks; e.g., Louis Leithold, *The Calculus with Analytic Geometry*, 2nd ed. (New York: Harper & Row, 1972).

7. Recall that $D_x = v^x l_x$. For the function $f(x) = v^x = e^{-\delta x}$, we have $f^{(1)}(x) = -\delta v^x = -\delta e^{-\delta x}$ and $f^{(2)}(x) = \delta^2 v^x = \delta^2 e^{-\delta x}$. Since $f^{(2)}(x)$ is greater than 0 for all x, the graph of $f(x) = v^x$ is concave upward. Figures 6.1 and 6.28 indicate the function $g(x) = l_x$ is concave downward at the most common IVA issue ages and for some years thereafter, then has a point of inflection, and thereafter is concave upward for the more advanced years of the mortality table. Figure 6.17 indicates the net effect of the $f(x) = v^x$ and $g(x) = l_x$ functions is a concave upward graph for $D_x = f(x) \cdot g(x) = v^x l_x$ for the age range shown.

8. Common assumptions regarding the nature of mortality patterns within a unit age interval are (1) UDD, (2) constant force of mortality, and (3) the Balducci hypothesis. These will be described in a later section. Note that in contrast to a uniform distribution of deaths within a unit age interval, a constantly increasing force of mortality would suggest that more of total deaths within a year occur nearer the end than during an equally long fraction of a year nearer the beginning.

9. The force of mortality, μ_x, is an instantaneous measure of the intensity with which mortality is operating at each moment in time, serving to decrease the number of lives l_x. This index measure of the instantaneous variation in intensity with which mortality operates will be described in detail later in this chapter.

10. The study of variable income annuities—to which actuarial science contributes a great deal—is more than musings in a "theorist's paradise." While elegant mathematics is involved, the breadth of practical application worldwide is staggeringly large.

11. "Then the Lord said, 'I will not allow people to live forever; they are mortal. From now on they will live no longer than 120 years.'" (Genesis 6:3) "Moses was a hundred and twenty years old when he died, yet his eyes were not weak nor his strength gone." (Deuteronomy 34.7)

12. Dr. Leonard Hayflick observed in the 1960s that certain cells wouldn't divide more than a finite number of times, suggesting aging to be a cellular process. Perhaps a "genetic clock" resides in the cell nucleus. Intervention into the Hayflick limit is possible (by repressing certain active genes or activating certain repressed genes). For example, certain types of cells (bone marrow, cancer) don't obey the Hayflick rule, so determining what makes these cells different provides clues.

   A Harvard Medical School and Children's Hospital study published in the June 2004 journal *Nature* describes this dynamism. Studies of 11,000 genes in brain tissue of deceased people showed about 400 genes that experienced significant changes in how hard they had been working before and after age 40. Slightly less than half of these 400 or so genes, including those associated with learning and memory, functioned at a lower level after age 40, possibly due to damage. The other half, including those associated with DNA repair, worked harder after age 40. This suggests a "genetic signature" to the aging process— one set of genes sustains damage that impedes its ability to instruct cells to make certain proteins, while another set works harder to repair that damage. These may serve as important physical markers to help scientists gain insight into the aging process and gauge its degree of advancement in individuals.

13. Aging is a byproduct of this repair deficit. Perhaps the architect of our universe allowed for such a dynamic nature of genetic material precisely to permit species to evolve in such a way as to continually acclimate to their changing environment. The level of the DNA repair rate—by the collection of enzymes within each cell that recognize and repair damage—programmed into different species has been experimentally shown to correlate highly with the maximum life span of different species.

14. Lower death rates among certain religious groups that strictly require certain healthy behaviors (e.g., abstention from alcohol, smoking) demonstrate that salutary lifestyles are indeed conducive to longevity.

15. *World Health Report 2002*, Annex Table 16, World Health Organization.

16. "Report of the Committee to Recommend a New Mortality Basis for Individual Annuity Valuation (Derivation of the 1983 Table *a*)," *Transactions of the Society of Actuaries* 33. © 1982 Society of Actuaries.

17. Omram, Abdel R. "The Epidemiologic Transition: A Theory of the Epidemiology of Population Change," *The Milbank Memorial Fund Quarterly* (October): 509–538 (1971).

18. Olshansky, S. Jay, and A. Brian Ault, "The Fourth Stage of the Epidemiological Transition: The Age of Delayed Degenerative Diseases," *The Milbank Quarterly* 64(3): 355–391 (1986).

19. Johansen, Robert J., "Annuity 2000 Mortality Tables," *Transactions of the Society of Actuaries, 1995–96 Reports:* 263. © 1998 Society of Actuaries.

20. National Center for Health Statistics *Monthly Vital Statistics Report* 43, no. 13 (October 23, 1995); and 44, no. 12 (July 24, 1996).

21. Note that technically the graph shows an increase in median survival age, rather than life expectancy per se.

22. Bell, F., *Social Security Area Population Projections: 1997*, Actuarial Study no. 112 (Washington, DC: Social Security Administration, 1997).

23. See Tindall, Drew, and Jess Mast, "A Credible Theory of Credibility," *Contingencies* (September/October 2003). © 2003 American Academy of Actuaries.

24. Johansen, Robert J., "Annuity 2000 Mortality Tables," *Transactions of the Society of Actuaries, 1995-96 Reports:* 263. © 1998 Society of Actuaries.

25. Ibid.

26. Metaphysically, some might say we are living in one universe that happened to explode in precisely such a manner as to produce particles and physical and chemical laws that permitted the evolution of complicated structures (humans) capable of contemplating themselves, their own longevity, and their own mortality. (And today, one might add, capable of contemplating optimization of financial management associated with the last two items!)

27. "It is not the strongest of the species that survive, not the most intelligent, but the one most responsive to change." Attributed to Charles Darwin, scientist.

28. Insurance companies need to guard against the opportunity for a consumer to arbitrage the difference in mortality assumptions between life insurance and immediate annuities. This can occur if (1) a very healthy individual buys a life insurance policy at preferred rates and an immediate annuity at standard rates or (2) an unhealthy individual buys a life insurance policy at standard rates (perhaps due to agent persuasion of the underwriter) and an immediate annuity at substandard rates.

    The consumer borrows money and buys an immediate annuity. Annuity benefit payments pay loan interest, with the remainder purchasing a life insurance policy with a face amount greater than the loan. The death benefit exceeds the loan amount, guaranteeing a gain. The mispricing of the mortality cost must be large enough to overcome product loads for expenses and profit. Capital markets can quickly amass and direct large sums of money to exploit such arbitrage opportunities resulting from uneven pricing.

29. Gompertz, Benjamin, "On the Nature of the Function Expressive of the Law of Human Mortality, and on a New Mode of Determining the Value of Life Contingencies," *Philosophical Transactions of the Royal Society of London,* Vol. 115 (1825):513–585.

30. Makeham, W. M., "On the Law of Mortality, and the Construction of Annuity Tables," *Journal of the Institute of Actuaries* 8 (1860).

31. Makeham, W. M., "On the Law of Mortality," *Journal of the Institute of Actuaries* 13:325–358 (1867).

32. The use of intercompany studies obviously allows for a greater amount of source data, improving credibility of results. Another benefit is that in a competitive marketplace, anomalies may occur peculiar to any single company. For example,

Company A may be selected for IVA business placement by financial advisers due to its favorable payout rates on nonrefund (i.e., straight life only) annuity options (single or joint), perhaps because it fails to price differently for this healthier class of business. As a result, mortality rates premised on a study of this company alone may be lower than for all companies writing this category of business.

There has been no *industrywide* individual immediate annuity mortality experience study for over a quarter century. The report "Mortality under Individual Immediate Annuities, Life Income Settlements, and Matured Deferred Annuities between 1971 and 1976 Anniversaries" published in the 1979 *Reports of Mortality and Morbidity Experience of the Transactions of the Society of Actuaries* represents the most recent available experience. (A more recent study covering the 1976–1986 experience period included only eight companies, none of which provided data for the entire period.) Because the 1971–1976 experience is approximately centered on 1973, the mortality results therein obtained were projected about 10 years to create the 1983 Table *a* used for individual annuity valuation. The Annuity 2000 Mortality Table was subsequently derived effectively by projecting the 1983 Table *a* forward 17 years. Since pricing and reserving for income annuities—and the related financial health of the annuity industry—depend on reasonably accurate and current annuitant mortality data, more frequent intercompany experience studies may emerge with the growth of income annuities and their concomitant importance to insurance company sales and earnings.

33. For example, Robert W. Batten's *Mortality Table Construction* (Englewood Cliffs, NJ: Prentice-Hall, 1978) is an excellent volume on the subject.
34. The minimum allowable statutory valuation reserves are *necessary* as a result of law but may not be *sufficient*, either because (1) the situation at hand demands higher reserves even if predicted mortality plays out in actual experience or (2) future experience deviates substantially from assumptions on which minimum valuation standards are premised today.
35. Greenwood, M., and J. O. Irwin, "The Biostatistics of Senility," *Human Biology* 11:1–23 (1939).
36. Wetterstrand, W. H. "Parametric Models for Life Insurance Mortality Data: Gompertz's Law Over Time," *Transactions of the Society of Actuaries* 33:159–179 (1981). © 1982 Society of Actuaries.

    A computer program uses mortality rates (q values) as input and produces a graph containing approximate values of the force of mortality (μ values) from which estimates of B and c are obtained. The exact methodology is described in the preceding reference. Briefly, the force of mortality can be estimated from mortality rates by the approximation $\mu_{x+\frac{1}{2}} \approx -ln(1 - q_x)$. Since $\mu_x = Bc^x = e^{\alpha + \gamma x}$, then $\ln \mu_x = \alpha + \gamma_x$, which is a linear equation. A least-squares linear regression line is fitted to $\ln \mu_x$, which yields values for α and γ. Since $B = e^\alpha$ and $c = e^\gamma$, estimates of parameters B and c from Gompertz's law result.
37. Scientists and mathematicians aspire to find broader, higher level, more general equations of which previously determined phenomena or equations merely happen to be special cases. For example, in the field of probability theory, the uniform probability distribution is a special case of the more general beta dis-

tribution, and the exponential probability distribution is a special case of the more general gamma distribution.

Albert Einstein particularly sought such simplifying general cases. One might have thought Einstein's discovery of the general theory of relativity reducing gravity and inertia to the same phenomenon would have been quite enough! Yet even after Einstein's proclamation of his general theory of relativity equating the (previously two) forces of gravity and inertia, he further wanted to remove complexity and move toward simplicity by uniting gravitational and electromagnetic fields by developing a "unified field theory" that would unite gravitation and electromagnetism in one set of mathematical equations. This desire went unfulfilled. (James Clerk Maxwell had previously unified electricity and magnetism in the late nineteenth century.)

In scientific theory, the principle known as *Occam's Razor* ("eliminate all unnecessary assumptions") states that of two theories supporting the same consequences, the superior theory is the one that involves the less restrictive assumptions. This extends to theories governing laws of mortality.

38. Heligman, L., and J. Pollard, "The Age Pattern of Mortality," *Journal of the Institute of Actuaries* 107: 49–75 (1980).

39. Peter Bernstein, author of *Against the Gods, the Remarkable Story of Risk*, in a CNN/*Money* interview, October 15, 2004.

40. Actuarial organizations conduct mortality experience studies, as do governmental organizations. These are based on a number of factors, especially the definition of the group under study (e.g., life insurance policyholders, annuitants, pensioners, general population). Within an immediate variable annuitant group under study, results may be subdivided by age, gender, and annuity payout option. For example, one might expect annuitants electing "life only" annuities to exhibit more favorable mortality experience than other life-contingent options, since annuitants with greater health impairments might tend to elect annuity options with stronger guarantees, such as certain periods or refund features.

41. It is actually the case that an annuity for a fixed period of time equal to life expectancy costs more (i.e., has a higher present value) than a lifetime annuity. In symbols, $a_{\overline{e_x}|} > a_x$ whenever the assumed interest rate $i > 0$. The proof is given in the section that follows this section.

42. Jordan, Chester Wallace, Jr., *Life Contingencies*, 2nd ed. (Chicago: Society of Actuaries, 1975), 173–175. © 1975 Society of Actuaries.

43. "Life Expectancy Hits Record High," CDC National Center for Health Statistics, February 28, 2005.

44. Bolnick, Howard J., "A Framework for Long-Term Actuarial Projections of Health Care Costs: The Importance of Population Aging and Other Factors," *North American Actuarial Journal*, 8, no. 4:1–29. © 2004 Society of Actuaries.

45. Ibid.

46. The maximum value occurs at the point i_0 such that the first derivative of equation 6.46 at i_0 equals 0; that is, where $f'(i_0) = 0$.

47. *Integration by parts* is used to evaluate the integral. The formula for the differential of a product of functions u and v is given by

$$d(uv) = u\, dv + v\, du$$

and thus

$$u\, dv = d(uv) - v\, du$$

on which integrating both sides we have

$$\int u\, dv = uv - \int v\, du$$

Let $u = y$ and $dv = l_y\mu_y\, dy$, in which case $du = dy$ and $v = -l_y$. Then

$$\int y l_y\mu_y\, dy = -y\, l_y + \int l_y\, dy$$
$$= -y\, l_y - T_y$$

Differentiation verifies that terms on both sides of the final equation are equal.
48. The so-called "broken-heart syndrome" or "mortality of bereavement" is the phenomenon whereby during the early months of bereavement following the death of a beloved spouse widows and widowers exhibit higher mortality rates. This mortality dependence of paired lives, if recognized, results in lower annuity prices and lower annuity reserves for last-survivor annuity options when compared to the same values assuming independence. Pairs of individuals, such as a husband and wife, can exhibit dependence in mortality because they share common environmental factors, for example, common lifestyles. Pairs of individuals, such as siblings, can exhibit dependence in mortality because they share common genetic factors as well as possibly sharing common environmental factors. Statistical tools are used to examine dependency between random variables, such as the mortality of a pair of annuitants.
49. For those who purchased a deferred variable annuity, this illustrates the difference between electing a variable annuitization and taking systematic withdrawals.

CHAPTER 7   Immediate Variable Annuity Subaccounts

1. Variable annuities must satisfy a multiplicity of rules—state insurance laws; SEC, Department of Labor, and Employee Retirement Income Security Act (ERISA) regulations; Internal Revenue Code; and so on—making simultaneous compliance a challenge for product design.
2. Requirements for insurance companies to be licensed in every state in which they transact business and to obtain approvals from each state to sell products in its jurisdiction that comply with the possibly unique rules of each state—which lengthen the time and cost of bringing products to market—place a costly regulatory burden on the industry. Proposals to grant insurance compa-

nies the alternative option of a single federal charter that could reduce cost and speed innovation meet some resistance, including some state reluctance to relinquish power.

3. For example, Section 27-1-12-2 of Indiana insurance law deals with limitations on investments; Subsection 22 states: "Investments in: (a) preferred stock; and (b) common stock; shall not, in the aggregate, exceed twenty percent (20%) of the life insurance company's admitted assets, exclusive of assets held in segregated accounts."

4. Bogle, John C., "As the Index Fund Moves from Heresy to Dogma . . . What More Do We Need to Know?" remarks to Washington State University, The Gary M. Brinson Distinguished Lecture, April 13, 2004.

5. The Dow Jones Wilshire 5000 Total Market Index represents the broadest index for the U.S. equity market. It reflects performance of all U.S. headquartered equity securities with readily available price data. While the index derives its name from the nearly 5,000 stocks it contained when originally created in 1974, it now includes more issues than this.

6. The term "duration" when used in the context of fixed-income securities has a technical meaning different from "maturity," the time when an investor receives back his entire principal. "Total duration" is a local, first-derivative measure of price sensitivity to a change in or shock to the entire yield curve of interest rates. "Partial duration" or "key rate duration" is a local, first-derivative measure of price sensitivity to a change in or shock to one particular point on the yield curve. "Convexity" is a second-derivative measure that looks at the rate of change of the rate of change of the price of a security to a change in interest rates. Fixed-income specialists find "duration" a more important concept than "maturity."

7. Internal Revenue Code Section 817(h); Reg. section 1.817-5.

8. Markowitz, Harry M., *Portfolio Selection—Efficient Diversification of Investments* (New Haven, CT: Yale University Press, 1959).

9. A *locus* is the set of all points satisfying specified conditions. In Figure 7.4, the condition is that an asset portfolio produce the highest expected return for a given level of risk. There are no portfolios above the efficient frontier curve. There are numerous inefficient, suboptimal portfolios in the shaded region below the curve.

10. An excellent orientation to the notion of random walks and related lemmas, theorems, and numerical illustrations is given in William Feller's *An Introduction to Probability Theory and Its Applications*, Vol. I, 3rd ed. (New York: John Wiley & Sons, 1968). For example, to the extent a random walk results from a sequence of independent Bernoulli trials, the system has "no memory," in the sense that the course taken to arrive at the current state yields no information about the future. The next state of the system depends only on the current state and the matrix of transition probabilities to possible outcomes in the next step.

11. Brinson, Gary P., L. Randolph Hood, and Gilbert L. Beebower, "Determinants of Portfolio Performance," *Financial Analysts Journal*, (January-February): 133–138 (1995).

12. © 2005 The McGraw-Hill Companies, Inc. Standard & Poor's, including its subsidiary corporations ("S&P"), is a division of The McGraw-Hill Companies, Inc.

13. Ibid. Reproduction of this data in any form is prohibited without S&P's prior written permission.
14. Milevsky, Moshe A., and Chris Robinson. "Self-Annuitization and Ruin in Retirement, with Discussion," *North American Actuarial Journal* 4(4): 112–129. © 2000 by the Society of Actuaries. Reprinted with permission.
15. Parikh, Alan N. "The Evolving U.S. Retirement Income System." *The Actuary* (March): 2–6. © 2003 by the Society of Actuaries. Reprinted with permission.
16. Young, Virginia R., "Optimal Investment Strategy to Minimize the Probability of Lifetime Ruin," *North American Actuarial Journal* 8(4): 106–126. © 2004 Society of Actuaries. Young finds the optimal dynamic investment strategy to minimize the probability of lifetime ruin. In contrast, Milevsky and Robinson (n. 14) calculate probability of lifetime ruin for various fixed investment strategies.
17. Ibid.

CHAPTER 8   Rate of Return

1. Kellison, Stephen G., *The Theory of Interest*. (Homewood, IL: Richard D. Irwin, Inc. 1970), pp. 36–38.
2. Note the similarity to—but not the identity with—leveraging an investment portfolio, where positive rates of return are amplified (i.e., made more positive) through leveraging whereas negative returns are made more negative. With a "life only" IVA with no refund feature, those who survive to advanced ages receive a more positive rate of return than achievable with only their own funds, while those who die shortly after issue receive a rate of return more negative than would have occurred with their own funds. One must value the protection element more than the investment element, however, since a high rate of return for a few years is meaningless if one thereafter runs out of income!
3. This is consistent with Milevsky and Robinson's introductory comment: "A retiree who decides to forgo the life annuity and instead withdraw a fixed periodic amount from wealth will find it difficult to compete with the very high 'mortality credits' at advanced ages." Milevsky, Moshe A., and Chris Robinson, "Self-Annuitization and Ruin in Retirement, with Discussion," *North American Actuarial Journal* 4(4): 112–129. © 2000 by the Society of Actuaries. Reprinted with permission.
4. Based on Annuity 2000 Basic Table, 5% AIR, and 5% actual rate of return, where a $100,000 single premium provides an annual benefit of $10,288.02.
5. McCrory, Robert T., "Mortality Risk in Life Annuities," *Transactions of the Society of Actuaries,* 36: 309–338. © 1984 Society of Actuaries.
6. Qualified Domestic Relations Orders (QDROs), created by the Retirement Equity Act, permit an employee's pension to be split at the source between the employee and a nonemployee spouse.
7. Projector, Murray, "Discussion of Robert T. McCrory's article, Mortality Risk in Life Annuities," *Transactions of the Society of Actuaries* 36: 345–346. © 1984 Society of Actuaries.

8. It has been only semi-jokingly stated that we now live in a "second-derivative world," where focus has shifted from the rate of inflation—a first-derivative measure—to change in the inflation rate—a second-derivative measure.

CHAPTER 9   Reserves and Risk-Based Capital

1. Reprinted with permission of the National Association of Insurance Commissioners.
2. To the extent that the law or regulation of a particular state differs from the NAIC model law or regulation, the former governs.
3. Same as note 2.
4. From a private conversation in 1997 with Ian M. Rolland, retired Chairman of Lincoln National Corporation, who in 1967 started the variable annuity business of The Lincoln National Life Insurance Company.
5. Becker, David N., "A Generalized Profits Released Model for the Measurement of Return on Investment for Life Insurance," *Transactions of the Society of Actuaries* 40, pt. 1: 61–98. © 1988 Society of Actuaries. This paper describes two distinct pricing models and introduces a methodology that resolves difficulties inherent in traditional return on investment (ROI) techniques for financial products with multiple changes in sign of book profits or products that require no initial investment.
6. Actuarial guidelines used with permission of the National Association of Insurance Commissioners, National Actuarial Guideline.
7. Hardy, Mary R., and Julia L. Wirch, "The Iterated CTE: A Dynamic Risk Measure," *North American Actuarial Journal*, 8, no. 4: 62–75. © 2004 Society of Actuaries.

CHAPTER 10   Immediate Variable Annuity Taxation

1. For tax-qualified plans, an increase in annuity payments resulting from variations in performance of the underlying assets in a variable annuity is one permitted exception to the requirement that annuity payments be nonincreasing. Treasury regulation section 1.401(a)(9)-6.
2. Prior to the most recent amendment, the definition of *immediate annuity* included the wording "which is one of a series of substantially equal periodic payments made for the life of a taxpayer or over a period extending for at least 60 months after the annuity starting date." As a result, the shortest non-life-contingent immediate annuity (fixed or variable) offered by most insurance companies was a five-year fixed-period annuity option.
3. Tax-qualified immediate variable annuities with a non-zero cost basis—such as a traditional individual retirement account (IRA) to which nondeductible contributions were made as a result of the taxpayer's income being too high to be deductible—similarly contain a tax-excludable portion.

4. Treasury regulation section 1.72-2(b)(3).
5. If the annuity start date was before January 1, 1987, the tax-excludable portion of each annuity payment continues to be tax-excludable even after the annuitant has fully recovered his or her cost basis.
6. Treasury regulation section 1.72-4(d)(3).
7. Treasury regulation section 1.72-11(c)(2), Ex. 4.
8. Internal Revenue Code (IRC) Section 72(b)(3)(A).
9. IRC Section 72(b)(3)(B).
10. IRC Section 2033.
11. IRC Sections 2039(a) and (b).
12. Kennickell, Arthur B., "A Rolling Tide: Changes in the Distribution of Wealth in the U.S., 1989–2001," Finance and Economics Discussion Series no. 2003-24 (Washington, DC: Federal Reserve Board, 2003).
13. Ibid.
14. NAVA's mission is "to promote the growth, acceptance and understanding of annuity and variable life products to retirement-focused Americans; to provide educational and informational resources to our members and the public; to protect consumers by encouraging adherence to the highest ethical standards by insurers, distributors, and all other participants in our diverse industry; and to protect and advance the interests of our members."
15. Krach, Constance A., and Victoria A. Velkoff, "U.S. Bureau of the Census, Current Population Reports, Series P23-199RV, Centenarians in the United States" (Washington, DC: U.S. Government Printing Office, 1999). Figures 10.3 and 10.4 show the percentage living in poverty for the 94.8% of the population age 65 and over for whom poverty status was ascertained; those living in institutions, such as nursing homes, did not have their status determined. The data are taken from special tabulations from the 1990 census sample files.

CHAPTER 11   Services and Fees

1. New Jersey requires reporting how each immediate variable annuity payment was determined, that is, how much of the total benefit is attributable to each subaccount.
2. Appendix O contains a list of some of the benefits conferred on contract owners.
3. The VARDS® Expense Ratio (VER) is one yardstick for examining comparative expense levels of variable annuity products. VARDS® is a registered trademark of Morningstar, Inc. Reprinted with the permission of Morningstar, Inc.
4. Gutterman, Sam, "2002 Inter-Company Expense Study of U.S. Individual Life Insurance and Annuities," *Product Matters*! Society of Actuaries Product Development Section Newsletter (November 2004).
5. In the 2002 study, termination expense was combined with the per policy in force data. (Termination expense reflects those activities performed on death of the last surviving annuitant.) In the comparable 2001 study that did split per policy in force and per termination expense, the values were per policy in force—$109.66; per termination—$444.93.

CHAPTER 12   Product Distribution

1. The trails could be paid on the "natural reserve," that generated by best-estimate pricing. If trails are paid on a more conservative statutory reserve—the natural reserve augmented by the insurer—the insurer effectively ends up paying trails on an asset base partially consisting of its own money, whereas it may desire to pay trails only on funds provided it through the financial adviser. Using the statutory reserve as a base may offer more comfort to financial advisers, not only because the base on which trails are paid may be higher but also because the base is derived from a state-prescribed formula.

2. Chalke, Shane, "Macro Pricing: A Comprehensive Product Development Process, with Discussion," *Transactions of the Society of Actuaries* 43: 137–230. © 1991 Society of Actuaries.

3. Reuters, "Fidelity Targets Retirees," June 10, 2004.

4. The Committee of Annuity Insurers, Survey of Owners of Non-Qualified Annuity Contracts (The Gallup Organization and Matthew Greenwald & Associates, 2005). Reprinted with permission of the Committee of Annuity Insurers.

5. Profile of Immediate Annuity Owners—Research Findings. Washington, DC: American Council of Life Insurers, April 2003.

6. If the contract owner worries that the beneficiary recipient may squander a lump sum, some policies allow contract owners the option to elect that the death benefit be paid only in annuity form—a so-called "gifting with strings" approach. Alternatively, a trust may be named as beneficiary, where the trustee is instructed to apply the lump sum proceeds to the purchase of an annuity; this results in the expense of an attorney and construction of trust documents for contract owners.

7. ACLI tabulations of National Association of Insurance Commissioners (NAIC) data. NAIC does not endorse any analysis or conclusions based on its data. Reprinted with permission of the National Association of Insurance Commissioners.

8. VanDerhei, Jack, and Craig Copeland, *The Changing Face of Private Retirement Plans.* Employee Benefit Research Institute (EBRI) Issue Brief No. 232 (April 2001), pp. 12–13.

9. This excludes annuitizations of insurers who do not proactively emphasize annuity payout provisions but provide variable annuity income payouts as an accommodation to clients or advisers who want them.

10. Ayers, Wm. Borden, and James R. Sholder, "Variable Payout Annuity Industry Study," The Diversified Services Group, Inc., 2004.

11. Parikh, Alan N., "The Evolving U.S. Retirement System," *The Actuary* (March): 2–6. © 2003 by the Society of Actuaries. Reprinted with permission.

12. For pension plans requiring some form of life-contingent annuity option, group (rather than individual) mortality may be used. Group mortality rates, which are higher and therefore allow higher payouts, may be safely used since mortality anti-selection such as that associated with IVAs in the non-tax-qualified market may be absent.

13. U.S. Department of Labor, Bureau of Labor Statistics, "Employee Benefits in Medium and Large Private Establishments, 1997," *Bulletin*, no. 2517 (September 1999).

14. In actual practice, *similar* (though perhaps not perfectly identical) annuity pay-out options would be compared. For example, single life only payout options with 60%, 70%, and 80% floors might be grouped. Even then, the definition of *floor* would need to be reviewed, since one percentage might apply to initial benefit (i.e., "level floor") while another percentage might apply to the highest benefit ever received (i.e., "ratcheting floor").

15. Noble intent sometimes leads to costly regulations. Truly valuable product designs will naturally register an attractive index value, while less valuable designs simply may be rearranged to display a better index value. As Plato quipped, "Good people do not need laws to tell them to act responsibly, while bad people will find a way around the laws."

CHAPTER 13   Individual Immediate Variable Annuity Underwriting

1. Mehr, Robert I., and Emerson Cammack, *Principles of Insurance*, 6th ed. (Homewood, IL: Richard D. Irwin, Inc., 1976), p. 576.

CHAPTER 14   Legal Issues

1. Note that blending resultant male and female payout rates 50%/50% does not produce the same result as blending the male and female q_x values that go into producing the ultimate payout rates 50%/50%. As a result, one needs to exercise caution in the derivation of unisex payout rates. While the differences may not be large, they can be important when product margins are thin due to competitive pressures.

2. Scahill, Patricia L., "U.S. Sex Discrimination Regulations as They Affect Financial Security Programs," *Education and Examination Committee of the Society of Actuaries, Part 6 Study Note.* © 1985 Society of Actuaries.

3. Twain, Mark, *Lecture on Christian Science* (1899).

4. Mehr, Robert I., and Emerson Cammack, *Principles of Insurance*, 6th ed. (Homewood, IL: Richard D. Irwin, Inc., 1976), p. 397.

5. Ibid.

6. Because insurance is at this time under the aegis of state regulation, to avoid the complexities and administrative expense of complying with 50 different sets of insurance laws, the National Association of Insurance Commissioners (NAIC) helps provide some degree of uniformity through approaches to make it easier for some or all of these 50 state insurance commissioners to act in unison. For example, a model law, such as a model nonforfeiture law, is drafted. States are encouraged to adopt this verbatim or with minimal changes.

     Most U.S. annuity regulation is done by the states. The Tenth Amendment to the Constitution declares that "powers not delegated to the United States . . . are reserved to the states." In 1944, the Supreme Court ruled that insurance is interstate commerce and therefore subject to federal law. In 1945, Congress passed the McCarran Act, which clarified the open question of federal versus state authority by providing that the business of insurance shall be subject to state law.

7. Meyer, William F., *Life and Health Insurance Law, A Summary* (International Claim Association, 1976), p. 175.

8. This rule of construction does not apply when contract language is statutorily prescribed. It is only true when the drafting party has free choice of words to be used.

CHAPTER 15   Securities Law

1. Justice McKenna, U.S. Supreme Court, opinion in *Hall vs. Geiger-Jones Co.*, 242 U.S. 539 (1917).

2. Rule 22c-1, promulgated under the Investment Company Act of 1940.

CHAPTER 16   Forms of Insurance and Insurers

1. Vilfredo Pareto was an Italian economist, engineer, and sociologist whose work influenced modern welfare economics.

2. Quirk, James P., *Intermediate Microeconomics* (Science Research Associates, 1976), pp. 227–245.

3. Brown, Robert L., and Joanne McDaid, "Factors Affecting Retirement Mortality," *North American Actuarial Journal* (April 2003): 24–43. © 2003 Society of Actuaries.

4. Further information on the issues of individual equity versus social adequacy can be found in Myers, Robert J., *Social Security* (Homewood, IL: Richard D. Irwin, Inc., 1985), 9–11. Robert Myers served as chief actuary of the Social Security Administration from 1947 to 1970.

CHAPTER 17   IVA Business Value to Annuity Company

1. Cost of capital is actually a duration-based vector of rates rather than a single, uniform rate over the entire project period. For example, as bond investors tie up their funds for progressively longer periods (with commensurately increasing uncertainty of events that may transpire over progressively longer periods), they tend to demand higher rental payments on their borrowed money in the way of interest rates.

2. Statutory valuation mortality typically is too conservative in actual practice to use as pricing mortality.

3. Much like physics migrated from a deterministic worldview in the days of Isaac Newton to a greater appreciation of randomness in the early twentieth century, with such theories as Max Planck's particle/wave duality and Werner Heisenberg's uncertainty principle, annuity modeling has migrated from use of a single, deterministic, best-estimate path to stochastic models, which incorporate measures that recognize a range of possible outcomes attributable to random variables such as investment returns and mortality.

4. The 3% value used here for illustrative purposes is higher than that actually used in practice for traditional immediate variable annuities, at least barring additional features that meaningfully increase the volatility of outcomes across potential scenarios.

5. C-1 to C-4 factors are discussed in "Discussion of the Preliminary Report of the Committee on Valuation and Related Problems," *Record of the Society of Actuaries* 5, no. 1: 241–284. © 1979 Society of Actuaries.

6. Differential geometry is a branch of mathematics that studies curves. For example, the Fundamental Theorem of Curves states that any regular curve with positive curvature is completely determined, up to position in space, by its curvature and torsion. *Curvature* measures bending within a plane, while *torsion* measures twisting out of a plane.

CHAPTER 18   Product Development Trends

1. Theoretically, just like stock and bond mutual funds, immediate variable annuity benefits can drop to $0. This would only occur if investments in every investment fund underlying the variable subaccounts chosen became totally worthless. Annuitants probably needn't worry about such an event because anything remotely similar to this probably indicates a doomsday scenario, such as a monumental catastrophe like nuclear disaster, a meteor hitting the earth, or civil war—in which case annuitants, if they're still alive, are probably sitting on lawn chairs on their front porch with a rifle across their lap guarding food and home from looters, and current investment valuations and performance of their retirement income program are the least of their worries!

2. Calling the feature by its generic name GPAF or by a more picturesque product-specific marketing name does not change its essential quality of being a long-dated, complex put option.

3. Technically, the contract owner owns and controls the contract and has the right to exercise its provisions, such as a provision to reallocate among subaccounts the performance of which dictate the level of variable benefit payments. Throughout this discussion, it may be helpful for the reader to make the simplifying (and often true), assumption that the contract owner and the annuitant are the same person. In reality, the contract owner(s), annuitant(s), primary beneficiary(ies), and contingent beneficiary(ies) can all be different people.

4. When $\sigma_{XY} = 0$, this implies that the covariability of X and Y is zero; that is, X and Y do not tend to vary together. The covariance σ_{XY}, however, is a measure of only *linear* covariability. It is possible that Y can be completely determined by X (nonlinearly) and still the covariance—and, hence, the correlation coefficient—is zero.

5. A high-kurtosis distribution has a sharper peak and fatter tails. Its acute peak around the mean indicates a higher probability than a normally distributed random variable of values near the mean. Its fat tails indicate a higher probability than a normally distributed random variable of extreme values. Higher kurtosis means more of the variance is due to infrequent extreme deviations, rather than frequent modest deviations; that is, such a fat-tailed distribution has higher

than normal chances of a big positive or negative realization. Such probability distributions with positive kurtosis are called *leptokurtic*.

A low-kurtosis distribution has a smaller, more rounded peak about the mean and thin tails. Such probability distributions with negative kurtosis are called *platykurtic*. In between are probability distributions with zero kurtosis, called *mesokurtic*, which include the normal distribution, irrespective of its mean or standard deviation.

Actuaries perform stochastic scenario analyses to determine minimum capital requirements for variable annuity products with guarantees, such as GPAFs. The model that generates equity market returns used in performing these analyses must be calibrated to ensure sufficiently fat tails, based on historical S&P 500 total return index experience.

While *kurtosis* is defined as μ_4/μ_2^2, or, equivalently, μ_4/σ^4, *excess kurtosis* is defined as $\mu_4/\mu_2^2 - 3$, where the minus 3 factor is introduced to make the excess kurtosis of the normal distribution equal to zero.

6. An "American option" can be exercised at any time up to the expiration date. A "European option" can be exercised only on a specified future date.

7. An excellent description of option strategies is provided in McMillan, Lawrence G., "Options as a Strategic Investment," New York: New York Institute of Finance, 1980.

8. Modigliani, F., and M. H. Miller, "The Cost of Capital, Corporation Finance, and the Theory of Investment," *American Economic Review* 48: 261–297 (1958).

9. Modigliani and Miller's (MM) first proposition is that market value of a firm is independent of capital structure. The firm generates cash flows. The capital structure defines their split between bond holders and stock holders. Changing the relative proportions of debt and equity financing doesn't change the cash flows that the firm generates, merely their distribution. While equities become riskier as a company issues more debt and increases leverage, a firm cannot increase enterprise value by changing its debt/equity ratio. This is sometimes referred to as the "irrelevancy proposition." An important implication is that financing decisions (sources of funds) and investment project decisions (uses of funds) can be separated. Real-world frictions like taxes and transaction costs do affect the MM first proposition.

10. Black, F., and M. Scholes, "The Pricing of Options and Corporate Liabilities," *Journal of Political Economy*, 81: 637–654 (1973).

11. Ibid.

12. Cox, J., S. Ross, and M. Rubinstein, "Option Pricing: A Simplified Approach," *Journal of Financial Economics* 7, 229–263 (September 1979).

13. Climatology and hydrology were the original applications of extreme value theory (EVT). Insurance loss modeling is a fairly recent application of EVT.

14. We earlier defined the *probability function* for X as the probability that the random variable X assumes the value a, denoted $p_X(a) = P\{X = a\}$. The *distribution function* (sometimes called the *cumulative distribution function*) for a random variable X, denoted $F_X(a)$, is a function of a real variable a such that (1) the domain of F_X is the whole real line and (2) for any real a, $F_X(a) = P\{X \leq a\}$. The distribution function associates with each real a the probability that X is less than or equal to a; it expresses the probability that X will equal a value in

the interval $(-\infty, a)$. The *probability density function* for a continuous random variable X, denoted $f_X(x)$, is a function of a real variable x such that (1) the domain of f_X is the whole real line and (2) for any real number a,

$$F_X(a) = \int_{-\infty}^{a} f_X(x)dx$$

For a continuous random variable X, the probability of X being equal to any specific value a in its range is zero; that is, $P\{X = a\}$ is 0. The probability function cannot therefore be used to compute the probability that $a \le X \le b$ if X is continuous. Hence the role of the probability density function, since

$$P\{a < X \le b\} = F_X(b) - F_X(a)$$
$$= \int_{-\infty}^{b} f_X(x)dx - \int_{-\infty}^{a} f_X(x)dx$$
$$= \int_{a}^{b} f_X(x)dx$$

A probability density function $f_X(x)$ of a continuous random variable X is nonnegative (i.e., $f_X(x) \ge 0$ for all x). Its integral, extended over the entire x-axis, is unity, that is,

$$\int_{-\infty}^{\infty} f_X(x)dx = 1$$

15. See n. 14 for the definition of the distribution function.
16. Further information about British actuary F. M. Redington's concept of immunization can be found in the discussion of duration at the close of Chapter 3.
17. Vega is not a Greek letter; hence the lack of symbol.
18. The class of regime-switching lognormal models permits the stock price process to switch randomly between k regimes, where each regime has different model parameters (μ_k, σ_k). Transition probabilities of moving from one regime (state) to another in any given period govern the evolution of which regime the stock price process is in at any time. Two- or three-regime models (i.e., $k = 2$ or 3) are generally sufficient for modeling monthly equity returns.
19. While no access to principal exists in the sense of being able to put the contract back to the insurance company issuer, it may be possible for the immediate annuity owner to assign the income payments to a third party in exchange for whatever lump-sum value may be agreed on with that party. In other words, under specified conditions, an annuitant can sell his rights to a future income stream from an insurer to anyone of his choosing in exchange for cash now. Immediate annuity contracts used to fund state lottery winnings and structured settlements typically contain a provision indicating that they are nonassignable. Prohibitions against assignment exist to protect the annuitant; for example, a structured settlement may have been custom tailored to provide specific payments on specific future dates—such as for a college education or a series of surgical procedures—and there is a desire to not permit easy disruption of the objectives of a well-conceived program mutually agreed on between plaintiff

and defendant. Yet there exist instances when a prohibition against assignment may be unaligned with the annuitant's needs, such as when a 95-year-old person is to receive lottery winnings annually for the next 40 years. Individual state laws govern the secondary market for lottery and structured settlement immediate annuities. Court approval must be obtained for the transfer of payment rights. For example, Illinois Lottery Law (20 ILCS 1605/13) states, "No prize, nor any portion of a prize, nor any right of any person to a prize awarded shall be assignable, except as provided in Section 13.1." Section 13.1 begins, "The right of a person to receive payments due under a prize that is paid in installments over time by the Department may be voluntarily assigned, in whole or in part, if the assignment is made to a person or entity designated pursuant to an order of the circuit court located in the county in which the assigning winner resides or in which the Department's headquarters are located." The circuit court is to issue an order approving a voluntary assignment if specific safeguards are met, such as that the assignment is in writing, the assignor is of sound mind and not acting under duress, the assigning winner has had the opportunity to receive independent financial and tax advice, and the assigning winner has been provided a disclosure statement that includes the rate of discount used to derive the purchase price. The situation for an IVA is more complicated because it involves transfers of value associated with a security.

20. For contracts issued and deposits made prior to August 14, 1982, the ordering of distributions from the contract for tax purposes is different, being nontaxable return of principal first followed by taxable appreciation.

21. For tax-qualified markets where neither principal deposits nor appreciation have ever been taxed, all distributions are 100% taxable.

CHAPTER 19 Conclusion

1. Topics covered in this volume rely on the mathematical fields of algebra; differential, integral, multivariate, and stochastic calculus; probability; statistics; numerical analysis; geometry and analytic geometry, and differential equations. Other optimization techniques—such as the linear programming simplex algorithm from operations research and quadratic programming—also have application to immediate annuities.

2. While immediate fixed annuities with *level* benefits will not keep pace with inflation, immediate fixed annuities with guaranteed *increasing* benefits—such as 4% or 5% per year—offer a better chance of keeping pace with inflation. Immediate fixed annuity purchases make the most sense when interest rates are at historically high levels. This is because annuity payouts are premised on the yields that insurers can achieve on a collection of fixed-income securities that replicate the projected benefit payments at time of purchase. Of course, it's only by coincidence that the time when an individual starts to require retirement income is contemporaneous with historically high interest rates!

3. The market basket of goods and services used by seniors tends to differ from the market basket used to determine the overall U.S. consumer price index (CPI). For example, seniors may consume higher levels of pharmaceutical prod-

ucts and healthcare services per capita than the aggregate population. To the extent that these products and services exhibit faster price increases (e.g., due to price inelasticity, meaning the quantity demanded is relatively insensitive to price) than the market basket of goods used to determine overall CPI values, the overall CPI index may understate inflation experienced by seniors.

4. Yet another reason that insurers have not aggressively offered CPI-adjusted immediate annuities is because the initial benefit amounts may be significantly lower than other annuity forms, making the sale challenging. Just as an immediate fixed annuity where benefits are guaranteed to increase by 3% annually starts with a lower benefit than the same annuity option that pays level (i.e., nonincreasing) benefits—because all annuity options have identical present value equal to the premium—CPI-adjusted immediate annuities start with a lower benefit than alternative, level-benefit annuity options also backed by bonds and other fixed-income instruments of comparable quality and duration.

5. Russell, Bertrand, "The Study of Mathematics," essay in *Mysticism and Logic*, (Garden City, New York: Doubleday, 1957), p. 84.

APPENDIXES

1. Johansen, Robert J., "Annuity 2000 Mortality Tables," *Transactions of the Society of Actuaries, 1995–1996 Reports:* 263. © 1998 Society of Actuaries.
2. Ibid.
3. Derivation of 1983 Table *a*, *Transactions of the Society of Actuaries* 33:721. © 1982 Society of Actuaries.
4. Cherry, Harold. "The 1971 Individual Annuity Mortality Table," *Transactions of the Society of Actuaries,* Volume XXIII, p. 496. © 1972 Society of Actuaries.
5. Derivation of 1983 Table *a*, *Transactions of the Society of Actuaries,* 33:708. © 1982 Society of Actuaries.

Glossary

Accumulation unit a measure used to calculate account value of a deferred variable annuity contract prior to any election to convert it into an immediate annuity contract.

Accumulation unit value the value of one accumulation unit on a valuation date, with valuation typically occurring once daily following the close of the market on each day that major stock exchanges are open for business.

Annuitant a person who receives immediate annuity income benefits; for life-contingent annuity options, a person on whose life annuity payouts are based.

Annuitization the process of converting a lump-sum dollar amount into a series of periodic income benefits through the purchase of an immediate annuity.

Annuity payment option any of the optional forms of payment of annuity benefits defined in the contract or otherwise made available by the insurance company; alternatively known as *annuity payout option*.

Annuity unit a measure used to calculate the amount of periodic immediate variable annuity benefit payments.

Annuity unit value the value of one annuity unit on a valuation date, with valuation typically occurring once daily following the close of the market on each day that the major stock exchanges are open for business.

Assumed investment rate (AIR) the investment return assumed in calculating the initial annuity benefit; future annuity benefits fluctuate based on actual subaccount performance relative to the AIR; alternatively known as *benchmark rate, hurdle rate,* or *target rate.*

Beneficiary a person designated to receive residual benefits, if any, following death of the annuitant; the annuity payout option chosen defines whether such benefits shall be payable in a lump sum or in continuing installments.

Conversion rate the factor that converts a lump-sum dollar amount into an initial periodic income benefit based on factors such as age, sex, annuity payment option, benefit payment frequency, and AIR; often expressed as dollars of monthly income per $1,000 of net premium; alternatively known as *annuity purchase rate.*

Deferred annuity an annuity contract purchased with a single premium, a schedule of periodic premiums, or flexible, ad hoc premiums used to accumulate retirement savings; ultimately, deferred annuity account value may be used to generate retirement income by conversion to an immediate annuity or via one or more withdrawals.

Fixed annuity an annuity contract that guarantees that a fixed rate of interest will be credited during the accumulation phase and that a fixed amount of periodic income will be paid following conversion to an immediate annuity.

Fund any of the underlying investment options into which the variable annuity premium may be invested through the separate account.

General account an account consisting of all assets owned by the insurance company other than those assets in separate accounts.

Immediate annuity an annuity contract, generally purchased with a lump sum, that provides periodic income benefits as defined by the annuity payment option; an immediate annuity may be fixed, variable, or a combination.

Net asset value per share the market value of one share of an investment fund underlying a variable annuity subaccount; calculated each business day by taking the closing market value of all securities owned, adding the value of all other assets including cash, subtracting all liabilities, and dividing the total net assets result by the number of shares outstanding.

Non-tax-qualified plan a retirement plan other than a tax-qualified plan.

Owner a person who has authority to exercise ownership rights within the annuity contract, such election of annuity payout option and designation of beneficiary, and, for variable annuity contracts, investment allocation and reallocation.

Premium the amount paid to purchase an annuity product, the terms of which are defined in writing in the annuity contract.

Separate account a segregated investment account into which the insurance company invests the assets for immediate variable annuities (and possibly also for deferred variable annuities and variable life insurance products); such assets are segregated from the general account of the insurance company.

Subaccount the portion of the separate account that reflects investments in accumulation units and/or annuity units of a particular fund available under the contract.

Tax-qualified plan a retirement plan qualifying for special tax treatment under the Internal Revenue Code of 1986, as amended, including Sections 401, 403, 408, 408A, and 457.

Valuation date a date on which (1) net asset value per share of funds underlying variable annuity subaccounts and (2) accumulation unit values and annuity unit values of variable annuity subaccounts are valued, which typically occurs once daily following the close of the market on each day that major stock exchanges are open for business.

Variable annuity an annuity contract that permits allocation of the premium to one or more variable subaccounts the performance of which govern account value for deferred annuities and periodic income levels for immediate annuities.

About the Author

Jeffrey K. Dellinger, a fellow of the Society of Actuaries and a member of the American Academy of Actuaries, is president of Longevity Management Corporation.

An author, speaker, mathematician, actuary, executive, and business consultant, Mr. Dellinger is a Phi Beta Kappa graduate of Indiana University, holding bachelor's and master's degrees in mathematics.

With over 25 years in the financial services industry, Mr. Dellinger provided successful leadership as Individual Annuity Profit Center Head for the third-largest U.S. annuity company, with $60 billion in annuity assets. Responsible for profitability, product development (product strategy, conception, design, pricing, investment strategy, patents), marketing, communications, investment company relationship management, distributor relationship management, asset/liability management, state compliance, interest crediting strategy, and in-force business management for individual annuities—deferred and immediate, fixed and variable—his extensive breadth of experience and strong analytic skills provide a unique vantage point for sharing insights about variable income annuities.

Index to Notation

Note: Page number indicates where notation is introduced.

Subject Index